THE EARLY FACTORY LEGISLATION

LEONARD HORNER

THE EARLY
FACTORY LEGISLATION

A STUDY IN LEGISLATIVE

AND ADMINISTRATIVE EVOLUTION

MAURICE WALTON THOMAS

1948

THE THAMES BANK PUBLISHING COMPANY LIMITED
1773 LONDON ROAD : LEIGH-ON-SEA : ESSEX

First published in 1948 by
The Thames Bank Publishing Company Limited
1773 London Road, Leigh-on-Sea.
Printed in Great Britain by
W. H. Houldershaw, Limited,
49 London Road, Southend-on-Sea.

TO MY WIFE

ACKNOWLEDGMENTS

I desire to express my warmest thanks to Mr. H. L. Beales, without whose help and guidance this book could not have been written; to the late Mr. H. E. Chasteney, formerly H.M. Chief Inspector of Factories, who placed at my disposal the minute books of the Factory Department; to Mr. F. N. Ball, my publisher, for his wise counsel and friendly criticism; and to my wife, for whose constant encouragement I can never be sufficiently grateful.

M. W. THOMAS

Enfield
1948

CONTENTS

CONTENTS

ILLUSTRATIONS

FOREWORD

Much has been written of the Industrial Revolution and the growth and evils of the factory system in this country in the late Eighteenth and early Nineteenth Centuries, but the evolution of factory legislation has not, in general, received the same detailed treatment from historians. Although many students of industrial history must have realised the onerous tasks which were imposed on the early Factory Inspectors, they have probably been unable through the medium of the ordinary textbooks either to assess accurately the part played by those officials towards establishing a basis upon which to frame our present Factories Act or to appreciate the influence of their pioneer work on the growth and development of the present-day system and methods of inspection. Mr. Thomas has laid particular emphasis on the activities of the Inspectors during the period from the date of their inception to the middle of the Nineteenth Century and portrayed their difficulties, their experiences and, moreover, their reactions as successive legislative measures, which often gave rise to acute controversy, were placed on the Statute Book. A great deal of information with regard to this period was comprised in the Home Office minute books which recorded the Inspectors' discussions at their bi-annual conferences, and their periodical reports. The author has now culled from these, as well as many other original sources, much that is intensely human and instructive and collated it in one volume. Industrialists and others no less than students of history and economics will find many new and interesting facts in this comprehensive survey of early factory legislation and inspection.

G. P. BARNETT
H.M. Chief Inspector of Factories

ROBERT OWEN

CHAPTER 1

THE BACKGROUND

THE ARCHITECTS of Britain's industrial fabric, the men who in the latter half of the eighteenth century, applied power to the textile trade, and in so doing achieved for their country a paramount place among the manufacturing nations of the world, were, for the most part, individuals of humble origin. Within a comparatively short span of years, James Hargreaves, the Blackburn weaver and carpenter, Richard Arkwright, the barber, Samuel Crompton, descendant of a line of Lancashire small-holders, and Edmund Cartwright, who had relinquished his Magdalen fellowship to minister to the spiritual needs of a small country parish, evolved a series of inventions which " accomplished what no conqueror by the power of armies and the force of decrees could have realized—they changed the personal and relative condition, and, consequently, the habits and character, of numerous sections of the people; they aggregated into a few districts what was formerly a widely spread cottage industry."[1]

Until the advent of machinery the textile trade, though organized to some extent on a capitalistic basis,[2] had been essentially a domestic industry. In many rural homes the two main processes, spinning and weaving, were carried on side by side— " the spinner and the weaver were to some extent synonymous "[3] —yet even so it was difficult to maintain that steady balance between the production of thread by the spinner, and its consumption by the weaver which was essential if the industry was to maintain its equilibrium. Dr. Ure described in picturesque phrase the work of the weaver and the difficulties he had to encounter. " The workshop of the weaver was a rural cottage, from which, when he was tired of sedentary labour, he could sally forth into his little garden, and with the spade or the hoe tend its culinary productions. The cotton wool which was to form his weft was picked clean by the fingers of his younger children, and was carded and spun by the older girls, assisted by his wife, and the yarn was woven by himself assisted by his sons. When he could not procure within his family a supply of yarn adequate to the demands of his loom, he had recourse to the spinsters of his neighbourhood. One

---

[1] " Alfred " (S. Kydd), *The History of the Factory Movement* (1857) Vol. 1, p. 8.
[2] P. Mantoux, *The Industrial Revolution in the Eighteenth Century* (1928) p. 209.
[3] P. Gaskell, *The Manufacturing Population of England* (1833) p. 40.

good weaver could keep three active women at work upon the
wheel spinning weft. It was found more easy to multiply weavers
than spinsters, and hence looms were often at a stand for want of
yarn. . . . Such was the competition he met with from other
weavers . . . that he was often obliged to treat the females with
presents in order to quicken their diligence at the wheel."[4]

In 1733, when John Kay invented the flying shuttle, the
balance between spinning and weaving was upset still further.
Hitherto the weaver had thrown the shuttle through the warp by
hand, and this not only limited the breadth of material that could
be woven by a single operative, but imposed a definite restriction
on the rate of work. Kay devised a shuttle that ran on wheels
in a small wooden groove, at either end of which was a spring-
loaded hammer. To each hammer was attached a string, the two
ends of which were tied to the " picking-stick." When the weaver
jerked his picking-stick the hammer struck the shuttle a smart
blow and sent it on its wheels through the warp, a jerk in the
opposite direction causing it to return. The flying shuttle thus
made it possible to weave broader fabric, and, more important, it
increased very considerably the speed at which the work could
be accomplished.

By the year 1760 the flying shuttle had been adopted almost
universally in the cotton and woollen industries, and so acute had
become the shortage of yarn that the demand for improvement in
the technique of spinning was insistent. As long ago as 1738 Lewis
Paul and John Wyatt had patented a machine in which rollers were
employed to draw out the roving (the rope-like mass or sliver into
which the cotton was formed after it had been cleaned and carded)
into thread; but their invention met with little success,[5] and it was
left to Hargreaves and Arkwright to evolve machines that revolu-
tionized the entire industry, by restoring the balance between the
operations of spinning and weaving.

The spinning jenny, which Hargreaves invented about 1765,
was a rectangular frame across which lay two wooden rails
mounted on a wheeled carriage. The rovings were wound upon
bobbins, passed through the rails, and attached to spindles. The
carriage carrying the rails was then moved away from the spindles,
the rovings were gripped between the rails by closing a clasp, and
the carriage was moved still further from the spindles, thus

---

4 A. Ure, *The Cotton Manufacture of* **Great Britain** (1836) Vol. I,
pp. 224-225.
5 " He [Paul] was of a gentle and passive spirit, little fitted to cope with
the hardships of a new manufacturing enterprise. It required, in fact, a man
of Napoleon nerve and ambition to subdue the refractory tempers of work-
people accustomed to irregular paroxysms of diligence . . . Such was
Arkwright." A. Ure, *The Philosophy of Manufactures* (1835) p. 16.

stretching the rovings into thread. At the same time, the spindles were revolved by means of a wheel, thus applying a twist to the thread. As the carriage was pushed back to its first position, the wheel was turned again, and the thread was wound upon the spindles.

The importance of the spinning jenny lay in the fact that one workman could spin a number of threads at the same time, so increasing the amount of yarn that was available for the weaver, but the thread it produced was not hard or fine enough for use as warp.

Arkwright's water-frame, patented in 1769, went far to remedy this defect. His machine embodied the roller principle, whereby the roving was stretched, not by being drawn out on a movable carriage, but by being passed between four pairs of rollers, revolving at progressively increasing speeds. As the thread emerged from the last pair of rollers it was wound on to vertical spindles, and in this way a twist was imparted. The water-twist, as it was called, produced a much stronger yarn than the jenny, indeed it was strong enough to be used as warp, though it was somewhat coarse in texture.

The mule or mule jenny, invented by Crompton in 1779, combined the advantages of the spinning jenny and the water-frame. The roving, having passed through rollers, was wound on to rapidly revolving spindles which were mounted on a moving carriage. The alternating motion of the carriage gave the necessary stretch as it travelled away from the rollers, and provided the twist as the spindles revolved on the return journey. The thread produced by the mule possessed a strength and fineness hitherto unknown; it could be used for the warp as well as the weft, and was soon being employed in the manufacture of the finest muslins.[6]

The result of this remarkable series of inventions in the spinning of yarn upset once more the balance of the textile industry. Thread was now being produced in enormous quantities by machinery, but weaving was still being done on hand-looms. Once again the cotton trade was faced with a crisis, and it fell to Edmund Cartwright to resolve the problem. A casual conversation with some Manchester manufacturers supplied the impetus, and in 1785 he took out a patent for the first power-loom. Within a few short years " the results were plainly visible. Two steam looms, looked after by a fifteen-year-old boy, could weave three and a half pieces of material, while in the same time a skilled weaver, using the fly shuttle, wove only one. Even though the textile industry had not yet found that organic balance, which successive inventions

---

[6] For a full and lucid account of these inventions see G. W. Daniels, *The Early English Cotton Industry* (1920).

had for sixty years sought to restore, the problem was now solved.
. . . Now all the essentials were there, and in that particular
branch of production the triumph of machine industry was an
accomplished fact."[7]

Within a very short space of time a vast flow of capital began
to be attracted to the textile industry, for the prizes that could be
won by energy and ruthlessness were dazzling beyond the dreams
of avarice. A spinner who could scrape together the few pounds
that were necessary to purchase one of Hargreaves' spinning jennies
might hope, in the course of a few years, to attain considerable
affluence, and many were the cottage workers who aspired to such
heights. "Many of the first successful manufacturers," said
Gaskell,[8] "were men who had their origin in the rank of mere
operatives . . . . The celerity with which some of these individuals
accumulated wealth in the early times of steam spinning and
weaving, are proofs . . . that they were men of quick views, great
energy of character, and possessing no small share of sagacity . . . .
But they were men of very limited general information . . . who
exercised very considerable influence upon the hordes of workmen
who became dependent upon them . . . . Master cotton spinners
and weavers then, at the commencement of this important epoch,
were in many instances men sprung from the ranks of the labourers,
or from a grade just removed above these—uneducated—of coarse
habits—sensual in their enjoyments—overwhelmed by success—
but yet . . . industrious men, and active and farsighted tradesmen."[9]
The founder of the great Peel fortune, 'Parsley Peel' as he
was called, because he used the pattern of a parsley leaf on his
fabrics,[10] started life as a humble calico printer in an old farmhouse
near Blackburn. At the close of the century his son employed

---

7 P. Mantoux, The Industrial Revolution in the Eighteenth Century
(1928) p. 250.
   8 P. Gaskell. The Manufacturing Population of England (1833)
pp. 53, 55.
   9 Leonard Horner, the factory inspector, writing to his daughter in
1837, related how he visited one of these cotton masters, Mr. Horsfield, of
Hyde, who was then nearly 70 years of age. He " is said to be worth at
least £300,000 and can hardly write his own name. . . He took me to his
house, as he was going to dine, it being twelve o'clock. He had a piece
of cold beef and potatoes, no wine; he keeps one woman servant, and his
daughter, whom I saw, was not much in appearance above the maid. He
told me that at eighteen years of age he had not five shillings in the world,
beyond his weekly wages; that out of his wages of fifteen shillings, he
saved £28, bought a spinning jenny, and made £30 the first year. In 1831,
he made £24,000 of profit; he employs about 1,200 people. His is not a
solitary case; there are many not very unlike him in this part of the
country."—K. M. Lyell, Memoir of Leonard Horner (1890) Vol. I, p. 333.
   10 W. Cooke Taylor, Notes of a Tour in the Manufacturing Districts of
Lancashire (1842) p. 93.

more than fifteen thousand hands, the entire population of Bury being dependent on his mills. Such instances could be multiplied almost indefinitely,—Oldknow of Stockport, the Horrocks of Preston, the four Greg brothers with their mills at Wilmslow, Macclesfield, Lancaster and Bury, Fielden and Brotherton—but pre-eminent among these great industrialists, at least in the eyes of the contemporary world, was Richard Arkwright himself, the erstwhile maker of wigs, who in due course became Sir Richard, Sheriff of Derbyshire, and who died leaving an estate of half a million sterling. In Arkwright were combined those qualities which were essential to success in that expanding epoch,—profound technical skill and knowledge, astuteness and a certain cunning, financial acumen, and a courageous daring. But the characteristic that gained for him most readily the plaudits of admiring observers, was his iron will, the driving force that enabled him to impose the harsh discipline of the factory upon a heterogeneous collection of operatives who had hitherto followed only their own whims. " Some authors, indeed," said Ure, " have comprehended under the title *factory*, all extensive establishments wherein a number of people co-operate towards a common purpose of art . . . . But I conceive that this title, in its strictest sense, involves the idea of a vast automaton, composed of various mechanical and intellectual organs, acting in uninterrupted concert for the production of a common object, all of them being subordinated to a self-regulated moving force . . . . To devise and administer a successful code of factory discipline, suited to the necessities of factory diligence, was the Herculean enterprise, the noble achievement of Arkwright."[11]

As the mechanization of the industry increased in impetus, as the rewards of success grew ever greater, and the consequences of failure ever more disastrous,[12] there emerged a generation of masters who asked nothing more than that they should be left to carve their way to fortune undisturbed. With a few honourable exceptions, these men were ruthless, hard, and selfish. They wielded enormous power, they amassed riches, they made their country prosperous, but they knew no scruples, they acknowledged no claims of humanity, they cared little, if at all, for the welfare of the men, women and children who came crowding to their mills. It was this indifference to the needs of the operative classes that made State intervention necessary, and the story of factory legisla-

---

[11] A. Ure, *The Philosophy of Manufactures* (1835) pp. 13, 15.
[12] Gaskell averred that few rich men who entered the cotton industry made a success of it. " They trusted too much to others—too little to themselves." It was the poorer man, as a rule, who pushed his way to success " by a series of unceasing exertions."—P. Gaskell, *The Manufacturing Population of England* (1833) p. 45.

tion during these early years is the story of the gradual imposition
of regulations and controls upon those who conceived that regulation and control would involve them in ruin.

The decade after the invention of the spinning jenny was a
period of rapid transition, for the new machine, being small and
comparatively inexpensive, was ideally suited to domestic use.
Its motive power was derived from the large wheel which the
spinner, taking up his position within the rectangular frame, turned
with his right hand. The old spinning wheels, the Jersey and the
Brunswick, that had served so many generations, were cast aside,
and the jenny was installed in their place. " Cotton, cotton, cotton
was become the almost universal material for employment, the
hand-wheels . . . were all thrown into lumber-rooms, the yarn was
all spun on common jennies."[13]
This period of domestic mechanization[14] was, however, of short
duration, for Arkwright's water-frame, as the name suggests, was
best worked by the power of a stream or river. The age of the
factory system, organized on a capitalistic basis, was at hand. In
1771 Arkwright and his partners built their first mill at Cromford,
on the banks of the Derwent near Derby.[15] Two years later they
set up weaving shops in Derby, and in 1776 a third mill was established at Belper. Thereafter progress was rapid indeed. Along the
banks of the swiftly flowing streams that found their way to the
sea east, west and south from the Pennines, rose the factories, and
the remote valleys became centres of thriving industry.
In these rural fastnesses Nature supplied cheap power in
abundance, but since they were remote from the great centres of
population, labour was not so readily available. The machines
were small and simple, and standing low on the ground they could
easily be operated by children.[16] Many parents were reluctant to
send their boys and girls to labour in these mills,[17] and so it was
to the workhouses of London and other great cities that the em-

13 W. Radcliffe, *The Origin of Power-Loom Weaving* (1828) p. 61.
14 This was the golden age of the hand-loom weavers, who were now
provided with an abundant supply of yarn. " The mule-twist now coming
into vogue, for the warp, as well as weft, added to the water-twist and
common jenny yarns, with an increasing demand for every fabric the loom
could produce, put all hands in request of every age and description. The
fabrics made from wool or linen vanished, while the old loom-shops being
insufficient, every lumber room, even old barns, cart-houses, and out-
buildings of any description were repaired, windows broke through old
blank walls and all fitted up for loom-shops. This source of making room
being at length exhausted, new weavers' cottages with loom-shops rose up
in every direction; all immediately filled."—*Ibid*.
15 See A. Ure, *The Philosophy of Manufactures* (1835) p. 14.
16 P. Gaskell, *Artisans and Machinery* (1836) p. 137.
17 " Alfred," *The History of the Factory Movement* (1857) Vol. I, p. 16.

ployers looked to provide the hands they needed. The parish authorities, anxious as always to keep the poor-rate as low as possible, were only too glad to be relieved of the necessity of supporting pauper children, and they were not slow to embrace the opportunity of sending the young people in their charge as apprentices to serve in the cotton mills of the north.

These apprentices, "the cheapest raw material on the market,"[18] were conveyed in batches by coach, waggon or canal boat, to the scene of their labours, where they were lodged in the gaunt and comfortless prentice houses in the neighbourhood of the mills.[19] Forlorn and friendless, they were left entirely to the mercy of their masters, and their labour was often limited only by their exhaustion. In low, ill-ventilated rooms they were kept at their monotonous tasks sometimes for fourteen or fifteen hours a day, and when the mill worked throughout the night, as it frequently did, the day workers occupied the sleeping quarters vacated by the night shift, so that the beds were never cool. Little attention was paid to their education, their morals, or their religious training, and the strain and fatigue they suffered caused ill-health and physical deformity.[20]

---

[18] *Ibid.* p. 16.

[19] See Peel's evidence before the Committee appointed in 1816 to report on the condition of factory children. " Mr. Arkwright was the inventor of machinery, of great national importance, which was employed at a time when steam-power was little known in large buildings, which were erected in situations commanding considerable water-power, but generally in country places remote from inhabitants: to work these machines, the surplus population of large towns was sought after, and many thousands of parish children were supplied from London, Birmingham and other populous districts."—*Report of the Minutes of Evidence on the State of Children Employed in Manufactories* (1816) p. 132.

John Moss, formerly master of the notorious apprentice-house at Backbarrow, gave the Committee a vivid account of the hardships endured by the children (*ibid.* pp. 178-185); but perhaps the most savage indictment of the system was contained in the pamphlet *A Memoir of Robert Blincoe, an Orphan Boy; sent from the Workhouse of St. Pancras, London, to endure the Horrors of a Cotton Mill, through his infancy and youth, with a minute detail of his sufferings, being the first memoirs of the kind published.* (1832).

[20] " Children of very tender age are employed; many of them collected from the *workhouses* in *London* and *Westminster,* and transported in crowds, as apprentices to masters resident many hundred miles distant, where they serve unknown, unprotected and forgotten by those to whose care nature or the laws had consigned them. These children are usually too long confined to work in close rooms, often during the whole night: the air they breathe from the oil, etc., employed in the machinery, and other circumstances, is injurious; little regard is paid to their cleanliness, and frequent changes from a warm and dense to a cold and thin atmosphere, are predisposing causes to sickness and disability, and particularly to the epidemic fever which so generally is to be met with in these factories."—J. Aikin, *A Description of the Country from thirty to forty Miles round Manchester* (1795) p. 219.

Considerations of humanity carried little weight at a time when the acquisition of wealth was set in the scale against human suffering, but a series of epidemic fevers in the Lancashire mills came as a sharp and salutary reminder that the community as a whole might have to pay a heavy price for imposing on large numbers of the population working conditions in which such diseases could flourish and spread. In Peel's own mill at Ratcliff Bridge, near Manchester, where night-work was common,[21] and where conditions were particularly bad, an unusually severe outbreak of the " putrid fever " caused general alarm in the neighbourhood, and in 1795 Dr. Percival, with other medical men, formed the Manchester Board of Health, the purpose of which was to make a full inquiry into the question.[22] On 25th January, 1796, they published their findings and recommendations, in these memorable words:—

" It has already been stated that the objects of the present institution are to prevent the generation of diseases; to obviate the spreading of them by contagion; and to shorten the duration of those which exist, by affording the necessary aids and comforts to the sick. In the prosecution of this interesting undertaking, the Board have had their attention particularly directed to the large cotton factories established in the town and neighbourhood of Manchester; and they feel it a duty incumbent on them to lay before the public the result of their inquiries:—

1.—It appears that the children and others who work in the large cotton factories, are peculiarly disposed to be affected by the contagion of fever, and that when such infection is received, it is rapidly propagated, not only amongst those who are crowded together in the same apartments, but in the families and neighbourhoods to which they belong. 2.—The large factories are generally injurious to the constitution of those employed in them, even where no particular diseases prevail, from the close confinement which is enjoined, from the debilitating effects of hot or impure air, and from want of the active exercises which nature points out as essential in childhood and youth, to invigorate the system, and to fit our species for the employments and for the duties of manhood. 3.—The untimely labour of the night, and the protracted labour of the day, with respect to children, not only tends to diminish

---

21 " It should be known to the Committee," said Peel, " that at that time the profits arising from the machinery of Sir Richard Arkwright were so considerable, that it frequently happened . . . that the machinery was employed the whole four-and-twenty hours; but the Committee are not to understand from that the children were worked twenty-four hours."— *Peel's Committee* (1816) p. 139.

22 See B. L. Hutchins and A. Harrison, *A History of Factory Legislation* (1926) pp. 7-9.

future expectations as to the general sum of life and industry, by impairing the strength and destroying the vital stamina of the rising generation, but it too often gives encouragement to idleness, extravagance and profligacy in the parents, who, contrary to the order of nature, subsist by the oppression of their offspring. 4.—It appears that the children employed in factories are generally debarred from all opportunities of education, and from moral or religious instruction. 5.—From the excellent regulations which subsist in several cotton factories, it appears, that many of these evils may, in a considerable degree, be obviated; we are therefore warranted by experience, and are assured we shall have the support of the liberal proprietors of these factories, in proposing an application for Parliamentary aid (if other methods appear not likely to effect the purpose,) to establish a general system of laws for the wise, humane, and equal government of all such works."[23]

Sir Robert Peel was sufficiently impressed by the urgency of the problem to introduce a bill in 1802. "The house in which I have a concern," he said, "gave employment at one time to near one thousand children of this description [e.g. apprentices]. Having other pursuits, it was not often in my power to visit the factories, but whenever such visits were made, I was struck with the uniform appearance of bad health, and in many cases, stinted growth of the children; the hours of labour were regulated by the interest of the overseer, whose remuneration depending on the quantity of work done, he was often induced to make the poor children work excessive hours, and to stop their complaints by trifling bribes. Finding our own factories under such management, and learning that the like practice prevailed in other parts of the kingdom where similar machinery was in use, the children being much over-worked, and often little or no regard paid to cleanliness and ventilation in the buildings; having the assistance of Dr. Percival and other eminent medical gentlemen of Manchester, together with some distinguished characters both in and out of Parliament, I brought in a bill in the Forty-second year of the King, for the regulation of factories containing such parish apprentices."[24]

Some pressure was brought upon Peel by people who, in his opinion, were governed more by humanity than by a knowledge of the business, to extend the scope of the measure beyond the apprentices, so that it might operate " through every cottage in the country." He resisted their persuasion, threatening to drop the whole matter unless he were allowed to have his way, and thereafter his proposals encountered surprisingly little opposition.[25] On 22nd

23 *Peel's Committee* (1816) pp. 139-140.
24 *Ibid.* pp. 132-133.
25 The debate is not even recorded in *Hansard*.

June, 1802, the Health and Morals of Apprentices Act became law.[26]

The Act was not limited to establishments employing apprentices, for it applied to all mills and factories in Great Britain and Ireland where three or more apprentices, or twenty or more other persons were engaged at one time. In all such establishments the walls and ceilings were to be washed at least twice a year with quick-lime and water, and the windows were to be sufficient to secure adequate ventilation.[27] If any infectious disease occurred in the factory the visitors appointed by the magistrates were empowered to call in a physician, who was to make periodical reports on the progress of the disorder. The medical fees were to be paid by the mill-owner.[28]

The provisions governing the treatment of apprentices afford some indication of the conditions under which they had been compelled to work. No apprentice was to be employed for more than twelve hours a day, exclusive of the time allowed for meals, and from 1st June, 1803, night work (between the hours of 9 p.m. and 6 a.m.) was forbidden.[29] Some provision was made for general welfare, for education, and for religious instruction. Every apprentice was to be supplied with two complete suits of clothing, one suit being delivered each year.[30] Separate sleeping apartments were to be provided for males and females, and apprentices were not to sleep more than two in a bed.[31] During the first four years of their apprenticeship they were to receive daily instruction, during working hours, in reading, writing and arithmetic, " or either of them, according to the age and abilities of such apprentices." A discreet and proper person, paid by the mill-owner, was to be engaged as a teacher; and a room was to be set apart for lessons.[32] Every Sunday, for at least one hour, the apprentices were to be instructed and examined in the principles of the Christian religion. If their parents were members of the Church of England they were to be taken at least once a year to be examined by the rector or vicar, and between the ages of fourteen and eighteen they were to be prepared for confirmation.[33]

---

[26] The full title was " An Act for the Preservation of the Health and Morals of Apprentices and others employed in Cotton and other Mills, and Cotton and other Factories." 42 Geo. III, c. 73.

[27] Sec. 2.

[28] Sec. 10.

[29] Sec. 4. In mills containing between 1,000 and 1,500 spindles, however, night work was permitted until 25th December, 1803, and in larger premises it was allowed to continue until 25th June, 1804. (Sec. 5).

[30] Sec. 3.

[31] Sec. 7.

[32] Sec. 6.

[33] Sec. 8.

Although the mill-owners were " strictly enjoined and required to pay due attention to and act in strict conformity to the said rules and regulations," some doubt was entertained as to the likelihood of their obeying so pious an exhortation. The magistrates were therefore required, at their midsummer sessions, to appoint two persons, one a Justice, and the other a clergyman of the established church, " not interested in, or in any way connected with any such mills or factories," to act as visitors. These visitors were invested with " full power and authority from time to time throughout the year, to enter into and inspect any such mill or factory, at any time of the day, or during the hours of employment, as they shall think fit." They were to make periodical written reports to quarter sessions of the conditions of the mills, and of the extent to which the Act was observed.[34] The penalty for obstructing them was a fine of not less than £5 and not exceeding £10.[35]

A register of factories was established, and the owners were required to enter particulars in a book kept for the purpose by the Clerk of the Peace.[36] Copies of the Act were to be hung in some conspicuous place where they would be accessible to the operatives.[37] The penalty for disobedience to the Act was a fine of not less than 40s. and not exceeding £5, half of which was to be paid to the informer, and half to the overseers of the poor.[38]

It is not easy to assess the significance of the Health and Morals of Apprentices Act. The objective, it is clear, was strictly limited, for, so far as the regulations concerning apprentices were concerned, its purpose was to remedy a precise and ascertained evil, in much the same way as the Act for the better Regulation of Chimney Sweepers and their Apprentices (1788) had aimed at improving the conditions of the climbing boys. In its wider application it was a health measure pure and simple, designed in this respect also to deal with a specific problem, that of epidemic fevers in the mills. What is really remarkable in this connection is that it applied to all mills employing more than twenty operatives, irrespective of whether apprentices were included.

This early example of State intervention in private enterprise does not appear to have aroused any uneasiness in the minds of those who were most closely affected. This may have been due to the fact that the measure was so narrowly limited in its scope; or the absence of controversy may have been attributable to the

---

[34] Sec. 9.
[35] Sec. 11.
[36] Sec. 14.
[37] Sec. 12.
[38] Sec. 13.

scattered nature of the industry and the consequent lack of organization among the owners. Crude in conception and unscientific in design as it was, the Act nevertheless contained some features of interest, for it showed that even in these days, when the problem of factory labour was only just beginning to emerge, it was recognized that certain fundamentals were inherent in any system of control—the regulation of working hours, the provision of education, facilities for inspection, and some method of publicity.

The Act was fore-doomed to failure, and it was in fact, totally ineffective. It would have been difficult in any circumstances to exercise any real control when the factories were so remote and scattered, but the inadequate system of inspection by a body of unpaid amateurs made it quite impossible to enforce the regulations. Some attempt was indeed made at first to inspect the mills, but the visitors performed their duties in a most perfunctory manner.[39] They had no incentive to carry out what must have been an onerous and difficult duty, and the owners were at pains to exclude them as far as it lay within their power to do so.[40] The

---

[39] Their reports, of which the following is typical, afford illuminating evidence of this. (*Peel's Committee*, 1816, p. 187).

Hundred of Scarsdale, December 20, 1802.

Gentlemen,

In pursuance of your appointment, to inspect the Cotton Mills in the Hundred of Scarsdale, we have visited those at Pleasley, belonging to Messrs. Hollins and Company, containing sixty apprentices, all girls, and employing about 240 other hands.

In our inquiries we closely followed the requisitions of the Act, and in every particular required by it found the most careful observance of its injunctions.

On the whole we are satisfied, from the remarkable healthful and clean appearance of the apprentices, and very wholesome conditions of this mill, and from the inspection of the domestic rules, and the writing and work in the school, that the great objects of the Act, the health, morals and instruction of the apprentices, have here been long and successfully attended to.

We are, Gentlemen,
Your obedient Servants,
Jos. Jebb.
Edward Otter.

To His Majesty's Justices of the Peace
 for the County of Derby, in their
 Quarter Sessions assembled.
A. L. Maynard,
Clk. Pac.

[40] One of the reasons adduced by the owners was the risk that manufacturing secrets might be revealed to their rivals. James Pattison, a silk manufacturer of Congleton, mentioned this to Peel's Committee (pp. 78-79).

"Would not the visiting inspectors be objectionable amongst manufacturers as tending to expose any particular improvement in the manufacture that you or any other person might possess?—I should think so, certainly; at a particular period, we were possessed of what we considered a secret, and we were very anxious to keep it as secret as possible, and very studiously kept strangers out of the mill." See also the evidence of Frederick Robinson. (*Ibid.* p. 228).

result was that before very long the visitors abandoned the unequal struggle, and any semblance of external control disappeared.[41].

In many parts of the country, it seems, the very existence of the Act was unknown. David Evans, a barrister, and stipendiary magistrate of Manchester, confessed that he was aware that an act had been passed to regulate the factories, but he had not had the curiosity to read it. He knew of no instance of the penalties being enforced, and the mills were certainly not visited—he himself had entered them occasionally, but only " to show them to a friend, as part of the curiosities of the town."[42]

It was not very long, however, before the problem of juvenile labour in the textile industry assumed an entirely different complexion. The era of the apprentices was rapidly passing away. A new motive power transformed the character of the factories, and in so doing threw into high relief a new social problem of much greater extent, and of unprecedented gravity.

[41] See the evidence of Henry Hollins, owner of the Pleasley mill, (*Peel's Committee,* 1816, p. 187) and of Richard Arkwright, son of the inventor, who said, " The Act has not been followed up, with respect to the visiting of magistrates, for these thirteen years. I think they visited my mills at Cromford twice." (*Ibid.* p. 227).

[42] *Ibid.* p. 319. James Moss, too, declared that he had never heard of the Act. (*Ibid.* p. 183).

CHAPTER 2

THE FREE CHILDREN

WHEN JAMES WATT took out a patent, in the year 1781, to convert the energy of steam to rotary power, a fresh vista opened up before the textile industry. The new invention was first utilized in a spinning mill at Papplewick in 1785; it was introduced in Manchester in 1789, in Bolton and Glasgow in 1792, and thereafter its progress was rapid.[1] No longer was it necessary for the factories to be established in lonely valleys, where they relied on the seasonal vagaries of the streams for their motive-power —they could move to the towns, where they were nearer to the markets and where a more abundant supply of labour was available. " Domestic manufactures," said Greg, the Bury mill-owner, writing in 1831, " are almost extinct. The population which was formerly scattered throughout the country is now congregated into large towns, and is impressed with a distinct character."[2] There was a considerable influx of workers to the new mills,[3] and in Lancashire, Yorkshire and the midlands the urban population increased at an unprecedented rate, as the mean dwellings hastily thrown up to house the workers sprawled in every direction under the shadow of the factory chimneys.[4]

The employment of steam as the motive power made it possible to increase considerably the size of the factories. " As soon as the steam loom was brought into operation, which was in

---

[1] G. W. Daniels, *The Early English Cotton Industry* (1920) p. 81. P. Mantoux, *The Industrial Revolution in the Eighteenth Century* (1928) p. 342.

[2] W. R. Greg, *An Enquiry into the State of the Manufacturing Population, and the Causes and Cures of the .Evils therein existing* (1831) p. 3.

[3] " The rapid growth of the cotton manufacture has attracted hither operatives from every part of the kingdom, and Ireland has poured forth the most destitute of her hordes to supply the constantly increasing demand for labour. . . The Irish have taught the labouring classes of this country a pernicious lesson. . . They have discovered, with the savage, what is the minimum of the means of life, upon which existence may be prolonged."—J. P. Kay, *The Moral and Physical Condition of the Working Classes employed in the Cotton Manufacture in Manchester* (1832) p. 21.

[4] See Appendix. In 1836 Leonard Horner described Rochdale as " a pretty country town, in a pretty situation "—(K. M. Lyell, *Memoir of Leonard Horner* (1890) Vol. I, p. 330)—but a foreign visitor painted a somewhat grimmer picture of Leeds, which must long have been typical of the manufacturing towns. " Le dimanche est le seul jour à Leeds où l'on puisse apercevoir le soleil. Dans la semaine et tant que fument les cheminées des manufactures, l'air, les eaux, le sol, tout est imprégné de charbon, les rues, couvertes de cette poussière noire, resemblent aux galeries d'une mine."—Léon Faucher, *Etudes sur l'Angleterre* (1856) p. 406.

1806, many of the first mills were either greatly enlarged, or abandoned for larger buildings, raised and fitted up for the spinning and weaving processes. Compared with the old buildings, these are much more comfortable and healthy for the workpeople. The rooms are much loftier, generally of large proportions, with numerous windows, so arranged as to afford good ventilation."[5] Enormous sums were spent in providing these new buildings, and equipping them with the necessary plant. Holland Hoole calculated that the cost of a cotton factory employing a thousand hands, built " upon the fire-proof principle," was £100,000,[6] and Orrell's great factory near Stockport, a model of its kind, with its 1100 power looms housed on six floors, in apartments 280 feet long and 50 feet wide, was stated to have cost £85,000.[7]

Charles Babbage, Lucasian Professor of Mathematics at Cambridge, believed that the increased size of manufacturing establishments was inherent in the very nature of the industrial process. " The great competition introduced by machinery," he said, " and the application of the principle of the subdivision of labour, render it continually necessary for each producer to be on the watch, to discover improved methods by which the cost of the article he manufactures may be reduced; and, with this in view, it is of great importance to know the precise expense of every process. . . . When (from the peculiar nature of the produce of each manufactory) the number of processes into which it is most advantageous to divide it is ascertained, as well as the number of individuals to be employed, then all other manufactories which do not employ a direct multiple of this number, will produce the article at a greater cost. . . . Hence arises one of the causes of the great size of manufacturing establishments, which have increased with the progress of civilisation."[8]

---

[5] W. Carpenter, *Machinery as it affects the Industrial Classes* (1844) p. 42.

[6] H. Hoole, *A Letter in Defence of the Cotton Factories* (1832) p. 5.

[7] A. Ure, *The Cotton Manufacture of Great Britain* (1836) Vol. I, p. 314. Ure gives some interesting details concerning the mill built by Fairbairn for Messrs. Bailey at Stalybridge:—

Buildings	... ...	...	£30,000
Engine house and boiler house		...	£3,000
2 steam engines, 110 h.p. each		...	£8,800
Steam pipes for heating	...	...	£2,400
40,000 mule spindles	...	...	£11,500
Preparation machines		...	£12,000
1,280 power looms ...	...	...	£18,000
Contingencies	...	...	£2,300
			£88,000

(*Ibid.* p. 316).

[8] C. Babbage, *On the Economy of Machinery and Manufactures* (1832) pp. 164, 172-173.

One of the advantages attendant upon the transfer of the textile industry from remote rural situations to the towns was the easing of the labour problem. It was no longer necessary, even if it had been possible, to rely on the labour of parish apprentices, for the native children, unrestricted by any measure of legislative control, were available in large numbers to perform those functions that were essential in the newly-developed processes. Even under the domestic system children had been freely employed by their parents in spinning and weaving, and the introduction of machinery created a still greater demand for their services. Some of them were employed as doffers, to collect the cotton as it came out of the carding machine; some as scavengers, whose duty it was to sweep the dust and flue (the fine particles of cotton) from under the machines; but the majority were piecers, who tied together the threads that broke during the stretch,[9] when the carriage with its revolving spindles moved away from the rollers.

The work of children and adults was closely integrated,[10] the running of the machines depending absolutely on the nimble fingers of the boys and girls, who, as a rule, were employed and paid by the adult operatives themselves. During the early years they had been engaged in large numbers because they were more amenable to the discipline of the factory,[11] but as the improved design of machinery simplified the various processes they took the place of adults in many departments of the manufacture.[12] It was this rigid interdependence of children and adults that made it so difficult to reform industrial conditions during the early years of the 19th century. No disinterested observer could have denied that young people were being grossly over-worked, but it was considered

---

9 " Children are soon very dexterous at connecting broken ends with prepared cotton at the rollers, their small fingers being more active and endued with a quicker sensibility of feeling than those of grown persons; and it is wonderful to see with what dispatch they can raise a system, connect threads, and drop it again into work almost instantaneously."— J. Aikin, *A Description of the Country from thirty to forty Miles round Manchester* (1795) p. 173.

10 " The old and the young are essentially necessary to each other, and form a whole, and make a full and beneficial division of labour."— V. Royle, *The Factory System Defended* (1833) p. 23.

11 See A. E. Dobbs, *Education and Social Movements, 1700-1850* (1919) p. 131.

12 " In proportion as machinery is improved in simplicity, and becomes more uniform in its action or motion, a lower class of labour is required for its management; and as women and children are thus enabled to produce those fabrics, which it formerly required all the ingenuity, skill, and labour of the very best workmen to furnish, the latter are set at liberty from the mere drudgery of manufacturing employment and are at leisure to engage in those more difficult and delicate operations, which the perpetual multiplication of machinery renders necessary.—J. Kennedy, *Miscellaneous Papers* (1849) pp. 43-44. See also A. Ure, *The Philosophy of Manufactures* (1835) p. 23.

impossible to limit their hours without either limiting the hours of the adults in like measure, or throwing the whole industry out of gear. " Children from nine to twelve years of age," said Dr. Gaskell, " are now become part of the staple hands, and are consequently subjected at this tender period to all the mischiefs incident to the condition of the older work-people."[13]

Vast sums of money had been invested in factories and machinery; vast fortunes were to be won by those who seized the golden opportunity; and it is not therefore surprising that the wheels were kept turning as long as possible each day. " Much labour and ingenuity and expense being incurred in the invention and construction of machinery," it was said, " the owner of a costly improvement naturally wishes to employ it as far as he can to his individual advantage."[14]

For this reason it was customary to work extremely long hours, adults and children being often confined to the mills for thirteen, fourteen, and even fifteen hours a day, with only short periods of intermission for meals. So great was the demand for juvenile labour that very young children were frequently employed, and the close confinement in over-heated rooms had disastrous results. The condition of the free children, indeed, approximated very closely to that of the apprentices, and in 1815 Sir Robert Peel was persuaded to introduce a bill to afford them some measure of protection. " Diffident of my own abilities to originate legislative measures," he declared, " I should have contented myself with the one alluded to,[15] had I not perceived, that, owing to the present use of steam power in factories, the Forty-second of the King is likely to become a dead letter. Large buildings are now erected, not only as formerly on the banks of streams, but in the midst of populous towns, and instead of parish apprentices being sought after, the children of the surrounding poor are preferred, whose masters being free from the operation of the former Act of Parliament are subjected to no limitation of time in the prosecution of their business, though children are frequently admitted there to work thirteen to fourteen hours per day, at the tender age of seven years, and even in some cases still younger. . . . Unless some parliamentary interference takes place, the benefits of the Apprentice Bill will soon be entirely lost, the practice of employing parish apprentices will cease, their places will be wholly supplied by other children, between whom and their masters no permanent contract is likely to exist, and for whose good treatment there will not be the slightest security. Such indiscriminate and unlimited employ-

---

13 P. Gaskell, *Artisans and Machinery* (1836) p. 66.
14 J. Kennedy, *Miscellaneous Papers* (1849) p. 42.
15 *e.g.*, the Act of 1802.

ment of the poor . . . will be attended with effects to the rising generation so serious and alarming, that I cannot contemplate them without dismay, and thus that great effort of British ingenuity, whereby the machinery of our manufactures has been brought to such perfection, instead of being a blessing to the nation, will be converted into the bitterest curse.

Gentlemen, if parish apprentices were formerly deemed worthy of the care of Parliament, I trust you will not withhold from the unprotected children of the present day an equal measure of mercy."[16]

These memorable and prophetic words were inspired by one who must ever occupy an honoured place in the great company of reformers, Robert Owen, the first of the humanitarian philosophers whose untiring zeal supplied the impetus that was the essential if not the sole ingredient of legislative regulation.[17] Owen, who had been engaged in the spinning industry since 1789, when he employed three operatives in one small room,[18] had, with his partners, purchased from David Dale the great mill at New Lanark, on the falls of the Clyde.[19] Dale was an enlightened master, his 500 apprentices being well fed, clothed and lodged, but even so, they were worked thirteen hours a day, including an hour and a half for meals. Owen, convinced that such a system was injurious, reduced the hours to twelve, and fixed the minimum age for admission to his mills at ten. Schools were established for children from three years of age and upwards, and here they were not merely taught the rudiments of reading, writing and arithmetic, but were encouraged to play, and to dance to the music of the pipe.[20]

Scouting the idea that a reduction of hours would involve the

---

16 *Peel's Committee* (1816) p. 133.

17 " It will for ever remain creditable to the judgment of the first Sir Robert Peel and of Mr. Owen, that they boldly raised the question,— whether a system which sacrificed man to aggregated productive power, health and morals to mammon, ought, unimpeded, to establish its iron sway over hundreds of thousands of human beings."—" Alfred," *The History of the Factory Movement* (1857) Vol. I, p. 41.

18 S. J. Chapman, *The Lancashire Cotton Industry* (1904) p. 60.

19 In 1799.

20 Owen also opened shops on the co-operative principle for his work-people, and tried to provide the adults, too, with opportunities for a wider culture. His efforts were not always well received, as Adam Bogle, the owner of a neighbouring mill, testified. Many operatives from New Lanark, he said, applied to him for employment. Upon enquiring the reason for this, he was told " that there had been a number of new regulations introduced. That they had got a number of dancing-masters, a fiddler, a band of music, that there were drills and exercises, and that they were dancing together till they were more fatigued than if they were working."—*Peel's Committee* (1816) p. 167.

manufacturers in financial loss,[21] Owen sturdily affirmed that the regulation of children's labour, the fixing of a minimum age for employment, and the provision of education would be of incalculable benefit, not only to the young people concerned, but to the community as a whole.

Peel was sufficiently impressed with the wisdom of these views to introduce, on 6th June, 1815, a bill[22] the purpose of which was to amend and extend the Act of 1802. It was to apply to all cotton, woollen, flax and other mills employing twenty or more persons under eighteen years of age. No child was to be employed under the age of ten,[23] and no person under eighteen was to work more than ten and a half hours a day, exclusive of half an hour for breakfast, an hour for dinner, and half an hour for instruction, making in all twelve and a half hours. To prevent working at night this labour was to be performed between five o'clock in the morning and nine o'clock at night, but if the machinery was stopped owing to the need for repairs, or by other unavoidable accident, the time lost might be made up by working not more than two additional hours each day.

During the first four years after their admission to the factory children were to receive instruction for half an hour each working day, in reading, writing, and arithmetic. A discreet and proper person was to be appointed and paid by the mill-owner, and a suitable room was to be set aside as a class-room.

The provision for inspection shows that even at this early date it was coming to be recognized that the appointment by the Justices of unpaid visitors was wholly ineffective.[24] It was therefore proposed that the former system should be abandoned, and that in future the magistrates should appoint as visitor the Clerk of the Peace or his deputy, or other properly qualified persons, who were to receive " a full and adequate compensation for their trouble and expenses " from the county rates. These visitors were to have the same powers and responsibilities as their predecessors under the Act of 1802, but, unlike them, they were to be paid.

Thus Peel's bill anticipated the trend of future legislation in one of its most important particulars. But this was not all, for

---

[21] He calculated that the price of the finished product would not be increased by more than a farthing a yard.—*Peel's Committee* (1816) p. 90.
[22] *Parl. Papers* (1814-15) II, pp. 735, 739.
[23] The age was to be ascertained by the register of baptisms or other satisfactory evidence.
[24] In his article " A Historical Survey of Factory Inspection in Great Britain " (*International Labour Review*, November, 1938) D. H. Blelloch suggests that since the apprentices were paupers the Act of 1802 rightly placed the onus of supervising their working conditions on the Justices. This was doubtless true, but it must be remembered that the Justices exercised a wide range of local functions, since there was nobody else to whom the central government could turn.

an attempt was made to secure that the regulations would be obeyed by imposing on the owners the obligation of depositing with the Clerk of the Peace each year a declaration in the following terms—

" I, A.B., do hereby Certify, THAT no Boy or Girl has been employed in any Mill, [Manufactory, *or* Building, *as the case may be*] during the preceding year, who was not Ten years of age; nor has any Persons under Eighteen been employed more than Ten Hours and a Half, exclusive of Two Hours, which were duly allowed for Meals and Instruction, except as this Act directs: And I also certify, That Instruction has been provided for the said Boys and Girls, according to the directions of an Act made in the Fifty-fifth year of the reign of His present Majesty. . . . I further certify, That the Mill, [Manufactory *or* Building] has been ventilated and white-washed, in conformity to an Act made in the Forty-second year of the reign of His present Majesty, intituled, ' An Act for the Preservation of the Health and Morals of Apprentices, and others, employed in Cotton and other Mills, and Cotton and other Factories.' "

The bill was not introduced until late in the session, and Peel, anxious to conciliate the mill-owners by giving them the opportunity of considering the proposals in some detail, did not press matters. The measure was accordingly dropped, and yielding to the solicitations of the owners, Peel moved, on 3rd April, 1816, for a Select Committee to consider the whole question of factory children.

The Select Committee, under the chairmanship of Sir Robert Peel himself, sat from 25th April to 18th June, during which time it examined forty-seven witnesses. Of these, eight were medical men, not all of whom had first-hand experience of factory conditions; and twenty-nine were manufacturers, the majority being engaged in the cotton trade in Scotland and Lancashire. There was nobody to present the views of the operatives.

As might have been expected, there was a sharp division of opinion concerning the effects of factory labour on children. The doctors were quite unanimous in declaring that the close confinement and the long hours must inevitably result in stunted growth and physical deformity. Dr. Baillie averred that nobody could be employed for thirteen hours a day without injury to health, and that children between the ages of seven and ten should certainly work less than ten hours. Children of seven, he thought, might perhaps work four or five hours a day; during the next two years, six or seven hours; thereafter they might labour for ten hours, but

never more.[25]   Sir Gilbert Blane agreed, observing that he had
noticed "the natural appetency of all young creatures to loco-
motive exercise, and the open air," the deprivation of which would
cause "rickets and mesenteric obstructions, weakness of body, and
imbecility of mind."[26]   Dr. Kinder Wood thought that lack of
adequate ventilation, and high temperatures in the mills were
exceedingly prejudicial, producing feverish disorders and general
debility.[27]

Archibald Buchanan, manager of Messrs. Finlay's cotton
mills in Glasgow, did not share these opinions.   Children aged six,
he maintained, could work from 6 a.m. to 7.30 p.m., with a break
of an hour and a half for meals, without hardship.   Parents were
most anxious to secure their admission to the mills, for the work
was light—"little or nothing with the young children, they have
merely to attend there."[28]

Adam Bogle, of Glasgow, expressed the belief that was
entertained by most manufacturers, when he said that if the hours
of work were reduced the output would be reduced in exact proportion.[29]   This, it was held, would expose the home industry to
unfair competition from foreign countries where no restrictions
were enforced, and much business would be lost.   Wages, too,
would necessarily be lowered, and this would inflict hardship and
suffering on both children and parents.

Robert Owen, recognizing that the work of children could not
be divorced from that of adults, suggested that the most satisfactory
way to improve their conditions would be to employ them in
double sets—"to be instructed one half the day, and the other
half to be initiated into the manufactories by parties employing
two sets of children in the day, on the same principle that two sets
of children were employed when proprietors thought it their
interest to work day and night."[30]   Peel agreed, though he thought
the practice would be attended with a little more expense, but
the other owners refused to entertain the suggestion, alleging that
there were not sufficient children available, that wages would be
decreased, and that it would be necessary to dismiss all those to
whom the regulation applied.[31]   "In the estimation of these mill-
owners," said Kydd,[32] "the beginning and the end of the duties
of a government consisted in protecting their property, and

25 *Peel's Committee* (1816) p. 29.
26 *Ibid*. p. 45.
27 *Ibid*. p. 192.
28 *Ibid*. pp. 6-7.
29 *Ibid*. p. 166.
30 *Ibid*. p. 21.
31 *Ibid*. p. 169.
32 " Alfred," *The History of the Factory Movement* (1857) Vol. I, p. 65.

allowing them to treat all those under their control as to themselves seemed best."

No report was issued by the Committee, but during the course of the discussion Peel intimated that he was prepared to make certain concessions. He proposed that the minimum age for employment should be reduced from ten to nine; that the hours of attendance should be increased to thirteen, inclusive of an hour and a half for meals; that restrictions should be limited to children between nine and sixteen; and that Inspectors should only be appointed by the Justices on complaint being made.[33]

On 19th February, 1818, Peel introduced his motion for the new bill,[34] which came up for its second reading on 23rd February. Applying only to cotton mills, it incorporated the amendments that he had already promised. The provisions concerning inspection were obviously designed to placate the mill-owners, for the machinery set up by the Act of 1802 was abolished, and it was now proposed that visitors should be appointed by the Justices only when some specific complaint had been registered.[35] If it appeared that the complaint was justified, the Justices were authorized to appoint visitors with full powers of inspection. They were to make their report to Quarter Sessions, and were to be compensated from the county rate.

When he brought in the bill of 1802, said Peel, he had been an advocate of free labour. He had not changed his views in this respect, but he could not think that little children, who had not a will of their own, could be called free labourers. He now proposed, therefore, that no child under the age of nine[36] should be employed in the cotton factories, and that until they reached the age of sixteen children should not be allowed to work more than eleven hours a day, exclusive of one and a half hours for meals. It was his intention, if possible, he continued, to prevent the recurrence of such a misfortune as that which had recently taken place—he alluded to the fourteen poor children who were lately burnt in the night in a cotton factory. He knew that the

---

[33] *Peel's Committee* (1816) p. 133.

[34] *Parl. Papers* (1818) I, pp. 87, 91.

[35] For a defence of this provision see the pamphlet *Answers to Certain Objections made to Sir Robert Peel's Bill* (1819) p. 17—" Sir Robert Peel has studiously endeavoured to avoid giving occasion for complaint . . . for the Bill contains an especial provision, that no inspection of a factory shall take place, but on information, verified by the oaths of two credible witnesses, that the law has been violated; and it further provides that the visit shall not be repeated, unless the allegation so made shall have been duly substantiated."

[36] The age was still to be ascertained by the register of baptisms or other satisfactory evidence.

iniquitous practice of working children at a time when their masters were in bed too often took place.[37]

Despite the opposition of Philips and Finlay the bill was read a second time, and when the debate was resumed on 27th April, 1818, Peel justified his proposals at considerable length, reminding the House that the Act of 1802 had long been a dead letter, largely because the changed conditions in the factories, due to the introduction of steam-power, had raised problems of an entirely different nature. The great majority of factory children were now congregated in towns, where they were totally unprotected, and subjected to excessive hours of work. Many petitions had been presented urging that reforms should be introduced, and if the House questioned the necessity of further legislation, he would suggest that the best procedure would be to ascertain the true conditions, by the examination of witnesses upon the spot.

Lord Stanley raised his voice in protest. The question, he said, concerned not merely the children, but the interests of the cotton manufacture, and the interests of the empire at large. In former days abuses had existed,—that was generally admitted— but the present measure was much more than a mere extension of the Act of 1802, for it was designed to protect all persons. Its professed object was to interfere between the parent and the child, the master and the juvenile work-person, and to hold out to the public that those whose duty and whose interest dictated affection and care to those about them, were indifferent to the first moral obligations they were bound to consider. The bill was an interference with free labour. It would destroy the cotton trade and, by compelling the masters to dismiss from their employment those who were subject to its restrictions, it would involve the children in hardship and their parents in ruin. The owners, who had had no opportunity of stating their case, desired to express their views, and asked that they should be represented by counsel. Lord Lascelles joined Stanley in warning the House that the precedent they were now proposing to establish was fraught with danger. " Be cautious what you are about," he pleaded, " as, if you interfere now in this instance with the regulation of labour, you will find it difficult to find out when to stop."[38]

The case that Peel had made out, however, was too strong even for so sustained an opposition, and by 91 votes to 26[39] the bill was passed and sent to the Lords, where it was introduced by Lord Kenyon on 7th May, 1818.[40]   In the Upper House progress

[37] *Hansard* (1818) XXXVII, 581-582.
[38] *Hansard* (1818) XXXVIII, 342-352.
[39] *Ibid*. 371.
[40] *Ibid*. 548.

was slow. The Earl of Lauderdale pressed for another inquiry, alleging that the evidence given before Peel's Committee two years ago " was perfectly unfit for being made the foundation of any legislative proceedings."[41] After a somewhat desultory debate it was finally agreed that a committee of the whole House should hear the evidence afresh, and that the parties interested should be represented by counsel.

The Lords' Committee, under the chairmanship of Kenyon, opened its proceedings on 20th May, 1818, the hearing being completed on 5th June. For the first time witnesses both for and against the bill were examined, cross-examined and re-examined; but although this improved procedure helped to establish an accurate survey of the whole problem, no useful purpose was served by the second inquiry, for little fresh evidence was adduced, and no report was made. Perhaps the most striking aspect of the investigation was the attitude adopted by the medical men who spoke on behalf of the manufacturers in opposition to the bill. Their determination to yield nothing to those who advocated reform involved them in statements that were little short of ludicrous. Dr. Holme, of Manchester, for instance, said that his attention had been first called to the condition of the factories by the increase of contagious fever in 1796. The infection was thought to be due to double sets of workers being employed, and " propagated chiefly by the Children of one Set sleeping in the Beds which had been recently occupied by the other," but his inspection had convinced him that night workers were not more unhealthy than day workers. He was not prepared to admit that even twenty-three hours of work each day would be inconsistent with health, unless it appeared on examination that injury had, in fact, been sustained, and he was unable to form any opinion, independently of the facts, as to how long a child should be allowed to work.[42]

Dr. Whatton thought that employment involving twelve hours' standing each day might be harmful for a child of six, but not for a child of ten, for " the Labour is so moderate it can scarcely be called Labour at all." He had no idea how many hours a child should be employed, but he was sure that spinning was not unhealthy, and that it might be carried on for more than twelve hours a day by a child under sixteen.[43] Dr. Hardie affirmed that the inhalation of cotton flue was not injurious " because the daily Expectoration throws off the cotton; there is no Accumulation takes place in the Lungs ";[44] while Dr. Wilson, who thought a

[41] *Ibid.* 579.
[42] *Lords' Committee* (1818) pp. 7, 20.
[43] *Ibid.* pp. 30-35.
[44] *Ibid.* p. 50.

lad of fifteen might well be expected to work twelve hours a day,. exclusive of meals, could not be prevailed upon to admit that recreation and amusement were necessary if young people were to maintain their health.[45]

The Lords' Committee accomplished little but to impose further delay on the progress of the bill, and it was not, in fact,. until 2nd July, 1819, that the measure finally passed into law. The Act to make further Provisions for the Regulation of Cotton Mills and Factories, and for the better Preservation of the Health of young Persons employed therein,[46] provided that after 1st January, 1820, no child should be employed in a cotton mill until he had attained the full age of nine years.[47] No person under the age of sixteen was to be employed in the spinning of cotton, or in cleaning or repairing the mill or the machinery, for more than twelve hours in any one day exclusive of the time allowed for meals, and such labour was to be performed between 5 a.m. and 9 p.m., thus making night work illegal for the protected class.[48] Half an hour was to be allowed each day for breakfast, and one hour, between 11 a.m. and 2 p.m., for dinner.[49] If in mills situated upon streams of water, time was lost owing to want of due supply or to excess of water, it was lawful to extend the hours of daily labour " after the Rate on one additional Hour per Day, until such lost time shall have been made good, but no longer."[50]

The ceilings and the interior walls of the mill were to be washed with quick-lime and water twice a year;[51] a copy of the Act, or a full and true abstract, was to be hung in a conspicuous part of the mill;[52] while the penalty for each offence was to be a minimum of £10 and a maximum of £20, half of which was to be paid to the informer and half to the overseers of the poor. Informations were to be laid within three calendar months of the commission of the offence.[53]

" The bill was passed, and the world called it mercy;" said the Quarterly Review,[54] " and mercy it was by comparison with the recognition of unlimited power over the labour of the children; but it was still a most inadequate measure. The law still *allowed*

[45] *Ibid.* p. 58.
[46] 59 Geo. III, c. 66.
[47] Sec. 1.
[48] Sec. 2.
[49] Sec. 3.
[50] Sec. 4.
[51] Sec. 5.
[52] Sec 6.
[53] Sec. 7.
[54] Vol. 57 (1836) p. 408.

seventy-two hours of weekly toil, amid all the grease and gas, and noise, and filthy atmósphere; and we may be assured that what the law allowed, the masters took." The Act was admittedly defective and it remained a dead letter, but it established the fundamental principle of State interference with free labour, as the *laissez-faire* school realized only too well. " The principle of that act (1802) was liable to little objection," it was said, " because those whom it protected had literally and really no protector except the public. . . . But those comprehended under the present bill have nothing in common with the former: they have never been dependent on the public either for support or protection. . . . The principle which is now struggling for admission is a new one, entirely distinct from that which Parliament recognized in regulating parish apprentices. . . . Another misconception arises from this, that the bill apparently limits the period of labour only in the case of those whose tender age is well suited, at first sight, to diminish the reluctance which every one must feel to adopt so violent a regulation. The truth, however, is, that it is a bill to limit the hours of labour of *all persons* employed in cotton factories, whatever may be their age. Every person acquainted with cotton spinning knows, that so soon as the younger persons employed cease working, the more advanced must cease likewise; their labour is so connected, that they must cease or go on together. . . . Thus the bill gains covertly what it does not aim at openly."[55]

Unlike the Act of 1802, Peel's measure was limited in its application to cotton factories. " It was in no invidious spirit," said Ashley, " that the textile fabrics were the first selected for legislative operation. Everything could not be done at once; the prominence of these fabrics, with the vast numbers engaged in them, had attracted the attention of everyone—and it was manifest, besides, that their order and discipline, the multitudes gathered under a single roof, whose toil was governed by the precision and publicity of steam-power, offered, for the enactment of legal restrictions, facilities which could not be found in employments of a less symmetrical and more widely spread character."[56] The cotton mills were singled out for regulation because it was thought to be easy to apply restrictions to them, but where, asked the opponents of reform, is this process to stop? " The proposed limitation of age is objectionable," they contended, " chiefly on the ground that it brands cotton factories, exclusively of other manu-

---

[55] *An Inquiry into the Principle and Tendency of the Bill now pending in Parliament for imposing Certain Restrictions on Cotton Factories* (1818) pp. 3-6.
[56] *Speeches of the Earl of Shaftesbury* (1868) p. v. See H. Hoole, *A Letter in Defence of the Cotton Factories* (1832) p. 4.

facturing establishments, with an unmerited reproach; that it recognizes a principle which may and will afterwards be carried most dangerous lengths; and that it establishes a precedent, which will be employed to justify every future restriction that the wildness of dreaming reformers and innovators may hereafter choose to patronise."[57]

It was because the Act of 1819 opened the way to further and more far-reaching reforms that it occupies so important a place in the development of factory legislation. It set up no machinery—even the primitive regulations concerning inspection and the verification of age proposed in the original bill had disappeared—it provided only the most meagre relief from excessive work, and it was partial in its incidence; but it broke down the barriers. The State had intervened between employer and employed, and on the narrow foundation of this fundamental principle the dreaming of the reformers and innovators was to rear a mighty fabric.

Six years elapsed before the next advance was made.[58]   On 6th May, 1825, Hobhouse, later Sir John Cam Hobhouse, moved in the Commons[59] for leave to bring in another factory bill.[60] The principle that he now proposed to extend, he said, had already been approved in 1819, and his aim was simply to carry into effect that excellent statute which had long been most shamefully evaded, and which had been almost entirely inoperative, for only two convictions had ever taken place under it. To those who objected that the bill would inflict injury on industry he replied that it would be better to give up the cotton trade altogether, than to draw wealth out of the blood, and bone, and sinews of these unfortunate children. He found a warm supporter in Sir Francis Burdett, who asserted that it could not upon any grounds be contended that these helpless children should be sacrificed to the avarice and cupidity of their unfeeling parents, and of those by whom their labour was purchased. Those parents, whatever their right might be to receive the profits of their children's labour, had no right to sell them. " We hear of slavery abroad," he said,

---

[57] An Inquiry into the Principle and Tendency of the Bill now pending in Parliament for imposing Certain Restrictions on Cotton Factories (1818) p.27.

[58] On 8th December, 1819, Peel introduced a bill (Parl. Papers 1819-20, I, p. 97) designed to afford some slight relief to the manufacturers. The amending Act, (60 Geo. III, c. 5) passed on 23rd December, 1819, provided that if a mill was destroyed by fire the proprietor might employ the persons thus thrown out of work in other mills belonging to him. Such persons were to be allowed to work during the night for a period not exceeding ten hours. Section 2 of the Act extended the time during which a dinner interval must be allowed to 4 p.m.

[59] Hansard (1825) XIII, 421.

[60] Parl. Papers (1825) I, pp. 297, 303.

" but, good God, have we ever heard of any such instance of over-working as has been published with respect to the labour of children in the cotton manufactories? These wretched little beings are, in many instances, employed day after day for more than twelve hours at a time. Why, has any man a horse that he could think of putting to such toil? It is shocking to humanity!" Mark Philips, then, as always, the spokesman of the manufacturing interests, contended that the effect of the bill would be to reduce the hours of adults to those of the children, who would, in consequence, be dismissed from their employment.[61]   His arguments, however, were unavailing, and on 22nd June, 1825, Hobhouse's Act became law.

The Act to make further Provisions for the Regulation of Cotton Mills and Factories, and for the better Preservation of the Health of young Persons employed therein[62] marked but a slight advance on the Act of 1819. The regulations concerning hours of work were made a little more rigorous, for it was now provided that the period during which night work was prohibited should extend from 8 p.m. to 5 a.m.,[63] and that only nine hours' labour, ending at 4.30 p.m., should be permitted on Saturday.[64] During the half hour allowed for breakfast (between 6.30 and 10) and the hour allowed for dinner (between 11 and 3) work was forbidden;[65] and the amount of overtime permitted to make up for broken periods of working due to irregularity in the supply of water was reduced from an hour to half an hour a day.[66] For the first time extended hours were permitted to make up for cessation of work consequent upon accident to the steam-engine, water-wheel, or mill-gearing. In such circumstances the period of labour might be increased by an hour a day during the six following days.[67]

Every occupier of a mill employing persons under sixteen years of age was to keep a book in which was to be entered the name of every child whom the occupier considered might be under the age of nine, together with the names of the parents of such children. The parent was required to append his signature to a statement that the child was, in fact, over the minimum age, and the employer was then exempt from proceedings if it was later shown that the child was actually too young to be employed.[68]

---

61 *Hansard* (1825) XIII, 643-649.
62 6 Geo. IV, c. 63.
63 Sec. 1.
64 Sec. 2.
65 Sec. 3. Hobhouse had alleged that children were kept in the factory during meal times three or four days each week to clean the machinery.
66 Sec. 5
67 Sec. 4.
68 Sec. 9.

This clumsy procedure was obviously open to abuse, but the provision is interesting as showing that even in these early days it was recognized that the problem of determining the age of the protected children was one that must be faced.

Another problem that was to cause considerable embarrassment in the future also began to emerge at this juncture. The magistrates, who were charged with the enforcement of the law, were frequently vigorous opponents of its provisions, particularly if they themselves were affected in their private interests. Hobhouse's Act attempted to deal with this situation by providing that if a magistrate was the proprietor of a mill, or the father or son of a proprietor, he should not be competent to adjudicate upon cases arising under the Act.[69]

The penalties under the Act of 1825 remained unchanged, a minimum of £10, and a maximum of £20 for each offence; but it was now further provided that no fine in excess of £100 was to be levied in respect of any number of offences committed on the same day, and that no person was to be prosecuted for more than one offence on the same day without the sanction of the Justices at Quarter Sessions. The time for laying information was also reduced from three months to two months.[70]

A technical difficulty that arose in connection with the laying of informations and the serving of summonses was dealt with by a short bill[71] that was introduced on 19th May, 1829, and passed into law on 19th June.[72] This amending Act stated that the provisions of 6 Geo. IV, c. 63 had frequently been defeated and set aside for want of form, and it was therefore declared that it was not necessary to include in the information or summons the names of all the partners of the firm concerned. It was to be sufficient to insert the name of the ostensible proprietor; and service of the summons on the principal manager during the usual working hours was to be deemed good.[73]

On 17th February, 1831, Hobhouse announced that he intended to introduce another bill[74] to amend the laws relating to labour in

---

[69] Sec. 10.

[70] Sec. 8.

[71] *Parl. Papers* (1829) I, p. 483.

[72] 10 Geo. IV, c. 51.

[73] This measure having been passed by the Commons, was sent to the Lords on 4th June. Certain amendments were inserted by the Lords, but by an oversight the measure was included among a batch of bills which received the royal assent on 19th June, before the amendments had been agreed to by the Commons. It was thus necessary to pass a short declaratory Act, rendering these amendments valid, on 24th June, 1829 (10 Geo. IV, c. 63).

[74] *Parl. Papers* (1830-31) I, pp. 121, 127, 135.

the cotton factories.[75]   The measure was read a first time, but no further action was taken until 30th June, when he presented petitions from working people in various parts of the country praying that the House would pass a bill to restrict still further the working hours of the children.[76]   His opponents relied on the old arguments—the price of cotton would be increased, children would be dismissed, and the labour of adults would be restricted— and endeavoured to delay progress by suggesting that Scotland and Ireland should be excluded from the operation of the bill.[77] Hobhouse resisted this proposal, and on 15th October, 1831, the new law was passed.[78]

After repealing all previous statutes except that of 1802,[79] the Act declared that it was still the practice to employ great numbers of young persons of both sexes late at night, and in some instances throughout the night.   After 1st November, 1831, it was to be illegal for persons under the age of twenty-one to work in cotton factories between 8.30 p.m. and 5.30 a.m.;[80] and no person under the age of eighteen was to work more than twelve hours a day (nine hours on Saturday).[81]   One and a half hours were to be allowed for meals, but no times were stipulated for these breaks for refreshment.[82]   Important changes were made in the regulations governing lost time.   When work was interrupted by deficiency or excess of water, or by reason of its being impounded in higher reservoirs, additional work was permitted between 5 a.m. and 9 p.m., but the time thus lost must be made up within six months.[83] Time lost owing to accidents to the machinery could be worked up at the rate of one hour a day for the ensuing ten days, Saturdays included.[84]   An entirely new ground for exceeding the normal hours was provided in cases where drought or flood prevented the whole of the machinery from being worked at one and the same time.

----

[75] *Hansard* (1830-31) II, 624.

[76] *Hansard* (1831) IV, 501.

[77] This amended bill was introduced on 4th July, 1831. The text is printed in *Parl. Papers* (1831) I, pp. 345, 353.   The debate is not recorded in *Hansard*.

[78] 1 & 2 Will. IV, c. 39.   An Act to repeal the Laws relating to Apprentices and other young Persons employed in Cotton Factories and in Cotton Mills, and to make further Provisions in lieu thereof.

[79] Sec. 1.

[80] Sec. 2.

[81] Sec. 3.

[82] Sec. 4.

[83] Sec. 5.   It was the common practice for mills operated by water power to build up reserves of water in small reservoirs.   When numerous mills were situated at intervals along the same stream, the machinery in those lower down would be unable to work if the factories nearer the source retained the water.

[84] Sec. 6.

Such parts of the machinery as were not worked during the day might be worked at night by persons over sixteen years of age, but those under the age of twenty-one were not to be employed more than sixty-nine hours a week.[85] The manufacturers who depended on water-power attached great importance to these provisions, which, in deference to their views, were retained in the Act of 1833. Evasion of the law was thus greatly facilitated, and one of the major problems that Parliament had to face was that of reconciling the legitimate interests of the owners with the strict observance of the statute.

The minimum age for employment was retained at nine,[86] but manufacturers were no longer required to keep a register of those children about whose ages they were doubtful. Instead, they were relieved from responsibility if they obtained from the parent a certificate that the child was old enough for employment, parents who furnished false certificates being liable to a penalty of £5.[87] An effort was made to prevent the working of excessive hours by the provision that the occupiers of mills should keep a Time Book, in which was to be entered a true and correct account of the time the machinery had been in operation each day, such book to be available for inspection by a magistrate on written notice being given.[88] The magistrates were empowered to convict if the machinery was kept in motion for manufacturing purposes before 5 a.m. or after 9 p.m. unless it could be proved, by the evidence of reliable witnesses, that no person subject to restriction had been employed.[89]

A magistrate who was himself the proprietor of a mill, or the father, son, or brother of a proprietor, was declared incapable of adjudicating under the Act;[90] the time allowed for the laying of informations was again reduced, this time to twenty-one days from the commission of the offence;[91] while the provisions of the Act of 1829 relating to the formality of information and summons were incorporated in the statute.[92]

Hobhouse had made a courageous attempt to grapple with a problem that was far too complex for the forces he was able to call in aid, but the Act met with but scant approval. " Many of its details," it was urged, " betray a sad want of acquaintance with

---

[85] Sec. 7.
[86] Sec. 8.
[87] Sec. 9.
[88] Sec. 17.
[89] Sec. 18.
[90] Sec. 10.
[91] Sec. 13.
[92] Secs. 12, 15.

the subject on which he undertakes to legislate; and it will be
utterly inefficient for the object it has in view."[93] The mill-owners
protested that although it might be desirable in theory to restrict
the working hours of children, and to exclude those under nine
from the factories altogether, such a reform was, in practice, not
only undesirable, but dangerous. "It is stated by some restric-
tionists," declared one manufacturer in a letter to Hobhouse, "that
eleven hours and a half per day is long enough for children to be
kept at work. Others state ten hours to be their favourite
maximum. For my own part, I do not scruple to state, that
considered as an ABSTRACT QUESTION AND PUTTING ALL THE
CIRCUMSTANCES OF THE CASE OUT OF CONSIDERATION as a practical
question—that I go beyond them all—and that I should like the
hours of labor for children to be reduced to six hours per day . . . .
I should be, indeed, rejoiced to see half the time now engaged by
the toil of the body, occupied by the culture of the mind . . . and
I know only *one reason* why the children of the poor *are not*
educated like the children of the rich. . . . And that reason is,
BECAUSE NECESSITY DEMANDS IT OF THEM. . . . The first and
immediate consequence of limiting the ages of children employed,
to 'under nine years,' will be to throw out of employment all that
class of hands. . . . I protest against this threatened invasion of
the rights of the parent over the child, as an infringement of the
liberty of the subject, and a direct violation of the homes of
Englishmen."[94]

Dr. Ure contended that within a few months of the passing of
the Act the cotton trade had been adversely affected by a steep
decline in prices;[95] while Holland Hoole complained that it was
unfair to confine regulation to the cotton industry. "An extension
of that Act," he said, "to the Linen, Silk, and Woollen Mills of the
Kingdom, would remove that just ground of complaint which the
occupiers of Cotton Mills now possess, that hitherto their branch
of Factory labour has been unfairly singled out as the only subject
for legislation."[96]

The Act of 1831, unscientific in its approach, limited in its
scope, devoid of any adequate means of enforcement, and making
no provision at all for education, was the last effort made by the
unreformed Parliament to improve conditions in the factories. Vast

---

[93] W. R. Greg, *An Enquiry into the State of the Manufacturing
Population* (1831) p. 30 n.
[94] *A Letter to Sir John Cam Hobhouse by a Manufacturer* (1832)
pp. 16, 36.
[95] A. Ure, *The Cotton Manufacture of Great Britain* (1836) Vol. II,
p. 338.
[96] H. Hoole, *A Letter in Defence of the Cotton Factories* (1832) p. 16.

changes in the political world were already imminent, new and mighty forces were about to be unleashed, and of the surge and turbulence that ensued a new system was to be born.

CHAPTER 3

THE TEN HOURS AGITATION

EVEN BEFORE the passing of the Act of 1831 the agitation for reform had begun to assume a new and more violent character. Popular feeling having been aroused by the revelations that had been made concerning the conditions that obtained on the slave plantations in the West Indies, the nonconformists were leading a movement designed to effect the abolition of a system which neither political expediency nor the Christian conscience could continue to defend. It was at this time, when public opinion was showing itself peculiarly sensitive to the hardships and ill-treatment suffered by the negroes, that Richard Oastler, an estate bailiff, of Fixby Hall, near Huddersfield, heard from the lips of John Wood, a Bradford woollen manufacturer, of the conditions under which English children worked in the mills of the West Riding.

Oastler, a man of simple habits, and strong religious convictions, easily moved to passion at the sight of suffering, and profoundly convinced of his mission to relieve it, was deeply stirred by what he had been told, and returning home the following day, 29th September, 1830, he wrote the first of a series of provocative and highly inflammatory letters to the *Leeds Mercury* denouncing "Yorkshire Slavery." Thousands of our English boys and girls, he cried, were suffering a far worse slavery than any that existed on the colonial plantations. "The very streets which receive the droppings of an 'Anti-Slavery Society' are every morning wet by the tears of innocent victims at the accursed shrine of avarice, who are *compelled* (not by the cart-whip of the negro slave-driver) but by the dread of the equally appalling thong or strap of the overlooker, to hasten, half-dressed, *but not half-fed*, to those magazines of British infantile slavery—*the worsted mills in the town and neighbourhood of Bradford!!!*

Poor infants! Ye are indeed sacrificed at the shrine of avarice, *without even the solace of the negro slave;* ye are no more than he is, *free agents;* ye are compelled to work as long as the *necessity* of your needy parents may require, or the cold-blooded avarice of your worse than barbarian masters *may demand*."[1]

Thus was inaugurated the Ten-hours movement, the agitation for 'Ten Hours a Day and a Time Book Bill,' which was to pursue its bitter and controversial course during the next quarter of a

---

[1] *Leeds Mercury*, 16th October, 1830, Quoted " Alfred," *The History of the Factory Movement* (1857) Vol. I, pp. 99-100.

century, and of which Hobhouse's Act was the first ineffective
fruit. Powerful and influential supporters quickly gathered under
Oastler's banner, the Rev. G. S. Bull, Vicar of Bradford, J. R.
Stephens and John Doherty, the Chartists, George Condy, the
journalist, together with Michael Thomas Sadler, John Fielden,
Lord Ashley, Charles Hindley and Joseph Brotherton, who waged
the battle on the floor of the House of Commons.

The ostensible purpose of the reformers was to limit the
working day of children and young persons to ten hours, but this
could not be achieved without seriously interfering with the work
of adults,[2] who were now demanding that their own hours should
also be restricted. They knew that " if they could obtain the
restriction of the labour of all young persons under 18, to ten
hours daily, their object would be gained, for . . . such a restriction
would be tantamount to one on the machinery itself.

The increasing strain and tension of long, unregulated hours,
due in no small measure to greater demands imposed by the
improvements in machinery,[4] were doubtless largely responsible for
the programme now put forward by the adults; but they also
believed that if there was a reduction in the amount of juvenile
labour available there would be an increased call for adults, whose
wages would consequently be raised.[5] Their opponents warned
them that a reduction in the hours of labour must inevitably result
in a diminution of their wages—" whatever time is subtracted from
the hours of labour must be accompanied with an equivalent
deduction from its rewards "[6]—but to these remonstrances they
turned a deaf ear. They professed themselves prepared to accept
lower wages as the price to be paid for a shorter working day,[7] but
they were not convinced that such a sacrifice would, in fact, be
necessary.[8]

---

[2] See L. Faucher, *Etudes sur l'Angleterre* (1856) Vol. I, p. 450. " La
question déjà bien assez grave du travail des enfants s'absorba dans la
question plus générale, mais infiniment moins pratique, du travail des
adultes."

[3] R. H. Greg, *The Factory Question* (1837) p. 20.

[4] " The vast improvements in principle and construction—the incredible velocity of the wheels, and the power of the engine, have added
five-fold suffering to a period of toil which : . . had already been pronounced well-nigh intolerable.—*Quarterly Review* (1836) Vol. 57, p. 432.
Cf. Speeches of the Earl of Shaftesbury (1868) p. 94.—" Machinery has
prodigiously multiplied the labour of those who are governed by its
fearful movements."

[5] W. Cooke Taylor, *Factories and the Factory System* (1844) p. 97.

[6] J. P. Kay, *The Moral and Physical Condition of the Working Classes*
(1832) p. 90.

[7] J. M. Ludlow, *Progress of the Working Class 1832-1867* (1867) p. 91.

[8] See E. von Plener, *The English Factory Legislation* (1873) p. 11.
A. Ure, *The Philosophy of Manufactures* (1835) p. 304. *Annual Register*
(1833) p. 205.

The confusion of thought that existed is well illustrated in the report of a great meeting of operatives held in January, 1831, at Mixed Cloth Hall Yard in Leeds, where some 12,000 people assembled to demand a ten-hours bill. One of their leaders, the Rev. R. W. Hamilton, told them plainly what the result might be. " There may be a diminution of your immediate wages in consequence . . . it is for you to say that you are willing to incur the risk that right may be done." He was greeted with cries of " We are! We will!" but a later speaker met with a somewhat different reception, as the report of the meeting shows. " Brother operatives," said Mr. Ellis, " I think that the idea which has gone abroad that the manufacturers will pay the same wages for ten hours' labour a day, as they do now for twelve is quite erroneous. (" *No, no.*" " *Ten hours is plenty to work.*") I know that; I know that ten hours is quite plenty for infants; but it is well known to many of you that if we turn out the infants at ten hours the adults cannot proceed with their business. Therefore, I mean to say that the masters, at this day, cannot give six days' wages for five days' labour. (" *They must!*" " *Down him!*")."[9]

Some of the more extreme advocates of the ten-hours day insisted that so far from wages being reduced, they would, in fact, be increased. " It is evident," they said, " that if the weavers . . . could, by any *restrictive* measure, reduce their labour *one-sixth* (the same demand continuing) the effect would be an *advance* of wages."[10] They argued that if 1,000,000 pounds of yarn could be produced each week by 50,000 hands working twelve hours a day, an additional 8,000 hands would be required if work was restricted to ten hours a day. On the principle that price is regulated by supply and demand, the greater demand for operatives would ensure increased wages, and they would get twelve hours' pay for ten hours' work.

The notion that restrictions should be directly applied to adults was wholly repugnant to the individualistic philosophy of the day. It may be questioned, said Gaskell, how far the interference of the government in labour matters is likely to prove beneficial, " and whether the parties, the masters on the one hand, and the workmen on the other, would not act most wisely by saying as the merchants of France once said to Colbert, when it was proposed to take measures of protection for their interests—' *Laissez nous faire.*' "[11] The true function of the government, it was held, did not extend to interference with the relationships into which individuals entered

9 *Report of the Proceedings at the Leeds Meeting* (1831) pp. 5-6.
10 *The Moral Reformer*, Vol. III, No. 3 (1st March, 1833) p. 82.
11 P. Gaskell, *The Manufacturing Population of England* (1833) p. 12.

one with another.[12] Whatever was most profitable for the individual was most profitable for all those with whom he was connected, and whatever was advantageous to an individual in practice, was advantageous to the nation considered as an individual state in the society of nations.[13] It followed, therefore, that men must be left free to pursue their own ends unhampered by State control, that neither the hours they worked, nor the wages they received, should be the subject of regulation. They were free agents, and each must be left to work out his own salvation.

In these circumstances the adult operatives realized that it would be idle to seek legislative protection for themselves; they must gain their ends by striving to secure protection for those upon whom their own work depended—the children and young persons.[14] This programme appealed especially to the evangelical humanitarians, who were led to espouse the ten-hours cause by their sympathy for the young. This fusion of two parallel but dissimilar interests supplied the driving force behind the agitation, and it was not unnatural, therefore, that, in the early days at least, the policy of the reformers should have been dictated rather by an appeal to the emotions than by a scientific and considered approach to the problem of juvenile labour as such. It was not until the Reform Act of 1832 wrought so profound a change in the political situation that it became possible to devise methods of control that afforded protection for the young while leaving the adult, in theory at least, free from regulation.

In the meantime the clamour for a ten-hours bill spread to Lancashire, to the midlands, and to London. Short-time Committees were set up, highly organized and adroitly managed, and strenuous efforts were made to enlist the support of members of Parliament. Prominent among those who sympathised with the cause was Michael Thomas Sadler, the member for Newark, a resident of Leeds, a close friend of Oastler, and a strong supporter of Hobhouse. True to his promise to raise the question in the Commons, he sought leave to introduce a ten-hours bill[15] on 15th December, 1831. " He was happy," he said, " in anticipating that his proposition would meet with no opposition, but that its success

---

[12] R. H. Greg, *The Factory Question* (1837) p. 2—" There are few subjects upon which more erroneous sentiments prevail, than as to the proper objects and limits of legislation. The '*trop gouverner*' is no less common than mischievous."

[13] " Alfred," *The History of the Factory Movement* (1857) Vol. I, p. 86.

[14] W. Cooke Taylor, *Factories and the Factory System* (1844) p. 28.— The agitation " was intended as a blind to the ulterior project of a Ten-hours' Bill, by which the operatives absurdly hoped to compel the masters to give them the same wages for ten hours that they usually received for twelve."

[15] *Parl. Papers* (1831-2) II, p. 1.

would be triumphant, as it was grounded upon principles of humanity and policy."[16]   Poulett Thomson assured him that the Government, though far from pledging their support, would not oppose its introduction, and after the first reading on 17th January, 1832, the bill came up for detailed consideration on 16th March.[17]

"It is necessary," said the preamble, "that the Hours of Labour of Children and young Persons employed in Mills and Factories, of whatever description, should be regulated, inasmuch as it has of late become a practice in many such Mills and Factories to employ a great number of Children and young Persons of both Sexes an unreasonable length of time, and late at Night, and in many instances all Night, to the great and manifest injury of the Health and Morals of such Children and young Persons."

It was proposed that no child should be employed under nine years of age; that no person under eighteen should work for more than ten hours a day or forty-eight hours a week; and that those under the age of twenty-one should not work at night, *i.e.,* between 7 p.m. and 6 a.m.   An hour and a half was to be allowed for meals (half an hour for breakfast and an hour for dinner) at such times, outside working hours, as parents and employers should agree.   In mills powered by water-wheels the working day might be extended from 5 a.m. to 8 p.m. if time was lost by want of, or excess of water, or by reason of its being impounded in higher reservoirs, but the hours of work were not to be increased.

Every mill-occupier was to keep a Time Book, in which he was to enter each day the length of time the machinery was operated, the time that children and young persons commenced work in the morning, the time they ceased at night, and the intervals they were allowed for meals.   This book was to be signed weekly; it was to be available at all times for inspection by the Justices; and it was to be exhibited at Quarter Sessions each year. The penalty for making a false entry was to be a fine of £20.   If it was proved to the satisfaction of the Justices that the machinery had been worked before 5.30 a.m. or after 7 p.m. a conviction might be registered, unless it could be shown that the persons alleged to have been overworked had not been employed contrary to the regulations.

The age of the children and young persons engaged in the factory was to be attested by the parents, and the occupier was to be absolved from liability if he held a signed statement that the persons concerned were of the appropriate age.   An attempt was made to overcome the manifest weaknesses of this system by

[16] *Hansard* (1831-2) IX, 255.
[17] *Hansard* (1832) XI, 340-385.

providing heavy penalties for fraud—a fine of £5 for parents who
produced false certificates, and a fine of £15 for an owner who
connived at the employment of any one possessed of a false
certificate.

It was proposed to take steps to check the fraudulent extension of hours by providing a reliable method of timing. " Whereas,"
said the bill, " a practice is known to exist in certain Mills or
Factories, of using Two or more different Clocks or Timepieces,
one being a common or Time Clock, and the other a Clock
regulated by the velocity of the Steam Engine or other Machinery,
and often called a Speed Clock, by which the period of daily
Labour, though nominally limited to a certain duration, is often
increased much beyond that limitation," the time of the working
hours was to be regulated either by the nearest public clock, or
by the factory time clock, which itself was to be regulated by a
public clock.

The terms of Sadler's bill are a sufficient indication of the
bankruptcy of the programme of the ten-hour partisans, for it was
in some respects a retrograde measure. The whole emphasis was
placed on the ten-hours day. There was not a word about education; the existing provision for inspection, rudimentary as it was,
was ignored; and children of nine were to be condemned to work
the same hours as those twice their age. It was not surprising
that the manufacturers condemned it as a piece of hypocrisy,
designed to limit the labour of adults while professing to protect
the children. " Scarcely had the second bill of Sir J. Hobhouse
been in operation twelve months," declared Greg, " when . . .
Mr. Sadler, emerging as if from a long entombment, with all the
political and religious prejudices of the olden times, comes forward
with a new proposition for limiting the labour, not of children only,
but of adults, employed in factories, to ten hours daily."[18]

That Sadler was moved by the highest motives, however, it
is scarcely possible to doubt, for he supported his bill in a speech
of singular pathos and eloquence. His purpose was, he said, to
rescue the factory children from a state of suffering and degradation
which he conceived the children of the industrious classes in hardly
any other country had ever endured. Admitting freely that all
legislative interference was an evil, only to be tolerated if its
purpose was to remove some greater evil, he denied that he was
attempting to impose restrictions on free agents, for the children
were not free. " Whoever has lived in a manufacturing town
must have heard, if he happened to be awake many hours before
light on a winter's morning the patter of little pattens on the

---

[18] R. H. Greg, *The Factory Question* (1837) p. 7.

pavement, continued, perhaps, for half an hour together, though the time appointed for assembling was the same." In moving words he described the physical cruelties inflicted on the children, the refined punishments, the beatings and whippings, and drew attention to the increase in delinquency, debauchery and premature mortality.[19]

This highly emotional appeal made little impression on the opponents of the ten-hours movement, however. Lord Althorp, the Chancellor of the Exchequer, advised the House to proceed with the utmost caution, and the bill was finally referred to a Select Committee under the chairmanship of Sadler himself. The Committee sat on forty-three days, examined eighty-nine witnesses, to whom it put 11,618 questions. No report was issued, but the minutes of evidence,[20] published on 8th August, 1832, created a profound sensation.

A state of affairs was revealed which, if typical of the manufacturing districts as a whole, cried to heaven for speedy redress. One after another the operatives, both old and young, appeared before the Committee, and recited the dismal story of the sufferings and hardships they endured. The lame and the deformed exhibited their tortured limbs, parents related the agonies of their children, and medical men testified to the evils of the system. " Providence, indeed, brought good out of evil: the result of this inquiry, instituted for delay, and the decencies of interment, was a revival of the question in all its breadth; a body of evidence, which, in depth, extent and science, has never been approached, alarmed and disgusted the world."[21]

That was the view of the reformers, but there were many who refused to accept the evidence adduced at its face value. The Parliamentary session came to an end before the Committee had finished its work, and the arrangements that had been made to hear the owners' case after the operatives and their supporters had delivered their testimony, had to be abandoned. Sadler, nevertheless, caused the evidence to be published immediately, thus laying himself open to the charge of producing a biassed and one-sided report.[22] Objection was taken, too, to the fact that the evidence itself was *ex parte,* and not on oath, and that it described a state of affairs that had long ceased to exist.[23] " A mass of *ex*

---

[19] See "Alfred," *The History of the Factory Movement* (1857) Vol. I, pp. 152-190.

[20] *Report from Select Committee on the Bill to regulate the Labour of Children in Mills and Factories. Parl. Papers* (1831-2) XV, p. 1.

[21] *Quarterly Review* (1836) Vol. 57, p. 409.

[22] *Hansard* (1833) XVII, 90. R. H. Greg, *The Factory Question* (1837) p. 8.

[23] C. Wing, *Evils of the Factory System Exposed* (1837) p.ii. V. Royle, *The Factory System Defended* (1833) p. 9.

parte evidence was received," said Baines, " which was full of the grossest exaggerations and misstatements,"[24] while Ure contended that the Committee had " published a mass of defamation against the cotton mills—a torrent of falsehood and defamation which lately overflowed the country, and had nearly converted its most productive fields of industry into *sloughs of despond*."[25] Even Engels, assuredly no friend of the owners, shared these views. Sadler, he said, " betrayed by his noble enthusiasm into the most distorted and erroneous statements, drew from his witnesses by the very form of his questions, answers which contained the truth, but truth in a perverted form."[26]

Stung to fury by the charges made against them, and apprehensive of the results they feared would follow, the owners and their supporters opened a campaign designed to demonstrate that the conditions of the children were not such as to render Parliamentary intervention necessary. Like Sadler, they made the mistake of trying to prove too much, and the picture they painted was equally remote from the truth. " The toil is not very great," said Taylor, " nor is it incessant. The heaviest part of the labour is executed by the steam-engine or the water-wheel; and there are so many intervals of rest, that I am under the mark when I assert that an operative in a cotton factory is at rest one minute out of every three during his period of nominal employment."[27] Nassau Senior bore similar testimony—" The work is merely that of watching the machinery, and piecing the threads that break. I have seen the girls who thus attended, standing with their arms folded during the whole time that I have stayed in the room—others sewing a handkerchief or sitting down. The work, in fact, is scarcely equal to that of a shopman behind a counter in a frequented shop—mere confinement, attention, and attendance."[28]

Baines considered that abuse was the exception and not the rule, for though the hours were long, the labour was light—only " attention and gentle exercise are needed."[29] It was maintained by Ure that if cruel punishments were inflicted the operatives themselves, who actually employed the children, were responsible,

---

24 E. Baines, *History of the Cotton Manufacture in Great Britain* (1835) p. 453. See also R. H. Greg, *The Factory Question* (1837) p. 7.
25 A. Ure, *The Philosophy of Manufactures* (1835) pp. 291, 298. It was said that only three witnesses were called from Manchester—one a delegate of the Lancashire Short-time Committee, one the keeper of a small tavern, and one an atheist.
26 F. Engels, *The Condition of the Working-Class in England in 1844* (1892) p. 170.
27 W. Cooke Taylor, *Notes of a Tour in the Manufacturing Districts of Lancashire* (1842) p. 24.
28 Nassau Senior, *Letters on the Factory Act* (1837) p. 15.
29 E. Baines, *History of the Cotton Manufacture in Great Britain* (1835) pp. 454-7.

but in the many factories he had visited he had never seen an instance of corporal chastisement   The children ·" seemed to be always cheerful and alert, taking pleasure in the light play of their muscles. . . . It was delightful to observe the nimbleness with which they pieced the broken ends . . . and to see them at leisure, after a few minutes' exercise of their tiny fingers, to amuse themselves in any attitude they chose. . . . . The work of these lively elves seemed to resemble a sport, in which habit gave them a pleasing dexterity."[30]

Amidst such a welter of conflicting evidence it is difficult to arrive at any satisfactory conclusion.   Conditions must have varied enormously from mill to mill, and in the smaller establishments there were probably many cases of extreme ill-usage.   Perhaps the most reliable estimate was that presented by the Commission of 1833,[31] but the very bitterness of the controversy illustrated the violence of the forces that were at work.   Mighty issues were in the balance both for masters and men, a new conception of the functions of the State was struggling for recognition, and the whole vast problem, intimately related as it was to fundamental principles of economic and social significance, was reduced to one single question—should juvenile labour be controlled or should it be left untrammelled by regulation?   And on that question the report of Sadler's Committee had focused a burning light.

Under the auspices of the Short-time Committees the agitation continued unabated.   Numerously attended meetings were organized in the manufacturing districts, and the leaders of the movement, inspired by Oastler and Bull, employed all their arts to work upon the feelings of the operatives.[32]   Petitions poured into Parliament,[33] and it was clear that the climax was fast approaching.

On 7th June, 1832, however, the great Reform Act had been passed, and in the following December a general election was held.   Sadler, standing for Leeds, was defeated at the polls by

---

[30] A. Ure, *The Philosophy of Manufactures* (1835) pp. 8, 299.

[31] See *post* p. 46.

[32] Kydd gives a vivid account of a great meeting held in April, 1832, at Castle Yard, York, attended by men, women and children who made their way thither on foot from places forty or fifty miles away.   " The appearance of the road was novel and impressive; it resounded with cheers, which were uttered ' by the *Pilgrims* at those who passed them in carriages of various sorts.   In some groups there were torches, composed of old ropes, and the undulations of the road afforded many views of illuminated groups, successively rising over the hills and disappearing the next instant, leaving a loud, long cheer behind, as they sank out of view. It was indeed a moving scene."—" Alfred," *The History of the Factory Movement* (1857) Vol. I, p. 241.   See B. L. Hutchins and A. Harrison, *A History of Factory Legislation* (1926) pp. 51-52.

[33] Lord Morpeth presented a petition 2,322 feet long, containing 138,652 signatures.

Macaulay, to the consternation of the reformers, who were thus
deprived of the services of their most able Parliamentary advocate.[34]
After a hurried consultation of the Lancashire and Yorkshire
delegates, Bull was instructed to proceed to London, where he
succeeded in persuading Lord Ashley to take over Sadler's work.
" In the autumn and winter of 1832," wrote Ashley, " I read
incidentally in the *Times* some extracts from the evidence taken
before Mr. Sadler's committee. . . . I was astonished and disgusted;
and, knowing Sadler to be out of Parliament (for he had been
defeated at Leeds) I wrote to him to offer my services in presenting
petitions or doing any other small work that the cause might
require. . . . The Houses met in the month of February; on the
second or third day I was addressed by the Rev. G. S. Bull, whom
till then I had never seen or heard of. He was brought to me by
Sir Andrew Agnew, and they both proposed to me to take up the
question that Sadler had necessarily dropped."[35] Thus it was that
Ashley became associated with the factory agitation, and with the
whole business of the reform of the working conditions of young
people that he spent his life trying to achieve.

Born in 1801, son of the sixth Earl of Shaftesbury, Ashley[36]
was educated at Harrow, and Christ Church, Oxford. He entered
Parliament in 1826 as member for Woodstock, the pocket borough
of his mother's family, the Marlboroughs, but in 1831 he was
returned for Dorsetshire, which he represented until 1846. Rigid
and uncompromising in his views, a devout churchman of the
evangelical school, a man of wide human sympathies and great force
of character, he was ideally fitted to assume the mantle of Sadler,
and he threw himself into the fray with ardour and gusto. The
fact that he was almost entirely ignorant of factory conditions
doubtless explained the eagerness with which he embraced
uncritically the views of Oastler and his disciples. In the early
days he was a ten-hours man pure and simple, but as the years
went by he came to realize that the problem was not quite so
straightforward—that co-ordinated, scientific, and centralized
control was, if anything, even more important than the mere
limitation of hours.[37]

[34] See A. V. Dicey, *Law and Public Opinion in England* (1905) p. 226.

[35] E. Hodder, *The Life and Work of the seventh Earl of Shaftesbury*
(1893) p. 81.

[36] He succeeded to the title by which he is better known in 1851.

[37] His erstwhile supporters did not spare him when he ultimately
strayed from the narrow path they had marked out for him. " Lord
Ashley has at length removed the mask of affected sympathy with the
sufferings of the unhappy children and women, whose cause he has for so
many years professed to uphold, and, under circumstances of the most
unparalleled baseness, has suddenly at the eleventh hour betrayed them
. . . into the hands of their enemies. What the immediate result of this
foul treachery will be it is impossible to say."—*The Champion*, Vol II,
No. 2, p. 25.

The bill[38] that Ashley introduced in the Commons on 5th March, 1833, was in many respects similar to Sadler's bill, but the increased severity of the penalties to which the owners were to be liable indicated a definite hardening in the attitude of the reformers. The fine for a breach of the law was to to be fixed at a maximum of £20 for a first offence; on a second conviction the fine could be doubled; on a third conviction the penalty was to be trebled, and in addition a term of imprisonment varying between three and twelve months might be imposed. An owner knowingly receiving a false certificate of age was to be liable to a fine of £100, while the penalty for making a false entry in the Time Book was increased to a maximum of £100. If an employee was injured by unfenced machinery there was to be a penalty of between £50 and £200, payable to the injured party. Should death result from an accident due to lack of fencing a coroner's jury were to inspect the machinery, and if they found that the owner had been negligent, he was to be committed for trial on a charge of manslaughter.

These harsh penalties were designed to secure obedience to the law, but there was no provision for any scheme of inspection, which alone was likely to prove efficacious.[39] No mention was made of education, nor was there any plan to differentiate the working hours of the younger and the older children. In one respect alone was there an attempt to break new ground. In order to prevent the fraudulent extension of hours it was provided that the same meal times should be observed throughout the factory, and that from the commencement of work in the morning to its termination in the evening, labour should be continuous except at meal times. This proviso would certainly have been inadequate to its purpose, even had it come into force, but it is nevertheless significant as constituting the first dim recognition of a principle that the efflux of time showed to be fundamental in all factory legislation— the principle that the mere enunciation of rules was of no avail unless adequate defences were set up against evasion.

In the meantime the owners had not been idle. Realizing the dangers with which they were confronted, they marshalled their forces, and opened the attack by presenting petitions asking for a Commission to be set up to clear them from the charges made against them by Sadler's Committee. On 14th March, 1833, their spokesman in the House, Wilson Patten, explained that this request

---

[38] *Parl. Papers* (1833) II, p. 263.

[39] Ashley's later assertion (*Hansard* (1833) XIX, 224) that he would have included such a proposal in his bill but for fear of giving additional offence to his opponents, was, to say the least, a little curious, since many owners favoured inspection, and all were incensed at the severity of the penalties prescribed.

was not meant to delay consideration of the measure now before
the Commons, but was rather " for the purpose of clearing the
characters of the masters from those imputations which seemed to
be cast upon them by the friends of this measure, but which further
evidence would prove to be utterly unjustifiable."[40] . Ashley
vigorously opposed the suggestion, asserting that it was merely a
manoeuvre to cause delay, but the masters continued to press for
a Commission with all the force at their command. Wilson Patten
contended that further inquiry was vital, since no reliance could
be placed on Sadler's evidence. He had taken statements, Patten
declared, only from those on whom he knew he could rely.
Fifteen of the twenty-one medical witnesses, he alleged, lived in
London, and had no knowledge of factory conditions. There was
no evidence about conditions in the midlands or the west, but
fifty-one witnesses were summoned from Leeds alone. These men
had been paid nine shillings a day in addition to their travelling
expenses, and much money had been spent in smuggling people out
of London so that they might not give evidence. He therefore
moved, on 3rd April, 1833, for a Commission " to collect information in the manufacturing districts with respect to the employment
of children in factories, and to devise the best means for the
curtailment of their labour."[41] The motion was carried by 74
votes to 73,[42] and on 19th April, 1833, the Commission was issued.

---

[40] *Hansard* (1833) XVI, 640. See H. Hoole. *A Letter in Defence of*
the Cotton Factories (1832) p. 16.
[41] *Hansard* (1833) XVII, 84. See " Alfred," *The History of the Factory*
Movement (1857) Vol. II, p. 31. E. von Plener, *The English Factory*
Legislation (1873) p. 10. E. Hodder, *The Life and Work of the seventh*
Earl of Shaftesbury (1893) p. 86. *Annual Register* (1833) p. 205.
[42] *Hansard, loc. cit.* 113.

CHAPTER 4

THE COMMISSION OF 1833

NO TIME was lost in setting up the machinery to institute the inquiry, for with Ashley's bill still before Parliament the matter was recognized to be one of some urgency. To each of the four great centres of the textile industry, the north, the north-east, Lancashire, and the west, were sent one medical and two civil Commissioners, with instructions to report their findings as soon as possible to the Central Board, who were to supervise the whole of the work from their headquarters in London. It was the task of the members of this Board to sift the evidence submitted to them, and then to frame their report, making such recommendations as they considered necessary. That the colour and content of the report would be decisively affected by the impact that the minds of these men made on the evidence, was, of course, apparent, and it was by no mere chance that Edwin Chadwick and Thomas Southwood Smith found themselves chosen, together with Thomas Tooke, to bear the burden of this responsibility.

Chadwick, a barrister of the Inner Temple, is perhaps best remembered as Secretary to the Board of Commissioners established by the Poor Law Act of 1834, and for the great work he accomplished in the sphere of public health, but not the least of his titles to fame is the contribution he made to factory reform. Like Southwood Smith, he was an ardent disciple of Jeremy Bentham, becoming in 1830 literary secretary to that rare genius whose teachings affected so profoundly the development of English legislation during the 19th century.[1]

The followers of Bentham regarded the business of law-making as a scientific process, logical in its inception, grounded on stable principles, and scrupulously co-ordinated in the details of its execution. It was necessary, in their view, that all the relevant factors and circumstances should be carefully examined and realistically assessed, that a definite plan should be worked out, and that adequate control and regulation should be imposed. This control, they held, could only be secured by a system of centralized administration, whereby paid officials, appointed by and responsible to the central government, replaced the unpaid magistrates, who had for so long been charged with the administration of the law. The " combination of an absolute centralization of legislative power

---

[1] M. Marston, *Sir Edwin Chadwick* (1925) p. 22.

with an utter absence of administrative centralization,"[2] typical
hitherto of the English system, they condemned root and branch.
Their philosophy " was not solely, nor even perhaps fundamentally,
a liberal system; it was at the same time a doctrine of authority
which looked to the deliberate and in a sense the scientific interference of Government to produce a harmony of interests."[3] The
bureaucratic despotism which they regarded as essential to the
ordered and progressive government of the country imported a new
and challenging conception into political philosophy, implying, as
it did, a breaking down of that peripheral exclusiveness and
isolation that had hitherto been so characteristic of the English way
of life. No longer was the magistracy to be the sole repository
of local executive power, no longer was the enforcement of the
law to be left in the hands of those who had no particular interest
in carrying out the decrees of the legislature. The whole system
was to be administered and controlled by the professional officers
of the central government, which would thus be enabled not only
to exert its power throughout the length and breadth of the land,
but also to acquire first-hand information concerning the practical
working of its schemes even in the most remote parts of the
country.

Such was the pattern of the ideal legal and administrative
system as the Benthamites saw it, but the area within which that
system should operate ought, they believed, to be severely circumscribed. For the most characteristic of their doctrines was that of
utility, summarized by Dicey in two propositions. " The right aim
of legislation is the carrying out of the principle of utility, or, in
other words, the proper end of every law is the promotion of the
greatest happiness of the greatest number."[4] " Every person is in
the main and as a general rule the best judge of his own happiness.
Hence legislation should aim at the removal of all those restrictions
on the free action of an individual which are not necessary for
securing the like freedom on the part of his neighbours."[5]

This implied, of course, a system of *laissez-faire*, and those
who were seeking to impose restrictions on the working hours of
adults could, therefore, expect little sympathy from the adherents
of Bentham's creed.[6] They were free agents, and both their own
interests, and the interests of the community at large, would best

---

2 L. Stephen, *The English Utilitarians* (1900) Vol. I, p. 30.
3 E. Halévy. *A History of the English People 1830-1841* (1927) p. 101.
4 A. V. Dicey, *Law and Public Opinion in England* (1905) p. 135.
5 *Ibid.* p. 145.
6 " The wiseacres are reluctant to legislate on such matters—they hold
all such interference to be an evil. They have learned a few words of
French, and each parrot from his perch, as he keeps swinging himself to
and fro in his glittering cage, ejaculates, ' Laissez nous faire!' "—*Blackwood's Edinburgh Magazine* (April, 1833) Vol. XXXIII, No. CCVI, p. 423.

be served by leaving them free to dispose of their labour, the only commodity they had to sell, in a free and open market.[7] It was otherwise with children. They were not free agents, and they rightly looked to the government to intervene on their behalf. It was for this reason that Chadwick and Smith held that restrictions on juvenile labour should not only be imposed, but imposed rigorously and effectively.

Although self-interest was their guiding principle, they believed that self-interest should be enlightened. Provision must therefore be made for education, and it was for this reason that Roebuck[8] endeavoured, in 1833, to secure the establishment of a universal system of education based on the Prussian model. His effort proved abortive, but nevertheless a limited scheme of education, applicable to factory children only, was shortly to become possible of achievement.

It was freely asserted that the setting up of the Commission was merely a device to delay legislation, and that the members had been instructed to present a report favourable to the owners.[9] The reformers poured scorn and contempt upon the proceedings. " What a piece of sheer mockery was this Commission!" they cried. " Here were three Government Hirelings and their Secretary with most philosophical coolness, sitting in judgment upon a cruel, murderous system—the criminal party whispering in their ears, and guiding their pens all the while."[10] Sadler entered his protest in

[7] The opponents of *Laissez-faire* held that the intrinsic nature of labour gave it a claim to protection, " for the working man . . . absolutely depends upon it for his subsistence from day to day and cannot withhold it from the market. He must sell it for whatever price it will bring, or suffer the agonies of want and hunger. Hence it is the most defenceless of every kind of property, and that which most needs protection."— J. Wood, *Right of Labour to Legislative Protection* (1832) p. 10.

[8] J. A. Roebuck had been introduced to the Utilitarian Society by John Stuart Mill in 1824. " My first visit to the Utilitarian Society," he said, " I shall never forget. It met in a low, half-furnished desolate sort of room—I believe the dining-room of the house, not Mr. Bentham's dining-room. The place was lighted by a few tallow candles. A desk was drawn across the end of the room, at which desk sat the chairman, and some half-dozen young men sat in chairs round the room, and formed the society."—R. E. Leader, *Life and Letters of John Arthur Roebuck* (1897) p. 27.

[9] E. von Plener, *The English Factory Legislation* (1873) p. 10. *Cf.* G. Crabtree, *Factory Commission : The Legality of its Appointment questioned, and the Illegality of its Proceedings Proved* (1833) p. 12—" If the Commission were bad in its inception, it is ten times worse in its execution. . . . The Factory party have broken in on the constitutional course of justice, and the Ministry will never be able to wipe out the stain of yielding to their unhallowed cupidity. . . The Government granted them, to purge themselves, a court of their own choosing. They, the delinquents ! have been consulted about the mode of procedure, and dictated more than half the proceedings which have been taken."

[10] *Address to the Friends of Justice and Humanity* (1833) p. 10.

quieter vein, addressing his remonstrance to the Commissioners who visited Leeds. " You appear to be quite ignorant of the subject of the inquiry, which to its due examination demands habits, talents, and experience far different from those requisite for mere legal investigations: and you come at a time of the year when the Factories . . . are usually in the best state; and after full notice of your approach, and abundance of time given to prepare for your reception. . . . I need not remind you that your whole plan met with the entire and indeed enthusiastic approbation of the Mill-owners. You heard from them expressions of the most unbounded confidence, and the warmest compliments to yourselves."[11] No opportunity was lost of hindering the Commissioners in their work, and of heaping ridicule upon them. " When your Honours arrive at, or near any large Manufacturing Town, give the postillion an extra half-crown . . . to drive you in the back way, and not to tell where you come from. If you come by the Coach, book yourselves by false names, and sit sulky all the way. Forewarn your worthy Masters, the Millocrats, not to meet you at the Coach, nor to let it be known on what day or hour the rogues are coming. By the by, have you all made your Wills? . . . There is no occasion to be very particular in asking about *recent* improvements—such as boxing off machinery—removing cripples—ventilation—cleaning—the speed of the Engine. Just say to some of the men ' I suppose all things are going on in the usual way?' ' Oh yes sir.' ' You swear that.' ' Oh yes, and anything else you please sir.' "[12]

The event demonstrated that these strictures were quite unjustified. There was certainly no delay, for the first report of the Central Board was presented on 25th June, some nine weeks after the Commission had been set up.[13] Nor could there be any legitimate complaint about the way in which the inquiry was conducted. The old procedure of calling witnesses to London to give their evidence was abandoned: instead the Commissioners were sent into the manufacturing districts to conduct their investigations on the spot. The most detailed instructions were given to them—they were to invite communications from both the supporters and the opponents of the bill for regulating factories,[14] they were to study the answers given by the owners to the series of questions

11 M. T. Sadler, *Protest against the Secret Proceedings of the Factory Commission in Leeds* (1833) pp. 10, 13.

12 *The Commissioners' Vade Mecum whilst engaged in collecting evidence for the Factory Masters* (1833) pp. 3, 5.

13 *Parl. Papers* (1833) XX.

14 " We were not favoured," said the Report, " with any assistance from any of the supporters of that Bill."—*Ibid.* p. 6.

which had already been circulated,[15] and they were to use their utmost endeavours to arrive at the truth. " The object of the Commission being to obtain the most authentic, accurate, and complete information within the shortest time, the Central Board entrust to your discretion the adoption of any additional other means for the better attainment of that object."[16]

When they arrived in their districts the Commissioners found that the Short-time Committees had organized resistance on the widest possible scale. The Manchester operatives flatly refused to co-operate in the inquiry, condemning the Commission as " partial, unjust, unnecessary and delusive, sued out on false pretences." The factory children were paraded on Peterloo Field, where they marched in procession, their banners emblazoned with the slogans " A muzzle for the steam giant," " Manufactures without child-slaying." At Bradford a long line of the halt and maimed passed before the Commissioners; while at Leeds some three thousand children, amidst a great concourse of sympathizers, many of them wearing round their hats the printed slips labelled " The Ten Hour Bill," sang their factory song:

> We will have the Ten Hour Bill,
> That we will, that we will;
> Or the land shall ne'er be still,
> We will have the Ten Hour Bill.[17]

These skilfully arranged demonstrations of popular feeling did not, however, deflect the Commissioners from their purpose. " The most active if not the best instructed supporters of this measure," said the Report, " have manifested a spirit of hostility to the progress of the present inquiry, to which we believe that few parallel instances are upon record on a subject of grave national importance. . . .We refer to that class of men who, while stating the present inquiry to be merely whether children ought to work more than ten hours a day, are exerting their whole efforts for the restriction of adult labour, and for the arbitrary stoppage of the moving power. . . . The interests of the children, which alone supply materials for popular excitement on the subject of the proposed measure, are, of all other considerations, that which appears to enter least into the councils of the operative agitators for that measure."[18]

Despite the difficulties under which the inquiry was conducted, the first report of the Central Board was a masterly review of the

---

[15] A copy of these questions was to be posted for at least one whole day in a room frequented by the operatives.

[16] *Ibid.* p. 9.

[17] " Alfred," *The History of the Factory Movement* (1857) Vol. II, pp. 39-46.

[18] *Parl. Papers* (1833) XX, pp. 48-49.

whole question, calm and dispassionate in tone, and revealing clearly the logical and scientific attitude with which its authors had approached their task.[19]   " From the whole of the evidence laid before us," they said, " we find—

1st—That the children employed in all the principal branches of manufacture throughout the kingdom work during the same number of hours as the adults.

2d—That the effects of labour during such hours are, in a great number of cases,

Permanent deterioration of the physical constitution;

The production of disease often wholly irremediable; and

The partial or entire exclusion (by reason of excessive fatigue) from the means of obtaining adequate education and acquiring useful habits, or of profiting by those means when afforded.

3d—That at the age when children suffer these injuries from the labour they undergo, they are not free agents, but are let out to hire, the wages they earn being received and appropriated by their parents and guardians.

We are therefore of opinion that a case is made out for the interference of the Legislature in behalf of the children employed in factories."[20]

The report then proceeded to examine the efficacy of the ten-hours bill, and the motives of its advocates, in the following terms.   " This bill does not accomplish the object at which it purports to aim.   Its professed object is the protection of children; but it does not protect children.   For the same evidence which shows that the legislative protection of children is necessary shows that the restriction of the labour of children to ten hours a day is not an adequate protection.

This bill, making no provision for the occupation of any part of the time of children for their own benefit, either before or after their hours of labour, and taking no charge of their education, elementary or moral, leaves the removal of a most important portion of the evil under which children suffer unattempted.

While this bill does and attempts to do so little for children, its operation, if it could be carried into effect, would be to restrict the labour of adults, as well as of children, to ten hours.   The most direct and undisputed consequence of the passing of the Ten Hour Bill would be the general limitation of the labour of adults within the same hours as those assigned to children and adolescents. . . . On the part of the manufacturers it is generally

---

[19] A second report, dealing largely with the medical evidence, was published on 13th July, 1833 (*Parl. Papers,* 1833, XXI) and was followed by two supplementary reports (*Parl. Papers,* 1834, XIX, XX).

[20] *Parl. Papers* (1833) XX, pp. 35-36.

taken for granted that such will be the first effect of the measure under discussion. With the operatives the same assumption is prominently put forward in the arguments of most of the leading advocates of the measure, and is generally dwelt upon as forming a principal item amongst the benefits which they expect to derive from the passing of the measure.

The point at which the opinions of the masters and the operatives begin to diverge is in the estimate of the ulterior effects to be anticipated from the passing of the proposed measure, and from the consequent reduction of the hours of work for children and adults, attended, as the majority of witnesses agree must be the case, with a corresponding diminution of production.

It appears to be the general opinion of the operatives, that though wages may in the first instance fall, from reduction of the hours of labour, the artificial scarcity of commodities thus occasioned will effect a rise of prices, and a consequent rise of wages, as well as an increase of work for hands which are now partially out of employ, by occasioning the erection of new establishments to supply the deficiency of production caused by the diminution of labour.

The process by which not only the operative supporters of the Ten Hour Bill, but some otherwise well-informed persons, appear to have been led to the conclusion that a restriction of the working hours for adults, and a consequent increase of the cost of production in this country, could have the effect of raising and permanently maintaining a range of comparatively high prices, appears to have been the general application to all products of labour of a proposition true with respect to particular articles only, which are kept in a state of artificial scarcity by monopoly."[21] It is true, observed the Report, that in the first instance a temporary scarcity might cause a rise in prices, and allow wages to be maintained at the former level, but these conditions would not endure, for the competition of foreign manufacturers would soon restore the former proportion of supply to demand, with disastrous consequences to owners and operatives alike.

The allegations of physical cruelties inflicted on the factory children, which had formed so prominent a feature of the evidence adduced by the witnesses examined before Sadler's Committee, were refuted. " It appears in evidence that in Scotland, and in the eastern district of England, where the harshest treatment of children has taken place, the greatest number of bad cases occur in small obscure mills belonging to the smallest proprietors, and that the bad treatment is inflicted by violent and dissipated workmen, often the very men who raise the loudest outcry about the cruelties to

21 *Ibid*. pp. 37-41.

which children are subject in factories. . . . All the respectable witnesses throughout Scotland agree in declaring, that whatever may have happened in the beginning of the factory system, at a period when coercion was far more resorted to even in public schools than now, they are ignorant of any instance of punishment attended with severity."[22]

It was the view of the Commission that the case for affording legislative protection to children should not, and indeed could not be based on the alleged cruelties to which they were exposed. The inhuman practices described with such a wealth of detail by the extremists made a strong appeal to popular sympathy, but they were not inherent in the factory system. What was inherent, and what was indeed universal under good and bad masters alike, was the physical disability resulting from gross overwork. " The effects of factory labour on children," said the Report, " are immediate and remote: the immediate effects are fatigue, sleepiness, and pain; the remote effects, such at least as are usually conceived to result from it, are, deterioration of the physical constitution, deformity, disease, and deficient mental instruction and moral culture. . . . The physical evil inflicted on children by factory labour, when commenced as early[23] and continued as long as it now is, is not the only evil sustained by them. . . . Even when the employment of children at so early an age, and for so many hours as is customary at present, produces no manifest bodily disease, yet in the great majority of cases it incapacitates them from receiving instruction. . . . The young children very generally declare that they are too much fatigued to attend school, even when a school is provided for them."[24]

The dangers were now attributable rather to the excessive length of the working day than to the conditions under which the children were employed, for the newer factories were, on the whole, better designed. " The large factories, and those recently built, have a prodigious advantage over the old and small mills. The working-rooms in the large and modern buildings are, without exception, more spacious and lofty; the buildings are better drained; more effectual expedients are adopted to secure free ventilation, and to maintain a more equable and moderate temperature. It is of the old and small mills that the report pretty uniformly is—' dirty; low-roofed; ill-ventilated; ill-drained; no

---

[22] *Ibid.* pp. 24, 27.

[23] " It appears in evidence, that in some rare instances children begin to work in factories at five years old; it is not uncommon to find them there at six; many are under seven; still more under eight; but the greater number are nine; while some, but comparatively few, branches of manufacture do not admit of the employment of children under ten years of age."—*Parl. Papers* (1833) XX, p. 19.

[24] *Ibid.* pp. 29, 33.

contrivance for carrying off dust and other effluvia; machinery not boxed in; passages so narrow that they can hardly be defined; some of the flats so low that it is scarcely possible to stand upright in the centre of the rooms.' "[25]

In buildings such as these the lack of floor space, and the consequent heavy concentration of machinery, had been responsible for many accidents.[26] The improved construction of the new buildings had tended to reduce the dangers to some slight extent, but there were still many mills in which no precautionary measures were attempted, and where serious accidents were consequently of frequent occurrence. In many instances the manufacturers sought to exculpate themselves by imputing the accidents to the carelessness of the operatives, but the Commission was not prepared to accept this view, and laid the blame squarely on the shoulders of the owners. " The greater the carelessness of the proprietors in neglecting sufficiently to fence the machinery," said the Report, " and the greater the number of accidents, the less their sympathy with the sufferers."[27]

Much of the investigation had been directed to discovering the extent to which previous legislation had been effective, and the Commissioners had no hesitation in declaring that it had been almost entirely nugatory. " We find that in country situations the existing law is seldom or never attempted to be enforced, that in several principal manufacturing towns it is openly disregarded, that in others its operation is extremely partial and incomplete, and that even in Manchester, where the leading manufacturers felt an interest in carrying the act into execution as against the evasions practised by the small mill-owners, the attempt to enforce its provisions through the agency of a committee of masters has for some time back been given up. On the whole we find that the present law has been almost entirely inoperative with respect to the legitimate objects contemplated by it, and has only had the semblance of efficiency under circumstances under which it conformed to the state of things already in existence."[28]

---

[25] *Ibid.* p. 20.
[26] See the evidence of Kinder Wood, the Oldham surgeon before Peel's Committee. In the low rooms of the small factories, he said, " the accidents are more common; the shafts and cylinders are lower, and the children are more likely to be caught up by them; sufficient room is not left for them to be carried round the shaft or cylinder. This arises from the shape of the room and the size of the cylinders, and therefore the workpeople involved are crushed to death. . . Where there is sufficient space between the top of the room and the cylinder, children will be carried once or twice round, and be very little injured."—p. 195.
[27] *Parl. Papers* (1833) XX, p. 35.
[28] *Ibid.* p. 36.

Having thus considered the problem in all its complexity the Central Board proceeded to outline its proposals for reform. Its recommendations, inspired by Chadwick, who took the predominant part in framing them, constitute the real point of departure in the history of factory legislation. Previous measures had accomplished little or nothing beyond the enunciation of general principles. It was left to the administrative genius of this young disciple of Bentham not to formulate a new code of law, but to devise a system of checks and controls that should render the existing law effective, to evolve the machinery that would make it possible for the Executive to carry out the purpose of the Legislature.

The Report recommended that no child under nine years of age should be employed in a factory, and that, until the commencement of the fourteenth year the hours of labour during any day should not exceed eight, night work, between 10 p.m. and 5 a.m. being forbidden. This was a striking innovation, for although it was proposed to lower the age of protection from sixteen to twelve, it reduced the working day of these children from twelve hours to eight. The Commission justified their choice of the fourteenth year as the time at which protection should end on the grounds that at this age the period of childhood has ceased, puberty is established, and the physical frame is capable of more protracted labour. When they reach their fourteenth year, it was said, young people cease to be under the complete control of their parents, they usually make their own contracts, and are, in the proper sense of the word, free agents, who may rightly be placed on the same footing as adults. There were, too, reasons of administrative convenience that made it desirable not to limit the work of the older children. " The grounds on which we abstain from recommending more than one limit," explained the Board, " are the facilities which every additional restriction would afford to fraud and evasion; and the impossibility, according to the evidence, of employing three sets of hands with different limitations. The nearer the approximation of the hours of one set to the hours of another, the greater would be the facilities and temptations of the lower set to run into the working hours of the higher set."[29]

Recognizing that an immediate limitation of those under thirteen to eight hours a day might cause serious embarrassment, especially in country districts where there was a shortage of hands, the Commission recommended that in the first instance, in order to allow time for preparation, the restrictions should apply only to those children who had not attained the age of eleven. Thereafter

---

[29] *Ibid.* pp. 56-57.

the restrictions should be extended by stages, at intervals of six or twelve months, to those under twelve and thirteen respectively.[30]

But this was not the only difficulty. If the labour of children was to be limited to eight hours a day, some scheme must be evolved to enable the adults to work their normal hours.[31] The Commission recommended, therefore, that the children should be employed in shifts or relays. "The great evil of the manufacturing system, as at present conducted, has appeared to us to be, that it entails the necessity of continuing the labour of children to the utmost length of that of the adults. The only remedy for this evil short of a limitation of the labour of adults, which would in our opinion create an evil greater than that which is sought to be remedied, appears to be the plan of working double sets of children." The masters, said the Report, were opposed to such a scheme because it was inconvenient and would involve them in the payment of increased wages. Some owners objected that double sets would be impracticable. "We find, however, in the course of our inquiry that the words 'impracticable' and 'impossible' are too commonly attached by many of the manufacturers to any regulation which may subject them to expense or to temporary inconvenience."[32]

The most far-reaching and revolutionary proposals concerned the provision of education for factory children. "Since the whole of our recommendations have for their object the care and benefit of the children, we have been desirous of devising means for securing the occupation of a portion of the time abridged from their hours of labour to their own advantage. We think the best mode of accomplishing this object will be the occupation, suppose of three (or four) hours of every day in education; and we are the more disposed to recommend this, since it will secure two ulterior objects of considerable importance: first, it will be the best means of preventing the employment of the same child in two different factories on the same day, or in any other kind of labour likely to be injurious to its health; and secondly, it will better qualify the persons so educated to adapt themselves to other employments, if in after life the vicissitudes of trade or other causes should render it desirable that they should find other means of support.

---

[30] *Ibid.* p. 61.
[31] Some of the more extreme reformers were, indeed, pressing for an eight-hours day for adults. See a pamphlet published at Bradford in 1833— *Catechism of the Society for Promoting National Regeneration* (p. 4): "Q.—What ought to be the Maximum of Time for daily labour? A.— Eight Hours a day—or from eight o'clock in the morning till mid-day, and from two o'clock in the afternoon till six o'clock in the evening . . . because it is the longest period that the human race . . . can endure, of physical exertion, so as to be healthy, intelligent, virtuous and happy."
[32] *Parl. Papers* (1833) XX, p. 57.

As a means of securing that the prescribed portion of every day should be devoted to the purpose of education, we recommend that every child on entering a factory be required to produce a ticket certifying that such portion of time has been spent in school; the afternoon set certifying that they have been at school during the prescribed number of hours on the forenoon of the same day; and the morning set that they had been at school during the same number of hours in the afternoon of the preceding day. And we further recommend that the inspector be required and empowered to direct the execution of such regulations and securities, adapted to local circumstances, as he may deem requisite for the accomplishment of this object."[33]

So far as the machinery of enforcement was concerned the Commission proposed two innovations which were destined to sway the whole course of future legislation—the appointment of factory inspectors, and the introduction of surgeons' certificates as a means of verifying age. " Several eminent manufacturers," declared the Report, " have represented to us, that the only certain method of ensuring obedience to any legislative measures on this subject would be by the appointment of officers charged with the powers and duties requisite to enforce their execution. The necessity of some appointments of this nature has indeed been urged from all parts of the country.

In general it is conceived that the officer ought to be resident, and should be charged with exclusive jurisdiction of complaints relating to the infraction of legislative regulations of manufactories. The prominent objection to such an establishment of resident officers is chiefly the expence; for the manufactories being spread all over the country, such officers must necessarily be very numerous and expensive, if they are adequately paid for their services. We consider that by giving to the magistrates a concurrent jurisdiction on complaints made before them, a comparatively small agency would suffice.

The necessity of the appointment of inspectors has been most urgently stated by those manufacturers who have had chiefly in view the restriction of the hours of labour in other factories to the level of their own. The greater necessity of the appointment of some special agency for the enforcement of the measures we have recommended must be admitted, when it is recollected that they relate solely to the children, and are not directly conducive to the immediate interests either of the master manufacturers, or of the operatives, or of any powerful class, and are not therefore likely to receive continuous voluntary support. On the whole, we recommend the appointment by the Government of three inspectors

---

[33] *Ibid.* pp. 75-76.

to go circuits of the chief manufacturing districts, at intervals as
short as may be practicable, and exercise the functions with which
they may be invested for carrying the law into force. For this
purpose each inspector should have the right of entering all
manufactories where children are employed, and of ordering
machinery to be fenced off, and directing arrangements of a sanitary
nature, compatible with the execution of the manufacturing processes; and he should also have cognizance of the arrangements
for the education of the children employed. He should have
power to hear and determine all complaints of infraction of the
provisions of the law, to give directions with relation to them to
peace officers, and fine for neglect. It should be the duty of the
inspectors to meet as a board, to report periodically to the Government for the use of the Legislature as to their proceedings and
as to any amendments of the law which they might find requisite
or which might be called for. For this purpose they should be
invested with the power of examining witnesses on oath, and of
compelling their attendance.

In several of the most important manufacturing districts the
resident magistrates are manufacturers; and the appointment of
officers of the character and the concurrent jurisdiction we have
recommended would enable a complainant to reserve his complaint, if he thought proper, until the period of the visit of the
inspectors. Some mills are so remotely situated in solitary places
apart from towns that it would be impracticable to visit them with
the same frequency. But in these places the difficulty of finding
a magistrate who was not a manufacturer, before whom a complaint
might be made, probably would not exist.

We consider that the performance of the function of reporting
periodically to the Government, by persons whose duty it should
be to examine the evidence on which allegations of abuse were
founded, and to whom all complaints might be referred for
examination, would be attended with considerable advantages, in
the security it would give against the occurrence of practices inconsistent with humanity, and in the protection which on the other
hand it would extend to the master-manufacturers against groundless complaints."[34]

The new realism that the Commission proposed to introduce
into the control of the factories led them to suggest the adoption
of a system of certificates which, it was hoped, would enable the
ages of children to be ascertained with some precision. " Any
measure," they said, " by which the enforcement of the law shall
be made chiefly dependent on those who have an interest in
breaking it may be expected to prove as inefficient as the provisions

---

[34] *Ibid.* pp. 72-73.

of the existing law. On the part of the parent, who, under the existing law, is called upon to give the certificate of the age of the child, (which certificate forms at present the main security against evasion on this point), we find a strong interest in the commission of fraud; . . . on the part of the immediate agents or overlookers, probably the friends of the parent, a willingness to connive at it; and on the part of the masters no especial motive to exert vigilance. . . .

On the consideration of the difficulties displayed in the testimony of the witnesses, we are prepared to recommend, that it should be declared unlawful to employ any child of the prescribed age without a certificate from a surgeon or medical man resident in the township where the mill or factory is situated, who shall certify, on inspection of the child, that he believes it to be of the full growth and usual condition of a child of the age prescribed by the legislature, and fitted for employment in a manufactory. This certificate should be given in the presence of a magistrate, provided that he also were satisfied that the child was of the average condition of a child of the prescribed age. The age would be fixed by the legislature, as one of the means of determining the physical condition, which alone is the proper qualification for employment. . . .

If the medical certificate alone were required, it is to be apprehended that in many neighbourhoods practitioners would be found whose practice is dependent on the labouring classes, and who would sometimes find a difficulty in refusing certificates to children below the proper standards as to age or condition.

The most important period for the exercise of vigilance is however that of admission to the period of full work. We propose that it should be guarded by a similar but a more special examination and certificate or indenture, to be given by an inspector who should also certify, on examination, that the child examined has received an elementary education of the nature which may be hereafter prescribed. This last provision may be made to serve as a check against evasions of such regulations as may be adopted with regard to attendance at schools, or misapplications of the previous time allowed by the reduced labour."[35]

The Commissioners gave careful attention to the problem of accidents caused by the machinery. Some owners had suggested that the inspectors should be empowered to direct that certain parts of the machines should be fenced, and that when that had been done the mill-occupier should be relieved from any further responsibility. " We concur in the proposition for giving such power to the inspectors," said the Report, " but we do not concur

[35] *Ibid.* pp. 68-71.

in the proposal to relieve the manufacturers from responsibility. . . . The proprietor of the machine is necessarily the person who can best foresee all the consequences incidental to its use, and can best guard against them. By throwing upon him a portion of the pecuniary responsibility for those mischiefs, we combine interest with duty, and add to the efficiency of both."[36]

The Report of the Royal Commission marks a decisive point in the evolution of factory legislation. This " volume of most repulsive magnitude,"[37] as the reformers scornfully termed it, cast an entirely new light on the problem of industrial control, and made possible a new and effective approach. The manufacturers welcomed it because it was " such as to dissipate the clouds of misrepresentation which declaimers had breathed forth on the subject,"[38] but their relief at being cleared of the more odious of the charges that had been levelled against them by Sadler's Committee was tempered by the reflection that if the recommendations of the Commission were adopted their long period of immunity from regulation was likely to come to an end.

---

[36] *Ibid.* pp. 76-77.
[237] *Quarterly Review* (1836) Vol. 57, p. 412.
[38] E. Baines, *History of the Cotton Manufacture in Great Britain* (1835), p. 435. *Cf.* R. H. Greg, *The Factory Question* (1837) p. 8—" An official and authenticated mass of evidence to which all must bow."

CHAPTER 5

ALTHORP'S ACT, 1833

O N 17TH JUNE, 1833, Lord Ashley's bill came up for its second reading in the Commons. Lord Althorp, speaking for the Government, declared that he would offer no opposition at this juncture, since the Report of the Royal Commission would be available in a few days' time, and the House would doubtless wish to consider its recommendations at the committee stage.[1] The Report was duly published on 25th June, and on 5th July, when the House was in Committee, Althorp suggested that the bill be referred to a Select Committee.

Ashley's proposals, he said, filled him with apprehension. The effects in the manufacturing districts would be disastrous, for foreigners would be enabled to compete in the English market, and the workers would, in consequence, be impoverished. He admitted that in view of the present state of feeling in the country, and of the excitement which so generally prevailed, it was necessary that Parliament should interfere, and legislate to protect children, properly so-called; but he thought that Ashley's measure carried protection too far, since adults would be unnecessarily deprived of the opportunity of making the most of their only property, their labour. Children of nine, ten or eleven, who had no choice of their own as to the duration of their labour, should, of course, be protected; but to say that regulation should necessarily extend to adults, who were masters of their own time, was to broach a proposition to which he hoped Parliament would not assent. The alteration that he desired to see was the insertion of a clause by which protection to children would be increased, while leaving adults unshackled and unrestricted. If the bill were referred to a Select Committee it should be an instruction that children under thirteen should not work more than eight hours a day. One great and paramount object must be kept in view—the promotion of education. Care should be taken that an interval at a seasonable period of the day should be reserved for instruction.

It was notorious, continued Althorp, that existing laws were ineffective. If a restriction was to be made it should be accompanied with adequate powers to secure its observance; for unless the law were enforced, those who obeyed would have to compete at a great disadvantage with those who managed to evade it. It was, therefore, his intention to propose an instruction to the

---

[1] *Hansard* (1833) XVIII, 914.

Committee to ascertain the expediency of a system of inspection throughout the mills where child labour was used.[2]

Ashley agreed that inspection was desirable, and that the hours of children under thirteen should be further limited, but did Althorp really believe that boys and girls, as soon as they reached that age, should be left to the mercy of the owners? The suggestion that double sets or relays should be employed had been recommended by the Commission in the face of all the evidence. Such a scheme was impracticable—there were not sufficient children available, and the reduction in their wages, which must inevitably follow, would cause serious injury.[3]

Brotherton supported his leader. All persons were agreed, he said, that some legislation was desirable. That was making great progress, for twenty years ago not a single master would allow that legislative interference was necessary. Now, the public, the masters, and the working men, all agreed in appealing to Parliament to make regulations for the labour of factories. They had different motives for demanding it. The masters demanded it because they desired to prevent some amongst themselves from working too long. The adults required interference as the only means of preventing them from being over-worked; and the public required the interference of the Legislature to protect the children.[4]

Althorp's proposal for a Select Committee was then put to the vote, and having rejected it by 164 to 141,[5] the House resumed the detailed consideration of Ashley's bill on 18th July. Althorp strenuously opposed the suggestion that all workers under eighteen years of age should be restricted to ten hours a day. The effect would be to impose this limitation of time on the running of the mills, and he emphasized once again the hardships in which this would involve the operatives, and the dangers that would arise from the competition of foreign countries, where manufacturers were unlimited and unfettered in conducting their business. For his part, he repeated, he would much prefer to afford a genuine protection to the younger children, who should be allowed to work no more than eight hours a day until they reached their fourteenth year. If this were agreed he would be quite prepared to extend the scope of the measure to a wider range of textile industries. The Government carried the day, and on the motion for a ten-hours limitation being put, Ashley was defeated by 238 votes to 93. He thereupon withdrew from the contest. Having taken up the subject fairly and conscientiously, he said, he found that the noble Lord had completely defeated him. He should therefore surrender the

[2] *Hansard* (1833) XIX, 220-223.
[3] *Ibid*. 224-227.
[4] *Ibid*. 233-234.
[5] *Ibid*. 254.

bill into the hands of the noble Lord; but having taken it up with a view to do good to the classes interested, he would only say into whatever hands it might pass, God prosper it.[6]

The Government bill[7] was ready on 9th August, 1833. It had been prepared by Chadwick,[8] who naturally enough had incorporated in it most of the recommendations of the Commission for whose findings he was so largely responsible. Althorp explained to an eager and expectant House that it was proposed to limit children under thirteen to eight hours a day, while young persons between the ages of thirteen and eighteen were not to work more than sixty-nine hours a week. No child was to be employed under the age of nine, and these arrangements were to be secured by the appointment of inspectors, in such a way that no evasion of the law could take place. The bill, he said, contained three principles—first, that children under thirteen years of age should not work more than eight hours a day,—secondly, that there was to be set up a system of inspection by which the bill would be carried into effect,—and, thirdly, it would establish a better and more general system of education among the class of persons employed in factories. He still entertained doubts, he continued, of the propriety of the Legislature's interfering between master and servant, but he would admit that if children were placed in a situation in which they could not protect themselves, it was the duty of that House to afford protection to them.[9]

In the debate that followed Althorp accepted the amendment moved by Gilbert Heathcote that the lace trade should be excluded from the operation of the bill,[10] but the suggestion that the manufacturers should be allowed to work the mills for twelve hours on Saturdays was rejected, on the ground that " it was intended that the children should have a little relaxation on the Saturdays, that they might be somewhat refreshed from their fatigues on the Sundays, and enabled to keep from sleeping while in school."[11] The extent to which the advocates of the ten-hours bill were really interested in the welfare of the children whose cause they pleaded so vehemently, was illustrated by the amendment, moved by Brotherton, that children under thirteen should

6 *Hansard* (1833) XIX, 883-913. See " Alfred," *The History of the Factory Movement* (1857) Vol. II, pp. 63-64. E. von Plener, *The English Factory Legislation* (1873) p. 15. E. Hodder, *The Life and Work of the seventh Earl of Shaftesbury* (1893) p. 89.
7 *Parl. Papers* (1833) II, p. 281.
8 *Transactions of the National Association for the Promotion of Social Science* (1860) p. 419.
9 *Hansard* (1833) XX, 449.
10 *Ibid.* 450.
11 *Ibid.* 452.

work not for eight, but for ten hours a day, since this would be better for masters and operatives. The Government, who in this respect at least had stolen the thunder of the reformers, opposed this suggestion, and carried the House with them.[12]   Further attempts to destroy the main principles of the bill were similarly rejected—the educational clauses, attacked by Thomas Attwood, were retained, the powers of the inspectors were left unimpaired, and the limitation of children's hours, involving as it did, the adoption of the relay system, was preserved, though with some hesitation, and after lengthy discussion.

Sir Henry Willoughby maintained that " the suggestion framed on the Report of the central Commissioners, with respect to double relays of children, was in the teeth of the great mass of evidence collected by those Commissioners who had gone through the country.   Commissioners, masters of mills, managers, all wonderfully coincided in declaring such a system ineffectual and impracticable. . . . The great objection to relays was the deficiency of supply, and the necessary fall in wages, what they gained in time being lost in diet and clothing. The clause would operate greatly to the prejudice of the children, and have a tendency to drive the factories into crowded and unhealthy places."   Althorp agreed that the question was difficult, " but he had always thought Parliament could not legislate on this subject without incurring the risk of producing mischief."   The only solution appeared to be that recommended in the Report of the Commissioners, namely, to secure that the restrictions on the working hours of the children should be introduced by progressive stages, and this was the course that the House finally decided to adopt.[13]

The Lords accepted the bill, but they introduced a modification that was to have the most unfortunate consequences. Chadwick, realizing that the educational provisions could not possibly be effective unless schools were available in the factory districts, had inserted a clause giving the inspectors power to establish such schools where necessary.[14]   "Wherever it shall appear to any Inspector that a new or additional School is necessary or desirable to enable the Children employed in any Factory to obtain the education required by this Act, such Inspector is hereby authorized and required to establish or procure the establishment of such School by contract or otherwise; and if the deduction hereinbefore authorized at the rate of One Penny out of every Shilling from the weekly Wages of such Children shall be insufficient to pay the expenses of such School, the Employer or Employers of such Children shall pay the deficiency, each in the ratio of the number

12 By 40 votes to 16. *Ibid.* 577.
13 *Ibid.* 528, 577.
14 Clause 20. *Parl. Papers* (1833) II, p. 287.

LORD ASHLEY

of Children in their employment, which deficiency shall be assessed by and paid to the Inspector; and every Sum so paid by any Employer, may be deducted by such Employer out of the Poor-rates which shall next become due from such Employer in respect of his Factory; and if such payment shall exceed the amount of the Poor-rates so due from such Employer, the excess shall be re-imbursed to him out of the Poor-rates of the Town, Parish or Place in which such Factory is rated."

The Marquis of Salisbury procured the rejection of this clause. " Nor can there be a doubt," said the *Westminster Review*,[15] " that it was advisedly done, in order to defeat this vital part of the measure. And the omission of this clause has established the magnificent purpose which its rejection was intended to effect."

Less than three weeks after its introduction in the Commons, on 29th August, 1833, the Act to regulate the Labour of Children and young Persons in the Mills and Factories of the United Kingdom[16] received the royal assent. The preamble stated that the hours of labour of children and young persons ought to be regulated, for there were great numbers employed, and their working hours were longer than was desirable, due regard being had to their health and means of education.

Accordingly it was provided that after 1st January, 1834, no person under 18 years of age, employed in or about any cotton, woollen, worsted, hemp, flax, tow, linen or silk mill or factory, where steam, water, or other mechanical power was used, was to work during the night, *i.e.* between 8.30 p.m. and 5.30 a.m.,[17] nor was any such person to be employed for more than 12 hours in any one day, or for more than 69 hours in any one week.[18]

After 1st January, 1834, no child was to be employed in the mills regulated by the Act until he had attained the age of 9, but an exception was made in favour of silk mills, which were still allowed to engage children regardless of their age.[19]

After the expiration of six months from the passing of the Act no child under 11 years of age was to work for more than 9

---

[15] October, 1836, p. 206. For Chadwick's view see *Transactions of the National Association for the Promotion of Social Science* (1860) p. 419. *Cf.* L. Faucher, *Etudes sur l'Angleterre* (1856) Vol. I, p. 457— " Par une singulière imprévoyance, en déclarant que les jeunes ouvriers des manufactures *seraient tenus de fréquenter les écoles,* on négligea d'établir partout des écoles à leur portée. La loi prescrivait l'impossible; on comprend qu'elle n'ait pas été obéie."

[16] 3 & 4 Will. IV, c. 103.

[17] Sec. 1. The Act did not apply to mechanics, artisans, or labourers under the prescribed ages working only in repairing the machinery or the premises (Section 46).

[18] Sec. 2.

[19] Sec. 7.

hours in any one day or for more than 48 hours in any one week. After 18 months the age limit was to be raised to 12, and after 30 months to 13, but in silk mills children under 13 years of age were to be allowed to work 10 hours in any one day.[20] Any child restricted to 9 hours' work a day who had been employed for less than 9 hours in one factory, might work the residue of the 9 hours in another factory on the same day, provided he was not employed for more than 48 hours in any one week.[21] A mill-owner was liable to a penalty if he allowed a child restricted to 9 hours' work a day to remain on the premises for a longer period, even if he was not actually employed during this additional time, but this did not apply to children who remained in a play-ground or school-room attached to the factory.[22]

In certain circumstances the Act allowed an extension of working hours. In mills relying on water-power the hours of labour could be extended in order to make up time lost through lack of, or excess of water, or by reason of its being impounded in higher reservoirs. Time thus lost could be recovered at the rate of three hours a week, and the working day could, for this purpose, be extended to the period from 5 a.m. to 9 p.m. The loss was to be made good within six calendar months.[23] During periods of drought or flood when the power of the water-wheels was interrupted, and time was consequently lost, the hours during which persons under 18 years of age could work might be extended even beyond the period 5 a.m. to 9 p.m., but no child or young person was to work more than the number of hours stipulated by the Act in any one day, and no child under 13 was to be employed between 9 p.m. and 5 a.m.[24]

When any extraordinary accident affected the steam-engine, water-wheel, shafting, gearing, or gas apparatus, by reason of which not less than three hours' work was lost at any one time, the loss

[20] Sec. 8. The interpretation of this section caused some difficulty. In a letter addressed to the owners (*Parl. Papers*, 1834, XLIII, p. 437) Leonard Horner, the Inspector for the northern district, explained that the first period of six months would expire on 13th February, 1834, since he had been advised that the word " month " in an Act of Parliament must be construed as lunar month, not calendar month. On 20th February, 1834, a short amending Act was passed (4 & 5 Will. IV, c. 1) section 1 of which provided that the periods of 18 months and 30 months mentioned in section 8 of the principal Act should be calendar months, not lunar months. It was not until 1889 that this confusion was finally resolved. In that year the Interpretation Act (52 & 53 Vict., c. 63) provided, by section 3, that in every Act passed after 1850, the word " month " was to mean calendar month.
[21] Sec. 10.
[22] Sec. 24.
[23] Sec. 3.
[24] Sec. 5.

could be made good by working an additional hour a day during the ensuing twelve working days.[25]

Persons restricted to twelve hours' work a day were to be allowed an hour and a half each day for meals.[26] Children and young persons whose hours were limited by the Act were to be entitled to the following holidays:—the whole of Christmas Day and Good Friday, and not fewer than eight additional half-days in each year.[27]

After six months from the passing of the Act no child under 11 years of age was to be employed without a certificate stating that he was of the ordinary strength and appearance of a child aged 9. Eighteen months and thirty months after the passing of the Act the age limit was to be raised to 12 and 13 respectively.[28] In order to obtain a certificate the child was to appear personally before some surgeon or physician in the neighbourhood of its residence, and when the certificate had been granted it was to be counter-signed within three months by an Inspector or Magistrate.[29] If the Inspector or Magistrate refused to counter-sign, he was required to state his reasons in writing, and the parents could then appeal to the Petty Sessions.[30]

Young persons between the age of 11 (rising to 12 after eighteen months, and to 13 after thirty months) and 18, were not to be employed for more than 9 hours in any one day, nor between 9 p.m. and 5 a.m. without a certificate testifying that they were above the age of 11 (or 12 or 13 as the case might be). The form of this certificate was to be decided by the Inspector.[31] No penalty, however, was to be levied if a young person was employed more than 9 hours a day without a certificate, if it appeared that at the time of the alleged offence he was, in fact, above the age of 11 (or 12 or 13 within eighteen and thirty months respectively.)[32]

Children who were restricted to 48 hours' labour a week were required to attend some school, which was either to be chosen by the parents, or appointed by the Inspector in the event of the parents' default. In the latter case the employer was authorized to deduct from the child's weekly wages a penny in the shilling, and this money was to be paid as the Inspector required towards the cost of the schooling.[33] Each Monday morning the child was

---

25 Sec. 4.
26 Sec. 6. This period was, of course, in addition to the 12 hours of actual work, *i.e.*, the working day extended over 13½ hours.
27 Sec. 9.
28 Sec. 11.
29 Sec. 12. For the form of the certificate prescribed by section 13, see p. 123.
30 Sec. 16.
31 Sec. 14.
32 Sec. 15.
33 Sec. 20.

to produce a voucher from the schoolmaster certifying that he had attended school (except when prevented by sickness) for at least two hours a day on six days of the preceding week.[34]

If additional schools were required to enable the provisions of the Act to be complied with, the Inspector was authorized to establish them, or to take the steps necessary to secure their establishment.[35] The Inspector was also given a certain measure of control in that he was empowered to disallow the order for the salary of any schoolmaster or schoolmistress who was incompetent.[36]

The interior walls of the factory (other than those that were painted) were to be lime-washed, and ceilings were to be white-washed once a year, unless the Inspector gave written permission to the contrary.[37]

Since, said the Act, the provision in the Health and Morals of Apprentices Act, 1802 (42 Geo. III, c. 73) requiring the magistrates to appoint two persons to visit the factories, had not been observed, and the law had, in consequence, been evaded, four persons were to be appointed to be Inspectors of Factories. These Inspectors were to carry out the terms of the Act, and for this purpose they were authorized to enter factories and factory schools at all times, and to summon any person to give evidence on oath.[38]

The Inspectors were required to make such rules, regulations and orders as were necessary for the due execution of the Act, they were to enforce attendance at school, and they were to see that there was kept a register of the children employed in the factory, and of their hours of attendance. The form of these registers was not prescribed.[39] Any orders or regulations that they made applying to more than one factory were to have the same effect as if they had been personally served on each occupier when they had been published during two successive weeks in the local newspaper, and they were to come into force seven days after the second publication.[40]

Upon the application of an Inspector, one or more superintendents might be employed to assist in carrying out the Act.[41]

The Inspectors were to have the same power and authority over constables and peace officers as magistrates,[42] and the penalty for wilfully obstructing them in the execution of their duties was

---

[34] Sec. 21.
[35] Sec. 22.
[36] Sec. 23.
[37] Sec. 26.
[38] Sec. 17.
[39] Sec. 18.
[40] Sec. 25.
[41] Sec. 19.
[42] Sec. 33.

a fine not exceeding £10.[43] They were authorized to administer
the oath to witnesses, and to summon witnesses to appear and give
evidence. In default they could commit the offender to prison foi
a term not exceeding two months.[44]

They were required to keep full minutes of all their visits and
proceedings, and to report them to the Secretary of State at least
twice a year. They were also to make general reports at similar
intervals, and to meet at least twice a year in conference so as to
secure, as far as possible, uniformity in practice and procedure.[45]

Parents who allowed their children to be employed contrary
to the provisions of the Act were liable to a penalty not exceeding
20s.[46] The penalty for an offence against the Act, or against an
Inspector's regulations, was to be the forfeiture of a sum not
exceeding £20, and not less than £1 at the discretion of the
Inspector or Magistrate before whom the offender was convicted.
If the Inspector or Magistrate considered that the offence was not
wilful or grossly negligent, the penalty might be mitigated below
the sum of £1, or the information might be dismissed.[47] The
agents or servants of the mill-owner were to be personally liable
for any offences against the Act, and the owner was to be freed
from responsibility if the offence was committed without his consent
or knowledge.[48] The Inspector or Magistrate was empowered to
pay to the complainant or prosecutor one half of any penalty
imposed, the remainder of the penalty, or the whole if it were
considered desirable, to be applied as the Inspector or Magistrate
directed, for the benefit of any school at which factory children
were educated.[49]

Proceedings under the Act could be taken before a single
Inspector or Magistrate.[50] Complaints for offences against the Act
were to be made at, or before, the time of the next visit of the
Inspector, and written notice of the intention to prefer a complaint
was to be given within 14 days of the commission of the alleged
offence. Not more than one penalty was recoverable for a
repetition of the same offence, except after the service of such a
notice.[51]

If a person adjudged to pay a penalty neglected or refused to
pay, the Inspector or Magistrate could distrain upon his goods,
and if there were no sufficient distress, the offender might be com-

43 Sec. 32.
44 Sec. 38.
45 Sec. 45.
46 Sec. 29.
47 Sec. 31.
48 Sec. 30.
49 Sec. 43.
50 Sec. 34.
51 Sec. 35.

mitted to prison for a term not exceeding two months.[52] No appeal was allowed against a conviction under the Act, except when the charge was the forgery of a certificate or voucher,[53] or other document required by the Act or by the Inspector's regulations.[54]

Section 27 provided that an abstract of the Act, and of the Inspector's regulations, signed by the owner or manager, was to be hung in a conspicuous place in each factory. The last section, the 48th, repealed the Act of 1831[55] as from 1st January, 1834.

Such were the terms of the Factories Regulation Act of 1833. Following the precedent of former legislation it was strictly limited in its scope, for it protected fully only the children and young persons employed in manufacturing processes in cotton, woollen, worsted, hemp, flax, tow and linen mills. It is true that this extension of control to other branches of the textile industry was a notable advance, for even Hobhouse's Act had applied only to cotton factories, but there were still departments of the industry that remained wholly or partly unregulated. Lace factories were specifically excluded by the first section, and the children employed in silk mills were afforded only a half measure of protection, for not only was it legal to work them for ten hours a day, but they were outside the scope of the educational clauses, which were limited to those whose labour was restricted to 48 hours a week.[56]

" This Act," said Leonard Horner, " has three great objects in view: *first*, to prevent children and young persons from being worked a greater number of hours than is believed to be safe for their health; *secondly*, to give time for the children to receive a suitable education, and to insist that their education shall not be neglected; and *thirdly*, to accomplish these ends without interfering with the generally established number of hours of daily work of adults."[57] It was because the Act was designed to improve the conditions of the children while leaving the working hours of adults unrestricted that the operatives offered such violent opposition to it. They alleged that it had been framed in accordance with the desires of the owners, who had secured the ear of the Commission.

---

[52] Sec. 41.

[53] This was an offence punishable by imprisonment for not more than two months. (Sec. 28).

[54] Sec. 42.

[55] 1 & 2 Will. IV, c. 39.

[56] This discrimination caused much dissatisfaction, especially in those towns such as Congleton, Derby and Sandbach, where silk mills existed side by side with those subjected to full regulation. Saunders in his report of 28th December, 1833 (*Parl. Papers,* 1834, XLIII, p. 481) mentioned the unfair competition thus caused, and stated. (August, 1835, *Parl. Papers,* 1836, XLV, p. 157) that both masters and operatives resented the exclusion of the lace mills.

[57] *The Factories Regulation Act Explained* (1834) p. 21.

" This Act, from the moment of its birth in the Chambers of the
Central Board of Factory Commissioners, (at which Mr. Poulett
Thompson assisted) to that of its passing the Houses of Parliament,
has been entirely under the care and direction of a few great Mill
Owners."⁵⁸ " We assert," said the Bradford operatives, " *that the
present Act is not that which we recommended, but it is that against
which we openly and vehemently protested,* as vexatious and
impracticable—we declared that it would injure the children—hurt
their parents, and *gall* their employers, and our words are proved
true at this day. . . . The Central Board had a Committee of large
Factory Proprietors at their elbows. These Gentlemen suggested
to the Central Board much of what had been passed into an Act."⁵⁹
     Althorp was denounced as the mere tool of the manufacturers
—" finding himself very much annoyed by the innumerable
petitions presented by the people to Parliament, he told the Mill-
owners, that the question could not be allowed to sleep, and that
an Act of some sort must be passed, *in order to satisfy the demands
of the people, and to put down the agitation, which was so annoying the Government.* After a good deal of ' back-stairs intriguing,'
the *Millowners and the Government* concocted a Bill, and . . . we
are informed that it was supported by the Millowners, *because
they knew it to be impracticable.*"⁶⁰ The Short-time Committees of
Ashton and Stalybridge also proclaimed their hostility, announcing
that they were " wishful to impress on the minds of the Operatives
and Friends of an effective Ten Hours' Bill, the succeeding facts—
that they disclaim in every participation in the now existing law
—that they petitioned, protested, and remonstrated against it—that
it was the Masters' Bill, drawn up and agreed to by ' the Bit of a
Cotton Parliament, in Palace Yard,' and it is no other than
bullock-breeding Lord Althorp's Factories Regulation Act—that
Meeting after Meeting in England, Ireland and Scotland, denounced
it as injurious both to masters and men."⁶¹
     It was asserted that the owners, realizing that legislation was
inevitable, had secured the passing of an Act that was foredoomed
to failure. " The measure," said the operatives, " was concocted in
the vilest spirit of hypocrisy and evasion, vicious in its origin, and
designedly inefficient for practical working,"⁶² while Ashley,
writing in the *Quarterly Review,* denounced it as " that precious
law which now regulates the factories; a law got up in haste to

⁵⁸ *Address to the Friends of Justice and Humanity* (1833) p. 6.
⁵⁹ *Protest of the Bradford Short-time Committee* (1835) pp. 1-2.
⁶⁰ R. Oastler, *The Rejected Letter* (1836) p. 13.
⁶¹ *On the Factory Question* (1836) p. 1.
⁶² *Blackwood's Edinburgh Magazine* (July, 1836) No. CCXLIX,
Vol. XL, p. 116.

serve a purpose; approved by none, yet supported by a large majority, all of whom knew it to be impracticable."[63]

" His Majesty's Government," said the Manchester operatives, " has involved itself in a labyrinth of difficulty and perplexity, in consequence of originally adopting a Bill which had no foundation of practical experience or knowledge on which to rest, and the leading principle of which (the employment of relays) was at variance with all the mass of evidence that from first to last has been laid before Parliament . . . a bill intricate in all its details and loaded with provisions obnoxious alike to masters, operatives, parents and children."[64]

So far from approving the Act, however, the manufacturers, once they had grasped its full implications, condemned it as bitterly as did the operatives. Dr. Ure, writing in March, 1836, asserted that Parliament had over-reached itself. " In my humble opinion," he told Hindley, " Parliament has already gone too far in restricting the labour of factories when it fixed the minimum age of children employed in them at 13 years. It has therefore done great injury to working people, burthened with a numerous family, whose children might be employed most beneficially to their parents and themselves, as scavengers and piecers, in mule spinning from their eleventh year."[65] Nassau Senior concurred. " To enforce ventilation and drainage," he said, " and give means and motives to education, seems to me all that can be done by positive enactment."[66]

A Scottish spinner, writing to Lord Althorp, stigmatized the Act as " indefensible in principle; invidious, oppressive, and absurd in its provisions; in its penalties harsh, ruinous, and tyrannical in the extreme,"[67] while Gaskell referred to it as " absurd in its details, complicated in its machinery, and worse than useless for the purposes aimed at."[68] Baines considered that all restrictions on industry should be imposed " with a delicate and cautious hand."[69] Many of the provisions of the Act, he held, were quite impracticable, and unless the measure was repealed, all children under twelve years of age would be dismissed in March, 1835, thus making it impossible for the mills to continue. " The commissioners had hoped that the manufacturers might obtain relays of children, each set working not more than eight hours a day,

[63] Vol. 57, p. 416.
[64] *Memorial of the Manchester Short-time Committee.* Parl. Papers (1837) L, p. 207.
[65] *Foreign Competition and the Ten Hours' Bill* (1836) p. 2.
[66] *Letters on the Factory Act* (1837) p. 27.
[67] *Letter to the Right Hon. Lord Althorp on the Factory Bill* (1833) p. 12.
[68] P. Gaskell, *Artisans and Machinery* (1836) p. 172.
[69] E. Baines, *History of the Cotton Manufacture in Great Britain* (1835) p. 480.

whilst those above thirteen years of age worked twelve hours. But neither can the children be obtained, nor will the masters submit to the inconvenience caused by the change of hands."[70]

Amidst this welter of contending factions the voices of those who supported the Act were but faintly heard. Realizing the strength of the opposition they had to face, confident that their plan of centralized control would, in the long run, be vindicated, the Benthamites prepared for the struggle, calling for vigilance and firmness. "'We repeat," they declared, "without watchfulness and exertion . . . the present law . . . will become a dead letter. For there are arrayed against it powerful interests which must defeat it, unless an agency be created adequate to enforce it. There is the interest of the parent, who, it is proved, cares only for the wages of his child, and who will do everything in his power to evade any provision made for its physical and moral improvement, if that improvement costs any portion, however small, of the child's wages. There is the interest of the workman on whom the care required by the law, of the health and morals of the child imposes considerable trouble and some expense. There is the interest of the master to whom the strict observance of the regulations necessary to insure the proper instruction of the child must cause still more trouble and expense. There is the interest of the advocate for imposing restriction on adult labour who, in order to demonstrate that there is no true remedy for the evils of the factory system but the Ten-hour Bill, will do anything in his power to counteract the working of a measure, the direct and immediate object of which is limited to the regulation of the labour, the protection of the health, and the security of the education of the young. . . . There is the interest of the ally, the chief active promoter of the Ten-hour project, the operative agitator . . . who avoids the necessity of labour by taking on himself the more easy employment of declaiming."[71]

It was generally admitted, albeit somewhat grudgingly in certain quarters, that the factory children ought to be prevented from working excessive hours, and that they should be afforded opportunities for education.[72] But how far was this principle to

---

[70] *Ibid.* pp. 479-480. *Cf.* P. Gaskell, *op. cit.* p. 168—"Of this Bill it may be truly said that it is an absurdity, being founded on the most singular ignorance of the interior economy of mills . . . If the children who are employed principally by the spinner are dismissed, his work ceases, and the mill is at a standstill."

[71] *The London and Westminster Review* (October, 1836) p. 206.

[72] Even Cooke Taylor, ardent opponent of legislative interference as he was, conceded this, speaking with approval of "the sound principle that it is the duty of a Government to protect the weaker part of its subjects against the possible abuse of power by the strong."—*Factories and the Factory System* (1844) p. 102.

be carried, and by what methods was it to be achieved? The problem of factory legislation in these early days was basically a problem of administration, and the importance of Althorp's Act, paradoxically enough, lay in the fact that its very defects enabled this aspect of control to be surveyed in all its magnitude. " The Act of 1833," said Horner, " has been productive of much good; it has put an end to a large proportion of the evils which made the interference of the legislature then necessary. But it has not done nearly all the good that was intended. The failures have mainly arisen from the defects in the law itself; not in the principles it lays down, but in the machinery which was constructed for the purpose of carrying the principles into operation. . . . There was this further source of error, that it was in some degree legislating in the dark; a great part of the mechanism adopted was entirely of a novel description, of a kind that had never been tried in former factory acts; and after it was set to work, much of it was found to have been ill-contrived, and some positively so bad that it obstructed, and to a great degree prevented, the attainment of the object."[73]

Neither manufacturers nor operatives hesitated to point out these defects. Both sides were highly organized, possessed of ample resources, and with powerful friends in Parliament; and the streams of conflicting criticism that they directed upon the Act revealed, as nothing else could have done, its inherent weaknesses. Diametrically opposed as they were, their joint efforts impelled Parliament to fresh, and eventually to more fruitful activity.

---

[73] L. Horner, *On the Employment of Children in Factories* (1840) pp. 1-2.

CHAPTER 6
REACTION

BEFORE THE year closed the four Inspectors had been appointed—Leonard Horner to the northern district, Robert Rickards to the midlands, Robert Saunders to the south and east, and Thomas Jones Howell to the west,[1] and assisted by their superintendents they began to make their first contacts with the mills. The opposition of the manufacturers having already begun to cause the Government some anxiety, instructions were issued to the Inspectors that, for the time being at any rate, they were to address themselves exclusively to the owners, adopting wherever possible a friendly and conciliatory attitude. " When first appointed Inspectors," said Saunders, " Mr. Rickards, Mr. Howell and myself (before we were joined by our first colleague, Mr. Musgrave) were directed in our earlier circuits to confer more immediately with the mill-occupiers, and to endeavour to reconcile them in any way that was practicable and reasonable, to the restrictions and regulations then first to be enforced."[2] Horner soon realized the implications of these instructions—that if the Act was to work successfully the co-operation of the operatives must also be secured—and accordingly, because as he said, he found the Act much misunderstood,[3] he published a small pamphlet explaining its main provisions.[4] " This publication," he said in the preface, " is intended chiefly for the Working Classes. In my visits to the Factories, I have an opportunity of explaining, in conversation, doubts as to the provisions of the statute, and of correcting misapprehensions as to their tendency, on the part of the Mill-owners; but as I can have only a very limited personal intercourse with the operatives, I take this mode of communicating to them, what I have said to their employers.[5]

But he did not abandon the policy prescribed by the Home Office, for he continued to meet the owners rather as a friend than as a government servant charged with the task of enforcing an unpopular law. " I have broke ground in my new vocation very auspiciously," he wrote in a letter to his daughter Mary, " as far as a good reception from the mill-owners goes. They naturally

---

[1] *Parl. Papers* (1834) XLIII, p. 423.
[2] Report, 31st October, 1848. *Parl. Papers* (1849) XXII, p. 239. Howell confirmed this in his Report of the same date. *Ibid.* p. 230.
[3] Report, 21st July, 1834. *Parl. Papers* (1834) XLIII, p. 429.
[4] *The Factories Regulation Act Explained, with some Remarks on its Origin, Nature and Tendency* (1834).
[5] *Ibid.* p. iv.

dislike the Act, like any other interference, but they say that as they were to have one, that which has been passed is very little open to objection, and they see no difficulty in carrying it into effect. . . . Nothing could be kinder than the way they have received me, and one of them, Mr. Lepper, has placed his little carriage at my disposal, and I am to dine with him to-day."[6] These buoyant hopes were similarly reflected in another letter, written on 14th April, 1834, to his other daughters, Frances and Susan. " You are anxious to know how I have been received by the mill-owners, who, in December, were very much disinclined to the Act, and who have hitherto been quite unused to any legislative interference. I have been agreeably disappointed,—wherever I have been . . . I have been met with the kindest reception, and found a very prevalent disposition to do the best they can to fulfil the intention of the legislature. . . . I have no fear but that in a short time the greater proportion of the mill-owners in my district, will view the Act, not only without dislike, but will even admit it to be in many respects highly beneficial."[7]

The instructions that Rickards issued to his superintendents explained precisely the policy that was to be followed. " Your best chance of success," he told them, " will be a courteous and con- ciliatory demeanour towards the mill-owners; and by impressing on their minds that the object of your visits is rather to assist them in conforming to the Act and Regulations thereon founded; and to explain what they may find it difficult, or require, to understand, rather than to fish out grounds for complaint. . . . It should be kept in mind that the Act itself is a novelty; that it was at first received in the manufacturing districts with great dissatisfaction, that part of it still presses heavily on certain parties; that on the whole, however, it has produced much good in regulating the labour of the young; that it is now considered much more favourably than at first; and that a gradual and quiet introduction of its observance by the body of manufacturers, is the most likely method to perpetuate its benefits; which would probably be defeated by a rigorous execution of conformity to all its details, before it shall be sufficiently rooted in the habits and goodwill of those over whom its operation is intended to extend."[8]

This was the spirit in which the Inspectors went to work, and for a short time the response was encouraging. Horner's first meeting with the manufacturers took place at Belfast, where a full

---

[6] 29th November, 1833—K. M. Lyell, *Memoir of Leonard Horner* (1890) Vol. I, p. 287.

[7] *Ibid.* p. 290.

[8] *Parl. Papers* (1835) XL, p. 698.

discussion of the terms of the Act led him to believe that no difficulties were likely to arise. On the whole, he thought, the owners welcomed it as an improvement, professing themselves willing to employ the system of relays, though, as they pointed out, the reduction in the children's wages would be severely felt by the parents. The educational clauses they considered most salutary, and they were quite prepared to complete the necessary registers.[9] The Glasgow manufacturers appeared equally anxious to co-operate. Early in December Horner met them, and explained the Act clause by clause. They expressed some doubts about the practicability of relays, and many of them thought it would not be easy to operate the educational clauses, especially when there were no schools attached to the factories, as was the case in most districts.[10] In Aberdeen the owners were well disposed towards the Act, but they, too, were uneasy about the schooling provisions, and about the feasibility of the relay system.[11]

These misgivings were echoed more insistently by the flax spinners of Dundee. They told Horner that they regarded the Act as a great interference, and that they proposed to remove themselves as far as possible from its operation by dismissing those children whose work was limited to forty-eight hours a week.[12]

Rickards reported that he found no disposition to comply with the Act in his district. The operatives condemned it because the wages of the children would be reduced, and the owners were restive because they considered many of the provisions impracticable. There were not sufficient children available, they declared, to make working by relays possible, and the only alternative left to them was to dismiss the younger hands. The educational clauses, too, presented a difficulty. Some of the manufacturers— Birley of Manchester, Thomas Ashton of Hyde, and Marshall of Leeds, who already had schools organized in conjunction with their mills, were quite prepared to carry out the provisions of the Act; but the great majority of the owners were not in this happy position, and they saw no alternative but to dismiss the younger workers.[13]

The principal owners in Manchester, said Rickards, obeyed the Act, but others, not only in Manchester, but in Stockport, Stalybridge, and Glossop were working beyond the permitted hours, " to the great annoyance and prejudice of those who strictly observed the law." Even in these days methods were devised to evade the regulations, and some masters continued to work their

---

9 Report, 28th November, 1833. *Parl. Papers* (1834) XLIII, p. 423.
10 Report, 4th December, 1833. *Ibid*. p. 424.
11 Report, 26th December, 1833. *Ibid*. p. 426.
12 Report, 8th December, 1833. *Ibid*. p. 425.
13 Report, 24th December, 1833. *Ibid*. pp. 446-447.

mills for 12½ or 13 hours a day, contending that they were not
infringing the law because they turned out of the factory the hands
under 18 years of age after they had completed 12 hours' work.
" The mill-owners who run their engines only 12 hours in the day,"
commented Rickards, " naturally conceive this over-working to be
taking an undue advantage of them," for it was impossible to check
whether the young persons concerned had in fact worked more
than 12 hours a day unless some authentic record was kept and
certified.[14]

Howell found much the same state of affairs. Except in the
silk-mills children were being dismissed, though the larger manufacturers were quite prepared to obey the law, even if they disputed
its policy, so long as their competitors fell into line.[15]

Saunders reported that he found the masters helpful and
courteous, and thought that most of them approved the Act, though
they objected to the machinery by which it was to be enforced.
But he anticipated that evasion would be common, for it would
be difficult to convict offenders, and heavy penalties would be
infrequent, " and not to be put into competition with the advantages
arising from unrestricted labour in large and extensive factories."[16]

The doubts expressed by the manufacturers very quickly
hardened into open opposition—an opposition which they sought
to justify on a wide variety of grounds, but which was fundamentally based on their dislike of legislative interference in their
private affairs.[17] The reduction in the working hours of children,
and the obligation to attend school threatened to upset the smooth
and easy running of the mills, and for this reason the owners
united in common hostility to the Act.

The need for education was universally acknowledged. " The
population employed in the factories of this country," said the
London and Westminster Review, " is in a state of gross and
barbarous ignorance. . . . The education of this class in Great
Britain, if they are to be educated at all, must be compulsory,

---

14 Report, 10th February, 1834. *Ibid.* pp. 449-450.
15 Reports, 20th December, 1833, and 28th July, 1834. *Ibid.*
pp. 442, 445.
16 Report, 28th December, 1833. *Ibid.* p. 482.
17 That this attitude was not peculiar to the early days of the factory
system is evident from the report of H.M. Chief Inspector of Factories
for the year 1945 (Cmd. 6992)—" The cessation of hostilities brought an
intensification of the process . . . of reducing the number of relaxations
of the Factories Act in regard to hours of employment. . . In many
cases employers had become so accustomed to the wider range and the
greater elasticity of the emergency provisions that they were loath to give
up the opportunities of working extended hours, even if they had no
intention of making regular use of them, and much persuasion and explanation was necessary in some cases." (p. 27).

because there is no natural and powerful interest to secure it."[18]
Gaskell contended that the only way to improve the working
conditions of the children was to establish a well-organized system
of national education,[19] while Kay complained that "those
politicians who propose a serious reduction of the hours of labour
. . . appear . . . not to have sufficiently reflected, that, if this
measure were unaccompanied by a general system of education, the
time thus bestowed, would be wasted or misused."[20] Ure considered it to be of paramount importance that the State should
provide education for the children of the poor, because in no other
way could they be protected against the devices of crafty
demagogues, and because education would enable them to produce
better work. "It is excessively the interest of every mill-owner,"
he declared, "to organize his moral machinery on equally sound
principles with his mechanical, for otherwise he will never command
the steady hands, watchful eyes, and prompt co-operation essential
to excellence of product. . . . There is, in fact, no case to which
the Gospel truth, 'Godliness is great gain,' is more applicable than
to the administration of an extensive factory."[21]

But the Act of 1833 was, in Ure's view, singularly ill-contrived
to achieve the purpose at which it aimed. "The twenty-first clause
of the Factories Regulation Bill," he wrote, "is an act of
despotism towards trade, and of mock philanthropy towards the
work-people who depend on trade for support. It requires every
factory child, twelve years of age, to produce every Monday
morning a certificate of having attended school for two hours at
least, on six days of the preceding week, on pain of dismissal from
the mill in which he earns his livelihood. Against this absurd law,
strong remonstrances have been made by the real friends of the
poor. Few mills, in fact, are situated near schools which are open
at hours convenient for these busy children, namely, early in the
morning and late in the evening; and therefore to make the requirements practicable, one or more factories should have a school, or
schools, subservient to them, open at suitable times of the day.
The school clauses exhibit an ingenious sample of legislative
wisdom; for they have had the diametrically opposite effect of their
avowed purpose. Instead of protecting and improving the position

----

[18] October, 1836, pp. 196, 200. The Radicals were staunch supporters
of State education. "I hope you will join us in a cry for schoolmasters
as a first step to Radicalism," wrote Cobden to his friend Tait. "Let me
pray you to strike a blow for us for education."—J. Morley, *The Life of
Richard Cobden* (1905) p. 127.
[19] P. Gaskell, *Artisans and Machinery* (1836) p. 172.
[20] J. P. Kay, *The Moral and Physical Condition of the Working
Classes* (1832) p. 91. See also W. R. Greg, *An Enquiry into the State
of the Manufacturing Population* (1831) p. 35.
[21] A. Ure, *The Philosophy of Manufactures* (1835) pp. 407, 417.

of the children, the supposed victims of the mill-owner's avarice, they have deprived them of the means of subsistence, causing them to be turned adrift to sympathize with the listless progeny of the farm labourer.

The mill-proprietor, after finding that this factory act, like its predecessors, was the fruitful parent of deceit and perjury to the young operatives and their guardians, and a law-trap to himself, has had no alternative but to dismiss from his works all children under twelve years of age—an event fraught with wide-spread privation. The children so discharged from their light and profitable labour, instead of receiving the education promised by parliament, get none at all; they are thrown out of the warm spinning-rooms upon the cold world to exist by beggary or plunder, in idleness and vice—a life woefully contrasted with their former improving state at the factory and its Sunday School.

After the 1st March, 1836, all children, even up to thirteen, will be in danger of being dismissed from factory employment, by a prospective ordinance which, under the mask of philanthropy, will aggravate still more the hardships of the poor, and extremely embarrass, if not entirely stop the conscientious manufacturer in his useful toil. This law will no doubt be evaded in many ways by the indignant artisans, whose families it tends to starve, and it will thus prove operative only for evil, by perverting their moral principles."[22]

Throughout their districts the Inspectors found the greatest reluctance to carry out the educational provisions of the Act. As soon as he arrived in the north the Glasgow mill-owners expressed themselves forcibly to Horner on this point. They agreed that it was desirable for children to attend school, but they pointed out the difficulty of making the necessary arrangements, especially when the factory had no school attached to it.[23] In Yorkshire many of the mills were remote from towns, neither schools nor schoolmasters being available,[24] and even in those districts where British or National schools[25] had been established it was usually impossible to arrange for the factory children to attend during the

---

22 *Ibid.* pp. 405-407.
23 Report, 4th December, 1833. *Parl. Papers* (1834) XLIII, p. 424.
24 Rickards' Report, 15th April, 1834. *Ibid.* p. 458.
25 Cf. J. P. Kay, *The Moral and Physical Condition of the Working Classes* (1832) p. 93—" Our present means of instruction are confined to Sunday Schools and a few Lancasterian and National Schools, quite inadequate to the wants of the population." In 1808 a society, later known as the British and Foreign School Society, had been founded to administer the undenominational schools organized by Joseph Lancaster; in 1811 the National Society had been inaugurated to provide Church Schools. In August, 1833, Parliament decided to make a grant of £20,000 to these bodies " in aid of private subscriptions for the erection of school houses for the education of the children of the poorer classes in Great Britain."

normal hours of opening, since they were only available early in the morning or in the late afternoon.[26] " Until proper schools are provided," said Horner, " in the neighbourhood of the factories, with a schoolmaster subject to the supervision of the Inspector, where the hours shall be adapted to the changes of the relay children, and where they may go in their working dress, this important part of the Act will always be imperfectly fulfilled."[27]

Had the Act been fully enforced[28] a very real, practical difficulty would have arisen. Children were indispensable in every mill—the work could not go on without them—yet if they did not produce, each Monday morning, a voucher from the schoolmaster, certifying that they had attended school on six days of the preceding week, their services would have to be dispensed with, and the working of the factory would, in consequence, be disrupted. The owners complained that this put them in an impossible position. They could not secure a child's attendance at school, yet they were made to suffer if it was absent.[29]

The Act had not been in operation for six months when many of the owners declared that the educational provisions were impracticable, and that they would be compelled to dismiss the children to whom they applied.[30] Horner reported[31] that the provisions of the Act were nowhere complied with, and Howell's testimony was similar. The successful operation of a mill, he said,[32] depended on regularity and precision at each stage of the process. In the woollen mills most children were employed in the preliminary stages of manufacture, carding and spinning, and if for reasons beyond the master's control they did not produce their vouchers of school attendance on Monday, they could not be employed, the spinners were short of assistance, and all the other departments suffered in consequence. Rickards could name only

---

26 Horner's Report, 21st July, 1834. *Parl. Papers* (1834) XLIII, p. 434. Howell reported that in Trowbridge the British School was ready to afford the woollen mills great help in carrying out the education clauses. Arrangements had been made for the factory children " to attend half time at half price, namely, 1½d. per week," yet of 435 children in the school, only two were factory children.—October, 1834. *Parl. Papers* (1835) XL, p. 693.
27 Report, 12th October, 1836. *Parl. Papers* (1837) XXXI, p. 63.
28 It was not strictly enforced however. *Cf.* Horner's Report, 21st July, 1834. *Parl. Papers* (1834) XLIII, p. 434. He exercised discretionary power, " and dispensed with the rigour of the 21st clause in those mills employing children under 11 years of age."
29 Horner's Report, 21st July, 1834. *Parl. Papers* (1834) XLIII, p. 434. The owners also complained that there was no obligation on the schoolmaster to certify the vouchers. In Glasgow some of the masters had refused to do so.
30 Horner's Reports, 4th December, 1833. *Parl. Papers* (1834) XLIII, p. 424; 26th December, 1833, *ibid.* p. 427.
31 21st July, 1834. *Parl. Papers* (1834), XLIII, p. 431.
32 Report, 20th December, 1833. *Ibid.* p. 442.

half a dozen instances in his district where the educational clauses
had been observed, and he confirmed the reports of his colleagues
that the children concerned were being dismissed.[33]   Saunders
agreed that education presented the greatest difficulty, and considered that a measure of financial assistance would be necessary.
The position would be eased, he thought, if masters were appointed
upon whom the Inspectors might rely for proper vouchers.[34]

The general verdict, to which inspectors,[35] owners, and outside
observers alike subscribed, was that some measure of education
was clearly necessary, but that the Government had failed to
provide the requisite means.   It was idle to enact that children
must attend school if there were no schools available, but in the
early thirties few men would have shared Horner's view that the
only solution lay in the establishment of a national scheme of
compulsory education.   Much had to be endured, and many
schemes tried before this truth, self-evident as it is to-day, was
generally realized.   For the time being the majority of the owners
were content to take no action, confident in their belief that an
Act which so clearly struck at the very foundations of factory
economy could not possibly survive.

It had been realized from the first that if children under the
age of 13 were to be restricted to 48 hours' labour a week it would
be necessary to evolve some plan whereby they might work in
shifts or relays, for the adults were required to work at least twelve
hours a day, and it was not possible for them to dispense with the
help of their young assistants.   It was because the work of the
children was intimately associated with that of the adult spinners
and weavers that the provisions of Althorp's Act stirred the textile
industry so profoundly.   Here was an example of State intervention
in private affairs on an unparalleled scale, and the great majority
of the owners viewed the new arrangements with the utmost alarm,
for they were convinced that they would be faced with ruin if they
were compelled to shorten the working day.

---

[33] *Ibid.* p. 461.   In answer to an enquiry made by Lord Duncannon
on 30th July, 1834, asking whether he thought the educational clauses
should be repealed.

[34] Report, 28th December, 1833.   *Ibid.* p. 482.

[35] Horner expressed himself forcibly on this. (Report, August, 1835,
Parl. Papers, 1836, XLV, p. 158).   He was convinced of the " paramount
necessity of legislative interference to prevent the children in factories
growing up in a state of barbarous ignorance; especially as the tendency
of improvements in machinery is more and more to substitute infant for
adult labour, and consequently the temptation to parents to neglect the
education of their children is daily on the increase."

Nassau Senior, indeed, contended that the entire profit of the mill was derived from the last hour of work.[36] He assumed that the whole capital was turned over in about a year, and that to make a net profit of 10 per cent., a gross profit of 15 per cent. must be earned, because the fixed capital, *i.e.* that sunk in buildings and machinery, was subject to deterioration through wear and tear. If a manufacturer invested £100,000 the annual return ought therefore to be £115,000, one twenty-third of which was produced in each half-hour of an eleven and a half hour day. In these circumstances it followed that the net profit of £10,000, representing approximately two twenty-thirds of the capital engaged, was earned in the last hour. If the factory could be kept working 13 hours a day instead of $11\frac{1}{2}$, the net profit would be more than doubled, but if working time was reduced by an hour a day the net profit would be destroyed. His reasoning, of course, does not bear examination, but it illustrates the prevailing idea that the longer the wheels were kept turning, the greater would be the profits.

There were three courses open to the mill-owners. They could employ children for eight hours each day, and manage as best they might, without their assistance, for the remaining four hours. This was a counsel of despair, and only a few mills met their difficulties in this way.[37]

Another plan was to dismiss all the children whose hours were restricted to 48 a week, and there is much evidence to suggest that many manufacturers followed this course. The advantage was two-fold: the mill could be run throughout the length of the normal day without interruption, and the onerous provisions of the educational clauses could be avoided. In its anxiety to temper the impact of the new regulations Parliament had decided that the restrictions should be introduced progressively. After March, 1834, protection was afforded to children between the ages of 9 and 11. On March 1st, 1835, the upper age limit was to be raised to 12, and on March 1st, 1836, to 13. This was intended to give the owners an opportunity of devising plans to employ children in relays, but in fact it had the opposite effect, since it served only to postpone the full operation of the Act and encouraged the manufacturers to delay formulating the arrangements that were necessary for its proper working. In many mills the owners decided to employ only those children who were outside the scope of the restrictive clauses, with the result that the relay system was not even tried. The Act had scarcely been passed when the manufacturers of Dundee told Horner that they proposed to dismiss the

---

36 *Letters on the Factory Act* (1837) pp. 12, 13.
37 Nassau Senior alleged (*Letters on the Factory Act* (1837) p. 18) that this was the usual plan, but the Inspectors' Reports nowhere confirm this view.

children under 11 years of age,[38] and Howell, too, reported that, except in the silk mills, the younger children were being discharged.[39] Saunders said[40] that in his district the effect had been "practically to exclude from factory employment all children under 11 years of age." In August, 1835,[41] Howell confirmed his previous findings. The masters, he said, had anticipated the regulations that would begin to operate on 1st March and had not engaged children who would be over 12 years of age on that date. For this reason few children were affected by the raising of the age limit, and of these the majority had been dismissed. This had affected the parents adversely, and many children had, on this account, entered unregulated occupations. The masters had not been seriously inconvenienced, for except in the more remote districts, there were plenty of hands available.

The third course which the factory-owners might have pursued was that which it had been assumed they would follow, that is to employ the children in relays or shifts. The scheme had all the appearance of simplicity, but in fact it was not easy to operate, and many owners, declaring that it was impracticable, refused to have anything to do with it. It is true that any plan of working by relays would seriously interrupt the steady and orderly running of the factory system, for it was necessary to make due provision for meal times[42] and for attendance at school. Horner, who was a staunch advocate of the scheme, went to much trouble to explain to the owners how they could put it into operation, but the two alternative plans that he laid before them were both extremely complex.[43] In each case it was necessary to make no less than four changes of hands each day, and though it was true that the switch-over usually coincided with the break for meals, the dislocation would in any case be considerable, if only because a detailed system of supervision and checking would need to be established.

In Scotland the manufacturers protested against the interruption of factory routine which the relay system would cause, and they complained also of the increased expense it would entail.[44] Howell encountered considerable opposition in his district, and asserted that only two of 330 establishments were working by

---

[38] Report, 8th December, 1833. *Parl. Papers* (1834) XLIII, p. 425.
[39] Report, 20th December, 1833. *Ibid.* p. 442.
[40] Report, 5th February, 1835. *Parl. Papers* (1835) XL, p. 691.
[41] *Parl. Papers* (1836) XLV, p. 159.
[42] This difficulty was specifically mentioned by Horner in his Report for 21st July, 1834. *Parl. Papers* (1834) XLIII, p. 433.
[43] See Appendix.
[44] Horner's Report, 8th December, 1833. *Parl. Papers* (1834) XLIII, p. 425.

relays.[45]   Rickards confessed that he despaired of being able to introduce the system in the midlands,[46] and was confident that in country districts " relays of children are absolutely not procurable." " The injury and inconvenience thus sustained," he continued, " will, it is said, and I fear with truth, be greatly enhanced after the 1st March, 1835, when these provisions shall apply to children under 12 years of age; and after the 1st March, 1836, when embracing children under 13 years of age, the evil, it is apprehended, will be intolerable."[47]   In February, 1835, Howell reported that one of the two mills that had tried the relay system had abandoned it, and that the general feeling was that the whole scheme was unworkable.[48]

It was commonly stated that there were not enough children available to operate the system, but as Horner pointed out[49] it was idle to contend that there were insufficient children, when those who were subject to regulation were being dismissed, and when many new factories were being built.   He was convinced[50] that the system would work if only the owners would give it a fair trial.   Messrs. Finlay & Co. in their mill at Deanston had 106 children in relays early in 1834, and altogether, in the spring of 1836, there were 65 mills in his district employing 776 relay children.   In Bradford Messrs. Wood and Walker were operating the scheme successfully with 300 children,[51] and he was confident that many more owners " would have adopted the system, but for a strong expectation that the law is to be altered."[52]

The manufacturers communicated their misgivings to such good purpose that the Inspectors had come to share their view that the law must be changed if disaster was to be avoided.   The Act had barely been in force a year when Saunders asserted that he was convinced that grave injury would ensue, both to owners and operatives, if children under thirteen years of age were restricted to 48 hours' labour a week.[53]   He had instituted no legal proceedings against the mill-occupiers, he said, because he anticipated that the law would shortly be amended, and its operation thus facilitated.[54]   Six months later, though admitting that the increased numbers who had become subject to regulation on 1st March,

45 Report, 28th July, 1834. *Ibid.* p. 445.
46 Report, 10th February, 1834. *Ibid.* p. 451.
47 Report, 15th April, 1834. *Ibid.* p. 458.
48 Report, 5th February, 1835. *Parl. Papers* (1835) XL, p. 693.
49 Report, 12th October, 1836. *Parl. Papers* (1837) XXXI, p. 60.
50 Report, 21st July, 1834. *Parl. Papers* (1834) XLIII, p. 433.
51 Nassau Senior, *Letters on the Factory Act* (1837) p. 34.
52 Report, February, 1836. *Parl. Papers* (1836) XLV, p. 167.
53 Report, 29th July, 1834. *Parl. Papers* (1834) XLIII, p. 486.
54 Report, 5th February, 1835. *Parl. Papers* (1835) XL, p. 691.

1835, had caused the mill-occupiers less inconvenience than they had anticipated, he urged that the law should be amended, especially in respect of the clause that was to come into operation on 1st March, 1836.[55] Howell stated that in his district both owners and parents resented the restrictions imposed on children between eleven and twelve, especially when trade was brisk, repeating that he viewed the next stage of control with great apprehension.[56]

In their Joint Report dated 28th July, 1834,[57] the Inspectors asked that the whole question should be reviewed. " We are very strongly impressed with the conviction," they said, " that it will be found extremely difficult in practice, if not wholly impossible, to limit the labour of children, who are 12 years of age, to 48 hours in the week, without a serious injury to the masters and work-people; as in many situations it will not be possible to find a sufficient supply of children to work by relays; and unless that plan of working be adopted, adult labour must necessarily be interfered with.

Mr. Howell and Mr. Saunders are of opinion that even children, who have attained their 11th year, may, under certain circumstances, be safely allowed to work more than 48 hours in the week.

We are of opinion that it will be expedient to allow children younger than nine to work in cotton, woollen, and flax mills, for if they are limited to 48 hours in the week, we see no ground for apprehending any injury to the health of children of eight years of age from factory employment, but are rather inclined to think they would in a great many cases have both their health and morals less exposed to injury in the factory, than in their ordinary course of living out of it."[58]

With such a lead from the Inspectors the mill-owners naturally pressed the case for the amendment of the law with increased energy and vigour. They sent numerous petitions to Parliament emphasizing the inconvenience to which they were being subjected, and calling for an alteration in the law. On 27th February, 1836, John Fielden, the member for Oldham, received a copy of a memorial which was submitted to the Privy Council for Trade by 72 mill-owners in his constituency. " The Act," said the memorial, " has prohibited the employment of children under twelve years of age for more than nine hours in any one day since the first day of March one thousand eight hundred and thirty five, and such

---

[55] Report, August, 1835. *Parl. Papers* (1836) XLV, p. 156.
[56] Report, February, 1836. *Ibid.* p. 167.
[57] *Parl. Papers* (1834) XLIII, p. 492.
[58] E. von Plener, *The English Factory Legislation* (1873) p. 18. E. Baines, *History of the Cotton Manufacture in Great Britain* (1835) pp. 479-480.

prohibition has tended greatly to injure the interests both of your Memorialists and the parents of such children, without any advantage resulting to the children themselves.

Your Memorialists are looking forward with great anxiety and alarm to the situation in which they will be placed on the first day of March next, by the working of children under thirteen years of age being restricted to forty-eight hours in one week, for that such restriction will have the effect of throwing all the children under thirteen years of age wholly out of employment, and will render it impossible for your Memorialists to work their respective mills with advantage, in proof whereof your Memorialists confidently appeal to the Factory Inspectors of the district for the truth of their assertion."[59]

The masters were confident that relief could not long be delayed. The new law had been proved to be impracticable, the further restrictions on the employment of children, due to be imposed on 1st March, 1836, would assuredly be abrogated, and once this had been accomplished, the rest would follow, when a large measure, at least, of the old freedom would be restored.[60]

Opposition to Althorp's Act was not the prerogative of the manufacturers alone—their hostility was shared, though for very different reasons, by the ten-hours party, who now came forward once again with proposals which, they claimed, could alone resolve the problem. On 15th August, 1835, at the instance of Oastler,[61] Charles Hindley, a wealthy mill-owner and member for Ashton-under-Lyne, and Joseph Brotherton introduced an amending bill,[62] the preamble of which declared that the provisions of the Act of 1833 " have been found to be injurious to the welfare of . . . Children and young Persons, harassing and vexatious to the Occupiers of Mills and Factories, and ineffectual in securing the objects contemplated by the Act."

The Act of 1833 was to be repealed. The new measure was to apply to cotton, woollen, worsted, hemp, flax, tow, linen and silk mills, where the hours of all persons under twenty-one years of age were to be gradually reduced until January, 1839, after

---

59 J. Fielden, *The Curse of the Factory System* (1836) p. 2.
60 *Cf.* P. Gaskell, *Artisans and Machinery* (1836) p. 67n.—" The ' Factories Regulation Act ' has caused multitudes of children to be dismissed, but it has only increased the evils it was intended to remedy, and must of necessity be repealed." E. Baines, *History of the Cotton Manufacture in Great Britain* (1835) p. 479—" The Inspectors state that the Act must be amended . . . and there can be no doubt that this amendment will take place next session."
61 E. von Plener, *The English Factory Legislation* (1873) p. 19. " Alfred," *The History of the Factory Movement* (1857) Vol. II, p. 86.
62 *Parl. Papers* (1835) II, p. 781

which they were to work not more than ten hours a day, exclusive of an hour and a half for meals, which were to be taken at such times as the Inspectors deemed proper. As a safeguard against overworking it was proposed that the machinery should not be run outside the permitted hours,[63] which were to be regulated by the nearest public clock. A wider range of powers was to be entrusted to the four Inspectors—they were to decide the circumstances under which lost time might be recovered, and they were to order the mill-occupiers to keep registers containing details of all children employed, of their sex, hours of work and periods of absence through illness.

The reformers, it seems, had learned little during the past two years, for in their anxiety to impose a ten-hours day they ignored completely those aspects of control that experience had already shown to be fundamental. They proposed to retain the minimum age for employment at nine, but they discarded the device of the certificate of age, and put nothing in its place. They proposed to extend the benefit of the shorter working day to all under twenty-one, but in order to achieve this they were quite prepared to increase the hours of children from 48 to 58 a week.[64] There were no provisions for education, for fencing, or for cleaning—in short the bill was a retrograde measure. Only when there developed a fusion of interests between those who advocated a ten hours day and those who sought to make regulation effective by the setting up of adequate machinery for enforcing the law, was any real progress possible.

Hindley's bill was short-lived: it had been printed and widely distributed when the Government announced that Poulett Thomson, President of the Board of Trade, would shortly introduce a measure repealing so much of Althorp's Act as prescribed that on 1st March, 1836, children under thirteen years of age should be restricted to forty-eight hours' labour a week.[65] On 15th March, 1836, a bare

---

[63] In his report for August, 1835, Rickards asserted that there was a universal cry for restriction on the moving power. He agreed that in no other way could the children be effectively protected. "The steam-engine," he said, "performs all the hard work, leaving to the hands . . . easy tasks. But a steam-engine in the hands of an interested and avaricious master is a relentless power, to which old and young are equally bound to submit . . . Their position in these mills is that of thraldom; 14, 15 or 16 hours per day, is exhausting to the strength of all, yet none dare quit the occupation, from the dread of leaving work altogether."—*Parl. Papers* (1836) XLV, p. 163.

[64] On Saturdays work was to be limited to eight hours.

[65] E. Hodder, *The Life and Work of the seventh Earl of Shaftesbury* (1893) p. 115. E. von Plener, *The English Factory Legislation* (1873) p. 19. "Alfred," *The History of the Factory Movement* (1857) Vol. II, p. 91.

fortnight after the restrictions had been applied to children under 13, Poulett Thomson moved[66] for leave to bring in his amending bill.[67] The reaction was immediate and violent. Charles Wing, in his book *Evils of the Factory System Exposed* examined the whole history of factory legislation. He recited numerous extracts from the evidence received by Sadler's Committee, gave a verbatim report of the Parliamentary debate on the bill of 1833, and criticized in detail the views expressed by Andrew Ure in *The Philosophy of Manufactures*. He made an impassioned plea for the preservation of Althorp's Act, and denounced those who were now seeking to amend it. "Ministers found themselves in a dilemma;" he declared, "either they must overwork the children, or underwork adults,—and they have got out of the dilemma by determining to overwork the children. In their alarm they have thrown consistency overboard; and the very same men who declared even ten hours' labour too long for a child in his thirteenth year, would now expose him to be worked twelve hours."[68]

Fielden, too, attacked the inconsistency of the Government. When they passed the Act of 1833, he said, "they were in this dilemma: the Committee had always discovered the same cruelties in practice; the same overworking, and the same horrifying results. . . . They could not refuse to protect the children. But they are 'political economists;' and though, *as men,* they could no longer screw up their minds and hearts so far as to sacrifice any more limbs and lives of infants, the science would not suffer them to invade the 'freedom of industry,' by involving the adult in that protection which they were obliged to give to the child. It is this absurd attempt to separate the adult from the child in its labour, that has rendered every Act that has ever been passed to give protection to children, almost void."[69] Like Wing, he taunted them with their present inconsistency. "The Ministers stand, therefore, in this position: they threw out Lord Ashley's Ten-hour Bill, because Commissioners of their own told them it did *not give protection to children,* whose labour ought to be restricted to *eight hours.* Then, as their Eight-hour Act will not work pleasantly, upon the advice of their Inspectors, they want to drive us back to *twelve hours,* because *that is adequate protection.* The very men who were sent down to put [the Act] in force, amuse themselves in writing up to the Government, suggestions, that a short Act may be passed to carry us back not to the time proposed by Lord Ashley, but to that of Sir John Hobhouse's Act."[70]

[66] *Hansard* (1836) XXXII, 273.
[67] *Parl. Papers* (1836) IV, p. 1.
[68] C. Wing, *Evils of the Factory System Exposed* (1837) p. ii.
[69] *The Curse of the Factory System* (1836) p. 17.
[70] *Ibid.* p. 24.

The Times was, if anything, even more virulent in its attack on the new bill.[71] " We are far from meaning to insinuate," said the leader, " that the President of the Board of Trade has been stimulated to this inhuman sort of legislation by the least desire to inflict pain upon children, or to harden the hearts of parents by administering to their avarice a barbarous temptation, and indulging it at the expense of their miserable and unprotected off-spring. We consider the right hon. gentleman a mere political economist . . . ignorant of all that lies beyond the precincts of that specious theory of which ' production ' is at once the subject and the idol. . . . A political economist is an animal with limited brains, and altogether destitute of bowels. With moral principles or results he never ventures to trouble himself. . . . The human race with such a philosopher are but necessary incumbrances to spinning jennies.

On any other ground it would be difficult, and might be cruel, to account for Mr. P. Thomson's endeavour to frustrate the operation of a law which only passed last session for reducing to eight hours the period of daily labour—*thereto-fore indefinite*—during which children under 13 years of age should be compelled to toil in our unwholesome manufactories.

But a description of manufacturers . . . found in Mr. P. Thomson a ready tool of their cupidity, and the right hon. gentleman, on looking at his primer, found that ' the less labour is interfered with the better.' Very well; then, it was quite monstrous that the State should inter-meddle between the master manufacturer and the young children whom he employed. ' By all means,' quoth Poulett, ' it is very barbarous and unscientific to prevent those children, *under 13 years of age,* from being worked to death, if they themselves like the process. We must not interpose between them and their liberal masters; leave the children *free* to perish, if it suits their fancy.'

The pretence that the law cannot be enforced is sheer nonsense. The Minister must see it executed at his peril, or let the law be amended. It is not on party considerations that we take up this question. We have never held any other opinion. We would not for all the earth have the weight on our consciences of upholding such a scheme as this of Mr. P. Thomson, any more than we would have tolerated the murder of the innocents by Herod."

In 1836 the *Quarterly Review* published a long article by Ashley on the factory system, the purpose of which was to demonstrate that the fears expressed by the opponents of legislation were, in fact, groundless. Poulett Thomson's proposals received no more generous treatment than that accorded them by *The Times*. " A more faithless proposal," it was said, " was never made to the

---

71 *The Times,* 11th May, 1836.

integrity and understanding of a legislature; the pledge to the
country, that children should be ' protected up to a certain point '
—the compromise between the masters and the operatives,
guaranteed by the interposition of the government—and the induc-
tions of common sense, which required at least the fair trial of so
solemn an enactment, were all equally violated."[72]

Robert Greg, speaking for the manufacturers, replied to
Ashley's " calumnious article," condemning its illiberal spirit, and
declaring that his opposition to the bill was merely a political
manoeuvre, designed to embarrass a Government rightly anxious
to mitigate the rigours of a harsh law. " In the month of July
last," he declared, " for the first time, the Act was put into full
operation; and by dint of great strictness and of some severities on
the part of the inspectors, and of much suffering on the part of the
operatives, and of inconvenience and loss on the part of the masters,
its provisions have at length been carried into effect. . . . Ministers,
on the remonstrances of the mill-owners, backed by the strongest
recommendations of the Factory Inspectors, brought in a bill to
repeal the clause. The question had, however, by this time been
taken up as a political one, and the merits of the case lost all
chance of a fair hearing, from the determination of Lord Ashley
and the Tories to throw Ministers into a minority."[73]

The opposing forces girded themselves for the fray, since it
was now plain that with such issues in the balance, the struggle in
the House would be bitter and prolonged.[74] The bill was debated
on the second reading on 9th May, 1836, when Poulett Thomson
defended his proposals on the ground that the Inspectors had
unanimously declared that " they had found it almost impossible to
enforce the law as it had stood since the 1st of March last," and
that both Inspectors and manufacturers were convinced that the
children between the ages of 12 and 13 would be thrown out of
employment. The Act had failed in Glasgow, Manchester, and
other large towns because it had proved impossible to find sufficient
children " to keep the manufactories going on the relay system."
He did not think it was necessary to restrict the labour of these
older children, and of the 48 medical men he had consulted, 43
concurred in this view. There were some who opposed the measure
for other reasons, men who desired to extend protection to adults

[72] Volume 57, p. 417. See also *Blackwood's Edinburgh Magazine,*
No. CCXLIX (July, 1836) Vol. XL, p. 113.
[73] R. H. Greg, *The Factory Question* (1837) pp. 12-13.
[74] " I suspect it will not pass quietly through," wrote Horner to his
daughter, " for there has been a meeting at Manchester of the operatives
to petition for a Ten Hours Labour Bill, and there is a deputation come
up on the subject."—K. M. Lyell, *Memoir of Leonard Horner* (1890)
Vol. I, p. 322.

as well as children, and to limit the labour of all to ten hours a
day. He protested that this " would be to inflict the most grievous
tyranny upon those who, having only their labour to sell, had a
right to make the most of it."[75]

Ashley was quickly on his feet. He denied the assumption that
35,000 children would be dismissed if the bill were not passed,
and quoted extracts from the Report of Sadler's Committee showing
the need for a diminution in working hours. Let hon. members
recollect that the Negro Emancipation Act contained a clause
providing that the negro population of the British colonies should
not work more than forty-five hours per week. Would the House
increase this time if the planters said this was not sufficient to
remunerate them? He suspected that the proposal was nothing
more than a feeler, and that if it were passed there would soon be
a request to repeal further clauses.[76]

Poulter supported Ashley. The law, he contended, should not
be amended but enforced—at the moment it was grossly violated.
If there were not enough Inspectors let the number be
increased.[77] Brotherton agreed that the law was not obeyed.
Those mill-owners who disregarded it gained enormous advantages,
for in many cases the working of an additional hour a day resulted
in an increased profit of £100 a week. " Persons engaged in these
manufactories," he declared, " were generally desirous of making
rapid fortunes, and the Legislature might as well expect to extract
oil from granite as to obtain anything from the humanity of the
worshippers of Mammon."[78]

Baines supported the bill, and scouted the idea that factory
labour was unhealthy. In his opinion there was " not a set of
children in this Kingdom better fed, better clothed, better lodged,
and more healthy than the children in the factories."[79] Sir John

---

[75] *Hansard* (1836) XXXIII, 737-739.
[76] *Ibid*. 742-748.
[77] *Ibid*. 749.
[78] *Ibid*. 758-760.
[79] *Ibid*. 763. The Inspectors had repeatedly urged this view. *Cf.*
Rickards (12th August, 1834, *Parl. Papers,* 1834, XLIII, p. 460) who
asserted that factory labour was light, and that children of 11 were strong
enough to work 69 hours a week. Saunders (29th July, 1834, *ibid.* p. 486)
said that his own observations made him think that the ill-health of factory
children had been exaggerated, and that he was convinced that a 69 hour
week would not be prejudicial to the health and spirits of a child of 11
(5th February, 1835, *Parl. Papers,* 1835, XL, p. 691). Howell and Saunders
(28th July, 1834, *Parl. Papers,* 1834, XLIII, p. 492) considered that children
of 11 might safely work more than 48 hours a week " under certain circumstances." " Mill labour," said Rickards, (August, 1835. *Parl. Papers,* 1836.
XLV, p. 162) " taken *per se,* is neither unhealthy nor exhausting," and he
mentioned how on quitting the mill on a fine summer's evening the children
showed life and vivacity, so that their playfulness and frolics reminded
him of youths leaving school.

Elley took up this point, and remarked grimly that " although he had not visited the manufacturing towns lately, he could not say he had ever witnessed in them a redundancy of health. . . . He would never go to a manufacturing district to select grenadiers."[80]

Feeling was running high, not only in the House, but in the country at large. When the count was taken the Government found itself with a majority of two only—178 having voted Aye, and 176 No.[81] In these circumstances the wiser plan seemed to be to abandon the measure, and Poulett Thomson announced that the Government intended to drop the bill.[82]

Nothing remained now but to enforce the terms of Althorp's Act, and when, on 23rd June, Hindley proposed to introduce another ten-hours bill, Lord John Russell, renewing an undertaking already given, promised in the name of the Government that the existing laws should be enforced with all the authority at its command.[83] Hindley accordingly withdrew his bill, and together with his fellow-reformers, awaited events.

---

[80] *Hansard* (1836) XXXIII, 765.

[81] It was freely asserted that the mill-owners had resorted to bribery to achieve their ends. Daniel O'Connell, who supported Ashley at first, but who later voted for the bill, was bitterly attacked by the ten-hour party. " The sordid Judas of these days betrayed them for gold. Three days after the traitor had fulfilled the conditions of the compact . . . a purse of L.700 from the Unitarian and Dissenting mill-owners and others was presented to him. It had been kept back until the noxious reptile had acquitted his engagement."—(*Blackwood's Edinburgh Magazine*, No. CCXLIX, Vol. XL, p. 116.) Richard Oastler, in his pamphet *The Factory Question and the Factory Agitation* (1836), repeated the charge— " He voted against the friends of the factory children and received his reward—the ' Blood-money,' paid to him by the ' Liberal ' tyrants." (p. 13). See also *The Sayings and Doings of Daniel O'Connell, Esq.* (1836) p. 4.

[82] *Hansard* (1836) XXXIV, 306.

[83] *Ibid.* 840. E. Hodder, *The Life and Work of the seventh Earl of Shaftesbury* (1893) p. 116.

CHAPTER 7
FACTORY INSPECTORS AND SUPERINTENDENTS

THE INSPECTORS had seriously misjudged the situation, as they afterwards admitted. "At that period," confessed Howell, " I had no practical experience of the factory system, or of the working of the Act of Parliament, which did not come into full operation till 1836, inasmuch as under our instructions we were at that period in communication exclusively with the employers, with the view of making the law acceptable to them, and from some of whom we unwarily adopted suggestions which appeared plausible enough on paper at the time, but which a very short practical acquaintance with the factory system in the cotton districts, when the law was afterwards fairly launched, caused me to repent, and which I gladly seize the present opportunity to repudiate."[1] Saunders made a similar admission. " I was led to believe," he wrote, " that a serious injury was about to be inflicted on all classes engaged in manufacture, especially on the mill-owners themselves, if the law, as it then stood, was fully carried out; and to avert this supposed evil, joined my colleagues in July, 1834, in recommending . . . that the maximum age of 13 should be altered, so as to include as children, who were to work by relays and attend school, only those under 12, or even *under certain circumstances,* under 11 years of age. It was not however long before we found we had been misled in various particulars, and that it was necessary for the interest of the working classes to modify our opinions."[2]

The blow to their prestige was felt all the more severely because from the very first their appointment had been viewed with suspicion and apprehension by masters and workers alike. The Act itself was anathema to both parties, and those who were responsible for its enforcement were exposed to the cross-fire of the conflicting interests. " The officers charged with administering the Factory Act," lamented Howell, "have a very ungracious task to perform: the masters as well as the parents of the factory children are equally opposed to them."[3]

---

[1] Report, 31st October, 1848. *Parl. Papers* (1849) XXII, p. 230.
[2] Report, 31st October, 1848. *Ibid.* p. 239. *Cf.* L. Horner, *On the Employment of Children in Factories* (1840), p.3—" The inspectors were appealed to by the Government, and they stated that the assertions had been so often and so confidently made to them, that they could not venture to set up their opinions and their then limited experience in opposition. . . . But happily Parliament was firm, and would not yield."
[3] Report, 31st March, 1840. *Parl. Papers* (1840) XXIII, p. 32.

Dr. Taylor voiced the opinion of many of the owners when he asserted that any system of inspection was to be resisted because all legislative interference in the details of trade was bad in principle. " Inspection by government agents has been recently established;" he said, " and though it is obviously a system open to objection . . . it has on the whole worked well. Still there is room to fear that as the mills improve, the inspection may become vexatious; it is a very common error for persons in authority to suppose that they can regulate the processes of manufacture better than the manufacturers themselves, and nowhere is this tendency to inter-meddling legislation greater than in England. Hence there is reason to fear that inspectors may fall into the error of exacting literal obedience to arbitrary rules."[4] He was apprehensive that the Inspectors would in time acquire a vested interest, and that once appointed they " would have substantial reasons for endeavouring to procure the continuance of their office, and would, therefore, be interested in keeping up the belief that there was somthing peculiar to the factory system which required authoritative supervision and parliamentary interference."[5]

The owners were particularly incensed at what they considered " the very wide and loose powers "[6] conferred upon the Inspectors, and Greg elaborated this point at some length. " It cannot be denied," he wrote, " that the powers of the Inspectors are already greater than were ever before committed to any individual in this country, and greater than ought to be entrusted to *any* individual in *any* country. In all matters not specially provided for by the Act, the Inspector's *will*, is *law without appeal;* his mere *ipse dixit,* proclaimed in two successive local newspapers, *is the law of the land;* it is subject to no discussion, no scrutiny in a committee, no first, second, and third reading, no transit through a second legislative chamber. Not only is the Inspector a maker of the law, but the administrator of it. His ' Superintendent ' is informer, witness, prosecutor, and expounder of the law to the magistrates, and, should the magistrates incline to mercy, the Inspector is their accuser before the Secretary of State. . . . Nor is this all; the Inspector and the Superintendent wield a power alien to the spirit and practice of English law—a power of *compelling a man to be witness against himself,* and of forcing his servants (should they prove unwilling) to appear in court against their master.

The Inspector can also, it appears, ' *convict on view.*' What could a Pacha of Three Tails desire more? What farther power

---

[4] W. C. Taylor, *Notes of a Tour in the Manufacturing Districts of Lancashire* (1842) p. 241.
[5] W. C. Taylor, *Factories and the Factory System* (1844) p. 36.
[6] P. Gaskell, *Artisans and Machinery* (1836) p. 168.

remains to be granted, unless it be that of hanging a mill-owner without trial, and leaving his body to the surgeons for dissection?"[7]

The friends of the operatives, on the other hand, contended that the arrangements for inspection were inadequate. " The vigilance of inspectors," said Wing, " is not a match for the money-getting spirit of the masters, and the stimulating effect of higher wages upon the workmen. The apparatus for carrying the present Act into effect is palpably inadequate; the few inspectors and superintendents that are appointed would need the eyes of Argus, the hands of Briareus, and the seven-league boots of Jack the giant-killer, with his coat of invisibilty, to discharge their duties effectually. . . . An Act, to be effectual, should resemble the machinery, and be in some measure automotive. The present Act enlists so many interests against itself, that it has been, and will continue to be, defied or evaded."[8]

There was general apprehension that the Inspectors would work in close concert with the owners, and that their powers would be invoked to oppress the workers—a fear that their attitude in the early days did little to allay. The 35th section of the Act, providing that complaints were only to be preferred at or before the time of the Inspector's visit, which was to be duly notified, was condemned as the " Grand Nullifying Clause." " He may visit without duly notifying it, to dine with the masters, to feast upon those luxurious viands which the labour of the poor children procures," and the effect of all this, it was urged, would be to enable transgressors to escape punishment. " We shall learn ' from high authority ' that the Law is effective—and in proof of it, there have been few, if any, *convictions*."[9]

Some of these objections were not entirely without foundation, for in their anxiety to make the Inspectors effective instruments for the enforcement of the law, the framers of Althorp's Act had vested them with powers hitherto unknown to the constitution. Primarily the servants of the executive, working under the direction of the Home Office, they were empowered to issue regulations having the force of law without submitting them first to Parliament for ratification, while the magisterial powers they wielded enabled them to exercise judicial functions in cases to which they them-

---

[7] R. H. Greg, *The Factory Question* (1837) pp. 129-130.
[8] C. Wing, *Evils of the Factory System Exposed* (1837) p. xxvii.
[9] *Address to the Friends of Justice and Humanity* (1833) pp. 2, 19. This address from the Short-time Committee at Birstall went on to speak in contemptuous terms of the Inspectors—" a briefless lawyer—a broken-down Merchant, a poor Aristocrat—and an intimate friend of Lieut. Drummond . . . incompetent for their task, but amply provided with most unconstitutional means of annoyance and mischief."

RICHARD OASTLER

selves were parties.[10]   Thus they combined in their own persons
the full range of governmental power, executive, legislative and
judicial, a weight of authority, which, as events were to show, was
far too heavy for them to bear.   Their functions were severely
curtailed by the great Act of 1844, by which time their true *métier*
had been more clearly defined, yet it remains true that the powers
they wielded during the intervening years, when the new system
was being slowly forged, enabled them to set a permanent mark
on the form and content of factory legislation.   The freedom they
enjoyed in the early days made it possible for them to experiment
freely, to adapt, to modify, and to reject, as their growing
experience of the problems of factory control dictated, and their
close liaison with the Home Office provided the Government with
the opportunity of translating the lessons derived from that experience into statutory form.[11]

In the meantime, their work was that of pioneers.   To them
was committed the onerous task of enforcing a new and unpopular
law, of devising, within the imperfect framework of the Act, such
rules and regulations as should best achieve the purpose of the
Legislature, of securing uniformity of procedure and practice
throughout the length and breadth of the land, and of advising the
Government of the defects of the system, and of the amendments
of the law that those defects showed to be necessary.

It was apparent that when Parliament limited the number of
Inspectors to four it had by no means envisaged the demands that

---

[10] "There have been four instances," said Horner, "in which I have
convicted upon view; they were cases of operatives whom I found employing children contrary to law, notwithstanding frequent warnings by the
master and manager."—Report, 18th January, 1837, *Parl. Papers* (1837)
XXXI, p. 100.   His journal contained records of these and other cases.
e.g., "In going through the mill . . . I saw a very young child piecing to
Wm. Fielden.   The child appeared to me about eight years old, certainly
not more than nine. . . I called the parties before me in the counting-
house; swore Mr. Platt to his having given repeated orders to his people
that the law was to be strictly obeyed . . . and thereupon I adjudged
Fielden to pay a fine of 20s." (*Parl. Papers*, 1840, X, p. 279). "There
was a great neglect of the books and notices, and I told Mr. Barnes that
I should fine him 40s. on view, this being a mitigated penalty for one
offence only." (*Ibid.* p. 280).   See also L. Horner, *The Factories Regulation Act Explained* (1834) p. 17.

[11] *Cf.* L. Faucher, *Etudes sur l'Angleterre* (1856) Vol. I, p. 457—"Cette
création devait froisser les moeurs de l'Angleterre, où tout citoyen con-
sidère sa maison ou son établissement comme un château fort fermé à
l'action de la puissance publique; elle n'a été acceptée qu'avec une extrême
répugnance, et pourtant, entre les mains d'hommes honorables et prudents,
elle a porté les meilleurs fruits.   S'il reste quelque chose de l'impulsion
donnée en 1833, si la loi n'a pas complétement échoué, si l'on a recueilli
des indications plus sûres pour les réformes à venir, c'est aux inspecteurs
des manufactures que l'Angleterre le doit."

were to be made upon them, nor did the division of the country
·nto districts[12] bear any relation to the relative concentration of
industry. To Robert Rickards[13] was assigned Yorkshire, Lancashire, Cheshire, north-west Derbyshire and north Staffordshire,·
together with Caernarvon, Denbigh, Flint and Anglesey; to
Leonard Horner,[14] the whole of Scotland, north Ireland, and the
four northern counties of England, Cumberland, Westmorland,
Durham and Northumberland; to Robert J. Saunders the eastern,
southern and south-western counties; and to Thomas Jones
Howell,[15] southern Ireland, the remaining counties of Wales, those
portions of Derbyshire and Staffordshire outside Rickards' district,
together with the counties of Hereford, Worcester, Warwick and
Gloucester.

Saunders, it is true, had a widely scattered area to cover, but
he had only to supervise some 300 mills containing 24,000
operatives. Rickards, on the other hand, was confronted with a
superhuman task, for his district contained some 2,700 factories
manned by more than a quarter of a million workers. It was not
long before he collapsed under the strain, and he was compelled
to resign on 9th June, 1836.[16] "His weak state of health," commented Fox Maule, the Under-Secretary of the Home Office,

---

12 *Parl. Papers* (1834) XLIII, p. 423.

13 Rickards had been a partner in the firm of Rickards, Mackintosh &
Co., East India merchants. " Mr. Rickards has resided some years in
India," said *The Times* (5th November, 1833). " His experiences in the
world, joined to his acknowledged talents and various acquirements,
peculiarly fit him for discharging the delicate and responsible office of
inspector."

14 The first Inspector appointed to the northern district was Musgrave,
about whom little is known. He died, or resigned in October or November,
1833, whereupon Francis Jeffrey, Lord Advocate for Scotland, offered the
post to Horner. (See K. M. Lyell, *Memoir of Leonard Horner* (1890)
Vol. I, p. 286). Horner, who was born in Edinburgh on 17th January,
1785, was the outstanding figure among the early Inspectors. The third
son of John Horner, a linen merchant, he was educated at Edinburgh High
School, whence·he proceeded, in August, 1799, to Edinburgh University
to study geology. At the age of 19 he became a partner in his father's
firm, but when the family removed to London in 1804, he turned to
scientific and educational work. Becoming a member of the Geological
Society in 1808, he was elected a Fellow of the Royal Society in 1813, and
in 1828 he was appointed Warden of the newly-established University of
London. His imperious temper brought him into conflict with the
authorities, however, and he resigned in 1831, to be appointed a member
of the Factory Commission two years later. He retired from the inspectorate in 1858, and died in London on 5th March, 1864. Short and stocky
in appearance with high forehead and deep-set eyes, his strong mouth and
determined jaw proclaimed him a man of ruthless energy and deep conviction—ideally fitted for the part he was called upon to play.

15 A barrister—formerly Judge-Advocate of Gibraltar.

16 *Home Office Papers*, H.O. 87 (1). p. 6. His work received but
scant recognition, for when he died shortly afterwards his widow received
a curt letter from the Home Office informing her that his salary would be
paid to the day of his resignation, and asking her to return the office seal.

" necessarily rendered his services not so efficient as they might have been,"[17] and five days later Horner was summoned from the north to take over his district, James Stuart being appointed in Horner's place a few weeks later.[18]

Despite his immense energies, Horner found the burden too great, and in March, 1837, he asked the Government to consider re-arranging the districts on a more equitable basis.[19] His plea was ignored, but matters were brought to a head the following July when, at the statutory half-yearly meeting of the Inspectors, Horner informed his colleagues that he had been instructed to take over, in addition to his existing area, the four northern counties forming part of Stuart's district.[20] He had said that it would be quite impossible for him to do this, whereupon Saunders suggested " that a plan should be submitted to Lord John Russell,[21] by which in his opinion, a more equitable division of the country might be made into Superintendencies."[22] The matter was deemed to be of such urgency that Horner and Stuart repaired to the Home Office at one o'clock the same afternoon (it was a Saturday) to discuss the matter more fully. They returned with the news that Stuart was to take over southern Ireland from Howell, and that the Inspectors were to prepare a plan for the reorganization of their districts by the following Monday. A long discussion resulted in the preparation of the new scheme, but Howell objected to certain of the details, and it was not until 3rd August that final proposals were submitted.

Stuart was to inspect the whole of Ireland and Scotland—600 mills in all. Horner was to take over from Stuart the four northern counties of England, giving up to Saunders most of the West Riding of Yorkshire, and parts of Derbyshire and Staffordshire, and to Howell north Wales (Flint, Denbigh, Caernarvon and Anglesey) together with the greater part of Cheshire and parts of Derbyshire and Staffordshire. This left him with 1,484 mills under his control. Howell received from Saunders Cornwall, Devon, Dorset, Somerset,

---

[17] *Parl. Papers* (1837) XXXI, p. 123.
[18] *Ibid.* p. 114. Stuart, born in 1775, attended Edinburgh University and became a Writer to the Signet. An enthusiastic Whig he was involved in a duel in 1822 with Sir Alexander Boswell, who had attacked him in a series of scurrilous articles in the Tory *Glasgow Sentinel*. Stuart had the misfortune to kill his opponent, but was acquitted of the charge of wilful murder. In 1828 he went to America, becoming editor of the London *Courier* on his return. He gave up this work on his appointment as Factory Inspector in 1836. He died of heart disease on 3rd November, 1849. (*Dictionary of National Biography*, Vol. LV, p. 90.)
[19] Report, 31st March, 1837. *Parl. Papers* (1838) XXVIII, p. 84.
[20] *Minutes*, 22nd July, 1837, Vol. I, p. 75. The instruction had been conveyed to him two days before. See *Home Office Papers*, H.O. 87 (1), p. 83.
[21] Home Secretary in Melbourne's administration.
[22] *Minutes, loc. cit.* p. 76.

and part of Wiltshire, so that his new district contained 1,006 mills, leaving Saunders with 1,193 mills.[23] The plan was approved by the Home Secretary on 8th August,[24] and on the following day the Inspectors went to their new territories. The scheme worked well, and in their Joint Report for July, 1838,[25] the Inspectors expressed their satisfaction that, as a result, they were able to enforce the law more effectively.

This was not the first difference that had arisen between the Inspectors and the Home Office. The previous September Horner had reported that upon his asking to be supplied with stationery, he had been told that the Home Secretary had decided " that the Inspectors are to find their own stationery, and that it was intended so from the beginning."[26] They resolved not to be satisfied with this, and Saunders was able to produce a letter that he had received from Lord Melbourne in October, 1833, saying that he had been pleased to give directions to the Comptroller of the Stationery Office that the Inspectors were to be re-imbursed for any stationery they purchased.[27] The question was not so trivial as it might appear, for the Inspectors were determined to establish the principle that any expenses they incurred in the discharge of their duties should be paid from the public funds, and in this they were successful.[28]

Their salaries were fixed at £1,000 a year, from which sum they were required to defray their travelling and hotel expenses.[29] In 1842 they asked that a portion of their remuneration should be assigned to cover these charges, so that only the residue should be liable for income tax, which was then chargeable at the rate of 7d. in the pound. Here, however, the Government was on firmer ground, and the Inspectors met with a somewhat curt rebuff. The letter conveying the refusal to accede to their request was read at

23 *Ibid*. pp. 90-93. The changes are recorded by the Inspectors in their Reports of September, 1837. *Parl. Papers* (1838) XXVIII, pp. 105, 108, 111, 114.
24 *Home Office Papers*, H.O. 87 (1), p. 88.
25 *Parl. Papers* (1839) XIX, p. 537.
26 *Minutes*, 22nd September, 1836, Vol. I, p. 28.
27 *Ibid*. pp. 36-37.
28 They were required, for instance, to insert in the newspapers advertisements setting out the regulations they had made. The minutes of their meeting held on 27th January, 1837, record that they sent to the Home Office a bill for £8. 7s. 3d., being the account for advertisements published in the *London Gazette*. " These expenses," they said, " were necessarily incurred by us in the discharge of our duties as Inspectors of Factories," and they asked that the bill should be paid by the Treasury.—*Minutes*, Vol. I, p. 63.
29 *Parl. Papers* (1834) XLIII, p. 423.

their half-yearly meeting, and pasted, without comment, in the minute book.[30]

The incidental expenses they were obliged to incur must have been heavy, for they usually made a complete tour of their districts three or four times a year.[31] In those days travelling was not only costly, but slow and tedious as well—the mail coach from London to Newcastle, for instance, taking forty-eight hours to complete its journey.[32] To this physical burden was added the labour of seeking out the mill-owners,[33] explaining to them their new obligations, and exhorting them to carry out their duties. Infractions of the law could only be detected by close personal vigilance,[34] and with the limited assistance available this was difficult to achieve, for rigorous and detailed investigations had to be conducted in every mill the Inspectors visited. " The chief inquiries in a visit to a factory," said Horner, " ought to be as follows: whether any child is employed at an earlier age than the law allows; if any child or young person is employed without a certificate of age; if any child or young person is employed for a longer time than the law allows; if the child attends school as required; if the proper time for meals is allowed, and if the interior of the mill has been whitewashed as the law directs. Now it is impossible to ascertain these facts without a personal examination of the workpeople, and without seeing the interior of the mill; and the children and young persons can only be met with in those parts of the mill where manufacturing processes are carried on."[35]

It had never been intended that the duty of enforcing the Factories Regulation Act should be confined to the four Inspectors who were appointed in compliance with the 17th section. They would obviously need assistance in maintaining that intimate contact with the mills that was essential if the law was to be enforced effectively, and accordingly it had been provided by the

---

[30] *Home Office Papers,* 87 (1), p. 263. *Minutes,* 5th July, 1842, Vol. I, p. 176.

[31] In 1839 Stuart travelled more than 5,500 miles.—Report, 31st December, 1839. *Parl. Papers* (1840) XXIII, p. 23.

[32] Horner first experienced the thrills of the railway in 1836. "We saw the country before us as we shot along," he wrote, " and were not at all annoyed with dust or smoke. We were an hour and forty minutes, in going the thirty-one miles; the motion is not only not unpleasant, but is far superior to most stage-coaches."—K. M. Lyell, *Memoir of Leonard Horner* (1890) Vol. I, p. 328.

[33] The obligation to report the occupation of factories was not imposed until later. In the meantime the district surveyors of taxes made returns of mills to the Inspectors.—Horner's Report, 21st July, 1834. *Parl. Papers* (1834) XLIII, p. 428.

[34] See Rickards' Report, August, 1835. *Parl. Papers* (1836) XLV, p. 161.

[35] Report, 31st March, 1838. *Parl. Papers* (1838) XXVIII, p. 138.

19th section that upon the application of an Inspector, one or
more Superintendents might be employed to help in carrying out
the provisions of the Act.[36] These subordinate officers were vested
with a range of powers much less extensive than those entrusted
to the Inspectors, who were empowered to enter all departments
of the factories at any time of the day or night. The Superintendents, on the other hand, were only authorized to enter " any
school-room, counting-house, or any part of any factory or mill,
excepting such part or parts as may be used for manufacturing
purposes."[37]

This limitation of the Superintendents' powers was a concession
to the views of the mill-occupiers, who from the first had expressed
their uneasiness at the appointment of " mill-wardens."   Within a
few months of the passing of the Act the Dundee manufacturers
told Horner that they felt great anxiety about the mill-wardens
" unless very discreet persons be nominated,"[38] an anxiety that was
shared by the owners in Glasgow and elsewhere.   There was great
alarm, said Horner, " from the fear that troublesome persons might
be appointed to exercise inquisitorial powers over the manufacturers,"[39] while Howell declared that the mill-occupiers would
object to the visitations of persons of inferior status to themselves.[40]
Rickards reported that in his district the owners anticipated great
annoyance from the mill-wardens,[41] and Saunders found much
speculation concerning their powers and duties.[42]

The real objection, however, was that the Superintendents were
in a position to exercise a closer measure of control than the
Inspectors, since they were resident on the spot and had less ground
to cover.   Nassau Senior feared that their visits would disturb the
smooth working of the mills.   " A strict and almost superstitious
discipline is necessary to keep this vast instrument going for a
single day," he declared.   " Now how, ask the mill-owners, could
this discipline be kept up, if the sub-inspectors were at liberty to
walk over our establishments at all hours; listen to the complaints
and jealousies of all our servants, and at their instigation summon
us as criminals before the magistrates?   Could the discipline, they
ask, of a regiment or of a ship be carried on, if we had sub-

---

36 In December, 1836, five Superintendents had been assigned to
Horner (Heathcote, Baker, Bates, Trimmer and Ewings); three to Saunders
(Kent, Bury and Marshall); three to Howell (Hicks, Webster and Brown)
and three to Stuart (James, Beal and Wood)—*Home Office Papers*, H.O.
87 (1), pp. 31-33.
37 3 & 4 Will. IV, c. 103, sec. 19.
38 Report, 8th December, 1833. *Parl. Papers* (1834) XLIII, p. 426.
39 *Ibid*. p. 427.
40 Report, 20th December, 1833. *Ibid*. p. 444.
41 Report, 24th December, 1833. *Ibid*. p. 446.
42 Report, 28th December, 1833. *Ibid*. p. 482.

inspectors of regiments, with power to ask all the privates for grievances, and summon their officers for penalties?"[43]

These, however, were not the only grounds on which the manufacturers were apprehensive. Mechanical processes were constantly being improved, the inventive genius of the engineer was rapidly introducing innovations in the design of textile machinery, and plant that had been laid down at great expense quickly became obsolete. It was, therefore, of the first importance that trade secrets should be well guarded, and there was reason to fear, it was alleged, that if the Superintendents were granted free access to the mills they might be tempted to communicate confidential information to rival manufacturers.

The Inspectors were unanimous in declaring that the powers of the Superintendents should be extended. They were the eyes and ears of the Inspectors, to whom they made their weekly reports, and Rickards emphasized that they were indispensable, pleading that they should be permitted to visit the interior of the mills, under the direction of the Inspector, for in no other way could the law be enforced.[44] If they were allowed access only to the counting-house they would, it was admitted, be able to examine the age certificates and time-books, but they would be precluded from making personal observation of working conditions, and in particular they would be unable to see the children and young persons at their tasks. The news of their arrival was quickly spread through the mill,[45] and it was not difficult for an unscrupulous occupier to take such steps as were necessary to conceal any infractions of the law.

Saunders reported a case in which one of his Superintendents, having entered a mill, " cast his eye round the room, and observed some person very busy about a bag of wool; he went up and found a boy who had been wrongly employed, in the act of being concealed therein; his head and body had already been enclosed, and the bag fastened over him, and Mr. Baker only discovered him by his feet protruding."[46] The practice of concealing children who were being illegally employed was not uncommon. Horner, too, had discovered them hidden in wool-bags; and on one occasion, he said, " I was told in a mill that I visited, believing children to be improperly employed there, after I was gone I was told, ' If you

---

[43] Nassau W. Senior, *Letters on the Factory Act* (1837) p. 27.

[44] Report, 12th August, 1834. *Parl. Papers* (1834) XLIII, p. 461.

[45] Neighbouring mills, too, were soon informed when a Superintendent was in the vicinity. For this reason it was often found advisable to visit on foot, rather than to make use of public conveyances.—*Minutes*, 6th June, 1845, Vol. II, p. 167.

[46] Report, 30th September, 1838. *Parl. Papers* (1839) XIX, p. 445.

had looked into the necessaries, you would have found them full.' "[47]

The mill-occupiers did not always exercise their right to exclude the Superintendents; indeed, Stuart said of Scotland, " Factory-owners in this country afford facilities in enforcing the Act far greater than the Act requires from them, on all occasions when they are applied to in conciliatory terms by the Inspectors and Superintendents."[48]   Full access, he said, was allowed in his district,[49] but the fact remained that the power to exclude existed, and when it was exercised it was by the very occupiers who most needed vigilant observation.[50]   It was possible for the Inspector to insist on the Superintendent's being admitted, but only if he accompanied him in person, and it was often necessary to resort to this device.[51]

But as Rickards pointed out, " Nothing can make a factory law really efficient but a constant inspection of the interior of mills,"[52] and the Inspectors chafed under a system that so reduced their efficiency.   As early as July, 1834, they made a formal protest to the Home Secretary,[53] and Horner continued to urge that the law should be amended.   " To retain, in an amending Act," he declared, " the right of excluding them from all those parts where manufacturing processes are carried on, would be to pass over one of the greatest defects in the existing law; and it would be nothing less than to reserve a power of defeating the intentions of the legislature to any mill-owner who might choose to avail himself of it."[54]   The Superintendents had been excluded originally, he said, because it had been the intention to appoint mill-wardens " selected from the humbler and less-educated classes of society, as constables often are . . . but officers appointed to carry a law into effect should have by law *a right* to do all that is necessary for the execution of the law."[55]   He did not think there was any danger of secret processes being disclosed, but suggested that if it was not felt desirable to place the Superintendents on an equal footing with the Inspectors

----

[47] Select Committee on the Act for the Regulation of Mills and Factories.   *Parl. Papers* (1840) X, p. 585.   *Cf.* R. Oastler, *The Unjust Judge* (1836) p. 8.—" It is quite common for the Factory-Masters to send the young hands out of the mill, or to shut them up in the privies, or to hide them under sheets, when the Inspector is coming."

[48] Report, 31st March, 1840.   *Parl. Papers* (1840) XXIII, p. 36.

[49] Report, 30th December, 1840.   *Parl. Papers* (1841) X, p. 193.

[50] Greg, for instance, one of the most vociferous opponents of the Act, invariably excluded the Superintendents from the working flats.—Horner's Report, 31st March, 1838.   *Parl. Papers* (1838) XXVIII, p. 137.

[51] Howell's Report, 31st December, 1837.   *Ibid.* p. 120.

[52] Report, August, 1835.   *Parl. Papers* (1836) XLV, p. 162.

[53] Joint Report, 28th July, 1834.   *Parl. Papers* (1834) XLIII, p. 492.

[54] Report, 31st December, 1838.   *Parl. Papers* (1839) XIX, p. 449.

[55] Report, 31st March, 1838.   *Parl. Papers* (1838) XXVIII, p. 138.

in this respect, they should at least be allowed free access if the Inspector made a written declaration that he had reason to believe that the law was being violated.[56]

To any suggestion that the powers of the Superintendents should be enlarged, the manufacturers offered an uncompromising opposition. " We are sorry to see," remarked Greg, " on the part of one of the Inspectors a call for *farther powers,* for authority to the Superintendent to enter the mills without the consent of the owner. . . . The Inspector has power to enter the interior of the mills at all times, but the Superintendent cannot go beyond the counting-house (where the time-books and certificates are at his command) without the consent of the owner. This limitation was one of mutual agreement between the Government which introduced the bill and the mill-owners. To give to the Superintendent an absolute right of entrance into the mills, would be extremely offensive to the proprietors, and probably defeat some of the most important objects of the bill. . . . Such a power, after the courting both Inspectors and Superintendents have experienced from the mill-owners, ought not to have been demanded. It is an ungracious return for that courtesy. If granted, hostility will be commenced, and all hopes of the Relay system, and any good arising from the bill, to balance its evil, will be gone for ever. The children will remain without food as well as education, the operatives will be extremely distressed, and the prosperity of the manufacturers seriously compromised."[57] Repeated efforts were made by the Inspectors during the ensuing years to secure the powers that were necessary if the Superintendents were to take a full part in the enforcement of the Act, but it was not until 1844 that the legislature conferred the full right of access.

The estimation in which the Government at first held these officers was reflected in the salaries that were paid to them. Their remuneration was fixed at £250 a year, from which sum they were required to pay their own travelling expenses, estimated by the Inspectors at not less than £200.[58] In arriving at this figure the Home Secretary had obviously been considering the appointment of persons of inferior status: he could certainly not have envisaged the responsible nature of the duties they were, in fact, required to undertake. The Superintendents themselves were dissatisfied—" My salary is 250*l.* per annum; and, in consequence of accepting this office, I have been deprived of my pension of 73*l.* per annum, as late paymaster of the Royal Montgomeryshire

56 Nassau W. Senior, *Letters on the Factory Act* (1837) p. 42.
57 R. H. Greg, *The Factory Question* (1837) pp. 129-130.
58 *Minutes,* 15th September, 1836, Vol. I, p. 13.

militia," said Charles Brown, one of Howell's Superintendents, who
covered some 1,600 miles a year visiting the 147 mills in north
Wales which were in his charge. " From the nature of the country,
and want of public conveyance, I am compelled to perform my
journies on horseback, for which I am obliged to keep two horses."[59]

On more than one occasion the Inspectors urged the Home
Office to increase these obviously inadequate salaries, and to the
formal representations they made at their meeting in September,
1836,[60] Lord John Russell replied that he was prepared to consider
appointing two classes of Superintendents, one to receive £250 and
the other £350 a year.[61] He could hardly do less, for it was already
becoming apparent that the Superintendents must be men of some
standing. Robert Baker, for instance, who was responsible for the
Leeds district, was a medical practitioner, who prior to his appointment, had been employed by the mill-occupiers, as he later affirmed,
" to stand between them and the public, with reference to the
effect of labour on their workpeople, with power to enter their
factories at all times by day and by night."[62] Russell himself
considered that " a surgeon or other medical man of intelligence "[63]
was particularly well fitted to act as Superintendent, and he could
not expect to employ men of this calibre at an unattractive salary.

The new rates came into force early in October, 1836.[64] In
each district two of the Superintendents were to receive £350 a
year, but the fact that they were still required to pay their own
travelling expenses being considered unsatisfactory, in July, 1837,
Saunders suggested asking the Government " to alter the mode
of paying the travelling and personal expences of those officers."[65]
No action was taken, however, and it was some years before this
difficult problem was resolved.

This more generous treatment went far to remove a legitimate
grievance, but the equivocal status of the Superintendents, and the
fact that their relationship with the Inspectors had never been
clearly defined caused a certain bitterness, and led to personal
squabbles, for it was too early for any professional code of conduct
to have been established, nor had there been an opportunity of
developing an *esprit de corps*. A further source of trouble lay in
the fact that some, at least, of the men appointed were quite un-
suited to posts of such importance. Daniel Webster, for instance,
who acted in Howell's district, was venal and irresponsible. The

[59] *Parl. Papers* (1838) XLV, p. 75.
[60] *Minutes, loc. cit.* pp. 12-13.
[61] 28th September, 1836. *Home Office Papers,* H.O. 87 (1), p. 11.
[62] *Transactions of the National Association for the Promotion of Social Science* (1859) pp. 554-555.
[63] *Home Office Papers,* H.O. 87 (1), p. 17.
[64] *Ibid.* p. 11. *Minutes,* 5th October, 1836, Vol. I, p. 40.
[65] *Minutes,* 22nd July, 1837, Vol. I, p. 76.

mill-occupiers complained that he did not enforce the law equally, that he retained for himself a proportion of the penalties inflicted by the magistrates, and that his general demeanour was light and frivolous.[66] He was called upon to reply to these charges, and his explanation being rejected as inadequate, he was summarily dismissed.[67] Within a week, however, yielding to his protestations and promises of amendment, Russell had agreed to rescind his former decision, and Webster was reinstated, being transferred to Stuart's district at the reduced salary of £250.[68] In less than two years, having, in the meantime, been transferred to Horner's district, he was in trouble again. Twice he was arrested for debt; he had accepted bribes from some mill-owners and borrowed money from others; and, most unwisely, he applied to a member of Parliament for a loan of £100. He went so far as to circulate a printed paper—" a most extraordinary Document " declared the Home Office—comparing the duties carried out by Inspectors and Superintendents respectively. Once again he was dismissed, but this time he was not re-engaged, despite his pleas, which extended over many months, and which sorely taxed the patience of the Home Office.[69]

Horner's Superintendents, too, were a source of trouble, for two of them, at least, showed themselves loath to carry out his instructions. In June, 1837, Charles Trimmer, who was stationed at Macclesfield, received a letter from the Home Office, informing him that Horner had reported " that you have refused to obey Mr. Horner's instructions that you should request the Magistrates to permit the Fines imposed for breaches of the Factory Act to be funded, in order that they may be afterwards applied in a more solid form, under the directions of the Inspector, for the benefit of Schools where Factory children are educated." The Home Secretary made it clear to Trimmer that he was determined to support the Inspector's authority, and the erring Superintendent was reprimanded, and transferred to Howell's district as successor to Daniel Webster. Heathcote, the Manchester Superintendent, who had adopted an equally insubordinate attitude, was cautioned, but allowed to remain in his district.[70]

Robert Baker's indiscretion, too, placed Horner in a difficult position. Accustomed to act as certifying surgeon, prior to his

---

[66] *Home Office Papers,* H.O. 87 (1), p. 58. It was alleged, said Fox Maule in a letter to Webster, that meeting an owner at the factory gate, " You said that you were just going in here to catch a bird for your dinner tomorrow."

[67] On 3rd June, 1837. *Ibid.* p. 63.

[68] *Ibid.* p. 68.

[69] *Home Office Papers,* H.O. 87 (1), pp. 157, 161. See Horner's Report, 30th September, 1839. *Parl. Papers* (1840) XXIII, p. 3.

[70] *Home Office Papers,* H.O. 87 (1), pp. 66-69.

appointment at Leeds, he continued to grant certificates of age after he became a Superintendent. The Manchester Short-time Committee seized upon this in the memorial they addressed to the Home Secretary, stigmatizing as highly objectionable the practice by which " Superintendents who are medical practitioners derive extra emolument by entering into private engagements and compacts with particular mill-owners," and declaring that such men should devote the whole of their time to the duties of their office.[71] Horner had already heard from an anonymous correspondent what Baker was doing, and had forbidden him to grant any more age certificates,[72] but although he had been called upon by the Home Office to report " upon the fact of your continuing to practise as a surgeon,"[73] Baker was in no hurry to comply with the instructions of his superior, though after an interval of six months he gave way.

At the meeting of the Inspectors in July, 1837, Horner and Howell having explained the circumstances " which had unhappily occurred in their respective districts relative to the conduct of certain Superintendents," a formal minute was adopted that all the Superintendents should be informed what had happened, and that they should be instructed " that they are to allow no other occupation to interfere with their official duties, but be at all times ready to perform any duty required of them by the Inspector which he shall deem necessary for the due execution of the Act."[74]

The letters to the Superintendents were sent out within the next few weeks.[75] The Inspectors, they were reminded, were acting under the direct orders of the Secretary of State, and the code of instructions now issued for their guidance must be rigidly followed. The confidential nature of their duties was stressed; they were given precise orders as to the manner in which they were to conduct prosecutions, and as to how they were to comport themselves towards the mill-occupiers; they were told how they were to frame their weekly reports, and what to look for when they examined the registers and other official documents during their visits to the mills.

It was not really surprising that difficulties such as these should have occurred, for it had been necessary to enlist men who had no previous experience of the public service. The whole conception of inspectorial control was new; standards of vigilance, propriety, and personal relationship were governed by no precedent, and it was the duty of the Inspectors to shape the plans and devise the

71 *Parl. Papers* (1837) L, p. 203.
72 *Ibid.* p. 209.
73 *Home Office Papers,* H.O. 87 (1) p. 84.
74 *Minutes,* 18th and 22nd July, 1837, Vol. I, pp. 68, 79.
75 See Appendix.

machinery that were essential to the due enforcement of the law.
There was as yet no tradition to guide them, no corpus of minutes
and decisions upon which they could rely—all this had to be
worked out slowly and painfully, and there were many setbacks,
for even the Inspectors themselves had still to establish a code of
professional conduct, particularly in their relationship with the
Home Office. They had already shown themselves able to adopt
an independent attitude, but the exigencies of the time involved
them in a course of action that might well have had the most
serious consequences, for they allowed themselves to be employed
in affairs that were clearly outside the range of duties contemplated
by the Act that had called them into being.

The country was in a state of unrest—the new Poor Law
system inaugurated in 1834 was extremely unpopular, the textile
industry was entering upon a period of severe depression, and
political agitation was rife. The Government was nervous, the
more so because it had no means of assessing accurately the state
of public opinion in those centres of unrest that were remote from
the metropolis. In its anxiety the Home Office, whose duty it was
to preserve public order, turned to those men whose intimate
knowledge of the manufacturing districts gave them a unique
opportunity of reporting upon the situation.

On 3rd May, 1837, each of the four Inspectors received from
the Under-Secretary of State for the Home Department a letter
couched in the following terms:—

" *Confidential.*

I am directed by Lord J. Russell to acquaint you, that
he is desirous of receiving from time to time, any information
which you may be able to furnish respecting the state of trade,
the wages of labour, and the state of tranquility or excitement,
in the district in which you act."[76]

No complaint could legitimately have been made against the
request for information about trade and wages, for these matters
were clearly concerned with the working of the Act. Nor was there
any need to ask for such details, since the Inspectors were already
alluding to these topics in their reports. But to ask them to report
on the state of political feeling was another affair altogether. They
had been appointed for a specific purpose, to enforce the provisions
of the Factories Regulation Act, and it was essential that they
should remain aloof from popular controversy.

Early in 1838 political agitation began to assume a more
definite and menacing shape. Under the guidance of Feargus
O'Connor the Chartists drew up detailed plans for revolutionary
changes in the Parliamentary system. Huge meetings were held

---

[76] *Home Office Papers*, H.O. 87 (1), p. 59.

in Glasgow and other Scottish towns, as well as in Newcastle, Birmingham and Northampton. Pikes were distributed at Norwich. At Rochdale firearms were handed out, and the Government marshalled its forces to meet the anticipated threat of revolution.[77]

It was against this background that the Inspectors, assembled at their statutory meeting, recorded in their minutes: "Monday, 29 July, 1839.—On Saturday last Mr. Horner had communicated to his colleagues, instructions from Mr. Maule to report weekly respecting the Chartist Meetings."[78] There was no further comment, and apparently the instructions were carried out. It was the indiscretion of Beal, the Superintendent at Dundee, that brought matters to a head. He had received secret orders from his Inspector, Stuart, against whom he entertained a bitter personal animosity, and he was unwise enough to allow them, accidentally or by design, to fall into the hands of a third party, who in turn communicated them to John Fielden, the member for Oldham.[79]

Fielden was a vigorous opponent of the Act, and here was his opportunity. In June, 1840, he was sitting as a member of a Select Committee to enquire into the working of Althorp's Act, and when Stuart was giving his evidence, Fielden startled his colleagues by asking him if he had ever employed Beal "in any other capacity than as a superintendent of factories?"[80] Stuart, taken by surprise, hedged. He had, he said, received confidential instructions from the Secretary of State to get information about the state of feeling of the working classes, the extent of the distress in the manufacturing districts, and the state of political feeling generally, but he could produce no documents, nor could he remember how the orders reached him, though he was clear in his recollection that he had been required "particularly to secure information about the proceedings of those misguided men (the Chartists) last year. I think Dundee was a place where there were meetings very frequently, and Kirriemuir."[81] He produced a letter that he had written from Dundee, to Fox Maule, the Under-Secretary, on 12th October, 1839—"The Chartist agitation has so completely ceased that I need no longer communicate with you on the subject. I have been all over that part of my district in the west of Scotland and here, where it was understood to have

---

[77] E. Halévy, *A History of the English People, 1830-1841.* (1927) pp. 302-333.

[78] *Minutes,* Vol. I, p. 137.

[79] "A gentleman," remarked Ashley, "of vast practical knowledge in every stage and department of the business."—*Quarterly Review* (1836) Vol 57, p. 399. His firm, it was said, worked up nearly 1% of all the cotton imported—in 1835, 330 million pounds. Like Brotherton, he had had early experience of factory conditions in his father's mill.—*Ibid.* p. 433.

[80] *Parl. Papers* (1840) X, p. 635.

[81] *Ibid.* p. 637.

flourished the most, but hear nothing of it. The revivals are now the prevailing hobby, and will spread. They keep the people from the alehouses and whiskey shops, and are, therefore, at least harmless."[82]

Fielden did not pursue the matter at that stage, but on 17th July, 1840, he rose in the House and moved for a Select Committee to consider the question of the employment of Inspectors and Superintendents " in other matters than those assigned to them by the authority of Parliament, and to ascertain how far they have been employed by the Government in the capacity of political spies." He read aloud the incriminating document which had come to him from Beal.

" *Confidential.*   345, Strand,
                                                                                            30th July, 1839.

Dear Sir,

       I have to acquaint you, for your own information alone, that I am especially instructed to watch and take measures for obtaining information as to any proceedings in any district relative to assemblages of workpeople, or Chartists, or circumstances calculated to disturb the public peace. You will, therefore, be so good as to make me weekly a confidential report on this subject. The newspapers from different parts of your district will generally point out to you any places requiring particularly to be noticed, but take care at Dundee and elsewhere to act with secrecy and prudence, so that you may escape observation, and not be suspected of giving information.

                                                        I am, dear Sir,
                                                                    Yours truly,
                                                                                James Stuart."

This showed clearly, said Fielden, that an odious system of spying had been resorted to by the Government, and he charged the Ministers with having employed men, appointed under an Act of Parliament to carry into execution a statute intended to benefit children and young persons, with having mis-applied the funds voted by Parliament to pay these men, and with having employed them in a pursuit that they themselves must consider odious and degrading. How did the House know, he demanded, that Poor Law Commissioners, police, and all who were in direct communication with the Government, and the officers under them, had not been similarly employed? The Government system of centralization naturally led to this, and to the establishment of a system of spying throughout the country. The Factory Act had not been carried out in Scotland. The powers possessed by the Inspectors had been used for purposes of oppression, and their time might

---

[82] *Ibid.* p. 642.

have been wholly taken up in this degrading occupation, instead of attending to their duties.

Fox Maule attempted a defence of the Government's action. It was the duty of the Factory Inspectors, he said, to acquire information about the condition and habits of the working classes, and to keep the Government informed. This was the object of the instructions, and he ridiculed the idea that the Inspectors had acted as political spies to denounce individual agitators. The young Disraeli characterized this explanation as " monstrous and pharisaical hypocrisy," but Ashley asserted that Fielden was mistaken, and that there was no question of political espionage. He was fully and solemnly convinced, he said, that if the impression were to go forth through the country that the Factory Inspectors were political spies or agents, they might as well wipe out all legislation on the subject.

Sir Robert Peel, whilst not admitting that the Inspectors had been employed as spies, was quite prepared to justify their obtaining political information for the Government. In times of great excitement and great distress, he reminded the House, it became a matter of expediency that the Government should resort to means of obtaining information, without which the public service could not be carried on.

Lord John Russell supported the Government's policy. The Inspectors and Superintendents of Factories, he emphasized, being resident in the great manufacturing towns, and well acquainted with the character and habits of the population, were the persons best calculated to form a correct opinion of what was going on. With respect to police,[83] in most of the counties there was no force of that description from which any information could be derived.

The House was satisfied, and resolved by 113 votes to 11 to take no further action.[84]   But these revelations had come as a severe shock to the Home Office, and the unhappy Beal was speedily called to account.   On 18th July Fox Maule wrote to him, " Mr. Fielden having read in debate last night, in the House of Commons, a Letter addressed to you by your Superior Officer, of a strictly confidential character, Lord Normanby[85] desires that you will immediately account to him for that letter being out of your possession."[86]   Beal's reply was held not to constitute a

---

[83] Following the successful establishment, by the Metropolitan Police Act, 1829, of a police system in London, counties had been empowered to set up police forces in 1839; but it was not until 1856 that the County and Borough Police Act made it compulsory for them to exercise their powers.

[84] *Hansard* (1840) LV, 785-802.

[85] Russell's successor as Home Secretary.

[86] *Home Office Papers*, H.O. 87 (1), p. 218.

"sufficient explanation of the most inexcusable breach of confidence. . . . It is of little consequence as to the contents of the
letter," continued Fox Maule, "which might be construed to imply
a course of proceeding, for which the Secretary of State had
certainly given no authority."[87]   Beal was thereupon dismissed,
but his case was later re-considered, upon his giving the name of
the person who had transmitted Stuart's letter to Fielden.   "Lord
Normanby is willing so far to absolve you in this affair," he was
informed, "as to believe that you did not connive at its falling
into Mr. Fielden's hands, but he cannot excuse the extreme carelessness that was the cause of your placing in the hands of persons
of whom you knew nothing, a paper of a confidential character."[88]
In October, 1840, Beal was accordingly reinstated, and transferred
to Horner's district at the reduced salary of £250.   His relations
with his new Inspector were satisfactory, and the following June,
on a favourable report from Horner, his salary was restored to
£350.[89]

Thus ended this singular chapter in the early history of the
inspectorate.   It is illuminating because it illustrates the pitfalls
that had to be avoided if the new system of centralized inspection
was to command confidence and work smoothly, for the fact was
that the central government was now armed with a weapon of
singular potency, and they had been tempted to misuse it.
Perhaps the most important of the many functions of the Inspectors
was to act as a channel of information, not in the political arena,
but in the narrowly circumscribed area within which their duties
lay.   On them was placed the responsibility of watching the
tremendous experiment of factory control at work, of observing
its weaknesses, of devising remedies, of securing uniformity in
practice and procedure, and of conveying their conclusions to the
Government in such a way that effective action could, in due course,
be taken by Parliament.   "The early factory legislation," it has
been said, "in its restricted application to textile undertakings,
was an experiment.   It was only when a proper system of factory
inspection had been instituted that the results of that experiment,
and the desirability of applying it to other industries, could be
assessed."[90]   The Inspectors made mistakes and involved themselves, from time to time, in embarrassing situations, but by and
large the part they played was a worthy one.   They were intelligent,

[87] *Ibid*. p. 219.
[88] *Ibid*. p. 230.
[89] *Ibid*. p. 247.
[90] D. H. Blelloch, *A Historical Survey of Factory Inspection in Great
Britain*. (*International Labour Review*, November, 1938) p. 628.

far-sighted men, with a tremendous appetite for work, and though they were called upon to face a bitter and sustained opposition, it was to them alone that the successful development of industrial control, with its ever-widening ramifications, was due.

CHAPTER 8

PROBLEMS OF ENFORCEMENT

FOLLOWING ITS virtual defeat over Poulett Thomson's amending bill, the Government took speedy action to fulfil the promise given by Russell that the Act should be stringently enforced. On 16th June, 1836, a letter having been addressed to Fox Maule from the Office of the Committee of the Privy Council for Trade, setting forth the principles on which the Inspectors should act in executing the provisions of the law, the Home Office communicated its instructions[1] to Horner, Saunders and Howell, who thereafter could be in no doubt as to what was required of them. They were reminded that " upon the urgent solicitations of parties connected with the great manufactures of this country, as well as upon the unanimous recommendation of the Factory Commissioners,"[2] the President of the Board of Trade, with the concurrence of the Home Office, had introduced a bill " suspending the operation of the progressive clauses relating to children between 12 and 13, which were to come into operation on the 1st March last." The bill had been withdrawn, since there was no hope of its becoming law, and an assurance had been given to the Commons that the Government would use every endeavour to bring the existing law into full operation. That pledge must now be redeemed.

It was true, continued the letter, that owing to the defective nature of some of the provisions of the Act it might not be possible to carry the law into full execution (more especially owing to the unwillingness of magistrates to enforce it, an unwillingness that must often make it difficult for the Inspectors to obtain convictions), but even so a great deal more could be done than had hitherto been the case. The difficulty that the operatives often declined to give evidence, and that the Superintendents were not allowed full access to the mills, was not insuperable—the evil could at least be mitigated by a more constant attention on the part of the Inspectors. Immediate supervision had been far less than was right or proper, especially in the Lancashire district, and in future the Inspectors were to devote their time unremittingly to visiting the mills. The education clauses must be strictly enforced. Great indulgence had been shown hitherto, and no doubt the strict execution of the law would cause serious difficulty, but no further latitude could be justified, in view of what had passed. The

---

1 On 25th June, 1836. *Parl. Papers* (1837) XXXI, pp. 123-125.
2 So in original, but " Factory Inspectors " is clearly meant.

Inspectors were to carry into effect, to the best of their ability, the whole of the provisions of the Act, unaffected by the inconvenience which their doing so might cause.[3]

Now that all doubts as to the intentions of Parliament were removed it became the duty of the Inspectors to regain some of the ground that had been lost, and as a first step Horner, Howell and Saunders inserted advertisements in the *London Gazette* and in the provincial newspapers setting out the existing provisions of the law, and warning the mill-occupiers that for the future a full measure of obedience would be exacted.[4] Horner and Howell followed up this general admonition with a circular letter which was sent to each manufacturer,[5] and as a result the Inspectors were shortly able to report that there was a decided change for the better, dislike of the Act having greatly subsided.[6] All the mill-owners, asserted Horner, were not so evil as report had painted them. Some, indeed, were selfish and negligent, but he knew of no description of persons of whom so many instances might be brought forward of active benevolent exertions and large pecuniary sacrifice to promote the welfare of the people they employed.

These optimistic reflections were, however, somewhat premature. During the period of uncertainty, when there had been every indication that the law was likely to be amended, there had been but little disposition to enforce the terms of the Act by bringing recalcitrant owners before the courts. Such action now becoming necessary, it became all too clear that the doubts recently expressed by the Home Office concerning the willingness of magistrates to convict were well-founded. The wise provision of the earlier statutes that Justices who were mill-owners, or the near relatives of mill-owners, were not to adjudicate, had been abandoned in Althorp's Act, with the unfortunate result, as Horner pointed out, that the purity of the administration of the law was called in question, for owners who were Justices must inevitably be suspected of bias, and their leniency was likely to be misconstrued.[7] Many of them flatly refused to impose adequate penalties for breaches of the law, and in the face of this attitude the Inspectors found themselves powerless. Elaborate regulations might be framed, the inspecting officers might be vigilant in their

---

[3] " We have learned," remarked Ashley, " that the proper authorities have issued an ukase, that England at last expects every inspector to do his duty."—*Quarterly Review* (1836) Vol. 57, p. 418.

[4] Horner's Report, 31st December, 1836. *Parl. Papers* (1837) XXXI, p. 56.

[5] *Ibid.* pp. 68, 79.

[6] Horner's Report, 18th January, 1837. *Ibid.* p. 92. Saunders' Report, 2nd January, 1837. *Ibid.* p. 111.

[7] Report, 31st December, 1836. *Parl. Papers* (1837) XXXI, p. 59.

duty, but in the long run the law could only be enforced by sanctions applied in the courts. So long as it paid an unscrupulous mill-occupier to ignore the Act, so long would restriction and control remain ineffective. Even had the penalties prescribed by the Factories Regulation Act been deterrent—and this was far from being the case—the whole structure would be threatened with collapse unless the Justices of the Peace performed their duties with energy and determination.

The day was past when the local Benches were recruited exclusively from the clergy and the landed gentry, for the manufacturing interests had been increasingly represented since the industrial revolution had called into existence a moneyed aristocracy. Lord Melbourne, the Whig prime minister, was suspicious of the new magistracy. " It is certainly true," he wrote to Russell, the Home Secretary, " that I always admitted a man's being a Trader to be an objection to his becoming a Magistrate, and I believe that it is upon this principle that the Commissions have been constituted generally, and particularly in the manufacturing Counties. The notion was that manufacturers would not be considered impartial Judges in cases between the Workmen and their employers."[8] But Russell, who favoured the appointment to the Bench of Whig dissenters and manufacturers, reminded his chief, " You must recollect that the power of a Magistrate does not begin and end with sending a sheep-stealer to jail. The county purse is in a great degree under his control, roads are turned, bridges made, the poor relieved by his decisions. . . . The landed gentry are very respectable . . . but they are certainly the class in this country most ignorant, prejudiced, and narrow-minded of any. The uneducated labourers beat them hollow in intelligence."[9]

Melbourne's doubts about the impartiality of those magistrates drawn from the ranks of the mill-owners were not without foundation, for they were, generally speaking, only too ready to avail themselves of the power of mitigating penalties allowed by the 31st section of the Act.[10] The result was that in many instances mill-owners were able to flout the law with impunity, and the efforts of the Inspectors to bring offenders to justice were rendered nugatory. " I am strongly impressed with the belief," said Horner, " that the continued violation of the law is, in no small degree, to be ascribed to what appears to me a very mistaken course on the part of many of the magistrates who, to an extraordinary extent, have availed themselves of the power given to them by the Act to

---

8 *Early Correspondence of Lord John Russell*, Vol. II, pp. 138-139.
9 *Ibid.* pp. 143-144.
10 " If it shall appear . . . that such offence was not wilful or grossly negligent, such Inspector or Justice may mitigate such penalty below the said sum of one pound, or discharge the person charged with such offence."

mitigate the penalties."[11]   In 458 cases in which convictions had
been recorded, he reported, the minimum penalty of 20s. had
been imposed in no less than 345 instances, and one mill-owner
who had rendered himself liable to fines of £300 had been called
upon to pay only £15. Such action could not but encourage fresh
violations of the law.[12] The magistrates, he asserted, gave him no
support, and in many mills the law was openly disregarded.[13]
Rochdale was the most difficult district to control—" The system
which the magistrates at Rochdale act upon, of mitigating the
penalties to so great an extent is a course which is not likely . . .
to bring about a better observance of the law."[14] Despite his
efforts Horner was unable to effect any improvement, and
he complained bitterly of the frustration to which he was exposed.
In September, 1841, he instanced a particularly bad case, again at
Rochdale, where his Superintendent, Beal, had prosecuted an owner
who admitted working young people for more than twelve hours
a day. A plea of guilty was entered, and a lawyer being employed
to plead in mitigation, " a train of futile excuses was advanced. I
pleaded the necessity of an example, as overworking was so unfair
to those who obeyed the law, and I was sorry to add, that I feared
it was an offence much practised at Rochdale. I was astounded at
the decision—5s. and costs. Mr. Beal has been but a short time
in his present district;" added Horner, " if he had referred to former
decisions by Mr. Clement Royds, the chairman of the Rochdale
Petty Sessions, his surprise would have been less. I have already
alluded to the difficulty of proving a case of over-working, and
therefore, when it is proved, it is more incumbent on the magistrates
to impose such a fine as will show that they will support the
inspecting officers in the execution of their duty; and not render
a prosecution nugatory, as it was in this case."[15]

The policy thus pursued by many of the magistrates aroused
the greatest resentment among the reformers, whose views on the
question were voiced by Richard Oastler in a typical piece of
vituperative eloquence, addressed to Mr. George Goodman, the
Mayor of Leeds. " A Criminal was brought before you, who was
proved to have been guilty of breaking an Act of Parliament, for
which the Law, very properly, awarded imprisonment in the House
of Correction. . . . You were assured that the Clause against which
he had sinned, was the main check against the infringement of

---

[11] Report, 18th January, 1837. *Parl. Papers* (1837) XXXI, p. 100.
[12] Report, 12th October, 1836. *Ibid.* p. 58.
[13] Report, 31st March, 1837. *Parl. Papers* (1838) XXVIII, p. 84.
During the current quarter, he said, there had been 362 convictions, and
in 245 cases the fine had been 20s. or less.
[14] Report, 30th June, 1838. *Parl. Papers* (1838) XLV, p. 57.
[15] Report, 30th September, 1841. *Parl. Papers* (1842) XXII, p. 340.

the whole Law—the Law against Child Murder. . . . There the delinquent stood: there you sat: you could not, as on some occasions, plead ignorance of the Law; the book of the Law was open before you; AND YOU SHUT IT! The *law* condemned him, *the unjust Judge acquitted him.* It may be the will of the Magistrates of Leeds, and of other places, to render the Factory Law inoperative; it is, however, the Law of the Land; it is the imperative order of Government, *that it shall be strictly enforced;* and it will very soon be *woe* to those Magistrates who make a plaything of it. The people are tired of seeing unstamped sellers, and poachers, sent by wholesale to prison; and then five shillings, and ten shillings, and twenty shillings, allowed to be paid as the price of ' Child Murder!' . . . The Factory Law is intended to prevent Infanticide; any professional man who wilfully betrays his ' sacred and solemn trust,' and any Magistrate who refuses to punish such an one, are alike disgraced, and are morally guilty of murder."[16]

The manufacturers, as was to be expected, regarded the 31st section as a beneficent provision designed to temper the full rigour of the law. Robert Greg was pained, he said, by the ungracious remarks of Horner. " At one time, they assume the shape of *fears lest such mistaken lenity* should encourage offences; at another time, of statements that *those fears have been realised.* Sometimes, they appear in the shape of contrasts of what *possible penalties the law might have yielded* with those the magistrates actually granted; sometimes, in exhibiting, as bright examples, the magistrates who had inflicted the extreme penalties, and in the good consequences resulting from such severity; and, again, in the expression of wishes that no magistrate connected with the mills, or connected with those who might be connected with mills, should sit upon the Bench when any prosecution under the Factory Act took place.

Now, the Inspector should remember that the unfortunate mill-owner is allowed *neither jury, nor a power of appeal,* however unjust he may consider his sentence to be. The humanity and equity of the magistrate, alone, stands between him and his prosecutor. How can the Inspector desire that this discretion, *universally and properly granted to judges,* should be taken away, or limited, in order that the extravagant powers of himself and his superintendents may be increased?

Besides, does the Inspector suppose that it is no punishment to a *man,* we will say nothing of a *gentleman of education and standing in society* equal to himself, to be dragged into a court of justice, tried and condemned, and to have his name entered on a

16 R. Oastler, *The Unjust Judge* (1836) pp. 4-7.

register of convicts?   But this appears to be entirely overlooked,
and the magistrates are reprimanded because they impose a penalty
of £2 instead of £10."[17]

Nassau Senior, writing in April, 1837, declared that he was
alarmed to hear it rumoured that the Government, " in compliance
with Mr. Horner's requisitions," was proposing to make the Act
more stringent by forbidding magistrates who were beneficially
interested in the mills to adjudicate.   Such a measure, he alleged,
would exclude all manufacturers and commercial men, leaving the
enforcement of the law to the clergy and country gentry, who were
opposed to the owners in habits and politics, and who had no
knowledge of factory conditions.   This would not matter so much
if only substantial offences were punishable, but many offences were
purely formal.[18]   Horner could not agree.   The manufacturers must
be swayed in their adjudication by a bias, he replied, and even
if that bias were unconscious the results were the same.   He had,
in point of fact, ample evidence that many magistrates were
actuated by conscious bias—he had seen a mill-owner sitting alone
to hear an information against his son, the tenant of his own mill;
in another instance a manufacturer heard an information against
his brother; and in both cases the minimum penalty had been
inflicted.[19]

There was little that the Inspectors could do to remedy this
unsatisfactory state of affairs, and in their perplexity they turned
to the Home Office in the hope that steps might be taken to bring
home to the magistrates the serious consequences that would ensue
if the law was not strictly enforced.   The ruling of the Home
Secretary, conveyed to Saunders in December, 1839, was clear and
explicit: —

" The cases may be separated into two

1st—Whether Magistrates were empowered under the 31st
section of the Factories Act to mitigate Penalties below the sum
of 20s. under either of the following cases

Because the Prosecution had not averred in the Information
that the offence was committed wilfully or through gross
negligence

or When the Defendant confesses the offence and does not
advance any Plea of mitigation

or When a plea of mitigation is advanced but not supported by
any evidence.

It appears to Lord Normanby that the Magistrates have taken
a mistaken view of the Act and his Lordship agrees . . . it is not

17 R. H. Greg, *The Factory Question* (1837) pp. 132-135.
18 Nassau W. Senior, *Letters on the Factory Act* (1837) p. 26.
19 *Ibid.* p. 41.

necessary the Prosecutor should state in the information that the offence is of a wilful or negligent character; *that* the discretion to the Magistrates under the 31st Sect. to mitigate below 20s. is not an arbitrary discretion, and when the Defendant offers no Plea or Evidence in mitigation the legal inference which the Magistrate is bound to draw is that the offence was wilfully committed, and therefore to convict in a penalty of 20s. in the least; and *that* the only cases in which a Magistrate can properly mitigate the Penalty below 20s. are

First: When the Prosecutor offers no evidence and the Defendant pleads ignorance which the Magistrate believes—and *secondly*: When the Magistrate is satisfied by evidence on the Defendant's part; or otherwise on the whole case proved; that the offence was not committed wilfully."[20]

The Home Secretary expressed the hope that his views might be brought to the attention of the magistrates, and in cases of particular difficulty representations were made by the Home Office direct to the Bench in question.[21] So long as the law remained defective, however, remonstrance was of little avail—the manufacturers found that it answered their purpose better to pay a small fine occasionally than to obey the law, and in many parts of the country, the Justices continued, as they said, to resort to the ' sovereign ' remedy, a fine of twenty shillings for each offence.[22]

The magistrates had also important duties to perform in connection with one of the most vital aspects of the Act, the determination of the age of children, and in this respect, too, the attitude that many of them adopted threatened to upset the whole scheme of control. From its very inception the code of factory legislation, so far as the regulation of the working hours of children and young people was concerned, had been obliged to grapple with a problem of formidable dimensions, for in the absence of any provision for the compulsory registration of births, reliable evidence as to the age of any particular individual was frequently unobtainable. Various devices had been suggested to overcome this difficulty. The bill introduced by Peel in 1815 had proposed to place the onus of ascertaining age on 'the employer; the bill of 1818 looked to the register of baptisms or other satisfactory evidence; the Act of 1819 ignored the whole matter; while the Acts of 1825 and and 1831 laid the responsibility on the parent.

---

[20] *Home Office Papers*, H.O. 87 (1), pp. 186-190. The second case mentioned dealt with the employment of children in reeling rooms.

[21] *Minutes*, 1st February, 1842, Vol. I, p. 168.

[22] Report of the Select Committee on the Act for the Regulation of Mills and Factories. *Parl. Papers* (1840) X, p. 581.

Such crude improvisations stood self-condemned from the beginning. Of the bill introduced in 1818 it was said " The age of the child is to be ascertained by the register of baptism, ' or other satisfactory evidence '; and to decide whether this ' other ' evidence is satisfactory, must of course be left to the master. Now there is an infinite variety of ways in which fraud may be successfully practised by those who are anxious that their children should be employed, and which the master cannot possibly detect. Wherever people are prohibited by statute from doing what they have a strong desire to do (as in the present case), and the statute at the same time by the inaccuracy and vagueness of its directions leaves a number of loop-holes, through which, by the help of a little ingenuity, those who are interested in escaping from the regulations can easily contrive to escape—in such a case, the statute has uniformly been found to fail, and has encouraged fraud, without in any respect gaining its end."[23]

The provisions of Hobhouse's Act were similarly condemned by Ure. " This bill," he said, " was soon found to be ineffectual towards protecting children from being worked over-hours under greedy operatives and needy parents: for it held out mutual temptations to collusion and perjury with respect to the ages of the children. . . . Had the preceding bills been simply inoperative, they would have deserved no blame; but they were instrumental in demoralizing both the parents and the children, by leading the former to commit perjury, and the latter to become habitual liars. In fact, the perjury of the witnesses placed an effectual barrier against conviction, and compelled the masters in Manchester to abandon all attempts to enforce by law the provisions of Hobhouse's Act."[24]

Kirkman Finlay, the Scottish cotton spinner, affirmed that the masters were powerless to enforce the law, and that those who endeavoured to do so were exposed to the unfair competition of their less scrupulous rivals. " It has been admitted by owners of Factories in Lancashire," he declared, " that the laws are not enforced, that various plans have been successfully adopted for their evasion, and that both with respect to the ages of children employed, and the hours of working, little attention is paid at some Factories to the legal enactments. . . . It is, I am confident, not the wish or interest of owners to have younger children in their works,

---

[23] An Inquiry into the Principle and Tendency of the Bill now pending in Parliament for imposing Certain Restrictions on Cotton Factories (1818) p. 25.

[24] A. Ure, The Philosophy of Manufactures (1835) pp. 289, 360. Cf. The Ten Hours Bill (1831) p. 15—" If we have any under seven, it is owing to the parents and children telling us an untruth," asserted the mill-owner, John Marshall, at the Leeds meeting in support of Sadler's Bill.

but they do not, and cannot, possess the means of *really* knowing, whether every one they employ is truly arrived at the age prescribed by law or not."[25]

It was typical of the scientific approach of Edwin Chadwick and his collaborators that in framing the Factories Regulation Act they should have aimed at substituting for the vague and illusory provisions of former measures a more precise and objective method of ascertaining age. They broke entirely fresh ground when they introduced a medical test, an intelligent and courageous experiment which, destined as it was, in many cases, to fail through the combined efforts of greedy manufacturers and selfish, thoughtless, or needy parents, nevertheless produced a result unforeseen by its authors—the close identification of the medical profession with the system of factory control.

By section 11 it was provided that no child was to be employed in cotton, woollen, worsted, hemp, flax, tow or linen mills,[26] unless he produced a certificate stating that he was of the ordinary strength and appearance of a child of the age of nine. In order to obtain this certificate the child was to appear personally before some surgeon or physician in the neighbourhood of his residence, and submit to an examination, after which the certificate, if granted, was to be counter-signed within three months by an Inspector or magistrate.[27] Young persons under the age of eighteen were not to be employed otherwise than as children unless they produced a certificate, in such form as was ordered by the Inspector, that they were more than thirteen years old,[28] but no penalty was to be imposed if a person employed without such certificate was, in fact, above the prescribed age.[29]

This was a genuine attempt to solve a problem that was fundamental to the whole system of regulation. " The absence

---

[25] K. Finlay, *Letter to the Right Hon. Lord Ashley on the Cotton Factory System* (1833) pp. 6, 13.

[26] The position of children in silk mills was obscure, but in view of the fact that they could be employed irrespective of their age, the Inspectors resolved not to require certificates from them.—*Minutes*, 16th September, 1836, Vol. I, p. 22.

[27] Sec. 12. The form of the certificate prescribed by Sec. 13 was as follows:—

I [*Name and Place of Residence*] Surgeon [*or* Physician] do hereby certify, That A.B. the Son [*or* Daughter] of [*Name and Residence of Parents, or if no Parents, then the Residence of the Child*] has appeared before me, and submitted to my Examination; and that the said [*Name*] is of the ordinary Strength and Appearance [*according to the Fact*] of a Child of at least Nine Years of Age [*or if apparently above Nine, say exceeding*].

[28] Sec. 14. This, of course, when the Act was fully operative, on 1st March, 1836. The upper ages of childhood were eleven and twelve respectively on 1st March, 1834, and 1st March, 1835.

[29] Sec. 15.

of every thing like a systematic registration of births, when the Factory Act passed," said Horner, "made it necessary that some other expedient for determining the age should be resorted to; and no other seemed better, or more readily available, than the opinion of a surgeon, who should attest the child to have 'the ordinary strength and appearance' of a child of the age certified. Had the spirit of the law been at all times faithfully observed, this substitute would have been a sufficient protection against fraud in most cases. The abuses have arisen in a great degree from defects in the Act, which contains little or no check upon the conduct of a surgeon."[30]   There were, he declared, powerful motives in existence which led to fraudulent evasion on an extensive scale. "As the law does not allow a child to work full time until he is thirteen years of age, if a piecer who is thirteen gets six shillings a week, one of ten, and one who wants some days of thirteen may have only the same sum, or three shillings. Hence the great temptation to parents to get their children passed for thirteen; a temptation to which the children themselves are by no means insensible; for there is this addition in their case, that, when they are allowed to work full time, they hold their heads higher in the factory, as being no longer in a state of pupilage. This is the great cause of the evasion of the law in this particular; and the force of the temptation seems not to have been duly appreciated, otherwise it would have been better provided for in the present act."[31]

The only check on the probity of the surgeon who granted the certificate was the requirement that his estimate of the child's age should be corroborated by an impartial third party—by an Inspector or magistrate, whose counter-signature was essential to the validity of the certificate. Here it was that the scheme broke down, for many Justices connived at the issue of false certificates, and many more omitted the elementary precaution of seeing the child for whose age they vouched, no personal inspection being required by the Act. "It has been a common practice," said Horner, "to send the accumulated certificates of three months, or more, to a magistrate, often to the Court-house, at Sessions time, and thus they have been countersigned *en masse,* without a child appearing or a question being asked as to the correctness of the matter certified."[32]   Howell also reported that in many instances the countersigning had degenerated into a mere matter of form. "Cases have in my District occurred," he declared, "in which the manufacturer, being a Magistrate, has countersigned the certificates

---

[30] L. Horner, *On the Employment of Children in Factories* (1840) p. 34.
[31] *Ibid.* p. 33.
[32] Report, 18th January, 1837. *Parl. Papers* (1837) XXXI, p. 95.

for his own factory; and two manufacturers, both being Justices, have reciprocated civilities in this matter, each countersigning the certificates of children employed in the factory of the other."[33]

When the Inspectors approached the Home Office for assistance in dealing with this matter, they received but little help or encouragement. "In the case of children employed between the ages of 9 and 13," wrote Fox Maule to Horner, "the Law Officers are of opinion that the Certificate is a nullity unless it be countersigned either by a Justice or an Inspector, and they further think that any Justice or Inspector countersigning a Certificate without taking reasonable care to ascertain its correctness is violating the plain intention of the Act, but they do not think that the Inspector can interfere on the subject of the certificate when it is in fact countersigned by the Magistrate even though the Magistrate may have acted wrong in so countersigning it."[34]

Quite apart from the fact that this check was in many cases wholly inoperative, evasion was all too easy. "From the great imperfection of the Act," said Horner, "in all that relates to the enactments for the determination of the ages of the children, it is impossible for the inspector to check the most palpable frauds. . . . I am persuaded that fully one half of the children now working under surgeons' certificates of thirteen, are in fact not more than twelve, many not more than eleven years of age."[35] Rickards was convinced that unless this difficulty could be surmounted "the fundamental objects of the Act must necessarily be defeated, and that the Act itself would, like its predecessors, necessarily become a dead letter."[36] Certificates, he alleged, were frequently sold or lent, and a single certificate might be used, without the possibility of detection, to pass into the mills hundreds of children, many of whom would be worked beyond the legal hours.[37] In numerous instances parents succeeded in smuggling children into mills without certificates; and Horner complained that the parents and the operative spinners who employed the children, were generally most active in trying to defeat the law.[38]

[33] Report, 31st March, 1837. *Parl. Papers* (1838) XXVIII, p. 85. It was the considered opinion of the Inspectors that the counter-signature of the magistrates was a mere matter of form in the great majority of cases.—*Minutes,* 19th July, 1837, Vol. I, p. 72.
[34] 23rd April, 1838. *Home Office Papers,* H.O. 87 (1), p. 120.
[35] Nassau W. Senior, *Letters on the Factory Act* (1837) p. 34.
[36] Report, 15th April, 1834. *Parl. Papers* (1834) XLIII, p. 457.
[37] Report, January, 1835. *Parl. Papers* (1835) XL, p. 695.
[38] Report, 30th June, 1838. *Parl. Papers* (1838) XLV, p. 55. "It is not at all improbable," said Horner, referring to an operative whom he had detected over-working a young girl, "that he was one of those who had sent up petitions calling on Parliament to interfere for the protection of the poor factory children, ' the white slaves,' who were so cruelly over-worked by ' the hard-hearted, avaricious masters '."—Report, 31st December, 1838. *Parl. Papers* (1839) XIX, p. 447.

In order to prevent certificates being used by children to whom they had not been granted Rickards suggested that they should be issued by the surgeon only in the mill where the child was actually employed,[39] a proposal that was later warmly endorsed by Stuart,[40] who informed the Home Office that he had made a regulation to this effect. His action was not endorsed " because," as he was reminded, " the Factory Act does not expressly prescribe such a regulation and does not afford the means of enforcing it."[41] The Law Officers also rejected, for the same reason, the suggestion made by Horner, that in order to identify the child to whom the certificate was granted, the form of the document should be amended so as to include a description of the child, *e.g.* the height, the colour of the hair, and the colour of the eyes.[42]

The position of young persons between the ages of thirteen and eighteen was even more difficult, for the Act did not prescribe any form of certificate for them. It was assumed that in the majority of cases baptismal certificates would suffice,[43] but Horner condemned this arrangement as " a fertile source of evasion," since no reliance could be placed on these documents. " Scraps of paper," he said, " dirtied and in tatters, purporting to come from Protestant Ministers or Roman Catholic Priests, in distant parts of the United Kingdom, have been produced as justification for the employment of children for twelve hours who were manifestly much under thirteen years of age."[44] The Inspectors accordingly devised a medical certificate similar to that required by the Act for children under thirteen years of age, and the approval of the Home Office having been obtained,[45] they imposed it uniformly throughout their districts.[46]

The obvious remedy for all these difficulties was to establish a system of registration of births, and Edwin Chadwick, whose researches in the field of life assurance had already convinced him of the necessity for such a system, prevailed on Lord Lyndhurst to introduce into the Lords a measure designed to provide for the appointment of a Registrar-General.[47] The Act, which came into operation on 30th June, 1837, set up a General Registry Office, and made it obligatory for the father or mother of any child born in England to give to the Registrar information about the birth within forty-two days upon being requested to do so. The local

39 Report, August, 1835. *Parl. Papers* (1836) XLV, p. 161.
40 Report, 31st December, 1836. *Parl. Papers* (1837) XXXI, p. 118.
41 28th March, 1837. *Home Office Papers*, H.O. 87 (1), p. 49.
42 Report, 12th October, 1836. *Parl. Papers* (1837) XXXI, p. 56.
43 *Home Office Papers*, H.O. 87 (1), p. 89.
44 Report, 18th January, 1837. *Parl. Papers* (1837) XXXI, p. 97.
45 *Home Office Papers*, H.O. 87 (1), p. 90.
46 *Minutes*, 20th July, 1837, Vol. I, p. 73.
47 M. Marston, *Sir Edwin Chadwick* (1925) p. 26.

Superintendent Registrar was to inform himself of every birth taking place in his district, and to register it, but there was no obligation on the parent to supply this information unless he was asked for it. The whole organisation was to be controlled by the Registrar-General, whose powers extended throughout the country.[48]

Some years must elapse, of course, before the new Act could affect the factory children, and in the meantime the Inspectors had to deal with the problem as best they could. " After a careful consideration of the difficulties in obtaining any authentic proof of real age," said Saunders, " I am . . . clearly of opinion that until proof of birth under the new Registration Act can be obtained, no more reasonable substitute for a certificate of age under the present law has been suggested than the one now used."[49]

It was very soon discovered that the test prescribed by the Act, that the child was of the ordinary strength and appearance of a child of at least nine years of age, was not sufficiently objective, since it lent itself to widely differing and conflicting interpretations, and therefore offered many loopholes for evasion and fraud. The chief concern of the Inspectors was to establish criteria which would allow a minimum of discretion to the certifying surgeons, thus making for uniformity and a greater degree of precision. The search for a single and reliable standard by which age might be ascertained was, as might have been expected, quite vain, but it illustrated forcibly one of the many problems that had to be faced at this stage in the development of industrial control.

In the first set of instructions that Horner issued to the surgeons he reminded them that it was their duty to see the child, and to satisfy themselves that the declaration they were making was true. They must not certify an age as exceeding a particular number of years—such an expression was too indefinite. Instead, they were to certify that the child had the ordinary strength and appearance of one of 9, 9½, 10, 10½, etc., as the case might be.[50] The surgeon's declaration, he explained, had no reference to the actual age of the child. The opinion must be formed from the

---

48 The original Act (6 & 7 Will. IV, c. 86) passed on 17th August, 1836, was to come into force on 1st March, 1837; but its operation was postponed until the following June by an amending Act (7 Will. IV, c. 1) passed on 24th February, 1837. Further minor alterations were included in yet another amending Act (7 Will. IV & 1 Vict., c. 22) passed on 30th June, 1837. It was not until 1874 that the registration of births became compulsory: in that year the Births and Deaths Registration Act (37 & 38 Vict., c. 88) made it obligatory for parents to inform the local Registrar of the birth within forty-two days.
49 Report, 30th June, 1838. *Parl. Papers* (1838) XLV, p. 62.
50 Report, 21st July, 1834. *Parl. Papers* (1834) XLIII, p. 441.

physical condition alone, indeed it was better not to make any enquiries about the child's real age, since a false reply would probably be given. If a child known to be thirteen had the strength and appearance only of a child of twelve, the age "twelve" should be inserted in the certificate. On the other hand, a child of twelve who had the physical development of one aged thirteen, should be certified as thirteen.[51] It was desirable that all surgeons should follow the same general principles, and he recommended them to look to the child's stature as being least likely to lead to error. No child under 3 feet 10 inches should be considered as having the strength and appearance of a child of nine, while for the ages ten, eleven, twelve and thirteen the minimum heights should be 3 feet 11½ inches, 4 feet 1 inch, 4 feet 2 inches, and 4 feet 3½ inches respectively, though these figures should be adopted as a general guide, not as an invariable rule.[52]

Horner's effort to establish some sort of objective test of age had the most unfortunate consequences, for his opponents seized upon his instructions as affording yet another proof that he was endeavouring to impose an interpretation of the law that would defeat the object of the legislature by pushing children into premature employment. "Such a public servant," declared the Manchester Short-time Committee, "is clearly unfit for so responsible an office as that of inspector. . . . The circumstances of the case call loudly for his dismissal."[53] The law, they contended, recognized no certificate but one of *actual* age, "but the instructions tell the surgeons in so many words, that if they find a child which they know with certainty to be not more than twelve years of age, they will be justified in inserting the word thirteen in the certificate." Horner was openly accused of deliberately conniving at the unlawful employment of children under thirteen, and for this reason, said the Short-time Committee, they were led to entertain a strong conviction "that an attempt, and hitherto a

---

51 Horner had already explained this as his interpretation of the law in his pamphlet *The Factories Regulation Act Explained* (1834) p. 12.— "Although a child be in fact 9 years old, yet if by ill-health it has not the ordinary strength and appearance of a child of that age, it is not entitled to be certified to be 9 years of age, as far as its power of working in a Factory is concerned. On the other hand, if a child be in fact less than 9, yet by unusual health and growth, has the ordinary strength and appearance of a child of 9, the Surgeon may certify it as such, and it may be employed in a Factory."

52 Report, 12th October, 1836. *Parl. Papers* (1837) XXXI, pp. 72-73.

53 *Parl. Papers* (1838) XLV, p. 80. Fielden said that of the 103 children under thirteen in his factory, 57 could, under these regulations, be certified as thirteen and worked twelve hours a day, "and thus what Poulet Thomson could not prevail on the legislature to do in the last session, has been far outdone by a superior law-maker, an inspector."— C. Wing, *Evils of the Factory System Exposed* (1837) p. xxv.

JOHN FIELDEN

successful one, has thus been made, by indirect and circuitous means, to accomplish that which the House of Commons, in the last session of Parliament, showed a reluctance to do, *viz.*, to reduce the maximum age, entitled to special protection, from thirteen to twelve; a reluctance which led to the final abandonment of Mr. Poulett Thomson's Bill, and to a distinct, solemn, and repeated pledge, on the part of His Majesty's Government, that the provisions of the existing law should thenceforward be faithfully and unflinchingly enforced."[54]   " What is the rank and position which this gentleman holds," they demanded, " who treats with equal contumely the law givers, the law expounders, and the executive? Who comes forward in the two-fold capacity of law-breaker, and law-maker?   Who is at this moment exercising, in this free country, more than kingly power?"[55]

Horner was quite unable to ride the storm.   In vain he protested that he had never intended the height of the child to be the sole criterion, and he told the surgeons explicitly that the figures he had mentioned were the minimum heights for the ages in question.[56]   The regulation he had issued was referred for the opinion of the Law Officers, who examined the whole question. " A surgeon," they said, " is not to certify a child to be or appear to be above a given age on any evidence except that afforded by personal examination.   But after all, the apparent age is sought for only as being likely to afford the best evidence of the real age, and the spirit and purpose of the Act would be better complied with by directing the surgeons never to certify the strength and appearance of a child to be that of an age beyond what they know or have good reason to believe is its real age.   The object of the certificate, the form of which is given in the 13th section, is merely to show that the child does not come within the meaning of the class of those whom it is unlawful to employ at all;—*viz.*, children under nine years of age, and the clause in question does not authorize a certificate to any other fact, than that of being or not being of the ordinary appearance of a child of nine years of age, and the form given by the Act should be strictly followed."[57]

When this opinion had been delivered, the true function of the certificate of age could no longer be in question; it was designed, not to establish the precise age of the child, still less its fitness for employment, but merely whether it was above the age of nine or not.   What the Law Officers did not do was to suggest any reliable test by which this fact might be verified, and the Inspectors

---

[54] *Parl. Papers* (1837) L, p. 205.
[55] *Parl. Papers* (1838) XLV, p. 81.
[56] Circular letter dated 7th November, 1836.   *Parl. Papers* (1837) XXXI, p. 104.
[57] *Parl. Papers* (1838) XXVIII, p. 89.

consequently felt it necessary to pursue their investigations in this
direction. They turned with interest to a monograph[58] published
in 1837 by Edwin Saunders, who declared that the most reliable
test of age was that afforded by the development of the teeth.
"From their great uniformity of configuration, size, and arrangement," declared the author, "the teeth possess characters more
definite and constant than any other parts; and their physiological
history is more precise, and subject to less variation, than that of
any other organ."[59]

Saunders was one of the first Inspectors to advocate this
method of determining age. In December, 1837, he reported that
he was employing it as an auxiliary test,[60] and two years later he
asserted that it was still being extensively used.[61] Horner, too, was
experimenting. "I am striving with the difficulty of ascertaining
the *real* ages of the children from physical characters," he said in
a letter to his wife, " and have had consultations with many doctors
upon the value of the teeth as a test. I mean the growth of the
second teeth, and I believe, from all they say, that it is the most
unerring we can use. I am becoming rather knowing in that way
for I have looked into 500 little mouths lately. I suppose it has
got wind, for when the doctors and I go round the mills, and call
any to us that appear too young for their work, they sometimes
come running up with their mouths open, and turn up their little
heads without being told."[62]

Such shifts and stratagems, ingenious as they were, would have
been superfluous had the Inspectors been able to rely on the un-
biassed testimony of properly qualified doctors. But the medical
profession was not yet clearly de-limited, and upon the fringes
there practised many men whose technical knowledge and skill
were of the slenderest.[63] Rickards reported that he had come
across instances of certificates having been granted by " a drunken
ale-house keeper who . . . had set himself up as a medical practitioner, and by a person who had been brought up as a druggist's

58 E. Saunders, *The Teeth a Test of Age, considered with reference to
Factory Children.*
59 *Op. cit.* p. 45. The presence of 24 teeth—4 incisors, 2 canines,.
and 6 molars above and below indicated, it was said, an age of eight;
28 teeth fully developed, an age of fourteen.
60 *Parl. Papers* (1838) XXVIII, p. 122.
61 Report, 31st December, 1839. *Parl. Papers* (1840) XXIII, p. 20.
62 K. M. Lyell, *Memoir of Leonard Horner* (1890) Vol. I, p. 352.
63 It was not until 1858 that the Medical Act established the General
Medical Council, whose duty it became to supervise the standards of
medical education, and to maintain a register of those who, having passed
the examinations of an approved licensing body, had obtained a registrable
qualification. See A. M. Carr-Saunders & P. A. Wilson, *The Professions*
(1933) pp. 75-83.

apprentice ";[64] while Horner registered his " firm conviction that an alteration in the law as regards the proof of the age of the child is greatly wanted. As any person practising surgery is entitled to grant certificates of age . . . a wide door is open to fraud."[65]

Even a properly qualified surgeon was likely to be placed in an invidious position, finding his public duty clashing with his private interest. " The surgeon," said Howell, " *is not to go into extrinsic evidence,* nor to certify a child to be above a given age, *on any evidence except that afforded by personal examination;* but his opinion as to its appearance is naturally biassed by the desire which he feels to comply with the wishes of the parent and of the master (one or both of whom he probably numbers among his regular patients), that the child should receive from him such a certificate as will admit it into the factory."[66] Strong pressure was frequently applied to persuade the surgeon to accept ancillary evidence of the child's age. " The parents, indeed, looking to their children in a great degree for support, resort to all kinds of expedients to induce the belief that the child is really of the lawful age : entries in Bibles and other books, some religious, others profane, are produced, which entries there is little reason to doubt have been made for the occasion."[67]

The experiences of the first few months convinced the Inspectors that only if they were allowed to exercise some measure of control over the certifying surgeons could the age regulations be enforced. Rickards took the initiative when, on 4th February, 1834, he issued a regulation, with the approval of the principal mill-owners, dividing the Manchester district into five areas, in each of which he appointed surgeons who alone were authorized to grant certificates.[68] " A certificate indiscriminately procured is of

---

[64] Report, January, 1835. *Parl. Papers* (1835) XL, p. 696.
[65] Report, 30th September, 1837, *Parl. Papers* (1838) XXVIII, p. 106.
[66] Report, 31st March, 1837. *Parl. Papers* (1838) XXVIII, p. 85.
[67] Howell's Report, 30th September, 1837. *Ibid.* p. 108. In the manufacturing districts, he said, where the surgeon is dependent for his livelihood on a semi-pauper population, it is difficult to resist the demands of the parent. If one surgeon refuses a certificate the parents send the child to another.—Report 30th September, 1836. *Parl. Papers* (1837) XXXI, p. 80. Saunders confirmed this. " A parent will go to one Surgeon with his child, clean and in his best clothes, and if the Surgeon does not think it 13, the parents immediately put on his working dress, higher shoes, and by the aid of the indigo complexion obtained in a woollen mill, will endeavour to get the child a certificate of thirteen from another Surgeon; if he fails in the second attempt, the parent will take the child into a flax mill, where a third Surgeon is employed, and if still thought too small and young, will try a fourth or fifth, till he finds that Surgeon who takes the lowest quantum of height and development as his guide in certifying a child or young person."—Report, 30th September, 1838. *Parl. Papers* (1839) XIX, p. 445.
[68] *Parl. Papers* (1836) XLV, p. 207.

no validity," he asserted, and he was confident that the arrangement would do much to remedy the abuses that had already become
evident.[69]   Horner followed his example, announcing in July, 1834,
that since it was obvious that fraud would be facilitated if certificates could be obtained from anybody calling himself a medical
man, he had appointed surgeons from whom alone he would accept
certificates.[70]

It could not be denied that Rickards and Horner[71] were acting
wisely in limiting the power to grant certificates to surgeons whom
they could trust, but it was clear, too, that they were exceeding
their powers, for the Act authorized *any* medical practitioner to
grant certificates.   Lord Melbourne accordingly intervened, and
issued an instruction that certificates granted by surgeons other
than those nominated by the Inspectors were not to be refused.
Rickards protested vigorously, justifying his action on the ground
that the grossest frauds had been committed by " persons of low
estimation and practice in the medical profession," and declaring
that the manufacturers approved the policy he had adopted.   He
proposed to continue with the plan, he said, though on a voluntary
basis,[72] and the following July he took the further step of arranging for the appointed surgeons to grant certificates at the mills.[73]

Although the Inspectors were thus thwarted in their efforts to
obtain control over the surgeons, they nevertheless made a further
effort to restrict the right of granting certificates to properly
qualified practitioners.   At their meeting on 18th July, 1837, Horner
mentioned that some of the more enlightened magistrates in his
district had refused their counter-signature to certificates granted
by persons who were really only apothecaries practising as
surgeons.   If such action could be upheld it would be possible to
restrict certification to those who were members of a medical
College, and it was resolved to submit a case for the opinion of
the Law Officers.[74]   Once again they were disappointed, for the
Law Officers expressed the view "that any person acting as a

---

[69] Report, 10th February, 1834. *Parl. Papers* (1834) XLIII, p. 450.
[70] Report, 21st July, 1834. *Ibid*. p. 431.
[71] Saunders and Howell did not adopt the plan for some time.—
Minutes, 8th September, 1836, Vol. I, p. 4.
[72] Report, 22nd February, 1834. *Parl. Papers* (1834) XLIII, p. 456.
[73] Report, 20th August, 1834. *Ibid*. p. 471.   By February, 1835,
Rickards had appointed 148 surgeons, who had granted between them
130,559 certificates. (Dr. J. G. Harrison, of Manchester, alone had issued
5,256.) Horner had nominated 79 surgeons in Scotland (23,684 certificates),
14 in Ireland (2,797 certificates), and 18 in England (1,912 certificates).—
Parl. Papers (1835) XL, p. 704.
[74] *Minutes,* Vol. I, p. 69.   Joint Report, 22nd July, 1837. *Parl. Papers*
(1838) XXVIII, p. 103.

Surgeon although not a member of any College of Surgeons is a Surgeon entitled under the Factory Act to grant Certificates."[75]

These difficulties were doubtless inherent in any newly conceived system of control. The accurate determination of age was an integral factor in the regulation of juvenile labour, and the Act of 1833 made a very real advance in looking to the surgeon to establish the age of a child as a matter of fact rather than of surmise. This appeal to medical opinion, however, was a mere expedient, adopted because no better test seemed available, yet it was fraught with the most important consequences. Horner had rightly assumed that age ought not to be the sole criterion for employment, but he had been wrong in supposing that it could be disregarded altogether. The only satisfactory test of employability was age combined with physical fitness, but it was as yet too early for this view to have won general acceptance. The imperfections of the existing law, in this as in so many other respects, suggested the trend of future reform, the establishment of the principle that factory labour should be confined to those who, having attained the minimum age prescribed by law, were certified as fit for employment by fully qualified medical men working under the control of, and responsible to the Factory Inspectors.

---

[75] *Home Office Papers*, H.O. 87 (1), p. 91.

CHAPTER 9

THE MACHINERY OF CONTROL

ASSEMBLED AT their statutory meeting on 24th January, 1837, the Inspectors addressed to the Home Secretary a formal memorandum summarizing the opinions that they had all expressed at frequent intervals in their reports concerning certain aspects of the detailed administration of the Act. " We beg leave," they said, " earnestly to direct the attention of your Lordship to those parts of our individual Reports, wherein we refer to certain enactments which render the attainment of the great object of the Act in many cases extremely difficult; and which make the restrictions it imposes tell very differently upon those who honestly fulfil the Law, from what they do upon others who seek to evade it and who can so often do so with impunity."[1]

The sections to which they referred were those designed to secure that the restricted hours prescribed by the statute were not exceeded, but which inexpert drafting had framed in such a fashion that they were inadequate for the purpose. Of these, the most difficult to enforce were the provisions concerning the extension of the working day, which were thus interpreted by Horner:—

" When the machinery is moved by a water-wheel, if time be lost in consequence of the want of a due supply or of an excess of water, or by reason of its being stopped in higher reservoirs, the lost time may be made up by working extra hours, at the rate of 3 hours a-week, but not more; and it must be done between 5 in the morning and 9 at night. If six months have elapsed since the period when the time was lost, it cannot be made up. (Section 3).

In dry seasons, and in floods, the power of a water-wheel is, on some streams, so much interrupted that all the machinery cannot be worked at the same time, and consequently the work-people lose a part of the day. In such cases, it is lawful to employ children under 13 years of age between 5 in the morning and 9 at night, provided those restricted to 9 and 10 hours[2] in any one day, do not work more than that in all; and it is also lawful to employ in such cases young persons between 13 and 18 years of age during the night, provided they do not work more than 12 hours in all in the twenty-four. (Section 5)."[3]

The effect of these two sections, together with section four, which provided that when time was lost through accidents to the

---

[1] *Minutes,* Vol. I, p. 55.
[2] Children employed in silk mills were restricted to 10 hours a day.
[3] L. Horner, *The Factories Regulation Act Explained* (1834) pp. 9-10.

machinery, an additional hour might be worked each day for the
ensuing twelve working days, was not to authorize an increase
in the number of hours prescribed, but to extend the period during
which those hours might be worked. As Horner pointed out, the
fact that children restricted to nine hours a day could be worked
at any time and at any intervals within a range of fifteen hours
(*i.e.* 5.30 a.m. to 8.30 p.m.) made evasion easy; but when the range
was extended beyond fifteen hours it became almost impossible to
detect over-working.[4] Rickards considered that the only effective
way to check this evil would be to restrict the moving power, for
it was impossible in practice, he asserted, to limit one class of
operatives to so many hours, and another class to a different
number. The fourth section, in any event, should be expunged,
since it opened the door to fraud on a wide scale.[5] Saunders
reported that many water-mills worked excessive hours even when
there was an abundant supply of water,[6] while Howell complained
of the loose wording of the Act. " Sufficient provision does not
appear to have been made," he said, " to prevent the loss of time
sustained on a *part* only of the machinery from being made the
pretext for working up the same time by the *whole* of the
machinery. . . . In none of the sections providing for the recovery
of lost time does the fact appear to have been contemplated, that
the machinery in very many factories is propelled by various
powers, by both steam and water, by more than one steam-engine,
and by more than one water-wheel."[7] Detection of offences was
rendered the more difficult because of the limited powers of access
to the interior of the mills granted to the Superintendents. " So
long as it is allowed to make up lost time," asserted Horner, " by
accidents to the machinery, fraudulent over-working will be
practised with impunity to a considerable extent; and until power
be given to the Superintendents to enter at once into the mill,
without the necessity of first obtaining leave, many working
illegally will escape detection."[8]

The sixth section of the Act, providing that young persons
restricted to twelve hours' labour a day should be allowed an hour

---

[4] L. Horner, *On the Employment of Children in Factories* (1840) p. 7.
Cf. L. Faucher, *Etudes sur l'Angleterre* (1856) Vol. I, p. 455.—" Un autre
vice de la loi consiste dans la faculté accordée aux manufacturiers
d'allonger la journée, toutes les fois que le manque ou l'excès d'eau
dans les manufactures mues par la force hydraulique, et qu'un accident
survenu à la machine, dans les manufactures mues par la vapeur, auraient
amené une interruption ou un chômage. Cette autorisation sert en effet
de prétexte à toutes les fraudes."
[5] Report, 12th August, 1834. *Parl. Papers* (1834) XLIII, p. 461.
[6] Report, August, 1835. *Parl. Papers* (1836) XLV, p. 156.
[7] Report, 31st March, 1838. *Parl. Papers* (1838) XXVIII, p. 141.
[8] Report, 30th September, 1841. *Parl. Papers* (1842) XXII, p. 339.

and a half for meals, afforded additional opportunities for over-
working.   Unlike similar regulations in the earlier statutes this
section said nothing about the times of the day at which the meal
interval was to be allowed, nor, strangely enough, were children
under thirteen within the scope of the provision, and, as the
operatives pointed out,[9] this omission made it possible for the
manufacturer to employ them for nine hours without a break.
Since the time allowed for meals was, in the case of young persons,
additional to the twelve hours of labour,[10] their actual working
day extended over thirteen and a half hours, and many employers
took advantage of this to keep them at their tasks during the meal-
times, or to set them to clean the machinery.[11]   Such over-working
was not by any means easy to detect, and the Inspectors, realizing
that the only effective safeguard was to forbid the young workers
to remain in the machine rooms during the meal interval, decided
that this prohibition should be universally enforced.   " It is the
practice in some Mills," they recorded in their minutes,[12] " for
breakfast and tea to be given in the Mills without the machinery
employed in the manufacture being stopped.   The Inspectors agree
to act in such circumstances as follows: That children under 13
years of age must not be allowed to take their meals or be allowed
to remain in any part of the Factory where there is machinery,
unless under special circumstances, where the exclusion from the
Mill would be clearly injurious to the health of the children; &
under no circumstances to allow children to take their meals, or be
allowed to remain in any part of the factory where the machinery
is at work; in both cases excepting those occasions when the time
allowed for meals is included in their restricted hours of labour."

Some mill-occupiers secured continuity in the manufacturing
process by arranging for meals to be taken outside the working
hours, thus raising a legal problem of some nicety, upon which the
Inspectors sought the guidance of the Law Officers.   " By the sixth
section of the Factory Act it is enacted that there shall be allowed
in the course of every day not less than one & an half hours for
Meals, to every person restricted to the performance of 12 hours
work daily.   By the first section the Factory Day appears to commence at half past 5 in the morning, and to terminate at half past
8 in the evening, between which periods the 12 hours work must
be performed.   It is desirable that the Inspectors should be

---

[9] *Address to the Friends of Justice and Humanity* (1833) p. 16.
[10] L. Horner, *The Factories Regulation Act Explained* (1834) p. 10.
[11] Their retention in the mill was justified on the ground that it was
better for them to take their meals in the warmth of the factory rather
than to traverse the streets twice a day.—*A Letter to Sir John Cam Hobhouse on the Factories Bill* (1832) p. 30.
[12] 16th September, 1836.   Vol. I, pp. 22-3.

instructed whether it is a sufficient compliance with the provisions of the sixth section that the Hours of Meals should be given in whole or in part before the work commences, or after it terminates; for example, whether it be lawful that the persons should take any portion of the day for breakfast before they commence work, and any portion of the day for dinner after they leave off, such portion being still within the hours of ½ past 5 a.m. & ½ past 8 p.m. And further whether intervals of cessation from work at any process enumerated in the first section may be lawfully considered as Meal Hours although the workers are employed during those intervals in cleaning machinery or any other occupation not enumerated in the first section."[13]

The Law Officers delivered their opinion a few days later. " The meaning of the Act was," they held, " that at least an hour and a half should be allowed for meals in the course of the Factory working day, and that no part of such hour and a half should be taken before the commencement or after the termination of the actual employment of the party, and further, that it is not lawful during meal hours to employ the children in any work whatever connected with the machinery or apparatus of the mill."[14]

It was not quite such an easy matter to arrive at a satisfactory interpretation of the 9th section of the Act, which provided that children and young persons were to be entitled to holidays on Christmas Day and Good Friday, and on not fewer than eight additional half days to be determined by the master.   In their anxiety to run the machines without intermission many manufacturers kept the mills open on these days, arguing that those operatives whose hours were limited need not attend unless they chose.   The Inspectors considered that they had no option but to accept this view,[15] but once again they asked the opinion of the Law Officers, who confirmed their interpretation.   " Under the 9th section of the Act, the master of a factory is not subject to a penalty for employing children on Good Friday and Christmas day *with their free consent;* at the same time the onus would be upon the manufacturer to prove that the children found working on those days preferred work to play, and that the Inspector ought to interfere in such cases without waiting for a complaint that the children have asked for a holiday and were refused.   Upon an information against a master for employing them on those days

---

13 *Minutes,* 3rd August, 1837, Vol. I, pp. 94-95.
14 11th August, 1837, *Home Office Papers,* H.O. 87 (1), p. 92.
15 *Minutes,* 16th September, 1836, Vol. I, p. 23.—" It is sufficient compliance with the law if the workers have the power of availing themselves of the holidays to which they are by law ' entitled '."

without their consent, it would be a *prima facie* case against him
that the children were worked in the mill on those days as on
ordinary occasions."[16]

The defective wording of the 9th section made it almost
impossible to enforce the law. Howell reported that in his district
the magistrates were not prepared to accept the ruling of the Law
Officers, the informations being dismissed on the ground that the
onus of proving that protected persons had been worked without
their consent lay on the Inspector. " If the interpretation put upon
the law in this case be correct," he added, " and it is incumbent on
the prosecutor not merely to prove that the children were working
on the holiday as on ordinary occasions, but also to prove that
they had asked for a holiday and had been refused . . . *i.e.* that
they were working under coercion, it is not to be expected that
any prosecutions for offences against the 9th section will be
successful."[17] Horner and Saunders also reported that it was
impossible to obtain convictions under the section,[18] since it was
universally held that there was no breach of the law if young
people had been given the opportunity of taking a holiday, and in
the great majority of cases the Inspectors were compelled to give
up the unequal struggle. But the lesson was well learnt. " In any
amending legislation," asserted Horner, " it will be of great consequence to look with a jealous eye upon all proposed changes of
phrases, and even of single words, by interested parties. . . . For
example: there is, I believe no doubt that it was intended, that
all mills should be closed on Good Friday and Christmas-day, the
same as on a Sunday, in England and Ireland; but in consequence
of a single word, the clause has been rendered almost nugatory."[19]

The intimate experience of the working of the Act which their
close contact with the mills provided made it abundantly clear to
the Inspectors that if these restrictions, inadequate as they were,
were to be enforced at all, it would be necessary to invoke the
powers conferred upon them by the 18th section to make " such
rules, regulations and orders as may be necessary for the due
execution of this Act." When the statute was framed it had been
realized that wide powers would need to be exercised independently
of the statute, since it was obviously impossible for Parliament to
provide in advance for all the contingencies likely to arise in the

16 Saunders' Report, 31st March, 1837. *Parl. Papers* (1838) XXVIII,
p. 89.
17 Report, 30th June, 1838. *Parl. Papers* (1838) XLV, p. 60.
18 Horner's Reports, 30th June, 1837. *Parl. Papers* (1838) XXVIII, p. 95;
30th June, 1840. *Parl. Papers* (1840) XXIII, p. 38; Saunders' Report, 30th
June, 1840. *Ibid*. p. 42.
19 L. Horner, *On the Employment of Children in Factories* (1840) p. 4.

enforcement of an extensive and hitherto untried system of control.[20] The short and chequered history of factory legislation had already demonstrated beyond question that the mere enunciation of general principles could achieve nothing. The fundamental and basic need was to provide for the establishment and development of machinery that would enable those principles to be carried into effect by making evasion, if not impossible, at least susceptible of detection.

This need could best be met by giving the fullest publicity to the restrictions that were to be imposed, so that neither operative nor master could be in ignorance of what was allowed and what was required; and by devising such records as would provide permanent evidence of the extent to which the law had been obeyed. Section 27 made it obligatory to display in some conspicuous place a copy of an abstract of the Act and of the Inspectors' regulations, and section 18 required a register of children to be kept in the mill where they were employed. These rudimentary provisions, however, were soon found to be quite inadequate, and it was left to the Inspectors to work out a fuller and better plan. That their early attempts should have been crude and cumbersome need occasion no surprise. The process was necessarily one of trial and error, and what was really remarkable was that within a very short time they had conceived and put into operation a system that provided the maximum of efficiency with the minimum of inconvenience.

The first regulations to be issued by Howell, Saunders and Horner showed that they had, as yet, only a vague conception of what would ultimately be needed, for they did little but remind the manufacturers of what the Act required.[21] Rickards, on the other hand, viewing the problem as one that could be solved only by the application of a scientific technique, elaborated a scheme of registration designed to furnish the Inspector with the information he needed if he was to enforce the Act. His agile and discerning mind was fully responsive to the demands of the situation, and he did not hesitate to revoke and amend his regulations as the need arose. Not unnaturally this brought upon him the wrath of the manufacturers. "This is drawing rather heavily upon the patience of the unfortunate mill-owner," complained Greg, "who, before he could well introduce one system and one set of time-books into his establishment, was compelled to abandon them in favour of others."[22] It must be admitted that the result of Rickards' experiments involved a measure of confusion

[20] See Horner's letter to Senior—Nassau W. Senior, *Letters on the Factory Act* (1837) p. 39.
[21] See Appendix.
[22] R. H. Greg, *The Factory Question* (1837) p. 128.

and uncertainty, but a consideration of far greater importance was that the regulations should not be allowed to crystallize into a permanent and rigid code until adequate experience of their practical working had been gained.

It was impossible, argued Rickards, to check the extent to which overworking was practised unless the manufacturers kept authentic records, to the accuracy of which they testified,[23] and for this reason he promulgated, on 29th January, 1834, a regulation requiring the mill-occupiers to keep two registers—Time Form No. 1, in which was to be entered each day a statement of the number of hours the machinery had been worked, and Time Form No. 2, which was to record day by day the working hours of protected persons. A fortnight later this arrangement was amended in respect of mills in which the machinery was worked not more than twelve hours a day or sixty-nine hours a week. In such establishments, where there could be no possibility of overworking young persons, Time Form No. 2 was to be used only for children, who were, of course, restricted to forty-eight hours' labour a week.

In July, 1834, the scope of these registers was extended. Time Form No. 1 was replaced by Time Book No. 1, so designed as to show not only the number of hours the mill was worked each day, but, in addition, the intervals allowed for meals, and the amount of time lost and recovered under sections 3, 4 and 5 of the Act, thus making it possible for the Inspector to check any evasions in these directions. Time Book No. 2, which was substituted for Time Form No. 2, did not introduce any material alterations, continuing as the daily record of the hours of children only, when the mill worked no more than sixty-nine hours a week, and of both children and young persons when these hours were exceeded. A few days later, on 19th July, 1834, another register was introduced, in which were to be entered the names and ages of the children and young persons engaged, together with details of their previous occupation, and of the date of their leaving their present employment.

Twelve months' experience of the working of these registers convinced Rickards that Time Book No. 2, showing merely the aggregate daily hours of labour was not sufficient to prevent young persons being overworked. He therefore introduced, for mills working more than twelve hours a day, Time Book No. 3, in which was to be recorded, for each person, each day, an accurate statement of hours, indicating the time of beginning in the morning, the interval allowed for each meal, and the time of stopping at night.

When Horner took over the district on 14th June, 1836, he found it necessary to introduce only minor changes. Time Book

---

23 Report, 10th February. 1834. *Parl. Papers* (1834) XLIII, p. 451.

No. 2, now limited to children, and still showing merely the total number of hours worked each day, was elaborated so that it should contain henceforth the more detailed statement of daily work provided for in Time Book No. 3.[24] As a matter of administrative convenience Horner also issued an instruction that at the beginning of Time Book No. 1 certain particulars should be entered—the name of the mill-occupier, the official designation and the address of the mill, the type of work carried on, and the nature and amount of the moving power.

Rickards had concentrated almost exclusively on the form of the registers, and that he had at length devised a scheme that was sound in principle was evidenced by the fact that Horner adopted his plan almost in its entirety. In the regulations that he issued on 6th July, 1836, however, Horner carried the process of administrative control a good deal further. Realizing the importance of full publicity in matters concerning the welfare of the operatives, he instructed the mill-occupiers that they must fix up in a conspicuous part of the factory the name and address of the surgeon authorized to grant certificates of age.[25] A notice printed in large, legible characters, signed by a person in authority, setting out the time work began in the morning, the intervals allowed for breakfast, dinner and tea, and the time work stopped at night, was also to be posted in a place where it could be easily read by all the work-people. A similar notice was to be displayed setting out the day and hour at which any time was lost, the cause of the loss, and the exact amount lost. So long as that time was being recovered, the notice was to be kept in position, and if the recovery extended over more than three days, the time actually made up was to be entered on the notice every third day.[26]

At the same time Horner made provision for an orderly and systematic scheme of records. In Time Book No. 1 were to be entered particulars of the statutory holidays, and of the dates when the mill was lime-washed. Certificates of age and school attendance vouchers were to be retained by the mill-occupier and pasted in a book kept for the purpose. When a new mill was opened particulars were to be sent to the Inspector within seven

---

[24] The less exacting record for children had been allowed to continue in deference to the wishes of the manufacturers. After the abandonment of Poulett Thomson's bill, the Home Office recommended that the more detailed register should be used.—*Parl. Papers* (1837) XXXI, p. 124.

[25] See *ante* p. 131. Any surgeon, whether nominated by the Inspector or not, could issue these certificates, but the Inspectors had followed the practice, initiated by Rickards, of appointing surgeons to each mill, by arrangement with the occupier.

[26] In addition to these three notices the mill-occupier was obliged to display an abstract of the Act, and a copy of the Inspector's regulations.

days, a regulation designed to meet a serious omission in the Act, which had made no provision for furnishing the Inspector with this vital information.

Horner's purpose was plain. When there were such powerful inducements to evade the law it was idle to rely on the personal observation of Inspectors and Superintendents to detect breaches of its provisions. Their visits to the mills were necessarily infrequent, and in many instances the manufacturer, fore-warned of an impending visit, was able to put his house in order before the tour of inspection began. What was required was a continuous record of extrinsic evidence, the accuracy of which, attested by the owner, could be checked by cross-examination of the operatives, who were given full opportunity of acquainting themselves with the provisions of the Act. Such evidence would usually be indispensable in any legal proceedings, and the manufacturers were therefore required to produce all time-books, registers, and other documents when informations were laid against them.

One of the main purposes of the Act being to secure uniformity of administration throughout the country, it was clearly desirable that the regulations in force in each district should be similar, and in September, 1836, Fox Maule informed Horner that the Government desired the Inspectors to frame a single code of regulations to be introduced into all four districts. The need for such a code had been apparent for some time,[27] and at their autumn meeting the Inspectors examined the whole question.[28] Howell, it appeared, had adopted Horner's regulations in their entirety; Saunders had followed his example, except that he had not introduced the Time Books; while in Stuart's district no regulations had been issued since January, 1834. It was the form the Time Books were to take that occasioned the most prolonged discussion. Of their usefulness there could be no doubt, but they were bitterly resented by the manufacturers who complained of the undue burden thrust upon them by the requirement that a detailed statement of the working time of each individual was to be entered each day.[29] " It was unanimously decided," recorded the minutes of the meeting, " these Time Books should be discontinued. New forms applicable to all the Districts were brought forward, considered, and provisionally agreed upon."

---

[27] Saunders' Report, 28th December, 1833. *Parl. Papers* (1834) XLIII, p. 483.

[28] *Minutes,* 8th December, 1836, Vol. I, pp. 1-3.

[29] *Cf.* R. H. Greg, *The Factory Question* (1837) p. 124.—" In the Time Book No. 2, or No. 3, it was necessary to make from *one to two thousand entries, and in one case, four thousand entries daily.* The time being entered, at which every child under 13, *came into and went out of the mill,* any mistake subjected the mill-owner to prosecution. This was found to be intolerably burthensome."

The new Time Registers, as they were called, though preserving the principle of the Time Books, were at once less cumbersome[30] and more comprehensive. For the requirement that there should be a detailed account of the working hours of each individual each day was substituted a statement of the hours of the whole body of children and young persons, so designed as to show the intervals allowed for meals, and preceded by a solemn declaration on the part of the mill-occupier that the statement was accurate in every particular. With this was incorporated a record of the holidays granted, details of lime-washing, and an account of time lost and recovered. The consolidated code contained little else that was new; since it was hardly possible to improve upon the regulations that Horner had already adopted, they were included without major alteration. In due course the new regulations were submitted to Lord John Russell, the Home Secretary, and to Poulett Thomson, President of the Board of Trade, and having been approved on 4th October, 1836, they came into operation at once.[31]

The new scheme promised to work well. Horner reported that the substitution of one general declaration for the daily entry in the Time Book " has removed a great practical difficulty,"[32] and at their meeting on 24th January, 1837, the Inspectors agreed to report to the Home Secretary, " We are induced to believe that the rules and regulations drawn up by us last October, and approved of by your Lordship, have tended very materially to render observance to the Law much more easy that it was before, by their having greatly diminished the trouble that attended the Time Books formerly required to be kept in order to show the hours when the Children and young Persons are employed."[33]

The manufacturers, however, were not so sanguine. Greg had complained of the burdens imposed by the old Time Books, and he now attacked the formalism of the new Registers. " Another Time Book has been introduced by the Inspectors," he declared, " in which the mill-owner enters, not at what periods daily, every child *actually comes into and goes out of the mill, but at what moment of time, every child shall make its entries and its exits for the next twelve months.* The mill-owner, therefore, guarantees matters over which he has little or no control, and thereby puts himself at the mercy, not merely of the Inspector and

---

[30] A full observance of the regulations, said Horner, " would, in the large majority of cases, be secured by one individual giving half-an-hour's attention to them once a week."—Report, 30th December, 1839. *Parl. Papers* (1840) XXIII, p. 9.

[31] Joint Report, 12th October, 1836. *Parl. Papers* (1837) XXXI, p. 86.

[32] Report, 18th January, 1837. *Ibid.* p. 97.

[33] *Minutes,* Vol. I, p. 55.

his Superintendent, but of every servant, or even common spy.
Who would not shrink from such a responsibility? If a mill-owner
employs only 50 *children,* which is a moderate number, he is liable
to prosecution, if 300 entries and exits are not punctually made
each day, and this exclusive of the schooling arrangements for the
same children. Neither are the fear and danger of prosecution,
by any means visionary."[34] Practised controversialist as he was,
Greg could hardly have expected that much weight would be
attached to objections such as these. The real gravamen of his
complaint was rather that the effect of the regulations would
inevitably fetter the manufacturer's freedom of action by increasing
the possibility that his evasions of the law would be detected. His
remarks in this connection were somewhat disingenuous. " It is
much to be regretted," he continued, "that the present Factory Law,
and the regulations of the Inspectors, tend to *destroy all good
feeling, and to aggravate misunderstandings where they exist.* The
Inspector's regulations are founded upon the principle of the master
being *a tyrant and a cheat;* and that the operatives must look to the
Inspector, rather than to *him,* for justice and protection. Mr.
Horner, in his directions to his Superintendents, dated July, 1836,
on entering upon his official duties, says : —
     ' You will, in like manner, be rigid in enforcing Rules 10 and
     11. You are aware that the work-people are often cheated
     of their meals, and grossly imposed upon, under pretence of
     making up lost time, &c.'
Regulations framed in such a spirit, necessarily throw the master
into a false position, from which he can with difficulty extricate
himself, and throw power into the hands of the work-people, of
which, it is too much to suppose, they will not sometimes avail
themselves."[35]

     Ashworth, the great Quaker cotton-master, confessed that
children were often employed without age certificates, since otherwise the machinery must remain idle. " It is utterly impossible,"
he asserted, " for any manufacturer to employ a moderate number
of hands without being liable to a penalty every day. . . . This plan
gives the superintendents great power of annoyance if we were to
thwart them." The general feeling, he said, was that the effect
of the regulations was to place the manufacturers in the hands of
the Superintendents, who often laid informations for purely formal
offences.[36]

     Senior, too, condemned the machinery established by the
Inspectors, holding with Ashworth that it tended to encourage
prosecutions for formal violations of the law. A master might

---

[34] R. H. Greg, *The Factory Question* (1837) pp. 124-125.
[35] *Ibid.* p. 127.
[36] Nassau W. Senior, *Letters on the Factory Act* (1837) pp. 50-51.

be fined for over-working, he said, because a child had remained in the factory a minute beyond his allotted time to shelter from the weather or to tie a bootlace; or he might be prosecuted for making a false entry in the Time Register if one of eighty children worked from 8.30 to 4.30 instead of from 8 to 4.[37]   Horner replied to these allegations with his customary vigour.   The masters, he said, were not prosecuted for formal offences.   " They have been prosecuted for allowing a child to remain in the factory longer than the law allows; not because they were humanely protecting the child from the inclemency of the weather, but because they were employing it *to clean the machinery,* while the adult was at his dinner, or after the mill had stopped at night. . . .   No mill-owner has been prosecuted for making a false entry, ' because one of 80 children has one day come at half-past 8 and remained till half-past 4,' but because he was working the 80 children twelve hours a day, and falsely stating in his Time Register that they worked only eight hours."[38]

The indignation of the owners was perhaps the best indication of the effectiveness of the revised regulations.   They stood the test of time and experience, and remained in force until 1844 when, modified to meet the changed requirements, they were embodied in a new Act which, at the same time, deprived the Inspectors of their subordinate law-making powers.   The arbitrary functions with which these servants of the Executive had been invested were admittedly indefensible on any grounds of constitutional propriety, but they had served their purpose.   Effective machinery was indispensable to the enforcement of the law, and it could only be evolved in the light of experience.   Rigidity at this stage of legistive evolution would have spelt disaster, and rigidity there must have been had a system of administrative regulation been incorporated in the statute.   As it was there was full freedom to experiment.   The Inspectors did not abuse this freedom, nor did they fail to take full advantage of the powers deputed to them, and so it was that they were able to impose shape, form and substance on this important department of factory law.

---

[37] *Ibid.* p. 20.
[38] *Ibid.* pp. 39-40.

CHAPTER 10

FOX MAULE'S BILLS

THE AVOWED determination of the Government, following the withdrawal of Poulett Thomson's bill, to enforce the provisions of the existing law, persuaded the Short-time Committees that it would be politic to hold their hands for a time to await the outcome of the new measures. " The present factory law having been passed," said Oastler, " as I knew there were many clauses in it which would very much annoy the factory masters, I foresaw that it was not possible that it should ' work well.' I knew also that if the friends of the factory children were to keep up an agitation, or were in any way to interfere with the working of the law, then that all the evils of the new system would be charged upon us. I therefore resolved to recommend stillness and quietness, in order that the law might take its course. The event has proved the wisdom of this plan. The law has been proved to be a failure; its authors, supporters, and friends have found it to be so; and they are now clamorous for its ' amendment.' "[1] Despite their abstention from Parliamentary agitation, however, the Committees remained vigilant and fully organized in the manufacturing counties, where Oastler and his disciples by public declamation and the written word, contrived to keep the interest at fever-heat. Oastler's condemnation of the masters became increasingly bitter,[2] and at a great gathering held in Blackburn in September, 1836, he threatened to show the factory children how to deal with those who derided ' Oastler's law.' " I assured the meeting," he said, " that if the Factory Masters were more powerful than the Law and the King, I would *then* teach the Factory Children, to defend themselves, to prevent themselves from being murdered, contrary to Law;—and so I will. I will, in that event, print a little card, about Needles, and Sand, and Rusty-nails, with proper, and with very explicit directions, which will make these Law-breakers look about them."[3]

[1] R. Oastler, *A Letter to the Bishop of Exeter* (1838) p. 6. See also W. R. Croft, *History of the Factory Movement* (1888) p. 107.

[2] *Cf. The Unjust Judge* (1836) p. 9.—" They have worked, and beaten, and starved the poor Factory Children to death by shoals. Yes, they have —Day and night! Night and day! Bloody Monsters are they!—Just now they are raving mad, because the Law forbids them to shed innocent blood. . . . They may be the props and pillars of ' the Cause ' in different denominations; they bribe the Almighty! but it won't do. . . . They are Bloody Murderers, and the God of the Innocents rejects their offerings, and mocks at their solemn assemblings."

[3] R. Oastler, *The Law or the Needle* (1836) p. 9. See also " Alfred," *The History of the Factory System* (1857) Vol. II, pp. 108-109.

The Government, conscious of the fact that its integrity would be impugned if the Act was not rigorously enforced, and swayed not so much by the virulence of the reformers as by the representations made by the Inspectors, was soon persuaded that steps must be taken to remedy some of the most obvious anomalies in the law. Accordingly, on 25th January, 1837, a letter was written to the Inspectors informing them that the Home Secretary would shortly be consulting them about the amendments they wished to suggest;[4] and on the following day they met Fox Maule and Labouchere to submit their proposals.[5] The problems discussed can be gathered from the letter addressed to Horner the day following the conference.—

" Sir,

I address you as the Inspector of the greatest number of mills and request you will convey to your colleagues the result of Mr. Labouchere and my own reflection on the Statement made by you yesterday.

It appears to us necessary to improve the machinery of the present Act, and we therefore request you will draw out the Heads of a Bill to be submitted to the Cabinet, in which you will provide for a more effectual system of Certificates of Age, and a better mode of making the Penalties for the infraction of the Law of more than the mere nominal effect they are at present. You will also insert a clause by which these penalties are to be applied as intended by the original Act.

You may likewise propose to extend the Powers of the Superintendents.

These seem to us to comprise the most necessary alterations, and we shall be happy to consider them & submit them to the Cabinet as soon as you can prepare them.

I am, Sir,

Yrs,

F. Maule."[6]

The task of considering the recommendations that were to be made was entrusted to Horner and Howell, and within a week their proposals had been submitted to the Home Office.[7] More than a year elapsed, however, before any action was taken, and it was not until 9th April, 1838, after further discussions with the Inspectors,[8] that the bill was introduced in the Commons in the

---

4 *Home Office Papers*, H.O. 87 (1), p. 38.
5 *Minutes*, 26th January, 1837, Vol. I, p. 57.
6 *Ibid.* pp. 61-62.
7 *Ibid.* pp. 63, 65.
8 *Ibid.* p. 108. *Home Office Papers*, H.O. 87 (1), p. 110.

names of Fox Maule and Labouchere.[9]   The Inspectors rejoiced
that the defects in the Act of 1833, against which they had for so
long inveighed, were soon to be remedied,[10] but the owners viewed
with foreboding this impending revival of legislative activity.   What
need was there, they asked, for this renewed agitation?   " Surely,
if the master manufacturers are content with their position, no
other party need take the field?   They have suffered a total defeat,
their characters have been blackened, the ' Short-time Committee '
has its spies in all their mills, Government has its spies in the
inspectors, they again, their inferior spies, in the sub-inspectors,
nay, the masters are compelled to be spies upon themselves, and
contrary to a well-known principle of English law, to keep a
register of their own offences."[11]

The bill bore the strong impress of the Inspectors' recommendations, for it went far to remedy many of the abuses of which they
had complained.   An entirely new form of surgical certificate was
to be introduced, the purpose of which was not merely to identify
the individual by incorporating a personal description (thus
adopting the suggestion made by Horner in December, 1836) but
also to secure the surgeon's testimony that he actually believed
the child or young person to be of the age certified.[12]   This
expression of medical opinion concerning actual age would have
been an invaluable safeguard against fraud had the power to grant
certificates been confined to surgeons appointed by the Inspectors,
but the Government did not feel able to take this decisive step,
though they agreed in principle with the view so frequently
expressed by Horner and his colleagues.   The expedient to which
they resorted was ingenious.   The Inspectors were to be authorized
to appoint surgeons and to fix their fees, while the mill-occupiers
were to be encouraged to concur in this arrangement by the proviso
that they might be licensed by the Inspector to employ a child or
young person for not more than thirteen days without an age
certificate if all the certificates in the factory were issued by an
appointed surgeon.   Such certificates were to become valid without
further formality, but a certificate granted by a non-appointed
surgeon was not to become effective until it had been counter-
signed by a magistrate in the presence of the child or young
person to whom it related.   If an Inspector had reason to believe
that a certificate was false, he was authorized to cancel it.

---

9 A Bill for regulating the Employment of Children and young Persons
in Factories.   *Parl. Papers* (1837-8) **IV**, p. 1.
10 Horner's Report, 31st March, 1838.   *Parl. Papers* (1838) **XXVIII**,
p. 136.
11 R. H. Greg, *The Factory Question* (1837) p. 16.
12 See Appendix.

The authority of the Inspectors was to remain unimpaired, though they were no longer to promulgate separate sets of regulations for their own districts. The advantages of a uniform code applicable to the whole country had already become apparent, and it was accordingly provided that any further regulations should be made by the whole body of Inspectors at their statutory meeting, such regulations to be approved by the Secretary of State and advertised in the *London Gazette* before they became operative.

Although the Inspectors had consistently urged that the law could not be effectively enforced unless the Superintendents were allowed to enter all parts of the mill at their discretion, the bill still maintained most of the existing limitations, authorizing the Superintendent only " to enter any counting-house, school-room, waiting-room, yard or playground belonging to any Factory, and every part of any Factory, except such parts which are used for any manufacturing process; and also to pass through any such manufacturing part for the purpose only of arriving at part of the Factory which he has authority to enter, but cannot enter otherwise; and also to summon any child or young person in the Factory to the counting-house . . . and to examine them either alone or in the presence of any other persons." The Superintendents were, however, to be allowed to apply to a magistrate for a warrant to enter the working rooms on making a written declaration that they had reason to believe that protected persons were being employed contrary to the Act. Such a warrant, when granted, was to authorize entry to the factory on any three specified working days, and the Superintendent was then to be vested with the full powers of an Inspector.

The bill proposed additional safeguards to ensure that working hours were not exceeded, that proper breaks for meals were allowed, and that holidays were granted. No child was to work in more than one factory on the same day, and the hours of children and young persons were to be regulated by a single clock, either a public clock, or a clock in the factory constantly regulated by a public clock, the situation of which was to be notified to the Inspector. Lost time was only to be made up if the whole of the machinery was stopped by accident or by interruption to the water supply, thus making it illegal for mills to extend the hours of labour when only a part of the machinery was out of action. Meals were to be taken between 7.30 a.m. and 7.30 p.m., and of the hour and a half allowed, one hour at least was to be given before 3 p.m. The difficulty that had arisen concerning holidays was to be removed by the provision that two full days and eight half days were to be obligatory, irrespective of whether the persons concerned elected to avail themselves of the holidays or not.

Section 35 of Althorp's Act had stipulated that written notice of intention to lay an information for breach of the law must be delivered within fourteen days of the commission of the offence. This provision frequently making it possible for offenders to escape prosecution, the Inspectors had repeatedly urged that the time limit should be extended,[13] and Fox Maule's bill met their wishes by allowing complaints to be made within three calendar months.

The proposed measure was thus concerned rather with improving the administrative machinery than with extending the scope of the existing law. It contained no provisions requiring the fencing of dangerous machinery, it still excluded lace-mills, and permitted children of any age to work in silk factories for ten hours a day, and it did not propose any alteration in the hours of children and young persons in other textile establishments. Ashley and his followers, convinced of the futility, in the present state of feeling, of trying to persuade the Government to consider the adoption of the ten-hours day, confined themselves to attacking the imperfections of the Factories Regulation Act, charging the authorities with indifference if not with overt hostility to the measure. No facilities having been afforded by the Government for expediting the progress of the amending bill since its introduction on 9th April, 1838, Lord Ashley himself moved the second reading on 22nd June.[14] Calling attention to the repeated violations of the provisions of the bill which had been suffered to pass unnoticed, and to the total neglect and contempt with which the Government had treated all the representations which had been made to them upon this subject, he urged the House to consider the pressing necessity of providing some means during the present session to afford relief to those miserable victims of the most abominable system that had ever prevailed in any civilised country. He himself had been deluded and mocked upon this subject by Her Majesty's Government in the most unwarrantable manner. The Government had invariably taken the matter out of his hands by the solemn promise that they would proceed with it themselves, but they had not moved, and now declared that it was too late in the session to proceed with the bill."[15]

Lord John Russell agreed that he had promised to operate the Act as efficiently as possible, but it was difficult to enforce the law

---

[13] Saunders' Report, February, 1836. *Parl. Papers* (1836) XLV, p. 165. Howell's Report, February, 1836. *Ibid.* p. 168.
[14] E. Hodder, *The Life and Work of the seventh Earl of Shaftesbury* (1893) pp. 118-120. "Alfred," *The History of the Factory Movement* (1857) Vol. II, p. 123.
[15] *Hansard* (1838) XLIII, 968.

against the short-sighted interests both of the parents of the children and of the factory proprietors. The greatest problem, he declared, was that of verifying age, " a point upon which much difference of opinion existed."[16] Poulett Thomson confirmed the Government's desire to enforce the Act as stringently as possible, reminding the House that instructions had been issued to the Inspectors " that they should carry out the spirit of the Act to its fullest extent, and that every precaution should be taken that the child's age should be ascertained as satisfactorily as possible." The Government, however, were determined to resist the agitation for a ten-hours day, since any restriction on the labour of adults would be fatal to the best interests of the country. It was only in due time, he asserted, and on deep consideration, that the question could be at all satisfactorily settled.[17]

Sir Robert Peel, speaking for the Opposition, held that the problem was urgent, and should be settled at once. He warned the Government that they had nothing to gain by delay; if they thought the matter too difficult, let them say so, but to pursue a policy of inactivity, session after session, was like " applying a perpetual blister to the sides of the country, and keeping up the fever and irritation of a dangerous sore."[18] A substantial proportion of the House agreed that early and decisive action was necessary, but on the division 119 voted for the Government and 111 for Ashley, and the matter was once more postponed for the time being. " The public attention," said *The Times*, " cannot be too forcibly directed to the scandalous conduct of the Melbourne Government with regard to the factory question as exposed by Lord Ashley on Friday evening in his most impressive and striking speech. It was not merely that the noble Lord . . . has himself been ' mocked and deluded ' in the prosecution of his benevolent schemes by the broken faith and callous feelings of this mercenary and jobbing clique, but that laws of their own making have been left unenforced. . . . The ministerial majority of 8 in a house of 234 members is a sufficient index of the real state of public feeling on this affecting question."[19]

On 12th July Ashley renewed his attack, but since there were only thirty-seven members present, the House was counted out, and nothing more could be done. The Government denied any responsibility,[20] but they could not escape the charge that they had been quick to take advantage of this fortuitous circumstance. " Lord Ashley deserves the highest credit," said *The Times*, " for

---

16 *Ibid*. 970.
17 *Ibid*. 973-974.
18 *Ibid*. 974-975.
19 *The Times*, 25th June, 1838.
20 *Hansard* (1838) XLIV, 190.

the steady resolution with which he has fought the battle of the friendless children in our factories, and in defiance of the most harassing and discouraging trickery resorted to by Ministers on all occasions for the simple purpose of defeating his Lordship's benevolent object. The last manoeuvre, of counting out the house, has however recoiled, we firmly believe, on the heads of its unworthy authors."[21]

It was now too late to proceed with the bill, but before the session closed Ashley brought the question once more before the House by moving, on 20th July, a resolution "that this House deeply regrets that the law affecting the regulation of the labour of children in factories, having been found imperfect and ineffective to the purposes for which it was passed, has been suffered to continue so long without any amendment." In a moving and eloquent speech[22] he drew the attention of the House to the extent of the problem. The returns made in 1835 showed that 354,684 persons were engaged in the cotton mills, and that of these 196,385 were females. When Peel's bill had been introduced in 1816 it was said that a child walked $8\frac{1}{4}$ miles in the course of its daily work; in 1832 that distance had increased to 20 and often 25 miles, while "in some mills the length travelled per day amounted to 30 miles, being a severity of labour exceeding that imposed upon soldiers in forced marches." It appeared from the mortality returns that in the factory districts as many persons died under 20 as under 40 in any other part of England. "In Birmingham one half of the population attained their 16th year, while in Manchester one half died within the first three years."

He did not, on this occasion, propose to discuss the relative merits of the ten- and twelve-hours day; he simply asked what the Government intended to do about their own law? If it were good, let them enforce it; if bad, let them mend it; if it were unnecessary or dangerous, let them repeal it. But to leave the law in its present condition was equally unwise and absurd. It not only withheld just protection from the factory children, but, by pretending to give protection, deprived them of the sympathy of a deluded public. The reports of the Factory Inspectors showed that the law had been systematically violated, yet the Government had remained inactive. Adequate powers were still denied the Superintendents, nothing had been done to remove the abuses inherent in the system of age certificates, and the magistrates continued to make a mockery of the Act by mitigating the penalties for offences. "The disreputable mill-owner," declared Ashley, "who is regardless of the discredit of a prosecution for violating

---

[21] *The Times,* 16th July, 1838.
[22] *Speeches of the Earl of Shaftesbury* (1868) pp. 1-9. *Hansard* (1838) XLIV, 383-395.

the law ... looks only to the amount of the penalty imposed on his neighbours, and finds, on casting up the account, that it is far more profitable to disobey than to observe the Act."

There was little that the Government could say in reply to criticisms that only reiterated what the Inspectors had been urging from the beginning. Fox Maule emphasized the steps that had been taken, by remodelling the districts and increasing the frequency of the Inspectors' visits, to render control more effective; but he admitted that the law was deficient on the question of surgical certificates.[23] Russell agreed that the Act was only partially enforced, but he remained unconvinced that a reduction of hours would provide the solution. Wages would be decreased if the ten-hours day was introduced, and foreign competition would wreck the industry. The problem must be tackled in other ways.[24]

Ashley's motion was lost by 121 votes to 106, but his effort had not been in vain, for it had drawn attention to the need for further reform, and had undoubtedly placed the Government in an embarrassing position, as being unduly sensitive to the influence of the manufacturers,[25] " so many of whom had been sent into the House by the Reform Act, and who possessed very powerful interests out of it."[26] The ministers, realizing the weakness of their position, and anxious to alienate neither the great manufacturing constituencies nor the powerful cotton lords, concentrated their efforts on discovering a solution that would be acceptable to both parties. During the autumn of 1838 the amending bill was re-drafted, and in the following January the revised text was sent to each of the Inspectors for consideration. At their winter meeting, which opened on 17th January, 1839, they devoted three entire days to a detailed examination of the new proposals, and after full consultation with Fox Maule had resulted in a substantial measure of agreement, the bill was ordered to be printed.[27]

The bill[28] introduced by the Under-Secretary of the Home Office on 14th February, 1839,[29] while preserving the main outlines of the previous measure, introduced modifications that afforded a

[23] *Ibid*. 399-405.

[24] *Ibid*. 429-430.

[25] " The debate on Lord Ashley's resolution," *The Times* had said that morning, " comes on this evening. We could wish that, ' for this night only,' the hostile mill-owners could be accommodated on the Treasury bench; their slaves, the Ministers, might sit upon one of the benches behind them."

[26] *Annual Register* (1833) p. 205.

[27] *Minutes*, Vol. I, pp. 113-116. Joint Report, 31st January, 1839. *Parl. Papers* (1839) XIX, p. 538.

[28] Bill for regulating the Employment of Children and young Persons in Factories. *Parl. Papers* (1839) III, p. 467.

[29] *Hansard* (1839) XLV, 434.

clear indication of the direction in which the current of opinion was beginning to flow. There was as yet nothing to suggest that any reduction of working hours could be seriously contemplated, nor was it considered feasible to extend the ambit of legislation by including any other branches of industry—these major reforms were still outside the realm of practical politics. The extreme radicals, it is true, were continuing to acclaim the ten-hours day as the panacea which alone could cure the evils afflicting industry, but for the moment their voice was hardly raised above a whisper. Even Ashley, now firmly established as the spokesman of the reformers, was inclined to abandon the unrealistic altruism that had characterized his policy six years ago, and was turning his attention to the more immediate problems of control. The chief emphasis was being laid on the improvement of the machinery by which regulation was to be effected, and although the bill was ultimately abandoned, many of its provisions came to be embodied in the fabric of political opinion.

The most notable advance was concerned with the status of the officers charged with the administration of the law. The oft-reiterated demand of the Inspectors that the Superintendents should be allowed free entry to every part of the mill was at last to be conceded, and henceforth these subordinate officials were to be permitted to conduct their investigations with full rights of access. The powers of the Inspectors themselves were to undergo a striking revision. They were no longer to exercise judicial functions, but were to be empowered to waive prosecution, and instead to accept from those who were alleged to have infringed the law a compounded sum which was to be applied towards the provision of factory schools.[30] They were to be authorized to summon witnesses before a court of summary jurisdiction, to take depositions on oath, and to demand the production of documents, while their right to promulgate regulations was to remain unimpaired.

The bill proposed a general tightening of control. Lost time was to be recoverable only in mills driven by water-power when the whole of the machinery had been out of action; the clauses regulating meal intervals prescribed that of the hour and a half that was to be allowed between 7.30 a.m. and 7.30 p.m. at least thirty minutes should be taken before six hours' work had been completed, and, a significant provision in view of subsequent developments, all young persons should have their time for meals at the same period of the day, a stipulation designed to facilitate the detection of evasion. The obligation to post notices and to keep registers, hitherto required only by the Inspectors' regulations,

---

[30] This suggestion had been put forward by Horner in a letter dated 18th January, 1837, addressed to Nassau Senior.—Nassau W. Senior, *Letters on the Factory Act* (1837) p. 40.

was now to be enforced by statute. Minimum penalties were laid down, and it was provided that each individual act of illegal employment was to constitute a separate offence, thus overcoming the defect in the existing law whereby only a single information might be laid, and a single fine imposed, in respect of the over-working of any number of persons on the same occasion.

The position of the certifying surgeons was also reviewed. The most perplexing problem was still that of determining age, and it was coming to be accepted that the only satisfactory solution was to leave the matter in the hands of medical men in whom full confidence could be reposed. The Government was still unwilling to confine the right to issue certificates to surgeons appointed by the Inspectors, but it was now proposed to remove the most obvious source of evasion and abuse by refusing to recognize the unqualified practitioner,[31] and limiting the right to certify to those " duly authorized by any University or College, or other public body having authority in that behalf, to practise surgery or medicine." Mill-occupiers were still to be encouraged to employ only duly appointed surgeons,[32] and in these circumstances it became possible to replace the cumbersome form of certificate proposed in the bill of 1838 by a simple declaration that the person concerned had been examined, and that the surgeon believed his age to be that certified.[33]

The bill having been read a second time on 25th February,[34] when Fox Maule outlined his proposals, the Committee stage was reached on 1st July.[35] Issue was at once joined on the question of the extended authority to be vested in the inspecting officers. Wilson Patten, still one of the chief supporters of the manufacturing interests, complained bitterly of the extraordinary powers that it was proposed to grant to the Superintendents. Greater powers than the local magistracy possessed, he declared, were to be entrusted to persons holding very subordinate situations under the Inspectors. Master manufacturers, who considered themselves rather hardly dealt with by this bill, wished that the Inspectors should be persons of such authority that they should be above suspicion of collusion with themselves or with any other party. Mark Philips said the owners objected to the intrusion of persons

---

[31] A person who was " often little better than a cow-doctor," said Fox Maule.—*Hansard* (1839) XLV, 881.

[32] The time during which a child or young person might work without a certificate was reduced to seven days, the period of thirteen days being allowed only when the surgeon resided more than three miles from the factory.

[33] See Appendix.

[34] *Hansard* (1839) XLV, 881 *ff*.

[35] *Hansard* (1839) XLVIII, 1063 *ff*. The debate was resumed on 6th July. *Ibid.* 1416 *ff*.

of inferior station, a circumstance which they, gentlemen of character and honour, had felt severely. There was a grave danger that the Superintendents might divulge technical secrets, and he suggested that they should be replaced by Inspectors resident in each district. Lord Stanley, the member for North Lancashire, holding that the status of the Superintendents should be improved, urged that it was unwise to pay men bearing such a weight of responsibility, so inadequate a salary as £350 a year. On the other hand he protested against the extensive powers wielded by the Inspectors, holding that it was impolitic and unnecessary to allow them to issue rules and regulations enforceable by penalty.

Lord John Russell supported the proposals of the Government on the ground that it was essential to entrust wide discretionary powers to the Inspectors. He was afraid that if the bill defined everything which the Inspectors would have the power of doing, they would be obliged, year after year, to come to Parliament and ask for new bills granting additional powers, as it was impossible at once to legislate upon all the points which might afterwards arise. Fox Maule was so perfectly convinced of the necessity of the Inspectors' powers in order to procure the proper administration of the Act that he was most unwilling, he declared, to depart from the clause bestowing those powers. Poulett Thomson agreed that the status of the Superintendents should be improved, but he did not think Parliament would agree to incur the expense of making them all Inspectors at salaries of £1,000 a year. He thought, however, that the House would rest satisfied when the Government declared that the course they wished to follow was to raise the salaries and characters of the sub-inspectors, to make three of the Inspectors resident in their respective districts, and to centralize the general inspection in London. This would take time, and the new arrangements could not be included in the present bill.

A somewhat half-hearted attempt on the part of Ashley to reduce the hours of young persons from sixty-nine to fifty-eight a week was defeated by 94 votes to 62, but his suggestion that silk mills and lace factories should be subject to the same regulation as other branches of the textile industry was carried, to the Government's consternation, by 55 votes to 49. A new issue of the first importance having been raised so unexpectedly, and the opposition of the manufacturers to the clauses dealing with Inspectors and Superintendents, and with the recovery of lost time continuing unabated, the Government decided to re-consider the whole framework of the bill. The Inspectors had been in close consultation with Fox Maule since 1st July, and during the next fortnight they met daily to consider the progress of the bill and to

discuss possible amendments.[36] On 20th July they recorded in their
minutes, " Conference with mill-occupiers. Their objections to the
appointment of officers continue, together with some few minor
points of which the principal is the recovery of lost time.   M.
occupiers approved of some further alteration which has been
suggested."[37] The account of the anxious and protracted negotia-
tions which follows indicates clearly the tense situation that was
developing. " Monday, 22 July, 1839.—Bill read. Deputation of
M.O. called & further conference held with them. Note on
alterations approved by Inspectors & objections still entertained
by the mill-occupiers were prepared for Mr. Maule. Additional
Schedule prepared in the event of any relaxation of the section for
Recovery of Lost Time. Mr. Stuart saw Mr. Maule & received
Instructions which were to be considered confidential. Note taken
respecting it by each Inspector.

Thursday, 25 July.—Deputation of mill-occupiers called to
know if Mr. Maule had consented to adopt any further of the
alterations urged by them. All the Inspectors to attend in the
Ho. of Commons this Evening.

Friday, 26 July.—The Inspectors attended the Ho. of
Commons last night & remained until ¼ after 1 a.m. of this day,
when the further consideration of the Bill was adjourned until this
Evening. Inspectors to attend again this Evening.

Saturday 27 July.—The Inspectors attended the House of Cm.
last night, some left earlier than others & one remained till ¼
after one a.m. this morning when it was impossible the subject of
Factories could be brought forward. At ½ past one a.m. this
morning Lord John Russell intimated the intention of Government
to withdraw the Bill for the session. This information confirmed
to the Inspectors."[38]

The bill had reached the report stage when Russell announced
that since Ashley had declared his intention of opposing it if it
were not extended to silk and lace mills, he had determined to
withdraw it.[39] This unexpected decision, dictated no doubt not
only by Ashley's insistence on extending the scope of the measure,
but also by the opposition of the manufacturers, came as a grievous
blow to the Inspectors, who had been confident that the reforms
for which they had pressed so long were at length to be achieved.[40]

36 *Minutes,* 16th July, 1839, Vol. I, p. 123.
37 *Ibid.* p. 131.
38 *Ibid.* pp. 132-136.
39 *Hansard* (1839) XLIX, 914.
40 There was no need to enlarge further on the insufficiency of the
present system, said Saunders, for it was now certain " that Her Majesty's
Government have decided to ask from Parliament such alterations in the
Factories Act as they deem necessary to enforce the principle of the
present law."—Report, 1st January, 1839. *Parl. Papers* (1839) XIX, p. 453.

" The provisions in the Bill recently before Parliament," they observed, " respecting certificates of age ... and authority to visiting officers, as well as the removal of much of the ambiguity in the present Act, and the insertion, as a part of the law, of what may be termed the machinery for carrying the principles into execution, which was left by the existing Act to be provided for by Rules and Regulations of the Inspectors, would have proved highly advantageous; and we earnestly hope that these great improvements may be brought forward in a Bill early in the next session of Parliament."[41]

The Inspectors were not alone in taking too optimistic a view of what the reformed Parliament could achieve during these early years of its existence. It had, indeed, embarked upon a remarkably ambitious programme. The Poor Law had been recast, the Municipal Corporations Act had changed the whole basis of local government, the system of tithes had been overhauled, and slavery had been abolished. Yet despite this unprecedented outburst of legislative energy it remained true that the Whig ministry had defined no long-term policy, had set for itself no ultimate goal. Its methods were empirical, its progress was slow and tentative.[42] The high hopes so freely entertained in 1832 had, in part at least, been dashed, because the means were not adequate to the end. " The general election," it had been said, " had proved most auspicious to the cause of liberal principles. . . . With the exception of a few, whose opinions were pushed to violent extremes, the bulk of the members returned were rational, though firm and determined, friends of political improvement—men resolved temperately, though strenuously, to promote such changes in our system of Government as the spirit of the age, and the state of the country demanded,—while they who resisted all reformation, seemed now to have shrunk into a space not more considerable than was filled by the party bent upon altering by wholesale and at once, every portion of our institutions in Church and in State. From a Parliament thus constituted, every thing was to be hoped: nor were they to blame who hoped all things and believed all things; but their error was in believing that all they had a good right to hope, could be all at once effected.

---

[41] Joint Report, 13th August, 1839. *Parl. Papers* (1840) XXIII, p. 24.
[42] Speaking of the Government's attitude to the Irish Coercion Bill, Russell had said, " Be the consequence what it may, . . . I am content to abide by these opinions, to carry them out to their fullest extent, not by any premature declaration of mere opinion . . . but by going on gradually, from time to time improving our institutions, and, without injuring the ancient and venerable fabrics, rendering them fit and proper mansions for a great, free and intelligent people."—Spencer Walpole. *The Life of Lord John Russell* (1889) p. 203.

Nothing, it must be confessed, could be more unpropitious, both to the Government and the House of Commons, than the commencement of their labours under the general expectations, thus raised to an extravagant pitch. Whatever was done must needs fall short of the wished for point; and that, because the point was not defined;—men reckoned upon a great deal, an immense deal, being done, but they could not tell what; and any thing how great soever that could be done, would have left them at liberty to say it was too little, for they had expected much more."[43]

Of all the measures proposed by the reformed Parliament, the amendment of the Poor Law, and the Factory Act aroused the bitterest and most sustained opposition, and for this reason, progress was inevitably slow. The conflict was all the more severe because the bureaucratic centralization that was the cardinal feature of both measures ran counter to all preconceived opinion.[44] Every foot of ground was sternly contested, every innovation was resisted, every advance was criticised, and the broader aspects of reform became submerged in the consideration of the immediate and pressing problems of detailed administration. " In the House of Commons legislation general principles are held in absolute distrust: nothing is deemed certain but what is individual and special. Every motive has therefore equal weight; every trifling inconvenience takes rank as an insuperable objection; and the question is carried by some side-wind—by some contingent induce- ment that has nothing necessarily to do with the merits of the case. This is the field in which every indirect manoeuvre can be practised, if not without detection, without inconvenient exposure."[45]

In such circumstances it was inevitable that major reforms should be deferred. Amid the sharp clash of conflicting interests progress was necessarily fragmentary and piece-meal. Yet that very clash subjected the new conceptions of authority and control to the decisive test of practicability. Centralized, efficient, and impartial administration was the bed-rock upon which the whole edifice of industrial regulation must be reared; if the foundations were insecure the structure would collapse under its own weight.

---

[43] The Reform Ministry, and the Reformed Parliament.—*The Edinburgh Review*, No. CXVII (October, 1833) p. 200.

[44] *Cf.* W. Page, *Commerce and Industry* (1919) p. 85.—" In the 18th century an absolute centralization of legislative power was combined with an utter absence of administrative centralization. The governing classes met in Parliament merely to distribute the various administrative functions among themselves. Such measures as the Amendment of the Poor Law in 1834 and the Factory Act of 1833 made necessary the centralization of authority in order to secure impartiality and freedom from local bias."

[45] Review of Sir Samuel Romilly's Memoirs. *The Athenæum*, 2nd May, 1840. Quoted L. Horner, *On the Employment of Children in Factories* (1840) pp. 2-3.

The years that intervened, therefore, between the passing of Althorp's Act in 1833 and the Factories Regulation Act of 1844, though devoid of legislation, were by no means barren, for they enabled those who were charged with the duty of enforcing the law to test, and where necessary, to modify, the machinery upon which success was, in the ultimate resort, dependent.

INSPECTORS' DISTRICTS
BEFORE REORGANIZATION

SAUNDERS

HOWELL

HORNER

STUART

CHAPTER 11

EDUCATION

" " I AM convinced," said Horner, " of the paramount necessity
of legislative interference to prevent the children in factories
from growing up in a state of barbarous ignorance;
especially as the tendency of improvements in machinery is more
and more to substitute infant for adult labour, and consequently
the temptation to parents to neglect the education of their
children is daily on the increase."[1]   The need for State intervention
was, indeed, universally admitted, for the conditions to which the
factory children were exposed were causing apprehension on all
sides. The crowding together in the mills of young people of both
sexes encouraged moral delinquency, while the breaking up of
family ties and the virtual severance from the restraining influence
of domestic example caused by excessive hours of work, served only
to intensify the evil. The overlookers, declared Gaskell treated the
children harshly, "often with brutal coarseness, making no allowance
for childish simplicity, bashfulness, delicacy, or female failings."[2]
Girls who were denied all training in the art of home-making
would, it was feared, lack the essential qualities of the good house-
wife when the time came for them to marry; boys who had grown
up without the influence of moral and religious education would
drift into crime. These forebodings were shared by men of all
views and of all political parties, and there were few who did not
agree that the remedy lay in providing educational opportunities
on a wider scale.

The Act of 1833, it would seem, had accomplished much when
it made employment in the textile mills conditional upon attendance
at school for two hours a day on six days of the week. The
principle, indeed, was impeccable, but the means adopted for
carrying it into effect were woefully inadequate, for apart from the
fact that children employed in the silk-mills were outside the scope
of the measure,[3] it proved in practice impossible either to enforce
school attendance universally, or to secure that adequate education
was provided for those who did attend. Some of the more

---

[1] Report, August, 1835. *Parl. Papers* (1836) XLV, p. 158.
[2] P. Gaskell, *The Manufacturing Population of England* (1833) p. 89.
[3] The Chairman of the Macclesfield Short-time Committee told
Saunders, " It is understood a decided opinion has been expressed at
Manchester, under the sanction of the Right Honourable P. Thomson, that
it was never intended children employed in silk mills should be educated."
—Report, 28th December, 1833. *Parl. Papers* (1834) XLIII, p. 481.

enlightened manufacturers, it is true, took their responsibilities seriously, and made every effort to ensure that proper buildings and suitably qualified teachers were available. The school attached to the Hollymount mill owned by Messrs. Whitehead was typical of many. " It was one of the most elegant and convenient buildings I have ever seen devoted to the purposes of education," declared Dr. Taylor. " It was well ventilated, and furnished with the best apparatus for being lighted with gas and heated with warm water. It could not have cost less than a thousand pounds. The children pay twopence per week for instruction, but the expenses are defrayed by the benevolent proprietors, and the weekly stipend is allowed to accumulate as a reserve fund, to be paid back to each pupil at twenty-one years of age."[4]

In such schools the results were all that could be desired, and the benefits derived by the children were unquestionable. " In some of the mills where schools have been established and the attendance regularly enforced," remarked Saunders, " the mill-owners have assured me that great improvements in the conduct and habits of the children had been early evident, and that the difficulties are not so great as they apprehended."[5] " I am assured," he added in a later report, " that the younger classes, in every case where their education is based on any sound and regular system, are deriving much benefit from it, and that the training consequent upon such order and regularity, is securing a greater degree of subordination than was expected."[6] It was Howell's experience that parents were willing to send their children to school, even at some cost to themselves, if the education provided was satisfactory, but, he added, " the worthlessness of the education, which is now to be obtained at such schools as may be casually accessible to factory children, effectually deters the parents of such children from co-operating to carry into effect the scheme of combining daily tuition in a school with daily employment in a factory."[7] Unhappily it happened all too frequently that where the manufacturer neglected to provide a school for his factory, no other was available, particularly in rural districts. In the early days the Inspectors had frequently waived the obligation to attend school in these circumstances, but after they had received specific instructions to enforce attendance, following the withdrawal of Poulett Thomson's bill,

---

4 W. Cooke Taylor, *Notes of a Tour in the Manufacturing Districts of Lancashire* (1842) p. 59. Horner stated that only in 95 of 657 factories had schools been established. In Manchester a few owners had fixed up commodious schoolrooms, " and had the teachers instructed in improved methods of tuition."—Report, 31st March, 1838. *Parl. Papers* (1838) XXVIII, p. 136.

5 Report, August, 1835. *Parl. Papers* (1836) XLV, p. 156.

6 30th September, 1838. *Parl. Papers* (1839) XIX, p. 442.

7 Report, 31st March, 1837. *Parl. Papers* (1838) XXVIII, p. 86.

they were often faced with a dilemma from which there appeared to be no escape. Stuart, for instance, mentioned the case of a small mill at Culroy, in Ayrshire, where only three children were employed, and where no school was available. The mill-occupier, pressed by the Superintendent to produce the vouchers of attendance, wrote to the Inspector in the following terms : —

" Mr. James has visited my factory this day, and has found fault with me for the want of school vouchers. I am sorry for this, but we have no school in the neighbourhood. I will continue to teach them myself, and with a clear conscience certify I have done so each succeeding Monday from this date in terms of the Act of Parliament, and the new rules and regulations."[8]

The dangers implicit in this purely nominal adherence to the mere letter of the law needed no emphasis, and the Inspectors were rightly sceptical of the policy that insisted on attendance at school while making no provision for schools to be established. " I have reason to believe," said Howell in 1833, " that in some of the very few instances in which the system of relays will be attempted, and schools for that purpose established, the schools will be in the factory, and the schoolmaster one of the workpeople."[9] Two years later he re-emphasized his anxieties. " If, from the impossibility of procuring a sufficient number of children above thirteen, the master should find himself compelled to attempt the relay system, and if there should be a sufficient number of younger children at his command for that purpose, ready to work short hours for short wages, he will, I apprehend, convert some part of his premises into what will be called a school, (wherein the children would be impounded to ensure the presence of the relays when wanted), and he will convert one of his workpeople into what will be called a schoolmaster; but beside the obvious facilities for increasing the hours of work which such a system would afford, the education so provided would be of little or no value."[10]

The schooling clauses were resented by both masters and parents. Nor can it be supposed that the children themselves acquiesced willingly in an arrangement that kept them confined to the school-room for a further two hours after their labour in the mill was finished. The masters complained of the interruption

---

[8] Report, 31st March, 1837. *Ibid.* p. 93.
[9] Report, 20th December, 1833. *Parl. Papers* (1834) XLIII, p. 443.
[10] Report, February, 1836. *Parl. Papers* (1836) XLV, p. 168. *Cf.* Howell's Report, 30th September, 1839.—" The facility of the children's transition from the school-room to the spinning- or to the throstle-room is obvious; and their transition from the spinning- or the throstle-room to the school-room, whenever the inspector or superintendent may appear at the factory lodge-gate, is not very difficult."—*Parl. Papers* (1840) XXIII, p. 5.

caused to the daily routine when they were forbidden to employ
children who did not produce their attendance vouchers on Monday
morning, and they also held that it was unjust that they should
be saddled with the expense of providing schools, maintaining that
if the State wished to shift the responsibility of educating children
from the shoulders of the parents, the State should see that the
schools were available.[11] In many instances parents connived at
the evasion of the law, appearing, as Horner believed, " to be
wholly insensible to the obligation they are under to set aside
that very small portion of their earnings which would be sufficient
to procure education for their children. . . . Even when schooling
is paid for by the mill-owner they take no pains to see that their
children attend school, and keep them at home on the most
frivolous pretences when they are set free from their work in
the mill."[12] So far as the children were concerned, Nassau Senior
asserted that the school appeared generally rather a place for
detaining and annoying them than of real instruction. " We found
a universal statement," he said, " that the children could not be got
into the school except by force; that they tried every means to
remain in the factory, or, if excluded, to ramble over the fields or
the streets."[13]

The Inspectors had emphasized from the beginning that it was
quite impossible to enforce the educational provisions of the Act
so long as the 22nd section giving them power to establish schools
remained inoperative.[14] It was true, said Horner, that a great
point had been gained, for it had been proved beyond dispute,
that working in a factory one part of the day and attending school
at another were quite compatible, by a very moderate sacrifice of
trouble and expense.[15] The results achieved, however, were comparatively worthless. Of 2,000 children between thirteen and
fourteen years of age employed in nineteen Manchester mills, he
found that 1,067 were unable to read, only 441 could sign their
names, 322 read the New Testament with difficulty, and only 611
could read with any degree of fluency.[16] This state of affairs was
profoundly unsatisfactory, and if the Government was not willing
to provide the schools, other possibilities must be explored. Horner
had no doubt what the ultimate solution must be. " I hail the
Factory Act," he said, " as the first legislative step in this country

11 Nassau W. Senior, *Letters on the Factory Act* (1837) p. 22. See
Saunders' Report, 30th September, 1839. *Parl. Papers* (1840) XXIII, p. 6.
12 Report, 30th June, 1837. *Parl. Papers* (1838) XXVIII, p. 96.
13 Nassau W. Senior, *Letters on the Factory Act* (1837) p. 19.
14 Joint Report, 28th July, 1834. *Parl. Papers* (1834) XLIII, p. 492.
15 Report, 18th January, 1837. *Parl. Papers* (1837) XXXI, p. 98.
16 *Ibid.* p. 99.

towards that to which, under some modification or other, we must sooner or later come—a compulsory education for all classes,"[17] but he well knew that the time for so great a reform had not yet arrived. Some action must be taken in the meantime, therefore, and in his report for December, 1837, he suggested that the mill-occupiers might be persuaded to pool their resources to set up the schools that were so urgently needed.[18]

The scheme for the establishment of joint schools was worked out in some detail. It was assumed that in a typical neighbourhood there was a number of factories employing 300 children by relays in such a way that whilst 200 boys and girls were at work in the mill, 100 were attending school. The cost of the building and equipment, estimated at £300, was to be raised by the issue of £10 shares, each factory subscribing in proportion to the number of children employed. Interest at the rate of 5% could be paid from school fees, which might be levied from the children at the rate of 3d. a week. The school could be open for an hour during the evening for young persons who were at work all day, and this would produce a revenue of some £40, so that the total annual income would amount to £235.

" The utmost caution," observed Horner, " is necessary in the choice of teachers. Moral and religious character, calmness of temper and general sobriety of deportment, and a thorough know-ledge of the subjects to be taught are indispensable qualifications." An adequate salary would have to be paid to secure suitable persons, and he suggested £80 a year for a master and £50 a year for a mistress. The total expenses of the school would be: —

	£
Salary of master	80
Salary of mistress	50
Salary of assistant master	20
Salary of assistant mistress	15
Fire and light	15
Books and stationery	20
Interest on capital	15
Ground rent, repairs and contingencies ...	20
	£235

The scheme seemed promising enough, but it was difficult to persuade the owners to co-operate. " I am sorry to say," lamented Horner, " that my efforts to accomplish this object have hitherto been unsuccessful," while Saunders reported that the plan had

[17] Nassau W. Senior, *Letters on the Factory Act* (1837) p. 37.
[18] *Parl. Papers* (1838) XXVIII, pp. 118-119.

failed in his district, chiefly because it had proved impossible to limit the expenses and to enforce the agreements made by the mill-occupiers.[19] " With some few exceptions," he said, " the occupiers of mills declare themselves unable to incur the expenses necessary for the building of school-rooms, and decline taking any active measures towards the establishment of joint schools; because they do not consider any further onus should be laid on them beyond what is prescribed by the law; *viz.*, to employ the children a limited number of hours, and to receive a certificate that they have attended some school during the previous week."[20]

The manufacturers were not opposed to education as such, indeed many of them considered it to be the only justification for regulating the labour of children at all.[21] Their objection was rather to the inconvenience and disturbance, to say nothing of the expense, in which the existing system involved them. An alternative scheme that found much favour was to place the responsibility not on the mill-owner but on the parent, by providing that the attainment of a minimum educational standard should be a condition of employment. No child, it was suggested, should be admitted to a factory until he could read, and no young person should be permitted to work full hours until he could read and write fluently.[22] This plan had been introduced in Thomson's print-works at Clitheroe, where children who desired to be apprenticed to pattern-drawing, engraving, block-cutting and block-printing were required to demonstrate their ability to read and write before being engaged. So great was the demand for apprenticeship, it was said, that a remarkable interest in education had been stimulated, and many new schools had been built. The substitution of an educational test for the obligation to attend school would encourage parents to provide for the education of their children, it was claimed, and the inconveniences inherent in the schooling clauses of the Factory Act would automatically disappear.[23] "We have abundant instances," said Thomson, " of parents who are anxious to get their children admitted into our employment, securing for them previously the required degree of instruction, when it is most probable every other

---

[19] Report, 31st December, 1837. *Parl. Papers* (1838) XXVIII, p. 123.
[20] Report, 1st January, 1842. *Parl. Papers* (1842) XXII, p. 432.
[21] R. H. Greg, *The Factory Question* (1837) p. 5.—" Reasonable doubts may be entertained of the propriety of interference with children resident at home, under the protection of their parents, except so far as securing to them an *education* . . . . We are satisfied that no protection of an effectual nature can be secured to children, *except by some general system of education, duly enforced.*"
[22] Nassau W. Senior, *Letters on the Factory Act* (1837) p. 22.
[23] *Ibid.* pp. 44, 46, 51.

means would have failed."[24]   Horner, however, was strongly
opposed to the educational test, considering that it would react
unfavourably on the parents of the younger children, who at the
age of eight or nine would be debarred from employment which
they could undertake with perfect safety.[25]   " It cannot be too
often repeated," he declared, " that a child who knows how to read
is not educated, but has only made the first step in that intellectual,
moral, and religious training, which alone constitutes education."[26]
Chadwick too, viewed the suggestion with disfavour, but on quite
different grounds.   He freely admitted that much of the teaching
provided under the Act was " of the lowest sort, evasive and
fraudulent," but he denied that the measure must be regarded as
having failed, since it accomplished what it set out to do,—to
provide bodily protection.   The attainment test, he averred, " overlooked the fact that the provision requiring that the child should
be . . . in a school, was a provision that it should not be in a
factory, and should be protected, by so many hours, from working
the full time of the adult."[27]

The bill introduced by Fox Maule in 1838 made no provision
for school attendance, proposing instead that no child should be
employed who was unable to read any portion of an easy book to
be published by the Secretary of State, and that no young person
should work more than forty-eight hours a week unless he could
read the New Testament.   The Inspectors, however, were to be
allowed to grant licences authorizing the employment of those who
were unable to satisfy these requirements if the mill-occupier was
able to prove that he was earnestly furthering the education of the
children and young persons in his employment by establishing a
school or by taking other steps to secure instruction for them.
These licences were to remain in force for not more than twelve
months at a time, and the Inspector was to attach such conditions
as he thought fit.

Had these proposals passed into law factory legislation might
well have developed along entirely different lines, but the Inspectors
understood only too well the dangers that would have resulted,
and they were soon to have an opportunity of influencing the
policy of the Government in accordance with their own ideas.   The

---

24 J. C. Symons, *Arts and Artisans at Home and Abroad* (1839) p. 171.
Symons proposed an educational test as the qualification for the franchise,
suggesting that claimants for admission to the register should be able to
write legibly not less than 70 words selected from the Gospels or from
any standard book.   (*Ibid.* p. 166.)
25 Nassau W. Senior, *Letters on the Factory Act* (1837) p. 40.
26 L. Horner, *On the Employment of Children in Factories* (1840) p. 17.
27 *Transactions of the National Association for the Promotion of Social
Science* (1860) p. 419.

time was opportune for a new survey of the educational problem,
and on 15th August, 1838, a few weeks after the fate of Fox
Maule's bill had been decided, Grote, the Radical banker, a sturdy
advocate of reform, moved that each Inspector be instructed to
report " on the effects of the educational provisions of the Factories
Act, as exemplified in not less than twelve of the schools situated
in his district in which the provisions have been observed in the
most effective manner," and that a joint report should be submitted
" as to any modification of the existing educational provisions of
the Factories Act, which may appear to them desirable."[28]   The
Inspectors embarked upon this welcome task without delay, and
having considered their several recommendations, they charged
Horner with the duty of framing the joint report, which, having
been approved and signed at their meeting on 26th January, 1839,[29]
was presented to Parliament the following month.[30]

     " I trust," said Horner, " that the educational clauses will
receive the special attention of Parliament, when the amending Act
is brought forward; for the good they have already done in their
present imperfect state, holds out great encouragement to
persevere in making daily attendance at school an indispensable
condition of the employment of children under 13 years of age."
The restrictions imposed by the Factory Act on the working hours
of children would have been of little benefit, he was convinced,
" had not the obligatory attendance for two hours daily at school
presented an obstacle to their being hired out to other occupations
for those portions of their day that remained beyond their eight
hours' work in the factory."   The chief difficulty in giving effect
to the educational provisions was encountered in districts where the
numbers of children concerned were so small as not to justify the
setting-up of factory schools.   " As the law has made it obligatory
on parents to send their children to school, if they are employed
in a Factory," he declared, " it is neither equitable nor consistent
legislation to impose this obligation without affording the means
of its being fulfilled, by providing suitable schools where none
exist."[31]

     The best school in his district was the factory school of
M'Connel & Co. of Manchester.   There was a large room, well-
warmed and well-ventilated, suitably and substantially furnished,
in which competent and zealous teachers taught reading, writing
and arithmetic.   The girls received instruction in needlework, and
preparations were being made to teach geography as well.   But
there was another side to the picture, for many of the factory

---

[28] *Parl. Papers* (1839) XLII, p. 353.
[29] *Minutes,* Vol. I, pp. 116-118.
[30] *Parl. Papers* (1839) XLII, pp. 355, 424.
[31] *Ibid.* p. 355.

schools were thoroughly unsatisfactory. " I have had to reject," he said, " the school voucher of the fireman, the children having been schooled in the coal-hole . . . and having been made to say a lesson from books nearly as black as the fuel, in the intervals between his feeding and stirring the fire of the engine boiler."[32]

Howell thought that the chief difficulty arose from the fact that the hours of the ordinary schools (9 to 12, and 2 to 4 or 5) did not fit in with the working hours of the factory children. " When, therefore, the master of a Factory determines to avail himself . . . of the full period allowed by law for the employment of children between 9 and 13 years of age, he must contrive to establish some kind of school which shall be accessible to his factory children at broken periods of the day, when ordinary schools are not available for them."[33] " Where good schools are open to Factory children," he continued, " I do not observe any reluctance on the part of parents that they should be sent to such schools; although the parents are, of course, disinclined to pay a twelfth part of their children's earnings, in order that they may remain two hours every day with a tattered spelling-book in their hands in some room which is called a school, under the valueless tuition of the over-looker's wife or daughter, or of some other ignorant person who is metamorphosed into a teacher for the purpose of a literal compliance with the educational provisions of the Factories Act."[34]

Saunders painted a vivid picture of the conditions that obtained in many of the factory schools in his district. Baker, his Superintendent, had been particularly distressed, he said, at the wretched buildings and the incompetent teachers. " The engine-man, the slubber, the burler, the over-looker, the wife of any one of these, the small shop-keeper, or the next-door neighbour, with six or seven small children on the floor and in her lap, are by turns found ' teaching the young idea how to shoot.' "[35] In proof of this assertion he instanced some of the vouchers of school attendance that he had met in the course of his inspection: —

" this to sertify that 1838 thomas Cordingley as atend martha insep school tow hours per day January 6."
" The above Named Children has Been twelve Hours in this School after the Manner of Scollers in the past week—Mary Collins."
" This is to Certify that Eliza Johnson & John Johnson have attended my school two hours each day for the last six days and have been teached by me."

---

[32] *Ibid.* pp. 357-358.
[33] *Ibid.* p. 370.
[34] *Ibid.* p. 372.
[35] *Ibid.* p. 412. See J. M. Ludlow, *Progress of the Working Class, 1832-1867* (1867) p. 15.

" This his to Certify that Christina Walker Comes to my School one halfe of the week—Hannah Hargreaves."[36]

The joint report was devoted to the consideration of the defects of the Act, and to the recommendations they desired to make. " In the 20th clause it is enacted," said the Inspectors, " that the school may be chosen by the parents or guardians of the child. Parents often choose, not the best, but the cheapest school; and it sometimes happens that, on this ground, they refuse to send their children to an excellent school at the Factory, at a moderate fee, because they can get what they call ' schooling ' elsewhere at a cheaper rate. . . . To meet such cases, as well as those where the mill-occupier employs a totally unfit person as a teacher on his premises, and those cases, also, where the children are taught in an unhealthy place, we think it desirable that the power conferred on the Inspectors by the 23rd clause,[37] which, from the preceding clause being inoperative, cannot be exercised, should be made effective; and that no certificate of school attendance should be valid that has been given by any person who shall have been declared by an Inspector unfit to teach children, or whose school-room shall have been declared by an Inspector unfit to be used as such; requiring, of course, an intimation to the mill-occupier of such a declaration, before the certificates become invalid."

The 20th section of the Act provided that if a child had neither parent nor guardian the Inspector might order the employer to deduct from the child's weekly wage a sum not exceeding a penny in the shilling to meet the cost of schooling. " We are of opinion," said the Inspectors, " that in order to secure his fees to the schoolmaster, which he very often loses when he has to look to the children for them, it should be enacted, that in every case the occupier shall be entitled to deduct from the wages of the child such sum as may be approved of by the Inspector, not exceeding 3d. in each week, to pay for the schooling, and that, upon demand, he shall pay the sums so deducted to the schoolmaster."[38]

Many schools to which factory children were sent, continued the report, were not open on Saturday. Those over thirteen years of age generally had a partial holiday on that day, so it was not unreasonable that the younger children should have a holiday from school too, especially as they usually worked the full period of eight hours on Saturday. " We do not, however, recommend," added the Inspectors, " that the total number of hours of weekly school attendance should be diminished, but that, after attending

---

36 *Ibid.* pp. 412-413.
37 Section 23 empowered the Inspectors to disallow the salary of an incompetent teacher. Section 22 authorized them to establish schools where necessary.
38 *Ibid.* p. 424.

at least two hours on each of five working days of the week, the remaining two may be made up, either by staying longer on all or any one of those five days, or by attendance at a Sunday School, producing a certificate of the same. What we now recommend amounts to no more than this, that the children shall have permission to have a holiday at school every Saturday, if they attend 12 hours the rest of the week."[39]

The Inspectors recommended that the form of the school attendance voucher should be set out in a schedule to the new statute, and not left to their individual discretion. It should state not only the number of days and hours of attendance, but also the periods of the day when the children were at school, " because it will afford . . . useful information as to the eight hours' employment of the children in the Factory, which may be either together or separately, at any time between half-past five in the morning and half-past eight in the evening, that is, within a space of 15 hours."[40]

One of the chief difficulties encountered by the Inspectors in enforcing the educational clauses had been due to the provision that a child was not to be employed unless he produced on Monday morning a voucher of school attendance for the previous week. " As the law now stands," they said, " if a child do not, on a fixed day of every week produce a certificate of his having attended a school for two hours at least for six out of seven days of the week next preceding, his master must discharge him. As this is very often productive of inconvenience to his master, and is in truth punishing him for the fault of the child, we think it only reasonable that he should have two weeks to look out for a substitute before being obliged to dismiss the offender, and that if the parent of the

---

[39] The fact that ordinary schools were usually closed on Saturday made it practically impossible for many children to attend six days of the week as prescribed by section 21. In order to meet this difficulty Horner had, by his 17th regulation, recognised attendance at Sunday School as part of the twelve hours' instruction, while in regulation 15 he had used the words " attend school twelve hours in each week." The Manchester Short-time Committee quoted this as another example of his conniving at the evasion of the Act. " An attempt was made," they said in their memorial to the Home Secretary, " to evade . . . the Act by means of certain printed instructions, to which was officially attached the name of Mr. Inspector Horner, those instructions suggesting in substance that the twelve hours of education . . . required to be equally distributed over six out of seven days of the week, might be made up without regard to such distribution, so long as the aggregate number of hours for the week was attended to: thus . . . enabling the mill-owners to transfer the greater part, if not the whole, of the twelve hours to the Sabbath day." Horner explained the position without difficulty, but considered it prudent to issue an advertisement setting out the true meaning of the regulations (26th July, 1836), *Parl. Papers* (1837) L, pp. 203, 208.

[40] *Parl. Papers* (1839) XLII, p. 425.

child is punished by a small fine, and the fault is not repeated, the child should not lose his situation. We recommend, therefore, that it should be lawful for the occupier of a Factory to employ a child without a school certificate during any time, not being more than two weeks together, on requiring from such child payment of the penalty of sixpence for each week during which such child shall be employed, without having attended school, as required by the Act; and that the occupier shall deduct the penalty from the wages next due to the child, besides the sum allowed to be deducted for payment of the schooling, and shall pay the amount of the penalty in the manner provided for the payment of other penalties."[41]

Section 22, continued the report, authorizing the Inspectors to establish schools where necessary, was wholly inoperative, since no provision was made for supplying the money which would be required. In the districts of Horner and Saunders several manufacturers had declared themselves willing to unite in supporting a school, and it was probable that some such plan would soon come into effect, especially if Government assistance was made available, and " if it were enacted that it shall be lawful for any number of persons to agree with each other for the establishment of a school for the use of the children employed in Factories, and to make rules for the management and for defraying the charges thereof, and to insert in their agreement penalties for the breach of conditions therein, and that the penalties may be recovered and applied as other penalties under the Act." When an Inspector thought that a new school was desirable it should also be made lawful for the Lords Commissioners of the Treasury to appropriate such sums as were necessary from any money granted by Parliament for the purpose of education.[42]

The Inspectors' observations and recommendations made a considerable impression, and many of them were incorporated in the new bill introduced by Fox Maule in February, 1839. All factory children (except those employed in silk mills) should, it was proposed, attend school for twelve hours a week, including at least two hours on each of five working days. The mill-occupier was to deduct from the wages a sum not exceeding threepence a week, which was to be paid to the schoolmaster.[43] Employment was still to be conditional on the production of a voucher of school attendance, the form of which was now prescribed, but it was provided that a child might be employed without such a voucher

---

41 *Ibid*. p. 425.

42 *Ibid*. p. 426.

43 Ashley proposed that the sum to be deducted should not exceed twopence, and succeeded in carrying this amendment by 96 votes to 51. *Hansard* (1839) XLVIII, 1091.

for not more than two consecutive weeks on payment of a penalty
of sixpence for each week he had not attended school. No voucher
was to be valid if it had been given by a person who had been
declared by an Inspector unfit to teach children, or whose premises
had been declared unsuitable.[44]

The 18th clause declared that it was to be lawful for factory
owners to agree together to establish schools, and that when the
agreement had been approved by an Inspector and deposited with
the Clerk of the Peace, any penalties incurred under the agreement
were to be recoverable as other penalties under the Act. This clause,
innocuous as it appeared at first sight, aroused much controversy.
Sir James Graham declared that it interfered with people's right to
combine for the purposes of education under the religious form
they chose. It would give arbitrary power to the Inspector to
approve the system agreed, and if the Inspector was a dissenter
and the mill-owners were churchmen, the Inspector would naturally
object to a system founded on their principles.[45] Mr. Slaney
supported this objection, asking what would become of the children
of dissenters or Roman Catholics if the factory school was based
on a national system, and if the Inspectors were not allowed to
meddle with the terms of the agreement made by the owners? The
matter was finally settled by the addition of a proviso that no
agreement for the establishment of joint factory schools should
authorize the education of a child in a religious creed other than
that professed by the parents.[46]

The bill of 1839 was ultimately withdrawn, but the attempt
it made to deal with the problem of educating factory children
marked a definite advance in all directions save one, and that the

---

[44] I hereby certify, That the undermentioned child [or, children] employed in the Factory of   situated in   has [or, have]
attended the School kept by me at   for the number of hours, and
at the time on each day specified in the columns opposite to his [her, or
their] name [or, names] during the week ending on Saturday, the
day of   One thousand eight hundred and   , and that
the causes of absence stated are true to the best of my belief.

Name of Child	Sun.	Mon.	Tues.	Wed.	Thur.	Fri.	Sat.	Total Hours	Causes of Absence
	Time	Time	Time	Time	Time	Time	Time		
	to	to	to	to	to	to	to		

(Signed)   Schoolmaster [or Schoolmistress].
                    the   day of   18   .

[45] *Hansard* (1839) XLVIII, 1416.
[46] *Ibid*. 1418.

most crucial. The omission to make provision from the public funds for the building and maintenance of schools was not due to inadvertence or to mere inertia, but to a basic difficulty that was to leave an abiding mark on the national system of education. The problem of religious teaching, which had aroused such anxieties when joint factory schools had been suggested, would clearly be the subject of even more bitter contention when the sphere of operation was extended. In the meantime a new conception of the educational needs of the factory children was beginning to emerge, a conception that was due partly to suggestions now being made by the Inspectors, and partly to Lord Ashley's determination to force once again the whole issue of industrial legislation.

CHAPTER 12

ASHLEY'S COMMITTEE, 1840

THE FAILURE of Fox Maule's bills in 1838 and 1839 was a cruel blow to the sanguine expectations of those who had hoped to see the speedy passing of an amending act to remedy what were now universally recognized as defects in the existing law. Hope, it is true, had again been deferred, but the delay afforded time for further reflection, and made it possible to build on firmer and more secure foundations.[1] Once again the initiative came from Lord Ashley, who on 3rd March, 1840, moved " That a Select Committee be appointed to inquire into the operation of the Act for the Regulation of Mills and Factories, and to report their opinion thereon to the House."[2] The suggestion met with general approval, and on 11th March, the Committee, presided over by Ashley himself, and including among its members Fielden, Hindley, Brotherton and Fox Maule, began its formidable task. When it rose on 14th July it had examined at length 26 witnesses,[3] whose evidence, set forth in six reports, covered 914 pages in the parliamentary papers.[4] The recommendations of the Committee were presented to the House on 18th February, 1841,[5] when Ashley recorded in his diary, " Concluded our Report to-day on Mills and Factories, and presented it to the House. To God above be all the glory! Great and signal has been the support I have received under great difficulties; may He continue it in the final difficulties of its passage through Parliament. Considering the nature of the Committee, its objects and members, we have been wonderfully harmonious."[6]

This report was of the first importance, not because it contained any strikingly original suggestions, but because summarizing the views of those who had first-hand experience of the working of the law, it offered for the consideration of Parliament a closely-reasoned, scientific programme of reform based on a careful and intelligent examination of all the available evidence. " It was not a new law that was required by the House," said the

---

[1] See L. Horner, *On the Employment of Children in Factories* (1840) p. 6.
[2] *Hansard* (1840) LII, 860.
[3] The four Inspectors, 7 Superintendents, 4 doctors, 7 mill-occupiers and 4 operatives.
[4] *Parl. Papers* (1840) X.
[5] *Parl. Papers* (1841) IX, p. 557 *ff*.
[6] E. Hodder, *The Life and Work of the seventh Earl of Shaftesbury*, (1893) p. 177.

Committee, " but the fulfilment of the intention of the existing law," and having investigated the operation of Althorp's Act section by section, they put forward recommendations the majority of which, incorporated in the Act of 1844, determined the whole course of future factory legislation.

The first section, forbidding persons under eighteen years of age to work between 8.30 p.m. and 5.30 a.m., was fairly well observed, declared the Committee, and it was now exceptional to find young people employed during the night.   They suggested that the age limit might well be raised to twenty-one, and in view of the fact that the spread-over of fifteen hours made evasion easy, especially in rural districts, they proposed that the working day should be reduced by one hour, *i.e.* from 6 a.m. to 8 p.m.[7]

The third, fourth and fifth sections, regulating the making up of lost time, were examined at considerable length.   The Inspectors complained that these sections were almost universally invoked to justify excessive working, the fourth section, authorizing an extension of the factory day when an accident stopped the machinery being, in the words of Horner, " productive of the grossest violations of the law, without the possibility of our checking it."[8]   Any trivial accident was held sufficient to bring the clause into operation—" a shaft broken or an escape of gas, or any small accident that may have occurred at a period some months before our visit."[9]   " We find," said Horner, " that the people have been working at a certain time 13 hours a day; we ask why?   He says ' Oh, the shaft broke.'   It is impossible for us to say that the shaft did not break, or that it was not broken, or a screw taken out on purpose."[10]   Howell's evidence fully confirmed Horner's allegations.   " I found," he stated, " at a cotton mill, that the people had been working over-time; I inquired the reason, and I was told that they were fetching up lost time.   It was entered, on a particular day, so many hours lost, in virtue of the 4th section, and in consequence of an extraordinary accident.   On questioning the hands, I said, ' You lost so much time on such a day?'—' Yes, sir.'   ' What was the cause?'—' There was a dinner to Mr. O'Connell, and we had a holiday.'   And therefore the fracture to the steam-engine was coincident with the holiday, and the gentleman who owned that mill had the credit of giving a holiday, and at the same time recovered the time afterwards by virtue of the 4th section."[11]

---

7 *Parl. Papers* (1841) IX, p. 565.
8 *Parl. Papers* (1840) X.   Qn. 230.
9 *Ibid*. Qn. 234.
10 *Ibid*. Qn. 241.
11 *Ibid*. Qn. 2204.

The operatives resented making up lost time after having worked twelve hours,[12] but the masters were strongly opposed to any alteration of the law. Henry Ashworth, whose spinning and weaving mills at Turton, near Bolton, were cited as models of what such establishments should be,[13] thought that great hardship would result if the section was cancelled. " Why should any man who has his property embarked in machinery be deterred from using it honestly and fairly?" he demanded,[14] while Birley of Manchester asserted that if the power to make up lost time was refused, " it would be a case of great hardship to the work-people; if we are not allowed to work up lost time, they will feel the inconvenience more than we shall, in loss of wages, because they are paid by the quantity of work they do."[15]

In the opinion of the Inspectors the best way to check evasions of section 5, permitting the making up of time lost through want or excess of water, would be to prohibit extended hours altogether if the mill had both water- and steam-power available. In these cases, said Horner, " frauds may be committed that are extremely difficult of detection or proof. . . . There may be such a stoppage of the water-wheel as may affect only a part of the machinery; the steam-engine is brought immediately in aid, and no time is really lost; but it is set down in the book, and truly, that the water-wheel was stopped from want or excess of water, and upon that not only is the time of work extended from the machinery driven by the water-power, but the whole mill is worked over-time.[16] " The 5th section," declared Howell, " is one which has given me a monstrous deal of trouble. . . . I have almost on every occasion found them working at night, under the plea of the 5th section. They have always either too much or too little water."[17]

The Committee was fully alive to the difficulty of framing regulations in such a way as to render the law effective while at the same time safeguarding the legitimate interests of the manufacturers. For this reason they did not feel able to make any specific suggestions, but contented themselves with bringing

[12] Evidence of John Lawton, a Manchester spinner. " They have expressed themselves strongly on that point, that they would rather lose their wages than work the time up." Qn. 8523.

[13] W. Cooke Taylor, *Notes of a Tour in the Manufacturing Districts of Lancashire* (1842) pp. 21,23.—" Fruit trees, unprotected by fence, railing, or palisade, are trained against the main wall of the building, and in the season the ripe fruit hangs temptingly within reach of every operative who goes in and out of the mill. There is not an instance of even a cherry having been plucked . . . . The working rooms are lofty, spacious, and well-ventilated, kept at an equable temperature, and scrupulously clean."

[14] *Parl. Papers* (1840) X, Qn. 4035.

[15] *Ibid.* Qn. 4355.

[16] *Ibid.* Qn. 404.

[17] *Ibid.* Qn. 2205.

the matter to the notice of Parliament, making a strong plea that this vexed question should receive the most careful consideration when the time came to amend the law as a whole.

The sixth section of the Act, regulating the time to be allowed for meals, was a classic example of imperfect drafting, for, while obviously intended to apply to all protected persons, it referred specifically only to those whose labour was limited to twelve hours a day, *i.e.* to young people between thirteen and eighteen years of age. Despite the opinion of the Law Officers " that it is not legal to employ children on any work whatever connected with the machinery or apparatus of the mill,"[18] at those times, the Inspectors found the utmost difficulty in securing a meal interval for children. Many of them were confined to the factory to clean the machinery during their meal-times,[19] and it was impossible to bring a successful action against the employer unless it could be proved that their work had been prolonged beyond the maximum of eight hours. Many mill-owners, too, reduced the meal-time by a few minutes, in order to secure increased production. " They generally infringe five minutes, sometimes six or seven; but, on a general scale, not less than five minutes at breakfast and dinner. . . . The engine starts before the expiration of the half hour, and when the engine starts, the people are expected to start with it."[20]

The Committee recommended that the section should be re-drafted in such a way as to make it clear that children as well as young persons were included within its scope. They considered that the first interval should not be earlier than 7.30 a.m., and the latest not after 7.30 p.m., one hour being allowed between 11 a.m. and 3 p.m. During meal-times it should be made illegal for any child or young person to remain in any room in which machinery was in motion, or in which any manufacturing process was being carried on. In order to prevent evasions of the law by the pretended employment of young persons by relays, all those between thirteen and twenty-one years of age should be required to have their meals at one and the same time—a point that had been strongly urged by Horner,[21] and incorporated in Fox Maule's bill of 1839.

The section prohibiting the employment of children under nine years of age was very generally observed, but the Committee noted Horner's opinion that there was " a very great disposition on the part of parents to encourage the working of their children

---

[18] Sanders' Report, 2nd October, 1837. *Parl. Papers* (1838) XXVIII, p. 113. *Parl. Papers* (1840) X, Qn. 2221.
[19] Horner's Report, 31st December, 1840. *Parl. Papers* (1841) X, p. 176.
[20] *Parl. Papers* (1840) X, Qns. 8537, 8538.
[21] *Ibid.* Qn. 1268.

under the prescribed age."²² All were agreed as to the expediency, under existing conditions, of keeping the minimum age for factory work at nine, even the owners of silk mills considering that to employ younger children would be unwise.²³ Those who had suggested that the age should be lowered had pre-supposed a further reduction in the number of hours worked, Horner being inclined to think that children might safely be employed at the age of seven if they were limited to six hours a day.²⁴

When they came to consider the 8th section, restricting children under thirteen to forty-eight hours' labour a week, the Committee, grappling with a problem that lay at the root of the whole system of limitation, proposed a remedy that was to have the most far-reaching results.²⁵ The law in its present form, they declared, was frequently and grossly violated. The number of convictions afforded no criterion of the number of offences—" a prosecution for over-working a hundred children on any one day would expose the offender to no more than a single penalty; which might be 20s., or less, at the discretion of the magistrate."²⁶ Remedial measures were necessary, if only in justice to those honest manufacturers who were anxious to obey the law, and who found themselves at a disadvantage in competing with less scrupulous rivals. The children, too, needed protection, for under existing conditions, said the Committee, they " may be employed eight hours a day, and those eight may be taken at any time of the fifteen hours between half-past five in the morning and half-past eight at night, and practically they are now employed at all hours within those limits; and they are, in a great proportion of instances, either in or about the factory the whole day, thus affording many opportunities for their being employed illegally."

The Committee considered that it would be much better to restrict the employment of those under thirteen years of age " to half the working day, divided by the general dinner-hour of the factory," but since it would be inconvenient to restrict to precisely six hours because the dinner-time did not always divide the day into two equal parts, they proposed a system of alternate morning and afternoon work. If the mill, for instance, started at 5.30 a.m., allowed half an hour for breakfast, and stopped for dinner at noon, it would be easy to arrange two periods of six hours each; but if the dinner-time was fixed at 1 p.m. it would be necessary for the morning set to work seven hours, and the afternoon set five

²² *Ibid.* Qn. 424.
²³ *Ibid.* Qns. 9263, 9590.
²⁴ *Ibid.* Qns. 413, 1270-1286.
²⁵ *Parl. Papers* (1841) IX, pp. 568-569.
²⁶ *Parl. Papers* (1840) X, Qns. 492-495.

hours. The two sets could be changed over each month, thus ensuring an average day of six hours without disturbing established customs.

For some time there had been much speculation as to the advantage of employing two sets of children for six hours a day instead of working them by relays for eight hours. Robert Baker asserted that when he was employed as medical adviser by the Leeds manufacturers as early as 1828 he had been empowered to put children on half-time employment if he thought the state of their health made such a reduction in working hours necessary. " This," he said, " was the origin of the half-time system; and these terms alone, independently of any other evidence, seem to me to practically prove that at that date there was an outcry, a cause for the course which these gentlemen adopted in defence of their reputation; and that they at least took steps voluntarily to remedy the evil complained of."[27] It was not until the Act of 1833 had been in operation for some years, however, that the proposal to adopt the half-time system universally was seriously considered. In June, 1840, Saunders reported that a number of mill-occupiers in Bradford had submitted a plan for reducing the labour of young persons between thirteen and eighteen years of age to eleven hours a day, and for employing those under thirteen for half the day only. " The principle of reducing the hours of labour of those children who work by relays," he said, " gives almost universal satisfaction to those who have hitherto employed them, and they are best able to judge of its effect on the operation of the mill." It was believed that an enactment that no child employed before noon should work after 1 p.m. on the same day would be advantageous both to mill-occupiers and to the children. There might be hardship in districts where there was a scarcity of labour, but this difficulty could be met by permitting children to work six hours a day at the age of eight.[28]

Horner thought that the half-time system had much to recommend it—it would be easier for the owners to administer, and it would facilitate the detection of over-working, since each set of children would leave the factory at the same time. The reduction in the children's wages which would inevitably ensue might inflict some hardship on individual families, but parents as a body would not suffer, because the same total of wages would be

---

[27] *Transactions of the National Association for the Promotion of Social Science* (1859) p. 554.
[28] *Parl. Papers* (1840) XXIII, p. 43. Saunders had at one time expressed the opinion that children under nine might safely be employed for eight hours a day (Report, 12th October, 1836. *Parl. Papers* (1837) XXXI, p. 83), but later he had suggested a maximum of six hours if the age limit was reduced. (Report, 1st January, 1839. *Parl. Papers* (1839) XIX, p. 453).

paid, though it would be distributed more widely as a result of the employment of children who would otherwise be debarred from working, " more particularly if they could be admitted as early as eight years of age, which, with the supposed limitation, could be done, not only without injury, but with great advantage to the children." But the suggested innovation, he thought, was not free from danger, and would " render caution still more necessary in guarding the entrance to the full day's work."[29]

He elaborated his view in his book *On the Employment of Children in Factories.*[30] " There appears to be but one practicable way," he said, " in which a limitation of the hours of the children's labour can be secured. . . . It is this, that no child under thirteen years of age shall be allowed to work more than half a day, the day to be divided by the general dinner hour of the factory. There would thus be a morning set and an afternoon set of children. The dinner is a marked break: it is the longest interval, and, in general, it is about the middle of the day. But in as much as the dinner hour varies, in different parts of the kingdom, that circumstance must not be lost sight of. In a great number of places in England it is from twelve to one o'clock; in others from half-past twelve to half-past one; in others, from one to two. Where they begin work at half-past five in the morning, and dine at twelve, allowing half an hour for breakfast, there is an equal division of the working day of twelve hours: where they begin at the same hour, but dine at one o'clock, the morning set would work seven hours, and the afternoon set five hours. Therefore, besides the enactment that no child shall work more than one half of the day, and that the other half day shall be either wholly before dinner or wholly after it, it will be necessary to declare that no child shall be allowed to work more than seven hours in any one day, or more than forty-two hours in the week. . . . If this plan were adopted, the limit of admission might safely be lowered to *eight* years instead of nine, as it is at present; for no child of eight years of age would get any harm by working half a day in the factory, especially in the afternoon; and it would make up to many parents for the diminution of the wages by the reduction from eight hours' work, by enabling them to have another child employed." The advantages of this system, added Horner, would be that the adult operatives would always have a full complement of young hands to assist them, the records of the children's working time would be simplified, and there would be less temptation to break the law.

The recommendations of Ashley's Committee followed closely the proposals of the Inspectors. Children under thirteen years

---

[29] Report, 31st December, 1840. *Parl. Papers* (1841) X, p. 176.
[30] pp. 8-11.

of age, they suggested, should work not more than seven hours a day, or forty-two hours a week; they should be employed " either before the commencement of the time allowed for the dinner of the workers in the factory, between 13 and 21 years of age, or after the expiration of that time; but no child who shall have been employed at all before the general dinner hour commences shall be employed after the said dinner-hour on the same day." If this scheme were adopted it would be possible to make much better provision for the children's education. The morning set would have the whole of the day, after dinner, for schooling and recreation, while the afternoon set could get up later and attend school before they commenced work. Both sets would be able to attend the National and British schools, which were usually open only between 9 and 5, and " other schools of a respectable kind would also be available, and thus the mockery of education, now so common to keep within the letter of the law, would be done away with."[31]

The evidence laid before the Committee led them to believe that the schooling clauses of the Act had been better observed in recent years, though many manufacturers were still opposed to them. The attendance vouchers were usually produced in accordance with the 21st section, and they were rarely fictitious, though they afforded no guarantee as to the adequacy of the education to which they testified. " In a great many instances," said Howell, " there is a nominal observance. The children attend two hours daily, but get no education that is worth having." In order to comply with the Act a room in the factory was often converted into a school-room, and one of the work-people into a schoolmaster —a practice which made it easy to work the children excessive hours.[32]

Horner drew attention to another weakness of the Act, which had omitted to grant the Inspectors power to enter schools that were outside the factory premises, and which gave them no effective control over the schoolmasters. No standards of education were prescribed, and he concluded that education was too often merely a mockery, not only in the factory schools, but in many of the

---

[31] Cf. L. Horner, op. cit. p. 10. " There would be no difficulty in getting them admitted to those good schools from which the masters now exclude them, on account of their dirty working dresses."

[32] Parl. Papers (1840) X, Qns. 2292-2296. In his report of 30th December, 1839, Horner mentioned the case of the school attached to one of the largest cotton mills in Lancashire. " About fifty children were crammed into a very small room as thick as they could stand, with the schoolmaster, a man with one arm only, in the midst of them, the atmosphere of the room being almost suffocating."—Parl. Papers (1840) XXIII, p. 14.

other schools that were open to the children of the working classes. He had come across instances of children being obliged to attend school between 5.30 a.m. and 7.30 a.m., before they began their work in the mill, or between 7.30 p.m. and 9.30 p.m., " when the children, as they themselves told me, after their day's work, almost constantly fall asleep."[33]

The Committee considered that if employment was limited to half a day, as they had suggested, the factory children would be able to attend the best day schools; but since the British and National schools were not open on Saturday, they recommended that the children should be required to attend not more than two and a half hours a day, on five days of the week only. No schooling certificate should be valid in respect of attendance before 7 a.m. or after 7 p.m., and the Inspectors and Superintendents should be authorized to refuse the certificates of teachers who were unfit to give instruction because of their gross ignorance, extreme age, or immoral character, or whose premises and equipment were unsuitable. The mill-occupiers should be required to deduct from the child's wages the school fee, not exceeding two-pence a week, which they were to pay to the schoolmaster.[34]

The problem of providing funds to establish schools was one that the Committee felt itself unable to solve. " The Committee feel," said the report, " that there must still exist cases in which, from the extreme remoteness and seclusion of their mills, many mill-owners will find a difficulty of access to established schools. For this evil they can devise no precise remedy. It might be dangerous, in many respects, to hold the Government responsible for providing schools in such cases; and they can only express their sincere and cordial hope, that the rapid progress of the prevailing feeling in favour of a moral and religious education of the operative classes will speedily come in aid of the difficulty."[35]

The problem of ascertaining the age of children and young persons was fully discussed, the evidence of the Inspectors in this connection being weighed with scrupulous care.[36] " There is no obstacle so great in the whole range of factory legislation," observed the Committee, " as that which is presented by the intricacies in the way of ascertaining correctly the ages of children; the baptismal register can render but slight service, as in some cases the children have not been baptized at all. . . . Not only is there the uncertainty whether the document relates to the individual child, but the inspectors must be on their guard against the

---

33 *Parl. Papers* (1840) X, Qns. 827-830.
34 *Parl. Papers* (1841) IX, pp. 573-576.
35 *Ibid.* p. 577.
36 *Ibid.* pp. 570-571.

forgeries and falsehoods of the parents themselves." Charles Trimmer, one of Howells' Superintendents, thought that in certain circumstances the baptismal certificate might have provided the best check, " but now," he added, " they are christening their children, and getting the day of their birth dated back."[37]   Horner said that the clergy were usually willing to give certificates from the register of baptisms, " but it is not always clear if it relates to the individual child."[38]   " To show the sort of thing that is some-times done," he said, " I may state that I found at Rochdale, I think it was last July, a boy working with his baptismal certificate, and upon looking at that baptismal certificate, I found that he had been baptized about a week before. He had been rejected by the surgeon; he went to the parish church, was baptized, an extract was given from the register, and, what appears to me an exceedingly improper thing, the clergyman had stated that the boy was born so-and-so. He put down upon his certificate the statement of the parents that the boy was born so-and-so, which made him 13, of course. I immediately brought the subject under the notice of the curate, a very respectable gentleman, and he said he was not the least aware of the object for which the certificate was wanted. . . . I told the mill-owner, ' I will not receive that; it is good for nothing, it is a fraud.' "[39]   The parents, who were usually anxious for their children to work the full twelve hours, resorted to every form of trickery in order to evade the law, and Howell cited, as one of the greatest obstacles he had met " the very prevalent habit of falsehood in which the factory children are trained; ' going 14 ' or ' passed 13 ' is the ready answer they have been taught to give."[40]

" There remains, then," said the Committee, " the physiological test alone, whereby a medical man may judge, from personal inspection, the age and capacity of the child for full labour. This, again, must be subjected to a threefold abatement; first, from the ignorance of some who set up for surgical practitioners; secondly, the dishonesty or negligence of others; and thirdly, from the defective state of science itself in this particular."[41]   The only remedy against fraud and evasion seemed to be to confine the power to issue certificates of age to those surgeons who had been appointed for the purpose by an Inspector. If a duly appointed certifying surgeon refused a certificate, recourse might be had to one who had not been appointed, but in this case the certificate

37 Parl. Papers (1840) X, Qn. 2692.
38 Ibid. Qn. 427.
39 Ibid. Qn. 630.
40 Ibid. Qn. 2239.
41 Parl. Papers (1841) IX, p. 570.

should be counter-signed by a magistrate, who should be required to testify that the child had actually appeared before him.[42]

Another safeguard that the Committee thought should be introduced was the amendment of the wording of the certificate. The present lack of precision often had the oppposite effect from what was intended, for it was frequently the means of forcing the child into premature employment.

Much evidence was adduced concerning the inadequacy of the penalties imposed by many benches of magistrates who used their powers of mitigation in such a way that in certain parts of the country the mill-owners were able to break the law with impunity. "Masters have told me," said Trimmer, "that it would answer their purpose better to pay a fine occasionally, when I came round, than to obey the law."[43]   In Saunders' district, during the period 1834-1839, of 703 penalties imposed, 543 had been 40s. or less, and 439 had been 20s. or less; while of the 20 convictions for over-working children obtained at Rochdale in the quarter ending July, 1838, a penalty of 20s. had been imposed in eight cases, and a penalty of 5s. only in seven other instances.[44]   Since section 43 of the Act provided that only one penalty should be recoverable for any one description of offence from any one person on any one day, there was no limit to the abuses that might be practised, for only one information could be laid at one time, no matter how many children were discovered to be overworking.

The remedy proposed by the Committee was that the provision in Hobhouse's Act should be revived, and that no magistrate who was the owner of a mill, or a near relative of an owner, should be allowed to adjudicate on cases under the Factory Act.   They also urged that there should be a distinct penalty for each offence, and that a scale of minimum penalties should be introduced.[45]

Recommendations were also made respecting other sections of the Act that experience had shown needed amendment.   Although the proviso that work should cease on Christmas Day and Good Friday was on the whole fairly well obeyed, the wording of section

---

[42] This proviso, it was considered, would put an end to the abuse of the magistrate's counter-signing in the absence of the child.   " I do not suppose," said Horner, " that in one case in a hundred the magistrate ever sees the child; I may state, what is a very common practice, that periodically the certificate-book containing perhaps a hundred certificates, is sent up to the petty sessions, and the magistrate as fast as he can sign, puts his name, without asking any questions whatever."—*Parl. Papers* (1840) X, Qn. 602.

[43] *Ibid.* Qn. 2626.

[44] *Parl. Papers* (1841) IX, p. 580.

[45] *Ibid.* pp. 580-584.

9 was vague. The observance of these holidays, said the Committee, should be made imperative, and the section should be
re-drafted so as to remove all doubts about its interpretation.[46]
The discretionary powers entrusted to the Inspectors had caused
much unnecessary friction, and their right to promulgate regulations
should cease, all requirements being contained in the Act itself.[47]
The salaries of the Superintendents were inadequate, and should
be increased substantially. Further appointments should be made,
so that the factories could be visited four times instead of three
times a year.[48] Section 26, providing that interior walls should be
lime-washed once a year, should be strictly enforced—it was a
proviso " extremely acceptable to the operatives."[49] Severe
penalties should be inflicted if the machinery was cleaned while
it was in motion, and dangerous parts of the machinery should be
boxed-off.[50]

Ashley's Committee concluded their investigations by considering the circumstances of children who were engaged in silk
mills and lace factories. The latter were outside the operation of
the Act altogether; the former were only partially protected, for
they were allowed to work ten hours a day irrespective of their
age, and they were not required to attend school. Within a few
months of the passing of the Act Saunders had drawn attention
to the dissatisfaction caused by the favoured position of the silk
and lace industries, and had stressed the unfair competition that
resulted when these mills were able to attract labour from the
textile factories that were fully regulated.[51] The Committee agreed
with the Inspectors " that these children both need and are entitled
to legislative protection," but owing to the unusual conditions
existing in the mills where silk was wound and thrown—conditions
that made it imperative to employ a considerable number of young
hands—they did not feel able to make any recommendation other
than that separate treatment should be considered.

The account[52] given by the Inspectors and Superintendents of
the working conditions of young people in the lace factories was
a grim indictment of the textile industry in its unregulated state.
" When the lace-machines are at work," said James Bury, a
Superintendent in Saunders' district, " they are generally at work
20 hours per day. When they give over at 8 o'clock on Saturday

---

46 *Ibid*. p. 569.
47 *Ibid*. p. 572.
48 *Ibid*. p. 584.
49 *Ibid*. p. 577.
50 *Ibid*. pp. 586-588.
51 Report, 28th December, 1833. *Parl. Papers* (1834) XLIII, p. 481.
52 *Parl. Papers* (1840) X, Qns. 3086-3326.

night, they lose of course 4 hours that day; then that is made up by their being worked the whole of the night on the Friday night; and the children from nine to fifteen years of age are obliged to be in the mills during the whole night and day too. Where the lace-mills are worked 24 hours a day, the children must be, during the whole of that 24 hours, either on the premises, or where they can be called out of bed whenever they are wanted." In Nottingham it was usual to run the machinery twenty hours a day, from four o'clock in the morning to midnight, and although the children whose duty it was to wind the bobbins and prepare the carriages, were not actually engaged the whole time, they had to be constantly available, ready to begin their work when the goods came off the machine.

"For similar reasons as those which have governed their opinion in the case of the silk trade," said the Committee, "and seeing the difficulties in bringing the lace manufacture under the same regulations as those which will apply to cottons, woollens and worsted, your Committee would recommend to the serious consideration of the House the condition of children and young persons employed in mills for the manufacture of lace, in order to their being placed under the regulations of a bill hereafter to be introduced."[53]

In their joint report dated 15th July, 1840,[54] the Inspectors made a strong plea for the early passing of an amending Act to remove those defects in the law exposed so fully in the report of Ashley's Committee. Early in 1841 Horner and Saunders having prepared for Fox Maule a digest of the evidence submitted to the Committee,[55] were charged with the task of drawing up a new bill, which received its first reading in the House on 26th March, 1841.[56]

The bill, introduced by Fox Maule, embodied the main recommendations of the Committee. The age of young persons,

---

[53] *Parl. Papers* (1841) IX, p. 595. The first attempt to regulate conditions in lace factories was made on 11th March, 1846, when T. S. Duncombe introduced a Bill to abolish night work. The measure was rejected on the second reading (20th May, 1846) by 151 votes to 66, the general feeling being that it would be impossible to impose control on an industry that was carried on, in many cases, in private houses; and that the complete prohibition of night work would affect the labour of adult males. (*Hansard*, LXXXIV, 975; LXXXVI, 914.) The provisions of the Factory Acts were not applied to lace manufacture until 1861, when the Lace Works Act was passed. (24 & 25 Vict., c. 117.)

[54] *Parl. Papers* (1840) XXIII, p. 47.

[55] Reports, 31st March, 1841. *Parl. Papers* (1841) sess. 2, VI, pp. 215, 218.

[56] Bill for Regulating the Employment of Children and Young Persons in Factories.—*Parl. Papers* (1841) II, p. 425.

who were restricted to twelve hours' work a day, was to be raised from eighteen to twenty-one; while children between the ages of nine and thirteen were to work not more than seven hours a day. The implications of the half-time system were recognized and accepted : no child employed before noon was to work after 1 p.m. on the same day, and attendance at school, between 7 a.m. and 7 p.m., was required for $2\frac{1}{2}$ hours a day on each of the five working days of the week. School holidays were not to exceed three weeks in the year, and the mill-occupier was to pay to the schoolmaster, in respect of each child, a sum not exceeding threepence a week, which he was authorized to deduct from the child's wages, the maximum deduction being fixed at one-twelfth of the total wages. Mill-occupiers were to be allowed to enter into agreements for the establishment of joint factory schools, but no further steps were taken to set up schools where none existed. It was proposed, however, to raise the standard of education in such schools as were available by authorizing the Inspectors to reject the certificates of any schoolmaster who was considered incompetent.

More stringent measures were to be adopted to prevent overworking. No young person was to be employed for more than sixty-nine hours a week, " or after the expiration of Twelve Hours from the time when any child or young person in the Factory first began to work in the morning, over and above the time allowed for meal times." The working day was to be reduced to fourteen hours, from 6 a.m. to 8 p.m., children and young persons being forbidden to work outside this period, except for the purpose of recovering lost time, in mills where the only moving power was the water-wheel. In these mills, if the machinery had been inactive owing to lack of, or excess of water, the time lost might be made up during the ensuing three months by employing children as early as 5 a.m. or as late as 9 p.m., provided they did not work more than the stipulated seven hours in any one day; but young persons might work at any time during the night, so long as they were limited to seventy-two hours a week, and thirteen hours in any period of twenty-four consecutive hours. All young persons were to have an hour and a half for meals at the same period of the day, between 7.30 a.m. and 7.30 p.m.; no child was to work more than five hours before 1 p.m. without a break of at least twenty minutes; and neither children nor young persons were to remain during meal-times in any room where a manufacturing process was being conducted. The factory hours were to be regulated by a public clock.

Drastic changes were to be made in the regulations governing the inspectorate. The four Inspectors were to continue in office, " one of whom shall be appointed by warrant under the sign manual, to be during Her Majesty's pleasure, Inspector-general of Factories." The Inspector-general was to be provided with a properly staffed office in London or Westminster; he was to make a report covering the whole field of inspection twice a year; he was to be consulted by his colleagues in drawing up rules for the guidance of the Sub-Inspectors (as the Superintendents were now to be called); and his concurrence was to be required when certifying surgeons were appointed. The Inspectors were to be assisted by not less than eighteen Sub-Inspectors, whose salaries were to be between £250 and £450 a year, in addition to travelling expenses. Both Inspectors and Sub-Inspectors were to have full right of access to factories and factory schools, and it was to be an offence to conceal any person from them when they were visiting the mills.

Certifying surgeons might be appointed by the Inspectors, but any other qualified medical man was to be allowed to grant certificates of age, providing such certificates were counted-signed, in the presence of the child, by a magistrate who was neither a mill-owner, nor the father, son, or brother of an owner. The Inspector was to fix the fees payable to the surgeon in accordance with the scale set out,[57] and a sum of 3d. was to be deducted from the wages of the child in respect of whom a certificate had been granted.

Ashley's Committee had recommended that silk mills should be the subject of a separate measure, and accordingly, on 30th March, 1841, Fox Maule introduced a bill[58] to regulate this branch of the industry. The administrative provisions were, for the most part, identical with those of the Factory Bill, but the peculiar circumstances of the silk trade made it necessary to incorporate certain features that departed in important particulars from the main trend of development in the textile industry as a whole. The minimum age of employment was to be nine, but until they attained the age of thirteen children were to be permitted to work for ten hours a day or fifty-nine hours a week, exclusive of the daily hour and a half to be allowed for meals. They were not to be required to attend school, but were instead to be subject to an educational test, which required them to produce, either from a

---

[57] The maximum payment to the surgeon was to be one shilling for each person examined, plus a shilling for each mile he travelled from his residence to the factory where the examination took place. His emolument was not to exceed five shillings in respect of any one visit, unless more than ten certificates were granted, in which case he was to receive sixpence for each certificate.

[58] A Bill for Regulating the Employment of Children and Young Persons in Silk Factories.—*Parl. Papers* (1841) II, p. 459.

clergyman of the established church, or from some other licensed minister, a certificate testifying that they were able to read any part of the New Testament. The child was to be re-examined each year to ensure that he had made satisfactory progress since the last test, and it was further proposed that no young person under fourteen years of age (*i.e.* during the first twelve months when he would normally be entitled to work sixty-nine hours a week) should be employed more than ten hours a day unless he could read fluently any part of the Bible, write a fair copy in large and small hand, and understand the first four rules in arithmetic.

These proposals, interesting as they were, were not destined to be the subject of debate in Parliament, for the days of Lord Melbourne's Whig ministry were numbered. On 3rd May, 1841, the Prime Minister had indicated to the House that he was prepared to consider a change in the Corn Laws. "There cannot be a doubt," wrote Ashley in his diary, "whatever be the final issue, the Ministers are thinking of a dissolution, and apprehending compulsory retirement. Successive defeats have loosened the cement, and a vigorous blow would batter down the wall. I believe they will 'go,' as the phrase is. . . . Horner writes me word that the Factory Bill is suspended indefinitely. . . . Suspended, forsooth! and thus another year is added to the period over which wrong and violence are to reign without control! The whole of last Session and the best half of this utterly lost; all the evidence will be stale, facts without point, and cases out of date; to say nothing of other opinions and other conduct in a succeeding Government."[59]
The blow fell on 4th June, 1841, when Sir Robert Peel's motion of "no confidence" received a majority of one in the House, and on 22nd June Parliament was dissolved. At the general election the Tories gained a substantial majority, and Peel took office, with Sir James Graham as his Home Secretary. How would the change of ministry affect the fortunes of the Factory Bill? The measure had never been a party issue, it is true, but Ashley was apprehensive, fearing that Peel would bow to the wishes of the manufacturers. In other quarters, however, there was a greater measure of optimism, for it had been observed that "the Whigs are most disposed to vote for popular measures, when on the bleak side of the Speaker's chair."[60] Any misgivings entertained by the reforming party were soon shown to be groundless, for Graham was determined to proceed with the factory question. He betrayed

---

[59] E. Hodder, *The Life and Work of the seventh Earl of Shaftesbury* (1893) pp. 179-180.
[60] "Alfred," *The History of the Factory Movement* (1857) Vol. II, p. 158.

little disposition to brook delays as his predecessor in office had done, and if, in the early days, he grasped the nettle a little too firmly, he was statesman enough to realize the fact, and by retreating from a position which was obviously untenable, he made it possible to achieve reform on the grand scale.

CHAPTER 13

GRAHAM'S BILLS, 1843 AND 1844

ON 28TH FEBRUARY, 1943, Lord Ashley moved "That an humble address be presented to Her Majesty, praying that Her Majesty will be graciously pleased to take into her instant and serious consideration the best means of diffusing the benefits and blessings of a moral and religious education among the working classes of her people." It had been estimated, he said, that there were over a million persons in the country who were denied the benefits of education, " but if we look forward to the next ten years, there will be an increase of at least 2,500,000 in the population; and should nothing be done to supply our want, we shall then have in addition to our present arrears, a fearful multitude of untutored savages." Despite the efforts of the National Society and of the dissenting bodies, there was still a great and terrible wilderness, as was evident from the reports of the Inspectors, who had quoted striking figures showing the extent of juvenile delinquency, ignorance, and moral depravity in the great manufacturing towns.[1]

It fell to Sir James Graham, the new Home Secretary, to reply on behalf of the Government. A man of deep religious convictions, and a staunch adherent of the established church, Graham was fully alive to the importance of education. " On this, both for children and for grown men and women, he placed his chief reliance for subduing the tendencies which he found strong and general to acts of violence—intimidation, rioting and insurrection."[2] But any general system of education required the provision of money from the public funds, and since teaching must be rooted in religion, sectarian differences might well cause difficulties. " A national scheme of education must be supported by national funds," he declared, " and recourse must be had at last either to parochial rates or to the public revenue. Religion cannot be separated from the system, and amidst the conflict of contending sects the State, if it make a choice, must prefer the established creed; and this preference is the signal for an attack on the measure, and for resistance to the rate or tax, which dissenters must pay, but the fruit of which they cannot share, if the religious instruction violate their belief. Experience proves that agreement on the fundamental

---

[1] *Speeches of the Earl of Shaftesbury* (1868) pp. 63-81. *Hansard* (1843) LXVII, 47-75.
[2] C. S. Parker, *Life and Letters of Sir James Graham* (1907) Vol. I, p. 336.

articles of the Christian faith as the basis of a mixed scheme of general instruction is delusive. . . . Religion, the keystone of education, is, in this country, the bar to progress."[3]

Despite these forebodings Graham hoped that in a matter of such vital import, sectional differences might be forgotten, and he therefore welcomed the suggestion put forward by Ashley. He hoped, he said, to induce the House to lay aside party feeling and religious strife, " and to endeavour to find out some neutral ground on which we can build something approaching to a scheme of national education, with a due regard to the just wishes of the established church on the one hand, and studious attention to the honest scruples of the dissenters on the other." Parliament had dealt with the education of factory children in so imperfect and unsatisfactory a manner as to render the provisions of the Act quite ineffective. Manufacturers were obliged to give some education, but there was no guarantee as to its quality or degree. A Roman Catholic mill-owner might establish a factory school, and make it a condition of employment that Protestant children should attend. His proposals, therefore, were designed not merely to raise the general standards of education, but to secure a religious basis for the teaching whilst safeguarding the rights of conscience.[4]

Lord John Russell warmly approved Graham's scheme, asking for a generous and sympathetic treatment of the problem of denominational instruction. " If it could be shown," he said, " that not one child of a dissenter need be excluded from these schools by the strictness of the rules imposed upon them—that there was no occasion for any parents to be alarmed for the religion of their children—then he should say that it would be far better to accept the regulations and not cavil at the parts of a scheme which they could not object to as a whole."[5] Sir R. H. Inglis sounded a note of warning, the first portent of the coming storm, when he insisted on the need for a full measure of sectarian instruction. He could not support any scheme of national and extended education, he averred, which, in the very first instance, would guard against the promotion of truth, and keep individuals from inculcating that which they sincerely believed to be the truth.[6] Hawes, the member

---

[3] Letter to Lord Brougham, 24th October, 1841. *Ibid*. pp. 338-339.

[4] *Hansard* (1843) LXVII, 75-89. Saunders, a staunch member of the Church of England, considered that the paramount duty imposed on him was " to afford every child at least the opportunity of being educated in the doctrine and principles of the Established Church." Many parents, he declared, were utterly indifferent to religious training. " Many would send their children to a school where the principles of Mahomet, or the worship of blocks and stones were inculcated, if only the school fee was less at such school than at the best school in the neighbourhood."—Report, 31st December, 1842. *Parl. Papers* (1843) XXVII, p. 322.

[5] *Hansard* (1843) LXVII, 93.

[6] *Ibid*. 104.

for Lambeth, was equally intransigent, holding that the proposals gave a preponderance of power to the established church. If the Home Secretary imagined that the protestant dissenters would acquiesce in any such arrangement, he was profoundly mistaken.[7]

Sir Robert Peel, pleading for a spirit of tolerance, and for a realistic approach to the whole question, reminded Inglis " that if they did rigidly abide by an exclusive system, the consequences must be, not a gain of converts to their faith, but that all must be left in the hopeless state in which they existed at present." If they said that they would establish no schools in which they did not attempt to gain converts to the established church, they " would utterly alienate from their side many whose support, under other circumstances, they might hope ultimately to gain."[8]

The House was not disposed, at this stage, to pay much heed to the discordant voices raised in protest against Graham's proposals and Ashley's motion was adopted without further debate.[9] On 7th March, the Queen's reply to the address was received. "The attention of my Government had been previously directed to the important object of increasing the means of moral and religious education among the working classes of my people. The assurance of your cordial co-operation in measures which I consider so necessary, confirms my hope that this blessing will be secured by legislative provisions."[10]

The broad outline of the pattern to which future legislation was to conform had by now begun to be fairly well defined, and the bill[11] that Graham introduced on 7th March, 1843, followed closely the proposals that Fox Maule had made two years before. The draft had already been submitted to the Inspectors the previous autumn,[12] and had the Government been able to settle the educational clauses to its satisfaction, the measure would doubtless have been brought forward earlier.[13]

Apart from the revolutionary proposals concerning the provision of schools, the bill differed from Fox Maule's measure in

7 *Ibid.* 112.

8 *Ibid.* 108-109.

9 *Ibid.* 114.

10 *Ibid.* 354.

11 A Bill for regulating the Employment of Children and young Persons in Factories, and for the better Education of Children in Factory Districts. —*Parl. Papers* (1843) II, p. 495.

12 Joint Report, December, 1842. *Parl. Papers* (1843) XXVII, p. 333.

13 *Cf. Minutes,* 7th February, 1843.—" The subjects waiting for the decision of the Government were the Educational Clauses and the Clauses involving any grants of money."—Vol. I, p. 180. Graham said that he had intended to introduce the bill in the spring of 1842, but he abstained because of the opposition of the Bishop of London.—C. S. Parker, *Life and Letters of Sir James Graham* (1907) Vol. I, p. 342.

that it fixed the minimum age for employment at eight years, and the maximum working day for children between eight and thirteen at six hours and a half. Children were to attend school, between the hours of 8 a.m. and 7 p.m., for at least three hours a day on five days of the week. Elaborate precautions were to be taken to ensure that an adequate standard of teaching was maintained, the Inspectors of Schools, working under the Committee of the Council on Education, being required to report to the Committee any cases where schoolmasters were incompetent or where premises were unsatisfactory. If arrangements could be made for the children concerned to attend a better school within two miles of the factory, the attendance certificates of the master upon whom the adverse report had been made were to be declared invalid.

Females were to be subject to the restrictions imposed on young persons until they attained the age of twenty-one; and the full range of regulations was to apply to silk mills. Of the one and a half hours allowed for meals, one hour was to be taken before 3 p.m., and no child or young person was to work for more than five hours before 1 p.m. without an interval of half an hour.

These provisions were the logical developments of what had gone before, but the educational clauses constituted an important, and indeed, a startling innovation. The schools to be established under the Act to cater for children employed in factories, and for other children part of whose family was so employed, were to be managed by bodies of trustees, each consisting of seven members. If the school served a single ecclesiastical district, the minister and two churchwardens were to be trustees *ex officio*; if it served more than one district the Bishop of the diocese was to choose a minister to act as clerical trustee, and he, in his turn, was to nominate two churchwardens. The four other trustees, two of whom were to be factory-occupiers, were to be chosen each year by the magistrates from those who were rated at an amount to be settled later, or who had contributed not less than one-tenth of the cost of the school building. A person who had given the site for a school was to be a trustee for life.

The trustees were to meet at least once a month under the chairmanship of the clerical trustee, who was to have a casting-vote. They were to decide the hours during which the school was to be kept open, the amount of the fee to be paid (not more than 3d. a week in the case of factory children), " the employment of each class during every hour of the day," the books and apparatus to be used, and the dates of the holidays, " which, exclusive of any holidays on any of the usual fasts and festivals of the Church," were not to exceed three weeks in the year. They were also to be responsible for the appointment of the schoolmaster, subject to the approval of the bishop " as regards the competency of such master to give religious instruction."

The master was to teach the Holy Scriptures, and was to employ no other book of religion whatever, but there was nothing to prevent the use of any part of the Church of England liturgy in divine worship in the school by the clerical trustee on Sunday, Christmas Day, Good Friday, and the usual fasts and festivals of the Church which the trustees had declared a holiday, so long as no scholar was required to attend contrary to the wishes of his parents. Instruction was to be given in the Catechism, and in such other portions of the liturgy of the established church as might be directed by the clerical trustee, who alone was to determine the mode of teaching, and the selection of the books, and who was authorized to require the schoolmaster to teach the Catechism and liturgy for not more than three hours on Sunday. No child was to be compelled to attend religious instruction if the parents objected, a provision which it was hoped would reconcile dissenters to the scheme.

The financial clauses proposed that part of the money necessary for the new schools that would be established should come from the central exchequer, the residue to be a charge on the local poor-rate. If the subscriptions raised in the district which the school was to serve were insufficient to enlarge an existing building, or to endow a new school, a memorial might be presented to the Committee of the Council on Education asking for assistance. The magistrates were then to submit a report to the Committee on the need for the school, and if their recommendations were approved, and if one-third of the necessary sum had already been obtained, a grant of a further third might be paid from the public funds, the balance being met by the issue of exchequer bills, repayable over a period of ten years from the poor-rate. The school thus provided was to look to local sources only for the income required to support it. The pupils were to pay fees not exceeding 3d. a week, and any deficit was to be met from the poor-rate, which could be increased by not more than 3d. in the pound for this purpose.

" I am afraid of elections by ratepayers, and of the presence of dissenting ministers on the Trust, side by side with the clergymen of the Establishment," wrote Graham on the eve of the first reading of the bill. " Mine is a measure of peace. I am afraid that such a compound would effervesce with one drop of acid, and the presence of sour ingredients must be anticipated."[14] When the terms of this measure of peace became known, however, the sour ingredients provoked not an effervescence merely, but an explosion, the

---

[14] Letter to the Rev. G. R. Gleig, 6th March, 1843.—C. S. Parker, *Life and Letters of Sir James Graham* (1907) Vol. I, pp. 343-344.

sustained and universal character of which shocked the complacency of the supporters of the bill though it did not altogether surprise the author.[15] Angry petitions poured in upon the Government by the thousand,[16] denouncing the proposals as an attempt to rivet the fetters of the established church on the dissenting bodies, which were particularly powerful in the manufacturing districts. " The worst part of the bill," declared one of its bitterest opponents, " is its daring attempt, not only to tax without the control, either direct or indirect, of the taxed, over the appropriation and management of their own money—but to aggrandise the secular power and lessen the spiritual and moral influence of the Church, by the oppression of other Christian forms of faith. . . . It is not right to compel support even for a worldly object from those who cannot conscientiously approve of that object. . . . Now this Bill does tax one creed, and many creeds, for the support of one which those creeds cannot approve. . . . If this Bill had been expressly devised for the purpose of arraying and uniting in one firm phalanx the hitherto severed bodies of the nonconforming community, of evoking the utmost strength of Dissent, and bringing it in direct collision with the Church, I will defy any measure to have more abundantly answered its end than Sir James Graham's Bill."[17]

" The Clerical Trustee," said another outraged evangelical, " has exclusive, unrestricted, irresponsible, and absolute power in directing the religious instruction to be given on Sunday and during the week, both as to manner and substance. . . . Many of the justices are clergymen, and nearly all are Tories; making it all but certain that the Trustees appointed will either be clergymen, or laymen favourable to the Established Church; and that an unnecessary number of schools under this Act will be authorised, to the prejudice of British and other non-Church schools already existing, and to a needless as well as unjustifiable increase of parochial burdens. Under pretence of excluding gentlemen from the exercise of authority in matters in which they have a personal or relative interest, probably nearly every magistrate of liberal

---

[15] See Graham's letter to Gladstone, March, 1843 (*Ibid.* p. 344).—
" By the education clauses, as they now stand, the Church has ample security that every master in the new schools will be a Churchman, and that the teaching of the Holy Scriptures, as far as the limited exposition may be carried, will necessarily be in conformity with his creed. But the enmity of the Dissenters is moved to the uttermost, and they will succeed in defeating the measure, at least in the sense which led me to propose it, as a scheme of comprehension and concord."
[16] In less than two months 11,611 petitions, bearing 1,757,297 signatures had been received.—E. Hodder, *The Life and Work of the seventh Earl of Shaftesbury* (1893) p. 245.
[17] J. C. Symons, *Light and Life for the People* (1843) pp. 10, 15.

political principles, or of Dissenting religious principles, is to be
got rid of."[18]

Introducing the bill on 7th March, 1843, Graham reminded the
House that the measure rested mainly on the report of Ashley's
Committee, its object being to remedy the defects of the existing
law. He proposed to include children engaged in silk mills, and
hoped later to bring in legislation to control the labour of those
employed in lace factories and in the printing of calico.[19] Ashley
approved the Government's proposals, though he regretted that
there was to be no further limitation of the hours of labour; but
Hume and Mark Philips launched a virulent attack on the principle
of compulsory education, which, they declared, was entirely wrong.
The manufacturers did not object to the factory clauses, but they
had strong scruples of conscience about the educational provisions,
and would much prefer to see these two topics the subjects of two
separate bills.[20]

When the debate on the second reading was opened on 24th
March, Hume and Philips renewed their attack on the bill. Were
all the expenses to be defrayed from the poor-rates? enquired
Hume. He disapproved of the entire system of management
provided under the bill, for great disapprobation would be
manifested if the rates were raised from all classes of the community and only a portion were to have the management. If
dissenters were to be taxed for the support of schools, and then
precluded from having a voice in their management, it would be
manifestly unjust.[21] Philips asserted that the great body of
dissenters, and the Roman Catholics too, were opposed to the
educational clauses. Under the guise of giving education to the
infant factory children they were recruiting for members of the
Church of England.[22] Hindley found himself in strange company
in supporting the views of so convinced a reactionary as Philips,
but he, too, considered that the interests of the dissenters had not
been sufficiently studied. " To those clauses which gave to a board
of education the management of the new system he had the most
positive objection."[23] Knight, the member for Nottinghamshire,
assured the House that many members of the Church were uneasy

---

18 *An Analytical Digest of the Education Clauses of the Factories Bill*
(1843) pp. 15, 19.
19 *Hansard* (1843) LXVII, 422.
20 17th March, 1843. *Ibid.* 1083. *Cf. An Analytical Digest of the
Education Clauses of the Factories Bill* (1843) p. 38.—" It is a tyrannical
stretch of power to compel parents to send their children to any school at
all, much more to do so without leaving them any choice as to the school,
and, most of all, both to compel attendance and exact the payment of a
school-fee."
21 *Ibid.* 1414.
22 *Ibid.* 1419.
23 *Ibid.* 1420.

about the proposed constitution of the trusts. "The *English Churchman*," he said, " had declared ' If this be the Conservative way to educate and bless the people, and to elevate the depressed Church, may God, in His goodness, shield us therefrom,' to which the *Nottingham Journal* devoutly added ' Amen.'"[24]

Ashley, dismayed at the prospect that the measure based on the recommendations of his own Committee was in imminent danger of collapse, implored the House to take a wider view and to compare what the present bill promised with what the Act of 1833 had achieved. Any system of education, he thought, must be preferable to that which had allowed the notorious coal-hole schools to flourish so freely. " A book was sent to him the other day quite black, and so rotten, that it went to pieces in his hands, and yet that had been one of the standard books of the school for the last two years." The bill fully safe-guarded the rights of those parents who objected to their children being taught the doctrines of a creed to which they could not subscribe. Let them sink their differences, and seize the opportunity that was before them.[25]

On 10th April, 1843, Lord John Russell tabled a number of resolutions which, he said, he intended to propose after Easter. His suggestions, designed to placate the opponents of the bill, included a proviso that ratepayers should be adequately represented on the trusts that were to manage the schools, and that the chairman should be elected by the whole body of trustees. The Authorized Version of the Bible should be used in the schools, but special provision should be made for Roman Catholics in this respect. The Catechism and Liturgy should be taught only to those children whose parents desired them to receive such instruction, and a schoolmaster should not be declared incompetent by reason merely of his inability to give religious teaching. Graham welcomed this intervention. He had received many deputations during the last few weeks, he said, and the Government had been considering the modifications which they might properly introduce in the hope of securing dispassionate discussion of the whole matter.[26]

These modifications were submitted to the House on 1st May, 1843, when Graham asked that they might receive calm consideration. " I cannot dissemble for myself," he said, " that although that spirit of calm forbearance prevails within these walls, much heat and excitement have arisen out of doors. The petitions which have been presented against those clauses of the Factories Bill to which I am about to advert have been numerous almost without a parallel.

[24] *Ibid.* 1422.
[25] *Ibid.* 1466-1468.
[26] *Hansard* (1843) LXVIII, 745-746.

. . . I am aware—for the symptoms are but too evident—that upon
this question the waters of strife have overflowed, and now cover
the land. This (here the right hon. Baronet placed the modified
bill upon the Table)—this is my olive branch. I tender it in the
hope that the harbinger of peace, ere long, may return with the
glad tidings that the waters have subsided. On the part of the
Government I tender this peace-offering in the spirit of concord,
and of Christian charity and goodwill."[27]

The amended bill[28] was designed to give an entirely new
character to the local bodies of trustees. A clergyman of the
Church of England was still to be appointed clerical trustee, but he
was only to choose *one* other member; those who had subscribed
to the school being allowed to nominate a trustee in place of the
second church-warden appointed by the incumbent under the
previous scheme. The four remaining trustees were no longer to
be chosen by the magistrates—instead they were to be elected by
those ratepayers occupying property assessed at £10 a year or more.

The clauses providing for instruction in the doctrines of the
Church of England during school hours had provoked considerable
controversy, because the children of dissenters would either have
to be withdrawn from these lessons, thus wasting their time, or
their parents would have to allow them to remain in school, so, as
Graham admitted, " exposing them to attempts which might be
made to instil into their infant minds the peculiar doctrines of the
Church of England."[29] The modification now proposed was that
denominational teaching should be given for one hour only on
three days a week during either the first or last hour of the session.

The opponents of the measure were not mollified by these
concessions, which, after all, did not touch the root of the problem.
Russell enlarged on the great services rendered to education by
the dissenters, who were numerically superior in the factory
districts. The new proposals, he maintained, were unacceptable
because they still placed the preponderance of power in the hands
of the Church. Hindley agreed, warning the Government that the
proposed constitution of the trustees would not give satisfaction
out-of-doors.[30]

Graham, sorely against his will, was compelled to admit defeat,
and when the discussion was resumed on 15th June, he announced
that the educational clauses would be withdrawn. " It was
evident," he told the House, " that the great body of the dissenters
of this country entertained insuperable objections to the bill in its
original form." The modified bill had been designed to meet their

27 *Ibid*. 1104, 1118.
28 *Parl. Papers* (1843) II, p. 549.
29 *Hansard* (1843) LXVIII, 1110.
30 *Ibid*. 1119, 1128.

wishes, " but," he added " I am bound to say that in that hope I have been entirely disappointed; the objections to the measure have not been removed or even mitigated by the modifications, and the opposition to my plan continues unabated. . . . The Government was anxious to bring Legislative powers and public funds to the aid of local exertion, but I am satisfied . . . that unless we should obtain general consent and willing co-operation in our mode of effecting this object, though we might carry the measure through Parliament, practically it would be inoperative."[31]

In the bill which was re-committed in its further modified form[32] on 19th June, 1843, all reference to the means of establishing new schools was excluded. Ashley deeply regretted the loss of the educational clauses, but for the sake of the rest of the bill, he could not but approve the Government's decision. Hindley, who himself had presented some two thousand petitions against the measure, expressed satisfaction that the controversial clauses had been dropped,[33] and amidst a general feeling of relief the bill went through the Committee. It was now too late in the session, however, to deal with so large a question, and on 30th June Graham outlined the proposals that he intended to put before the House when the time was more opportune.[34]

On 6th February, 1844, the Home Secretary introduced the promised measure,[35] pointing out that although it was identical in most respects with the bill that had been discussed last session, it contained some important new provisions.[36] For the first time it was proposed that adult women should be limited to the hours worked by young persons between the ages of thirteen and eighteen; silk mills were to come under the same regulations as the other textile factories;[37] and lost time was only to be recovered when there had been a complete stoppage of the machinery, and then only in mills worked solely by water-power. In the past, declared Graham, there had been " frequent excuses for exceeding the law, where the double powers of water and steam are employed. I propose that no facility shall be given for making up lost time excepting where the power is water exclusively."[38] So far as

[31] *Hansard* (1843) LXIX, 1567. See C. S. Parker, *Life and Letters of Sir James Graham* (1907) Vol. I, p. 345.

[32] *Parl. Papers* (1843) II, p. 607.

[33] *Hansard* (1843) LXX, 94, 97.

[34] *Ibid.* 483.

[35] A Bill for Regulating the Employment of Children, Young Persons and Women in Factories.—*Parl. Papers* (1844) II, p. 149.

[36] *Hansard* (1844) LXXII, 277.

[37] Children engaged in winding and throwing raw silk were, however, to be allowed to work ten hours a day.

[38] *Ibid.* 279.

education was concerned, he continued, the existing enactments were illusory. Teachers were poorly qualified, there was a lack of books and apparatus—" in fact, the system, as far as it has yet gone, has been one not of education, but of confinement in a schoolroom, without imparting to the children any knowledge or instruction whatever."[39] He therefore proposed that the arrangements envisaged in his first bill (7th March, 1843) should be revived, and that children should be required to attend school for three hours on each of five working days, except those engaged in the mornings, who need attend only two and a half hours a day during the winter months (*i.e.* between 1st November and 28th February).

Clause 59 broke new ground in seeking to establish evidence of employment, providing " In any complaint of the employment of any person in a Factory for a longer time in any one day than is allowed by this Act, the time of beginning work in the morning, which shall be stated in any notice fixed up in the Factory . . . shall be taken to be the time when all persons in the Factory, except children beginning to work in the afternoon, began work on any day subsequent to the date of such notice, so long as the same shall continue to be fixed up in the Factory, unless the contrary shall be proved." The full implications of this proviso were apparently not appreciated, for the debate turned not so much on the administrative machinery, as on the renewed attempt made by Lord Ashley to introduce the ten-hours day.

The bill having been read a second time on 12th February, 1844,[40] the Committee stage was reached on 15th March, when Ashley moved " That the word ' night ' shall be taken to mean from six o'clock in the evening to six o'clock in the following morning; and the word ' meal-time ' shall be taken to mean an interval of cessation from work for the purpose of rest and refreshment, at the rate of two hours a day, with a view to effect a limitation of the hours of labour to ten in the day."[41] He entertained no hostility towards the factories, he assured the House, but he had begun with the textile mills because they loomed large in the public eye, comprising the wealthiest and most responsible proprietors, and presenting the greatest facilities for legislation. That the State had a right to watch over the moral and physical well-being of the people was recognized by all civilised governments, and nowhere was the problem more acute than in this country, where the numbers engaged in the textile industry approached half a million. The improvements in machinery had increased the severity of the labour, and had resulted in the substitution of women and children

---

[39] *Ibid*. 280.
[40] *Hansard* (1844) LXXII, 518.
[41] *Hansard* (1844) LXXIII, 1073.

for adult males.[42]   Working conditions in the factories caused
scrofula, phthisis and eye-strain, and the weight of medical opinion
was undoubtedly in favour of the ten-hours day for those under
eighteen.   "We ask but a slight relaxation of toil," he concluded,
" a time to live, and a time to die; a time for those comforts that
sweeten life, and a time for those duties that adorn it; and therefore,
with a fervent prayer to Almighty God that it may please Him to
turn the hearts of all who hear me, to thoughts of justice and of
mercy, I now finally commit the issue to the judgment and
humanity of Parliament."

This moving appeal was coldly received by the Government.
It was not a question of principle, but of degree, declared Graham,[43]
and he felt bound to offer a most decided opposition to Ashley's
motion.   It was certainly a violation of principle that Parliament
should interfere in a case of this kind at all; that, however, was
decided by the Legislature in 1833.   " What is the general tenor," he
asked, " of the measure which I propose, as it relates to children?
A mitigation of time from eight to six and a half hours, a limitation
of margin from fifteen hours to fourteen, still leaving twelve hours
for work. . . . Adult labourers, stimulated by the honest desire of
earning as much as they are able, because wages are generally paid
by piece-work—so far from going to those masters where time is
limited, invariably prefer the establishments where most work is
done." Milner Gibson, the member for Manchester, supported this
view.[44]   Many operatives, he asserted, said that they considered
it would be an interference with the only property they had to
dispose of, namely their labour, for to enact that no young persons
or women of any age should work more than ten hours was, in
point of fact, to enact that no factory engines should be kept in
operation more than ten hours.   Nassau Senior had demonstrated
that the entire profit of a factory was gained in the last hours of
work, and that if the mills were restricted to ten hours a day they
would be run at a loss.[45]   He did not understand why the textile
industry should have been singled out for special treatment.   Other
industries, too, needed regulation, and " he knew not a more likely
case for investigation than that which might be furnished by the
large establishment in Printing-house-square."

---

[42] The self-acting mule, patented in 1825, provided for the automatic
return of the carriage, and for the winding, as well as the spinning of the
yarn.   The duty of the spinner was thus reduced to supervizing the head-
stock, and piecing the broken threads.   See S. J. Chapman, *The Lancashire
Cotton Industry* (1904) p. 69.
[43] *Hansard* (1844) LXXIII, 1102.
[44] *Ibid*. 1111.
[45] See Nassau W. Senior, *Letters on the Factory Act* (1837) pp. 12-13.

When the debate was resumed on 18th March, 1844,[46] the House divided on the question that the word 'eight' should stand part of the clause, *i.e.* that the working day should extend from 6 a.m. to 8 p.m. The motion was lost by 179 votes to 170,[47] and on Ashley's original amendment being put, it was carried by 161 votes to 153.[48] "Sir," said Graham, when the result was announced, "the decision of the Committee is a virtual adoption of a Ten-hours Bill without modification. To that decision, with the utmost respect for the opinion of the Committee, I have an insuperable objection." He did not feel it consistent with his duty, however, to drop the bill, suggesting that the question should be re-considered in the debate on Clause 8, which provided that young persons and women should not work for more than twelve hours a day.[49]

Excitement was mounting rapidly, for it seemed that the ten-hours day was at last to be achieved. "The greatest enthusiasm prevailed," wrote Ashley's biographer. "Meetings were held, pamphlets were scattered broad-cast, and all the paraphernalia of agitation was set in motion with a vigour that had never been known before. Twelve delegates were despatched to London to assist Lord Ashley in his labours, and nobly they worked. London and Westminster were divided into districts, and every Member of Parliament in these districts was canvassed, the working of the factory system explained, and its evils exposed."[50]

On 22nd March, 1844, Graham opened the debate on the 8th clause, enlarging on the fact that never before had the legislature considered regulating the labour of adult women. He certainly felt, he said, that it was a restriction questionable on principle, and an exception to all legislation on such subjects, but he supported the clause as being necessary for the health of those concerned.[51] He opposed Ashley's suggestion that women and young persons should be allowed to work only ten hours a day, declaring that a large and early reduction of wages would result, that this would lead to enmity between master and man, and that strikes for higher wages would be the inevitable consequence. "There is no effort I would not make," he declared, "there is no odium I would not incur, rather than run the risk of occasioning such disappointment, and of fostering delusions which must end in ruin." When the House divided on the question that the clause

---

46 *Hansard* (1844) LXXIII, 1202.
47 *Ibid.* 1263.
48 *Ibid.* 1266.
49 *Ibid.* 1266.
50 E. Hodder, *The Life and Work of the seventh Earl of Shaftesbury* (1893) p. 290.
51 *Hansard* (1844) LXXIII, 1378.

should stipulate twelve hours' work, there was an adverse majority of three, 183 having voted Aye, and 186 No. The question was then put that ten hours should be the period of labour, and this, too, was rejected by 188 votes to 181.[52]

This astonishing result not unnaturally threw the House into confusion, and Graham announced that since the Committee had decided against both ten hours and twelve hours, he proposed to postpone further proceedings until the following Monday. On that day, 25th March, he re-stated his reasons for refusing the demand for a ten-hours day.[53]   After rehearsing the classic arguments he proceeded to consider the wider implications that were involved.   " I pass on," he said, " to another argument, hardly less terrifying and alarming—I allude to the argument, that we have now arrived at a new social state; that we should therefore depart from the fixed principles which have hitherto guided the wisest men of this and every other country, and meet our alleged new social condition by new principles and new schemes of legislation. Hitherto interference with the free market for labour has been considered dangerous, and only to be justified by some very strong reasons in certain cases of exception.   That rule is now to be inverted; it is proposed to make legislative interference the general rule, and to acknowledge no limit—not even the necessity of the case—but only the possibility of interference.   Sir, a more dangerous course was never suggested for the adoption of a legislative assembly. . . . I do not think that it is an exaggeration to say that this is the commencement of a ' Jack Cade ' system of legislation."   He therefore asked leave to withdraw the present bill, promising to introduce a new measure containing modifications likely to be approved.

The amendments incorporated in the bill[54] that Graham introduced on 29th March, 1844, were important, but they were not such as to satisfy the ten-hours party, and on 18th April Ashley gave notice that at a later stage he intended to move the addition of clauses limiting the hours of labour, after 1st October, 1844, to eleven hours a day, and after 1st October, 1847, to ten hours a day.[55]   The bill was read a second time on 22nd April,[56] the Committee stage being reached on 26th April, when the House began the consideration of the administrative clauses.

---

[52] Ibid. 1460.   The five members who voted " No " in both divisions were W. Aldam, Capt. M. Archdale, W. Ewart, J. Martin and G. Palmer.
[53] Ibid. 1482.
[54] Bill to amend the Laws relating to Labour in Factories.—Parl. Papers (1844) II, p. 187.
[55] Hansard (1844) LXXIV, 89.
[56] Ibid. 130.

The regulations governing the Inspectors and the Sub-Inspectors, as the Superintendents were now to be known, were substantially the same as those contained in the bill introduced by Graham a year before. A central office was to be established in London, and the Sub-Inspectors were to have full rights of access to the mills, but the Inspectors were now to be deprived of their power to make regulations, nor were they, in the future, to be allowed to exercise the judicial functions of magistrates. Mark Philips complained bitterly of the increased powers to be given to the Sub-Inspectors, powers which, he warned the Government, " would not be at all liked by the manufacturers." He did not see the necessity for appointing Inspectors at all, he said, but if they were to continue, the Superintendents, at least, should be abolished.[57] Bright, the member for Durham City, supported this contention. " It was not an agreeable thing," he declared, " to have more persons than were absolutely necessary in possession of the power of going through manufactories whenever they pleased,"[58] while Hume considered " it was melancholy to witness this new attempt to put additional shackles upon commerce. They proposed to undertake that which they never would be able to carry out, and they were about to commence an interference that was quite unnecessary and uncalled for. He looked upon the whole Bill as a nullity and a disgrace to the country."[59]

The clause was carried without a division, but there was considerable opposition to the 5th clause providing for the establishment of a central office in London. " If they established such an office," asserted Bright, " before two years they would witness the appointment of an inspector-general at the head of it. In one of the Factory Bills it had been shadowed forth, and he believed that an inspector-general had been spoken of."[60] Philips argued that there was no need for such an office—" it was only the commencement of a future office of extended operation and increased expense,"—and he considered that the returns made by the Inspectors could be superintended by the Board of Trade. These apprehensions of the dangers of increased centralization were shared by those who were alarmed at the ever-widening range of State intervention, but Graham reduced the question to one of practicability and administrative convenience. He agreed that it would be possible for the Inspectors' returns to be made to the Board of

57 *Ibid*. 335.

58 *Ibid*. 335.

59 *Ibid*. 336.

60 The reference was to the bill introduced by Fox Maule on 26th March, 1841. In a letter to the Bishop of London, dated 27th December, 1842, Graham had referred specifically to Horner as " the Inspector-General of Factories."—C. S. Parker, *Life and Letters of Sir James Graham* (1907) Vol. I, p. 343.

Trade, but in that case it would be necessary to transfer the Factory Department from the Home Office to the Board, since it would clearly be undesirable for two government departments to share responsibility. The volume of work was growing rapidly, and it would be greatly to the public benefit to appoint two or three clerks to arrange and take care of the mass of information afforded by the Inspectors. The House agreed, the clause authorizing the establishment of a central office being carried by 157 votes to 104.[61]

The 30th and 31st clauses of the bill introduced important innovations in the regulation of the working hours of children under thirteen. By the former it was provided that no child was to be employed more than six and a half hours a day, unless the dinner-time of young persons between thirteen and eighteen years of age began at 1 p.m., in which case a child starting work in the morning might be employed for seven hours; by the latter clause a system of working on alternate days was envisaged in certain cases. In factories where the labour of young persons was restricted to ten hours a day, children might be employed for ten hours on three alternate days, attending school for five hours a day on the week day preceding their day in the factory. These arrangements, designed to secure greater flexibility in the interior economy of the mills, were accepted without discussion, but Fielden urged that it was cruel and impolitic to allow children to work at eight years of age. Graham justified the proposal on the ground that the hours of work had been substantially reduced, and the House agreed to the lowering of the age limit by 137 votes to 40.[62]

On 10th May, 1844, on the third reading, Lord Ashley moved his promised amendment, the effect of which would have been to introduce a ten-hours day by October, 1847.[63] On this occasion he made no reference to the physical and moral aspects of the question, holding that it was generally admitted that the hours of labour should be reduced if it could be shown that no hardship would result either to the operatives on the one hand, or to the manufacturers on the other. He confined himself, therefore, to a consideration of the four main contentions of his opponents—that the ten-hours day would result in a diminution of produce, that it would cause a reduction in the value of fixed capital, that wages would fall, and that foreign competition would jeopardize the home market because of the rise in prices. In a lengthy and reasoned discourse he examined each of these arguments in detail, quoting figures of comparative rates of wages, capital involved, aggregate production both in this country and abroad,—all designed to refute the prognostications of those who asserted that the shorter working

---

61 *Hansard* (1844) LXXIV, 337.
62 *Ibid.* 757.
63 *Ibid.* 899.

day would involve the textile industry in ruin. " Sir," he cried in conclusion, " it may not be given to me to pass over this Jordan; other and better men have preceded me, and I entered into their labours; other and better men will follow me, and enter into mine; but this consolation I shall ever continue to enjoy—that, amidst much injustice, and somewhat of calumny, we have at last lighted such a candle in England as, by God's blessing, shall never be put out."

The Government was shaken, but grimly determined not to yield the ground upon which they had taken their stand. Both Graham and Peel announced that they would resign in the event of an adverse vote, and when the debate was resumed on 13th May, Ashley's motion was negatived by 297 votes to 159.[64] In the face of such a decision there was no point in prolonging the conflict. The Commons finally passed the bill by 136 votes to 7,[65] and the Act to amend the Laws relating to Labour in Factories came into force on 6th June, 1844.

---

[64] *Ibid*. 1104.
[65] *Ibid*. 1108.

CHAPTER 14
THE ACT OF 1844

THE ACT of 1844[1] marked the opening of the third great chapter in the history of factory legislation. In 1802 the principle of State intervention in industry had been established; in 1833 the scientific approach of the Benthamites had resulted in the inception of a closely-knit, centralized system of control, the technical imperfections of which, however, rendered many of its provisions worthless. Derided by the operatives, resented by the manufacturers, and criticized by the Inspectors, it had been universally condemned, yet it had afforded an opportunity for experiment on an extensive scale. The technique of factory regulation, with its acute problems of human relationship raising such complex issues, could not be worked out in a moment of time; it had to crystallize slowly from long experience, from false starts, and from mistaken conceptions. Many plans had to be tried, many devices rejected, but gradually and inevitably the pattern developed, assuming in the course of years, and under the constant fire of criticism, a well-ordered shape and form. The Act of 1844 was the logical outcome. Profiting by the lessons of the past decade, its authors were able to devise an administrative system which, in its main aspects at least, was to be an enduring monument to their sagacity, and which, when the efflux of time had demonstrated beyond question the necessity for extending the ambit and increasing the measure of control, was to become the *point d'élan* for an ever-widening range of legislation.

New limitations were now imposed on the working hours of children, young persons, and women. No child was to be employed in a factory for more than six and a half hours in any one day, unless the dinner-time of the young persons in the factory began at 1 p.m., in which case children beginning to work in the morning might be engaged for seven hours a day. A child who had been employed in a factory before noon was not in any circumstances to work after 1 p.m. the same day, unless the system of alternate days had been introduced[2]. If the factory occupier had notified the Inspector that he intended to restrict young persons to ten hours a day, he might employ children for ten hours a day on three alternate days of the week, provided they

---

[1] 7 & 8 Vict., c. 15.
[2] Sec. 30.

did not work on two successive days, nor after 4.30 p.m. on Saturday.[3] The provisions of the Act of 1833 were to continue in force so far as the hours of young persons were concerned, and women above eighteen years of age were also to be restricted to twelve hours a day or sixty-nine hours a week.[4] The minimum age for employment was reduced to eight, and children who had completed their eighth year and obtained a surgical certificate were allowed to work under the same conditions as those between the ages of nine and thirteen.[5]

The hours of work of children and young persons were to be reckoned from the time when any child or young person began work in the morning, the time to be regulated by a public clock, or a clock open to public view and approved by the Inspector.[6] Registers were to be kept of young persons, of children employed before noon, and of those employed after 1 p.m., the Inspector being authorized to demand extracts from these registers to facilitate the discharge of their duties.[7] In cases of complaint of employment contrary to the Act the time of beginning work in the morning stated in the notice fixed up in the factory, and signed by the occupier or his agent, was to be taken to be the time when all persons in the factory (except children beginning work in the afternoon) began work on any day subsequent to the date of the notice. If a person was allowed to enter or remain in the factory it was to be evidence, unless the contrary was proved, that he was actually employed, the only exceptions being in respect of those who were on the premises at meal-times, during the total stoppage of the machinery, or between 4 p.m. and 5 p.m., if they had come to bring in tea or food.[8]

The severity of the regulations concerning the making up of lost time was considerably increased. No time lost by accident or otherwise was to be made up by extending the hours of labour except in factories where the machinery was moved by water power. In such establishments time lost from total stoppages caused by deficiency or excess of water might be recovered within six months between the hours of 5 a.m. and 9 p.m., and children and young persons might be employed one hour a day in excess of the time to which their daily labour was restricted (except on

---

[3] Sec. 31.

[4] Sec. 32.

[5] Sec. 29.

[6] Sec. 26. It was still the bitter complaint of the operatives that the factory clocks were fraudulently manipulated. For an account of this system of " genteel robbery," see W. Rashleigh, *Stubborn Facts from the Factories* (1844) pp. 14-15.

[7] Sec. 27.

[8] Sec. 52.

Saturday, when work was to cease at 4.30 p.m.).[9] No lost time was to be recovered until due notice had been sent to the Sub-Inspector, and particulars posted in a prominent position on the factory premises.[10]

If there was a partial stoppage of water-driven machinery, children were forbidden to make up lost time, but young persons who would have been employed on the machines might work during the following night, so long as they were not employed during any period of twenty-four consecutive hours a greater number of hours than that to which their daily labour was restricted.[11]

The time allowed each day for meals remained at an hour and a half, between 7.30 a.m. and 7.30 p.m. One hour at least was to be given before 3 p.m., and no child or young person was to be employed more than five hours before 1 p.m. without an interval of at least half an hour. During the break for meals children and young persons were not to be employed or allowed to remain in any room where manufacturing processes were being carried on; and it was further provided that all young persons should have the time for meals at the same period of the day, unless the Inspector had sanctioned a different arrangement.[12]

The ambiguity of the 1833 Act in relation to the holidays to be granted was removed by the express provision that no child or young person was to work on Christmas Day or Good Friday. No young person was to be employed in the factory on any of the eight statutory half-holidays, four of which were to be granted between 15th March and 1st October.[13]

The surgical certificate was retained as an integral element in the system of control, but it now underwent important modifications. Possession of a certificate was still to be a condition of employment, but its scope was enlarged, the surgeon being required not only to certify that the child or young person concerned was not incapacitated, by disease or bodily infirmity, from working in the factory, but to testify his belief that the age stated was correct. The erstwhile stubborn problem of determining age became of decreasing importance as, year by year, a new group of children became subject to the terms of the Registration of Births Act; indeed it now became possible to provide that if there was a dispute about the age of a child, a certified copy of the entry of birth might be obtained from the Registrar on payment of a fee

9 Sec. 35.
10 Sec. 33.
11 Sec. 34.
12 Sec. 36.
13 Sec. 37.

of one shilling, but this alone was not to authorize employment unless the surgeon also affirmed that the child was physically fit.[14]

The surgical certificate was to be valid only for the factory at which it had been granted, or at another factory in the occupation of the same owner if such factory was in the district of the same surgeon.[15] No certificate was to be granted otherwise than upon personal inspection, which was to take place at the factory where the child or young person was to be employed,[16] a form of certificate now being scheduled in respect of young persons between thirteen and sixteen years of age. A certificate might be dispensed with for seven working days (or, if the surgeon lived more than three miles from the factory, for thirteen working days) provided that all the certificates for the factory were granted by a duly appointed surgeon. This concession was not to be interpreted, however, as dispensing with certificates of school attendance during this interim period, nor did it authorize the employment of those to whom a certificate had already been refused.[17]

Certificates granted under the Act of 1833 were to remain in force so long as the place of employment remained unchanged, but the Inspector was authorized to cancel any certificate if he had good reason to believe that the age stated was greater than the real age, or if the surgeon deemed the young worker to be of deficient health or strength, incapacitated for labour by reason of disease or bodily infirmity, or likely to suffer injury by continued employment.[18]

The Inspectors were at last vested with the power for which they had clamoured so long, the power to appoint certifying surgeons, to issue regulations for their guidance, and to specify the factories or districts in which they were to act. No such surgeon was to be the occupier of a factory, or to have a beneficial interest in a factory.[19] The certificates granted by these appointed surgeons did not require the counter-signature of an Inspector or a magistrate,[20] but those granted by non-appointed surgeons (who must be licensed to practise surgery or medicine by a university, college, or authorized public body) were to be counter-signed by a magistrate, who must not be the occupier of a factory, nor the father, son, or brother of an occupier. The certificates were not to be counter-signed in the absence of the person to whom they related, and proof was to be required that the person who

---

14 Sec. 15.
15 Sec. 16.
16 Sec. 11.
17 Sec. 17.
18 Sec. 14.
19 Sec. 8.
20 Sec. 9.

appeared before the magistrate was, in fact, the person to whom the certificate was granted.[21]

The Act authorized the occupier of a factory to enter into an agreement with the certifying surgeon stipulating the payments that were to be made in respect of examinations, and if such agreement was approved by the Inspector, any penalties incurred by either party could be recovered like other penalties under the Act.[22]   If the occupier required him to do so, the Inspector was to fix the fees to be paid to the surgeon, and the times when he was to visit the factory. If more than one person was examined, the maximum fee for each examination was not to exceed a shilling, plus sixpence for each half mile the surgeon's residence was distant from the factory, no charge being made in respect of the first mile.   The total fee, including mileage, was to be not less than one shilling, and not more than five shillings for any one visit, except when more than ten persons were examined, when there was to be a fee of sixpence for each examination, no charge being made for mileage.   When the factory was less than one mile from the surgeon's residence, the maximum fee for each visit was to be two shillings and sixpence, except when more than five persons were examined, in which case the surgeon was to receive sixpence for each examination.

The fees were to be paid by the occupier of the factory, who was entitled to deduct not more than threepence from the wages of the person examined. The surgeon was not required to visit a factory less than three miles from his residence more than once a week, nor a factory more than three miles distant more than once a fortnight.[23]

Perhaps the most dramatic of the many reforms achieved by the Act of 1844, was the inauguration of the half-time system, whereby factory children were required to attend school during half the day as a condition of being employed in the factory the other half.[24]   It was provided that the parent, or the person having the direct benefit of the child's wages, was to cause him to attend school on the day following his first employment, and thereafter on each working day of every week during any part of which he continued in such employment.   The child was to attend school for a period of three hours each day from Monday to Friday, between 8 a.m. and 6 p.m., those working in the morning, however, being required to attend for two hours and a half only between

---

21 Sec. 10.
22 Sec. 12.
23 Sec. 13.
24 The half-time system was not abolished until 1918. In that year there were still some 70,000 "half-timers" employed in the factories.

the first day of November and the last day of February. Non-attendance was to be excused if the schoolmaster certified that it was due to illness or other unavoidable cause, if the child was taking one of the statutory holidays, if the Inspector consented to the absence, or, in the case of schools situated within the outer boundary of the factory, if the school was closed because the factory had ceased to work during the whole day.[25]

Attendance at school was to be certified by the schoolmaster, whose voucher was to be obtained each Monday by the mill-occupier. The Inspector was to fix the remuneration of the school-master, and to this end he was authorized to direct the mill-occupier to deduct from the wages of each child a sum not exceeding two-pence a week, or one-twelfth of the wages paid. The Inspector was also able to insist on reasonable standards of teaching, for he was empowered to annul the certificates granted by any school-master who was unfit to instruct children " by reason of his Incapacity to teach them to read and write, from his gross Ignorance, or from his not having the Books and Materials necessary to teach them Reading and Writing, or because of his immoral Conduct, or of his continued neglect to fill up and sign the Certificates of School Attendance required by the Act." Such disqualification was not to be imposed unless there was a suitable alternative school within two miles of the factory, and provision was also made for appeal to the Home Secretary against the Inspector's decision.[26]

There was, of course, no provision for the establishment of schools from the public funds, but the Inspectors were not left entirely destitute of resources, as they had been by the Act of 1833, for it was arranged that fines inflicted for breaches of the law should be paid into a banking account to be applied by the Inspector for the establishment or support of day schools for factory children.[27]

The Factory Inspectors were no longer to have the power to act as magistrates, or to make rules and regulations,[28] though they were authorized, as were the Sub-Inspectors, to summon offenders and witnesses to appear before the courts.[29] Both Inspectors and Sub-Inspectors were to have the right to enter every part of any

---

[25] Sec. 38.   Children working alternate days were to go to school for five hours a day on each week-day other than Saturday preceding the day of employment. (Sec. 31.) Children over eleven years of age employed in winding and throwing raw silk were exempt from the schooling clauses. (Sec. 72.)

[26] Sec. 39.

[27] Sec. 66.

[28] Sec. 2.

[29] Sec. 50.

factory, by day or night, when any person was employed therein;
to enter, by day, any place they had reason to believe was a
factory; and to enter any school where factory children were
educated. They could examine persons found in the factory or
school, and it was declared an offence to hinder their admission,
or to conceal children from them.[30]

A central office was to be provided for the Inspectors in
London or Westminster, and the Home Secretary was to appoint
the necessary clerks and servants, and to fix their salaries.[31] Every
person beginning to occupy a factory was required, within one
month, to send to this office a written notice giving the name and
address of the firm, the nature of the work carried on, and the
nature and amount of the moving power.[32]

A scale of minimum and maximum penalties was prescribed
for offences under the Act. For illegally employing any person,
or for employing a child without a certificate of school attendance
there was to be imposed a fine of not less than 20s. and not
exceeding £3 for each child or young person so employed, the
penalties for offences committed during the night being increased
to a minimum of 40s. and a maximum of £5.[33] The parent, or
the person having any direct benefit from the wages of a child or
young person employed illegally, or neglecting to cause a child
to attend school, was to be liable to a minimum penalty of 5s.
and a maximum penalty of 20s., unless he could prove that the
offence had been committed without his consent, connivance, or
wilful default.[34]

Complaints were to be preferred within two months of the
offence, and it was provided that no person was to be liable to a
larger penalty for any repetition from day to day of the same
kind of offence than the highest penalty prescribed for that offence,
unless the repetition was committed after the issue of an information, or unless the offence was that of employing two or more
children or young persons contrary to law.[35]

Proceedings were to be taken before two or more magistrates,[36]
who were not to be occupiers, nor the father, son or brother of the
occupier of the factory in which the offence was committed,[37]

---

[30] Sec. 3. The maximum and minimum penalties for obstruction
were respectively £10 and £3 (Sec. 61); for obstruction at night, £50 and
£20 (Sec. 62).
[31] Sec. 5.
[32] Sec. 7.
[33] Sec. 56.
[34] Sec. 57.
[35] Sec. 44.
[36] Sec. 45.
[37] Sec. 71.

Inspectors and Sub-Inspectors being declared competent witnesses, even when the prosecution was brought at their instance.[38]

An abstract of the Act of 1833, as amended by the present Act, was to be affixed to a movable board at the entrance to the factory, together with particulars of the names and addresses of the Inspector, the Sub-Inspector and the certifying surgeon, the clock by which hours were regulated, the times of beginning and ending daily work, the amount of time allowed for meals and the periods when meals were taken, time lost and intended to be recovered, and time actually recovered.[39]

" I was at Grahambury," wrote Horner, " when the division on the Factory Bill took place, and Government got the extraordinary and unexpected majority of 135. Nothing could exceed the universal astonishment, and many of their supporters grumbled much at having been compelled to vote with them or stay away, without any necessity. But they were wrong, for it was of great consequence to get such a majority as should put an end to the question, which this has done."[40]   Their long-deferred hopes realized, the Inspectors were as one in hailing the new Act as the remedy for those abuses and evasions which they had never ceased to denounce.   " These malpractices may, and probably will," declared Horner in his report for June, 1844,[41] " continue during the current quarter: but I trust no longer. The Amending Act has cut off many ways of evasion, has greatly increased the means of detection, and makes a heavy penalty so much more probable, that the profit of illegal working will not be so clear as it is at present." The full right of access to the factories now granted to the Sub-Inspectors, the power to get evidence without compromising the workers, the provisions concerning clocks and meal-times, the restrictions on adult women, and above all, the repeal of the clause giving power to make up lost time in case of accident to the machinery, would, he considered, all help to check over-working. Twelve months' experience of the operation of the Act confirmed his anticipation. " I have," he said, " had repeated, and in some cases quite voluntary testimony borne to the improvement of the laws by which the labour in factories is now regulated, to what they were previous to the late amending Act; the most ready admissions that, with a moderate, and not more than a reasonable degree of attention, all its provisions may be observed, and in so

[38] Sec. 48.
[39] Sec. 28.
[40] Letter to his wife, 26th May, 1844.—K. M. Lyell, *Memoir of Leonard Horner* (1890) Vol. II, p. 67.
[41] *Parl. Papers* (1844) XXVIII, p. 575.

far as regards the younger classes of the workers, I have heard the Act even eulogized by the occupiers of factories. I consider that it may now be safely affirmed, that the nearly twelve years' experience of the Factory Act has solved a very important problem, by proving that, under a judicious adaptation of means and with special reference to the nature of employments, it is practicable to check, by legislative interference, the excesses and moral evils which an unrestrained pursuit of gain has a tendency to create, more particularly as respects children and adolescent females, without injury to commercial interests."[42]

The revised arrangements for schooling were especially welcomed by the Inspectors. A few manufacturers had set up really good schools—M'Connell of Manchester, Cooke, Hyde & Co. of Manchester, and Openshaw of Bury for example[43]—but conditions throughout the country had not improved since the Inspectors had made their report on education in 1839. In the summer of 1843, when Horner made a survey of his district, he found that 45% of the children were receiving their education in factory schools, while 39% attended private schools, " small assemblages of children in cottages, brought together by indigent old men or old women, who nominally keep a school, they being incapable of earning a livelihood in any other way; but without any qualification for teaching." Of the 117 factory schools only 16 were efficient; in the others, he said " there is a mere nominal compliance with the law, and it is an entire misapplication to call such places schools." The Inspectors had no power to interfere to put a stop to this " discreditable mockery of education," mainly because the law had allowed children to work for eight hours a day at any time between 5.30 a.m. and 8.30 p.m., thus making it impossible for them to attend good schools, even in the few places where they were available. " It will be useless," he asserted, " to establish any schools for factory children, or those employed in any other kind of work, unless their labour be restricted to half a day; so that they may be able to attend at the usual school hours, and have a due allowance of exercise and play."[44]

Saunders corroborated Horner's views. The private or dame schools he condemned out of hand, and the majority of factory schools, he held, were little better. In one such school he found that the teacher was " an old, disabled soldier, who had been a comber, but has been long unable to work at his trade. He now takes 35 factory children, and attends to some little mill work.

---

[42] Report, 31st October, 1845. *Parl. Papers* (1846) XX, p. 568.
[43] Horner's Report, 30th December, 1839. *Parl. Papers* (1840) XXIII, p. 15.
[44] Report, 30th June, 1843. *Parl. Papers* (1843) XXVII, pp. 346-347.

The school-room connected with the mill is small and very filthy. When I entered the room I found three of the children employed at a winding machine, and one girl washing the floor, the remainder were sat on benches, some with an old tattered Testament on their knees, but more without." Many manufacturers, he thought, had been reluctant to set up schools because they were uncertain what the law would require when it came to be amended. " The conduct of some factory masters," he said, " has been most praiseworthy. . . . The conduct of other mill-occupiers may be justly condemned, yet it must not be denied that they may plead, as a ground of excuse, the uncertainty as to what is ultimately to be the law (for since 1837 notice has been given every year in Parliament of the intention to amend the Factory Bill)."

The remedy for this lamentable state of affairs was, in Saunders' opinion, to simplify the law, reducing the working hours of children from eight to six and a half a day; and to improve the schools by giving the Inspectors power to cancel the attendance certificates granted by schoolmasters whom they considered incompetent. It was true, he said, that objections had been urged against the half-time system on the grounds that it would reduce the wages of the children, that it would increase the expenses of the owners, who would need either to employ more adults or to raise the wages of the children if there was a shortage of hands, and that it would result in more children being trained to factory work than could be absorbed after they had reached the age of thirteen. But where the system had been tried, notably at Leeds, Bradford, Bingley and Keighley, it had proved an unqualified success, and had resulted in the establishment of good schools, in places where the competition and jealousy of the manufacturers had prevented them from combining to set up schools.

The advantages of the half-time system were that there would be less over-working of children, the complicated plans of changing hands on the relay system would be avoided, there would be more efficient instruction during a greater number of hours, and children would be able to attend better schools.[45]

When the Act came into operation it seemed that these hopes were to be fulfilled. Horner reported that education was generally improving, the grosser cases of mock schooling being less frequently encountered,[46] while Howell affirmed that the Inspectors' power to annul the certificates of incompetent teachers had resulted in children going to better schools.[47] " The number of children," said Saunders, " attending schools conducted by trained and

[45] Report, 30th June, 1843. *Ibid.* pp. 355-363.
[46] Report, 30th April, 1845. *Parl. Papers* (1845) XXV, p. 244.
[47] Report, 1st May, 1845. *Ibid.* p. 262.

efficient teachers, under the supervision of a committee or of trustees, is gradually increasing."[48] It was now easier for the factory children to attend the ordinary day schools, since they could be present for the whole of the morning or afternoon session. " This," he said, " induces the managers of National, of British, and of other schools to admit them, which was not always practicable or convenient when their attendance was limited to two hours, as the change of relays in the middle of school hours interrupted the whole of the scholars, and the order and regularity of school business."[49]

But the cry was still for cheap schools,[50] and so long as parents could comply with the requirements of the law by sending their children to *any* school, so long would education continue to be ineffective. " I seize the opportunity," said Howell, " of urging the importance of providing good schools, into which factory children can be admitted, at as cheap a rate as at the dame's and other low-priced private schools, which are at present necessarily preferred by the parents, merely because they are the cheapest at which the certificate of their children's daily attendance for the statutory number of hours can be obtained."[51] Although the numbers attending the British and National schools had increased there was still a substantial proportion of children to be found in the private schools, and nothing short of a fully state-aided system of education could remedy this state of affairs.[52]

---

[48] Report, 30th October, 1845. *Parl. Papers* (1846) XX, p. 588.

[49] Report, 1st May, 1845. *Parl. Papers* (1845) XXV, p. 270.

[50] *Cf.* F. Thorpe, *The Factory Bill* (1843) p. 12.—" I don't think the crotchetty schemes of the new Factory Bill, the most suitable to offer a hungry man and his family, they require something a little more substantial than the Schoolmaster will give them."

[51] Report, 30th April, 1847. *Parl. Papers* (1847) XV, p. 496.

[52] Saunders, in his report for October, 1846 (*ibid.* p. 461) supplied figures illustrating the position in 1843 and 1846:—

				Numbers in 1843	Numbers in 1846
Type of School					
National	...	...	...	1,547	4,434
Dissenting		...	...	243	2,272
Factory	...	...	...	3,367	3,038
Dame	...	...	...	4,159	6,037

In Horner's district the figures in 1847 were:—

National	...	...	4,355
British		...	1,211
Undenominational	...		2,020
Factory		...	3,746
Dame	...	...	3,908

" Not more than one-third," he said, " are receiving any education that can have any influence on the formation of their character . . . . In regard to private schools, as there is no control, any one, however, incompetent, may open a school; and, while professing to deal in education, he vends a commodity wholly worthless."—Report, 30th April, 1847. (*Ibid.* p. 491.)

Chadwick was undoubtedly right in contending that the Act of 1844, considered as an educational measure, was a failure; but the half-time system achieved another, and not less important purpose, in that it reduced the working hours of the children.[53] The task of the Inspectors in checking over-working was also greatly facilitated, for it was now impossible to bring children into the mill for short periods on the relay system, thus spreading their allotted span of hours over the whole of the legal working day. " The simpler arrangement under the amended Act of 1844 for the employment of children," said Saunders, " affords the officers great facility in discovering when they have been employed too long."[54]

The regulations concerning the appointment of certifying surgeons, and the granting of certificates of age were warmly welcomed by the Inspectors. The permission to employ children and young persons for a limited period before they were certified, in those cases where all the certificates for the factory were granted by the appointed surgeon, had the effect, in the majority of cases, of inducing the mill-occupier to resort to such surgeon.[55] The resulting advantage was two-fold: the Inspectors could exercise a full measure of control over the surgeons, and the position of the surgeons themselves was considerably strengthened, for they could now assume an independent and impartial attitude, free from the pressure that had so often been exerted by both parents and owners.[56] The manufacturers' interests, however, were not entirely ignored, for as Saunders pointed out, " the provisions of the Act enable a mill-occupier who has any private or political objection to the appointed officer, to procure other certificates, without any grave inconvenience or hindrance to his business."[57]

Evasion was now much more difficult. " The enactments respecting proof of real age are very generally and clearly understood," remarked Saunders. " Mill-occupiers are prevented employing either children or young persons on proof of real age alone; and any certificate of birth or baptism which is put forth by a parent, must be examined by the surgeon before the person to whom it refers can be admitted to permanent employment. This has operated in a very wholesome manner to check a practice which

[53] *Transactions of the National Association for the Promotion of Social Science* (1860) p. 419. For a critical assessment of the effects of the educational clauses see G. Anderson, *The Half-Time System and the Educational Test.—Ibid.* pp. 381-382.

[54] Report, 31st October, 1846. *Parl. Papers* (1847) XV, p. 456. See also Horner's Report, 30th April, 1846. *Parl. Papers* (1846) XX, p. 614.

[55] Howell's Report, 1st May, 1845. *Parl. Papers* (1845) XXV, p. 258.

[56] Stuart's Report, 31st October, 1846. *Parl. Papers* (1847) XV, p. 474.

[57] Report, 1st May, 1845. *Parl. Papers* (1845) XXV, p. 267.

had before very generally prevailed, of producing as proof of real age, documents of various descriptions, many of little or no value, and too often expressly obtained for the purpose of deceiving the mill-occupier."[58] Such efforts as were still made to employ those who were too young served to demonstrate the wisdom of the provision that the surgeon must not only testify his belief as to the child's real age, but must also certify that there was no physical incapacity for work. " The continued attempts to evade the law in respect to the ages of persons employed, show the absolute necessity there was to provide some mode of testing the correctness of these extracts from registers, and of proving the ages of children and young persons by surgical certificates in the form prescribed by the amended Factory Act."[59]

For the Act as a whole the Inspectors had nothing but praise. " The amending Factory Act," said Horner, " came into operation on the 1st of October last, and I have the satisfaction of being able to report very favourably of its operation. The objects of the Legislature in restricting and regulating the labour of children and young persons in factories, have unquestionably been more generally and effectively attained during the last seven months, than they have ever been since Parliament first began to correct the great moral evils that had taken root and extensively spread in these branches of industry."[60] Saunders reported that the Act was well received in the manufacturing districts,[61] and that the half-time system, involving as it did only one change of hands at dinner-time, was generally welcomed.[62] The number of cases in which it was necessary to resort to prosecution dropped considerably, partly because, as Horner observed " it is evident that there is a more general disposition to pay strict attention to the law, and that the occupiers of factories and their servants find, that all which the Factory Acts require may be performed with a very moderate degree of regular attention."[63]

It is true that the passing of the Act of 1844 was the occasion of no such outburst of indignation on the part of the manufacturers as had marked the inception of effective legislation eleven years before, but this was due rather to acquiescence in the inevitable than to any change of heart. The owners still maintained that child labour was " a national blessing, and absolutely necessary

58 Report, 30th October, 1845. *Parl. Papers* (1846) XX, p. 587.
59 Saunders' Report, 30th April, 1846. *Ibid.* p. 624.
60 Report, 30th April, 1845. *Parl. Papers* (1845) XXV, p. 243.
61 Report 30th June, 1844. *Parl. Papers* (1844) XXVIII, p. 578.
62 Report, 30th October, 1845. *Parl. Papers* (1846) XX, p. 588.
63 Report, 30th April, 1847. *Parl. Papers* (1847) XV, p. 490.

for the support of the manifold fiscal burthens which have been placed upon the industry of this country"; that the result of the Factory Act had been to throw the younger classes out of employment, their places being taken by older hands from Wales, Ireland and the agricultural counties; that inspection was unjust and unnecessary.[64] Nassau Senior contended that the extension of protection to adult women was uncalled for, and wrong in principle. " I believe them to have as clear a perception of their interest," he said, " and as much determination and as much power to follow it as belong to their brothers or to their fathers. I utterly disapprove therefore of the principle of the Act of 1844."[65]

It is no less true of the factory acts than of other legislative measures that they achieve success in proportion as the machinery of control is effective. The experience of the last decade had enabled those who framed the statute of 1844 to avoid most of the pitfalls that had encompassed the feet of their predecessors, and to set up machinery that was, in most respects, adequate to its purpose. But in the battle of wits that must always ensue between those who devise the safeguards imposed by the legislature and those whose interest it is to evade the law, the prize goes to the quicker mind and the more nimble intelligence. For the moment the manufacturing interests were quiescent, rejoicing in the short-lived boom in trade that had followed the long period of depression.[66] The Short-time Committees, too, though remaining fully organized, were content to bide their time, awaiting a suitable opportunity to strike the next blow. When, three years later, their cause had triumphed, and the ten-hours day had been won, it was discovered that the Act of 1844, too, could be circumvented, and that the shorter working day was a delusion. It was then that the opposing forces met in a clash the violence and bitterness of which recalled the controversies of earlier days. From the resulting turmoil there emerged further legislation, but six years elapsed before the residual weaknesses of Graham's Act were finally removed.

[64] W. Cooke Taylor, *Factories and the Factory System* (1844) pp. 21, 24, 103.
[65] M. Bowley, *Nassau Senior* (1937) p. 269.
[66] The depression, which continued from 1837 to the spring of 1843, reached its nadir in 1841 and 1842, when mills which cost over £70,000 sold for half that sum, and machinery normally worth £20,000 fetched no more than £7,500.—K. M. Lyell, *Memoir of Leonard Horner* (1890) Vol. II, p. 36.

CHAPTER 15

HEALTH AND SAFETY

"DURING THE whole course of the struggle that has been made in behalf of the Factory Children," said Michael Sadler, "it has been invariably asserted by those who have interested themselves in their unhappy condition, that the early and excessive labour to which they have been doomed, has not only been injurious to their morals and health, but, in multitudes of cases, destructive of life itself, at an age when of all others the human frame is the most tenacious of existence, and when to destroy it by any other means than direct violence involves a degree of long-suffering and sorrow which it is distressing to contemplate, even in imagination."[1] It was the excessive working hours to which young people were exposed that made the strongest appeal to the emotions of the humanitarian reformers: so dramatic were the results of an evil which was apparent to every sympathetic observer that this particular aspect of factory employment was in danger of swamping all other considerations. The shorter working day was held to be the remedy, which, once achieved, would reconcile the public conscience to the employment of young children and adolescents, while, at the same time, conferring upon the adult operatives the boon for which they were agitating with such persistence.

This preoccupation must be held, in part at least, to account for a most remarkable omission in the early factory legislation— the neglect to make any adequate provision for health and safety. That first essay in industrial regulation, the Health and Morals of Apprentices Act, had prescribed only rudimentary standards, yet the fact remained that the requirements of that statute, that interior walls should be lime-washed twice a year, and that sufficient windows should be installed to provide proper ventilation, were considerably more stringent than those laid down in the Act of 1833.[2]

In these days, before Edwin Chadwick and Southwood Smith had aroused the nation to a realization of the vital importance of sanitation and the science of public health,[3] it was not, perhaps, to

---

[1] M. T. Sadler, *Factory Statistics* (1836) p.4.

[2] The Act of 1819 made no reference to ventilation; the Acts of 1825, 1831 and 1833 provided for lime-washing once a year only.

[3] Chadwick played a leading part in the inquiry instituted in 1839 by the Poor Law Commissioners into the sanitary conditions under which the labouring population lived. He was associated with Southwood Smith in the Duke of Buccleugh's Commission in 1842, and was largely responsible for the Public Health Act of 1848, passed as a result of the report of that Commission. See M. Marston, *Sir Edwin Chadwick* (1925) p. 103 *ff*.

have been expected that adequate precautions to provide reasonably healthy working conditions should have been taken, but there were other dangers not less menacing. The day of the low, wooden machines, operated by the hand of the worker, was over; the small water-wheels that had been so typical a feature of the remote rural mills were being replaced by giant structures similar to that installed in the Quarry Bank factory of Messrs. Greg, where there was " an elegant water-wheel 32 feet in diameter, and 24 feet broad, equivalent in power to 120 horses."[4]   Between 1801 and 1804, steam had begun to replace water as the motive power,[5] with the result that factories increased in size, and the machinery itself became more efficient and more complicated.   In 1819 there were only 344 cotton establishments in England and Scotland; in 1835 there were 1,262.   In 1812 there were 4,988,330 spindles; in 1835 the number had increased to 11,152,990, and in Manchester alone plans were being made to install an additional seven thousand horse-power.[6]   These prodigious developments staggered the imagination of contemporaries, many of whom came to regard the new machines with superstitious awe and reverence.   " The fine spinning mills at Manchester," said Ure, " are the triumphs of art and the glory of England.   In the beauty, delicacy, and ingenuity of the machines, they have no parallel among the works of man; nor in the orderly arrangement, and the value of the products. When 350 hanks are spun, containing only one pound of cotton, they form an almost incredible length of thread, extending 294,000 yards, or 167 miles, and enhancing the price of the material from 3s. 8d. to *twenty-five guineas*. . . . It is delightful to see from 800 to 1,000 spindles of polished steel, advancing and receding in a mathematical line, each of them whirling all the time upon its axis with equal velocity and truth, and forming threads of surprising tenuity, uniformity and strength."[7]

There were not wanting, however, those who regarded these developments with deep misgiving.   Every advance in technical performance enabled the machinery to be driven at a greater speed, as the thinner driving shafts and smaller drums or pulleys revolved at an ever-increasing rate.   The dangers to which the operatives were thus exposed were not diminished by the growing congestion of work-rooms, where the maximum of machinery was packed into

4 A. Ure, *The Philosophy of Manufactures* (1835) p. 346.   The mills of Messrs. Strutt at Belper were driven by eighteen water-wheels, totalling 600 horse-power.—*Ibid.* p. 343.
5 P. Gaskell, *The Manufacturing Population of England* (1833) p. 179.
6 *Quarterly Review* (1836) Vol. 57, p. 429.
7 A. Ure, *The Philosophy of Manufactures* (1835) pp. 312, 365.

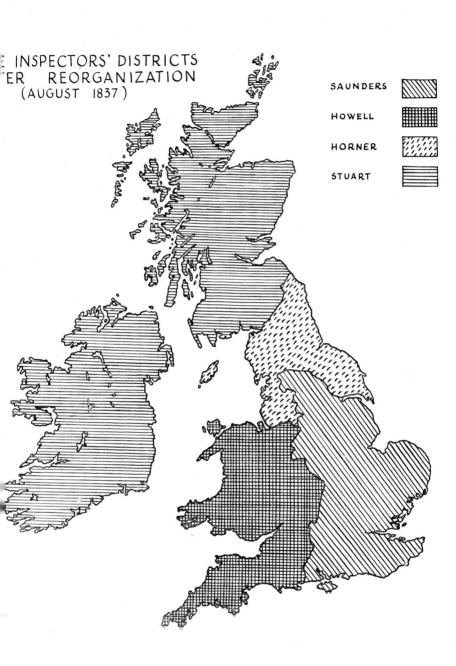

INSPECTORS' DISTRICTS
ER REORGANIZATION
(AUGUST 1837)

SAUNDERS

HOWELL

HORNER

STUART

the minimum of space.[8]   But few precautions being taken to fence the moving parts, accidents involving life and limb became common. " Besides the deformed persons," said Engels, " a great number of maimed ones may be seen going about in Manchester; this one has lost an arm or a part of one, that one a foot, the third half a leg; it is like living in the midst of an army just returned from a campaign."[9]

Prominent among those stirred by these conditions was Lord Ashley, who made the first proposals for reform in his bill of 1833.[10] Clauses 29 and 30 provided that if an operative was killed owing to an accident from unfenced machinery, the coroner should be required to summon a jury (from which any owner, or the father, brother or son of the owner should be excluded) to examine the machine.   If it appeared that there had been negligence in fencing, the mill-owner responsible was to be committed for trial on a charge of manslaughter.   If the worker had suffered non-fatal injury he was to be allowed to apply to the magistrates for an enquiry to be held at the petty sessions, which might inflict a penalty of between £50 and £200 to be applied for the benefit of the injured party.

These drastic proposals aroused dismay and apprehension in the minds of the manufacturers.   " I shall scarcely be able to speak of sections 29 and 30 with moderation," declared a Scottish spinning master. "Indeed, I have no hesitation in saying that, if passed into a law, it would be utterly impracticable for any man to conduct an establishment where machinery is used.   To think that the proprietor or occupier of a mill, for an accident over which he has no control, should be at the mercy of a jury who would be utterly incompetent to determine which of the machinery should or should not have been fenced in is altogether an invidious, harsh, and unwarrantable proposition. . . . Every practical man knows the absolute impossibility of fencing in all the machinery in a spinning-mill which may come under the denomination of ' dangerous.'   In fact, the work could not be carried on if every part were fenced in. The 29th and 30th clauses must therefore be expunged, or the title of the Bill had better be altered at once to ' A Bill for annihilating the Manufactures of Great Britain.' "[11]

It was commonly asserted that when accidents happened, they were due to the carelessness of the operatives rather than to the

---

[8] The manufacturers adduced this fact in proof of their contention that the operatives were not unduly crowded.   Each worker, it was said, had on an average, 12 square yards of floor space for himself and his machine.—H. Hoole, *A Letter in Defence of the Cotton Factories* (1832) p. 7.
[9] F. Engels, *The Condition of the Working Class in England in 1844* (1892) p. 164.
[10] *Parl. Papers* (1833) II, p. 263.
[11] *Letter on the Factory Bill* (1833) pp. 8, 11.

negligence of the master. In Henry Ashworth's mill at Turton, for instance, declared Cooke Taylor, the dangerous machinery was boxed-off, and accidents were very rare, but " when they did occur they were the result of the grossest negligence or of absolute wilfulness."[12] " Any one who reflected for a moment," he said, " could not fail to discover that an accident which destroyed life or limb must also derange the machinery, and, however careless he might suppose master manufacturers to be of their workmen, he cannot imagine them to be equally regardless of their own property. Now, however true it may be, that accidents were of frequent occurrence when machinery was a novelty, it is certainly untrue that they are equally common now. . . . No one can examine a cotton-mill without seeing, not only that its operations can be conducted with perfect safety to the operatives, but that there must be an utter disregard of ordinary precautions—a total want of prudence, and not a little perverted ingenuity to get into danger."[13]

Taylor was writing some ten years later, but he reflected the views of the owners who, in 1833, had been successful in securing the omission from Althorp's Act of any clauses concerning fencing or accidents. The Commission of 1833, while rejecting the suggestion in Ashley's bill regarding fatal accidents, had recommended a scheme of compensation for those who were injured. " We propose," said the Report, " that in the case of all accidents whatsoever from machinery occurring to children under fourteen years of age, the proprietor of the machinery shall pay for the medical attendance on the child, and all the expences of the cure, until medical attendance is no longer required; and also during the same period shall continue to pay wages at the rate of half the wages enjoyed by the individual in question at the time of the occurrence of the accident." Similar regulations, the Commissioners suggested, should govern those over fourteen years of age, but only if injury had been sustained in the ordinary course of employment, and if there had been no culpable temerity on the part of the injured worker.[14] These proposals, conferring on the younger workers an absolute right to compensation, and providing also for the older operatives if the accident was not the result of their own negligence, would have formed the basis of an interesting experiment had they been carried into law, for they would have left it to the mill-occupier to devise such measures as were necessary, thus absolving the legislature from the unenviable task of framing a safety code. But

---

12 W. Cooke Taylor, *Notes of a Tour in the Manufacturing Districts of Lancashire* (1842) p. 22.
13 W. Cooke Taylor, *Factories and the Factory System* (1844) p. 17.
14 *Parl. Papers* (1833) XX, p. 77.

the recommendations of the Commission were ignored, and the Act of 1833 made no provision for fencing, it gave the Inspectors no power of control, and it did not even require accidents to be reported.

Early in 1835 Saunders drew attention to the serious consequences to be anticipated from these omissions. In a number of factories, he said, the machinery was obviously dangerous, little care being taken to protect the operatives from injury, but he was powerless to intervene, and since there was no need for accidents to be reported to him, there was little he could do.[15] Everything depended on the whim of the individual owner. " Sufficient ventilation," he declared, " protection from dangerous machinery, general cleanliness, and the removal of noxious effluvia, cannot be secured under the present law, where there is no inclination on the part of the Mill-Occupier to adopt the necessary steps."[16]

The case of Cotterell v. Stocks, tried at the Liverpool summer assizes in 1840, brought the whole question of factory accidents into prominence. The plaintiff, a girl of seventeen, suing by Lord Ashley as her next friend, alleged that she had been caught by a revolving shaft, and hurled to the ground, sustaining broken limbs and severe bodily laceration. Her employers, who had been unwise enough to deduct from her wages the sum of eighteen pence for that portion of the week during which she had been unable to work, were ordered to pay damages of £100, and costs amounting to £600.[17]

The report of the Select Committee sitting under Ashley's chairmanship to consider the operation of the Act of 1833, was published a few months later, on 18th February, 1841. The problem was examined afresh, and for the first time specific and detailed proposals to ensure the safety of the workers were made. The cleaning of machinery in motion, it was recommended, should be prohibited under the severest penalties. The dangerous parts of the machinery should be boxed off—upright shafts to a point seven feet above the floor, while horizontal shafts revolving within seven feet of the floor should be totally enclosed if the operatives passed beneath them. Those pulleys on the main shafting which revolved in passages or gangways should also be boxed within seven feet of the floor. In cases of accidents due to the machinery's

[15] Report, 5th February, 1835. *Parl. Papers* (1835) XL, p. 691.
[16] Report, 30th September, 1838. *Parl. Papers* (1839) XIX, p. 442.
[17] Horner's Report, 30th September, 1840. *Parl. Papers* (1841) X, p. 167. E. Hodder, *The Life and Work of the seventh Earl of Shaftesbury* (1893) p. 187.

being negligently left uncovered some speedy and cheap method of
recovering compensation should be devised.[18]

The Government was impressed with the need for action, but
desiring further information as to the practicability of the proposals
made by the Committee, they resolved to obtain fuller information
from the Inspectors. Accordingly, on 2nd March, 1841, Fox Maule
issued the necessary instructions—

" I am to desire that you will as early as possible collect
information and report to His Lordship as to those parts of
the machinery in mills which, without impeding the work, it
is practicable to box off or fence, so as to diminish the risk
of danger to the workers.

His Lordship is of opinion that the information may be
more speedily obtained, if you desire the Superintendents who
act under your direction to make the inquiry at one or more
Cotton, Flax, Woollen, Worsted & Silk Mills, and to report
to you the result of such inquiries, distinguishing the following parts

The steam engine and water wheel
The main shafting or gearing & driving belts
The manufacturing machinery peculiar to the above five
branches.

The Select Committee of the House of Commons having
in their report recommended that the cleaning of machinery
while it is in motion should be prohibited, His Lordship
further desires that you will ascertain and report, whether
there are not certain parts of the machinery used in the above
named mills that must of necessity be wiped or cleaned while
they are in motion; and if so, you will in your report point
out what these are."[19]

Horner submitted his report on 2nd April, 1841.[20] The
subject, he said, had engaged his attention for some time,[21] for he
had long been surprised at the recklessness with which dangerous
machinery was left unguarded in some mills, while in others it was
carefully fenced.[22] After full consultation with manufacturers,

18 *Parl. Papers* (1841) IX, pp. 586-588.
19 *Home Office Papers.* H.O. 87 (1), p. 242.
20 *Parl. Papers* (1841) X, p. 206 *ff*.
21 On 30th April, 1840, he had written to his wife—" I am making an
inquiry with the view of finding out whether it be possible to frame a
clause for the new Factory Act that can be enforced, to prevent or diminish
the risk of those frightful accidents from the machinery which are so constantly happening by not enclosing the dangerous parts. It is a very difficult matter to deal with, but so far as I have gone in my inquiry my hopes
of being able to do something are great."—K. M. Lyell, *Memoir of
Leonard Horner* (1890) Vol. II, p. 13.
22 *Cf.* Saunders' Reports, 12th October, 1836. *Parl. Papers* (1837)
XXXI, p. 83. 30th June, 1838. *Parl. Papers* (1838) XLV, p. 63.

overseers, and machine makers he had come to the conclusion that it was possible to frame and enforce enactments prohibiting the cleaning of rapidly moving machinery, and requiring dangerous parts to be fenced.

The main gearing, including upright, horizontal or oblique shafts, cogged wheels, drums and pulleys, straps or belts revolving on pulleys on the main shaft—in short all those parts connecting the main moving power with the manufacturing machinery—could not, as a rule, be cleaned without some degree of motion. It might be sufficient to enact that no part of the main gearing within six feet of the floor should be cleaned whilst it was in motion, without so reducing the speed of the principal moving power that no accident could occur. So far as the cleaning of the manufacturing machinery was concerned, the chief danger could be removed by prohibiting the cleaning of the frame gearing[23] if it was being moved by the principal moving power. Special regulations would be necessary in the case of the self-acting spinning-frame or mule, which moved with great force. It should be declared illegal to clean the carriage or traverse part of the mule, the roller beam, and the floor space over which the carriage travelled, without stopping the machine entirely.

The master, added Horner, was often unable to control the cleaning, which was done at all odd times, but if he gave orders in contravention of the law, he should be fined heavily. The more immediate responsibility lay with the workman in charge of the machine, for he could prevent his piecers or scavengers from cleaning it if he took the trouble. If he was negligent he should be fined, but the penalty should not be excessive, since the forfeiture of a small sum would be a heavy punishment.

Much could be done, Horner thought, to reduce the risk of accidents by fencing the dangerous parts of the machinery, and he considered that it would be perfectly feasible to enumerate those parts in a schedule to any amending Act. The principal moving-power was usually in a detached part of the factory to which the workers had no access; but in the few instances where this was not the case, the steam-engine and the water-wheel should be adequately guarded, as should the water-way and wheel-race, and any flywheel directly connected with the moving power. The upright and oblique shafts of the main gearing should be strongly cased to a height of seven feet from the floor, and all parts revolving near a passage or gangway within seven feet of the floor should be so fenced that nobody could come into contact with them.

The frame gearing, he thought, should also be fenced, especially the vertical shafts and the parts of the machine where

---

[23] The frame gearing included minor shafts, pulleys and straps which distributed motion from the main gearing.

two wheels worked inward, or where a chain or screw motion propelled a wheel. The pulleys should be guarded if they revolved next to a passage less than two feet wide between the working parts of two machines, or less than eighteen inches wide between the machine and the wall. The worst accidents, in his experience, were caused by the driving belts, especially when they were fastened by buckles instead of laces, for they were apt to catch the clothing or the hair of the women, and drag them up bodily. The remedy, he suggested, was to secure that every belt should be so arranged that it did not pass across a gangway at a height of less than seven feet, and that a belt passing through the floor should be cased to a height of at least six inches. The pulley on which the belt worked, if not connected with a loose pulley and guide-hook by means of which the belt could be transferred from one pulley to the other, should be provided with a strap-hanger or catch-hook on either side, so that if the belt left the pulley it would not come in contact with the driving shaft.

Since it would not always be possible to comply strictly with the regulations that might be made, Horner thought the Inspectors should be allowed some discretion to accept alternative arrangements, but he was strongly opposed to the suggestion that instead of specifying the parts of the machinery that should be fenced, the whole matter should be left to the Inspector. To give any public officer so arbitrary and undefined a power would, he was convinced, give rise to serious difficulties.

This was the antithesis of the view entertained by Howell,[24] who, submitting the report of his Superintendent, Charles Trimmer, the leading witness in this matter before the Select Committee, held that " steam-engines and water-wheels were beyond the pale of legislative interference." Apart from the upright and horizontal shafts, which were only dangerous within six or seven feet of the floor, it was quite impossible to specify the parts that should be fenced, since conditions varied so greatly. The owners, he said, knew perfectly well that no Act could define all the dangerous parts of the machinery, and they would much prefer a system by which the Inspectors were empowered to order fencing to be carried out, if it could be done without hindrance to the work.

Stuart's report[25] had but little contribution to make to the solution of the problem. He agreed that the steam-engine, water-wheel, and flywheel should be completely enclosed, and that the shafting should be cased to a height of seven feet, but suggested that machinery near to which the operatives passed should not be completely boxed, but guarded by iron hoops, since it would be

---

24 *Parl. Papers* (1841) X, p. 227 *ff.*
25 *Ibid.* p. 269 *ff.*

impossible to carry out the necessary maintenance work if the manufacturing machinery was totally enclosed.

Saunders took the view that it would be impolitic to allow the Inspectors to order the fencing of any machinery they considered dangerous. " It has often been suggested," he said in his second report,[26] " that the Inspector and Sub-Inspector, might have the power to order the boxing-off of any machinery which he should deem dangerous, and thus, as it is said, ' avoid this minute regulation,' forgetting that unless minute regulations are made for limiting the authority of these officers, and for protecting the mill-occupier against unnecessary expense, such a regulation would be much more arbitrary, oppressive and vexatious than any of the other enactments to which these terms are applied." He therefore proposed a set of regulations[27] which, though following in the main the recommendations put forward by Horner, took the form of a detailed code to be incorporated in the statute. Saunders admitted, however, that he had been unable to provide for every contingency, and he considered it essential that some discretionary powers should be entrusted to the Inspectors.

This was precisely what had been proposed in the bill introduced by Fox Maule on 26th March, 1841,[28] clause 46 of which provided that an Inspector or Sub-Inspector should be authorized to give written notice to a mill-occupier if he saw " any machinery or parts of machinery not adequately enclosed, boxed-off, or secured, which he shall deem to be dangerous." The effect of such notice was not to be understood as placing any obligation on the owner to fence, but merely to render him liable to penalties if an operative was injured after the notice had been disregarded.[29]

Fox Maule's bill, of course, never reached the statute book, and the Inspectors remained powerless to deal with a problem the urgency of which was being constantly brought to their attention. In his report for September, 1841,[30] Horner alluded to the case of a young girl who, while working within ten inches of an unfenced shaft " was caught by her apron, which lapped round

---

[26] *Parl. Papers* (1841) X, p. 240. His first report (*Ibid.* p. 229 *ff*) had been revised after consultation with Horner.

[27] See Appendix.

[28] *Parl. Papers* (1841) II, p. 425.

[29] Clause 66 provided that if a person suffered injury " in consequence of the occupier of a Factory having grossly or wilfully neglected to arrange, inclose, box-off, or secure any part of the machinery in the Factory, of which he shall have received notice in writing from an Inspector or Sub-Inspector, that the Inspector or Sub-Inspector deemed the same to be dangerous," the occupier was to be liable to a penalty of not less than £10 and not more than £80.

[30] *Parl. Papers* (1842) XXII, p. 341.

the shaft, and being tight round her body, she was whirled round, and repeatedly forced between the shaft and the carding engine," her severed right leg being found some distance away. " This accident," he said, " shows the necessity of enactments to enforce the boxing of upright shafts in all circumstances, whether apparently harmless or otherwise, for they become dangerous whenever a fixed body is placed near them. The wanton careless manner in which dangerous machinery is often left exposed, which might be guarded at an expense of a few shillings, without any impediment to the working, is perfectly inexcusable."

The most serious accidents were caused by the straps connecting the manufacturing machinery with the main moving power, but it was extremely difficult to devise a set of regulations that should secure their being properly guarded. " Such is their complexity," declared Horner, " from the infinite variety of ways in which they are applied, modified by the nature of the machinery, and the dimensions of the room in which it is placed, that I do not believe it is in the power of language to define the belts which shall be fenced off, without the description having the effect, in numerous instances, of entirely stopping the operation of the mill."[31]

The anxieties of the Inspectors were reflected in their reports, which never ceased to urge the need for legislation. Descriptions of accidents that had come to their notice were given increasing prominence, and the grim facts that they so ruthlessly exposed had a profound effect on the public mind. " On the 23rd November," recorded Howell, " Mary Ann Lees, aged 24, a married woman, the mother of one child, and in an advanced state of pregnancy, carried her husband's dinner to him, in a room in Messrs. T. & G. Marshall's mill (at Stockport) where he was employed as a dresser. She remained with him for a short time after the expiration of the dinner hour, and having inadvertently approached too near an upright shaft, revolving with considerable rapidity, her shawl was caught by it, and she was consequently dragged against the shaft, from which she was with much difficulty released after her left arm had been torn completely off above the elbow joint, so as to render amputation necessary close to the shoulder. . . . If the trifling sum of three shillings had been expended in boxing off this shaft, the accident could not have happened; and this might have been done without the least impediment to the work carried on. . . . This accident, I think, affords another strong proof of the necessity for legislative interference, since it is obvious that some mill-owners will not take the precaution of fencing off dangerous machinery until compelled to do so by a stringent enactment."[32]

---

[31] Report, 31st December, 1841. *Ibid*. p. 354.
[32] Report, 31st December, 1841. *Ibid*. p. 430.

If universal agreement as to the measures to be employed had not as yet been reached, there was, nevertheless, a growing mass of opinion that Parliament should take vigorous action to minimize the dangers arising from unfenced machinery. But how was this to be accomplished? The Inspectors had no desire to be saddled with the sole responsibility of making decisions that could hardly fail, in many instances, to arouse the antagonism of the manufacturers; on the other hand it was generally recognized that it would be beyond the competence of the legislature to draft regulations that, in so highly technical a field, could be applicable to all cases. Common prudence suggested that before embarking on such a venture, a much greater body of evidence should be available. Saunders thought it would be helpful if a register of accidents could be kept at each mill,[33] and Horner, adopting the suggestion of a mill-occupier in his district, proposed that an account of every accident should be sent at once to the Inspector, who should then direct the certifying surgeon to investigate the circumstances and submit a report. In this way, he considered, " in the course of two or three years, a mass of authentic evidence would be collected, upon which Parliament might proceed to legislate, if necessary, with safety."[34]

This plan met with general approval, and it was incorporated in the bill introduced by Graham on 7th March, 1843.[35] It was proposed to prohibit children and young persons from cleaning machinery whilst it was in motion, and from working between the fixed and traversing parts of self-acting machines. Since it was beyond question that certain parts of the machinery were inherently dangerous, the 21st clause provided that the flywheel directly connected with the steam-engine or the water-wheel, every part of the engine or wheel near which children and young persons were liable to be employed, and all parts of the mill gearing, were to be securely fenced, while the wheel-race was to be guarded close to the edge.

The provision first made in Fox Maule's bill that Inspectors and Sub-Inspectors should serve written notice of machinery that they considered dangerous was retained, but the maximum penalty to which a mill-occupier rendered himself liable if an operative was injured after this warning had been disregarded was increased from £80 to £100. Any accident sufficiently serious to cause an interruption in the continuance of a worker's normal employment in the factory was to be reported the same day to the certifying

[33] Report, 31st March, 1842. *Ibid.* p. 458.
[34] Report, 31st December, 1841. *Ibid.* p. 354.
[35] *Parl. Papers* (1843) II, p. 495.

surgeon, who was to investigate the occurrence, and make a report to the Inspector immediately. The Inspectors were also authorized to institute an action for damages on behalf of any person injured, any sums recovered as the result of such action to be paid to the party concerned.

An important modification was introduced at the committee stage, on 1st May, 1843,[36] when it was considered desirable to provide for an appeal from the Inspector's notice requiring machinery to be fenced. If the mill-occupier dissented from the Inspector's opinion he could apply for the question to go to the arbitration of two examiners, one nominated by the Inspector, and one by himself. The experts thus appointed were to examine the machinery alleged to be dangerous, and if they considered that fencing was unnecessary or impossible, the Inspector was required to cancel the notice he had issued.

These provisions remained substantially unaltered in the new bill that Graham introduced on 6th February, 1844,[37] though it was now proposed to insist on the fencing of hoists and teagles as well. The Inspector was also required to give an occupier four days' notice of his intention to prefer a complaint, while the mill-owner was to give the Inspector two days' notice if he intended to produce a skilled witness when the case was heard.

On more than one occasion the Inspectors had drawn attention to the unsatisfactory conditions encountered in many factories engaged in the wet spinning of flax, a process which exposed the worker to the drenching effects of the hot water that was constantly sprayed over the material. In some mills, it was true, great care was taken to protect the operatives from wetting by erecting iron frames in front of the spindles to contain the water,[38] but the Inspector had no power to insist on such precautions.[39] In many instances the spinning apartments were full of steam, the feet of the workers were always wet, and " their bodies at the waist saturated with hot water and spray thrown on them."[40] Graham's bill proposed to remedy this by providing that no child or young person was to be employed in the wet spinning of flax, jute, hemp or tow, unless adequate precautions were taken to protect the operatives from wetting, and to prevent the escape of steam into the working-room.

[36] Parl. Papers (1843) II, p. 549.
[37] Parl. Papers (1844) II, p. 149.
[38] Stuart's Report, 31st December, 1836. Parl. Papers (1837) XXXI, p. 120.
[39] Stuart's Reports, 30th June, 1837. Parl. Papers (1838) XXVIII, p. 103. 30th September, 1841. Parl. Papers (1842) XXII, p. 351.
[40] Stuart's Report, 31st March, 1843. Parl. Papers (1843) XXVII, p. 343.

The provisions that had been gradually worked out over the past three years were finally incorporated in the Act of 1844. Section 20 provided that no child or young person was to clean any part of the mill-gearing whilst it was in motion, or to work between the fixed and traversing parts of a self-acting machine whilst it was mechanically propelled.

Every flywheel directly connected with the steam-engine, water-wheel, or other mechanical power, every part of a steam-engine or water-wheel, and every hoist or teagle near to which children and young persons were liable to pass or to be employed, and all parts of the mill-gearing, were to be securely fenced. Every wheel-race not otherwise secured was to be fenced close to the edge, and the protection was not to be removed whilst the parts were in motion by mechanical power.[41] The penalty for non-compliance was a fine of not less than £5, and not exceeding £20.[42]

If an Inspector considered that dangerous machinery or driving bands were not securely fenced he was to give written notice to the factory-occupier in the form set out in the schedule.[43] The occupier could, if he so desired, and on giving 14 days' notice, have the matter referred to two skilled arbitrators, one to be nominated by himself and one by the Inspector. Should these experts disagree they were to appoint a third arbitrator, and if it was reported to the Inspector that fencing was unnecessary or impossible, the notice was to be cancelled.[44] If any person suffered bodily injury because the mill-occupier had not boxed-off the machinery or driving bands after having received notice from the Inspector, the occupier was to be liable to a penalty of not less than £10, and not exceeding £100, to be applied in whole or in part for the benefit of the injured party.[45]

When an accident caused bodily injury to any person employed in the factory, so that he was unable to resume work before 9 a.m. the following day,[46] the factory-occupier or his principal agent was to notify the certifying surgeon within 24 hours of the absence, and the surgeon was to inform the Sub-Inspector of the district.[47] After such notification the surgeon, with the least possible delay, was to visit the factory and investigate the nature and cause of the injury. Within the next 24 hours he was to send a report to the Inspector of the district, by whom it was to be transmitted to the office of the Factory Inspectors. For the purpose of these

---

41 Sec. 21.
42 Sec. 59.
43 See Appendix.
44 Sec. 43.
45 Sec. 60.
46 This time limit was first proposed in the bill introduced by Graham on 29th March, 1844. *Parl. Papers* (1844) II, p. 187.
47 Sec. 22.

investigations the surgeon was to have the same power, authority
and protection as an Inspector. His fee was not to exceed ten
shillings, and to be not less than three shillings, at the discretion
of the Inspector.[48]

Six months after the passing of the Act no child or young
person was to be employed in any part of a factory in which wet-
spinning of flax, hemp, jute or tow was carried on, unless precautions were taken to prevent the workers from being wetted. Where
hot water was used, steps were to be taken to prevent the steam
from escaping into the work-room.[49]

The inside walls, ceilings, tops of rooms, passages and stair-
cases which had not been painted with oil within the last seven
years, were to be limewashed at least once every 14 months. The
inside walls, ceilings and tops of rooms in which children and
young persons were employed, and which were painted with oil,
were to be washed with hot water and soap every 14 months.[50]

The Secretary of State could empower an Inspector to direct
an action to be brought in the name of and on behalf of any person
injured for the recovery of damages.[51] Any sums so recovered were
to be applied for the benefit of the injured party; but if the verdict
was for the defendant he was to recover his costs from the
Inspector, the expenses of the action being paid as other expenses
incurred under the Act.[52]

It was further provided that written notice, four days prior to
the hearing, must be given of intention to prefer a complaint that
a child or young person had been employed in a factory without
sufficient protection against wetting or against the escape of steam
into the room used by the workers, or that machinery required to
be fenced had not been properly guarded. If the defendant intended
to call a skilled witness in his defence he was required to give
48 hours' notice to the Inspector or Sub-Inspector.[53]

" It should never be forgotten," declared Horner, " that sound
limbs are a main part of the working man's capital, and that it
should be exposed as little as possible to the risk of irrecoverable
diminution."[54]   Hitherto Parliament had steadfastly refused to
introduce legislation regulating the hours and conditions of adult
males, such limitations as were the inevitable corollary of the
enactments concerning children and young persons being regarded

48 Sec. 23.
49 Sec. 19.
50 Sec. 18.
51 Sec. 24.
52 Sec. 25.
53 Sec. 42.
54 Report, 31st October, 1846. *Parl. Papers* (1847) XV, p. 442.

as the regrettable consequence of over-riding necessity.[55] It was indeed true that adults had benefited from the lime-washing of internal walls that had been required by Althorp's Act,[56] but they were now, for the first time, to be protected from some at least of the dangers of their daily avocation. The prohibition of the cleaning of machinery in motion, and the protection against wetting in the flax mills applied only to children and young persons, but the other safety provisions were of universal application.[57]

The new code was acclaimed by the Inspectors,[58] whose close contacts with the mills never failed to remind them of the dangers encountered there. " When I view the complicated machinery amongst which the people work," said Horner, " the infinite number of wheels and other mechanisms, with projections to catch, sharp edges to cut, and vast weights to crush, the crowded state in which the machines are often packed together, and the great velocity and force with which they move, it often appears to me a marvel that accidents are not of daily occurrence in every mill."[59] Specific instructions were issued to owners " that every part of the machinery from which danger may arise, even to the heedless, to which a guard can be applied without impeding the working of the machine, ought to be securely fenced,"[60] but it soon became clear that such general directions were of little avail. " The terms and definitions used in these enactments," asserted Saunders, " are very vague and indefinite. Any individual at all acquainted with the complicated movements of machinery, as well as the infinite variety of names by which the several parts are called, will at once understand the difficulty of being more precise."[61]

One of the chief difficulties lay in the fact that it was often impossible to decide whether or not it was feasible to fence the

---

[55] For an expression of the then impious view that even wages should be regulated see J. Wood, *Right of Labour to Legislative Protection* (1832) p. 10.

[56] Horner's Report, 31st December, 1841. *Parl. Papers* (1842) XXII, p. 353.

[57] The Inspectors were doubtful whether section 60, providing penalties if injury was sustained by unfenced machinery, extended to adult males. Replying to their enquiry (*Minutes,* 29th November, 1844, Vol. II, p. 75) Manners Sutton said that the Law Officers " are of opinion that the language of the 60th Section of the 7 & 8 Vict., c. 15 is sufficiently comprehensive to include all persons whatsoever, whatever may be their age, and whether employed in the Factory or not." (*Minutes,* 17th February, 1845, Vol. II, p. 131.)

[58] " The enactments in the Act of last session requiring dangerous machinery to be securely fenced, will, I have no doubt, prove a great boon to the workers in factories, and I shall spare no pains to enforce their strict observance."—Horner's Report, 30th September, 1844. *Parl. Papers* (1845) XXV, p. 234.

[59] Report, 30th April, 1845. *Parl. Papers* (1845) XXV, p. 246.

[60] *Ibid.* p. 247.

[61] Report, 1st May, 1845. *Parl. Papers* (1845) XXV, pp. 271-272.

machinery without impeding its working, and in this connection the policy pursued by the Inspectors was to refrain from insisting that guards be provided until sufficient evidence had become available from the accident reports of the surgeons.[62]   Many injuries were caused by the cog-wheels at the ends of the throstle-frames, still more from attempts to clean the machinery when it was running at full speed, and from adjusting the driving straps on the pulleys whilst the shaft was still revolving.[63]   The advice of the Inspectors was that all gear-wheels should be fenced by a case of wood, iron, strong tin, or strong wire, covering all the wheels, or the ingathering parts of all gearing-wheels, and so fixed to the frame by a nut or screw that no person could remove or open the case without the assistance of the overlooker; while the danger from loose straps lapping round the shaft should, they suggested, be minimized either by casing the shaft between the pulleys, or by providing a strap-hook on either side of the pulley, so fixed as to prevent the strap from resting on the shaft, even if it should fall off accidentally.[64]

The mill-occupiers, however, were under no obligation to follow such advice, nor could they be compelled to heed the written warnings served on them by the Inspectors.[65]   The only remedy was to impose a statutory obligation in such cases, and the Inspectors, convinced of the inadequacy of the existing law, recommended the incorporation of additional clauses in an amending Act as follows:—

" I.—That the sides of every driving-drum or pulley over which any strap or band is employed in communicating motion to another drum or pulley shall be so securely fenced as to prevent the strap coming in contact with a revolving shaft, when it is removed, in any manner whatever, from the driving drum to which it belongs.

II.—That every driving strap or band by which any part of the machinery is set in motion, and to which a fixed and a loose pulley are attached, shall be provided with a guide-hook or fork, by which alone it shall be capable to move such strap or band from one pulley to the other.

III.—That when two cog-wheels of any machine, working inwards, are so exposed that any person is liable to come in

[62] Horner's Report, 31st October, 1845. *Parl. Papers* (1846) XX, p. 570.
[63] Howell's Report, 31st October, 1845. *Ibid.* p. 581.
[64] Saunders' Report, 30th April, 1846 *Ibid.* p. 626.
[65] *Minutes,* 10th December, 1845, Vol. II, p. 211.—" Mr. Howell brought before the meeting a Letter from one of the Sub-Inspectors of his district respecting the effect of a Notice of Dangerous Machinery, and all the Inspectors agreed that it is perfectly optional with the occupier of a Factory to disregard such notice with impunity until an accident shall have happened in which case he will subject himself to the penalties of the 60th clause."

contact with them, the parts of such cog-wheels as work inwards shall be securely fenced."[66]

The certifying surgeons were now much more closely associated with the general system of factory control, and this was destined to have important, though not immediate, consequences. In 1833 they had been called in not because there was any idea that they could make a contribution to problems of health and safety, but because their services were essential in ascertaining age. Their functions were now extended—they were required to vouch for the physical fitness of the younger workers, and to investigate accidents, while the fact that they were now definitely appointed by the Inspectors served to identify them even more closely with the industry. The Inspectors were fully convinced of the importance of establishing their authority, a matter not entirely free from difficulty, since many of them were reluctant to pay the stamp duty of £2 on the document by which they were appointed. " I hope," said Howell, " the legality of the mode of appointment will be clearly ascertained beforehand with a view more particularly to the powers to be exercised by the Certifying Surgeons, because it is very probable that the Surgeon's appointment may be disputed on the ground of illegality, in cases where we may have reason to complain of Parties for not giving notice of accidents to the Certifying Surgeon. It is the quasi judicial examinations he is empowered to conduct in cases of accident which, in my opinion, render it so very important that his appointment should be free from doubt."[67] This legal difficulty having been surmounted by appointing the surgeons otherwise than in writing,[68] it became possible for them to undertake their duties without undue qualms, and the great mass of evidence they collected as they submitted their accident reports was sufficient testimony to their zeal.

In order to secure uniformity of practice the Inspectors agreed that these reports should be framed in the same manner in each of their districts, and a circular letter was therefore sent to the surgeons requiring them to insert the name and age of the person injured, with full details of the operation upon which he was employed; whether the surgeon had visited the factory to examine the place where the accident had occurred, and whether he had seen the injured person or not.[69] At the central office of the Inspectors the records were to be kept for each district under the following heads: —[70]

Number of each accident for reference.

66 Joint Report, 31st December, 1846. *Parl. Papers* (1847) XV, p. 486.
67 *Minutes,* 14th August, 1844, Vol. II, p. 37.
68 *Ibid.* 20th August, 1844, Vol. II, p. 45.
69 *Ibid.* 29th November, 1844, Vol. II, p. 80.
70 *Ibid.* 17th December, 1844, Vol. II, p. 89.

Date of accident.
Name of Firm and Locality of Factory.
Christian and Surname and age of person injured.
Nature of accident.
Cause of accident.
Name of Surgeon.

The work involved in investigating accidents and drawing up reports was responsible and exacting, and the Inspectors, anxious that the surgeons should receive adequate remuneration, proposed that they should be paid a minimum fee of 5s. for each case. Sir James Graham, however, considered that the cost would be excessive, and despite the contention of the Inspectors that the sum of £800 a year, which seemed likely to be involved, was money well spent, since the knowledge that accidents were now reported induced manufacturers to fence their machinery, he insisted that the surgeon's fee should exceed 5s. only if he had to travel more than three miles to make his enquiries.[71]   The surgeons acquiesced in this arrangement, albeit somewhat unwillingly, and the Inspectors bore testimony to the fact that the parsimonious attitude of the Government had not diminished the value of their work.   " The amount of annual charge for the Reports (about 700 *l.*) appears large;" said Saunders, "but, I am convinced, no part of the expenses incurred in carrying out the Factories Act has been of greater service to the operatives."[72]

There were already indications that the functions of the surgeons could with profit be extended to include not merely the granting of age certificates and the investigation of accidents, but a much wider range of duties embracing the oversight of the health and the working conditions of the operatives.   The owners of the North Shore Mill at Liverpool, employing over 800 hands, arranged for the certifying surgeon to act as medical attendant, at a salary of £200 a year.   He attended the surgery provided on the premises from 12 to 1 daily, visiting the homes of the sick if the need arose.   For this attention those earning more than 4s. weekly paid one penny a week, while the lower paid workers were treated for nothing, the owners making up the deficiency.[73]

---

[71] See Appendix.

[72] Report, 31st October, 1848.   *Parl. Papers* (1849) XXII, p. 249.

[73] Horner's Report, 31st October, 1845.   *Parl. Papers* (1846) XX, pp. 574-577.   At this mill, said Horner, there was also an excellent school, a savings bank, and a brass band of 24 instrumentalists.   A fire escape was also provided.   " The knowledge of there being such an escape at hand would frequently encourage men to work effectually in the extinguishing an incipient fire, instead of hurrying away in alarm on the first outcry to save themselves.   To prevent this sort of confusion on such occasions," said the owners, " we have organized a species of ' Fire Brigade,' consisting of a few steady hands from each room who practise together monthly with the various water pipes, taps, hoses, buckets, &c., with which each room is provided, so as to be expert and steady if called upon to act."

There were, of course, few mills in which such enlightened counsels prevailed, but the unhealthy conditions encountered in many of the factories were beginning to cause grave concern, as the Inspectors called attention to the inadequacy of the existing law. "There are," said Saunders, "sources of injury which in many mills grievously afflict the workers—such as insufficient or no ventilation at all, and effluvia of the most disgusting and offensive nature. It was the object of a Factory Act still in force, 42 Geo. III, c. 73[74] to provide against these evils. That Act, which is the only Factory Act passed previous to 1833 not repealed, is, however, quite inoperative. It required a yearly appointment of two persons by the magistrates at quarter sessions, for the purpose of enforcing its provisions; but if these were ever appointed, they have long since been discontinued."[75]

The heavy incidence of epidemic diseases, especially in the large towns, convinced the Government that steps must be taken to deal with the appalling sanitary conditions that were the prime focus of infection, and in the years 1846 and 1847 some attempt was made to deal with the situation.[76] The Public Health Act of 1848[77] centralized the whole system of control, but it was not until the passing of the Factory Acts Extension Act[78] in 1864 that specific regulations governing the ventilation and cleanliness of factories were imposed.

The difficulties experienced by the Inspectors in interpreting and applying the fencing clauses were a source of considerable embarrassment. "Unless the legal opinions which may be given, on the cases now under consideration from Halifax and Huddersfield, shall have the effect of lessening the difficulties experienced as to the construction of the law, and thereby give greater uniformity to the proceedings of magistrates, I fear," declared Saunders, " it will be ultimately necessary to have recourse to some explanatory or amending Act of Parliament as regards these provisions of the amended Factory Act, before the Inspectors can enforce them satisfactorily."[79]

Section 24 of the Act had provided that the Inspectors might bring an action to recover damages on behalf of a person who had been injured by machinery, but there was no provision for compensation when death ensued. In their Joint Report for June,

---

[74] The Act of 1802.
[75] Report, 30th April, 1848. *Parl. Papers* (1847-8) XXVI, p. 184.
[76] An Act for the more speedy Removal of certain Nuisances (1846) 9 & 10 Vict., c. 96. The Towns Improvement Clauses Act (1847) 10 & 11 Vict., c. 34.
[77] 11 & 12 Vict., c. 63.
[78] 27 & 28 Vict., c. 48.
[79] Report, 30th April, 1846. *Parl. Papers* (1846) XX, p. 625.

1846, the Inspectors called attention to " the somewhat inconsistent provisions of an Act that makes the occupier of a factory, by whose neglect an accident occurs, which causes only a slight injury, liable to a fine of 100*l*; whereas it now appears that when instant death ensues from any such accident, the occupier is not liable, under the same provisions, to any pecuniary penalty whatever."[80]

The Inspectors had already discussed this anomaly on 30th June, 1845, suggesting that the bill then passing through Parliament should be amended so as " to enable the Inspectors of Factories to bring an action for the recovery of damages for and on behalf of the families of persons killed by machinery in Factories."[81]   In the meantime Saunders recommended that in cases of instant death due to accident any penalty levied under clause 60 of the Factory Act should be applied for the benefit of the relatives of the deceased.[82]   Sir James Graham agreed that this course should be adopted, though it was obvious that the discretion granted to the Home Secretary had never been intended to cover such cases. Parliament having refused to amend the Fatal Accidents bill as the Inspectors had proposed, the whole matter came up for further consideration as the result of a fatality that occurred in the mill occupied by Joseph Nichols of Halifax.

This case was particularly important, not only because it settled the law concerning compensation for death, but because it illustrated the difficulty of enforcing the fencing clauses in factories jointly occupied by a number of manufacturers.   The case as presented for counsel's opinion was as follows:—

" A. occupies a small room in a building other parts of which are let to other parties totally unconnected with A. who employ power transmitted to their several rooms from the Engine.   One shaft passes through the room in A's. occupation but he derives no power from it, the only machinery in his room being a warping mill worked by a woman only (37 years of age) by hand.   A child, who has no earthly business in the room, gets in, is caught by the shaft and is instantly killed.   The Inspector lays an Information against the occupier under Sec. 60 c. 15, 7 & 8 Vic. which imposes a penalty of £100 upon the occupier of a Factory for neglecting to case off his gearing shafts.

---

[80] *Ibid.* p. 639.

[81] *Minutes,* Vol. II, p. 182.   The Bill which was passed into law as the Fatal Accidents Act, 1846 (9 & 10 Vict., c. 93), granted for the first time to the personal representatives of a servant killed through the negligence of his master, the same rights of action as the deceased would have enjoyed had he lived, providing they could prove that they had sustained a pecuniary loss, arising from their relationship with him.

[82] *Minutes,* 4th July, 1845, Vol. II, p. 185.   Section 60 provided that the penalty should be applied for the benefit of the injured person, " or otherwise as the Secretary of State may determine."

1st.—Is the room so occupied a Factory within the meaning of the Act?

2nd.—If it is, is it the duty of an occupier or of the owner to protect shafts from which the occupier derives no advantage and if of the owner is there any means of punishing him for negligence in not doing so?

3rd—Death having instantly ensued, does the accident come within the limits of the 60th Sec., or does the expression ' bodily injury ' exclude accidents in which sudden death occurs which are cognizable under other Acts?"

The opinion delivered by James Stansfield inclined to the view that the room in question could not be regarded as a Factory.[83] " Whatever be the true answer to the first question," continued counsel, " the present case may be clearly disposed of upon the last.—For the words of the 60th Sec. ' if any person shall suffer any bodily injury ' would alone at least in a penal act like the present exclude the case of immediate death from the province of the enactment more particularly as any case of Death is otherwise cognizable by the Law—while the intention of the Legislature is shewn without doubt to have been thus restricted by the subsequent provision for the application of a given portion of the penalty ' for the benefit of the injured person.' "

This opinion, dated 17th February, 1846, was, of course, most unwelcome to the Inspectors, who made their remonstrance to the Home Secretary, but without result. " I am directed by Sec. Sir J. G.," Saunders was informed on 20th May, " that the Law Officers of the Crown are of opinion that the 60th Sec. of the Factory Act 7 Vic. c. 15 appears not to be intended to apply to cases where instant Death ensues from the accident."[84]

The decision, though undoubtedly correct in law, had unfortunate consequences, as Saunders observed in his report for October, 1846.[85] Section 21, he said, required mill-gearing to be fenced, section 59 prescribed penalties for neglecting to fence machinery, while section 60 imposed heavier penalties when accidents occurred because machinery was not fenced after warning. But there were parts of the mill-gearing so situated as not to be dangerous unless persons came into immediate contact with them, *i.e.* horizontal shafts eight or ten feet above the floor. In these cases it had been customary not to require fencing, but to serve notice that the shafts were dangerous, and then to proceed under section 60 in case of accident. The ruling in the Halifax case precluded action under this section if death resulted, and so it

---

83 See Appendix.
84 *Minutes*, 2nd June, 1846, Vol. II, pp. 241-244.
85 *Parl. Papers* (1847) XV, p. 466.

became necessary to proceed under section 59, with the result that the occupier escaped penalty since the magistrates held that it was not necessary to fence these horizontal shafts.

The scope of the 60th section was further considered in the Huddersfield case. On 10th March, 1846, in a factory occupied by Messrs. Walker and Sons, one Luke Dyson was severely injured because part of the mill-gearing, an upright shaft, was not securely fenced. Two informations were laid, one under section 59 " for not fencing part of the machinery required by the 21st section of the Act to be securely fenced "; and one under section 60 " for that a young person did suffer bodily injury in consequence of the said occupier having neglected to fence a part of the machinery (to wit an upright shaft) required by the Act to be securely fenced." The magistrates convicted on the first information, imposing the minimum penalty of £5, but they were divided in their views on the second charge. The defendants argued that in order to justify a conviction under section 60 it was necessary that due notice should have been served that the machinery was dangerous, and no such notice had been given. The complainants contended, on the other hand, that in the case of bodily injury caused by any part of the mill-gearing required by the 21st section to be securely fenced, no notice of danger was necessary.

The magistrates having submitted the facts to the Home Secretary, the case was considered by the Law Officers, whose opinion was transmitted to the Huddersfield bench on 20th May. " The Law Officers," wrote Manners Sutton, " are of opinion that the occupiers of a Factory are liable to the penalties prescribed by the 59th section for not fencing Machinery required to be fenced by the 21st section: and that they are also liable to the further penalties prescribed by the 60th section, which applies as well to accidents by Machinery absolutely required to be fenced, as to Machinery which is considered to be dangerous and as to which notice to fence has been given under the 43rd section."[86]

The whole problem of securing safe working conditions was intricate and difficult to a degree unrealized by those who were not charged with the duty of operating the fencing clauses of the Act. For some nine years the provisions were enforced only spasmodically and imperfectly, until in 1853 Lord Palmerston, alarmed by the increasing frequency of accidents, resolved that the Act must be strictly obeyed. The Inspectors then took vigorous and decisive action that convulsed the manufacturing interests, arousing a storm of controversy that equalled, if it did not exceed in bitterness, anything that had gone before.[87]

---

[86] *Minutes*, 2nd June, 1846, Vol. II, pp. 245-246.
[87] See H. Martineau, *The Factory Controversy* (1855).

CHAPTER 16

DEVELOPMENT OF THE INSPECTORATE

THE PERIOD that followed the débacle of 1836 witnessed a striking development in the powers and functions of the inspecting officers. The shock administered to their prestige by the rejection of Poulett Thomson's bill might well have daunted men of lesser calibre, persuading them that a policy of caution was the best guarantee of survival. The Inspectors, however, emerged from the ordeal shaken, it is true, but resolved for the future to place less confidence in the views put forward by interested parties, and with a renewed determination to make the Factory Act, despite its admitted imperfections and limitation, a living reality. In pursuit of this policy they closed their ranks, presenting, as the occasion required, a solid front not only towards owners and operatives, but towards the Home Office as well.

In this they were assisted by one of the most characteristic features of the Benthamite programme—the urge towards an increased measure of centralization, with all that such a plan involved, close and well co-ordinated uniformity of action, speedy and decisive enunciation of policy, and the power to take prompt and effective measures when the need arose. In the estimation of the more extreme of Chadwick's followers the sharing of authority between four Inspectors involved consequences that could not fail to weaken the whole system of control. The experience of each Inspector, it was said, was limited to one part of the field over the whole of which the law had to be applied, and each must, of necessity, be but little acquainted with circumstances which were not prominent in his own district, a fact which made it difficult if not impossible for him to survey the problem as a whole. "The consequence is," it was declared, "that each inspector adopts a different view, necessarily a partial, and so far an incorrect one, as to what is expedient or inexpedient, practicable or impracticable. . . . Were all these men highly intelligent, perfectly well qualified for their office, and zealously devoted to their duty, they would be precluded, by the very occupation of their time and thoughts in the discharge of their specific functions, from the means and opportunities of discriminating and considering the circumstances common to the whole manufacturing body and those peculiar to particular localities; and they would, therefore, be incapable of forming a correct judgment of the regulations practicable and expedient for all. This can only be done by minds which see the whole, and by a body which is responsible for the working of the entire measure."

Personal contact between Inspectors and mill-occupiers, and the mutual courtesies arising from such contacts could hardly fail, it was thought, to induce in the minds of the Inspectors a bias in favour of the manufacturers. "To such influences all men placed in such a position must be exposed: but from such interests, which are sinister interests, a central authority is free. Accordingly, when a measure is to be enforced, which is opposed to established interests, it is uniformly found that that measure is best worked by an authority which never comes into direct contact with the interests that are to be operated upon." It was therefore expedient to set up a central authority to which the Inspectors should report, and which should frame regulations for their guidance. Such a plan would have the overwhelming advantage that the regulations would be founded on accurate knowledge of all relevant data, and the system would, in consequence, be enforced uniformly throughout the country.

The creation of one central, superintending body would also serve to concentrate responsibility. "The factory inspector is responsible only for what takes place in his own district," it was said. "No one inspector, nor all the inspectors together, are responsible for the proper working of the statute in all the districts; nor are they bound to report to a competent authority why it does not work, if it does not, and to suggest the remedies which their observation and experience may have led them to discover. Next to the Poor Law Act, there is no legislative measure opposed to so many interests as the Factory Act; but hostile as the Poor Law Act is to numerous and powerful interests, yet with the exception of these individual interests, and with the exception of paupers, the whole community has a direct pecuniary interest in its being carried into full effect: on the other hand, the Factory Act is directly advantageous only to a number of helpless children, and cannot be carried into operation without immediate disadvantage to large classes—parents, masters, operatives, the pretended friends of the operatives, and their mistaken friends. If, then, the Poor Law Act could not be worked without a central authority to frame and enforce the necessary regulations, still less can the Factory Act be carried into operation without some similar authority. For the working of the Poor Law Act, the Legislature has appointed a Central Board of Poor Law Commissioners and a body of Assistant Commissioners, the duty of the latter being personally to inspect the different parishes in the kingdom, and to report to the Central Board; and the office of the former being to frame regulations which it is the part of the latter to enforce. For the working of the Factory Act, the Legislature has appointed only what is analogous to the Assistant Commissioners, and has omitted to appoint a Central Board, a superintending and controlling body."

The Home Office, it was contended, was quite incapable of controlling and superintending the working of the Act, partly because the Home Secretary was too fully occupied in other directions, and partly because the fact that he was a politician exposed him to the pressure of interested parties. " An authority wholly removed from all political contentions and influence, and responsible only to Parliament should," it was urged, " be constituted, to which the visiting inspectors should report, and from which they should receive their instructions. There is every reason to believe that the appointment of such functionaries . . . would ultimately accomplish, in a very complete degree, every object contemplated by the Legislature in the recent Act."[1]

These were the views of those who held that effective action was only possible if the supreme power was entrusted to a small, select body of men whose aloofness from the political arena would enable them to follow a firm and independent policy. But the problems of the poor-law unions were not the problems of the factories, and though uniformity of direction was clearly necessary, close, personal contact with the mills was no less essential. The Benthamites advocated centralization of power and authority : the Inspectors preferred rather the centralization of administration, of function and of procedure.

The suggestion put forward by Poulett Thomson in 1839 that an Inspector-General should be appointed to centralize the work of inspection drew the strongest objections from the four Inspectors, who declared that such an officer would be quite incapable of making those close contacts with the mills that were essential to the due enforcement of the law. The existing scheme of a limited number of Inspectors " having the weight and influence of a Commission from the Crown," was, in their opinion, best designed to supervize and control the work in the districts.[2] Centralization of administration was, however, quite another matter, and they had no hesitation in affirming that the establishment of a central office would do much to promote uniformity, and that it would greatly improve the existing organization.

The local office that had been opened in Manchester was abandoned in July, 1836,[3] and the suggestion that a room should be provided for the Inspectors when they were transacting business

---

[1] *The London and Westminster Review* (October, 1836) pp. 207-213.

[2] Joint Report, 13th August, 1839. *Parl. Papers* (1840) XXIII, p. 24. The Inspectors were determined to yield not a jot of their individual authority. When Saunders proposed that one of their number should act as chairman of their meetings, and supervize the work of the office staff, his suggestion was decisively rejected.—*Minutes,* 28th November, 1844, Vol. II, p. 71.

[3] *Parl. Papers* (1837) L, p. 40.

in London was rejected by Lord John Russell, who thought it " not advisable to provide a room for that purpose."[4] They were thus left without a permanent headquarters, accommodation being found for them in the office of the Privy Council, or, when that was occupied, in a waiting room at the Home Office.[5] The minutes of the spring meeting held on 14th January, 1840, recorded that Fox Maule had given directions that the Inspectors should have the use of a room at the Home Office, " provided Mr. Hall, the Police Magistrate, did not require it,"[6] but such a makeshift arrangement was obviously far from satisfactory, for the greatly increasing volume of work was making it imperative that a permanent office should be established.[7] The necessary provision having been made by section 5 of the Act of 1844, the Inspectors were informed on 18th November that two rooms had been set apart for their use in a house at No. 15, Duke Street, Westminster. A clerk and a messenger were to be appointed, and the Inspectors were instructed to prepare draft regulations for the management of the office.[8]

They submitted their proposals to the Home Office in a letter dated 29th November, 1844. " We have taken into consideration your Letter of the 18th Inst. in which you intimate to us your desire that we should prepare a draft of such Regulations for the management of the Factory Inspectors Office &c. as we may think best calculated for carrying out the provisions of the Factory Acts.

There are two descriptions of records which it is desirable to have made out; the one an abstract (and in many instances copies) of the Reports of accidents that have been received by the Inspectors; the other, Lists of all the Factories in the United Kingdom, setting forth such particulars as to the nature of the manufacture, the nature and amount of the moving power; and such other details as the Inspectors are empowered by the Act to have recorded in the Registers kept at the Factories. The reports of accidents are coming in daily, and in the last two months that

---

[4] Home Office Papers. H.O. 87 (1), p. 17. ((20th October, 1836).

[5] Minutes, 6th July, 1838, Vol. I, p. 109.

[6] Vol. I, p. 143. In June, 1842, when Horner was suffering from an affection of the leg that confined him to the house, the statutory meeting was held at his residence, No. 2 Bedford Place.

[7] In their Joint Report for January, 1839, the Inspectors drew attention to the " very considerable portion of the time of ourselves and of the Superintendents " that was consumed in preparing the returns for which Parliament asked.—Parl. Papers (1839) XIX, p. 538.

[8] Minutes, 26th November, 1844, Vol. II, p. 55. Domestic problems caused the Inspectors some concern. Mrs. Jones demanded 12s. a week " for lighting fires, cleaning the office, and other incidental work connected with the duties of Housekeeper "; but since she was receiving an allowance of 5s. a week from the Board of Woods and Works, it was decided that £20 a year would be adequate remuneration, a figure confirmed after some heated passages with her husband, Sergeant-Major Jones. (Minutes, 3rd and 22nd January, 1845, Vol. II, pp. 105, 119.)

have elapsed since the Act came into operation about 400 Reports have been received by the four Inspectors.

The making out the general Record of accidents and the Lists of Factories will be full occupation for the Clerk for several weeks, and before the expiration of that time we shall have other work ready for him. In the mean time, besides the above employment he will have to make copies of papers which each Inspector ought to be possessed of, such for instance, as when one Letter from the Home Office has been addressed to ' The Inspectors of Factories ' or when a Letter has been sent to an individual Inspector, on a subject in which his Colleagues are also concerned, and will have to attend to other ordinary business.

We have to suggest that the hours of attendance of the Clerk and Messenger should be regulated by us in such way as the public service appears to require; and with regard to the Messenger, it is very desirable that he should be able to write as well, in order that he may be employed in addressing and delivering Letters.

We shall be glad if the Clerk and Messenger were appointed soon; for we could set them to work immediately that the rooms are ready for occupation, that the Stationery Office has had directions to supply the Stationery that will be required, and that an arrangement has been made for defraying the current expenses of the Office."[9]

The messenger, James Syrett, was appointed by the Home Secretary on 5th December, 1844, but some difficulty was experienced in finding a suitable clerk. Sir James Graham had offered the post to Alexander Redgrave, who declined the office at first, but who subsequently agreed to serve at a salary of £150 rising to £400 a year.[10] The Inspectors moved into the new Factory Office on Thursday, 12th December. Redgrave took up his appointment four days later, and without further delay the staff were assigned their duties.[11] Redgrave was instructed to keep four separate sets of records, one for each of the districts, to write up the minutes of the meetings in the indexed folio book which was to be bought for the purpose, to make a list of the factories in each district, and to keep a register of accidents.[12] This was a formidable task, and despite his industry, Redgrave was unable to keep his returns up to date. The Inspectors were constrained to ask for extra assistance, and in February, 1846, they were granted

---

[9] *Minutes*, Vol. II, pp. 72-73.
[10] Redgrave had been in the service of the Home Office since 17th February, 1834. On 1st October, 1847, he was appointed Sub-Inspector, and on 4th May, 1852, he was promoted Inspector. He became Chief Inspector of Factories in 1878, resigning in 1891.
[11] *Ibid.* pp. 85-87.
[12] *Ibid.* pp. 89-90.

permission to engage a temporary copying clerk from 10 to 5 each day, at a daily wage of five shillings. " We feel it due to Mr. Redgrave to state," they explained, " that there has been no want of industry on his part, and we gladly avail ourselves of this opportunity to bear testimony to his zeal, diligence and ability."[13]

The premises at Duke Street were retained for rather less than three years, the Factory Department then being removed to the newly built wing of the Home Office. On 26th August, 1847, Sir Denis Le Marchant, the Under-Secretary, wrote to the Inspectors— " I am directed by Secretary Sir George Gray to inform you, that with the view of saving the rent of the apartments which you at present occupy, rooms have been appointed for your use on the third floor of the new part of this Building, and the requisite directions have been given to the Commissioners of Woods &c. for the fitting up and furnishing the rooms."[14] This change of venue was significant, for although it was apparently dictated by motives of economy, its effect was to identify the Inspectors even more closely with the Home Office, thus accelerating a process of development that had been discernible for some time.

The relations of the Inspectors with the Home Office had never been clearly defined, indeed in the early days it was by no means certain that they were to work under the sole direction of the Home Secretary, the President of the Board of Trade conceiving that he had some interest in factory inspection.[15] The wide powers conferred on the Inspectors by the Act of 1833 had placed them in a position of exceptional strength, and it soon became obvious that some limitations would need to be imposed, particularly in the making of regulations, and in the exercise of magisterial functions.

The consolidated code of regulations that had been drawn up in compliance with the Home Secretary's instruction of 8th September, 1836,[16] had secured uniformity of procedure, thereby removing the chief ground of complaint on the part of the manufacturers, who had been incensed at the multiplicity of rules that had previously been issued. So carefully had this code been evolved that no subsequent amendment was deemed necessary,[17] and when the majority of the regulations were incor-

---

[13] *Ibid*. 10th February, 1846, Vol. II, p. 232.

[14] *Ibid*. 13th December, 1847, Vol. II, p. 329.

[15] See *ante* p. 115.

[16] *Minutes*, Vol. I, p. 1.

[17] *Cf. Minutes*, 29th June, 1841, Vol. I, p. 164.—" The present Regulations have been in force since October, 1836, and do not at present in the opinion of the meeting require any alteration." See also Joint Report, 2nd July, 1841. *Parl. Papers* (1841) VI, p. 228.

porated in the Act of 1844 it became possible to deprive the Inspectors of their subordinate law-making power.[18]   In the meantime their discretion in the issue of instructions, as opposed to formal regulations, had also been curtailed, a direction having been sent to them on 13th March, 1837, that " no instructions should be issued by any Inspector until they have been submitted to the Law Officers of the Crown."[19]

A further limitation on their powers had been imposed about the same time in a letter sent to Howell, in which Lord John Russell intimated that they should only adjudicate in cases of breaches of the Factory Act in exceptional circumstances.   The Home Secretary, they were informed, " does not think it desirable that, in the first instance, an Inspector of Factories should hear informations preferred by his Superintendent, assisted by an attorney.   Lord J. Russell thinks it better that the information should be heard by the Magistrates of the district, who he has no doubt will decide each case according to its merits—& that it will be proper only in the event of their failing to do so, that subsequent informations should be heard by the Inspector."[20]   The Act of 1844 specifically forbade the Inspectors to act as magistrates : they were for the future to be confined to the exercise of what was, after all, their true function, the enforcement of the Factory Acts.[21]

The Inspectors were by no means loath to have their powers curtailed in this way, for the plenitude of authority with which they had been invested had proved an embarrassment rather than a help in carrying out their duties.   Doubtless there had been much to be said for giving them power to issue regulations and to act as justices in the early days when the whole system of control was in the embryonic stage, but experience had taught them that their real strength lay in their position as servants of the Executive, charged with the duty of administering the law, rather than as legislators, or as interpreters of the law.   After 1844 they began to assume their true rôle—that of the administrator, relying on the opinions of competent authority, aloof and disinterested.

---

[18] 7 & 8 Vict., c. 15, Sec. 2.

[19] *Home Office Papers*, H.O. 87 (1), p. 45.   See also *Parl. Papers* (1837) XXXI, p. 125.

[20] *Home Office Papers*, H.O. 87 (1), p. 43.   10th March, 1837.

[21] Shortly afterwards their relations with the magistrates were still further regularized.   The practice by which the justices had applied to the Home Office through the Inspectors for the elucidation of difficult points of law was condemned as " irregular and attended with serious inconvenience." (*Minutes*, 20th May, 1846, Vol. II, p. 247.)   In July each Inspector sent to his Sub-Inspectors a circular saying " in all cases wherein Magistrates entertain doubts as to the construction of any Section of the Factory Acts, you will state that the Secretary of State for the Home Department expects they will communicate such doubts directly to him, and not through the Inspector of the District." (*Ibid.* p. 269.)

This more formalized attitude was dictated in part by the fact that magistrates were more inclined to pay heed to the views of recognized legal authorities than to the opinions of the Inspectors. " H.M. Sec. of State," they declared, " should be requested to furnish them with an opinion from such legal authority as would carry weight with Magistrates when adjudicating on Factory cases,"[22] a plea which they reiterated when the interpretation of sections 13 and 60 of the Act of 1844 was in question.[23]   When they were asked to prepare an abstract of the Act of 1844, as required by the 28th section, they demurred on the ground that the magistrates would attach more importance to an abstract prepared by the Law Officers.   They reminded Graham that their powers had now undergone a change—" It has been our duty," they wrote, " to consider what steps should be taken preparatory to the coming into operation of the Act respecting Factories passed in the present Session of Parliament.

By the 28th section of the recent Law it is enacted, that such abstract of the Factory Act, as amended by this Act, as directed by one of H.M. Principal Secretaries of State, should be fixed on a movable board, and hung up in every Factory.

By the 2nd section of the amending Act the Inspectors are divested of the power of issuing any order or direction for the enforcement of the Acts, as they had under the Factory Act.

The enforcement of the Law by prosecutions is committed to us, and to the Sub-Inspectors who act under our directions.   It is therefore very desirable, that the Abstract should shew distinctly the extent to which the Factory Act has been repealed or altered by the amending Act for the information and guidance of ourselves and the Sub-Inspectors as well as of the mill-occupiers, and their workpeople.

Upon a full and anxious reconsideration of this subject we have come to the resolution of requesting respectfully that you will be pleased to give directions that such Abstract shall be prepared by your legal advisers with as little delay as possible, being of opinion that it should be prepared and emanate from a source, the weight of whose authority would be deferred to in questions arising in the interpretation of the two statutes.   Thus, when prosecutions take place, we should be able to refer to the Abstract as containing not our interpretation of the Law, but that which proceeds directly from the Law Advisers of the Crown, whereby

[22] *Minutes,* 28th November, 1844, Vol. II, p. 71.
[23] *Ibid.* 29th November, 1844, Vol. II, p. 75.—" We respectfully submit the necessity of the opinion being furnished us in such form as will carry with it that weight of legal authority to which the Magistrates would pay deference."

much misconstruction will be avoided, and greater uniformity in the decisions of magistrates secured."[24]

Their representations were unavailing, however, for on 20th July they were instructed to proceed with the preparation of the abstract.[25] Howell having undertaken the ungrateful task, the draft was considered at their meeting on 26th July, when they resolved to submit it to the Home Secretary with a covering letter in which they drew attention once more to the importance of an independent legal opinion. " As it is in the province of the Sec. of State alone to direct what abstract shall be hung up in the Factories and as he is consequently responsible for its faithfulness we think it our duty to address to you some observations on this subject . . . the more especially, because, as the Inspectors have no longer as formerly, any power to make rules, regulations or orders, no authority attaches to the Abstract from its being prepared by us, as Inspectors of Factories. . . . We therefore beg that before adopting this Abstract it may undergo the careful revision of the Law Officers of the Crown, as to its accuracy and sufficiency, whose opinion would be received as decisive on points of doubt and difficulty."[26]

There can be no doubt that the Inspectors were correct in their view of the respective functions of the Home Office and of themselves in this matter. It was probably convenient that those who had such intimate experience of the practical working of the Factory Acts should draft the new abstract, but in insisting that the Inspectors should undertake this duty the Home Secretary was ignoring a principle that had steadily been gaining ground during the past ten years, that had been enshrined in the Act of 1844, and that was fully realized by the Inspectors themselves—the principle that the officers whose duty it is to administer the law act wisely if they refrain from interpreting it.[27]

Inspectors and Home Office were agreed, however, that one of the most significant functions of the inspectorate was that of advising the Government on the detailed working of factory legislation, and of making recommendations concerning its amendment. The Home Secretary lost no opportunity of availing himself of their expert knowledge; and whenever a new proposal was being

---

[24] *Minutes,* 17th July, 1844, Vol. II, pp. 5-6. See Joint Report, 17th July, 1844. *Parl. Papers* (1844) XXVIII, p. 583.

[25] *Minutes,* 22nd July, 1844, Vol. II, p. 14.

[26] *Ibid.* 26th July, 1844, Vol. II, pp. 21-22.

[27] The Inspectors were not asked to draft the abstract of the Print Works Act, 1845 (*Minutes,* 25th November, 1845, Vol. II, p. 201) but despite their remonstrance they were instructed to prepare the abstract of the Act of 1847 (*Minutes,* 10th June, 1847, Vol. II, p. 310).

considered the advice of the Inspectors was sought.[28] They had
full access at all times to the Under-Secretaries, with whom they
were in constant communication, and if the matter was sufficiently
urgent they had no difficulty in securing audience of the Home
Secretary himself. Their personal relations were friendly and even
cordial (though they were inclined to be somewhat stiff in their
attitude to subordinate officials)[29] but this did not prevent them
from putting their point of view with vigour and persistence when
the occasion demanded.[30] In their reports they discussed fully the
defects of the existing laws, thus providing Parliament with a wealth
of material on which policy might be framed, and in the light of
which legislation could be shaped.

Section 45 of the Act of 1833 had provided that these reports
should be presented at least twice a year, but on 8th October, 1836,
directions were issued that quarterly reports should be submitted.[31]
This practice continued until 1844, when the Inspectors having
drawn attention to the inconvenience that was caused by the need
to report at such short intervals, and to the fact that the reports
were printed and presented to Parliament only at half-yearly
intervals, it was agreed that they should make their reports every
six months.[32]

The Inspectors had been allowed considerable latitude in the
framing of their observations, so much so that on occasion they
made it clear that in the course of their business they had exceeded
the limits that the Home Office considered desirable. If it had been
necessary to regulate their relationship with the magistrates by
forbidding them to act as a channel of communication with the
Home Secretary, it was even more important to define what their
attitude should be towards mill-owners and operatives. In October,
1844, Stuart reported that he had approached the secretary of a
Short-time Committee, asking him to find employment for a boy

---

[28] Cf. Minutes, Vol. I, pp. 4, 5, 11, 12, 13, 17, 18; Vol. II, pp. 57, 70,
71, 77, 89, 90, 91-96, 101, 142-145.

[29] On one occasion Bethune, Counsel to the Home Office, wrote to
Saunders suggesting an interview.—" Dear Saunders, I can't conveniently
leave my den, but I shall be happy to see you and your colleagues here.
I will have a basket outside of the window to hoist you upstairs." This
light-hearted missive was coldly received, and Redgrave was instructed to
reply, " The Inspectors of Factories present their compliments to Mr.
Bethune, and regret that they will be unable to call upon him, but they
will be here and glad to see him at 1 o'clock today."—Minutes, 4th June,
1846, Vol. II, p. 249.

[30] The prolonged struggle to secure adequate remuneration for the
Sub-Inspectors was a notable illustration of their pertinacity.

[31] Home Office Papers, H.O. 87 (1), p. 14.

[32] The new arrangement came into force in 1845, the first reports in
that year covering the seven months from 1st October, 1844 to 30th
April, 1845.—Parl. Papers (1845) XXV. p. 243.

who had been dismissed because he had given evidence in a case against his employer. This called forth a remonstrance from the Home Office, in a letter dated 25th November, 1844. " I am directed by Secretary Sir James Graham to call your attention to that part of your report of 1st Oct. in which you recount a conversation which you have had with Mr. McFadyen on the subject of the dismissal of a boy named Henderson from his employment, after giving evidence in a case of alleged overwork by his employers; and you state that you expressed to Mr. McFadyen who had described himself as the Secretary of the Short-time Committee for the Eastern District, a hope that that Committee would make every exertion within power to procure another situation for the boy.

Sir James Graham is fully aware that your conduct in this case was actuated by benevolent motives alone, but he desires me to call your attention to the injurious effect on the public service which would inevitably result, were the Master Manufacturers or the Operatives to have reason to believe that the Inspectors of Factories were in any way connected with the Short-time Committee, or with any body of persons associated together for objects in dispute or respecting which a difference of opinion may arise between employers and employed.

It is the manifest duty of the Inspectors whenever they may receive information of an alleged violation of the Law immediately to make enquiry into the facts of the case, and if necessary to bring to trial the accused parties, but it is very desirable that the Inspectors of Factories should abstain from any communication with the parties composing the Committees or associations of the nature to which I have referred except in the character of private individuals."[33]

Since the reports of the Inspectors were freely quoted during the course of debates in Parliament it was obviously desirable that they should touch as lightly as possible on matters of current controversy, or if that was impossible, that they should confine themselves in the main to the objective presentation of facts. It was not easy for the Home Office to lay down any strict line of principle in this respect, but there was no hesitation in declaring that allusions to confidential communications passing between the Home Secretary and the Inspectors, and to Parliamentary debates, were entirely out of place. In June, 1846, Sir James Graham having taken grave exception to the form in which the Inspectors had submitted their joint report for the previous half-year, Manners Sutton, the Under-Secretary, set out in a letter the considerations

[33] *Minutes*, 29th December, 1846, Vol. II, pp. 277-278.

that should guide them in the future. " At the interview which
Mr. M. Sutton had with the Inspectors he stated to them by
direction of Sec. Sir James Graham, that if their Joint Report is
intended for the information of the Sec. of State, it is unnecessary
to insert in it Letters sent to them from the Home Office or other
Documents, of which the Sec. of State has knowledge before he
receives their report. That if on the other hand their report is
intended for the information of Parliament and the Public, it would
be irregular and inconvenient that it should contain the correspondence of the Sec. of State with the Inspectors, or documents
which they have received from him—the propriety of publishing
such correspondence or documents being a matter for the consideration of the Sec. of State.

Mr. M. Sutton declines to express an opinion as to the form
in which it will be advisable for the Inspectors to prepare their
reports—but he is confident that they will give due attention to
Sir J. Graham's suggestions, and that their Report will be submitted
to Sir J. Graham in an unobjectionable form."[34]

The Inspectors could not but acquiesce, but the bitterness of
the controversy that followed the Ten-hours Act of 1847, and the
dissensions that existed between them concerning the manner of
its enforcement, were so strongly reflected in their reports as to
cause the Home Secretary once more to intervene. " With respect
to your several reports," they were told, " I am to recall your
attention to the letter addressed to you on the 25th June, 1846, by
direction of Sir J. Graham, a copy of which is enclosed. In the
opinion conveyed to you in that letter Sir G. Grey[35] entirely
concurs, and he thinks it desirable that the practice therein
adverted to, of inserting in your Reports copies of correspondence
between the Sec. of State and the Inspectors, should be avoided.
He has also observed with regret, that while much valuable and
interesting information is contained in your Reports, there is in
some parts of them a controversial tone, which appears to him to
be inconsistent with the character which such Reports ought to
bear. It is perfectly right that the Inspectors should read and
confer together on their Reports; but Sir G. Grey thinks it very
inexpedient that the result of such conference should be to make
their several reports the medium of argumentative discussion
between the Inspectors on points wherein they differ in opinion,
instead of their being restricted to a Report of the state and
condition of the Factories within their Districts, illustrated by a
statement of such facts as they feel it their duty to record.

[34] *Minutes,* 26th June, 1846, Vol. II, p. 263.
[35] Grey was Home Secretary in the ministry formed by Russell in
July, 1846.

I am to add, that a reference to Debates in Parliament, together with extracts from the reported Speeches of particular Members in Debate, appears to Sir G. Grey to be out of place in your Reports.

Sir G. Grey has no wish to check the free expression of opinion on the part of the Inspectors, and he will be always desirous of having the benefit of their experience and suggestions in reference to any points of doubt or difficulty which may arise in carrying into effect the provisions of the Factory Act, but as such suggestions may in some cases be properly considered as confidential, it is not expedient that when of this nature they should be transmitted to the Sec. of State in a printed form and embodied in a Report to be forthwith laid before Parliament. I am therefore to request that you will revise your reports with reference to the foregoing observations."[36]

This was not the first occasion on which the Home Secretary had reminded the Inspectors that any observations they wished to address to him on matters outside the scope of their normal duties should be submitted in such a way that they would not come before Parliament as printed papers. The great weight attaching to any utterances of the Factory Inspectors made it desirable that they should put forward no official pronouncements on matters of policy as would be likely to embarrass the Government if they were quoted in Parliamentary debate. This principle had already been accepted by the majority of the Inspectors, who, as long ago as 1837 had declined to accede to Saunders' suggestion that representations should be put forward concerning the division of the country into districts, on the ground that it was inexpedient to submit to the Home Secretary any proposition on matters in which their opinion had not been asked.[37]

Saunders was impatient of this restriction, and in 1846 he sent in a printed report containing some highly controversial views on education. The Home Secretary took a strong line, and on 26th June, Manners Sutton addressed a stiff letter to the Inspector— "Sir James Graham desires me to say that he would not wish to preclude you from addressing the Secretary of State on matters not strictly within the limits of your official duties as Inspector of Factories, but no communication of this nature should be transmitted to him in a printed form; and he requests you therefore to take the necessary steps for having the type of your special Report broken up and for destroying any copies of the report which may have been struck off; inasmuch as Sir James Graham is not pre-

---

[36] *Minutes*, 22nd January, 1849, Vol. II, pp. 418-419.
[37] *Minutes*, 22nd July, 1837, Vol. I, p. 76.

pared to publish this report, which is to be considered as a confidential communication."[38]

Slowly but inexorably the Home Office was imposing its will on the Inspectors, indicating the standards of professional conduct and propriety to which they should conform, whilst leaving them the greatest possible latitude in the discharge of their proper duties. It remained for the Inspectors themselves to work out the code governing their relationship with one another.

This might well have presented almost insuperable difficulties, for they were men of widely differing characters and temperaments, each supreme and independent in his own district, and each determined to maintain his independence. Horner, a competent, even a ruthless administrator, dour, purposeful and often domineering, might well have found it irksome to run in harness with Saunders, whose keen mind and incisive intellect revealed a spirit equally disinclined to compromise. In strong contrast were Howell, methodical but uninspired, attaching more importance to the routine of inspection than to the consideration of the wider problems of factory legislation, and Stuart, who must ever remain something of an enigma. Amongst the advocates of reform he had been suspect from the first. "There is indeed a report," said the *Westminster Review*, "we do not know how far it may be true, that in the present instance Mr. Stuart has been forced in on the Home Office on the shoulders of the Scotch Members. It is pretty certain that the Scotch members have exerted themselves very earnestly in his behalf."[39]

Stuart was flatly accused of pandering to the Scottish millowners. "It appears that in Glasgow," declared O'Connell, "the Factories Act is totally neglected; it is observed by nobody, and violated by everybody. They there find it too inconvenient to work with, and have in practice repealed it."[40] Stuart reacted sharply, indignantly denying these accusations, and asserting that the Act was fully operative in Glasgow, as in other parts of his district.[41] He examined on oath no less than 186 witnesses, including mill-occupiers, overseers, clerks, surgeons, spinners and piecers, all of whom corroborated his statement that the Act was observed in all its details.[42]

When he took over the northern district from Horner in 1836, he said, he found the owners disposed to obey the law, and he had acted on the principle enunciated by his predecessor, that

[38] *Minutes*, 29th December, 1846, Vol. II, p. 278.
[39] *The London and Westminster Review* (October, 1836) p. 212.
[40] *Hansard* (1838) XLIII, 978.
[41] Report, 30th June, 1838. *Parl. Papers* (1838) XLV, p. 65.
[42] Report, 31st December, 1838. *Parl. Papers* (1839) XIX, p. 460 *ff.*

the Inspector must endeavour to work in harmony with the mill-occupiers. During Horner's inspectorship there had been only 8 prosecutions in the district, compared with the 177 informations that had been laid in the Lancashire division, and he stated his conviction that " the humane intention of the Legislature would be best fulfilled by never having recourse, except in extreme cases, to suits for penalties or coercive measures of any kind." For this reason he had instructed his Superintendents that they should never initiate a prosecution without first consulting him, and that they should only make a special report when, *on leaving a factory*, they could not certify that the law was substantially enforced.[43]

Such an attitude raised profound questions of policy. Was it the duty of an Inspector to prosecute every time he observed a breach of the law, or should he endeavour to adjust matters before leaving the factory, having recourse to the magistrates only when the law was openly and consistently defied? His colleagues pursued the former, Stuart the latter course, and in so doing it may well have been that he was in advance of his time. If this was the case he certainly had authority on his side, and it is instructive to compare his notions of the Inspectors' functions with those of Redgrave, who in later years affirmed, " In the inspection of factories it has been my view always that we are not acting as policemen, that it is our object to be the friend of the manufacturer as much as the friend of the employé and the friend of the parent, and that in enforcing this Factory Act . . . we do not enforce it as a policeman would check an offence which he is told to detect. We have endeavoured not to enforce the law, if I may use such an expression, but it has been my endeavour since I have had anything to do with factory administration that we should simply be the advisers of all classes, that we should explain the law, and that we should do everything we possibly could to induce them to observe the law, and that a prosecution should be the very last thing that we should take up."[44]

One of the main objects of Althorp's Act had been to secure uniformity in practice and procedure,[45] and despite their personal differences the Inspectors addressed themselves tirelessly to this end. The inevitable result was that realizing their dependence upon each other they took such steps as were necessary to secure the appearance, if not the reality, of a common policy and purpose. There can be little doubt that Stuart's colleagues disapproved his attitude to the mill-owners, but they did not hesitate to lend him

---

[43] Report, 30th December, 1840. *Parl. Papers* (1841) X, pp. 186-190.
[44] Report of Factory and Workshops Act Commission (1876) Vol. II, Qn. 495. Quoted D. H. Blelloch, *A Historical Survey of Factory Inspection in Great Britain.—International Labour Review* (November, 1938) p. 654.
[45] Sec. 45.

their support when his position threatened to become untenable. The differences in their modes of procedure, they declared, " are mainly to be attributed to the vague and highly unsatisfactory nature of the Law, first from the loose manner in which many of the enactments are worded, and secondly because some of the enactments are rendered altogether useless; either by contradictory enactments or by the want of a sufficient provision for carrying them into effect. It appears further evident to the Inspectors from the details entered into that one great cause of apparent difference in the proceedings of the Inspectors is to be found in the varying class of persons who occupy factories in the different towns and manufacturing districts. This remark relates more immediately to the comparison drawn between the prosecutions in Scotland and in Lancashire from the first enactment of the general Law. The Inspectors are strongly impressed with the advantages which would be derived from their proceedings being uniform. They have endeavoured to attain this object & they consider with great success in respect to all the more important provisions of the Law as well as to all those enactments the meaning and intents of which are obvious.

It has long been a matter of regret to them that the state of the Law has prevented that entire uniformity which is so highly necessary both as to the proper interpretation to be assigned to each enactment, & as to the mode of conducting the details of Inspection."[46]

When the establishment of the factory office had made it possible for them to centralize more effectively their administrative procedure, particularly so far as the Home Office was concerned, the Inspectors were able to take steps to secure a greater measure of uniformity between themselves. At their meeting on 20th December, 1844, they considered the expediency of adopting standing orders concerning the transmission and circulation of information relative to any one district that might affect the proceedings in any other district;[47] and a week later they agreed that each Inspector should send to the office copies of any written communications passing between himself and any department of the government in matters relating to his duties, which would be useful to, or which might influence the proceedings of his colleagues. A memorandum of all verbal communications was also to be sent to the clerk, who was instructed to forward copies of such material to the other Inspectors.[48]

---

[46] Minutes, 3rd February, 1841, Vol. I, pp. 158-160.
[47] Ibid. Vol. II, p. 92.
[48] Ibid. 31st December, 1844, Vol. II, p. 100.

Two years later this policy was carried a stage further in consequence of the strictures that had recently been passed upon their joint report. Impressed with the importance of keeping each other informed of the substance of the observations contained in their individual reports, they discussed, on 8th December, 1846, " the mode and period at which the half yearly Reports should hereafter be sent in, and it was agreed that unless under any special order from the Secretary of State (which should be forthwith communicated to all his Colleagues by any one receiving such order) the half yearly Reports should not in future be sent in until after the same shall have been read at the Statutory Meeting of the Inspectors next after the date of such report."[49]

To have reached such a degree of unanimity was no mean achievement, indicating, as it did, the realization that a common policy was desirable, if only on the score of expediency; but the fundamental differences of outlook that divided the Inspectors sometimes made it impossible to preserve even the semblance of uniformity. On the question of further reducing the hours of work of young persons Stuart was diametrically opposed to his colleagues, and when towards the end of 1846 this highly controversial matter was again under discussion, the whole subject of the relationship of the Inspectors with the Home Office and between themselves was raised in acute form, as the Minutes bear witness.

At the statutory meeting held on 31st December, 1846, it is recorded, " Mr. Saunders informed his colleagues that he intended to send to the Secretary of State as a special report in manuscript the observations he had read to his colleagues, recommending a reduction in the hours of labour of young persons in Factories to eleven hours in each day, and that labour in Lace Mills should be placed under the same regulations as in other Factories.

Mr. Stuart with reference to the communication made by Mr. Saunders represented to his colleagues that it was his present intention to inform the Secretary of State by Letter, that he had refrained from making any report respecting a limitation of hours of labour in Factories because he thought it inexpedient for an Inspector to make reports unless required on any subjects as to which the Acts of Parliament by virtue of which they are appointed do not require or authorize them to enquire and report; because Mr. Stuart's colleagues are aware that there is a difference of opinion among them on the question to which Mr. Saunders' special Report relates, and because he holds himself not at liberty to enter at all on the important question respecting any further limitation of the hours of labour, on which great differences of opinion exist between the employers and the employed, by the express and implied instruc-

49 *Ibid*. Vol. II, pp. 269-270.

tions issued by Secretary Sir James Graham and contained in Mr. Under Secretary Manners Sutton's Letter of 25th November, 1844."[50]

Saunders considered the matter during the next few days, and when the meeting was resumed on 7th January, 1847, he informed his colleagues that he had sent his report to the Home Office, with a confidential letter in the following terms—" I have the honour to forward you a special Report on some matters relating to employment in Factories. . . . This report has been read to my Colleagues and one of them (Mr. Stuart) has intimated an intention to express to the Secretary of State his reasons for not making a report on the subject of the hours of labour in Factories. As one of the reasons assigned by Mr. Stuart is that he deems it inexpedient an Inspector should report on this subject unless required to do so I desire to explain that in expressing my opinion on this and other matters I have adopted a course which has received the implied and express sanction (I believe) of every Secretary of State since the Inspectors were appointed. In proof of this I could refer to several reports laid before Parliament which have contained individual opinions on the very subject and which reports have been referred to and quoted by the Secretary of State for the time being and by other Members of Parliament when Factory matters have been under discussion.

In submitting my opinion in the form I now lay them before you I consider I am moreover acting in strict conformity with the directions which I received last June from Mr. Manners Sutton.[51]

The instructions Mr. Stuart received in Nov., 1844, which he conceives as precluding him from reporting on this matter have always appeared to me as pointing out simply the injurious effects of Inspectors ' being in any way connected with the Short-time Committees or with any body of persons associated together for objects in dispute or respecting which a difference of opinion may exist between Employers and Employed,' a course I have at all times carefully avoided.

I would further observe that I was quite aware a difference of opinion existed among the Inspectors respecting the hours of labour in Factories and have therefore been careful only to express my own individual opinion with reference to my own District. I have not even quoted the expressed opinion of any Colleague which might appear to favour the same views while by reading my report at all to my Colleagues before I submitted it to the Secretary of State, I afforded any of them that might wish it the forwarding at the same time the reasons why he entertained a different opinion."

50 *Minutes*, Vol. II, pp. 280-281.
51 See *ante* p. 257.

The subsequent proceedings were stormy. "Mr. Stuart was surprised to learn," proceeded the Minutes, "that Mr. Saunders had sent a Letter to the Secretary of State commenting on a Letter from Mr. Stuart to the Secretary of State which Mr. Saunders had not seen, which had not yet been dispatched, and the general purport of which Mr. Saunders only knew from Mr. Stuart having from courtesy mentioned it to his colleagues and especially to Mr. Saunders that he might be aware generally of the grounds which led him (Mr. Stuart) to think that the Inspectors ought not to make reports to the Secretary of State respecting the limitation of hours of work in Factories.

It seemed to Mr. Stuart not only to be premature but irregular in Mr. Saunders to take this step, most especially as Mr. Stuart had not at the last Meeting by any means pledged himself to send his proposed Letter to the Secretary of State, nor if he did, to confine his statements or arguments to those communicated to his Colleagues at the last Meeting, as those which occurred to him.

In reply to the above observations on the part of Mr. Stuart, Mr. Saunders stated that he did not consider his letter as either premature or irregular, inasmuch as in that Letter he has offered no comment whatever except in the minute entered at Mr. Stuart's suggestion in the proceedings of the Inspectors at their Meeting held on 31st December last: and on the reasons assigned in that minute by Mr. Stuart for not making a special Report on the hours of labour in Factories."[52]

If this evidence of disunity and dissension was insufficient to demonstrate the need for a higher degree of centralization the different policies pursued by the Inspectors in enforcing the Ten Hours Act of 1847 were to provide ample grounds for supposing that supreme direction was sooner or later inevitable if the administration of the factory laws was to be anything but fragmentary and chaotic. The application of control to a limited section of the industry had already raised problems of the utmost complexity: the extension of control to other departments of manufacture could not fail to aggravate the difficulties in years to come. So long as there was no central co-ordinating authority, charged with the duty of formulating a common policy, with leisure and opportunity to survey the needs of the country as a whole, maintaining close touch with the districts, but free from the exacting routine of visits and inspections, so long would harmony and cohesion be lacking.

The Benthamites had accurately assessed the situation when they insisted that the Home Office was quite unfitted to discharge

---

[52] *Minutes*, Vol. II, pp. 283-285.

this onerous duty, for the reluctance of a succession of Home Secretaries to give the Inspectors a definite lead on major matters of policy and interpretation was to be ascribed not solely to the maladroit drafting of the Acts, but also to the fact that a government department was incapable of grappling with the highly technical issues involved. The solution lay in the appointment of a Chief Inspector, but to this there was, as yet, unshakable opposition.

Nevertheless it remains true that Horner and his three colleagues performed a great work. In a field previously unexplored, in circumstances of considerable difficulty, they laid the foundations for their successors, they established precedents, and they built a noble tradition, following unswervingly the dictates of conscience and common sense, unwavering in their devotion to the public service.

CHAPTER 17

PRINTWORKS AND ROPEWORKS

THOSE WHO were engaged in the branches of the textile industry as yet free from legislative control had for some years been convinced that it could only be a matter of time before they, too, became subject to regulation. Upon the urgent representations of the silk manufacturers as to the dire results to be apprehended if they were to be required to submit to the full restrictions proposed in 1833, the Government had been induced to permit them to employ children of any age for ten hours a day without provision for education,[1] while the occupiers of lace factories remained outside the scope of the factory acts altogether. It was small consolation to manufacturers who were exposed to the full rigour of the law to be told that their departments of the industry had been singled out for control because their establishments employed such vast numbers, and worked with such regularity that it was easier to impose regulation upon them, and they never ceased to resent the preferential treatment enjoyed by rivals who were competing with them for the labour of the younger hands.[2]

Despite its many imperfections Althorp's Act had wrought a great improvement in the conditions of those to whom its operation extended. Even its bitterest opponents could not deny that, nor could they deny that the prophecies that it would involve the manufacturers in ruin and the operatives in a standard of living still further reduced had been entirely falsified, for despite the depression that prevailed between 1837 and 1842, the volume of trade had increased, and a steadily growing number of hands had found employment in the mills. Expansion of trade and legislative control were obviously not incompatible, and there was at least a *prima facie* justification for enquiring into the possibility of enlarging the sphere of regulation.

In 1837 Nassau Senior recorded a conversation that had taken place between Ashworth, the Quaker cotton-master, Thomson, and himself.[3] Thomson, the owner of a printworks at Primrose, near Clitheroe, said to be the most extensive in the kingdom, stated that

---

[1] See Saunders' Report, October, 1846. *Parl. Papers* (1847) XV, p. 457.

[2] Stuart stated that these owners were particularly anxious that the printworks should be subject to regulation, since the increased wages paid for night-work induced parents to send their children to the print-grounds rather than to the factories.—Report, 31st March, 1843. *Parl. Papers* (1843) XXVII, p. 343.

[3] Nassau W. Senior, *Letters on the Factory Act* (1837) pp. 43-51.

he had long been interested in the legislation governing cotton factories, because he was convinced that in due time similar restrictions would be imposed on those engaged in calico-printing. This branch of the textile industry was, he thought, more obnoxious to reproach than spinning, for children were employed at an earlier age than in the cotton mills, and they worked harder and for longer hours. The ordinary day's labour in the print grounds extended over ten hours, but during the busy seasons of spring and autumn, and during the shipping months, the hours of work were increased to twelve or fourteen a day, and relays were frequently employed throughout the night. It was this seasonal variation that made it so undesirable, in Thomson's opinion, to extend regulation to calico-printing. He was convinced that if the law interfered, employment would be affected, for, he averred, " time is an element in the calculations of a manufacture dependent on season, taste, and fashion. That which one month fetches a high profit, in the next is sold for none at all, and, in the following, to a heavy loss. A calico printer cannot work to a stock as a spinner or weaver, whose production being the same from year to year, is saleable some time or other. The consequence is, that the printer is often idle for weeks, and often has double the work he can perform in the ordinary hours of labour. .... It is irremediable : and the law that imposed restrictions on the hours of labour in calico-printing would destroy the trade, and involve masters and labourers in common ruin."

The factory system of education, he maintained, was quite inapplicable to calico-printing, where the child was part of the machine.[4] Children would go to school dirty from their work, and unprepared for mental labour; and apart from this it was extremely difficult, especially in rural areas, to find suitable schoolmasters. " In the lower classes," observed Thomson, " when a man can do nothing else for his livelihood, he becomes a schoolmaster; men whose failure in life is often to be attributed to their own improvident and vicious habits."[5]

Thomson, an acute and far-sighted man, and in some respects an unusually enlightened master, was not alone in perceiving the dilemma. The principle of regulating child labour had long been conceded, and there could now be only one justification for allowing the major textile industries to remain in their unenvied isolation, condemned to accept restriction when others went free. That justification was one not of principle, but of expediency and practicability. It was not denied that the working conditions of children should be controlled, and that ideally control should

---

[4] " A tier-boy absent stops his master."—*Ibid.* p. 43.
[5] *Ibid.* p. 46.

extend to all departments of industry, to agriculture, to lace-
making, to iron and coal, tobacco and paper. But how, it was
asked, is regulation to be enforced? The well-ordered routine of
the cotton and woollen mills might have been expected to afford
unique facilities for the successful intervention of the legislature,
but the machinery that had been evolved was plainly inadequate.
Upon what grounds could it now be asserted, with even the
remotest degree of confidence, that it was possible to legislate for
industries carried on, in many instances, in small, widely-dispersed
establishments, where, by the very nature of the process, hours were
irregular and variable, and where conditions of employment bore
no relation to those existing in the great mills?

  If these objections carried weight with those whose interest
it was to limit any further legislative encroachment, they made
little impression on Lord Ashley, who was determined not to pause
from his labours until he had secured for the children in unregulated
callings some such degree of protection as was enjoyed by those
already subject to the Factories Regulation Act. On 4th August,
1840, he rose in the House to move " that an humble address be
presented to Her Majesty, praying that Her Majesty will be
graciously pleased to direct an inquiry to be made into the employment of the children of the poorer classes in Mines and Collieries,
and in the various branches of trade and manufacture in which
numbers of children work together, not being included in the
provisions of the Acts for regulating the employment of children
and young persons in Mills and Factories; and to collect information as to the ages at which they are employed, the number of
hours they are engaged in work, the time allowed each day for
meals, and as to the actual state, condition, and treatment of such
children; and as to the effects of such employment, both with
regard to their morals and their bodily health."[6]
  " I had long resolved," he told the House, " that so soon as
I could see the factory children, as it were, safe in harbour, I
would undertake a new task," and he proceeded to sketch a grim
and vivid picture of the conditions in which children worked in
many of the unregulated industries, pin- and nail-making, earthenware and pottery, in the iron foundries and glass-works, and in
the bleach-works and collieries. Several thousand workers, he
asserted, were engaged in calico-printing, where they sometimes
started at five years of age. They frequently took their meals in
the workrooms, they had no facilities for washing, and they were
grievously over-worked. " The House will with difficulty," he

  6 E. Hodder, *The Life and Work of the seventh Earl of Shaftesbury*
(1893) p. 164.

exclaimed, " believe for how minute an addition to the daily wages parents will doom their children to excessive labour," and he demanded a full inquiry into the circumstances of their employment.

Ashley had no difficulty in persuading the House to agree to his motion,[7] and on 20th October, 1841, the Commissioners, Thomas Tooke, Thomas Southwood Smith, Leonard Horner and Robert Saunders were appointed to form the Central Board which was to supervize and co-ordinate the work of the sub-commissioners, who were to collect evidence in different parts of the country. The scope of the inquiry was wide, for full investigation was made into the conditions obtaining in all the important industries free from regulation.[8]

The Report of the Children's Employment Commission on trades and manufactures, published on 30th January, 1843,[9] afforded ample evidence, if such were needed, of the urgency of the problem that Parliament was now called upon to face. " In Trades and Manufactures," said the Commissioners, " we find—

That instances occur in which Children begin to work as early as three and four years of age; not unfrequently at five, and between five and six; while in general, regular employment commences between seven and eight. . . .

That in the great majority of the Trades and Manufactures the youngest Children as well as the Young Persons are hired and paid by the workmen, and are entirely under their control; the employers exercising no sort of superintendence over them, and apparently knowing nothing whatever about them. . . .

That the work in which Children and Young Persons are employed is seldom in itself oppressive, or even laborious; and very few indeed of the processes in the care and management of which Children take any part are in their own nature injurious; but to this there are some lamentable exceptions in certain processes connected with the Manufacture of metal wares, of earthenware, and of glass.

That in some few instances the regular hours of work do not exceed ten, exclusive of the time allowed for meals; sometimes they are eleven, but more commonly twelve; and in great numbers of instances the employment is continued for fifteen, sixteen, and even eighteen hours consecutively.

---

7 " I was most attentively and kindly received," he said.—*Ibid*. p. 165.

8 The inquiry embraced metal manufactures, earthenware, porcelain, glass, fire-brick, lace, hosiery, calico-printing, bleaching, dyeing, calendering, paper-making, tobacco, rope- and twine-making, fustian cutting, glove-making, straw-plaiting, printing and book-binding, dress-making and needlework.—*Parl. Papers* (1843) XIII, p. 326.

9 *Parl. Papers* (1843) XIII.

That in almost every instance the Children work as long as the adults; being sometimes kept at work sixteen, and even eighteen hours without any intermission.

That in the Trades and Manufactures (and these constitute the great majority) in which the master is considered to be exonerated from all care and charge of the Children, because they are hired and paid by the workmen, the hours of work for the Children are almost always the longest, and their labour is performed under the most oppressive circumstances; it being the common practice with many of these workmen to work most irregularly; remaining idle during the early part of the week, and then working excessively at the latter end of it; and by their hours of work, whatever they may be, those of the Children must be regulated. . . .

That in all these occupations, in all the districts, some of the Children are robust, active, and healthy, although in general even these are under-sized; but that, from the early ages at which the great majority commence work, from their long hours of work, and from the insufficiency of their food and clothing, their ' bodily health ' is seriously and generally injured; they are for the most part stunted in growth, their aspect being pale, delicate, and sickly, and they present altogether the appearance of a race which has suffered general physical deterioration. . . .

That the diseases which are most prevalent amongst them, and to which they are more subject than Children of their age and station unemployed in labour, are disordered states of the nutritive organs, curvature and distortion of the spine, deformity of the limbs, and diseases of the lungs, ending in atrophy and consumption."

So far as the moral condition of the young workers was concerned, the Commissioners observed—

" That there are few classes of these Children and Young Persons ' working together in numbers,' of whom a large portion are not in a lamentably low moral condition. . . .

That the parents, urged by poverty or improvidence, generally seek employment for the Children as soon as they can earn the lowest amount of wages, paying but little regard to the probable injury of their Children's health by early labour, and still less regard to the certain injury of their minds by early removal from school, or even by the total neglect of their education; seldom, when questioned, expressing any desire for the regulation of the hours of work, with a view to the protection and welfare of their Children, but constantly expressing the greatest apprehension lest any legislative restriction should deprive them of the profits of their Children's labour; the natural parental instinct to provide, during childhood, for the Child's subsistence, being, in great numbers of instances, wholly extinguished, and the order of nature even reversed—the Children supporting, instead of being supported by, the parents. . . .

That the means of secular and religious instruction, on the efficiency of which depends the counteraction of . . . evil tendencies, are so grievously defective, that, in all the districts, great numbers of Children and Young Persons are growing up without any religious, moral, or intellectual training; nothing being done to form them to habits of order, sobriety, honesty and forethought, or even to restrain them from vice and crime. . . .

That, were schools ever so abundant and excellent, they would be wholly beyond the reach of a large portion of the Children employed in labour, on account of the early ages at which they are put to work.

That great numbers of Children and Young Persons attend no day-school before they commence work; that even those who do go for a brief period to a day-school are very commonly removed to be put to labour at five, six, seven, and eight years old; and that the instances are extremely rare in which they attend an evening-school after regular employment has begun."

It was no part of their duty, observed the Commissioners in conclusion, to suggest remedies, " but," they added, " the information we have collected appears to us to require the serious consideration of Your Majesty's Government and of the Legislature."[10]

The task of investigating conditions in printworks, where designs were applied to the fabric either by hand-blocking or by passing the material through machines, had been entrusted to John L. Kennedy, who conducted his inquiries in Lancashire, Cheshire and Derbyshire. He reported[11] that some 20,000 operatives were engaged in the industry, more than half being under the age of 18. Many children were employed at four or five years of age, the great majority, however, beginning work at eight or nine.

" The youngest children employed in every print-field," he said, " called ' teerers,' are assistants to the block-printer. The employment of these children is to spread the liquid colour evenly on a floating sieve with a small hand-brush; this done, the block-printer places his block in the sieve, and serves it with colour; he then applies it to the cloth, giving it a slight tap with the mall or mallet which he holds in his left hand. During the time which is occupied in applying the block to the cloth, the teerer draws his brush over the sieve and lays the colour evenly as before, to be ready for the next serving of the block. There is one teerer to

---

10 *Parl. Papers* (1843) XIII, p. 519 *ff*.
11 *Parl. Papers* (1843) XIV, p. 336 *ff*.

each block-printer." This work called for comparatively little muscular exertion, but it required unremitting attention. The teerer's arm was constantly in motion as he spread the colour, and he was compelled to remain upon his feet the whole time.

When the printing was done by machinery children were employed as ' hookers ' at the plaiting machines, helping the adult workmen to lay the calico in folds; while the ' lashers ' sewed together the ends of the pieces of fabric. The ' dryers ' were engaged in passing the damp material through steam-heated tin rollers, and many children were also employed in the singeing rooms, drawing the cloth over red-hot cylinders to burn away the nap from the surface.

" There is, perhaps, no description of manufacture in which the convenience and comfort of the places in which the various operations are carried on differ so materially in different establishments, and even in different departments of the same establishment as in that of calico-printing " remarked Kennedy. " In the rooms in which several of the processes are carried on, great care is necessary to render the place of work unoppressive, and even to prevent it from seriously injuring the health. With the view of lessening, as far as practicable, the noxiousness of these operations, some proprietors spare neither trouble nor expense to secure proper ventilation, temperature, and drainage; but in great numbers of cases these conditions of the place of work are deplorably neglected."[12] In the rooms where the colours were prepared, and in the dyeing rooms, ventilation was usually adequate, but the lashing-out and hooking rooms were often full of dust, while in the singeing rooms the atmosphere was charged with small burnt particles that irritated the eyes and nostrils. Much of the work was done in the open air. " They have to clean the blocks," wrote a doctor to Ashley. " This is done at the margin of the brook on which the works stand. I often see these little creatures standing up to the calves of their legs in the water, and this, even in the severest weather, after being kept all day in rooms heated to a most oppressive degree."[13]

Perhaps the worst feature of the calico-printing industry was the irregularity of the hours that were worked. In cotton and woollen mills the demand for the finished product was on the whole fairly steady; if the market slackened at any time it was always possible to maintain output against future needs. The printworks, however, were of necessity organized on a different

---

[12] *Ibid.* p. 361.
[13] *Speeches of the Earl of Shaftesbury* (1868) p. 23. In the machine-printing rooms, where it was necessary to dry the colours quickly, the cloth was passed through a stove often heated to 260°, and the atmosphere was consequently extremely oppressive.

basis, for the commodity in which they dealt was subject to the
fluctuating demands of fashion and season. "A large order arrives,"
explained Kennedy, "from a correspondent in London for a
particular pattern which happens to have taken, or which particularly suits the season; or perhaps a large quantity of a particular
style of goods is wanted for shipment by a certain vessel; perhaps
certain hands amongst the printers are alone capable of performing
the particular work well, or only a limited number of blocks have
been cut with this particular pattern : in either case the whole work
falls upon a small number of hands, the rest of the shop not
participating at all in the exertion to complete it."[14]   In many
instances the printer was supplied with cloth by the customer,
and frequently he worked only to specific orders that had been
placed.   The fact that the hand-block printers were independent
of machinery made it easy for them to adapt themselves to so
irregular and varying a demand.   The adult printers were paid by
the piece, and during busy seasons they worked unremittingly,
keeping their young hands fully engaged for fourteen or sixteen
hours a day. "Whilst we are now writing (March 29th, 1844)," said
a Manchester operative, " some of the master-printers are running
their machines 16 and 18 hours a day, and infants of a tender age,
many of them from 7 to 9 years old, are compelled to work the
whole of the time, whilst their fathers, who, but a short time ago,
could have earned from 25s. to 30s. per week, are now walking
about idle, in rags and wretchedness, while their children are toiling
these long and unnatural hours at those machines that have
supplanted the labour of their natural protectors."[15]

The report of the Children's Employment Commission on
trades and manufactures aroused but slight interest in the country,
partly because the evils there disclosed paled into insignificance in
comparison with the truly terrible state of affairs that their earlier
report had shown to exist in mines and collieries;[16] and partly
because the range of industries investigated was so vast that it
was difficult to know where to begin.

Ashley's instinct suggested the wise course.   He resolved to
start with calico-printing, an industry which, though differing in
important respects from those trades already regulated, was one

---

[14] *Parl. Papers* (1843) XIV, p. 385.
[15] W. Rashleigh, *Stubborn Facts from the Factories* (1844) p. 84.
[16] The first report, on the mines (*Parl. Papers*, 1842, XV) described in
grim and measured terms, conditions so appalling and inhuman in all their
stark terror, that Parliament was shocked into instant action.   Introduced
into the Commons by Lord Ashley on 7th June, 1842, the Bill to regulate
conditions in the collieries (*Parl. Papers*, 1842, III, p. 275) was passed into
law the following August. (5 & 6 Vict., c. 99.)   Women and girls, and
boys under ten years of age, were prohibited from working underground.

which offered the best promise of success. It was closely related to the main textile industry, it employed a large number of workers, and it could easily be supervised by the existing Factory Inspectors.

On 18th February, 1845, he moved for leave to introduce his bill.[17] Reminding the House of the findings of the Commission, he quoted extensively from the reports and evidence submitted by the sub-commissioners. "Robert Crawford, block-maker, states, that in the kiln, where the block runs through on rollers to dry the colours, no one can work above three, or at most five minutes. Mary Moody and Mary Maxwell, stove-girls, state that the girls often faint from exhaustion caused by the heat. John Rodgers, machine-printer, states that the girls who attend on the dash wheels have to stand with the feet and petticoats always wet, and that this in severe weather causes great hardship." The hours of work, he said, were rarely less than twelve a day, and during the ' pushes ' or ' flushes ' children aged five or six were often employed fourteen or sixteen hours without pause or respite. Thomas Sidbread, a block-printer, had told the sub-commissioner, " I began to work between 8 and 9 o'clock on Wednesday night, but the boy had been sweeping the shop from Wednesday morning. I never left the shop till 6 o'clock on the Saturday morning, and I had never stopped working all that time; I was knocked up, and the boy was almost insensible." Henry Richardson had given similar evidence. " At 4 o'clock I began to work, and worked all that day, all the next night, and until 10 o'clock the following day. I had only one teerer during that time, and I dare say he would be about 12 years old."

Such protracted labour, declared Ashley, could not but cause moral degradation, for the children were denied any opportunities of education. "The facility of obtaining early employment for children in the print-fields," the Commissioners had said, " empties the day-schools. Parents without hesitation sacrifice the future welfare of their children through life for the immediate advantage or gratification obtained by the pittance derived from the child's earnings."

His proposal was that night-work should be abolished for all females, and for boys under thirteen years of age; and that the hours of children should be restricted to eight a day, or twelve on three alternate days. These regulations should, in his opinion, apply not only to printworks, but to establishments engaged in the allied processes of dyeing, bleaching, and calendering. " Sir," he concluded, " it has been said to me more than once, ' Where will

17 Bill to regulate the Labour of Children in Calico Print Works.— *Parl. Papers* (1845) I, p. 227. *Hansard* (1845) LXXVII, 638 *ff*.

you stop?' I reply, without hesitation, ' Nowhere, so long as any portion of this mighty evil remains to be removed.' I confess that my desire and ambition are to bring all the labouring children of this empire within the reach and the opportunities of education."[18]

Sir James Graham, speaking for the Government, said he felt unable to oppose the introduction of the bill, but he thought it right to draw the attention of the House to the fact that there were several marked and striking distinctions between calico-printing, and other departments of the textile industry already regulated.[19] On the whole the occupation was not unhealthy, the high temperatures incidental to certain processes being only of short duration. It would be extremely difficult to regulate the hours of work because it was impossible to stop the machinery at pre-determined intervals—once the work had been begun it must be carried to completion without intermission. The labour of children was indispensable, for the block-printer could not work without his teerer; and if the masters were unable to employ the younger and cheaper hands, higher wages would have to be paid, and the profits would disappear. Another consideration that should be kept in mind was that the print-fields were widely dispersed, and that evasion would be easy.

He begged the House to pause before embarking on this new venture. " I see the impossibility, if we now advance on this line, of stopping here " he exclaimed. " The noble Lord tells us he will not stop here, and that he proposes applying legislative interference to the whole working population of the country. I cannot view that alternative without a serious apprehension that a fatal effect will be produced on the trade and manufactures of the country."

Leave to introduce the bill having been obtained, the first reading took place on 12th March, 1845.[20] The Government were as yet undecided what policy they should pursue, for although nobody could deny that some measure of control was desirable, the attitude of the manufacturers was not yet known with any certainty. Graham accordingly resolved to consult the Factory Inspectors, and on 20th March Horner, Saunders and Howell were recalled from their districts with instructions to meet the Home Secretary on Saturday, 22nd March.[21] Graham kept the Inspectors waiting nearly three hours, but when they were at last admitted to his presence he told them that he wanted to see them about the Printworks Bill which was to be debated on the second reading on

[18] *Speeches of the Earl of Shaftesbury* (1868) pp. 152-166.
[19] *Hansard* (1845) LXXVII, 656 *ff*.
[20] *Hansard* (1845) LXXVIII, 723.
[21] *Minutes*, Vol. II, p. 151. Stuart, who was in Glasgow, was not summoned to the meeting. His orders were sent to him by post.

2nd April. He said " that the Government had determined not to decide upon what course they should take until they had obtained more information, and that it was his desire that the Inspectors should proceed forthwith to their respective districts, and by personal enquiries and with the aid of the Sub-Inspectors collect as extensively as possible the opinions of those whose Trades are included in the Bill how far the several enactments contained in it will affect them." A circular letter had been prepared for each Inspector to issue in his district, and when the requisite information had been obtained they were to meet him again on Monday, 31st March.

At this second conference the matter was discussed in all its aspects, and the final decision was taken. When the House met on 2nd April, Graham announced that, since the first reading, he had made extensive enquiries as to the probable effects of the bill. " Under my direction," he said, " the inspectors repaired to their different districts, and having assembled the sub-inspectors engaged under them, they directed them to proceed with a copy of this Bill in their hands, and to enter into communication with all the leading parties connected with these branches of industry in their respective districts."[22] He had also received deputations from the masters, and he now had to announce that though he dissented from certain provisions incorporated in the bill, he had come to the conclusion that some regulation was necessary, though he was not prepared to extend the operation of the measure to dyeing, bleaching, and calendering. He agreed that children under eight years of age should be prohibited from working in the print-fields —that was a wise and humane measure; he agreed, though with some hesitation, that all females, and children under thirteen years of age should be forbidden to work during the night; he agreed that provision must be made for education, though in this connection there must be some flexibility. " In deciding on the question of the time to be allowed for the education of children employed in these works, I would prefer looking to the analogy between their condition and that of the children of agricultural labourers, rather than to that of factory labour regulated by machinery. In the north of England and in Scotland, where it is well known the children of agricultural labourers are, practically speaking, well educated, there are certain periods of the year when, in consequence of the greater demand for labour, there is a suspension of education. . . . We could secure a provision under this enactment, that during one hundred days throughout the year, being about one third of the whole working year, all children employed in these works from eight to thirteen years of age should attend a school daily, as in

---

[22] *Hansard* (1845) LXXVIII, 1369 *ff.*

the case of factory children, say for three or four hours a day; and I would also recommend, in order that there should be no evasion of the intentions of the Legislature, that this period should be divided into fifty days in each half year."[23]

Ashley having stated that he was prepared to make concessions in order to expedite the passage of the measure, the bill was read a second time. The report stage was taken on 11th, 17th, and 28th April,[24] the third reading on 30th April,[25] and after an uneventful passage through the Lords, it received the royal assent on 30th June, 1845.[26]

Although it had been decided not to legislate by reference to the Factory Acts,[27] the Act to regulate the Labour of Children, Young Persons, and Women, in Print Works[28] was in some respects identical with the Act of 1844, many of the sections being reproduced word for word. The provisions of the new Act were to be enforced by the Factory Inspectors, the certifying surgeons were to grant certificates of age, and practically the whole of the existing machinery of administration was incorporated in the statute.

After 1st January, 1846, no child under the age of eight was to be employed in a printworks,[29] and no child between the ages of eight and thirteen, and no female was to work at night, i.e. between 10 p.m. and 6 a.m.[30] The hours of work of young persons between thirteen and sixteen years of age were not restricted, the only requirement in their case being that they must possess a surgical certificate testifying that they were at least thirteen years old, and that they were not incapacitated by disease or bodily infirmity from working daily in a printworks.[31] There were no stipulations concerning the intervals to be allowed for meals, and no provision was made for holidays.

These less onerous restrictions were designed to afford the printworkers that degree of flexibility in conducting their business that the peculiar problems they had to face demanded; and it was for the same reason that the educational clauses differed fundamentally from those governing the factories. From 1st July, 1846, every child employed in a printworks was to attend school for at

---

[23] *Ibid.* 1373-1374.
[24] *Hansard* (1845) LXXIX, 494, 859, 1369.
[25] *Ibid.* 1439.
[26] *Hansard* (1845) LXXXI, 1341.
[27] *Hansard* (1845) LXXVIII, 1374.
[28] 8 & 9 Vict., c. 29.
[29] Sec. 19.
[30] Sec. 22.
[31] Sec. 21.

least thirty days[32] between 1st January and 30th June, and for thirty days between 1st July and 31st December. No period of daily attendance was stipulated, but at least 150 hours were to be spent in school during each six-monthly period.[33] The schoolmaster was to keep a record of each child's attendance, and he was to enter in a School Certificate book, provided by the parent, details of attendance and absence week by week.[34] Before taking a child into employment the occupier of a printwork was to obtain from the schoolmaster a certificate testifying that the child had attended school for at least six months, ending 30th June or 31st December, prior to his engagement, and a similar certificate was to be procured at the beginning of each subsequent six-monthly period.[35]

In the spring of 1846, when he had visited all the printworks in his district, Horner was able to report that the Act was well observed.[36] "The occupiers of these works," he said, "have evidenced the greatest readiness to fulfil the Act to the utmost of their power; they have met this new law, which for the first time has interfered with the workers in their employment, in the best spirit, and I look forward with confidence to their cordially co-operating in the humane purpose of the Legislature." Saunders, whose district contained only 48 printworks, was also well satisfied, though he thought the educational clauses might cause some difficulty. "The result of this first tour of inspection," he said, "affords a satisfactory assurance that the provisions of the law will be readily obeyed; and that the only enactments which can operate prejudicially, will be the peculiar mode in which school attendance is required and enforced in the case of children under 13 years of age."[37]

Howell was not so hopeful, indeed he was frankly critical of an Act that made no provision for fencing, for meal-times, or for holidays, that permitted children between the ages of eight and thirteen to be worked continuously from 6 a.m. to 10 p.m., and that placed no restrictions at all on the hours of boys over thirteen. The educational clauses, he was convinced, would cause serious

---

[32] The section actually stipulated "fifty" days—an error that necessitated the passing of an amending Act (9 & 10 Vict., c. 18) substituting the word "thirty."
[33] Sec. 23. No attendance above five hours on any one day was to be reckoned as part of the 150 hours.
[34] Sec. 24.
[35] Sec. 25.
[36] Report, 30th April, 1846. *Parl. Papers* (1846) XX, p. 617. He complained bitterly, however, of the increased burden thrust upon him. "The factories I have myself to attend to, 1519 firms, occupying 2,068 factories, were already more than enough; and now 114 printworks have been added."
[37] *Ibid.* p. 622.

difficulty, for the proviso that children must qualify for employment by attending school during a period of six months before that employment could begin, would cause great hardship and embarrassment. " Upon this," he observed, " it has been remarked to me, on behalf of the occupiers of printworks, that in the ensuing and in each succeeding half-year, they will be prevented from employing any but certain individual children, who will thus have a monopoly of employment, as being the only ones who will be provided with the Parliamentary Certificate of qualification for admission into a printwork."[38]

Six months later Saunders recorded that his first forebodings had proved only too well-founded. " I fear it will be wholly impracticable to carry out or enforce the law, as it is now framed. One serious error in the principle on which the school clauses of the Printworks Act are framed, is, that the attendance of children at school is required before (and long before) they are enabled to earn any wages to pay even the school fee. Nothing can make such a provision equitable, except the State shall provide schools at which the children whose parents can only earn the ordinary wages of a labourer, shall be able to receive a gratuitous education."[39] Another defect was that no provision had been made requiring attendance at school for a minimum number of hours each day. One hour's attendance was sufficient to comply with the statute, and, as Saunders remarked, " it would be preposterous to suppose good schools can admit children who are to be permitted to attend for one hour, and who probably, if the printing trade becomes brisk, do not return to their classes for days or weeks afterwards."

Stuart agreed with his colleagues, emphasizing the injustice of requiring parents to incur expenses before their children could enter employment. " The injustice of requiring expenses to be previously incurred, in some cases, for more than half a year before employment, is quite obvious; and, above all, the injustice of requiring the child, previous to employment, to insist on a schoolmaster to do that, which he, the schoolmaster, is not bound by law to do."[40] The cumbersome and complicated form of attendance register drew loud complaints from the unhappy schoolmasters, who were compelled to devote much of their leisure to the compilation of the weekly returns. " I may state," wrote Archibald Russell of Dalmonach, " that I have more work filling up the registers required by the Act, than in teaching the children. Besides the usual day-book which the schoolmaster must keep,

[38] Report, 30th April, 1846. *Parl. Papers* (1846) XX, p. 618.
[39] Report, 31st October, 1846. *Parl. Papers* (1847) XV, p. 455.
[40] Report, 31st October, 1846. *Ibid.* p 480

and in which is inserted the day's attendance of each pupil, we are forced to have a certificate book for each child. In this book, not only the particular hours of daily attendance must be written, but there must be a superfluity of unnecessary repetitions; such as inserting weekly the name of the child, names of parents, place of abode, the name of the particular school, parish, county, &c., all of which must be repeated in every page of the book, a page serving for a week. You will observe from this that the teacher has a great deal of unnecessary labour from such a process as is required, and that there is something radically wrong in the formation of such a plan."[41]

At the statutory meeting of the Inspectors held in June, 1846, Horner and Howell announced that they had received a number of letters from the occupiers of printworks complaining of the difficulty caused by their inability to employ, between July and December, those children who had not made the requisite attendances at school during the previous six months.[42] Many of the owners were uncertain what was required of them, as two of the letters read at the meeting clearly showed. Horner had just received from Messrs. Reddish & Bickham, of Oswaldtwistle, a communication in the following terms—" As we have been scarce of work from the commencement of this year till the present time, the children employed in our establishment have completed their period of Schooling without any difficulty. But as a number of them have left us and gone to work at the Cotton Mills, we stand much in need of new hands as we shall shortly be very brisk. Four have presented themselves to-day but they have been at no day school and it is impossible for them to finish the 30 days or the 150 hours which the Act requires for this half year. They come from a district where the people are quite ignorant of the Printworks Regulation Act. What am I to do with them? Will it be sufficient if they attend School this month (June) the number of hours which will constitute a sixth part of the time for one who has been employed from the 1st of January to the 30th of June? I will thank you to answer this application as soon as convenient."

Horner's reply was clear, but unhelpful. "I have this day your Letter of the 3rd Inst., and in reply have to inform you, that by the 25th Sec. of the Printworks Act you cannot employ any child between the 1st July and 31st December next without having in your possession a Schoolmasters Certificate that such child had attended School for at least Thirty days (Fifty is a misprint) and not more than 5 hours in any one day, between the 1st of Jan. and 30th June, 1846. I have no power to allow any deviation from what the Act prescribes in this matter."

41 *Ibid.* p. 482.
42 *Minutes,* 5th June, 1846, Vol. II, p. 251.

The letter addressed to Howell was from Messrs. J. & C. Yates, of New Mills, near Stockport. " We shall be much obliged to you if you will give us your opinion on clause 23 in the Print-works Act. We have in this neighbourhood two readings of the clause.

One: that if a child goes 30 days to School beginning on the 1st of July, 1846, and going to the 5th Aug., 1846, and then presents its book to the Sub-Inspector it may be employed (with a Surgeon's Certificate) on a Printground for the remaining part of the year say from Aug. to 31 Decr. We are aware that if a child has been at School for 30 days before the 1st July 1846 it can be allowed to work. The other reading is that if a child does not go to School 30 days before the 1st of July it cannot be employed in a Print-ground till Jan. 1847 and then it must have been at School 30 days prior to that time. This last reading is so very severe on the parents that are poor that we think it a hardship that cannot be intended by the framers of the Act. We may have for instance a widow sent to our Township with 5 children all under 13 years of age but 3 of them above 8, but if they cannot bring a Certificate book of their having been at School for 30 days before the 1st of July none of these children can be employed in a printwork for 6 months after they come to us—and many cases of a similar kind will arise."

" In reply to your Letter of yesterday," wrote Howell, " I have the honour to call your attention to the provisions of the 25th Sec. of the Printworks Act whereby you will perceive that a child cannot be employed after the 1st July next unless the occupier of a Printwork shall have obtained a certificate that it has attended School for at least 30 days as required by this Act *during the half year* ending on the 30th of June; and consequently that attendance at School in the month of July will not be available to justify its employment until the half year commencing 1st Jan. 1847."[43]

That the educational clauses would need to be amended was generally admitted, but no alternative plan had as yet won universal acceptance. The Inspectors discussed the problem afresh at their meeting on 8th December, 1846, but since they could not reach agreement, further consideration of the subject was postponed.[44] Horner had already expressed his own views in his report for the previous October. " It obviously was a mistake in framing this enactment; and the remedy I would recommend is this: that, without abating the amount of school attendance either as to days

---

[43] *Minutes*, 9th June, 1846, Vol. II, pp. 254-256.
[44] *Minutes*, Vol. II, p. 270.

or hours, and still making preliminary education necessary, the required attendance during *any* six months, before the first day of employment should be sufficient. . . . From the uncertain and irregular nature of the employment of the children, and their frequently changing from one Printwork to another, I consider a preliminary attendance at a school, to the extent required by the present law, indispensable; without it, many children employed in this branch would get no education at all." He rejected the suggestion that preliminary education would be unnecessary if schools were provided on the premises. " I know very well what that would come to. We should have some hole or shed, with a table and some benches, called a school, and some workman carrying on some odd jobs, and just able to read and perhaps sign his name, would be called a schoolmaster, and the children in their dirty clothes, smeared with colour, would be running in and out at all times, between six in the morning and ten at night. This would only be a counterpart of many Factory Schools on the premises that existed until the amending law fixed the working of the children to half a day, either forenoon or afternoon."[45]

Stuart, on the other hand, was not convinced that a period of preliminary education was either necessary or desirable; he supported the view of the most influential Scottish print-workers that a better plan would be to insist that the children should attend school, after 6 o'clock at night, for an hour and a half a day on five days of the week.[46]

Saunders thought that if sufficient children were available it would be more satisfactory to adopt the arrangements in force under the Factory Acts, with such modifications as the differing conditions in the printworks made desirable. He therefore proposed that children should work either alternate days or alternate weeks, and that they should attend school during the intermediate periods.[47]

On 27th February, 1847, Sir George Grey summoned the Inspectors to the Home Office, and told them " that he wished to see them because the Government intended to introduce into Parliament this Session a Bill to amend the Educational Clauses of the Printworks Act, and he would therefore be glad to hear in their opinion, how the occupiers could be relieved from the inconvenience to which they are now subject, retaining for the children the advantages of schooling as contemplated by the present Act."[48] The Inspectors explained the difficulties that they had encountered, but declined to suggest any amendment of the law, since they were

---

[45] *Parl. Papers* (1847) XV, p. 446.
[46] Report, 31st October, 1846. *Ibid.* pp. 479-482.
[47] *Ibid.* pp. 454-456.
[48] *Minutes*, Vol. II, p. 292.

not agreed as to the best course to follow. It was therefore decided to postpone further discussion until their next meeting, when they would have had an opportunity of studying conditions afresh in their districts.

When they re-assembled on 20th May, 1847, Horner recounted to his colleagues what had transpired at an interview he had had with the Home Secretary towards the end of April. " Sir George Grey asked Mr. Horner what alterations he thought would meet the obstacles that had been found in practice to the working of the education clauses, and took a pen and paper to write down Mr. Horner's replies. Mr. Horner said that he should much prefer to lay a proposal before Sir G. after consultation with his Colleagues, that the Statutory Meeting was to take place on the 1st June and asked whether that would be in time for his purpose. Sir George replied that he feared it would be in time, meaning that parliament would continue sitting long after that date and he assented to Mr. Horner's proposal. Mr. Horner asked Sir George to address a Letter to that effect to the other Inspectors but Sir George said that if Mr. Horner would convey his wishes to them it would be enough, as he had so much to attend to. Mr. Horner then observed, that before he and his colleagues could usefully enter upon the consideration of the subject, there was a point of principle to settle, which Sir George alone could decide upon, as there was a difference of opinion between him and some of his colleagues on the question of School attendance being a necessary preliminary to employment. Sir George's answer was to the following effect— that he would do no more than propose such alteration as would remove the difficulties that had been found to interfere with the working of the education clauses in the Act, that preliminary education is a principle settled by the Act and that he should not disturb that but only endeavour to render it more easy of being carried into effect."[49]

These instructions clearly limited the field in which the Inspectors could make their recommendations, the plan originally proposed by Horner being the only one which admitted the principle of preliminary education. Saunders and Stuart remained unconvinced that this principle ought to be preserved, and accordingly, although they agreed that Horner's plan was the best that could be evolved if the Government adhered to its present policy, they insisted that their own alternative schemes should be submitted formally to the Home Office. The letter containing their proposals was forwarded on 25th May;[50] three days later they conferred personally with Grey, and received his assurance that

---

[49] *Minutes*, Vol. II, pp. 296-297.
[50] *Minutes*, Vol. II, pp. 299-304.

he would consider their suggestions in the light of any observations that his legal experts felt inclined to make.[51]

The Government, pledged already to the principle of preliminary education, was reinforced in its decision by the cogent arguments advanced in its favour by Horner. There was no difficulty in persuading the House that reform on the lines suggested was desirable, and on 22nd July, 1847, the Act to amend the Law as to the School Attendance of Children employed in Print Works was passed.[52] Sections 23, 24 and 25 of the original Act were repealed, a new form of School Certificate was devised, and it was now provided that after 1st August, 1847, a child should be qualified for employment if he had attended school on at least 30 days for not less than 150 hours during the half-year immediately preceding the day upon which he began work, the minimum daily attendance to be two and a half hours.

"The Act of last session," said Horner in his report of October, 1847,[53] " has universally throughout my district been held to be a great improvement; while it interferes much less than the enactments of the original Act did with the convenience of the occupiers of the print works, and removes an objection which parents unreasonably made, it has rendered the attendance of the children at school much more likely to prove beneficial; has very considerably lightened the labour of the schoolmaster in making out certificates; and has made a close inspection of this important part of the legislative interference much more practicable." Stuart agreed that the new measure was an improvement on the old, but he found the Scottish owners still considered it a great hardship that they should have to submit to the absence of children for two and a half hours a day while they were completing their school attendance.[54]

To have insisted that children employed in calico-printing should attend school was no small achievement, while their exclusion from night work went far to temper the hardships of the conditions under which they worked; but, despite the fact that the elaborate and well-tried machinery of the Factory Acts was embodied in this new code, the provisions of the Printworks Act were woefully inadequate, especially in the measure of protection afforded to young persons over the age of thirteen. " I do think," observed Saunders, " that the employment of these classes might be placed under better regulations than at present, and that, if it be deemed right to permit employment at certain seasons when the

[51] *Ibid.* 28th May, 1847, Vol. II, p. 306.
[52] 10 & 11 Vict., c. 70.
[53] *Parl. Papers* (1847-8) XXVI, p. 117.
[54] Report, 31st October, 1847. *Ibid.* p. 147.

printing of goods is very brisk (periods technically called *pushes*), to be extended beyond the hours prescribed for factory labour, a register of the young persons and children thus employed, and of the extent of the overtime so worked, might as reasonably be required of the occupiers of Print Works as the record now required of the occupiers of factories when recovering lost time at night by the 34 sec. and Schedule C. of the 7 Vic., c. 15. Such a register would, moreover, prove to what extent such evils do exist, and whether they might not very safely be altogether prohibited."[55]

This was the invocation of a principle that was fundamental to any extension of legislative control. To what extent was the industrial code to adapt itself to the widely-varying conditions obtaining in those branches of manufacture as yet unregulated; to what extent were these industries to be required to modify their working to enable them to fulfil the requirements of the law? That was the problem that was now to be faced.[56] The true significance of the Printworks Act must be sought, not in its intrinsic provisions, but rather in the fact that it was the first attempt to break new ground, to advance from the narrow and rigidly circumscribed terrain of the major textile industries, where it was comparatively easy to impose control, into a new and more difficult territory in which the existing machinery would need to be modified to meet very different conditions.

Not the least of the perplexities that had confronted the Inspectors had been the problem of deciding to which establishments the Factory Acts applied. Ure held that the term factory system " designates the combined operation of many orders of work-people, adult and young, in tending with assiduous skill a series of productive machines continuously impelled by a central power . . . but it excludes mills in which the mechanisms do not form a connected series, nor are dependent on one prime mover."[57] The Act of 1833 had defined a factory, with greater precision, as a place where steam, water, or other mechanical power was used

---

[55] Report, 30th April, 1847. *Parl. Papers* (1847) XV, p. 499.

[56] In a paper entitled *The Half-time System and the Educational Test,* George Anderson emphasized the dilemma. The danger was, he contended, that separate legislation would be conceded to each industry, " each with its vexatious disabilities, whimsical exceptions, unfair discrepancies, and special perils of punishment and fine . . . The Factory Acts are full of all these things, and I fear no such Act can pass the Legislature without being so crippled by hostile factions, so mutilated by the ingenuity and pressure of private interests, that, however honest its first intention, it comes out of the ordeal with a very different aspect."— *Transactions of the National Association for the Promotion of Social Science* (1860) p. 383.

[57] A. Ure, *The Philosophy of Manufactures* (1835) p. 13.

to propel or work the machinery,[58] thus, as Howell pointed out,[59] embracing small establishments containing perhaps a single carding engine worked by a water-wheel, and employing only half a dozen hands. These factories were often situated in remote spots where no school was available, and since the occupiers were frequently quite illiterate it was impossible to enforce school attendance or to insist that registers be kept.[60] "This kind of rural occupation," said the Inspectors, "cannot be identified with the factory system; and although, strictly speaking, these mills come within the letter of the law, we have considered that we exercise a sound discretion in directing the various Sub-Inspectors not to consider them as requiring that same degree of supervision as establishments where the factory system, properly so-called, prevails."[61]

It was not such a simple matter, however, to exercise discretion when children were employed in rooms where no mechanical power was used, though the rooms formed part of a factory as defined by the Act. If it was held that these young workers were not subject to regulation, the door would be opened to evasion on an extensive scale, for they could easily be transferred from rooms where the Act did not apply to apartments where it did. The Inspectors recognized the danger, and as early as 1836 they resolved that children under thirteen years of age should not be employed at any description of work in any room attached to a factory without becoming subject to all the provisions of the Act applicable to children, whether there was machinery moved by power in that room or not.[62] This view was later endorsed by the Home Office in a letter to Saunders, who had enquired whether the Act applied to children employed at reeling frames which were worked by hand in rooms having no internal communication with any room containing mechanically operated machinery. The reply was that to all intents and purposes such children were employed in a mill as defined by the Act, and were therefore subject to all the provisions of the Act.[63]

An attempt was made to clarify the position in the Act of 1844, section 73 of which defined factories as all buildings or premises wherein or within the close or curtilage of which steam, water or any other mechanical power was used to work the machinery employed in preparing, manufacturing or finishing cotton, wool, hair, silk, flax, hemp, jute or tow. Any room situated within the outward gate or boundary of any factory

---

58 3 & 4 Will. IV, c. 103, sec. 1.
59 Report, August, 1835. *Parl. Papers* (1836) XLV, p. 159.
60 Stuart's Report, 31st December, 1836. *Parl. Papers* (1837) XXXI, pp. 116-117.
61 Joint Report, 27th May, 1847. *Parl. Papers* (1847) XV, p. 518.
62 *Minutes*, 16th September, 1836, Vol. I, p. 24.
63 *Home Office Papers*, 26th December, 1839, H.O. 87 (1), pp. 190-191.

wherein children or young persons were employed in any process incidental to the manufacture carried on in the factory was to be taken to be a part of the factory, even though it did not contain any machinery.

A net so widely cast could hardly fail to cause difficulty and embarrassment, especially when a building was jointly occupied by independent owners, any one of whom, it seemed, might, if he installed power-driven machinery, render his fellows subject to all the provisions of the Factories Regulation Act, including liability for accidents.[64]   In certain industries, too, power-spinning was a subsidiary part of the main manufacturing process, and the occupiers of ropeworks in Scotland made strong representations that they should be exempt from the provisions of the Act.   In order to meet these objections a bill was prepared, the object of which was to exclude from the operation of the Factory Act all ropeworks that did not employ mechanical power, and that had no internal communication with premises forming part of a mill within the meaning of the Factory Act.[65]

The Ropeworks Act did not define the phrase "internal communication," and the Inspectors, obliged to interpret it themselves, resolved that if a ropeground opened into the same court as a power-loom factory, the whole being in the same close or curtilage, the ropework was to be regarded as subject to the Factory Act.[66]   The Inspectors, said Saunders, were unable to understand distinctly what meaning was to be attached to these words; they could only assume that they were intended to apply to those works where no facility existed for removing regulated persons from the rope-walk to other departments where the processes of spinning and weaving were conducted.   Certain occupiers of ropeworks had lodged objections to the ruling of the Inspectors, he continued, holding "that if the doorway into a spinning or weaving mill is situated a few feet from the doorway into a rope-walk, so that persons going from the one to the other have to pass through the outer air, such communication, though both doors are within the same private premises, cannot be termed ' internal communication.' "[67]

The question was referred to the Attorney-General, who delivered an opinion with some hesitation.   "Has the Ropery," he said, "any internal communication with any building used as a Factory, or with any building or erection situate within the close

---

[64] For the contrary view see counsel's opinion in the Bradford case. Appendix.

[65] The Ropeworks Act (9 & 10 Vict., c. 40) came into force on 3rd August, 1846.

[66] *Minutes*, 28th January, 1847, Vol. II, p. 287.

[67] Report, 30th April, 1847.   *Parl. Papers* (1847) XV, p. 500.

or curtilage of a building used as a Factory? The term 'internal communication' has no doubt various meanings according to the context of which it forms a part—and frequently means a direct communication between the interior of one building and the interior of another building, in which case no such communication could probably be said to exist here, but looking to the nature of Roperies (which frequently cannot be said to constitute buildings at all and therefore cannot be ordinarily capable of internal communication in this sense with other buildings) and looking to what probably would be considered to have been the object of the legislature in exempting Roperies not having such internal communication (*viz.*, that the exemption should not apply where children employed in the Factory could be passed over into the Ropery without falling under observation) the inclination of our opinion is that the Ropery in this sense would not be deemed exempt from the operation of the Acts.

We must however add, that it is purely a question of construction, and one of very considerable difficulty, and we are far therefore from wishing to express any confident opinion on the subject."[68]

This was not very illuminating, and the Inspectors pressed for a greater measure of precision. They placed on record their view that "the wording of the Act 9 & 10 Vic., c.40 'To declare certain Ropeworks not within the operation of the Factory Acts' is very confused and difficult to understand, and that if Ropeworks are to be exempted from the Factory Acts some provision should be passed in such terms as shall clearly exempt all bonâ fide Ropeworks from the operation of that Act, but which shall not extend such exemption to any parts of those premises in which the processes of spinning or other manufacturing process is carried on for the production of the same articles that are manufactured in other Mills which are subject to the Factory Acts."[69]

Similar difficulties of interpretation arose in the administration of the Printworks Act, section 2 of which had defined a printwork as a building or shed within which persons were employed to print designs, by means of blocks or cylinders, upon woven fabric. In the neighbourhood of London there were some twenty factories in which patterns were printed on floor cloth. "The hours of labour in all these," observed Saunders, "are more limited than those prescribed by the Printwork Act, and are regulated by a law which operates as strictly and uniformly as any the Inspectors can enforce, *viz.*, the conditions imposed on them by the insurance offices, which

[68] *Minutes*, 13th December, 1847, Vol. II, p. 335.
[69] *Minutes*, 9th June, 1848. Vol. II, pp. 356-357.

provisions prevent the carrying on any operation in such premises, except during broad day-light. The only provisions of the Printwork Act to which the attention of the officers will have in these cases to be directed are those relating to the necessary registers and surgical certificates, with the attendance at school of those under 13 years of age, if any such should be employed, which is very unlikely."[70]

The occupiers of these factories, nevertheless, desired to secure formal exemption from the Act, and two of them wrote to Saunders pointing out that the regulations did not touch them, since they printed the designs, not on the fabric itself, but on a coat of paint that had been previously applied to the fabric. "They print their Patterns on Fabrics previously prepared by a coat of paint or other matter so that the Block or instrument in which the Pattern or design is cut or engraved does not come in contact with the woven or felted fabric." The Inspectors agreed that such an ingenious plea was inadmissible,[71] an opinion in which the Law Officers of the Crown concurred when the case was submitted to them.[72]

Early in 1846 the Inspectors were called upon to consider the position of establishments where dyeing was carried on as ancillary to calico-printing. Stuart consulted his colleagues about a letter he had received from a Scottish firm, who said that Balfour, the Sub-Inspector, was uncertain whether their dye-works came within the scope of the Printworks Act. "The Dye-works in question are on the same grounds as the Printworks; but tho' adjacent to the latter, they are carried on in separate and distinct buildings; and the processes are quite different in their nature from those of a Printwork. . . . Mr. Balfour has some doubts on account of their contiguity to the Printworks, and the *apparent* connection arising from the circumstances of some portion of the dyed cloth being afterwards printed upon in the Printworks, although it is well known in the Trade, and throughout the Globe, that Turkey red calico is a finished article of merchandize."   •

A memorandum from Balfour revealed the reason for his uncertainty. "They have operations going on within the bounds of that Establishment for dyeing Cloths and Yarn Turkey red— but the greater portion of it is sent away in that state, while only a small part of such cloth after being so dyed is subject to a discharging process in the Printwork whereby figures are formed. Now they wish to know if persons employed in such dyeing operations come within the Statutory Regulations."

The Inspectors were unanimous. "It was agreed that the Dyeworks described in that correspondence as lying adjacent to

[70] Report, 30th April, 1846. *Parl. Papers* (1846) XX, pp. 622-623.
[71] *Minutes*, 13th January, 1846, Vol. II, p. 223.
[72] *Minutes*, 28th January, 1847, Vol. II, p. 287.

the Printworks and forming part of the Establishment where the chief process of printing is carried on are obviously a part of the ' Printworks ' as defined by the 8 & 9 Vic. c. 29, and the persons employed therein are therefore subject to the provisions of that Act."[73]

These finer shades of interpretation, applying as they did to a limited range of manufactures, and those not of the first importance, were, from one point of view, comparatively insignificant, but they foreshadowed a problem that was to increase in complexity as the area in which legislative control operated was extended. To impose discipline on a highly-centralized and compact industry was difficult enough, but when the time came to regulate other branches of trade, where working conditions and manufacturing processes differed fundamentally from those existing in the textile mills, the ingenuity of Parliament and of the Inspectors was taxed to the uttermost. The pressure exerted by vested interests had secured for the printworks and the roperies some mitigation of the stern code applicable to cotton and woollen mills, and Parliament could hardly fail to follow the precedent that it had set when the rising tide of public opinion made further extensions of regulation inevitable. " The word writ large over English factory legislation," it has been said, " is ' piece-meal',"[74] and it can scarcely be doubted that the *ad hoc* nature of the measures that were imposed on industry during the nineteenth century was due not only to the empiricism that was characteristic of contemporary political philosophy, but to the tender regard paid to the claims of the manufacturing interests.

---

[73] *Minutes,* 10th February, 1846, Vol. II, pp. 229-231 .
[74] C. R. Fay, *Life and Labour in the Nineteenth Century* (1920) p. 268.

CHAPTER 18

TEN HOURS AND THE NORMAL DAY

ALTHOUGH THEIR hopes had ultimately been dashed in 1844, the advocates of the ten-hours day had come within an ace of success, and with grim determination and dogged perseverance they continued their campaign. The Short-time Committees renewed the agitation, and in their weekly journal, the *Ten Hours Advocate,* they published full details of their activities, calling upon their supporters to make even greater efforts to secure the victory for which they had striven so long. The political situation was not unpropitious. They had little to hope from Peel and the Tories, but the Government was sailing through stormy waters, and if it should fall they might look with greater confidence to the Whig leader, Lord John Russell, who had for some time declared his sympathy with their aims.[1]

On 29th January, 1846, Lord Ashley moved for leave to introduce a bill limiting the hours of young persons and women to ten a day.[2] He would not weary the House, he said, by rehearsing all the old evidence. "The question now is narrowed to a single proposition—can this be done without injury to the manufacturers, and without a serious diminution of the wages of labour?" He confidently affirmed that it could. Mr. Gardner, who owned large mills in Manchester and Preston, had been working an eleven hours day during the past twelve months, and so far from involving himself and his operatives in ruin, he had demonstrated quite conclusively that both master and workers had benefited. There had been no diminution of production, the quality of the finished goods was better, the health of the operatives had improved, and earnings had not decreased. Gardner himself had borne testimony to this, for in a letter addressed to Ashley he had said, " I am quite satisfied that both as much yarn and power-loom cloth may be produced at quite as low a cost in 11 as in 12 hours a day. All the arguments I have heard in favour of long time appear based on an arithmetical question; if 11 produce so much, what will 12, 13 or even 15 hours produce? This is correct as far as the steam-engine is concerned; whatever it will produce in 11 hours it will produce double the quantity in 22; but try this on the animal—horse—and you will soon find that he cannot compete with the engine, as he requires time both to rest and

---

1 S. Walpole, *The Life of Lord John Russell* (1889) p. 455.
2 *Hansard* (1846) LXXXIII, 378 *ff*. *Speeches of the Earl of Shaftesbury* (1868) p. 198 *ff*.

feed. It is, I believe, a fact, not to be questioned, that there is more bad work made the last one or two hours, than the whole of the first nine or ten hours." Other manufacturers who had reduced the length of the working day reported equally satisfactory results —Horrocks and Jackson of Preston, Knowles of Bolton, and others both in Scotland and the West Riding were as enthusiastic as Gardner.

Those who had so confidently affirmed that the textile industry would be ruined when the Act of 1833 was passed, continued Ashley, had been confounded. The volume of manufactured goods had increased, wages had not been reduced, and the numbers employed had not diminished. Nothing but good had resulted from the restrictions imposed upon the labour of children, but little had been done for young persons, the majority of whom were females. " I think I may appeal to the House," he declared, " to say whether it is not cruel to take a young female on the very day on which she has passed the age of thirteen, at the most tender period of her life, and to demand of her practically the same work in duration, and frequently the same in intensity, which is demanded from ripe and vigorous manhood?"

The reply of Sir James Graham, the Home Secretary, was singularly unconvincing. If it were true, he said, that certain manufacturers had reduced the length of the working-day without suffering loss and inconvenience in the process, what better argument could be adduced for leaving matters as they were? " Nothing," he urged, " can be more satisfactory; and, so far from legislation being necessary, it appears to me a conclusive argument against calling on the Government to interpose."[3] " The restriction on the labour of young persons," he affirmed, " is virtually and completely to restrict the working of the machinery itself, and the labour of adult males, to the same period of twelve hours; and, thus the practical result of our legislation is this—that in the four great staple manufactures of cotton, woollen, silk and flax, it is not permitted, by law, that any man shall work his machinery, whatever power it may be worked by, for a greater period than twelve hours per day." Further interference, he was convinced, would be a dangerous experiment, and he counselled the House to postpone its decision upon the principle of the bill until " opinion has been pronounced upon the great proposition of my right hon. Friend at the head of the Government, in respect to the supply of corn, and the laws which regulate that supply." Whatever might be the opinion of the House in that connection he would remain unalterably opposed to any interference with adult labour, but he was nevertheless prepared to assent to the introduction of Ashley's bill.

[3] *Hansard* (1846) LXXXIII, 395.

Joseph Hume protested that the measure was wrong in principle. " The noble Lord," he cried, " now proposes a different law to operate upon those masters who have embarked their capital in machinery and mills; and by that law to restrict them in the employment of the capital so invested. This I cannot but designate as an invasion of the property of the master. . . . Industry and capital ought to be free; and no individual possessing either the one or the other should be restrained, except on the single rule of doing no injury to his neighbour, from exercising his right over that which he possesses. . . . I am confident that the time is fast approaching when, from the exposure of the errors committed, the necessity of repealing the whole system will be manifest."[4]

The bill was brought in and read the first time. Two days later, on 31st January, 1846, Lord Ashley applied for the Chiltern Hundreds.

For some years Richard Cobden had led the Anti-Corn Law League in agitating for the repeal of the Corn Laws, which imposed a duty on corn imported into this country from abroad. When the failure of the Irish potato crop in 1846 made it apparent that the peasantry would have to be fed largely on corn, Peel became convinced that the duty must be abolished, even if abolition meant disrupting his own party. His announcement, towards the end of January, 1846, that he intended to move the repeal of the Corn Laws, caused the utmost consternation among the Tories and the landed gentry, and induced Ashley to resign his seat, since he had been sent to Parliament to uphold a law that he now felt could be defended no longer. His resignation was a bitter blow to the ten-hours movement, but a worthy successor was found in John Fielden, who moved the second reading of the Short-time bill on 29th April, 1846.[5]

With becoming modesty he donned the mantle of his illustrious predecessor, taking up the struggle where Ashley had been compelled to abandon it. Parliament, he declared, had totally disregarded the interests of those factory operatives whom the law designated young persons. The period between the ages of thirteen and eighteen was well known to be most critical, when the maximum amount of rest was required for growing bodies. Why were these young people kept at work to the utmost limit compatible with the strength of an adult? The real reason was that the Government had always been so jealous of any interference that could possibly lead to a diminution of the labour of the adult that it had not scrupled to sacrifice the child who worked by his

4 *Ibid.* 400-401.
5 *Hansard* (1846) LXXXV, 1222.

side. He was convinced that a reduction of hours would diminish neither production nor profits, and he based his opinion on a lengthy and practical experience of the textile industry. He had been engaged in the cotton manufacture all his life, and was now employing between two and three thousand hands. " If the Bill be so destructive as its opponents have represented it," he declared, " it is a Bill to abolish the business of myself and my family. Let me remind the House, that no Factory Bill was ever yet passed without the House being stunned with predictions of the ruin that would ensue to manufacturers; and all these predictions have been falsified by experiment. . . . I urge on the House the necessity that there is for giving the young children, whose labour I seek to shorten, time for personal relaxation and religious instruction, without the knowledge of which it is vain to hope that they will be a creditable or even a safe community."

Ainsworth, seconding the motion, urged the Government to meet the operatives half-way, and to seize the opportunity afforded by the present movement, when the workers were quite willing to abandon a Ten-hours Bill if, as he was commissioned to say, Her Majesty's Government would come forward and propose an Eleven-hours Bill.[6]

The ensuing debate illustrated clearly the direction in which opinion was slowly but surely moving. Never, declared Sir George Strickland, had the moment been more auspicious; never had there been a better chance of success, for a great change had taken place in the minds of the master manufacturers. Many of them had adopted the eleven-hours day with the most gratifying results, while the operatives gladly submitted to any slight loss in wages as the price of the increased leisure they were able to enjoy.[7] Colqhoun, proposing that an eleven-hours day be introduced experimentally for a period of two years, admitted that in the past he had opposed Lord Ashley. Now, however, the experience, not of three only, but of very many succeeding years, had served to convince him that it was an error to entertain any apprehension of evil consequences either to the employees or to the manufacturers. The honest and humane manufacturer knew that he would benefit by the rational restriction of labour, and consequently did not resist it.[8]

Fielden found another and more influential ally in Sir George Grey, who asserted that the prognostications of those who had opposed reform in the past had turned out to be unjustified. He could understand the argument that the market for labour should

6 *Ibid*. 1229-1234.
7 *Ibid*. 1239.
8 *Hansard* (1846) LXXXVI, 467.

be free, he said, but that was really not the question under discussion. The question before the House was whether after they
had upon former occasions adopted a certain course of legislation
as to factory labour, they had reached the limits to which it was
safe to advance. It was, in fact, a question of degree, and there
was no evidence to show that they had advanced to the precise
point beyond which they could not with safety venture.[9]

But the Government was to be won neither by argument nor
by the offer of compromise, and the Home Secretary, Sir James
Graham, bluntly declared that the bill would be resisted. " If we
adopt the measure now proposed," he warned the House, " and if
it be erroneous, it is no trifling error we are about to commit. It
touches our staple manufactures; it hampers our foreign trade; it
affects the industry of half a million of our population; it bears
upon wages amounting to nearly a quarter of a million paid week
by week."[10] This was decisive, and when, on 22nd May, 1846,
the House divided, the bill was lost by the narrow margin of 203
votes to 193.[11]

Peel's long reign was nearly over. On 15th May, 1846, he
had carried the third reading of the bill repealing the Corn Laws;
on 25th June the measure passed the Lords; and on the same
night, the Government, assailed by a heterogeneous body of
protectionists, Whigs and Radicals, was defeated by a majority of
73 on the Irish Coercion Bill. Two days later Sir Robert Peel
tendered his resignation, and the Whigs, under Lord John Russell,
took office, Sir George Grey being appointed Home Secretary.

The auspices were favourable, and on 26th January, 1847,
Fielden once more moved for leave to introduce the Ten-hours
Bill, declaring that the factory hands were more determined than
ever to secure its passage.[12] Despite the opposition of Peel, the
House agreed to the first reading, and when the second reading
was taken on 10th February,[13] Grey lent his support to the
measure, reiterating the view that he had expressed the previous
year, that the question was not one of principle but of degree.
" I ask any hon. Gentleman," he cried, " however strenuous an
opponent he may have been to legislative interference in this
matter, whether he can affirm that the restrictions imposed on
factory labour have produced prejudicial results, and whether he
is prepared, on the ground of experience, to resist further interference?" The Legislature, he continued, had failed in its duty

---

9 *Ibid.* 521.
10 *Hansard* (1846) LXXXV, 1243.
11 *Hansard* (1846) LXXXVI, 1080.
12 *Hansard* (1847) LXXXIX, 487.
13 *Ibid.* 1073.

towards young persons. " When I see children of 13 years of age, who, from being allowed to work only six hours a day in a factory —the rest of their time being devoted to purposes of education and recreation—suddenly transferred, without any restrictions to the class of adults, and employed during the same period of time for which adults of all ages are employed, I must say it appears to me that our legislation is defective."[14]

The debate was resumed on 17th February, 1847,[15] and two days later the second reading was agreed to without a division.[16] On 3rd March the House resolved, by 190 votes to 100 to go into Committee,[17] and a fortnight later Lord John Russell, intervening in the debate for the first time, urged that there should be no further delay. The principle involved in the Bill, he said, had already been accepted, and Parliament should face the implications courageously. It appeared to him that an endeavour to limit the labour of young persons to hours to which their strength was equal, was a perfectly legitimate object for the House to pursue. The labour of adults would also be restricted, it was true, but that was the inevitable result of the main purpose.[18]

The end was fast approaching. The Committee accepted the bill by 144 votes to 66;[19] a final effort by Hume and Philips to delay the measure on the report stage (21st April) was defeated by 104 votes to 46;[20] and on 3rd May the Ten-hours Bill was finally passed by 151 votes to 88.[21] There was no delay in the Lords, and on 8th June, 1847, the Act to limit the Hours of Labour of young Persons and Females in Factories[22] received the royal assent.

Having recited the provisions of the Acts of 1833 and 1844, section 1 continued: " And whereas it is expedient to alter the said Acts for the purpose of further restricting the Hours of Labour of young Persons and Females in Factories, be it enacted that from the First Day of July one thousand eight hundred and forty-seven no Person under the Age of Eighteen Years shall be employed in any such Mill or Factory, in such Description of Work as in the said first-mentioned Act is specified, for more than Eleven Hours in any One Day, nor for more than Sixty-three Hours in any one Week, except as in the said Act is provided; and that from the First Day of July one thousand eight hundred and forty-seven the said Two Acts before mentioned shall in all respects be

14 *Ibid.* 1083-1094.
15 *Hansard* (1847) XC, 127.
16 *Ibid.* 297.
17 *Ibid.* 819.
18 *Hansard* (1847) XCI, 118.
19 *Ibid.* 146.
20 *Ibid.* 1122.
21 *Hansard* (1847) XCII, 306.
22 10 & 11 Vict., c. 29.

construed as if the Provision in the said first-mentioned Act contained, as to Persons under the Age of Eighteen Years working in Mills and Factories, had been confined to Eleven Hours instead of Twelve Hours in any One Day, and to Sixty-three Hours in any One Week instead of Sixty-nine Hours."

Section 2 provided " From the first Day of May one thousand eight hundred and forty-eight no Person under the Age of Eighteen Years shall be employed in any such Mill or Factory, in such Description of Work as in the said first-mentioned Act is specified, for more than Ten Hours in any One Day, nor more than Fifty-eight Hours in any One Week, except as in the said Act is provided; and that from the First Day of May one thousand eight hundred and forty-eight the said two Acts shall in all respects be construed as if the Provision in the said first-mentioned Act contained, as to Persons under the Age of Eighteen Years working in Mills and Factories, had been confined to Ten Hours instead of Twelve Hours in any One Day, and to Fifty-eight Hours in any One Week instead of Sixty-nine Hours." By section 3 it was provided that restrictions imposed on persons under the age of eighteen were to extend to females above that age; while the 4th section provided that the Act was to be construed in conjunction with the Acts of 1833 and 1844.

Ashley's joy knew no bounds. " News that the Factory Bill has just passed the third reading," he recorded in his diary. " I am humbled that my heart is not bursting with thankfulness to Almighty God—that I can find breath and sense to express my joy. What reward shall we give unto the Lord for all the benefits He hath conferred upon us? God, in His mercy, prosper the work, and grant that these operatives may receive the cup of Salvation, and call upon the name of the Lord! Praised be the Lord, praised be the Lord, in Christ Jesus!"[23] To the Short-time Committees he wrote—

" My Good Friends,—Although there is no longer any necessity to name you collectively and as united together for the purpose of obtaining a reduction of the hours of working in factories, I will address a few words to you . . . on questions of the highest and dearest interest.

First, we must give most humble and hearty thanks to Almighty God for the unexpected and wonderful success that has attended our efforts. We have won the great object of all our labours—the Ten Hours Bill has become the law of the land; and we may hope, nay, more, we believe that we shall find in its happy results, a full compensation for all our toils. . . .

23 E. Hodder, The Life and Work of the seventh Earl of Shaftesbury (1893) p. 369.

I need not, I know, exhort you to an oblivion of past conflicts, and to hearty endeavour for future harmony. I trust that there will be no language of triumph, as though we had defeated an enemy. Let us be very thankful that the struggle is over, and that we can once more combine, not only the interests, but also the feelings, of employer and employed, in a mutual understanding for the comfort and benefit of each other, and for the welfare of the whole community. . . .

Although the final completion of this great measure has been achieved by another, I could not, after so many years of labour, take leave of it altogether without a few words to you of advice and congratulation. To no one could the lot have fallen so happily as to our friend Mr. Fielden. He joined me in 1833 in the introduction of the first Bill, and has been ever since, as you well know, your able, energetic, and unshrinking advocate.

In bidding you farewell, I do not retire from your service. I shall, at all times, hold myself in readiness to aid you in any measures that may conduce to the moral and physical welfare of yourselves and your children."[24]

The manufacturing districts gave themselves up to a frenzy of rejoicing; festivities were held on an unheard-of scale; Ashley and Fielden were fêted wherever they went. Broadsheets, elaborately and expensively printed in black and gold, setting out the terms of the new Act and commemorating the leaders of the struggle, were widely distributed. Medals were struck in honour of the great occasion, and the Queen herself accepted a gold medal presented to her by Lord Ashley on behalf of her grateful subjects in the mills and factories.

The Times, in its leading article of 4th May, cited the Act as a notable example of enlightened legislation. " A great event came off in the House of Commons last night in a very quiet way. The Ten Hours Bill was read a third time and passed without much ado. It is only three years since a powerful Ministry staked its existence against a similar measure. Had the Commons persevered in the spring of 1844—had a few dozen country gentlemen stood a few weeks longer to their opinions and votes on this subject, instead of calling that black after Easter which they had declared to be white just before, another body of statesmen would probably have had the glorious but fatal distinction of emancipating the food and alienating the affections of the aristocracy. History presents no example of retributive justice so striking or so speedy as that which avenged the wrong and insult then done to a powerful and almost speechless body of sufferers. . . .

---

[24] *Ibid.* pp. 369-370.

The spectacle of several hundred thousand women and young persons working twelve hours a day presents too striking an anomaly to the spirit of modern legislation to be long endured. It must be considered that twelve hours' actual work involves a day's work of fourteen hours long, including intervals for meals. Reckon that period from 5 to 7, and for eight months of the year the operative goes to work before the sun rises, and works till after sunset, never having half an hour's liberty while the sun is above the horizon. Reckon it from 6 to 8, and for half the year the operative sets to work before sunrise, and except for barely two months works on till after sunset. . . . Is it in keeping with such an era that the most industrious, most useful, and at the same time most dependent and helpless portion of the people, who are really the chief pillar of the state, should be cruelly and slavishly overworked and made the martyrs for the whole?"

The trade depression, the first signs of which had been noticed in the autumn of 1845, reached its climax in 1847. The Inspectors reported that conditions were worse than any they had known,[25] that many factories were working only half the permitted hours, and that consequently the introduction of the shorter day had caused little difficulty.[26] Saunders found many occupiers in his district apprehensive of the effects of the Ten-hours bill when trade revived,[27] but for the moment the reduction of hours, he reported, "has been carried out, on the whole, very satisfactorily."[28] Horner thought it was too early to estimate the results of the Act, "but," he added, "I have already seen indications of a disposition in some quarters to resort to plans for evading the law—such as employing young persons to clean the machinery at extra times, instead of within the eleven hours, and cutting off portions of the periods fixed by law for meal-times."[29]

Saunders, too, had observed cases of attempted evasion. "There are some few instances," he said, "in which total ruin is foretold, as the inevitable result of the reduction to 11 hours, and various expedients have been consequently suggested, and some of them practised, in order to enable parties to keep their machinery at work for 12, or even 13 hours a day. . . . The modes generally proposed to me, for effecting this object, have involved the employment of young persons and women, by relays—a system practised with much injury to young persons, before the passing of the

25 Saunders' Report, 30th April, 1847. *Parl. Papers* (1847) XV, p. 504.
26 Stuart's Report, 31st October, 1847. *Parl. Papers* (1847-8) XXVI, p. 145.
27 Report, 30th April, 1847. *Parl. Papers* (1847) XV, p. 504.
28 Report, 31st October, 1847. *Parl. Papers* (1847-8) XXVI, p. 132.
29 Report, 31st October, 1847. *Ibid.* p. 111.

Amended Factory Act in 1844."[30]   The same plan had been tried
in Horner's district, " some factories having begun to work their
machinery more than eleven hours, by relays of persons whose
labour is restricted to that time."[31]   Horner accordingly inserted
in a number of provincial newspapers a warning notice in the
following terms—

" Factory Act.—Hours of Work.—Having received communications from several occupiers of factories proposing modifications
of their previous modes of employing children, young persons, and
adult women, which they supposed would be legal, but which I
found to be otherwise: in order to prevent similar mistakes being
made . . . I think it advisable to call attention to the following
provisions of the Act 7 Vict. c.15." [An explanation of sections
26, 32 and 36 of the Act of 1844 was then given].   " It will thus
be seen, that it is the intention of the above-named Act, that all
young persons and adult women employed in a factory shall work
at the same time.   Thus, for example, in the case of a factory
allowing not more than an hour and a half for meals, if any kind
of work begins in the factory at half-past five in the morning, in
doing which any one child, young person, or adult woman is
employed, no child, young person, or adult woman can be legally
employed in that factory after six o'clock in the evening of that
day . . . and between the hours of $7\frac{1}{2}$ a.m. and 6 p.m. an hour
and a half must have been allowed for meals, of which time one
hour at the least must have been given before three o'clock."[32]

Horner himself had been the chief advocate of the relay system
in the early years of his inspectorship, when it had seemed that
there was no other way of keeping the machinery at work throughout the day, since children were limited to forty-eight hours' labour
a week.   The scheme he had favoured had involved the employment of three children for eight hours to do the work formerly
done by two children in twelve hours, and to this there could have
been no objection had each set been dismissed from the factory
when the period of labour was completed.   The manufacturers,
however, found that it suited their purpose better to set up a
complicated arrangement whereby the children worked in sets
throughout the day for relatively short periods, the sum total of
which, however, did not exceed their permitted hours.   " Various
ingenious expedients are resorted to," said Howell in his report
for May, 1838, " by the master, who prolongs the operation of his
mill beyond 12 hours daily, in order to command the services of a
sufficient portion of his younger workpeople during the whole of
his working day. . . . One class of the persons under 18 years of

---

30 Report, 31st October, 1847. *Ibid.* p. 132.
31 Report, 31st October, 1847. *Ibid.* p. 111.
32 *Ibid.* p. 119.

age commence at half-past five o'clock in the morning, and finally leave off working for the day at a quarter-past eight o'clock in the evening; but as in the interval they have one hour for breakfast, *viz.,* from eight to nine in the morning, an hour and a quarter for dinner, from half-past twelve to three-quarters past one, and half an hour for tea, from four to half-past four in the afternoon, they do not, in fact, work more than the lawful number of 12 hours in the course of the factory working-day, but the commencement and termination of their working day includes a space of time amounting to 14¾ hours. Where the system of working which I have described is resorted to it is extremely difficult to ascertain that the children and young persons are relieved from work at the different broken periods of the day assigned for the purpose, because the great irregularity of the clocks renders it in many cases impossible to ascertain at what particular time of the day offences are to be detected, in the mills in which the periods for rest and refreshment are broken into so many fractions."[33] " A part of the workers under 18 years of age is sent out of the mill at different times of the day," explained Horner, " and although it is notorious that the mill has worked 13 hours, it is rarely possible to fix upon the individuals who have worked more than 12; and without we do this they are beyond the reach of the Act. To cut off this subterfuge, I recommend that it be made illegal to employ, in any description of work in the mill, any person under 21 years of age after the expiration of 13½ hours from the first movement in the morning of any part of the manufacturing machinery on five days, or after the expiration of 10½ hours on Saturday, of which 1½ hour shall, on each day, have been allowed for meals."[34]

The dangers inherent in the false relay system were two-fold: the children, although not called upon to work in excess of their permitted time, were detained on the factory premises for twelve, and sometimes for thirteen or fourteen hours a day, so that they might be ready to resume when their turn came; and it was thus impossible for the Inspectors to check over-working, for although they might be convinced that certain persons had worked excessive hours, they were told that they had come late, or that they had been sent out during the day. " Indeed," said Horner, "it is obvious that, with a power to work by relays of hands, and of giving meal-times at various periods of the day, and of changing the hours of work and meals of every hand employed, arbitrarily from day to day, no restriction of the hours of work could be enforced in the factories of artful men."[35]

33 Quoted, *Parl. Papers* (1849) XXII, p. 220.
34 Report, 31st March, 1842. *Parl. Papers* (1842) XXII, p. 444.
35 Report, 30th April, 1848. *Parl. Papers* (1847-8) XXVI, p. 159.

The Act of 1844 was designed to defeat these abuses, though not in the way Horner had suggested, by forbidding children and young persons from working after the expiration of 13½ hours from the time the machinery commenced in the morning. Instead it was provided, by section 26, that the hours of the protected classes should be reckoned from the time when any child or young person first began to work in the morning; by section 36 that all the young persons in a factory should have their meal-time at the same period of the day; by section 28 that a notice should be displayed showing the times of beginning and ending daily work; and by section 52 that the time of beginning work stated in such notice should be taken to be the time when all persons, except children employed in the afternoon, began work.

The full implications of these provisions were apparently not realized until the introduction of the ten-hours day. " The factory occupiers," said Stuart, " maintain, that until now they were never aware that any other restrictions as to the employment of young persons and females were imposed on them, and least of all, that restrictions prevent them from employing *at such hours as they choose* . . . young persons and females, *for shorter periods than 10 hours a day,* and which are of such description as to limit the moving power of the machines to 10 hours. This Act [1844] was passed in a period of great manufacturing prosperity . . . and as soon as it was made known in the discussions, before it was passed, that the hours of work, and of course, the duration of the moving power, were to remain unchanged, the factory occupiers ceased, as they conceived, to have much interest in the enactments merely of ordinary regulation, and have only since the Act limiting the hours of work has been enforced, been referred by those appointed to see the law observed, to provisions contained in the Act of 1844, which must, as they state, subject them, according to the construction put on those provisions, to most inconvenient and harassing restrictions as to the employment of young persons and females, with which they were previously unacquainted."[36]

When trade began to revive in 1848 the temptation to extend the working hours to the utmost possible limits became overwhelming, and the system of false relays was re-introduced, gradually at first, but with increasing momentum as the difficulties in the way of enforcing the law became more and more apparent. The Inspectors were convinced that this mode of working was illegal, for early in 1845, having asked the views of the Home Secretary, they had been informed that under the Act of 1844 a factory could not be permitted to work more than twelve hours a

---

[36] Report, 30th April, 1848. *Ibid.* p. 194.

day, reckoned from the time when any child or young person first began work.[37]   Accordingly, they instituted prosecutions whenever they found the system in operation, but, to their dismay, many benches of magistrates refused to convict. Here was a problem of the utmost gravity and complexity. " If the checks against working by relays of young persons and women, provided by the Act of 1844, were removed," declared Horner, " no practical system of inspection could prevent extensive fraudulent overworking; thereby seriously injuring the mill-owners who obey the law, and rendering the object of the law to a great extent nugatory."[38]

The operatives, naturally, were watching developments with keen interest and anxiety. " If this system must be carried out," it was said, " the Ten Hours Bill will be a complete humbug."[39]   All the machinery of agitation, so joyfully abrogated when the ten-hours day had been won, was once again revived : the stalwarts of the cause organized the Fielden Society, with branches at Todmorden, Clitheroe, Rochdale, Stalybridge and other great centres of the textile industry, to promote resistance on the widest possible scale; Richard Oastler once more took the field, and from his head-quarters at Ashton-under-Lyne, poured out anew, in his weekly journal The Champion, the terrible floods of invective that recalcitrant manufacturers had years ago learnt to fear. " In this very Lancashire," he cried, "magistrates, not a few, have ruled their own will to be higher than the law, saying in effect that they would work their mills as they thought fit, in spite of queen, lords, commons, bishops or anybody else. For nearly twelve months Lancashire cotton-masters have made pipe-lights of the statutes of parliament and the government of the mightiest empire of the world has for the same space of time allowed them to have everything pretty much their own way."[40]

The inactivity of the Government was due not to apathy or indifference, still less to any hostility to the Ten-hours Act. The simple fact was that neither the Home Office, nor, for that matter, the Factory Inspectors, had realized that in seeking to impose on certain classes of operatives a restricted working period of ten hours in a day that extended over fifteen hours, from 5.30 a.m.

---

[37] Joint Report, 9th June, 1848. Ibid. p. 202.

[38] Report, 31st October, 1848. Parl. Papers (1849) XXII, p. 138.

[39] Howell's Report, 30th April, 1848. Parl. Papers (1847-8) XXVI, p. 171.

[40] The Champion, 10th November, 1849. Cf. Minutes, 6th December, 1848, Vol. II, p. 398.—" Mr. Saunders reported that there has been great excitement existing in his District . . . that since he has been in town some of the Sub-Inspectors have described the excitement as much increased."

to 8.30 p.m., the legislature had attempted a task far beyond the measure of its ingenuity. Parliament had endeavoured to fuse two conceptions that were fundamentally opposed, and the result was an unavailing and unworkable compromise. Horner's suggestion that no young person should work after the expiration of a prescribed number of hours would, in practice, have reduced the working day of adult males to ten hours, and in 1847 such a policy would have been impossible of achievement. The alternative was to devise a set of regulations that would safeguard women and young persons, leaving the men free from control, but the formula adopted, though it appeared adequate to its purpose at first sight, was so complex, and capable of such different interpretations, that it had finally to be abandoned.

The Inspectors, cognizant as they were of the evils attendant upon the system of so-called relays, had assumed, albeit after some hesitation, that the combined effect of sections 26, 28, 36 and 52, was to render illegal the employment of young persons and women after the expiration of $11\frac{1}{2}$ hours from the time work started in the morning.[41] In this assumption they were supported by the Law Officers of the Crown, who on 9th June, 1848, had stated their opinion to be "that the time of working for young persons, women and children (except children beginning to work in the afternoon) begins to run from the time specified in the Notice fixed up in the Factory as the time for beginning daily work."[42] The local magistrates, however, took a different view, and a week or two later, to Horner's mortification, the justices at Atherton dismissed an information that had been laid by his instructions against Messrs. Jones, who were working by relays. Worse was to follow, for when on 7th July, 1848, a second information came up for hearing by the neighbouring Tyldersley justices, the Atherton magistrates turned up in force and swamped the Bench. Their purpose in so doing was all too obvious, and the court, in these circumstances, declined to proceed with the case.[43]

This apparent vindication of the false relay system had repercussions not in Lancashire alone, but throughout the country, where the proceedings in Horner's district were being watched with the closest attention. "The several benches of magistrates to whom such cases have been referred," said Saunders, "have all agreed as to the proper interpretation of the law, with the exception of the bench ordinarily meeting at Atherton, in Mr. Horner's district. The magistrates at Colchester, Loughborough, Leeds,

---

[41] An interval of $1\frac{1}{2}$ hours had to be allowed for meals.
[42] *Minutes*, Vol. II, p. 361. See Joint Report, 9th June, 1848. *Parl. Papers* (1847-8) XXVI, p. 202.
[43] Horner's Report, 31st October, 1848. *Parl. Papers* (1849) XXII, p. 138.

Manchester and Stockport, have all had the case of relays distinctly
and clearly canvassed and discussed before them, and the bench
in each case decided that the practice was illegal. The Law
Officers of the Crown have also given the same opinion; and
among the Inspectors no difference of opinion has ever existed as
to its illegality."[44]

The result of the cases against Jones & Co., however, was
seriously perturbing Horner. He was convinced that the relay
system was indefensible, but the arrangements contrived by another
firm, that of John Bright & Co., of Rochdale, were such as made
him apprehensive that he would not be able to secure a conviction
against them for working by relays. On 20th July he wrote a long
letter[45] to his colleagues asking their advice. John Bright & Co.,
he said, employed adult males, as they were fully entitled to do,
from 6 a.m. to 7.30 p.m., with an interval of an hour and a half
for meals. The majority of the young persons and women were
engaged for ten hours a day, from 6 a.m. to 8 a.m., from 8.30
a.m. to 12.30 p.m., and from 1.30 p.m. to 5.30 p.m., and a notice
as required by section 28 was duly posted. There were, however,
about 50 young persons who assisted the adult weavers, and in
order that these men might be deprived of their help for as short
a time as possible, the hours of this particular set were from 6 a.m.
to 8 a.m., from 8.30 a.m. to 11.30 a.m., and from 1.30 p.m. to
6.30 p.m. A second notice containing the names of these young
persons set out their hours of work.

Horner admitted that the hours of work of both groups of
protected persons were reckoned, in accordance with section 26,
from the time when work first began, namely 6 a.m.; and that in
accordance with section 36, all had their meal interval at the
same time of the day; yet one set finished an hour later than the
other. Two questions of great complexity thus arose. Was it
legal to display two notices showing different times of work;[46] and
could the different lengths of the midday breaks be justified?
Horner had objected to the duplication of the notices on the
ground that Schedule C of the Act of 1844 specified only one
notice setting out the hours of *all* young persons, no provision
having been made for a supplementary notice specifying different
times for named individuals. So far as the meal interval was

---

[44] Report, 31st October, 1848. *Ibid.* p. 246.
[45] *Minutes*, Vol. II, pp. 376-379.
[46] Howell reported a case where twelve sets of relays were employed.
Instead of the hours being presented in tabular form, occupying a few
inches, and legible to all entering the factory, he said, " the hours of work
and lists of names of the different shifts cover a board from 15 to 20 feet
long, and some 15 inches wide, the upper part being fully 20 feet from the
ground "—an arrangement useless for the purpose contemplated by the
Act.—Report, 30th April, 1850. *Parl. Papers* (1850) XXIII, p. 286.

concerned, he held that the intention of the Act was that all young persons should have their meals at the same time, and that they should also have the same number of minutes, neither more nor less, though he agreed that in the last resort everything would depend on the interpretation of the word " period."

The Inspectors, enclosing a copy of Horner's letter for the information of the Home Office, asked that they might be given guidance on these " points of very great legal nicety." The reply, dated 26th July, 1848, was singularly unhelpful, for the Home Office, declining to make any general pronouncement, went no further than to offer to submit any particular points to the Law Officers if the difficulties were specifically stated.[47] In the meantime Horner had decided to lay an information against Messrs. James Kennedy & Co., of Manchester, who were following Bright's plan, though they had four sets working between 5.30 a.m. and 8.30 p.m. This case aroused the greatest interest, and when it was heard on 2nd August by the Manchester Stipendiary, sitting with ten other magistrates, the court was crowded with representatives of the operatives, and with mill-owners, prominent among whom was Jones, who had so recently been summoned before the Tyldersley Bench. Counsel appeared for both sides, and after a lengthy hearing the Court, by a narrow majority, decided to convict. Horner was satisfied. - " This decision," he said, " will probably carry great weight throughout my District."[48]

Messrs. Jones, however, announced that despite Kennedy's conviction, they did not intend to abandon relays, and Horner, therefore, enquired of the Home Office what action he should take in their case. Sir George Grey's reply came as a severe shock. He had no instructions to give, he said, for he did not wish to interfere with the discretion vested in the Inspectors. He would only observe that he considered it inexpedient to lay informations against mill-owners for a breach of the letter of the law when it appeared that young persons had not actually worked more than ten hours.[49]

Nothing could have illustrated more forcibly the Government's failure to grasp the true issue, and Horner hastened to point out what such a policy would imply. It was his firm conviction, he said, that the employment of young persons by relays would render nugatory the Ten-hours Act. Permission to work by relays, and a law restricting labour were two things which could not co-exist. Was he to enforce the law, or was he to cease to interfere with millowners who were working by relays?[50]

---

47 *Minutes*, Vol. II, p. 380.
48 *Minutes*, Vol. II, p. 382.
49 *Ibid.* p. 383.
50 *Minutes*, Vol. II, pp. 384-387.

Howell also entered his protest, explaining at length what the relay system really involved. " I would beg you with the utmost deference," he wrote, " to submit to Sir G. G. that I have never known in my District an instance of any Young Person working by relays in the proper sense of the word, *i.e.*, by dividing the hands into separate and equal classes to work like the crew of a merchantman in distinct watches, each watch keeping the machinery going for a given period. This is my, and I believe the general, understanding of the word ' relay,' an expression borrowed from the phraseology of the road, where it means a complete change of the team at the end of a stage; and hence it has been not inappropriately applied to the young class of children employed in Factories whose hours of work are limited to the morning or the afternoon (as the case may be) so that they must work in two distinct and complete sets, one relay relieving the other at the dinner hour.

But reverting to the phraseology of the word, by the term relay it is not meant that you should put each horse of your team in a different place at the end of every mile, diversifying the station by the temporary substitution of a spare horse (which accompanies you through the journey for this purpose) to take the place first of one and then of another of the original team, each of which again resumes its own place or takes that of some other after a brief interval: this however is not an inapt representation of what is meant by those Millowners who mystify their real meaning by misapplying the term relays to their plans for employing Young Persons; for the system which they seek to introduce in the guise of relays is some one of the many plans for shuffling the hands about in endless variety, and shifting the hours of work and rest for different individuals throughout the day by such incessant changes that you may never have one complete set working together in the same rooms at the same time."[51]

There was no middle way, declared Howell. The law must be fully enforced, or it must be abandoned. If the Home Secretary instructed him to allow working by relays he would, of course, obey, but he warned Grey that tension in the manufacturing districts was growing, and that the operatives were in an ugly mood. The issue could not have been stated more bluntly. If the Government was not prepared to stand behind the Inspectors in their endeavours to put down relays, the Government must accept responsibility for the consequences. This Grey was not prepared to do, and on 12th August, 1848, he assured Horner that he had no intention of interfering with the discretion of the

[51] *Minutes*, Vol. II, pp. 395-396.

Inspectors, nor would he think it consistent with his duty to instruct them to refrain from initiating prosecutions in cases where they conceived that the law was being broken.[52]

A new difficulty was introduced during the closing months of 1848, when Stuart announced that he proposed to take no action against those owners in his district who employed the relay system. The law, he held, was not sufficiently precise to justify his trying to prevent manufacturers working their hands for the longest possible time, and on 14th August, 1848, he announced that no prosecutions would be initiated if young persons and women worked by relays, provided their hours of actual labour did not exceed ten.[53]

Stuart's attitude was a source of serious embarrassment to his colleagues, and when, on 14th December, Horner told them that the Manchester Bench had on the previous day dismissed another charge against Messrs. Kennedy for operating relays,[54] it seemed that their position was no longer tenable. It was therefore agreed that representations should be made to the Home Secretary urging upon him " the expediency of Government taking some decided step for the removal of these difficulties."[55] Accordingly in their joint report dated 11th January, 1849, they explained the difficulties that had arisen in consequence of the policy adopted by Stuart, adding, " In this situation it does not appear to us that we have any other alternative but to submit these circumstances to you, that you may adopt such course, with a view to render our proceedings uniform in relation to the question of employing young persons and females by relays, as you may, on consideration, think right."[56]

Grey, however, had already taken his decision. Two days before the joint report was published Horner had met Cornewall Lewis, Under-Secretary of the Home Office, and had learnt from him that Grey had come to the conclusion that the only way of settling the question was to enact fresh legislation, and that an amending bill was to be introduced early next session.[57]

The task of drafting clauses that would prevent employment by false relays, while being acceptable at the same time to the mill-occupiers, was more formidable than had been anticipated. Grey's plan was to legalize the employment of women and young persons in two separate sets, but the Inspectors condemned this as impracticable. " Mr. Horner, Mr. Howell and Mr. Saunders," they

---

[52] *Minutes,* Vol. II, p. 387.
[53] Report, 31st October, 1848. *Parl. Papers* (1849) XXII, pp. 260-264.
[54] *Minutes,* Vol. II, p. 401.
[55] *Minutes,* 21st December, 1848, Vol. II, p. 405.
[56] *Parl. Papers* (1849) XXII, p. 281.
[57] *Minutes,* 9th January, 1849, Vol. II, p. 412.

wrote, " have considered the draft of a Bill sent to Mr. Horner & submitted by him to his colleagues, professing to amend the existing law, relative to working by relays of young persons and women, are of opinion that the plan proposed of allowing Mill-owners to employ such persons in two separate sets will not be acceptable to the Millowners in their respective Districts who have sought to work by relays, and still less to the workpeople; and that they cannot imagine the possibility of legalizing any plan of relays of such persons which will not be generally evaded."[58] Discussion was protracted, but no satisfactory conclusion was reached, despite the fact that things were going from bad to worse in the manufacturing districts. In January, 1849, the magistrates dismissed an information against John Leach of Stalybridge, who had four women working in relays from 6 a.m. to 7.30 p.m. " This decision was, of course," said Horner, " equivalent to their granting a licence to all the mills in that district to work by similar shifts . . . and the licence has been most extensively used." A similar prosecution against Henry and Edmund Ashworth of Bolton was likewise dismissed, and Horner at last gave up the struggle. " I consider it useless to prosecute more for this evasion of the law," he reported. " That part of the Act of 1844, which was framed for the purpose of securing uniformity in the hours of work is no longer in force in my district."[59] Howell, too, announced that he would institute no further prosecutions, " in the hope that some higher authority might interpose ";[60] and in their joint report of 12th June, 1849, the Inspectors urged the Government to delay no longer. " We venture to express our anxious hope that Her Majesty's Government may be soon enabled to provide a remedy for the inconvenience which has arisen from this conflict of authority; more especially considering the number of factories, both in Lancashire and in Scotland, in which the system of working by shifts or relays is adopted, has considerably increased since the date of our last Report, and appears to be further increasing."[61]

The Home Office and the Inspectors were still seeking a formula which would enable the mills to be run for the maximum number of hours, while at the same time imposing effective restrictions on the labour of women and young persons. Saunders had already declared that there was only one solution. " Nothing," he asserted, " but one uniform set of hours for all persons employed in the same mill, in each of the protected classes, can effectually

---

[58] Minutes, 29th January, 1849, Vol. II, p. 422.
[59] Report, 30th April, 1849. Parl. Papers (1849) XXII, pp. 286-287.
[60] Ibid. p. 304.
[61] Ibid. p. 346.

guard such operatives from overwork."[62]   Uniform hours for protected persons, however, meant uniform hours for the whole body of operatives, and although Grey was prepared to introduce fresh legislation, he was not, as yet, prepared to take this decisive step. There seemed to be only one escape from the dilemma, and that was to secure the ruling of a superior court that relays were illegal under the existing enactments.

Horner, Howell and Saunders had no doubt about the efficacy of the relevant sections of the Act of 1844, and they would gladly have submitted a case for the decision of the High Court had they been free to do so.   Their hands were tied, however, for the 69th section of the statute, designed to prevent frivolous appeals by mill-owners, had the unfortunate effect of depriving the Inspectors, too, of the right of appeal, for it provided that there should be no appeal from the decision of the magistrates except in the case of offences punishable at discretion by fine or imprisonment, or in respect of which a penalty in excess of £3 might be levied.   The Law Officers had advised the Home Secretary that the only way to bring the question before a superior court would be for the parties to arrange for a magistrate to refuse to convict, and on 9th June, 1848, Sir George Grey advised the Inspectors to take this course.[63]

But it was not easy for the Inspectors to make such an arrangement, as Horner explained in a letter he wrote to Cornewall Lewis on 15th November.   " I have never lost sight of the following paragraph in your letter to the Inspectors of the 9th June last— ' as it appears that conflicting decisions upon the 26th Section have been made by different benches of Magistrates, Sir G. Grey thinks it would be desirable that the question should, if possible, be raised in such a manner as to obtain the opinion of a Superior Court upon it.'   Very soon after the receipt of that letter I called on the Solr. of the Treasury for the purpose of learning from him in what way I could proceed in order to bring a case before the Court of Q.B.   I saw Mr. Reynolds, who referring to the 69th Section of the 7 Vict. C.15 which limits the power of appeal to certain cases, informed me that he did not see how the case in question could be brought before that Court, except in the event of Magistrates refusing to hear a case, that an application might be made for a Mandamus that the case should be heard. . . .

My understanding of the 69th Sec. is this : that a conviction for employing a Young Person more than 10 hours a day cannot be appealed from, because the maximum penalty for that offence is £3—and that altho' I lay an Information for so illegally employ-

[62] Report, 31st October, 1848.   *Ibid.* p. 237.
[63] *Minutes,* Vol. II, p. 362.

ing *five* persons, and the gross minimum penalty awarded upon a
conviction be £5 this would be held *in law* to be five distinct
convictions, in no one of which the penalty could be more than
£3 & therefore that there could be no appeal.

I request the favour of you to obtain for me such a legal
opinion as I shall be justified in acting upon, whether I am right
in interpreting the 69th Sec. in the manner stated above, or if I
were to lay an Information against a M.O. for so illegally employing 5 young persons, all the 5 being named in one information (a
frequent but not universal practice as some Magistrates require a
separate Information for each individual) and if upon conviction
the gross penalty awarded were £5, whether the M.O. would have
a right to appeal to the Court of Q.B."[64]

The Law Officers agreed that Horner's interpretation of the
69th section was correct—" that although a larger penalty than
£3 may be awarded in one connection for cumulative offences, yet
that as each offence could only be the subject of a penalty not
exceeding £3, the conviction would be held to be for distinct
offences and the right of appeal taken away."[65]

The need for action was becoming increasingly urgent, for
tempers were rising in the manufacturing districts. " The excitement throughout my district, arising from the continuance of
relays and shifts in other districts," reported Saunders, "continues
unabated. Indeed, I am assured that recently the cotton-spinners
and doublers about Huddersfield have determined on more active
measures to raise a discussion on the subject."[66] The only way
to secure a decision that would be binding on the local magistrates
seemed to be to bring a collusive action, and this was the course
Horner ultimately decided to pursue. His Sub-Inspector, Ryder,
had found David Mills of Heywood working his factory by relays
more than ten hours a day, and posting allegedly illegal notices
of the hours of employment. An information was laid, and when
the case came to be heard on 31st October, 1849, the solicitor
for the prosecution[67] announced that " he was happy to have it in
his power to state that . . . it had been arranged that the defendant
should consent to a conviction in this case in a penalty of 5*l*. A
conviction to this amount, and in this form, would give to the
defendant the opportunity of appealing to a court of superior
jurisdiction, and thereby obtaining a decision upon this important
question."[68] Mills was duly fined £5, and on 2nd November he
gave notice of appeal.

---

[64] *Minutes,* Vol. II, pp. 390-392.
[65] *Ibid.* p. 392.
[66] Report, 31st October, 1849. *Parl. Papers* (1850) XXIII, p. 225.
[67] J. M. Cobbett (son of William Cobbett) later M.P. for Oldham.
[68] Horner's Report, 31st October, 1849. *Ibid.* p. 193.

At last the question was to be settled, and there could surely be no doubt how the day would go. The operatives were jubilant. " A few days more," cried Oastler, " and the freebooters of Lancashire will stand before the judges in the queen's court at Westminster. What a sight! We cannot picture to ourselves the possibility of an English court of King's bench sanctioning an interpretation of the law, which would consign thousands to a lingering death. The relay system is illegal; the practice must be put down, and those who have resorted to it ought to be most severely punished."[69] Ashley, however, was less hopeful. On 1st February, 1850, he wrote in his diary, " Judges will decide adversely on factory case submitted to them, and thus legalise relays. The Attorney-General said to me this afternoon, ' They will give judgment, not according to law, but on policy. Judge Parke,' he added, ' observed to me ' I have no doubt that the framers of the Act intended that the labour should be continuous, but as it is a law to restrain the exercise of capital and property, it must be construed stringently.'' Might not this judge have said and thought, with equal justice and more feeling, ' This is a law to restrain oppression and cruelty, and alleviate an actual slavery under a nominal freedom. I will, therefore, construe it liberally!' "[70]

The judgment in the case of Ryder v. Mills was delivered by Mr. Baron Parke in the Court of Exchequer on 8th February, 1850. The Act of 1844, he observed, was penal, and it must therefore be construed strictly. It was not enough to conjecture what the intention of the legislature might have been,—the onus on the prosecution was to prove that the acts complained of were explicitly forbidden by the statute. This they had failed to do.

Both parties were agreed that the working time of women and young persons was to be computed from the time when the first woman or young person began work in the morning; but whereas the defendant contended that the other limit, the time of finishing work, was not prescribed, the prosecution maintained that this could be gathered from other parts of the Act, despite the fact that it was not expressly provided for by section 26. The use of the word " reckoned " in this section, they said, was a clear indication that Parliament had intended the hours of work to be continuously reckoned from the time of commencement, i.e., that all should cease when the first woman or young person had completed ten hours' work. But that was not the ordinary meaning of the word : it meant only that the computation of time should then begin.

---

69 *The Champion,* 10th November, 1849, p. 10.
70 E. Hodder, *The Life and Work of the seventh Earl of Shaftesbury* (1893) p. 372.

The prosecution relied also on the wording of the schedules as showing the intentions of the framers of the Act. No provision was made in the first schedule for the insertion of individual names, and it was therefore clear, it was argued, that it had never been contemplated that the names of those comprising different sets working at different hours would be entered on this form. In other words it had been assumed that all would begin and end at the same time. This view was untenable, declared Parke, for it would mean that no factory owner could employ young persons for shorter periods than ten hours. The schedule as it stood was not adapted to such cases, and there could be no valid objection to amending it.

The Acts of 1844 and 1847 stipulated that women and young persons should not work for more than ten hours between 5.30 a.m. and 8.30 p.m.; that the time of all was to be computed from the time of the first beginning work; that an hour and a half should be allowed for meals, for all at the same time. No other restrictions were imposed, and therefore, concluded the judgment, young persons were " at liberty to agree together for working less than for the whole of that time within the limits before-mentioned, ending at half-past eight, or any previous time that they please, and with any intervals of leisure that may be thought convenient."[71]

This decision spread dismay throughout the manufacturing districts. " The disappointment created . . . by that judgment," said Horner, " is so well known, that it is quite unnecessary for me to enter into any details of the proceedings that have taken place in my own district;"[72] but on the whole he was persuaded that it was as well that the matter had been brought to a head, for the Government would now be compelled to take some effective action. " There is a very great degree of excitement among the Factory operatives," he wrote in a letter to his daughter on 23rd February, " by the cruel disappointment to their hopes by the decision of the Court of Exchequer. I am inclined to think that it is as well that things have taken the turn they have done, because there must be now an Act of Parliament to settle the question. I do not think that the judgment will much increase the evil of relays, for it had got to a great length, and had the judgment been different we should have been struggling on with a doubtful, uncertain law upon a point which should be clear and unequivocal. The Government has behaved in a very discreditable way in this matter; so soon as doubt was thrown on the true meaning of the Act, by the contradictory decisions of the magistrates (and that was the case twenty months ago) they should

71 See Appendix.
72 Report, 30th April, 1850. *Parl. Papers* (1850) XXIII, p. 264.

have brought the subject before Parliament. If they attempt to infringe upon the Ten Hours' Act, they will be assuredly beaten sooner or later, for it has taken deep root in the good opinion of the operatives."[73]

"The Barons of the Exchequer," said *The Times*,[74] "have decided that the millowners may time the hours of work for women and children as they please, provided they keep within the limits $5\frac{1}{2}$ a.m. and $8\frac{1}{2}$ p.m. In other words, owing to the clumsiness or carelessness of the framers of the statute the 'shift-system' turns out to be a perfectly legal one. For fifteen hours out of every twenty-four the factory women and children must remain at the beck and call of the millowners. The Factory Act is practically a nullity, and the interference of the Legislature is again needed, unless the evils against which the statute was directed are to remain entirely without check or remedy. Will Lord Ashley look on quietly while the humane principles of the Factory Bill are practically nullified?"

In July, 1847, Ashley had been returned to Parliament as the member for Bath, and he was therefore in a position to renew the struggle in the Commons. He was no longer, however, the unquestioned champion of the operatives, for it was rumoured that in the summer of 1849 he had engaged with the owners in conversations designed to effect a compromise by increasing the working-day to ten hours and a half, between six o'clock in the morning and six o'clock at night. John Fielden, who had piloted the Ten-hours Bill through the House of Commons, had just died, and to many of the extreme advocates of the measure it seemed that Ashley had chosen this moment to sell the pass. "Alas!" lamented *The Champion*, "that we should be driven to say that this melancholy moment appeared to be eagerly embraced as most propitious for the degraded proposal made to the factory workers by Lord Ashley to compromise matters with the masters . . . by actually conceding a portion of their sacredly guaranteed rights as the stipulated means of preserving the remainder."[75]

Samuel Fielden, son of the dead leader, espoused his father's cause, and gathering his supporters in the Fielden Society, he vigorously denounced those who advocated compromise with the masters. They demanded a meeting with the Central Short-time Committee, which was inclined to come to terms with the factory occupiers, but since the Committee had already decided to entrust to Ashley the task of introducing a new Factory Bill in the event

[73] K. M. Lyell, *Memoir of Leonard Horner* (1890) Vol. II, p. 158.
[74] 11th February, 1850.
[75] Vol. I, p. 174.

of an adverse decision in the Court of Exchequer, the conference proved abortive, and Samuel Fielden and his friends declared that it was no longer possible for them to work with Ashley.

On 12th February, 1850, Ashley asked the Home Secretary if, following the decision in Ryder *v.* Mills, the Government intended to introduce a measure declaring what had been the intention of the legislature in passing the Act of 1844. Grey replied that he had only just seen the judgment, and that he was not yet in a position to make any announcement. He had been anxious, he said, to introduce a bill last year, " but he found that the persons who held extreme opinions on both sides were averse to any such interposition, and that they were anxious to have the decision of a superior court of law."[76]

Thomas Maudsley, secretary of the Central Committee, had already written to Ashley that a meeting of delegates was to be held on Sunday, 17th February. They were anxious, he said, to take the advice of the friends of the cause, and would be glad to have any observations that Ashley cared to make. Since it was apparent that the Government had not yet defined their policy, Ashley was free to offer his counsel, and on 15th February he urged the Committee to stand fast. " I advise you firmly, per-severingly, and respectfully to maintain your rights—the rights of a limitation of labour to ten hours a day for all young persons; and that such labour be not given by fits and starts, by shifts and relays, but continuously from the hour at which it is begun. I advise you to send up petitions, memorials, and every other authentic expression of feeling to the Houses of Parliament and to people in authority. I advise you, also, to send up a deputation which shall see, if possible, every member of the Legislature, and state your just claims."[77]

A month later, on 14th March, 1850, after a conference with the legal experts of the Central Committee, Ashley moved in the House for leave to bring in a bill to amend the Act of 1847.[78] It was proposed to enact that in computing the hours of labour (including the intervals allowed for meals) the time should be reckoned continuously from the moment when any young person, female, or child first began work in the morning. In the Act of 1844, said Ashley, there was a clause providing that the labour of young persons should be reckoned from the time that work commenced, and working by shifts was consequently abandoned. When the Act of 1847 came into force, however, it was discovered that this section was not so stringent as to preclude relays, which

76 *Hansard* (1850) CVIII, 712.
77 *The Times,* 20th February, 1850.
78 *Parl. Papers* (1850) III, p. 1.

were again introduced. The magistrates gave contradictory decisions, causing discontent and confusion, for nobody knew what the law really meant. The adverse decision recently given in the Court of Exchequer made further legislation imperative, and he now proposed a bill that should carry out the intentions of Parliament.

The evils attendant upon the relay system were plain for all to see, but he drew the attention of the House to some of the more serious consequences, quoting in support of his case a letter that he had just received from a visitor to the mills. " I have been to-day to see some factories where the so-called relay system is in full work, and have seen such evidence of the evils of that mode of working the people that I cannot refrain from pouring out my feelings to you. In one factory I found 335 young persons and women working by relays; they are sent out at different times of the day, so as to bring their actual working to ten hours. They are sent out of the mill without any regard to the distance of their homes or the state of the weather. Some of them, I ascertained, lived two miles off, and thus the half hour, or one hour, or two hours, can be turned to no good account. The lads of 13 up to 18, and the young girls and women, are wandering about the streets, and to what temptations of vice and profligacy they are exposed I need not say."[79]

Sir James Graham, who had been responsible for the Act of 1844, assured the House that it had been intended " to prohibit absolutely and peremptorily the shift and relay system in any form whatever." Having been advised by the Inspectors, he said, that the twelve-hours Act worked unequally and unjustly because of the employment of relays, he had directed Mr. Horner to have a clause framed giving effect to the views which the Inspectors entertained. Such a clause was, in fact, embodied in the bill, but a change took place. He could not remember how it had come about—perhaps he had yielded to the remonstrances of the masters, but he had certainly intended to introduce adequate safeguards.[80]

There was less opposition to Ashley's proposals than might have been anticipated, and leave to introduce having been granted, the bill was read a second time on 19th March.[81] Serious doubts were being entertained, however, as to the efficacy of the measure in its existing form, and when the report stage was reached on 22nd March, certain amendments were included. The revised bill[82] provided that the hours of work in any one day of all young persons and females, and of all children (except those beginning work in the afternoon) should be reckoned continuously from the

---

[79] *Hansard* (1850) CIX, 883 *ff*.
[80] *Ibid.* 928 *ff*.
[81] *Ibid.* 1089.
[82] *Parl. Papers* (1850) III, p. 5.

earliest time when any one of the children, young persons or women
first began to work in the morning, excluding from such reckoning
only such times as were actually given at the same periods of the
day for meals.

Samuel Fielden's party were loud in their expressions of dis-
approval.[83]   To them nothing seemed easier than to frame a simple
enactment making the relay system illegal, but those who were
charged with the task of devising a form of words that should
limit the day's labour to ten continuous hours, found that even
the most subtle and ingenious phraseology was inadequate for the
purpose. The four Queen's Counsel who had worked upon the
draft in collaboration with Cobbett, the solicitor who had
prosecuted in Ryder v. Mills, confessed themselves at a loss, and
were driven to the conclusion that some other way out of the
dilemma must be sought.[84]

The time was ripe for a fresh approach to the problem, and
on 25th April *The Times* took the plunge by publishing a letter
signed " A Manufacturer," containing new proposals. " A plan
has been suggested to the Government by some millowners, who
are desirous that this act should be honestly carried out, and that
the system of working by shifts and relays should be prevented,
which would effect the object more simply and more certainly than
the plan proposed in Lord Ashley's bill, now before the House of
Commons. It is this,—that none of the persons whose labour is
now regulated by the Factory Acts shall be employed before 6
o'clock in the morning, nor after six o'clock in the evening; and
that, between those limits, an hour and a half shall be allowed for
the meals of young persons and women; and, further, that they
shall not be employed after 2 o'clock on Saturdays, with half an
hour for breakfast on that day. This makes exactly 60 hours per
week, or an average of 10 hours per day,—thus giving, in truth,
all that was originally contended for, but in a better way.

The important point of an early stopping of work in the
evening is secured, and, what is of very great importance to the
workpeople, a long afternoon on Saturday is also gained. Two

---

[83] See *The Champion,* Vol I, p. 349.—" The bill was carefully drawn
and placed in his lordship's hands, but, whether from ignorance, conceit,
pride, or something worse, it is not for us to say, Lord Ashley refuses to
avail himself of the aid thus tendered by the delegates, and he lays a bill
upon the table of the House which, for the purposes it professes to have
in view, is so wretchedly defective that both master and man, lawyer and
civilian, friend and foe, as soon as they have read it, lift up their eyes and
look at one another in amazement, exclaiming with an ominous smile—
' Why what in the name of wonder is this? Put down relays, eh! Why,
this is a Bill to legalise and regulate them.' "
[84] *The Times,* 14th May, 1850.

hours and a half are taken off the 10 hours of Saturday, and distributed equally over the other five days, and that without the necessity of beginning work before 6 o'clock in the morning.

At present, the workers subject to the law must stop at half-past 4 o'clock on Saturdays, but they may be employed from half-past 5 a.m., with an hour and a half off for meals,—making nine hours and a half, to make up 58 hours a week,—if they have worked less on the preceding days.

The plan proposed makes 60 hours a week, and while the additional two hours will be a gain to the masters, and to the workpeople who are paid by piecework, they will in no degree interfere with the primary—indeed the sole object of the Factory Acts, *viz.,*—full leisure for the moral and social improvement of the great mass of the persons employed in that description of labour.

It is very much to be wished that Lord Ashley would substitute this plan for his own, or that Government should bring in a bill to carry it through."

This was substantially the proposal that had already been made to the delegates of the operatives by Mr. Walter of *The Times* a few days previously; and although the authorship of the letter was never disclosed, it was obviously an inspired document. The leading article declared that it had been published " with the view of ascertaining if any such compromise . . . would be judged by the operatives themselves to be a satisfactory working out of the Ten Hours Bill, to the benefits of which, in the very spirit in which it was passed, they are clearly and indisputably entitled."

" We cannot but say," continued the leader, " that the proposal appears to emanate from a spirit of temperance and moderation. We will not anticipate the decision of the operatives upon this point, but thus much at least we will venture to say, yielding as we do to no one in hearty sympathy with their cause—' If it be possible, by a fresh arrangement, to secure yourselves in possession, substantially, of all the advantages for which you are contending, do not stickle upon a mere point of form. . . . Do not be imprac-ticable upon mere matters of arrangement, however determined you may be to obtain substantial justice.'"

The letter created a profound sensation in the manufacturing districts. The local committees in each town were hurriedly summoned to consider the proposed compromise, and the result was a universal determination never to yield a single moment of the leisure time gained by the Act of 1847. The Lancashire Central Committee met the same night that the letter was published, and called a delegate meeting at the Cotton Tree Tavern for Sunday, 28th April. The discussion was long and anxious. Some delegates thought that Ashley's bill in its present form would not prevent relays; many considered that he should no longer be entrusted with the conduct of the measure; while all were deeply perturbed by the letter he had sent to Maudsley, their secretary. Various attempts, Ashley had written, had been made to draw an effective clause for prohibiting relays, but without success. A new clause had been drafted containing more detailed provisions for the regulation of meal times, but if this were adopted it would inevitably cause further delay, and postpone the whole measure until next session. What course did the meeting advise?

From this dilemma there seemed to be no escape, and the meeting, declining to give Ashley any definite instructions, did no more than pass a resolution declaring their determination not to effect a compromise. " This meeting," they affirmed, " having been rendered necessary by a letter which appeared in *The Times* of Thursday last, signed ' A Manufacturer,' suggesting to the operatives the propriety of surrendering two hours per week, . . . we, the delegates here assembled, avail ourselves of the present opportunity to declare to the Government, the Legislature, and the British public, both for ourselves and those whom we represent, that we never will submit to anything involving in the slightest degree a departure from the principle of the Ten Hours Act, for which we, the factory workers, have at an enormous expense struggled so many years."[85]

Ashley was now in a most difficult position. The Short-time Committee had insisted that some formula should be devised whereby the ten-hours day should be preserved, and relays prohibited, but they were quite unable to suggest what that formula should be. Ashley, convinced that they were seeking the impossible, could discern but one solution—acceptance of the compromise offered by the manufacturers, involving, it is true, two additional hours of labour each week, but involving also the establishment of the normal day.

He had already ascertained that the Government was prepared to support such a plan, for when the debate on his bill was resumed on 3rd May, he asked whether the Government intended to propose any scheme of their own. The Home Secretary in reply said that it would be extremely difficult to carry out the object of the bill while the range of fifteen hours, during which work could be carried on, was left untouched. He therefore had to propose a plan that would be more acceptable to the manufacturers, and also to the great body of operatives. " The plan," he said, " will be this—to substitute for the existing restrictions on the number of hours during which women and young persons may be

85 *The Times*, 30th April, 1850.

employed, a new limitation or definition of the hours within which they shall be employed." For five days of the week work should begin at 6 a.m. and finish at 6 p.m., the hours on Saturday to be from 6 a.m. to 2 p.m. "Perhaps," continued Grey, "this plan would be better understood, if I were to state what would be its effect. At present the class of young persons and women may be employed ten hours in the day during five days, and eight hours upon the Saturday, making altogether fifty-eight hours in the week. Under the alteration in the law—if it should be consented to by Parliament—they would be liable to be employed between six in the morning and six in the evening, which would be ten hours and a half, deducting the hour and a half for meals. They, therefore, might be employed during five days in the week fifty-two hours and a half instead of fifty, and on Saturday half an hour less than under the existing law, the day ending at two o'clock." It was true, he added, that by this plan longer hours would be worked, but there were counter-vailing advantages—the factory day would begin half an hour later in the morning, the operatives would cease work earlier in the evening, and they would be released from the mills at 2 o'clock on Saturday afternoon.[86]

What better solution could be found? Ashley could see none, and four days later, on 7th May, he addressed his famous letter to the Short-time Committees of Lancashire and Yorkshire.

"Gentlemen,—It has become my duty to state to you, without further delay, the course that I would advise you to pursue in the present position of the Factory Bill in the House of Commons.

I am bound to act as your friend, and not as your delegate; and I counsel you, therefore, to accept forthwith the propositions made by Her Majesty's Government as the only means of solving the difficulties in which we are now placed.

I wish most heartily for your sakes that they contained an unqualified limitation to 10 hours daily; but I am induced, nevertheless, for the following reasons to give you that counsel:

(1) The dispute is now limited to a struggle about two hours in the week—whether the aggregate toil shall be 58 or 60 hours; the Government plan requiring the two additional hours, but giving an equivalent in exchange.

(2) The plan imposes a most important and beneficial limitation of the range over which the work may be taken, reducing it from 15 to 12 hours in the day, thereby preventing all possibility of shifts, relays, and other evasions—a result which cannot be obtained by any other form of enactment. This has always been my strong conviction, and I carried the question by the separate divisions in 1844.

---

[86] *Hansard* (1850) CX, 1133-1134.

(3) It secures to the working people, for recreation and domestic duty, the whole of every evening after 6 o'clock.

(4) It provides for a later commencement of work by half an hour in the morning.

(5) It ensures additional leisure time on every Saturday.

(6) Because this arrangement would secure, I believe, the co-operation of the employers—a matter of no slight importance in the good working of any measure, and essential to the harmony and good feeling we all desire to see in the vast districts of our manufactures.

But there are other reasons, drawn from the embarrassments of our present position. I have already described to you in a former letter the necessity I have been under (after making many essays and taking many learned opinions) of introducing a clause to prohibit relays which contains new matter and imposes fresh restrictions. This unavoidable step on my part sets at liberty many members who considered themselves engaged to maintain the honour of Parliament, and thus endangers the success of the measure ultimately, and certainly the progress of it in the present session. Its progress, even were the bill unopposed, would be difficult under the heavy pressure of public business; but, opposed at it would be, postponement would be inevitable. Now, I greatly fear delay; I refrain from stating my reasons; but I repeat, I greatly fear delay, as likely to be productive of infinite mischief, and which may possibly completely alter your relative and actual position.

I have tried to discover the bright side of postponement, but I cannot conceive any advantage in it whatsoever. You will stand no better in the next session than you do in this; you may possibly stand worse.

The two hours are, I know, your unquestionable right; but, on the other hand, the range of 15 hours is the unquestionable right of the employers: the exchange they offer is fair, and the gain is on your side.

In giving this counsel, I know that I shall be exposed to sad misrepresentations; but it is my duty not to do that which will secure applause to myself, but that which will secure protection to your families and children. I should be overjoyed to obtain for you the full concession of the two hours in the week, but such an issue seems to my mind next to impossible; and in the protracted struggle to reach the 10, you incur the hazard of being brought to 11 hours. Postponement must follow the conflict; division among the operatives will follow postponement; and when once you are a divided body your cause will be irretrievably lost.

It will be necessary to insert the word 'children' into the clause introduced by Sir George Grey, in order that the youngest workers may be sure to enjoy the benefit of the close of the daily labour at 6 o'clock.

With this view I shall accept the amendment proposed by the Minister, in the humble but assured hope that the issue will be blessed to the moral and social amelioration of your great community.

I am, Gentlemen,
Your very faithful friend and servant,
Ashley."[87]

The choice confronting Ashley was a cruel one. Nothing could have been simpler than to win the easy plaudits of the unthinking mob by following, at their behest, a policy that could serve only to perpetuate indecision and frustration. To stand four-square for the ten-hours day would be to court disaster, for the House that had vented its anger on Peel and the Anti-Corn Law League by passing the Act of 1847, was not at all disposed to meet the demands of the operatives by limiting the manufacturers to a working day of 11½ hours—and in no other way could the object of the Short-time Committees be achieved. Ashley, realizing this, took a statesmanlike and realistic decision, counselling compromise even though he was fully conscious of the odium in which such a course must involve him. " Harassed exceedingly by Factory affair," he wrote in his diary on 8th May, "—resolved to adopt clauses of Government, and wrote letter to *Times* announcing it. Expect from manufacturing districts a storm of violence and hatred. I might have taken a more popular and belauded course, but I should have ruined the question; one more easy to myself, but far from true to the people."[88]

The storm, indeed, burst with unexampled fury. His long service to the cause forgotten, Ashley was now branded as a traitor, a deserter, a hypocrite. " How far the conduct of his lordship is attributable to a character naturally weak, mean and shifty, or how far other and more criminal instincts and purposes have led to a dishonourable abandonment of the best and holiest of causes we shall not stay to inquire " declared *The Champion*.[89] " Suffice it to say, that Lord Ashley's reputation as an able or as an upright statesman is irrecoverably gone." The *Constitution and Church Sentinel* joined in the attack. " And of Lord Ashley's conduct in this matter, what shall we say? He who presented the medal to the Queen—who solemnly declared he ' would die in the last ditch ' rather than give up the advocacy of the ten hours'

---

[87] *The Times*, 9th May, 1850.

[88] E. Hodder, *The Life and Work of the seventh Earl of Shaftesbury* (1893) p. 373.

[89] Vol. II. p. 123.

clause—did *he* fulfil his word? Henceforth his philanthropy will savour of hypocrisy, his benevolence of cant."[90]

The Bradford Short-time Committee, meeting on 12th May, affirmed its unwillingness to depart from the 58 hour week, and resolved to entrust the conduct of affairs to Lord John Manners, who had pledged himself to press for a day ending at 5.30 p.m. On the same day the Manchester Committee decided to accept the Government measure, reserving the right to apply next year for a further reduction of two hours.[91]

The Times, in its leading article of 9th May, placed the problem in perspective. "It appears that Lord Ashley finds his present Parliamentary position with regard to the Ten Hours Bill utterly untenable. He therefore recommends the operatives to accede to the Government proposition, which is substantially the same with that brought forward by 'A Manufacturer' in the columns of *The Times* some short while back. . . .

When this matter first came under our notice, we conceived that nothing would be simpler than to frame a short bill declaratory of the intention of the Ten Hours Act. It seems that this is not so. Lord Ashley has endeavoured, with the assistance of the most competent persons, to frame a clause which should entirely prohibit the system of shifts and relays, without importing into the act of Parliament any fresh restrictions upon the millowners not contained in the original Ten Hours Act. . . . Now, upon a trial, it has been found impossible to frame a clause which shall destroy the system of shifts and relays and at the same time not interfere with the full period of fifteen hours, during which the millowners may work their mills." The owners, it was said, welcomed the proposal because they would be freed from the constant supervision of the Inspectors. "It requires no very strained attention, no very shrewdly devised system of *espionage*, to ascertain if the doors of a factory be opened at six a.m. and closed at six o'clock p.m. The policeman on duty on the beat at the hours named could report upon the matter just as satisfactorily as the best paid inspectors who could be appointed."

When the text of the Government proposals was published on 13th May,[92] it was at once apparent that there was a serious omission, for although it was provided that women and young persons should be employed only between 6 a.m. and 6 p.m., there was no reference to the hours of children. It is true that when Grey had first outlined his plan he had said nothing about including

---

[90] Quoted, *The Champion*, Vol. II, p. 154.
[91] *The Times*, 14th May, 1850.
[92] *Parl. Papers* (1850) III, p. 9.

them in the new regulations, but this had aroused no particular comment. Ashley had, indeed, mentioned the matter to the Home Secretary, who after waving his protest aside, had finally promised that children should be placed on an equal footing with women and young persons in this respect.[93] Relying on the good faith of Grey, Ashley formally proposed, on 6th June, that the provisions of the bill should extend to children,[94] but to his consternation he was told that the omission was not accidental. The Government had decided to exclude children because their hours of work were not continuous. They were to be left as they were prior to 1847, for the regulations then in force had worked admirably and could not be improved. This policy was warmly supported by Bright, on the ground that if children ceased work at 6 p.m. the adult males also would be compelled to finish at that time. Had anything so monstrous ever been proposed, he asked, as that strong, robust boys of 12 or 13 years, should be prevented by statute from working more than five and a quarter hours per day at an employment confessedly the least laborious? Ashley's proposal was lost by 102 votes to 72,[95]—a further effort to secure the inclusion of children being defeated, five days later, by 160 votes to 159.[96]

This was sharp practice indeed, for those who supported the compromise had been led to expect that the measure would apply to children equally with young persons and women, and that the mills would, in fact, close at six o'clock at night. It now appeared that work could continue until 8.30 p.m., for there was nothing to prevent children employed in the afternoons from being kept at work, by relays if necessary, until that hour.

It was now too late to withdraw, however, and Lord John Manners, true to his promise, moved that the working day should not extend beyond 5.30 p.m. Grey opposed. It was his firm conviction, he said, that the object of the Act of 1847 would be better secured by keeping the time to 6 p.m., for that would command the assent of the owners. "The Government," he declared, "have derived information from various trustworthy quarters, and the result is a conviction that the benefits which the honest advocates of the Act of 1847 seek to obtain will be better secured by this Bill, and that when passed into a law the measure will prove satisfactory to the operatives themselves." Manners'

93 *The Times*, 14th May, 1850.
94 *Hansard* (1850) CXI, 846.
95 *Ibid*. 855.
96 *Ibid*. 1240.

amendment was lost by 181 votes to 142,[97] and on 20th June the bill was read a third time and sent to the Lords.[98]

" The House of Commons," declared Oastler, " has repealed John Fielden's Ten Hours' Factory Act. The meanness of the Manchester school has triumphed over the honour of the English gentleman. So much for the *lower* House, including Lord Ashley, who did not even give the poor children a God help-them, much less a vote. Now for the *upper* House. Let no time be lost in seeking to reverse in the Chamber of Peers the cruel decision come to *in another place*."[99]

Such hopes were vain. Despite the endeavours of the Earl of Harrowby to secure the inclusion of children, the bill passed the Lords without amendment, and on 5th August, 1850, the Act to amend the Acts relating to Labour in Factories[100] received the royal assent.

Section 1 provided that so much of the Acts of 1833, 1844 and 1847 as restricted the hours of labour of young persons, and of females over eighteen years of age was repealed, and henceforth these classes were not to be employed, except to recover lost time, before 6 a.m. nor after 6 p.m., and they were not to be employed in any circumstances after 2 p.m. on Saturday. Between 30th September and 1st April they might be employed between 7 a.m. and 7 p.m. (except on Saturdays) provided the mill-occupier gave the Inspector notice of his intention to alter the hours for a period of at least one month, and provided a notice was displayed setting out the necessary details.[101]

Young persons and adult females were not to make up time lost through excess of, or want of due supply of water after 7 p.m., nor were they to be employed for this purpose for more than an hour before 6 a.m. or after 6 p.m.[102] They were to take their meals between 7.30 a.m. and 6 p.m.,[103] and they were forbidden to remain, during meal-times, in a room where a manufacturing process was carried on.[104]

Children engaged solely in winding and throwing raw silk could be employed in all respects as young persons if they had a surgical certificate testifying that they had completed their eleventh year.[105] The provisions of the Act of 1844 requiring the posting

---

97 *Ibid.* 1283.
98 *Hansard* (1850) CXII, 130.
99 *The Champion*, Vol. II, p. 112.
100 13 & 14 Vict., c. 54.
101 Sec. 6.
102 Sec. 4.
103 Sec. 3.
104 Sec. 8.
105 Sec. 7.

of notices of the times of beginning and ending work were repealed.[106]

Many of the operatives were extremely bitter in their denuncia-
tion of the Compromise Act, as it was called, and they taunted
Ashley with his baseness in deserting their cause. But such feeling
was not by any means universal. *The Champion* recorded that at
Stalybridge " the abolition of the ' shift system ' by the government
has caused much joy amongst the factory-workers, even though it
entails an additional half hour's work per day."[107]   At Cheetham's
New Mill they buried two brush stales with full ceremony, thus
burying the shifts; at Leach's mill some of the weavers had tea
and rum on the strength of the abolition of relays, while others
arranged a mock funeral, regaling themselves with rum or gin,
and biscuits and wine.

Horner was convinced, even before the Act was passed, that
it would bestow substantial benefits. " The merit of the plan
chiefly dwelt upon," he said, "is that by the limitation of the factory
day to twelve hours, from six to six, out of which the hour and
half for meals must be given, it will secure an uniformity in the
hours of work in all mills, so far as concerns the employment of
young persons and women. It is an early stopping in the evening
that the workpeople chiefly value; and if the free evening hours
from six to nine be secured, the great object sought for by the Ten
Hours Act will be attained. . . . The intended general stopping of
the mills at two o'clock on Saturdays has given especial satisfaction."[108]

In October, 1850, he reported that since relays were now
impossible there was comparative quiet and contentment in his
district. Some still contended for the Ten Hours Act in all its
integrity, but they were few in number, the majority agreeing that
the masters " had made a concession which they are fairly entitled
to deduct from their share of the profit to be derived from the two
additional hours of work in each week."[109]   Captain John Kincaid
(later Sir John Kincaid), who had been appointed Factory Inspector
on 17th December, 1849, following the death of Stuart, declared
that the Act had given very general satisfaction—" not so much,
perhaps, from any particular benefit arising out of the measure
itself, as for its having brought to a happy settlement what had
been so long a source of very great vexation to all parties—the
disputed hours of labour."[110]

---

106 Sec. 2.
107 Vol. II, p. 287.
108 Report, 30th April, 1850. *Parl. Papers* (1850) XXIII, p. 265.
109 *Parl. Papers* (1851) XXIII, pp. 219-220.
110 *Ibid.* p. 255.

Kincaid noted, however, that the exclusion of children from the protection of the normal day was having serious results, especially in the woollen mills in the south of Scotland. Some owners were running the machinery after six o'clock at night by employing children to take the places of the women and young persons who left the mill at that hour. These children continued until 8.30 p.m., and many men were thus kept at work for thirteen hours a day. There were comparatively few instances of the practice in his district, but Horner and Saunders found considerable numbers of children employed in this fashion.

To the problem thus raised there could be but one solution— to reverse the policy for which Grey had stood in 1850, and include children within the scope of the normal day. The Parliament that had been elected in 1847 was dissolved on 2nd July, 1852, and in the coalition government of Lord Aberdeen, Palmerston became Home Secretary. When, on 5th July, 1853, J. M. Cobbett, now member for Oldham, moved for leave to introduce a bill limiting the hours of work of children, young persons and women to ten a day, and providing that children should work only between 6 a.m. and 6 p.m., Palmerston declared that although he could not undertake to support any proposal designed further to reduce the hours of women and young persons, he had already determined to bring in a bill to limit the working day of children. " I really think," he said, " that to have little children from eight to twelve years of age brought out on a drizzling winter's morning at five or half-past five, when they perhaps live three or four miles distant from the place where they work, and then in the evening to have them walking back, perhaps alone, to their homes in the dark, with perhaps snow on the ground, is a practice which must entail such evils that no one can be surprised at the extreme mortality among the children of the factory operatives. To limit the children will be to limit the adults, but all I can say is that I think it is so essential to protect these children from being overtasked that I cannot consider the results which it may be imagined will flow from it."[111]

So it was that once again pity for the young and defenceless provided the motive force. Nothing more was heard of Cobbett's proposal for a ten-hours day, but instead there was introduced, on 18th July, 1853, the Employment of Children in Factories Bill. Backed by Palmerston the bill was rushed through the Commons without debate; it went to the Lords on 4th August, and received the royal assent on 20th August.[112]

---

[111] *Hansard* (1853) CXXVIII, 1268.
[112] *Hansard* (1853) CXXIX, 1834.

The Act further to regulate the Employment of Children in Factories[113] was short but decisive. " It is expedient," recited the preamble, " that children should not be employed in factories at times during which young persons and women may not now by law be employed," and the four brief sections, while not extending the time during which children might work, provided that they, too, should be employed only between 6 a.m. and 6 p.m., or between 7 a.m. and 7 p.m. subject to the conditions laid down in the Act of 1850.

It would be difficult to over-estimate the significance of the principle of the normal working day, now finally established without any loopholes for evasion. No longer were the operatives condemned to excessive and unreasonable prolongation of their hours of labour, for they were now free to leave the mill at six o'clock at night, and for the first time they were able to enjoy a period of respite on Saturday afternoon. Such an addition to the sum of human happiness was in itself a sufficient justification for so far-reaching a reform, but the administrative consequences were not less important. Those who, in the early days, had urged that the only effective way to check over-working was to restrict the moving power,[114] had discerned the solution to the ultimate problem of factory control. So long as the machinery could be run for a longer period than the protected classes were permitted to work, so long would the inspecting officers be compelled to dissipate their energies in a battle of wits with mill-owners whose ingenuity was constantly directed to discovering methods of evasion. The institution of the normal day did not by any means preclude the possibility of evasion, but it was now a comparatively simple matter to detect overworking, and the Inspectors were thus able to devote their time to other and more important aspects of their work.

The Act of 1853 marked the close of an epoch in the history of factory legislation. What had been accomplished during the past fifty years? Perhaps the most striking achievement was the establishment of the principle that it is the right, and indeed the duty of the State to intervene between employer and employed, to impose control and regulation, in order to protect those who were unable, in the highly individualistic and competitive industrial system, to protect themselves. When once this basic principle had won general acceptance progress became possible on a wide front, and reform could proceed with increasing momentum. Elaborate

---

113 16 & 17 Vict., c. 104.
114 *Cf.* H. Hoole, *A Letter in Defence of the Cotton Factories* (1832) p.16.—" If the Act of last session required a more general enforcement of its provisions, the Legislature can secure its universal observance by fixing the time upon the moving power."

administrative machinery had been devised, tested, and improved; a system of inspection had been instituted to co-ordinate and administer the new code; surgeons had begun to play an increasingly important part in securing minimum standards of health and general well-being; provision had been made for education; and a vast fund of experience had been acquired.

Much remained to be done, for the field of action had hitherto been rigidly circumscribed. The great non-textile industries were still unregulated, provisions for health and safety were still rudimentary, while educational arrangements were primitive and unsatisfactory to a degree. As the nineteenth century moved onwards to its close the social conscience of the nation became increasingly sensitive to the needs of the operatives, and the demand for wider and more far-reaching reforms grew ever more insistent. Fresh problems emerged as each successive advance was made, problems of personal and domestic relationship, of control and organization, of expediency and policy. But the territory had been well surveyed, the foundations well laid, and the fundamental principles of industrial regulation that had been evolved so slowly and painfully during half a century were found to be so flexible, so adaptable, and of such universal application that they served as the basis for the major developments of the future.

APPENDIX

I.—RETURN OF FACTORIES SUBJECT TO REGULATION, 1835.

NUMBER OF MANUFACTORIES ENGAGED IN

Cotton	...	...	1,250
Wool & Worsted	...		1,315
Flax	...	...	352
Silk	...	...	237
		Total ...	3,154

NUMBER OF OPERATIVES

Under 11		11 —18	
Male	Female	Male	Female
4,811	5,308	67,203	89,822

TOTAL OPERATIVES ENGAGED IN

Cotton ...	...	...	100,258	119,124
Wool & Worsted	...		31,360	27,369
Flax ...	...	...	10,336	22,526
Silk ...	...	...	9,969	20,438
	Total ...		151,923	189,457

Returns made by the Inspectors to an order of the House of Commons dated 19th March, 1835.

(*Parl. Papers* (1836) *XLV*, p. 51 ff).

II.—RETURN OF CHILDREN SUBJECT TO REGULATION.

FEBRUARY, 1836.

District	Description of Factories in which the children are employed	Number of Children of the Required Age			Number of children to be discharged or restricted to 48 hours of labour per week	Number of children enjoying the benefit of the Educational clauses (1)
		12	13	14		
...nard Horner ...	In 176 cotton factories	1430	4327	3107	1770	742
	In 104 woollen factories	384	788	366	493	154
	In 192 flax factories	999	2984	2086	916	180
	In 5 silk factories	72	98	63	—	—
	477	2885	8197	5622	3179	1076
...omas Jones Howell...	In 11 cotton factories	54	179	133	50	none
	In 355 woollen factories	1014	1753	1164	694	110
	In 5 flax factories	88	89	143	84	30
	In 26 silk factories	111	138	96	—	—
	397	1267	2159	1536	828	140
...ert Rickards ...	In 1071 cotton factories	10470	20260	16997	12644	1625
	In 598 woollen factories	1996	3086	3953	4168	436
	In 249 worsted factories	1457	2503	2511	3063	761
	In 84 flax factories	515	895	1681	933	283
	In 140 silk factories	2001	1860	1634	—	—
	2142	16439	28604	26776	20808	3105
...ert J. Saunders ...	In 64 cotton factories	506	1039	791	373	258
	In 107 woollen factories	368	622	430	264	323
	In 43 flax factories	72	168	142	49	56
	In 71 silk factories	925	883	781	—	—
	285	1871	2712	2144	686	637
	In 3301 factories	22462	41672	36078	25501	4958

(1) These children had attendance certificates from the schoolmaster.

(*Parl. Papers* (*1836*), *XLV, pp. 204-213*).

III.—INSPECTORS' REGULATIONS.

Regulations made by Leonard Horner. 6th July, 1836.

A surgeon or physician is specially authorised to issue the certificates of age for the children and young persons in each particular mill.

1.   A notice containing the name and address of the surgeon or physician who issues the certificate of age for the mill, is required to be fixed up by the mill-occupier, and permanently kept in a conspicuous part of his factory.

2.   All certificates of age are required to be retained in the custody of the mill-occupier, so long as the person to whom it applies remains in his employment, and for three months after the person has left his employment.

3.   All certificates of age are required to be pasted in a book specially kept for the purpose, arranged in the order of the alphabet, according to the first letter of the sirname of the person certified; or in the order of a series of running numbers, with an alphabetical index of names referring to the number of the book against each certificate.

4.   When a person having a certificate of age has ceased to be employed in the factory, distinct lines are required to be drawn with ink across his or her certificate, in order that the inspector and superintendent may thereby be able to distinguish readily the certificates of those actually in employment.

5.   Spinners and others who have authority from their masters to engage children as piecers or as assistants for other purposes, without his previous sanction, are hereby required to deliver the certificates of each child, so engaged, at the office or counting-house of the factory, within 24 hours of the child being employed, whether as a learner or otherwise.

This rule must not be understood as in any degree relieving the master from the responsibility which attaches to him of seeing that every child working in his mill has a certificate.

6.   Overlookers are required to give notice at the office or counting-house of the factory, of the name of every person under 18 years of age whom he overlooks, who shall cease to be employed under him, and that within 24 hours of the person leaving.

[7 & 8.   Time Registers. See Appendix, pp. 341-343.]

9.   If any mill-occupier shall employ persons in his factory more than twelve hours in any one day, professing that they are above eighteen years of age, he is required to keep a separate register of all persons so employed more than twelve hours, in the same form as that for his workers under eighteen years of age, as given under rule No. 7.

10.   The time fixed for beginning work in the morning, the hours and amount of time allowed for breakfast, dinner, and tea, and the time fixed for giving over work at night, written, printed, or painted, in large, legible characters, signed by the mill-occupier, his manager, or overlooker, is hereby required to be fixed up and permanently kept in a conspicuous part of every mill, where it can be easily read by all the workers employed therein.

11. If time be lost, and if the mill-occupier intends to make it up, he is hereby required on each occasion, previously to fix up, in a conspicuous part of the mill, accessible to all the workers, a notice stating the date, day, and hour, when the stoppage took place; the cause of that stoppage, and the amount of time lost; and that notice is required to remain fixed up so long as the mill-occupier shall be making up the said lost time. And if the making up of lost time shall be continued beyond three days, the time recovered is required to be marked upon the said notice after every third day of continuance.

[12. Time Registers. See Appendix, p. 343.]

13. All the holidays and half-holidays given in the course of the year, are required to be recorded together in a distinct place in Time-Book, No. 1.

14. The dates when the mill is limewashed and whitewashed, with the signature of the overlooker, or other person responsible for the correctness of the entry, and the dates of any exemption of limewashing and whitewashing granted by the inspector, are hereby required to be recorded in a different place in Time-Book, No. 1.

15. All the children under thirteen years of age, belonging to one factory, who are required to attend school twelve hours in each week, and who go to the same school, may be certified in one paper weekly. The form of certificate of school attendance is for the present left to the decision of the mill occupier.

16. The certificates of school attendance must be pasted in a book in the order of their dates.

17. Attendance at a Sunday School will be held as part of the twelve hours above mentioned.

18. Any mill occupier commencing work in a new mill, or taking or recommencing work in an old mill, is hereby required, within one week of employing any person under eighteen years of age, to give written notice to the inspector, or superintendent, of the name of the factory, the place, township, parish and county where it is situate, and the nearest post town; the nature of the work, the nature and extent of the propelling power, and the firm under which the work is to be carried on.

19. In all and every proceeding relating to any alleged offence or offences against this Act, or against the rules and regulations of the inspector, the mill-occupier is hereby required to produce all the registers, time-books, and certificates of age or attendance at school, which may relate to the alleged offence, or offences, at the time and place appointed for the adjudication of the same, before the magistrate or inspector by whom the case is to be heard, although such registers, time-books, and certificates be not specially required by the summons to be produced.

20. The copy or copies of these rules and regulations transmitted to each mill occupier, are required to be signed by him, or by his manager or overlooker, and to be pasted upon a board, or otherwise preserved from injury, and to be fixed up, within one week of the receipt of the same, and permanently kept in some conspicuous place in the factory, so that these rules and regulations may be easily read at all times by the work-people. If the copy, so transmitted, be at any time accidentally destroyed, or be so injured as to be illegible, in any part thereof, the mill occupier is hereby required to provide another true copy, either written or printed, in large, legible characters.

LEONARD HORNER,
Inspector.

(*Parl. Papers (1836) XLV, p. 215 ff*).

The Uniform Code.

Rules and Regulations made in pursuance of the authority vested in the Inspectors by the Act of 1833.
4th October, 1836.

I. The time fixed for beginning and ending the regular hours of work of all persons employed in the factory, whether children, young persons, or adults; and the periods of the day and amount of time allowed for their several meals, written, printed, or painted, in large legible characters, signed by the mill-occupier, are hereby required to be fixed up and permanently kept in a conspicuous part of every mill, where they can be easily read by all the workers employed therein.

II. Mill-occupiers being entitled to recover time lost from want of water and other causes specified in the Act, it is hereby required that, if time be so lost, and if the mill-occupier intends to make it good, he shall, previously to working at any other than the regular hours, fix up, in a conspicuous part of the mill, accessible to all the workers, a notice stating the date, day, and hour, when the stoppage took place; the cause of that stoppage, and the amount of time lost: and that notice is required to remain fixed up so long as any persons shall be employed making up the said lost time. And if the making up of lost time shall be continued beyond three days, the time recovered is required to be marked upon the said notice after every third day of continuance.

III. A notice containing the name and address of the surgeon or physician, or of the surgeons or physicians, by whom the certificates of age received at the mill or factory have been granted, is required to be fixed up by the mill-occupier, and permanently kept in a conspicuous part of the factory accessible to all the workers.

IV. The certificate required as a proof that a young person has completed his or her thirteenth year of age may either be an authentic extract from a legal register of the baptism of the person, or a medical certificate of the same description as that required from children under 13 years of age.

V. Every certificate of age is required to be retained in the custody of the mill-occupier so long as the person to whom it applies remains in his employment, and for 14 days after the person has left his employment.

VI. All certificates of age, whether medical or baptismal, are required to be pasted into a book specially kept for the purpose, successively as received, and in the order of a series of running numbers, with a number against each certificate. There must also be kept an alphabetical index to this book, according to the first letter of the surname of the person certified, with a reference to the number against the person's certificate in the aforesaid book.

VII. If the children under 13 years of age belonging to the factory go to the same school, their daily attendance required by the Act may be certified together in one book, or on a separate paper; but if the vouchers or certificates of school attendance be on separate papers, either for one child or several, they must be pasted into a book specially kept for the purpose, in the order of their dates. Attendance at a Sunday-school, if properly certified, may be taken as attendance at school for one of the six days required by the Act.

[VIII, IX, X. Time Registers. See Appendix, pp. 344-345.]

XI. The register of workers, the certificate book and alphabetical index, and the time-registers, must not be locked up during the time the mill or factory is at work, in order that they may be seen at any time by the Inspector or Superintendent, whether the occupier be absent or present; and which register of workers, certificate book, index, certificate of school attendance, and time-registers, shall be produced at all times in the factory to the Superintendent, when required by him.

XII. In all and every legal proceeding relating to any alleged offence or offences against this Act, or against the rules and regulations of the inspector, the mill-occupier is hereby required to produce all the registers, time-books, and certificates of age or attendance at school, which may relate to the alleged offence, or offences, at the time and place appointed for the adjudication of the same, before the magistrate or inspector by whom the case is to be heard, although such registers, time-books, and certificates be not specially required by the summons to be produced.

XIII. Any mill-occupier commencing work in a new mill, or taking or recommencing work in an old mill is hereby required, within one week of employing any person under eighteen years of age, to give written notice to the inspector, or superintendent, of the name of the factory, the place, township, parish and county where it is situate, and the nearest post town; the nature of the work, the nature and extent of the propelling power, and the firm under which the work is to be carried on.

XIV. Such abstract of the Act, and such copy or copies of any rules or regulations, as may be transmitted by each Inspector to any mill-occupier in his district, for the purpose of being hung up in a factory, are hereby required to be pasted upon a *moveable* board, or otherwise preserved from injury, and to be fixed up, within one week of the receipt of the same, and permanently kept in some conspicuous place in the factory, so that those rules and regulations may be easily read at all times by the work-people. If the copy, or copies, so transmitted, be at any time accidentally destroyed, or be so injured as to be illegible, in any part thereof, the mill-occupier is hereby required to provide another true copy, or other true copies, either written or printed, in large, legible characters.

> LEONARD HORNER,
> T. JONES HOWELL,
> ROBERT J. SAUNDERS,   } Inspectors.
> JA. STUART,

(Parl. Papers (1837) XXXI, p. 88 ff.)

IV.—DEVELOPMENT OF THE TIME REGISTER.

Rickards' Regulations.

29th January, 1834.

The 18th clause of the Act 3 & 4 Guliel. IV., c. 103, requiring inspectors to make such rules, regulations and orders as may be necessary for the due execution of the Act; and it being of importance that an accurate register should be kept of the persons employed in each factory, and of the time or period of labour performed on each day, Notice is hereby given, that in pursuance of the aforesaid section, and of the authority thereby vested in the inspector, it will be requisite for the owners of mills or factories to keep for the future an accurate register or time-book of the information thus prescribed; in which should be carefully inserted, a true and correct account of the time which the steam-engine or water-wheel and machinery of such mill or factory shall have been in operation during each day; and such book to be at all times open and written up for the inspection of the inspector himself, or any justice of the peace for the division in which such mill or factory may be placed, or of any other official person duly authorised by the inspector to examine the same.

Where registers or time-books such as above described are now kept, the same form (with such additions as may be necessary under the present order) may be continued; where no such registers exist, the following form will be found convenient, and suffice for the purposes hereby required:—

TIME FORM, No. 1.

The number of hours the mill is worked each day to be entered as below.

	1824	January	1st	2nd	3rd	4th	5th	6th		
Number of Hours	the Mill									Total number of
worked each day	...		12	12	12	12	12	9	... 69	hours in the week

TIME FORM, No. 2.

Showing the Time each Person worked during the Week.

January 1st, 1834	Age	M.	T.	W.	T.	F.	S.	Total Time during the week
NAMES OF THE PERSONS								
J. S.	10	8	8	8	8	8	8	48
J. G.	12	10	12	12	12	12	9,	67¼
J. L.	15	10	12	12	12	12	9;	67½
P. C.	17	10	12	12	12	12	9:	67¾

For each $\left\{ \begin{array}{ccc} ¼ & ½ & ¾ \\ , & ; & : \end{array} \right\}$ of an hour

(*Parl. Papers* (1836) XLV, pp. 206-7.)

12th February, 1834.

To explain more clearly the intention of the inspector, in regard to the time-books required to be kept in the mills . . . it is hereby notified that in mills working only twelve hours in any one day, or sixty-nine hours in any one week, the first time-book, or that in which the moving power is registered, need only be kept, together with a time-book for children, if any, under eleven years of age, (and in silk mills under 13 years of age) showing the exact time of their daily employment in each day; but where the engine, or moving power, runs more than 12 hours in any one day, or 60 hours in any one week, the other time-book must contain the whole number of young persons under 18 years of age, in each mill, and show in like manner the exact time of their daily employment. Both these time-books are required to be duly certified, as to each day's work, under the signature of a responsible officer or officers in each mill.

(Parl. Papers (1836) XLV, pp. 207-8.)

5th July, 1834.

The 18th clause of the Act requires that registers of the young persons employed in mills, distinguishing their sex, &c., should be kept by mill-owners, and copies taken for the use of the inspector, together with other information and details, as to the persons employed or labour performed in such mills; all of which mill-owners would find it difficult or troublesome to keep, and to furnish in the forms required: but a certificate book, kept on the plan proposed, will be as complete a register as can be desired of all the young hands so employed, specifying their names, age and sex; and, with the Time Books, Nos. 1 and 2, will furnish all the information required by the Act, with the least possible trouble and inconvenience to the mill-owner.

Where the preceding arrangements may not be concurred in, it will, however, be requisite for the owners of mills to prepare and keep the registers of children, and to furnish the other documents and information particularised in the aforesaid section.

Time books are required to be kept in the following form:—

TIME BOOK, No. 1.

Showing the Number of Hours the Mill has been Worked each Day.

Date	Day of Week	Engine starts in the Morning	Breakfast		Dinner		Tea		Engine stops at Night	Total of Hours	Time lost		Time gathed		Occasion of Time Lost	Signature of Person taking Time
			Engine stops	Engine starts	Engine stops	Engine starts	Engine stops	Engine starts			h.	m.	h.	m.		

TIME BOOK, NO. 2.

Showing the Time each Person worked during the Week.

Name	Age	Mon.	Tues.	Wed.	Thurs.	Fri.	Sat.	Total time during the week

(Signature of Overlooker or Manager, as to each day's work in each week).

The Time Book, No. 1, is intended to record the working of the engine, or moving power; and it follows, that if the engine or water-wheel, &c., only runs 12 hours in each day, the hands employed in such mill cannot work more than 12 hours: it is therefore, the only time-book necessary to be kept by the mill-owner, provided, at the same time, he employs no hands in his mill under 11 years of age.

But when children under 11 years of age are employed in any mill, it is requisite that an authentic record should be kept in the mill, to show that the labour of such children does not exceed the time limited by the Act, viz., nine hours in any one day, or 48 hours in any one week. For this purpose the names of such children, their ages, and the times worked in each day, must be recorded in the Time Book, No. 2.

For the same reason, should the moving power in any mill run more than 12 hours in any one day, the names of the young persons, between 11 and 18, should also be inserted in the Time Book, No. 2, that an authentic record may be similarly preserved of the period of labour of this class of persons not exceeding the time prescribed by the Act, viz., 12 hours in any one day, or 69 hours in any one week

(Parl. Papers (1836) XLV, pp. 210-11.)

19th July, 1834.

Complaints having been made, that on the changes of children and young persons, which occur in mills, many are employed without certificates, to the serious inconvenience and prejudice of those who, in this respect, strictly observe the existing law . . . it is hereby further required, that each overlooker or other proper officer in a mill be ordered to keep a book, to record the changes, as they occur, of children and young persons employed in mills, according to the following form:—

NUMBER OF THE ROOM, WHEELS OR LOOMS, OR CARDER'S, SPINNER'S

OR WEAVER'S NAME.

1.	2.	3.	4.	5.	6.
Date of Certificate or of Employment	Name of Children and Young Persons	When Certificate received	Age	Where worked last	Date of leaving present Employment

N.B.—Every carder, overlooker, or other proper officer in a mill, who has the superintendence of a room, or a given number of cards, or wheels, or looms, should be provided with one of these books, so ruled that each carder, spinner or weaver, having a certain number of children or young persons under him, may, with the said children, be included in a distinct or separate page. The observance of this form will be a convenience to the person keeping the book, who may thus, once in every week, easily and quickly ascertain the changes which occur.

(Parl. Papers (1836) XLV, p. 212.)

5th August, 1835.

In mills which work more than 12 hours per day the inspector has experienced much difficulty in ascertaining the exact time which young persons, under 18 years of age, have been actually employed therein, and numerous complaints having been made to the inspector by mill-owners working the regular time, that the overworkers employ their young hands longer in each day than is allowed by law, it is hereby ordered and required, that in all mills so working above 12 hours per day, a time-book, according to the subjoined form, be kept, to show the daily commencement and duration of each young person's labour, and the time of their final discharge from the mill at night.

TIME BOOK, NO. 3.

Showing the time each person between the age of 12 and 18 years has worked during the day.

N.B.—This book is ordered to be kept in all mills where the engine or water-wheel runs more than 12 hours per day.

Date	Name of Young Person	Begins Work in the Morning	Breakfast		Dinner		Tea		Stops at Night	Signature of Overlooker
			Stops	Begins Work	Stops	Begins Work	Stops	Begins Work		

(Parl. Papers (1836) XLV, pp. 212-13.)

Howell's Regulations.

(Issued prior to April, 1836).

I direct that an account of time lost and made up in virtue of sections 3, 4 and 5, and a register of all children and persons under 18 years of age employed in the mill or factory, their sex, age, hours of weekly attendance and of meals, and absence on account of sickness, be kept by you in such form as may be most convenient, provided the necessary information be distinctly shown.

(Parl. Papers (1836) XLV, p. 205).

Saunders' Regulations.

30th January, 1834.

A register to be kept in every mill or factory of all children and young persons subject to restricted hours of labour employed in such mill or factory, stating the sex, ages, hours of weekly attendance, and of absence from the mill on account of sickness.

The hours of work and of meals, appointed by the mill-owner or his agent, for all such children and young persons employed in the mill or factory, to be registered in like manner.

An account of time lost and made good, in virtue of sections 3, 4 and 5, to be entered in a register in such manner as to show the day of the month on which any stoppage occurs, the nature of the stoppage, and the time lost; also the days of the month and the hours in which the time so lost shall be made up.

The above registers may be kept in such form as shall be most convenient to the manufacturer, provided the information be distinctly shown.

(*Parl. Papers* (*1836*) *XLV, pp. 213-14.*)

Horner's Regulations.

30th January, 1834.

A register to be kept in every mill or factory of all children and young persons subject to restricted hours of labour, employed in such mill or factory, stating the sex, ages, hours of weekly attendance, and of absence from the mill on account of sickness.

An account of time lost and made good in virtue of sections 3, 4 and 5, to be entered in a register in such manner as to show the day of the month on which any stoppage occurs, the nature of the stoppage, and the time lost; also the days of the month and the hours in which the time so lost shall be made up.

The above registers may be kept in such form as shall be most convenient to the manufacturer, provided the information be distinctly shown.

(*Report: 21st July, 1834. Parl. Papers* (*1834*) *XLIII, p. 438.*)

[Horner took over the district of Rickards on 14th June, 1836. He was succeeded in the northern district by Stuart, who was appointed on 16th August, 1836.]

6th July, 1836.

A register of workers is hereby required to be kept in every factory, containing the christian, sirname, and age of every person employed, who is under 18 years of age, together with the dates of their coming to and ceasing to be employed at the factory; and the form to be as follows:—

Name	No. of Certificate	Age	Came			Left		
A. B.		12	July	1	1836	August	3	1836
C. D.		15	—	2	—	September	5	1837
E. F.		10	October	3	—	November	4	1836

The following Time-books are required to be kept; and any omission or irregularity in the keeping of these time-books, or of the register of workers will be considered a violation of the Act, and will be proceeded against accordingly.

TIME BOOK, No. 1.

Showing the Number of Hours the Mill has been Worked each Day.

Date	Day of Week	Moving Power Starts in the morning	Breakfast		Dinner		Tea		Moving Power Stops at Night	Total of Hours	Time lost		Time gained		Occasion of Time Lost	Signature of Person taking Time
			Moving Power Stops	Moving Power Starts	Moving Power Stops	Moving Power Starts	Moving Power Stops	Moving Power Starts			H.	M.	H.	M.		

TIME BOOK, No 2.

Required to be kept where Children between Nine and Thirteen Years of Age are employed, to show the Time each Child under Thirteen Years of Age has worked during the Day.

Date	Name of Child	Begins Work in the Morning	Breakfast		Dinner		Tea		Absence from Other Causes		Stops at Night	Signature of Overlooker
			Stops	Begins Work	Stops	Begins Work	Stops	Begins Work	Stops	Begins Work		

TIME BOOK, No. 3.

Required to be kept in all Mills where the Engine or Water-Wheel runs more than 12 Hours per day, to show the Times each Person between the Age of 13 and 18 Years has worked during the Day.

Date	Name of Young Person	Begins Work in the Morning	Breakfast		Dinner		Tea		Absence from Other Causes		Stops at Night	Signature of Overlooker
			Stops	Begins Work	Stops	Begins Work	Stops	Begins Work	Stops	Begins Work		

At the beginning of Time-Book, No. 1, the following particulars are hereby required to be entered:—

1. The name of the occupier or firm.

2. The name of the factory, the place, township, parish, and county, where it is situate, and the nearest post town.

3. The nature of the work carried on.

4. The propelling power, whether steam or water, and the extent of the same expressed in the amount of horse-power.

(Parl. Papers (1836) XLV, p. 215 ff.)

Inspectors' Minute.

    8th September, 1836.

The Inspectors examined the rules and regulations prepared last July and now enforced in Mr. Horner's district. They compared them with those in force in the districts of Messrs. Saunders and Howell. The only material difference they found in the several Regulations related to a Register of Workers and the form of Time Books, of which the Time Books Nos. 1, 2 and 3 ordered by Mr. Horner, were in force in his and Mr. Howell's district, but in neither of the other districts.

It was unanimously decided these Time Books should be discontinued. New forms applicable to all the districts were brought forward, considered, and provisionally agreed upon.

(Minutes, Vol. I, p. 2.)

The Uniform Code of Regulations.

4th October, 1836.

VIII.—REGISTERS REQUIRED TO BE KEPT.

At the beginning of the register of workers, and of the time-register, hereinafter required to be kept, the following particulars must be entered:

1. The name of the occupier or firm.

2. The name of the factory, the place, township, parish, and county where it is situate, and the nearest post town.

3. The nature of the work carried on.

4. The propelling power, whether steam or water, and the extent of the same expressed in the amount of horse-power.

5. The name of the principal manager; and if the manager be changed, the name of his successor, and the date of his entering upon the management, is hereby required to be recorded in the same place within three days.

IX.—REGISTER OF WORKERS.

A Register of Workers is hereby required to be kept in every factory, containing the christian and surname of every person employed in or about the factory, and subject to this Act, who is under 18 years of age, in the form following:—

No. in Certificate Book	Name (Example)	Age at date of Entry		Came			Left		
		Years	Months	Month	Day	Year	Month	Day	Year
34	Adams, John ...	10	9	Aug.	5	1835	May	2	1836
35	Andrews, Mary	11	7	Sept.	4	1836			
36	Arkwright, Richard	13	6	May	9	1836	Sept.	3	1836

N.B.—If the names in this Register of Workers be entered in alphabetical order, it will save the necessity of keeping the separate Alphabetical Index for the Certificate-Book required in Rule VI.

With regard to persons in employment at the time of publication of these regulations, it will be sufficient for the purpose of this order if they be expressed as having come at the date hereof. New workers must be entered at the respective dates of their first doing any kind of work in the factory.

X.—TIME-REGISTERS.

A Time-Register is hereby required to be kept in every factory according to the instructions and in the precise forms hereinafter set forth, containing a record of the hours of work of all persons under 18 years of age employed in the factory, and subject to this Act; and of the times allowed for meals to all persons restricted to 12 hours' work daily.

The holidays and half-holidays required by this Act to be given in the course of the year are hereby ordered to be recorded together in a distinct place in the Time-Register.

The dates when the mill is limewashed and whitewashed, and the date of any exemption from limewashing and whitewashing granted by the Inspector, are hereby required to be recorded in a distinct place in the Time-Register.

When the mill-occupier intends to recover all or any part of the time which has been lost from either of the causes enumerated in sections 3, 4, or 5 of this Act, a record of the same must be kept in the manner hereinafter set forth.

In all the declarations in the Time-Register the day of the month and the year of the date must be inserted in WORDS, and not in figures; and in all cases where the occupier of a factory is required to sign a declaration or statement it will be sufficient in his absence if the principal manager or agent sign by his authority.

INSTRUCTIONS AND EXAMPLE for Registering the Hours of Labour and Meals of Young Persons between Thirteen and Eighteen Years of Age.

In a distinct page of the Time-Register the following declaration shall be made and signed by the mill-occupier:—

Declaration of the Hours of Work, and of the Times allowed for Meals, for all the Young Persons who are above Thirteen and under Eighteen Years of Age, employed in this Factory, and subject to restricted Hours of Labour.

I (or We) hereby declare that the hours of work and the time allowed for meals for all the young persons who are above 13 and under 18 years of age, employed in this factory, and subject to restricted hours of labour, shall be as follows, from this date, *viz.*—the   day of   183 , until a change of their hours of work shall be entered under a subsequent date, always excepting those occasions when time lost shall be recovered conformably with the provisions of the Factories Regulation Act, and which deviations from the following regular hours of work shall appear in the " REGISTER OF TIME LOST AND RECOVERED," kept for this factory, under the respective dates.

HOURS OF WORK (Example)							TIME ALLOWED FOR MEALS (Example)	
On Mon., Tues., Wed., Thurs., and Fri.	H.	M.	On Saturday	H.	M.		On Mon., Tu., Wed. Th. & Fri.	On Saturday
From 6 to 8 a.m.	2	—	From 6 to 8 a.m.	2	—	Breakfast	8 to 8½	8 to 8½
8½ to 12	3	30	8½ to 12	3	30	Dinner	12 to 1	12 to 1
1 to 4 p.m.	3	—	1 to 4½	3	30	Tea	4 to 4½	None
4½ to 8	3	30						
Total ...	12	—	Total ...	9	—			

....*Occupier.*

N.B.—Whenever a change of hours shall take place, a new declaration in the same words, with a statement of the new hours, in a similar form to that above, must be entered and signed.

INSTRUCTIONS AND EXAMPLE for Registering the Hours of Labour of Children under Thirteen Years of Age.

In a distinct page of the Time-Register the following declaration shall be made and signed by the mill-occupier:—

Declaration of the Hours of Work for all the Children under Thirteen Years of Age employed in this Factory.

I (or We) hereby declare,

1.—That this book shall contain the name of every child under 13 years of age, who shall be employed in or about this factory subsequent to this date, *viz.,* the   day of   , 183 .

2.—That no one of the said children shall work for a longer time than* hours in the week, nor more than* in any one day, except on occasions of making up lost time; which deviations from the regular hours of work of the factory shall appear in the "REGISTER OF TIME LOST AND RECOVERED" kept for this factory.

> * 48 or 9 in cotton, woollen, worsted, hemp, flax or linen mills.
> 60 or 10 in silk mills.

3.—That the said children shall be employed in this factory at the several periods of the day affixed to the last entry of each of their respective names and numbers of reference in this book, until a change of hours shall take place, when their names and daily periods of employment shall be entered anew in this book, under a subsequent number of reference and date; or until they shall have ceased to be employed in this factory as children, from their having completed their thirteenth year, or shall have been discharged from our employment.

....*Occupier.*

FORM IN WHICH THE REGISTER OF CHILDREN'S WORK IS TO BE KEPT.

Date M'th	Dy	Names of Children with explanation of the days of the week to which their hours of work refer	Morn. From To	Foren'n From To	Aft'n'n From To	Even'g From To	T't'l H.	M'th	Dy	Year	
183 6		*(Examples)*									
July	1	George Smith — Every	6 to 8	8½ to 10	3 to 4	4½ to 8	8	Dec.	8	1836	D
,,	,,	Mary Smith — Day	Ditto	Ditto	Ditto	Ditto	8	Aug.	5	,,	7
,,	,,	Robert King } in the	6 to 8	8½ to 12	1 to 3½		8	Nov.	3	,,	C
,,	,,	Charles Scott — Week	Ditto	Ditto	Ditto		8	Sept.	3	,,	8
,,	,,	Mary Turner } Every day		10 to 12	1 to 4	4½ to 8	8½				
		David Hart } except Saturday		Ditto	Ditto	Ditto	8½				
		The two children immediately preceding } Sat.		Ditto	Ditto		5				
Aug.	5	Mary Smith—Except Sat.		10 to 12	1 to 4	4½ to 8	8½				
		Ditto —On Sat.		Ditto	1 to 4		5				
Sept.	3	Charles Scott—Every day	6 to 8	8½ to 10	3 to 4	4½ to 8	8				

Mills where all children are employed regularly at the same hours, one entry, as follows, will be sufficient until a change takes place:—

Date M'th	Dy		Morn. From To	Foren'n From To	Aft'n'n From To	Even'g From To	T't'l H.	M'th	Dy	Year
July	1	All the children under 13 years of age entered in the Register of Workers are employed each day thus:—								
July	1	Ditto ditto	6 to 8 or, as in Silk Mills	8½ to 10 / 8½ to 12	3 to 4 / 1 to 4	4½ to 8 / 4½ to 8	8 / 10			

N.B.—The number in the last column indicates the new number of reference to be prefixed to the subsequent entry of the name, when the hours of work of the child have been changed; the letter C indicates that the thirteenth year has been completed; the letter D indicates that the child has been discharged.

INSTRUCTIONS AND FORM for Registering Time Lost and Recovered.

In a distinct page of the Time-Register the following declaration shall be made and signed by the mill-occupier:—

I (or We) hereby declare that this book shall contain a true account of all time which shall have been lost from all or either of the causes enumerated in the 3rd, 4th, and 5th sections of the Factories Regulation Act, with the date of the occurrence, and also the time of the day, at any time subsequent to this date, *viz.*, the day of   , 183 ; provided we shall intend to recover any part of the said time so lost; and further, that this book shall also contain a true account of all dates and periods of the day or night when the said lost time shall be in part or in whole recovered, and upon which days the children and young persons employed in this factory shall have worked for a longer time than the regular hours of work set forth in the declaration made by us respecting the employment of children and young persons.

...........................*Occupier.*

	Time lost from some one of the Causes enumerated in Section —					Time recovered under the authority of Section —				
Date	Cause of Loss	Time of day when lost	Amount lost		Explanatory Remarks	Date	Time of day when recovered	Amount recovered		Explanatory Remarks
			H.	M.				H.	M.	

In those cases where a part only of the machinery has been stopped, it will be necessary to give such an explanation, in the column headed "Explanatory Remarks," both as to the time lost and time recovered, as will show that only those young persons, etc., who did lose time were employed in recovering it.

N.B.—As lost time may be recovered under different conditions, according to the cause of loss, the entry must be made in a separate page or folio for each of the three sections under the authority of which the lost time shall be recovered.

If it should be deemed more convenient to keep the record of time lost and recovered in a separate book from the other register, it may be done, and must then be called " Time-Register, No. II."

Joint Report.

24th January, 1837.

We are induced to believe that the rules and regulations drawn up by us last October, and approved of by your Lordship, have tended very materially to render observance to the Law much more easy than it was before, by their having greatly diminished the trouble that attended the Time Books formerly required to be kept in order to shew the hours when the Children and Young Persons are employed.

(*Minutes, Vol. I, p. 55.*)

Factories Regulation Act, 1844. 7 & 8 Vict., c. 15.

SCHEDULE (B).

REGISTERS.

FORM FOR THE REGISTER OF YOUNG PERSONS.

List of Young Persons employed in this Factory.

No. of Reference to Age Certificate Book	NAMES		Date of first day of being Employed or Re-employed			When any Person ceases to be employed insert opposite the name the word "Left"; and when any Person completes his Eighteenth Year of Age, the word "Eighteen"
	Surname	Christian Name	Month	Day	Year	

This Register shall contain the Names of every Young Person employed in the Factory, to be entered successively when engaged to work, whether for the first time, or, after having left, when re-engaged to work.

At the beginning of this Register shall be inserted:—

1. The Name of the Occupier or Firm.

2. The Name of the Factory, the Place, Township, Parish, and County where it is situated, and the Post Office to which the Occupier desires his letters to be directed.

3. The Nature of the work carried on.

4. The Nature of the Moving Power, the whole Amount of Horse Power of the Steam Engine or Water-wheel, and also the Amount of Horse Power employed by the Occupier or Firm.

5. The Clock by which the Employment of the Workers in the Factory is regulated.

Every Alteration in any of the above Particulars shall be inserted immediately after the Alteration shall have been made.

6. The Holidays and Half Holidays which shall have been given in conformity with this Act shall be recorded together in a distinct Place in the Register.

7. The Dates when the whole of the Factory, if done at one Time, and the several Parts if done at different Times, shall have been limewashed or painted in Oil, and, when painted in Oil, the Dates of their having been washed as required by this Act, and the Names and Residences of the Persons by whom the Factory was limewashed or painted in Oil, shall be recorded in a distinct Place in this Register within Six Days after they have been so limewashed, painted, or washed; and this Declaration of the Times of limewashing, painting, and washing shall be signed by the Mill Occupier or his principal Agent.

8. The Visits of the certifying Surgeon to the Factory shall be recorded in this Register in the manner following:—

Date of Visit	Number of Persons presented for Examination	Number of Certificates granted	Signature of Surgeon

FORM FOR THE REGISTER OF CHILDREN.

To be kept in those Factories only where Children under Thirteen Years of Age are employed.

Names of the Children employed in this Factory before Twelve o'Clock at Noon, or the Morning Set.

No. of Reference to Age Certificate Book	NAMES		Date of first day of Employment or Re-employment			When any Child ceases to be employed, insert opposite its name the word "Left"; or if transferred to the Afternoon Set, the word "Changed"; or the words "Young Person," when a child completes its Thirteenth Year
	Surname	Christian Name	Month	Day	Year	

Names of the Children employed in this Factory after One o'Clock in the Afternoon, or the Afternoon Set.

No. of Reference to Age Certificate Book	NAMES		Date of first day of Employment or Re-employment			When any Child ceases to be employed, insert opposite its name the word "Left"; or if transferred to the Morning Set, the word "Changed"; or the words "Young Person" when a child completes its Thirteenth Year
	Surname	Christian Name	Month	Day	Year	

This Register shall contain the Names of every Child under Thirteen Years of Age employed in the Factory, to be entered successively when engaged to work, whether for the first time, or, after having left, when re-engaged to work.

If any Child be removed from the Morning Set to the Afternoon Set, or vice versâ, the Name of such Child must be entered as a new Comer in the Register for the Set to which it is removed, and the Number of its Certificate of Age must be placed against its Name, but no new Certificate shall be required for such Child.

If the Mill Occupier desires to change the Time of working of the Two entire sets of Children at stated Periods, (as for instance) to make a Change every Month, so that the Children who worked in the Morning one Month shall work in the Afternoon of the next Month, and vice versâ for the other Children, alternately throughout the Year, it will not be necessary to enter the names of the Children anew, but the Mill Occupier or his Agent shall only be required to make and sign the following Declaration, in addition to the other Details hereinbefore required:—

1. The Children entered in this Register as belonging to the Morning Set work in this Factory before Twelve o'Clock, and not after One o'Clock on and after the First Monday of the months of—

January, March, May, July, September, and November; and after One o'Clock, and not before Twelve o'Clock, on and after the First Monday of the Months of—

February, April, June, August, October, and December.

2. The Children entered in this Register as belonging to the Afternoon Set work in this Factory after One o'Clock, and not before Twelve o'Clock, on and after the First Monday of the Months of—

January, March, May, July, September, and November; and before Twelve o'Clock, and not after One o'Clock, on and after the First Monday of the Months of—

February, April, June, August, October, and December.

Signature of ....*Occupier or Agent.*

When a Change in the Time of Working of the Two entire Sets of Children is made at other stated Periods allowed by this Act the necessary Alterations shall be made in the above Declaration, to the Satisfaction of the Inspector or Sub-Inspector of the District.

In any Silk Factory in which Children above Eleven Years of Age are employed more than Seven Hours in any One Day a Register of the Names of such Children shall be kept in the above Form, distinct from the Register of the Names of the Children who are employed in Morning and Afternoon Sets.

In all Mills where more than Twenty Children or Young Persons are employed an Alphabetical Index shall be kept, according to the first Letter of the Surname, of the Names of all the Children and Young Persons employed in the Factory, adding to each Name the Number of the last Certificate under which the Age of the Child or Young Person is employed, or if more than Sixteen Years of Age, the Letters XVI.

SCHEDULE (C).

NOTICES TO BE FIXED UP IN THE FACTORY.

FORM FOR THE NOTICE to be fixed up of the Names and Addresses of the Inspector and Sub-Inspector, the certifying Surgeon, the Clock for regulating the Factory, and the Hours of Work of all Young Persons and Females employed in the Factory

Name and Address of the Inspector of the District...........................

Name and Address of the Sub-Inspector of the District......................

Name and Address of the Surgeon who grants
Certificates of Age for the Factory ....

Clock by which the Hours of Work are regulated..............................

THE HOURS OF WORK OF ALL YOUNG PERSONS AND FEMALES ABOVE EIGHTEEN YEARS OF AGE EMPLOYED IN THIS FACTORY.

Days of Week	Morning		Forenoon		Afternoon		Evening		Total Hours
	From	To	From	To	From	To	From	To	

....

Signature of the Occupier of the Factory or his Agent.

FORM FOR THE NOTICE TO BE FIXED UP OF THE TIMES ALLOWED FOR MEALS.

The Times allowed for Meals in this Factory

Days of the Week	Breakfast		Dinner		Tea	
	From	To	From	To	From	To

....

Signature of the Occupier of the Factory or his Agent.

These Notices of the regular Hours of Work fixed up in a Factory are not required to be altered when Young Persons are only employed at other Hours for the Recovery of lost Time as authorized by this Act, provided the Notice required to be fixed up when recovering lost Time be fixed up, and provided on such Notice it is stated at what Time of the Day it is intended to recover the Time so lost.

FORM OF THE NOTICE to be fixed up when the Occupier of the Factory intends to recover all or any Part of the Time which has been lost by the Stoppage of the Machinery in the Factory, as allowed by the Act.

ACCOUNT OF TIME LOST AND RECOVERED

	TIME LOST					TIME RECOVERED			
Date	Cause of Loss	Time of day when lost	Amount lost		Explanatory Remarks	Date	Time of day when recovered	Amount recov'r'd		Explanatory Remarks
			H.	M.				H.	M.	

....
Signature of the Occupier of the Factory or his Agent.

No lost Time is required to be entered except such as it may be intended to recover.

The Entries of all the Details in this Notice relating to any Time lost or recovered shall be made in conformity with the Provisions of the Act.

FORM OF THE NOTICE to be fixed up when Time has been lost by partial Stoppage of the machinery by Drought or Floods, and is intended to be recovered during the following Night.

NOTICE OF TIME LOST AND RECOVERED

Description of the Room where the Stoppage took place and of the Machinery stopped	TIME LOST				Signature of the Person taking Time	TIME RECOVERED			
	Time of the Day when the Stoppage took place	Amount of Time lost				Time of the Night when the young Persons are employed	Amount of Time recovered		
		Hrs.	Mins.					Hrs.	Mins.

NAMES OF THE FEMALES AND YOUNG PERSONS WHO HAVE LOST TIME BY THE STOPPAGE OF THE MACHINERY AT THE DATES AFFIXED.

Date when time was lost	Surname	Christian Name

The Entries of Time lost, and of the Names of the Females and Young Persons who have lost Time, shall be made in these Notices before any Part of the Time can be recovered.

All Notices of Time lost and recovered, except when they are kept hung up in the Factory, as required by this Act, shall be preserved in a Book in the Order of their respective Dates, and be open for the Examination of any Inspector or Sub-Inspector; and all such Notices shall be kept for Six Calendar Months after the lost Time entered therein shall have been recovered.

V.—SURGICAL AND SCHOOL CERTIFICATES.

The form of the Surgical Certificate of Age prescribed by the Act of 1833 is printed on page 123.

The Certificate proposed in the Bill of 1838 was as follows:—

I [*Name and Place of Residence*], Inspecting Surgeon, appointed on the [*Date of Appointment*], by [*Name of the appointing Inspector*], one of the Inspectors of Factories, do hereby certify, That the Child hereinafter described, has been personally examined by me, on the day and year underwritten, for the alleged purpose of enabling him [*or her*] to be employed as a Child by [*here insert the Name of the Factory or Description of the Employer*], and that he [*or she*] is of the ordinary size, strength, and appearance of a boy [*or girl*] of at least [*here insert the least age to which this description applies, which must not be less than Nine*] years of age, and that I believe him [*or her*] to be at least [*here insert the same age*] years of age.

Dated this   day of   18   .

(Signed) *A.B.*,

Inspecting Surgeon.

Name and Surname	Sex	Place of Residence	Barefoot Height		Colour of Eyes	Colour of Hair
			Feet	Inches		

The form adopted in the Act of 1844 was as follows:—

FACTORIES REGULATION ACT, 1844.

SCHEDULE (A).

CERTIFICATES

(*To be written or printed on White Paper.*)

No.......... CERTIFICATE OF AGE for a Child to be employed in the Factory of   situated at   in   .

I,   of   duly appointed a certifying Surgeon, do hereby certify, That   Son [*or Daughter*] of   and   residing in   has been personally examined by me this   Day of   One thousand eight hundred and   and that the said Child has the ordinary Strength and Appearance of a Child of at least Eight Years of Age, and that I believe the real Age of the said Child to be at least Eight Years; and that the said Child is not incapacitated, by Disease or bodily Infirmity, from working daily in the above-named Factory for the Time allowed by this Act.

(Signed).................................Certifying Surgeon.

The Form of Surgical Certificate to be given to a Child who has obtained a Certificate of real Age shall be the same as above, omitting the Words " and that the said Child has the ordinary Strength and Appearance of a Child of at least Eight Years of Age, and that I believe the real Age of the said Child to be at least Eight Years," and substituting these Words in their Place: ": and that a Certificate of the Birth [or Baptism] of the said Child has been produced to me in the Form required by this Act, proving that the real Age of such Child is at least Eight Years."

The Form of Surgical Certificate to be given to Children employed in Silk Mills in proof that a Child is Eleven Years of Age shall be the same as the above, substituting the Word " Eleven " for the Word " Eight."

(*To be written or printed on Coloured Paper.*)

No............ CERTIFICATE OF AGE for a Young Person to be employed in the Factory of   situated at   in   .

I,   of   duly appointed a certifying Surgeon, do hereby certify, That   Son [or Daughter] of and   residing in   has been personally examined by me this   Day of   One thousand eight hundred and   and that the said Young Person has the ordinary Strength and Appearance of a Young Person of at least Thirteen Years of Age, and that I believe the real Age of the said Young Person to be at least Thirteen Years; and that the said Young Person is not incapacitated, by Disease or bodily Infirmity, from working daily in the above-named Factory for the Time allowed by this Act.

(*Signed*) ....*Certifying Surgeon.*

The Form of Surgical Certificate to be given to a Young Person who has obtained a Certificate of real Age shall be the same as above, omitting the Words, " and that the said Young Person has the ordinary Strength and Appearance of a Young Person of at least Thirteen Years of Age, and that I believe the real Age of the said Young Person to be at least Thirteen Years," and substituting these Words in their place, " and that a Certificate of the Birth [or Baptism] of the said Young Person has been produced to me in the Form required by this Act, proving that the real Age of such Young Person is at least Thirteen Years."

The Form of Surgical Certificate to be given in either case by any Practitioner who is not a certifying Surgeon must be the same as the corresponding Form above given, omitting the Words " duly appointed certifying Surgeon," and substituting the Words " duly authorized by the University [or College, *or other public Body having authority in that behalf*] of   to practice Surgery [or Medicine]," and making the following Addition, which must be signed by a Justice of the Peace or Burgh Magistrate:—

The Child [or Young Person] named in the above-written Certificate has been this Day brought before me; and the Appearance of the said Child [or Young Person] agrees with the Description therein given; and I believe the real Age of the said Child [or Young Person] to be at least [*here insert the Word " Eight" or " Eleven" in the case of a Child, or " Thirteen" in the case of a Young Person*] years; and I declare that I have no beneficial Interest in and am not the Occupier of any Factory; and that I am not the Father, Son, or Brother of the Occupier of any Factory.

Dated this   day of   One thousand eight hundred and   .

(*Signed*)................................*C.D., Justice,*
[or *Burgh Magistrate.*]

CERTIFICATE REFUSED.

I,   of   duly appointed a certifying Surgeon, do hereby declare, That   Son [*or* Daughter] of   residing in   has been personally examined by me this   day of   One thousand eight hundred and   and that in my Opinion the said [Child *or* Young Person] has not the ordinary Strength and Appearance [of a Child of at least Eight Years of age (*or* of a Young Person of at least Thirteen Years of age) or (*or* and) is incapacitated by Disease and bodily Infirmity from working daily in a Factory for the Time allowed by this Act].

(*Signed*)................................*Certifying Surgeon*.

N.B.—The Words within Brackets shall be in the Handwriting of the certifying Surgeon, who shall insert the Reason of his Refusal, to be either on account of deficient Age or bodily Infirmity, or both, as the case may be.

SCHOOL CERTIFICATE.

I hereby certify, That the under-mentioned Child [*or* Children] employed in the Factory of   situated in   has [*or* have] attended the School kept by me at   for the Number of Hours and at the Time on each Day specified in the Columns opposite to his [her *or* their] Name [*or* Names] during the Week ending on Saturday the   Day of   One thousand eight hundred and   , and that the Causes of Absence stated are true, to the best of my Belief.

Name of Child	Monday		Tuesday		Wednesday		Thursday		Friday		Causes of Absence
	Time		Time		Time		Time		Time		
	From	To	From	To	From	To	From	To	From	To	

(*Signed*) ....*Schoolmaster* [*or* *Schoolmistress*].

the   Day of   18   .

Under the Column headed " Time " the Periods of the Day that each Child attends school shall be stated, as thus, from Nine to Twelve, or from Two to Five, or any other Time, as the case may be; and all the Children employed in the same Factory who attend School before One of the Clock in the Afternoon shall be entered together, distinct from those who attend School after One of the Clock.

The Time when each Child attends School shall be stated in the Column for each Day, in the Handwriting of the Schoolmaster, and no Certificate shall be valid unless the Schoolmaster shall, in his own handwriting, subscribe to it his Christian and Surname in full.

In the case of any Child who has been absent from School, the Letter (A) shall be inserted under the Day or Days of Absence, and the Cause of Absence shall be inserted in the Column headed "Causes of Absence," so far as the same can be ascertained; and when any Day has been a Holiday at the School the Word "Holiday" shall be entered in the Column of the Day.

All School Certificates, if given on loose Sheets, shall, as soon as received, be fixed in a Book, to be called "The School Certificate Book," in the Order of their respective Dates. Copies of the above Forms may be bound together in a Book for each Factory.

VI.—RE-ALLOCATION OF THE INSPECTORS' DISTRICTS.

31st March, 1837.   Quarterly Report.

Horner suggested that consideration should be given to the problems arising from the unequal distribution of districts.

(Parl. Papers (1838) XXVIII, p. 84.)

20th July, 1837.   S. M. Phillips to Horner.

The Home Office instructed Horner that in future he was to visit factories in that part of England hitherto in Stuart's district.

(H.O. 87 (1) p. 83.)

22nd July, 1837.   Inspectors' Minute.

Mr. Horner reported to his colleagues that he had received an order to take over the four northern counties of England, and that he had informed Mr. Phillips that it would be impossible for him to do this.

It was proposed by Mr. Saunders that a plan should be submitted to Lord John Russell, by which in his opinion, a more equitable division of the country might be made into Superintendencies.

Mr. Phillips, Mr. Howell and Mr. Saunders to confer on the best method of relieving Mr. Horner of a portion of his district.

(Minutes, Vol. I, pp. 75-77.)

24th July, 1837.   Inspectors' Minute.

Mr. Horner and Mr. Saunders submitted the following plan: Mr. Horner gives up to Mr. Saunders the greater part of the mills in the West Riding of Yorkshire partly in the superintendency of Mr. Baker, and partly in that of Mr. Bates amounting to 900 mills.

He gives up to Mr. Howell the mills under his inspection in North Wales, Staffordshire, part of Derbyshire and the greater part of Cheshire amounting to about 260 mills.

Mr. Horner receives from Mr. Stuart about 60 mills in Northumberland, Durham, Cumberland and Westmorland. Mr. Horner's district will therefore stand as follows, viz.: —

he has at present about		2,780
and receives from Mr. Stuart		60
making a total of		2,840
and gives up to Mr. Saunders 980, to Mr. Howell 260		1,240
	leaving ...	1,600

which with his present number of five Superintendents he hopes to be able to manage to inspect efficiently.

Mr. Saunders gives up to Mr. Howell Cornwall, Devonshire, Somersetshire and a few mills in each of the counties of Wilts, Stafford and Derby, amounting to about 140 mills. He receives 980 from Mr. Horner as above, and his district will stand thus: —

He has at present about 300 and receives 980=1,280 and gives up 140 leaving 1,140 which Mr. Saunders believes he will be able to inspect efficiently with four Superintendents.

Mr. Howell receives from Mr. Horner 260 mills as above, and from Mr. Saunders 140. His district will stand thus—he has at present 500, he receives from Mr. Horner 260 and from Mr. Saunders 140=900. He gives up to Mr. Stuart in the southern half of Ireland about 50, leaving 850.

Mr. Stuart has at present about 600 mills and his increase in Ireland is nearly balanced by what he gives up in England.

The Inspectorships will stand thus:—

Mr. Horner, 1,600 mills
with 5 Superintendents

- Mr. Heathcote
- Mr. Bates
- Mr. Ewings
- Mr. Hudson
- Mr. Webster

Mr. Saunders, 1,140 mills
with 4 Superintendents

- Mr. Baker
- Mr. Bury
- Mr. Marshall
- Mr. Trimmer

Mr. Howell, 850 mills
with 3 Superintendents

- Mr. Kent
- Mr. Hickes
- Mr. Browne

Mr. Stuart, 600 mills

- Mr. James
- Mr. Beale
- Mr.   (to be appointed)

to whom an additional Superintendent must be appointed who is to have charge of the whole of Ireland and to be resident.

(Minutes, Vol. I, pp. 84-86).

[On 27th July, 1837, Howell wrote to his colleagues dissenting from this plan, and accordingly the four Inspectors met on 1st August, 1837, when they agreed to a scheme which was sent to the Home Office on 3rd August, 1837.]

3rd August, 1837. Inspectors' Minute.

Memorandum of a Plan by the Factory Inspectors for a new division of their districts in compliance with the instructions of Lord J. Russell, proceeding upon the assumption that the whole of Scotland and the whole of Ireland are to be assigned to one Inspector and that an additional Superintendent is to be appointed and to constantly reside in Ireland.

Mr. Stuart will have about 500 mills in Scotland with his Superintendents Mr. James and Mr. Beale. He will have about 100 mills in Ireland with the Superintendent to be appointed, making together about 600 mills in his Inspectorate.

Mr. Horner receives from Mr. Stuart the mills in the 4 northern counties of England and the North Eastern part of Yorkshire which are under his inspection at present together with the Superintendent who has that part of Mr. Stuart's district under his charge. He gives up nearly all the mills in the West Riding of Yorkshire and parts of Derbyshire and Staffordshire to Mr. Saunders, together with his Superintendents Mr. Baker and Mr. Bates, amounting together to 1,018 mills.

Mr. Horner gives up to Mr. Howell all the mills in North Wales and nearly all the mills in Cheshire and a part of Derbyshire and Staffordshire which are under his inspection, amounting together to 436 mills. He will then have 1,484 mills left under his inspection with 4 Superintendents, viz., Mr. Heathcote, Mr. Ewings, Mr. Hudson, recently appointed to his District in the room of Mr. Trimmer but who has not yet acted, and Mr. Webster, transferred to him by Mr. Stuart together with his mills in the north of England. Mr. Webster has not yet acted in that Division having been only recently transferred to Mr. Stuart from the District of Mr. Howell.

Mr. Saunders gives up to Mr. Howell all the mills in Cornwall, Devon, Dorset, Somerset and part of Wilts with his Superintendent Mr. Kent amounting to about 125 mills. He receives from Mr. Horner as above. Thus he will have 1,193 mills under his inspection with four Superintendents, viz., Mr. Bury and Mr. Marshall and Mr. Baker and Mr. Bates transferred to him from Mr. Horner's District.

Mr. Howell gives up about 55 mills in the south of Ireland to Mr. Stuart, and receives from Mr. Horner 436, and from Mr. Saunders 125. He will thus have about 1,006 mills under his inspection with four Superintendents, viz.:—

    Mr. Hicks and Mr. Brown.
    Mr. Kent, transferred to him from Mr. Saunders' district and
    Mr. Trimmer, transferred to him from Mr. Horner's ditsrict.

The four Inspectorships are at present thus arranged, viz:—

    Mr. Horner, about 2,860 mills with 5 Superintendents
    Mr. Howell   „   500   „   „ 3   „
    Mr. Saunders „   300   „   „ 3   „
    Mr. Stuart   „   600   „   „ 3   „

By the arrangement now proposed they will stand thus:—

    Mr. Horner   1,484 mills with 4 Superintendents
    Mr. Saunders 1,193   „   „ 4   „
    Mr. Howell 1,006   „   „ 4   „
    Mr. Stuart   600   „   „ 3   „

(Minutes, Vol. I, pp. 90-93).

8th August, 1837. S. M. Phillips to the Inspectors.

Lord John Russell having considered the plan proposed by you for a new division of your several Districts—I am directed by His Lordship to inform you that he approves of the arrangements which you have submitted to him, and that directions have been given for transferring Mr. Hudson to Mr. Stewart's District with the view to his being stationed as Resident Superintendent in Ireland.

(H.O. 87 (I), p. 88).

VII.—HORNER'S INSTRUCTIONS TO HIS SUPERINTENDENTS AUGUST, 1837.

Sect. 1.— VISIT TO THE FACTORIES.

I.   Continue the practice, hitherto followed by the superintendents in all the inspectorships, of visiting the interior of factories, unless admittance be refused.

II.   Report to the inspector every case where you are refused admittance to the interior of the factory, and the reason assigned.

III.   At each visit of inspection inquire into the observance of all the enactments of the law, and especially of those respecting the restricted ages of children and young persons, and their hours of work, the meal hours, and the school attendance of the children; inquire also as to the observance of the rules and regulations of the inspectors, ascertaining as follows: —

1.   If the register of workers, and the time-register, ordered by the regulations of the inspectors of the 4th October, 1836, either in the authorized printed forms, or in manuscript according to those forms, be kept.

2.   As regards the Register of Workers.

(a)   If the blanks for the name of the occupier, etc., be filled up.

(b)   If the names of all the workers under 18 years of age be entered, with a number of reference to the certificate book affixed to each name, and other particulars required.

(c)   If the names be not entered in alphabetical order, ascertain if there be an alphabetical index to the certificate book.

3.   As regards the Certificate Book.

(a)   Send for some of the children and young persons who have been taken into employment since your former visit, and see whether their strength and appearance justify the ages mentioned in the certificates. If they do not, call the attention of the surgeon to the cases. If the surgeon appear to you to be in the habit of granting certificates improperly, bring the subject under the notice of the Inspector.

(b)   Ascertain if the certificates of age be fixed in a book in the order of their dates, or of their having been received; and if a number, in a consecutive series, be affixed to each certificate.

(c)   See that the certificate is worded in conformity with the opinion of the Crown lawyers.*

(d)   If the certificates have been granted by a surgeon whose name and address is fixed up in the mill.

(e)   If the certificates be countersigned by a magistrate within three months of their dates.

---

* The certificate for children under 13 years of age must not express the age in any other words than these: "of at least nine," or "exceeding nine," according to the fact.
When, in default of a regular baptismal certificate, a medical certificate is got for a young person between 13 and 18 years of age, it must not express the age in any other words than these: "above thirteen."

4. As regards the Time Register.

(a) If the blanks for the name of the occupier, etc., be filled up.

(b) If the holidays which have been given be entered.

(c) If the dates of whitewashing be entered, or the date of the letter of exemption (if any), with the term granted.

(d) If the declaration of the hours of work, for young persons between 13 and 18, be made, signed, and dated as required; and if the hours of work at the time of the visit and those fixed up in the mill correspond with the declaration.

(e) If children under 13 be employed, if the declaration of their hours of work be made, signed, and dated as required, and if the periods of the day when they work be entered as required.

(f) If lost time has been made up, if the entry thereof has been made and in the proper place, and if the notice thereof required by Regulation II has been fixed up.

5. As regards School Certificates.

(a) If there be a school certificate book, and if not, if the school vouchers on separate slips of paper be pasted into a book in the order of their dates.

(b) If there be a certificate of school attendance for every child under 13 employed.

(c) Inquire what is done when the teacher reports absences without cause allowed; what steps, short of dismissal, have been resorted to to enforce school attendance.

(d) Take every opportunity of seeing the teachers, and impress upon them the necessity of requiring daily attendance for at least two hours; and point out to them the danger they run if they give a certificate setting forth what is untrue.

6. In going through the Factory.

(a) Take down in your memorandum book the names and ages of some of the children and young persons, and afterwards examine if they are entered in the register of workers, and if they have certificates of age.

(b) In like manner ask some of the workers as to the hours of work, of meals, and of school attendance, and ascertain whether their statements correspond with the entries in the books, etc.

(c) If making up lost time, inquire as to the cause of the loss, the length of the stoppage, the daily extra time worked, and then ascertain whether these correspond with the entries in the time-register.

7. If the abstract of the Act, and the rules and regulations of the inspectors, in a clean legible state, be fixed upon a moveable board, be signed as required, and be hung up in a conspicuous part of the mill, accessible to all the workers.

8. If the hours of work, the times for meals, and the name and address of the certifying surgeon be fixed up in distinctly legible characters, in a conspicuous part of the mill, accessible to all the workers.

9. Take a special note of having seen the abstract of the Act, and the rules and regulations of the inspectors in the possession of the mill-occupier, or on the premises, so as to be able to swear to that fact in case of need.

If the mill-occupier states that he has not received a copy, deliver one to him, if you have a copy with you; but if not, on your return home send one to the certifying surgeon, and request him to deliver it himself at the mill, and to keep a note of the date of such delivery.

IV. At each visit of inspection take a note of the number of children under 13 years of age employed, males and females; if they work by relays; if they do so, whether by a double set or by three for two, or by irregular changes; also if the school be or be not upon the premises.

V. If all the enactments of the law, and the regulations of the inspectors be duly observed, the letter R. in your memorandum book against the name of the mill-occupier, will be a sufficient record of your observations; but each description of irregularity must be noted down.

VI. At each visit of inspection have with you a note of the state of the mill at the preceding visit.

VII. Enter in the blank page at the beginning of the register of workers in each mill, or in any other convenient place in it, or in the time-register, the date of each visit; thus,—" Mill visited by the Superintendent, 5th January, 1837, 10th May, 1837, 3d September, 1837."

Sect. 2.—PROSECUTION OF OFFENCES.

I. Where irregularities are met with, it is but justice to be slow in imputing them to wilful or gross negligence; nevertheless, the length of time which has elapsed since the Act came into operation, the explanations which have been given, and the numerous prosecutions which have taken place and have been reported, remove all reasonable excuse for a plea of ignorance of the law.

Show, by a close examination, that obedience to the Act, and compliance with the regulations of the inspectors, will be required; but endeavour, as much as possible, to effect this by explanation, respectful admonition, and warning: make it evident that when you find things wrong, you do so with regret, and that the punishments of the law will be employed only against wilful and obstinate offenders.

When you discover offences which appear to you to deserve the penalties of the law, represent them to the mill-occupier in person, or by letter if you cannot see him, or if he be non-resident, to his acting manager, in order that you may hear what can be said in mitigation, and to satisfy yourself whether the offences can be fairly considered as unintentional oversights, or are clear cases either of wilful disobedience of the law, or of gross and culpable negligence.

II. When you have found things wrong, take an early opportunity of again visiting the mill, more especially if you have passed over the faults on promise of amendment, in order to see whether the promise has been fulfilled.

III. In no case claim for yourself, or accept, if offered, any part of the penalties that may be awarded, for any purpose whatever; and take care to let it be known that you have no personal interest in bringing forward the prosecution.

IV. When penalties are awarded in a place where there is no school, open daily, at which the children employed in the factories are educated, apply to the magistrates to defer the appropriation of the penalties in the manner pointed out in the letter on this subject, addressed to you by the inspector, and a copy of which is annexed to these instructions, and, if necessary, read that letter to the magistrates when you make the application.

V. Endeavour to prevent the appropriation of the penalty to a private school attached to or connected with the factory of a convicted party, and supported at his expense.

VI. Take a note, at the time, of the christian and surnames, and the designations of the magistrates who hear the cases, and of the name and address of the magistrates' clerk, and report the same to the inspector.

VII. Except for drawing the notice, information, and summons, no attorney must be employed without special leave from the inspector.

SECT. 3.—GENERAL INSTRUCTIONS.

I. Act upon the interpretation of the law which you receive from the inspector of the district; and if you are doubtful upon any point, apply without delay to the inspector to get his instructions how to act.

II. In all your intercourse with mill-occupiers and their work-people show the utmost courtesy and forbearance consistent with a firm and honest discharge of your duty.

III. Every mill in your district should be visited at least twice* a year; and those which require it, more frequently, until they can be reported as conducted in perfect conformity with the law.

IV. Visit the several parts of your division, as you shall be directed by the inspector, from time to time; but should you receive information which appears to you to require your immediate presence in any place, go there without waiting for instructions from the inspector.

V. In order to secure the most prompt communication with you, which may sometimes be of importance, on all occasions when you are to be absent from your place of residence for more than four days, inform the inspector of your address.

* Changed afterwards to three times.

VI. In your rounds of visits, always try to see the appointed certifying surgeon, to ascertain whether he has any information to give you.

VII. Always visit with a copy of the Act and of the rules and regulations of the inspectors in your pocket.

SECT. 4.—RECORDS OF PROCEEDINGS, AND CORRESPONDENCE WITH THE INSPECTOR.

I. Keep full notes of your visits to the mills, and of all the official business in which you are engaged.

II. Keep copies of all the letters you write on official business.

III. Enter your visits to the mills weekly in the visiting book supplied to you by the inspector, in the manner directed by him, when you are at home, if inconvenient to travel with the visiting book.

IV. As a general rule, subject to exceptions when travelling, employ Saturday in writing up books and other records, and in correspondence with the inspector.

V. Make a weekly report to the inspector of your visits and other official employment, in the form prescribed by him.

VI. Unless the inspector asks for an earlier reply, you may defer to your weekly report answers to letters received from him in the interval.

VII. Make a monthly return of prosecutions, filling up the schedule supplied by the inspector for that purpose; this return to include all prosecutions in the month next but one before the time of making the return: thus, the return of the 1st March should contain all the prosecutions which took place in the January preceding. If no prosecutions have taken place, make the following entry in the first weekly report of the month: " No prosecutions in the month of ——."

VIII. Enter in your visiting book every new mill-occupier you may hear of, and all alterations of firms; and in your next weekly report send notice thereof, in order that similar entries may be made in the books kept by the inspector.

IX. The Home-office franks must not be used for any other purpose than official business.

(Parl. Papers (1840) X, pp. 154-156).

VIII.—SALARIES AND ALLOWANCES OF SUB-INSPECTORS.

CORRESPONDENCE BETWEEN THE FACTORY INSPECTORS AND THE HOME OFFICE.

15th September, 1836. The Inspectors to Lord John Russell.

My Lord,

We have on former occasions taken the liberty to call your Lordship's attention to the Salaries of our Superintendents, which we have long felt to be inadequate; and we are urged by a sense of public duty and in justice to zealous and meritorious officers, most respectfully to request that your Lordship will again take the subject into consideration.

Their allowance is £250 a year, out of which sum they must pay their travelling expenses. Now we are satisfied from minute inquiries which we have made that in order to make the necessary visits to the different factories in their divisions, in aid of the Inspectors, and to perform the duties attendant upon cases of prosecution, they must travel over so many miles, and spend so many days in Inns, that their travelling expenses cannot be less than £200: and as the duty cannot be safely entrusted except to persons of education and character on whom the Inspectors may fully rely, we are convinced that your Lordship will see that the sum they now receive is far too small.

The duty is an arduous one; they are exposed to considerable bodily fatigue in going through the retired parts of the country over bad roads in all weathers;—they must be away from home nearly the whole year, and they are exposed to considerable obloquy (Mr. Trimmer was last month mobbed by the Factory people in a country situation near Oldham); so that the employment is attended with many disadvantages . . .

It has been considered that it would be proper the Superintendents besides a salary, should receive an allowance of a guinea for each day they are travelling on duty. To that mode of remuneration there is the strong objection that it holds out a temptation to them to prolong their stay in places more agreeable as a residence and less irksome in point of work . . . We are of opinion it will be better to give them a larger salary, or a certain salary with the amount of their actual expenses for travelling.

(Minutes, Vol. I, pp. 12-16).

Extract from Minutes, 29th June, 1842.

" The Inspectors conferred particularly on that part of Mr. Saunders' report in which he adverts to the situation of the Superintendents, in relation to the disappointment of their hopes of having their salaries increased, in consequence of the amending Factory Act not having been brought forward in the present session."

(Minutes, Vol. I, p. 173).

15th January, 1844. The Inspectors to Sir James Graham.

The Inspectors of Factories recommend to the consideration of Sir James Graham an alteration in the amount and in the mode in which the Superintendents or Sub-Inspectors are at present paid and beg leave to remind Sir James Graham that the Committee of the House of Commons on Factories in 1841 recommended that the remuneration of the Sub-Inspectors should be raised. The Inspectors consider that the two items of salary and expenses necessarily incurred attending the discharge of their duties should be kept distinct. Among other reasons for this more or less urgent they would draw more particular attention to the fact that great differences must necessarily arise in the amount of these expenses in the several superintendencies. Thus Superintendents inspecting Factories that are not concentrated but are widely scattered must be liable to a much greater amount of expense not only by miles travelled but by longer absence from home than a Superintendent (at Ashton for instance) who is able to visit any Mill in his district without going to a greater distance than 10 miles from his own home. The expenses in each district are moreover liable to fluctuate according as a greater or a smaller number of Mills are in operation as Trade is more or less brisk or as Factories spring up in a new direction. All these circumstances concur in inducing the Inspectors to recommend that a Separation of Salary and contingent expenses shall be distinctly recognised in the Bill so that this department may be placed on the same footing as analogous branches of the public service in regard to salary and expenses.

(Minutes, Vol. I, pp. 192-194).

Extract from Minutes. 16th January, 1844.

" Sir James Graham decided that no estimate of expenses would fix a higher salary for each Superintendent than 300£."

(Minutes, Vol. I, p. 197).

17th January, 1844. The Inspectors to Sir James Graham.

Sir,

We beg leave respectfully to call your attention to the remuneration of the Gentlemen who act as Superintendents of Factories under our direction which we have long felt to be inadequate in the amount and defective in the mode. Out of a very moderate salary they pay heavy travelling and other expenses in the discharge of their duties which require a great deal of travelling and living at Inns throughout the year and involve many incidental expenses. The more active they are in the public service the more they are subjected to pecuniary loss.

We therefore earnestly recommend that they should be paid a fixed yearly salary together with such reasonable travelling and other expenses as they must incur in the discharge of their duties. There are at present 15 Superintendents for the United Kingdom 12 of whom receive £350 a year each, 1 £300 and 2 £250, making together £5,000.

We would suggest that each Superintendent should receive a salary of £300 together with travelling and other expenses but that these should in no case exceed £150.

From the diversity of circumstances and situations it is impossible to equalize the amount of travelling and other expenses in each Superintendency, an approximation is all that can be obtained and as far as we can judge from our knowledge of our several districts we think that we cannot be greatly in error nor understate the case materially by saying that the average amount for each would be about £120—making together £1,800 or an addition of £1,300 to the present charge.

If this proposal should be acceded to the expenses of each Superintendency would have to be regulated by some scale fixing by what modes of conveyance he should be allowed to travel under different circumstances and the occasions when Tavern expenses would be allowed as well as a maximum per day.

We presume also as a matter of course, the Treasury would require the Bills of expenses to be attested and that they would inform us as to the rules they usually follow on such occasions.

(*Minutes, Vol. I, pp. 199-201*).

20th June, 1844. Leonard Horner to Manners Sutton.

My dear Sir,

At the approaching meeting of the Inspectors we shall have to consider how we may make our proceedings under the new Act as uniform as possible. The most important matter is the regulation of the visits of the Sub-Inspectors, and particularly as to the frequency of their visits to the Mills in their several divisions. At present there is a great diversity in this respect in the different districts, nor can it be otherwise under the present mode of payment. For instance, one Sub-Inspector has all Ireland to look after with Mills at the extreme of N. & S., E. & W., and one of my Sub-Inspectors, with above 400 Mills to superintend has not one of them more than 12 miles distant from his residence.

Mr. Stuart I know is anxious that our meeting in July should be prolonged as little as possible, because he wishes to commence his autumn circuit of inspection soon, and it is inconvenient to Mr. Howell to be kept long in London. It would considerably shorten our proceedings if we knew beforehand whether it is the intention of Sir J. Graham to adhere to the principle that was contained in the Bill that was withdrawn, viz., to pay the Sub-Inspectors a fixed salary and their travelling expenses separately. If it is so intended it would be very useful if we were informed on what principles the allowance for travelling is to be made; because between this time and the 16th July we might be severally considering the subject, how the plan is to be carried out in detail.

(*Minutes, Vol. II, pp. 2-3*).

12th July, 1844. Manners Sutton to Leonard Horner.

Sir,

I have laid your letter of the 20th ult. before Secretary Sir J. Graham and I am to inform you that he is prepared to recommend to the Treasury that hereafter the Sub-Inspectors of Factories should receive a fixed salary together with the amount incurred by them in travelling upon official duty. It will be desirable that this subject should be taken into consideration by the Inspectors at their annual meeting.

(*Minutes, Vol. II; p. 4*).

17th July, 1844. Resolutions of the Inspectors.

1. The Sub-Inspectors should be paid a fixed annual salary of not less than £300.

2. They should be entitled to personal expenses of not less than 12/- a day when necessarily sleeping from home.

3. They should be paid the actual cost incurred in locomotion.

4. In such cases as may appear necessary to the Secretary of State as for example when a Sub-Inspector keeps a horse and gig as some of them do at present as the more economical and convenient mode of travelling on his public duty, the Sub-Inspector be allowed either in part or in whole a fixed money payment in lieu of all other charges for locomotion.

These recommendations were communicated to Manners Sutton on 18th July, 1844.

(Minutes, Vol. II, pp. 8-10).

4th September, 1844. Manners Sutton to the Inspectors.

I am directed by Sec. Sir J. G. to inform you that in pursuance of an arrangement which has been sanctioned by the Lords of the Treasury each Sub-Inspector of Factories will from next Quarter day receive a Salary of £300 per ann., together with the sums actually expended in conveyance on official tours of Inspection. The Sub-Inspectors should be informed that where a Railway is available, they should use it; failing a Railway they should travel by Coach, and failing a coach, they may hire a gig or Horse. The accounts of these expenses are to be transmitted Quarterly to the Inspectors to be examined and certified as correct to the best of their belief by the Inspectors and to be forwarded by them to the Sec. of State.

(Minutes, Vol. II, p. 56).

24th September, 1844. Manners Sutton to the Inspectors.

I have laid before Sec. Sir J. G. your Letter of the —— inst. on the subject of the remuneration of the Sub-Inspectors of Factories, and I am to inform you that Sir J. G. is not prepared to recommend an allowance, as you propose, for the personal expenses of the Sub-Inspectors whilst absent from home. The Inspectors of Prisons receive fixed salaries, and are repaid the sums which they expend in travelling from place to place, but no allowance is made to them for personal expenses, unless employed out of their respective districts or upon some special service not included in the ordinary course of duty. If a Sub-Inspector of Factories should prefer to retain his present Salary and not to receive his travelling expenses, Sir J. G. does not see any objection to his doing so: but no complaint can be made respecting the number of journies which he may have to travel in the performance of his duty.

(Minutes, Vol. II, p. 57).

September, 1844. The Inspectors to Manners Sutton.

We beg leave to state unless it [the allowance of 12/- a day] be given in addition to the sums actually expended on conveyance, the same evil will to a very great extent continue to exist, which formed one of the main reasons why we deemed it to be our duty to recommend that the Salary of the Sub-Inspectors should be distinct from his Tavern and Travelling expenses.

We beg leave also to add, that our recommendation of a reduction of the Salary from £350 to £300 a year was founded on the assumption that an adequate allowance for personal expenses when necessarily absent from home on official duty, would be awarded to the Sub-Inspectors.

(Minutes, Vol. II, p. 58).

28th November, 1844. The Inspectors to Sir James Graham.

Sir,

We thought it advisable, that so soon as our more pressing engagements in our respective districts would admit of it, we should meet for the purpose of deliberating together upon the arrangement for the payment of the Salaries and travelling expenses of the Sub-Inspectors of Factories, contained in Mr. Manners Sutton's Letters of the 4th and 24th of Sept. last, as we are unanimously of opinion that the public Service, and the interest of the Sub-Inspectors would be greatly promoted by some changes in that arrangement, which we have to suggest. And we have now the honor to submit to you our views upon this subject which we have reason to believe accord generally with those of the Sub-Inspectors.

We beg however in the outset respectfully to assure you, that notwithstanding the importance of the subject to the public interest, as well as its importance to the Individuals affected by it, we should not have felt ourselves justified in adopting this course, had not Mr. Manners Sutton in his Letter of 24th Sept., been so good as to tell us that you would be ready to consider any further observations on the subject we should be desirous of offering, and had we not been unanimously of opinion, that while the arrangement in question in a pecuniary point of view very considerably disappoints the expectations of the Sub-Inspectors it will not be attended with any corresponding advantages to the public.

In the reply we had the honour to make to Mr. Manners Sutton's Letter of 4th Sept., we stated, that our recommendation of the reduction of the Salary of the Sub-Inspectors from £350 to £300 a year was founded on the assumption, that they were to be re-imbursed the sums actually expended in conveyance, and their personal expenses to the extent of 12/- a day, when absent from home on official business; and it still appears to us, on the fullest and most deliberate consideration we can give to the subject that if an arrangement of that description were approved by you, and carried into effect under our direction, as to the times and number of the Journies to be undertaken, the payments to the Sub-Inspectors for locomotion and personal expenses, would not be materially greater than they would be according to the arrangement which has been intimated to us, whereas by re-imbursing them their expenses for board and lodging at Inns when they sleep from home, the Sub-Inspectors would not have that inducement to be as much as possible at home, which Individuals in their circumstances possessed of a very limited fixed income must otherwise have. We are acquainted with the position of every Factory in our respective districts, and with the access to them, and know with tolerable precision the time the ordinary Journies of the Sub-Inspectors required by us should occupy. We are therefore persuaded no abuse could follow the adoption of the arrangement we suggested of £300 a year besides travelling expenses, including personal expenses, when travelling. A sum might be fixed, which the travelling and personal expenses of any one Sub-Inspector should in no case exceed. The districts of the Sub-Inspectors are so various in respect of the situation of Factories in some of which they are aggregated in dense masses, in others scattered over a wide extent of country, frequently difficult of access, that no uniform allowance could be fixed; but we believe, that practically the average would be found to be about £120 per annum. The first year would give a pretty correct view of the necessary travelling and personal expenses of each Sub-Inspector, and they probably would be found to vary from £80 to £150.

Mr. Sutton has in his letter of 24th Sept. referred to the mode of paying the Inspectors of Prisons. We are aware, that they receive no allowance for personal expenses in their ordinary Tours of Inspection, but their Salaries are of so much larger amount than those of the Sub-Inspectors of Factories that their position and that of the Sub-Inspectors, hardly admits of a comparison. The usefulness of the Sub-Inspectors is to a considerable degree dependent upon their being able to occupy respectable positions in society, especially when it is considered that they are officially brought into frequent intercourse with Magistrates and professional men. Many of the Sub-Inspectors are married men and some of them we believe have no other resource than their official income of £300 a year: some of them too have large families, so that the expense of Housekeeping is very little diminished by their absence on their Tours. The actual consumption of food of the Sub-Inspector as a member of an economical family would probably not amount to more than 2/- a day, whereas for three moderate meals at an Inn he must pay at least 6/- or 7/-. Then he has his bed and servants at home, at the same time that he is paying for his bed and service at the Inns. The excess of his expenses at an Inn above what his board would cost at home cannot be fairly estimated at less than 10/- a day. The Sub-Inspectors are generally obliged to live in the Chief Towns of their districts, Manchester, Leeds, Macclesfield, Glasgow, Dundee, Belfast, etc., where House-rent and Taxes form large deductions from Salaries so limited in amount as theirs.

There cannot we conceive be any doubt, that if the Sub-Inspectors be not repaid their personal expenses when travelling on official business, they will endeavour in every possible way to lighten those expenses. Instead of proceeding on their Tours from Town to Town, and from place to place, they will whenever practicable return home at night, without entering an Inn and subsisting during the day on provisions carried from home with them. In the Towns too distant from their residences to admit their returning home at night, they will of course from their anxiety to curtail their expenses at Inns, discharge their duty with the least possible delay, and it may be supposed less satisfactorily. We cannot therefore but entertain considerable doubt, whether the expenses of conveyance alone may not be quite as great as that of conveyance and personal expenses united, should the Sub-Inspectors adopt the plan of returning home at night whenever practicable, by which the expense of mere conveyance will be prodigiously increased. On this account, as well as on account of the powerful motive they will have to hurry over the discharge of their duty when absent from home, and thus to perform it in a less satisfactory manner, we cannot but think it most unlikely, that the public should reap any advantage from the limitation of travelling expenses to those of conveyance alone. The greatest number of important Factories out of the Chief Towns of Manchester, Leeds, Halifax, Preston, Stockport, Glasgow, Dundee, and Belfast are situated within a radius of 20 miles around those Towns. All of them may be inspected Piece-meal by a Sub-Inspector starting in the morning in a hired conveyance with a Sandwich in his pocket and returning home to a late dinner. The expense of repeating such short journies to and fro will in very many cases be much greater, than if he were to remain at an Inn during the night as was his practice when the expense of conveyance was defrayed by himself.

In country districts the same inconvenience and increased expense cannot fail to occur. Instances might readily be given in every one of our districts of the greatly increased expense of conveyance that will be one of the consequences of the proposed limitation. Suppose for example, that a Sub-Inspector should make arrangements for visiting a number of Factories scattered round his residence to a distance of 20 miles, he might by starting early in the morning in a gig, visit a considerable number and return home to a late dinner, and he might do the same every day for a considerable time, running up a very heavy account of mileage, to say nothing of the loss of his time in going over so much ground uselessly.

Our Colleague Mr. Stuart has given us an example from his district which may serve as an illustration of what we are now urging in the districts of all his Colleagues. Suppose that the Sub-Inspector for Dundee should make arrangements for visiting the Factories in the County of Fife, about 50 in number, separated from his residence at Dundee only by a Steamboat ferry not two miles across. The factories lie scattered in all parts of a large County few at any one place, and above 40 of them within such distance from Dundee, that the Sub-Inspector leaving Dundee early in the morning, hiring a gig on the Fifeshire side of the Ferry, and visiting two or three Factories may return home every night without incurring any Tavern expenses whatever. His whole expense would be that of gig hire, a gig being with its contingent expenses the only carriage, by which he could in any view most cheaply reach the Factories, which are generally impelled by water, and not in the vicinity of public roads, or of Stage-coaches. In this way, the Sub-Inspector might inspect 40 of these Factories in 12 or 15 days, the necessary inspection of which formerly occupied three days, when he went regularly through them, travelling in his own gig and sleeping each night at an Inn. The expense of conveyance would thus be increased certainly to the extent of three-fourths, and the necessary duty not at all better discharged. It ought to be particularly observed that in the country districts, where a large proportion of the Factories are of small size and situated often at the distance of 6, 8 or 10 miles from each other, many of which abound in all parts of the United Kingdom where there are streams of water, public conveyances are of no use—the pauses for inspection are so frequent, that the cheapest way of travelling is in cars, gigs, or droskies, or on horseback.

We hope we may have said enough to induce you to re-consider the propriety of that limitation of travelling expenses, to which we have now the honor of directing your attention, as well with reference to the interest of the public as of the individuals affected by it, before we are called on to revise the accounts of travelling expenses to be submitted to us by the Sub-Inspectors.

The Act lately passed it should also be observed, imposes various additional duties on the Sub-Inspectors, especially the duty of visiting every Factory, altho' no child or young person under 18 years old be employed in it, and also imposes the duty of visiting Schools. Formerly the Sub-Inspector at Belfast could not make one Tour of factories in his division without travelling 1,250 miles. Now he will have to travel 1,520, and in almost every division there will be a considerable addition to the miles formerly travelled.

Mr. Hudson who has resided at Belfast as Superintendent, now Sub-Inspector for several years, and discharged his duty entirely to the satis-faction of the Inspector of the District, has in a Letter to the Inspector of the 4th Nov. communicated his sentiments as to the effect on him of the new arrangement in terms so clear and interesting, that we hope we may be permitted to lay them before you in his own words, as follows:—

" The offer made to the Sub-Inspectors to allow them to retain their present Salaries, and not to receive the travelling expenses would seem to permit me to submit to your notice some particulars which I would humbly hope may have escaped the consideration of Sir J. Graham in deciding upon the present arrangement. It is easy to conceive that at first view, personal expense or expenses incurred at Hotels on official Tours of Inspection may be deemed distinct from travelling expenses, but the Sub-Inspector of Factories who has at the same time a residence at head-quarters, and perhaps, as in my case, with a large family to support there, has practical and fearful experience to the contrary, his present Salary not admitting of an expenditure when at home that could in any way be commensurate with the charges which are made and cannot be avoided at hotels.   It is therefore his peculiar hardship, that having on his official circuit the responsibility of enforcing the Law, devolving entirely upon him, he can on no occasion vindicate it, without inflicting a penalty on himself for there can be no prosecution, whether conviction follow or not, no enquiry or investigation, that may cause detention on his journey, which will not put him to additional expense.   These considerations it may be supposed, determined the Select Committee on Mills and Factories, of which Lord Ashley was Chairman 1840, to recommend in their Report, that the Salaries of the Sub-Inspectors should be increased, and in accordance with this recommendation, the Bill brought in in 1841 appeared to provide by the 27th Sec. that the Salaries of the Senior Sub-Inspectors should be raised to £450 a year with such travelling expenses as should be judged proportioned to the extent of their district.   Thus assured that something would eventually be done for us, I have to the present time, struggled with the greatest difficulty to support that position in society which I believe essential to an efficient discharge of the duties of my appointment; but I am now constrained to say, that your communication of the intention of the Government has filled me with the most painful anxiety and apprehension, for whether I retain my present Salary of £350 a year or receive merely the expenses of conveyance with a reduced allowance (perhaps the preferable arrangment of the two) my situation would be such, that encumbered as I am by past obligations, I dare not venture to contemplate.   That this Statement may not appear overdrawn I should mention, that to complete but one entire circuit of my division, which extends to the four extreme points of the Island, I have now to travel 1520 English miles, and when it is shewn, that every day I am delayed on this journey, either prosecuting my official duties, or by accidents to which we are continually exposed, I am incurring the fearful expenses of an hotel, my house rent going on, and a large family to support and educate, to say nothing of other expenses incident to the duties of my appointment I earnestly hope, that I shall not be considered importunate in again soliciting you, should an opportunity be given to represent to Sir J. Graham the facts which I now lay before you of the inadequacy of our Salary and truth of every word of this Statement, you, I am sure, are perfectly aware, and I feel most sincerely grateful to you for the efforts that I know you have already made in our behalf."

We have the honor to be, etc.

L.H.—T.J.H.—R.J.S.—J.S.

(*Minutes, Vol. II, pp. 62-69*).

28th November, 1844.   *Inspectors' Memorandum on Travelling Expenses.*

1. In calculating travelling expenses the distance should be reckoned from a central point in the town where the Sub-Inspector resides.

2. No travelling expenses should be payable on visiting factories within a radius of three miles of this point.

3. The Sub-Inspector should not visit, except for special cause, factories both within and beyond this boundary on the same day.

4. When the Sub-Inspector visits factories in a town beyond the boundary, no travelling expenses should be payable when the factory is within a radius of one mile of a fixed point in such town.

5. The Sub-Inspector should travel by the nearest convenient route.

6. The Sub-Inspector should wait a reasonable time (but not stay overnight) for a cheaper conveyance before resorting to one more expensive.

(Minutes, Vol. II, p. 70).

2nd December, 1844. The Inspectors to Sir James Graham.

Conveyance and lodging expenses should be so restricted that they shall not indirectly become a source of income.

(Minutes, Vol. II, p. 82).

19th December, 1844. The Treasury to the Home Office.

Copy forwarded by S. M. Phillips to the Inspectors 24th December, 1844.

Sir,

The Lords Commrs. of H. M. Treasury have had under consideration Sir J. Graham's recommendation of an allowance for Subsistence for the Sub-Inspectors of Factories when actually engaged from home on the business of inspection, contained in your Letter of the 5th Instant, and I have received Their Ldps commands to acquaint you for the information of the Sec. of State, that where the duties imposed on a public officer are such as absolutely to require a frequent or constant removal from place to place in order to their discharge, My Lords consider that the Salary must be assumed to be fixed with reference to the expense of living at the several places, which by the tenure of his office, he is bound to visit, and that a further allowance for subsistence while travelling is neither more nor less than an addition of Salary.

Viewing Sir J. G.'s proposition in this light, and considering, as my Lords have done, the expense to which the constant locomotion of the Sub-Inspectors of Factories necessarily exposes them, Their Ldps are disposed to think that the fixed Salary of £300 a year is not altogether adequate, and they are therefore prepared to admit in this case (what they should not think admissible in cases in which a higher Salary is paid) an allowance of 12/- for lodging and Subsistence for every night during which a Sub-Inspector may necessarily be absent on duty from his own residence.

S. M. Phillips, Esq.

I am, &c.,

C. E. Trevelyan.

(Minutes, Vol. II, pp. 93-94).

15th January, 1845. Inspectors' Minute.

The Treasury regulations do not require Sub-Inspectors to travel by 2nd or 3rd class carriages, or on the outside of the Coach, but provide only that the claim shall be for the amount that is actually expended.

(Minutes, Vol. II, p. 112).

IX.—FEES PAYABLE TO THE CERTIFYING SURGEONS.

THE FORMULATION OF THE SCALE.

The Factories Regulation Act, 1844, (7 & 8 Vict., c. 15) provided as follows:—

If an accident caused bodily injury to any person employed, so that he was unable to resume work before 9 a.m. the following day, the factory occupier or his principal agent was to notify the certifying surgeon within 24 hours of the absence, and the surgeon was to notify the Sub-Inspector of the district. (Sec. 22).

After such notification the surgeon, with the least possible delay, was to visit the factory, and investigate the nature and cause of the injury. Within the next 24 hours he was to send a report to the Sub-Inspector, who was to transmit it to the office of the Factory Inspectors. For the purpose of these investigations the surgeon was to have the same power, authority and protection as an Inspector. The Surgeon's fee was not to exceed 10/- for each case, and was not to be less than 3/-, at the discretion of the Inspector. (Sec. 23).

29th November, 1844. Inspectors' Minute.

The Inspectors agreed as reasonable and moderate that the surgeon's fee for examining and reporting upon each accident should be 5/- if the factory and the injured party he has to visit are within one mile of his residence; 7/6 if they are more than one mile but less than three miles from his residence; and 10/- if they are more than three miles from his residence.

(*Minutes, Vol. II, p. 74*).

3rd January, 1845. The Inspectors to Sir James Graham.

The practical working of a part of the new Factory Act gives us some anxiety on account of the heavy expense it is likely to occasion to the public, an expense greater than may have been originally contemplated, and we do not think it advisable to allow any longer time to elapse without calling your attention to it. What we allude to is the clause respecting reports of accidents by the Certifying Surgeons.

By the 22nd Clause if *any* accident occurs in a Factory which shall cause any bodily injury to any person employed of such a nature as to prevent him from returning to his work next morning, a notice must be sent by the occupier of the Factory to the Certifying Surgeon who by the 23rd Sec. must investigate and report upon it, for which trouble he is to receive a fee varying from 3/- to 10/- at the discretion of the Inspector, and which Fee is to be paid by the State.

The trouble of the Surgeon is considerable; he must send a copy of the notice he receives of the accident to the Sub-Inspector, he must examine the injured person at the person's own home or at whatever place he may have been taken to, he must go to the Factory and investigate the cause of the accident, and he must send a written report to the Inspector of the nature and cause of the accident.

The Inspectors consulted together recently as to the Scale of Fees they should adopt, and they came to the conclusion that for so much trouble the minimum fee ought not to be less than 5/-; if the Surgeon has to go more than one and less than three miles, 7/6; and if more than three miles, 10/-.

We have waited for the completion of one Quarter before bringing the subject under your notice, and during the first quarter of the Act being in operation the number of accidents reported to us has been as follows:—

In Mr. Horner's District ...	...	...	356
Mr. Howell's ...	...	...	...	89
Mr. Saunders' ...	...	...	...	130
Mr. Stuart's ...	...	...	...	160

Total 735

Several of them are of a nature which must perhaps be considered as an inevitable accompaniment of employment on complex machinery.

Now at the minimum fee which appears to us only a reasonable compensation to the Surgeon, and supposing the reports to come in in the same proportion, or say 800, in other quarters, the charge will amount to about £800 a year.

We have thought it our duty to make you acquainted with these facts; at the same time we must add that we feel it to be a very difficult subject to deal with. The good effect which we have already experienced to have arisen from the reporting of the accidents in making the employers place guards upon dangerous machinery left exposed, thus saving the limbs and sometimes lives of the workers and saving them even in the minor accidents from heavy losses of wages by being temporarily off work may be thought to be well purchased even at the cost we have mentioned.

(Minutes, Vol. II, pp. 103-104).

[On 12th February, 1845, the Inspectors received a letter informing them that in the opinion of the Home Secretary the scale of fees which they proposed was too high. Sir James Graham suggested that if the Surgeon had to travel less than 5 miles the fee should be 3/-; between 5 and 10 miles, 5/-; and over 10 miles, 7/6. The Inspectors were to be authorized to recommend a fee of 10/- only " in peculiar circumstances."

(Minutes, Vol. II, p. 131)]

24th February, 1845. The Inspectors to Manners Sutton.

Being anxious to pay every attention in our power to any suggestion the Sec. of State may please to communicate to us, we have again gone carefully over the subject, and we beg leave respectfully to submit to you the result of our deliberation.

By the 23rd Sec. of the Act the Surgeon is to receive such Fee " not exceeding 10/-, or such part thereof not being less than 3/- as the Inspector of the district may consider a reasonable remuneration for his trouble."

The responsibility of determining what is a reasonable remuneration is thus thrown by the Act entirely upon the Inspector of the district. Although thus left to our individual responsibility we were desirous of framing, subject to Sir J. G's. approval, a general Scale of fees; so that there might be an uniformity in this particular in all districts.

In our Letter of the 3rd Jan. we expressed our anxiety on account of the heavy expense likely to be occasioned by these investigations of accidents by Surgeons. But whatever anxiety we feel on this head, we must consider solely what will be a fair remuneration to individual Surgeons for the time, trouble and professional skill they must give to the public in performance of the duty in question; taking into account the Station of the Surgeons, and the customary Fees, in their line of practice, and perhaps also the public responsibility which attaches to them in the performance of this rather anomalous duty.

Considering the responsible nature of the several duties that devolve upon Certifying Surgeons, it is essential that those only should be appointed on whose independence reliance can be placed; men who hold a respectable position in the district in which they are to act, from character, education and professional standing.

The duties to be performed by Certifying Surgeons in relation to accidents are defined in the 22nd & 23rd Sections of the Act, and are as follows:—

1st.—He must write out a copy of the notice of the accident which he receives from the occupier of the Factory, and must send that copy to the Sub-Inspector of the district, and by the first post after he receives it.

From specimens of these notices which we have seen he may sometimes have to write a page of Letter; and from being called upon to give immediate attention to the business, he may be called away from other remunerating duties.

2nd.—He must go " with the least possible delay " to the Factory where the accident happened.

3rd.—He must there " make a full investigation " both as to the nature and cause of the accident, and for the purpose of this quasi judicial enquiry he is expressly armed with the same powers of examining witnesses and compelling them to give evidence as those which are given to an Inspector. The discharge of this somewhat invidious duty must obviously consume much more time than the ordinary professional call of a medical man.

4th.—Inasmuch as the Surgeon investigates only those accidents by which the person injured is prevented from resuming work in the Factory, it follows that he must in the great majority of cases visit the place where the person injured—the principal witness—may be seen and examined.

5th.—Within 24 hours of the investigation he must send to the Inspector of the district a report of it, a copy of which report must be registered in this office, and this becomes a public document.

The Inspectors have prepared a form for such reports, a copy of which is sent herewith, by which will be seen the several points which the Surgeon has to investigate and report upon.

Although not required by law it is most probable that most Surgeons will deem it incumbent on them, as a measure of ordinary prudence to keep copies of their reports, which as public documents, are liable to be canvassed in Courts of Justice as well as elsewhere.

The Act itself has in the 13th Section laid down a scale of fees for the remuneration of the Surgeon for his time and trouble in granting Certificates of age, and it would not be irrelevant for the Surgeon to expect that the Inspectors in deciding upon a reasonable remuneration in the matter of accidents would keep in view the remuneration which the Legislature has deemed to be reasonable in the matter of Certificates.

In the duty of granting Certificates the Surgeon must

1st.—Go to the Factory where the Person to be examined for a Certificate is to be employed, and this he can generally do at a time convenient to himself in his ordinary rounds.

2nd.—He must judge the age of the child or young person by the physical character of age, and whether the person is not incapacitated by disease for factory employment, and

3rd.—He must if he is to grant a Certificate, fill up a printed form he finds at the Factory.

For this trouble if the Factory be situated within one mile of the Surgeon's residence, the Inspector may award him 2/6, and if he examines more than 5 persons, he is entitled to have 6d. more for every additional person examined.

If the factory be at a greater distance, say for example, 4 miles from his residence, and if he examine two persons, the Inspector may award him 1/- for each person and 6d. for every half mile of the distance over the first mile from his residence: Thus he might receive for a visit of this kind,

for examination	...	...	2/-
for mileage	...	...	3/-
			5/-

and if he were to examine more than 10 persons, he would be entitled to 6d. more for every additional person examined.

You will thus perceive that the remuneration you have suggested for accidents would fall far short of that which the Act gives for certificates of age, and which has to be paid by the Occupiers of Factories; although the time and trouble in the former is by much the greatest in amount, even in the case of those accidents which occupy the least time in the investigation.

Having thus brought under your notice for the information of Sir J.G. the nature of the duties cast upon the Surgeons, and the probable amount of time and trouble involved in writing and in visiting two places, together with the responsibility attending the prosecution of these enquiries, We respectfully beg you to inform us, whether upon a revision of the details submitted Sir J.G. is disposed to consider that the Scale of Fees proposed by us in our Letter of the 3rd Jan. is more than a reasonable remuneration to the Surgeons, or is of opinion that we ought to adopt that Scale of fees which is specified in your Letter to us of the 12th Instant.

(*Minutes, Vol. II, pp. 135-138*).

25th February, 1845.   Manners Sutton to the Inspectors.

Sir J.G. understands that the appointment of *Certifying Surgeon,* by whom this duty is to be performed is eagerly sought by the most respectable Practitioners in the different manufacturing Districts, and he sees no reason to fear that the Scale of Fees suggested by him (in my Letter of the 12th Instant) as a sufficient remuneration for examining into and reporting on accidents, will throw this appointment into the hands of less independent Practitioners.

The Legislature when enacting that a Fee of 3/- should be the minimum Fee, clearly intended that that sum should be the amount of the Fee in cases where the least trouble and time were expended by the Surgeon in making the enquiry and framing the report; and that a Scale of Fees should be framed, rising from this amount in proportion to the distance to be travelled and the intricacy of the case.

(Minutes, Vol. II, p. 139).

1st April, 1845.   The Inspectors to Manners Sutton.

We beg leave respectfully to acquaint you, that in our recent visits to our several districts, we have had representations from nearly all the Certifying Surgeons whom we have seen, that the Scale of Fees for investigating and reporting accidents, which by your direction we sent to the Certifying Surgeons on the 3rd March last, is an inadequate remuneration for the trouble to which they are subjected in that duty.   Besides these verbal representations, we have had many Letters to the same purpose, and the inadequacy is more particularly insisted upon by Surgeons in remote districts.

As the best way of bringing their statements and opinions before you, we beg leave to send you copies of some of the Letters we have received which we particularly request you to read.   We further request that after having read them you will be pleased to inform us whether you are disposed to make any alteration in the Scale of Fees.

(Minutes, Vol. II, p. 154).

14th April, 1845.   Manners Sutton to the Inspectors.

I am to inform you, that any definite proposals for the alteration of the present Scale of Fees, if submitted by you, will receive Sir J.G's. consideration; but as at present informed, he is not prepared to say that the existing Scale is not sufficient or that its retention will prejudice the public service.

(Minutes, Vol. II, p. 161).

2nd June, 1845.   The Inspectors to Manners Sutton.

We beg to state that our attention has been directed by your Letter of the 25th Feb. last to the circumstance, that the Legislature when enacting that a fee of 3/- should be the minimum fee clearly intended that that sum should be the amount of the Fee in cases where the least trouble and time was expended by the Surgeon in making the enquiry and framing the report and that a Scale of Fees should be framed rising from this amount in proportion to the distance to be travelled and the intricacy of the case.

We have in consequence drawn up the following scale with an anxious desire to carry out the above principle and we now beg respectfully to submit for the consideration of Sec. Sir J.G. the adoption of the Fees contained in this Scale instead of those laid down in your Letter of the 12th Feb. last.

SCALE OF FEES.

For examination and report on any accidents which do not require the Surgeon to proceed a greater distance from his residence than one mile, a fee of 3/-

For the examination and report on any accident which may require the Surgeon to proceed a greater distance than one mile and not more than two 4/-

— — — a greater distance than two and not more than three miles 5/-

If any examination or report shall require a Surgeon to proceed a greater distance than three miles, he shall be allowed a further sum of 6d. for each half-mile that such distance shall exceed three miles.

That in any intricate case, or when any peculiar circumstances shall arise either in making the enquiry or framing the report, the Inspectors may recommend a higher fee than those stated above, so that no fee be assigned for an accident exceeding 10/-, and provided the reason for recommending such higher fee be stated by the Inspector.

(Minutes, Vol. II, pp. 163-164).

[On 6th June, 1845, Manners Sutton wrote to the Inspectors informing them that the Home Secretary approved the scale of fees they proposed.

(Minutes, Vol. II, p. 170).

25th June, 1845. Circular Letter from the Inspectors to the Certifying Surgeons.

In a Letter which the Inspectors received from the Sec. of State, in reply to a communication they made to him on the 3rd April last, respecting the Scale of Fees to be paid to Certifying Surgeons, for investigating and reporting Accidents in Factories, he was pleased to say, that any definite proposal for an alteration of the Scale of Fees he had formerly suggested . . . . which the Inspectors would submit to him should receive his consideration. A letter which the Inspectors received from the Secretary of State, dated the 25th of Feb. last, contained the following passage: "The Legislature when enacting that a Fee of 3/- should be the minimum fee clearly intended that that sum should be the amount of the fee in cases where the least trouble and time were expended by the Surgeon in making the enquiry and framing the report; and that a Scale of Fees should be framed, rising from this amount, in proportion to the distance to be travelled, and the intricacy of the case."

Under these circumstances, the Inspectors took the earliest opportunity at their Statutory Meeting, which commenced on the 27th ult., to submit to the consideration of Sec. Sir J.G. an amended Scale of Fees, calculated to carry out the principle to which their attention had been directed, and briefly calling his attention to the statements, respecting the duties and responsibilities which devolve on Surgeons in respect to Accidents . . .

I have now to inform you that the following Scale has been adopted; it having been sanctioned by the Sec. of State:—

SCALE OF FEES.

1. For the examinations and report on any accidents which do not require the Surgeon to travel a greater distance than one mile ...   3/-

2. For the examinations and report on any accidents which may require the Surgeon to travel a greater distance than one mile, and not more than two miles 4/-

3. For the examinations and report on any accidents which may require the Surgeon to travel a greater distance than two, and not more than three miles 5/-

If any examination or report shall require a Surgeon to travel a greater distance than three miles, he shall be allowed a further sum of 6d. for each half-mile that such distance shall exceed three miles.

5. In any intricate case, or when any peculiar circumstances shall arise, either in making the enquiry or framing the report, the Inspectors may recommend a higher Fee than those stated above, so that no Fee exceeding 10/- be assigned for one accident, and provided the reason for recommending such higher Fee be stated by the Inspector.

REGULATIONS UNDER WHICH DISTANCES ARE TO BE CALCULATED.

In the Letter of the Sec. of State, approving of the above Scale of Fees, it is stated,—" That the Scale of remuneration, which is calculated on distance from residence, should be held to apply to that distance which a Surgeon is compelled to travel to make the examinations, taking the shortest way in his power."

The distances mentioned in the above Scale refer only to that which a Surgeon has to pass over in proceeding *to* the Factory, together with any additional distance which he may have to travel, to examine the person injured. The distance which he has to travel in *returning* either from the investigation at the Factory or from the examination of the person injured, is not to be added to the mileage: nor must the distance travelled to the place where the injured person is examined be added, unless he had to travel a greater distance than he would have done in returning from the investigation at the Factory direct to his residence.

(Minutes, Vol. II, pp. 178-180).

8th December, 1846. Inspectors' Minute.

Mr. Horner submitted to the consideration of his Colleagues whether it would be possible to reduce the expenses incurred in respect to Surgeons' Fees by preventing the necessity of Mill occupiers reporting the least important and most trifling accidents, inasmuch as these formed a large proportion of the aggregate number for which the Certifying Surgeons receive a Fee. Subject discussed but no satisfactory mode occurred at the meeting—further consideration to be hereafter resumed.

(Minutes, Vol. II, p. 270).

X.—TRAVELLING AND PERSONAL EXPENSES OF SUB-INSPECTORS.

QUARTER ENDED 30TH JUNE, 1848.

	£	s.	d.
Horner's District.			
Graham	23	13	5
Ewings	20	13	6
Ryder	13	3	10
Davies	17	16	3
Jones	27	17	1
	£103	**4**	**1**
Howell's District.			
Trimmer	41	11	7
Hickes	46	2	5
Kent	19	9	10
Redgrave	15	8	0
	£122	**11**	**10**
Saunders' District.			
Baker	14	6	10
Bates	24	5	0
Bury	12	5	8
Hart	18	7	8
	£69	**5**	**2**
Stuart's District.			
Balfour	12	0	1
Walker	48	19	10
Hudson	16	2	1
	£77	**2**	**0**

Total ... £372 3 1

—Minutes, Vol. II, p. 372.

XI—ACCIDENT FEES PAYABLE TO SURGEONS.

SIX MONTHS ENDING 31ST DECEMBER, 1845.

		£	s.	d.
Horner's district ...	...	223	12	0
Howell's district ...	...	59	7	6
Saunders' district ...	...	68	7	6
Stuart's district ...	...	117	14	6
		£469	1	6

—*Minutes, Vol. II, p. 224*

SIX MONTHS ENDING 30TH JUNE, 1848.

		£	s.	d.
Horner's district ...	...	95	10	0
Howell's district ...	...	38	5	6
Saunders' district ...	...	44	4	6
Stuart's district ...	...	61	8	0
		£239	8	0

—*Minutes, Vol. II, p. 373.*

XII.—EXPENSES OF THE CENTRAL OFFICE.

QUARTER ENDING 30TH JUNE, 1845.

	£	s.	d.
Salary to Mr. Redgrave, Clerk ...	37	10	0
Salary to John Syrett, Messenger	13	13	0
Allowance to G. Jones, in charge of office	5	0	0
Dorset, for Firewood, Candles, etc.		10	0
Wm. Stark, for a small lamp ...		5	0
Postage and Sundries	1	2	3
	£58	0	3

—Minutes, Vol. II, p. 178.

QUARTER ENDING 30TH JUNE, 1848.

	£	s.	d.
Salary to Mr. A. Redgrave	48	15	0
A. R. Willis ...	13	13	0
Postages incurred by Mr. Howell	1	10	0
Saunders ...		9	5
Stuart ...	2	3	0
Travelling Expenses by Mr. Stuart in visiting Printworks	11	0	7
Postages, &c., at the office	7	6	8
	£84	17	8

—Minutes, Vol. II, p. 372.

XIII.—ESTIMATED EXPENSES OF THE FACTORY DEPARTMENT.

YEAR ENDING 31ST MARCH, 1847.

(Minutes, Vol. II, p. 217).

	£	s.	d.	£	s.	d.
Four Inspectors at Salaries of £1,000 per ann. each, which sum includes Travelling expenses and contingencies	4,000	0	0			
Deduct pension received by one Inspector ...	500	0	0			
				3,500	0	0
Fifteen Sub-Inspectors at Salaries of £300 per ann. each, as in Estimate of last year ...	4,500	0	0			
Additional Sub-Inspector at same Salary for Printworks	300	0	0			
				4,800	0	0
Allowances to the Sub-Inspectors for Travelling and personal expenses in visiting Factories as in Estimate of last year	1,800	0	0			
Allowance for travelling expenses to the Inspector and Sub-Inspectors in visiting Printworks	400	0	0			
				2,200	0	0
Sum required for the payment of Fees to Certifying Surgeons, appointed under the Factories Acts, for reporting accidents in Factories				1,300	0	0
Clerk to the Factory Office	165	0	0			
Messenger to do.	52	12	0			
Housekeeper	20	0	0			
Coals, Candles, &c.	30	0	0			
				267	12	0
Expense of printing rules and regulations for Factories, with the sanction of the Sec. of State, Postage of Letters on Factory Business and sundry small incidental charges, as calculated in former estimates	300	0	0			
Estimated addition on account of Printworks ...	50	0	0			
				350	0	0
Allowances for printing rules, &c., as above for the year ending 31st March, 1846, omitted in the estimate for that year and directed by the Lords of the Treasury to be included in this estimate				300	0	0
				£12,717	**12**	**0**

The estimates for subsequent years were as follows:—

Year ending 31st March, 1848	...	£12,134 12 0 [1]
31st March, 1849	...	£11,614 12 0 [2]
31st March, 1850	...	£10,979 12 0 [3]

(1) Minutes, vol. II, p. 272. The Inspectors expressed their satisfaction that they were able to reduce the expenses of visiting Printworks from £400 to £300, and the accident fees from £1,300 to £1,100.

(2) Minutes, vol. II, p. 333. The accident fees were further reduced to £1,000, and postage and incidental charges to £150.

(3) Minutes, vol. II, p. 390. The Home Office had asked "that this Estimate may be prepared with the most rigid economy, excluding every charge whatever, which is not indispensably necessary for the due performance of the public service." Accordingly the Inspectors reduced the estimate for travelling expenses by £300; accident fees by £250; and postage and incidental charges by £100.

XIV.—PERSONNEL OF THE FACTORY DEPARTMENT—1847.

Return submitted by the Factory Inspectors to the Home Office on November 10th, 1847, in compliance with a resolution of the House of Commons calling for a return of all persons receiving £100 a year and upwards of public money, dated July 20th, 1847.

(Minutes, Vol. II, p. 331).

ALPHABETICAL LIST OF ALL PERSONS EMPLOYED IN THE FACTORY DEPARTMENT WHO RECEIVE £100 AND UPWARDS OF THE PUBLIC MONEY.

Name	Office	Average Annual Salary	Amount of other allowance	Date of first appointment in the public service
Baker, Robert ...	Sub-Inspector of Factories	£300	Actual cost of travelling with 12/- per night when absent from home on duty	22 Oct., 1834
Balfour, Charles ...	,,	,,	,, ,, ,,	Dec., 1839
Bates, James ...	,,	,,	,, ,, ,,	24 Oct., 1834
Bury, James ...	,,	,,	,, ,, ,,	23 April, 1836
Davies, Edward ...	,,	,,	,, ,, ,,	10 April, 1840
Ewings, Joseph ...	,,	,,	,, ,, ,,	1 July, 1836
Graham, William ...	,,	,,	,, ,, ,,	10 Feb., 1845
Hart, Richard ...	,,	,,	,, ,, ,,	1 April, 1841
Hickes, Weston ...	,,	,,	,, ,, ,,	29 Jan., 1836
Horner, Leonard ...	Inspector of Factories	£1000	Out of which sum he has to pay his travelling expenses	14 Nov., 1833
Howell, Thos. Jones	,,	£500	Mr. Howell also receives £500 per ann. as retired Judge Advocate at Gibraltar	1 Oct., 1833
Hudson, Percival ...	Sub-Inspector of Factories.	£300	Actual cost of travelling with 12/- per night when absent from home on duty	1 Mar., 1837
Jones, David ...	,,	,,	,, ,, ,,	1 Mar., 1846
Kent, Saml. Savill ...	,,	,,	,, ,, ,,	11 April, 1836
Redgrave, Alexr. ...	Clerk to Inspectors and Sub-Inspectors of Factories	£280	,, ,, ,,	17 Feb., 1834
Ryder, Thos. Dudley	Sub-Inspector of Factories	£300	,, ,, ,,	Oct., 1847
Saunders, Rob. J. ...	Inspector of Factories	£1000	Out of which sum he has to pay his travelling expenses	1 Oct., 1833
Stuart James	,,	,,	,, ,, ,,	Aug., 1836
Trimmer Charles	Sub-Inspector of Factories	£300	Actual cost of travelling with 12/- per night when absent from home on duty	14 Nov. 1834
Walker, Daniel	,,	,,	,, ,, ,,	2 Feb., 1838

Since their appointment under the Factory Act 3 & 4 Wm. 4 c. 103 the Inspectors were required to inspect Printworks, under the Act 8 & 9 Vict. c. 29, and they are repaid for their actual travelling charges on this extra duty.

XV.—THE PRINTWORKS ACT, 1845.

8 & 9 Vict., c. 29.

EDUCATIONAL PROVISIONS.

Sec. 23.—After the first day of July, 1846, the parent or person having any direct benefit from the wages of any child employed or intended to be employed in a printwork shall cause such child to attend some school for at least thirty days, together or separately, exclusive of Sundays, during the half-year between the first day of January and the thirtieth day of June, both days inclusive, and in like manner for thirty days during the half-year between the first day of July and the thirty-first day of December, both days inclusive, in each year, during any part of which it shall be employed in a printwork, such attendance being after the hour of eight o'clock in the morning and before the hour of six o'clock in the evening, and such attendance shall not be less than one hundred and fifty hours during each half-year; but no attendance above five hours on any one day shall be reckoned as part of the said one hundred and fifty hours.

Sec. 24.—That so soon as a child shall be employed in a printwork the parent or person having direct benefit from the wages of such child shall notify to the occupiers of the printwork the school which such child is to attend during the time it is employed in such printwork, and the occupiers of the printwork shall enter in the register of children hereinafter required to be kept the name of the schoolmaster and the situation of the school so notified to him; and the parent or person having direct benefit from the wages of such child shall provide a School Certificate book, according to the form and directions given in the Schedule annexed to this Act, and shall deliver the same to the master of the school where such child is to attend, and the said master shall enter therein, week by week; and shall produce such Certificate Book, while in his custody, to the Inspector or Sub-Inspector of the District, when required; and the master of any school which shall be attended by children employed in a printwork shall keep a register of their names and attendance, and if the Inspector of the District shall disapprove of the form of register adopted by the schoolmaster, it shall be kept in such other form as the Inspector shall direct.

Sec. 25.—After the first day of July, 1846, the occupiers of every printwork shall, before employing any child therein, obtain from a schoolmaster a certificate, according to the form and directions given in the Schedule to this Act annexed, that such child had attended school for at least fifty[1] days, as required by the Act, during the half-year ending on the thirtieth day of June or the thirty-first day of December next before the beginning of such employment and the like certificate at the beginning of each following period of six months during which the employment of such child shall be continued in that printwork; and such occupier shall keep every such certificate so long as such child shall continue in his employment for twelve months after the date thereof, and shall produce the same to any Inspector or Sub-Inspector, when required during such period.

Sec. 26.—If an Inspector, on his personal examination, or on the report of a Sub-Inspector, shall be of opinion that any schoolmaster who grants certificates of the school attendance of children employed in a printwork is unfit to instruct children by reason of his incapacity to teach them to

---

(1) 'Fifty' was a mis-print for 'thirty.' A short amending act (9 Vict., c. 18) made the necessary correction.—Minutes, 10th February, 1846. Vol. II, p. 231.

read and write, from his gross ignorance, or from his not having the books and materials necessary to teach them reading and writing, or because of his immoral conduct, or of his continued neglect to keep the registers, and fill up and sign the certificates of school attendance, as required by this Act, the Inspector of the District may annul any certificate granted by such disqualified schoolmaster, by a notice in writing addressed to the occupier of the printwork in which the children named in the certificate are employed, or his principal agent, setting forth the grounds on which he deems such schoolmaster to be unfit; and after the date of such notice no certificate of school attendance granted by such schoolmaster shall be valid for the purpose of this Act, unless with the consent in writing of the Inspector of the district; but no Inspector shall annul any such certificate unless in the aforesaid notice he shall name some other school situated within two miles of the printwork where the children named in the certificate are employed: Provided always that any schoolmaster whose certificate shall have been annulled, or the occupier of the printwork in which the children named in the certificate are employed, on behalf of the schoolmaster, may appeal to the Secretary of State against any such decision of the Inspector, and the Secretary of State may, if he think fit, rescind such decision: Provided also, that every Inspector shall in his annual report to the Secretary of State state the instances (if any) in which he shall have had occasion to annul any such certificate, together with the reasons which he had in each case assigned for so doing.

Schedule A.

School Certificate Book.

I hereby certify, That the Child *A.B.*, Son [*or* Daughter] of *C.D.* and *E.F.*, residing in　　　　　　　　　　attended the School kept by me at　　　　in the Parish and County of　　　　　　for the Number of Hours and at the Time on each Day specified in the Columns opposite to his [*or* her] Name.

During the Week ending on Saturday the　　　　　Day of　　　　　18　.

Monday		Tuesday		Wednesday		Thursday		Friday		Saturday		Total No. of hours during this week
From	To	From	To	From	To	From	To	From	To	From	To	

[Each Certificate Book, containing 26 forms as above, was valid for six months, either from 1st January to 30th June, or from 1st July to 31st December. At the expiration of six months the child's parent was to deliver the book to the occupier of the printwork].

THE INSPECTORS' RECOMMENDATIONS.

Letter from the Inspectors to the Home Secretary. 25th May, 1847.

We beg leave to submit the following alterations to your consideration, embracing three distinct modes by which the object of the legislature may be fulfilled leaving it to the occupier of the Printwork to select that mode he considers best suited to the local and other circumstances of his works.

These three modes, are,

    I.—Attendance at School preliminary to employment.

    II.—Attendance at School five days a week during employment.

    III.—Attendance at School alternately by days or by weeks with employment.

I.—As to attendance at School preliminary to employment, it is proposed

1. That Section 24 should be repealed with the exception of the following paragraph

" and the master of any school which shall be attended by children employed in a printwork shall keep a register of their names and attendance, and if the Inspector of the District shall disapprove of the form of register adopted by the schoolmaster, it shall be kept in such other form as the Inspector shall direct."

2. That section 23 of the present Act 8 & 9 Vict. c. 29 be repealed.

3. That section 25 be altered in manner following:—

" And be it enacted that after the first day of August one thousand eight hundred and forty-seven the occupier of every printwork shall, before employing any child therein, obtain from a schoolmaster a certificate, according to the form and directions given in the Schedule (A) to this Act annexed, that such child had attended School for at least 30 days and not less than 150 hours during the year immediately preceding the first day of the employment of such child, or if it has left the said printwork and is again employed therein, the said School attendance shall have been during the half year immediately preceding the first day of re-employment and such School attendance shall be after the hours of 8 of the clock in the morning and before 6 o'clock in the evening, but no attendance of less than $2\frac{1}{2}$ hours or more than 5 hours on any one day shall be reckoned as part of the said 150 hours and a like certificate shall be obtained at the beginning of each following period of six months during which the employment of such child shall be continued in that printwork; and such occupier shall keep every such certificate so long as such child shall continue in the employment for twelve months after the date thereof, and shall produce the same to any Inspector or Sub-Inspector, when required during such period."

4. That Section 26 should remain unaltered.

5. That the part of Schedule A which relates to the Certificate of School attendance should be altered in manner following:—

FORM OF SCHOOL CERTIFICATE FOR ONE CHILD.

I hereby certify, That the Child A.B., Son [or Daughter] of C.D. and E.F. residing in   attended the School kept by me at   in the Parish and County of for the Number of Hours and at the Time on each Day specified in the Columns opposite to his [or her] Name

DURING THE WEEK ENDING ON SATURDAY THE   DAY OF   18   ,
AS STATED IN THE FIRST COLUMN.

Week ending	Monday		Tuesday		Wednesday		Thursday		Friday		Saturday		Total No. of hours during this week
	From	To	From	To	From	To	From	To	From	To	From	To	

Under the Column headed with the Days of the Week the Periods of the Day that each Child attends School shall be stated, as thus, from Nine to Twelve, or from Two to Five, or any other Time, as the case may be, and under the column headed "Week ending" the Schoolmaster shall in his own handwriting fill up the date when the week ends during any part of which the child shall have attended his School.

The Time when each Child attends School, or the word "Absent," shall be stated in the column for each Day in the Handwriting of the Schoolmaster; and no Certificate shall be valid unless the Schoolmaster shall, in his own Handwriting, subscribe to it his Christian and Surname in full.

That no part of the School attendance certified shall be valid for a longer time than six months after the date of such attendance, and if a child for whom this form of Certificate has been given shall cease to be employed in the Printwork to the Occupier of which such School Certificate was delivered the child's Parent or any person having direct benefit from the wages of such child shall be entitled on demand to have the said Certificate restored to him.

In order to avoid unnecessary trouble it is desirable when two or more children employed in the same Printwork attend the same School that their names may be entered in one Certificate: We therefore recommend that the following form should also be given in the Schedule.

II.—FORM OF SCHOOL CERTIFICATE WHICH MAY BE USED WHEN TWO OR MORE CHILDREN EMPLOYED IN THE SAME PRINT-WORK ATTEND THE SAME SCHOOL.

I hereby certify, That the Children whose names are underwritten, employed in the Print-Work of   at in the parish of   and county of attended for the number of hours and at the time specified in the columns opposite to their respective names at the School kept by me at in the parish of   and county of

DURING THE WEEK ENDING ON SATURDAY THE   DAY OF   18   .

Child's Name		Monday		Tuesday		Wednesday		Thursday		Friday		Saturday		Total No of hours during this week
Surname	Christian Name	From	To	From	To	From	To	From	To	From	To	From	To	

The same directions that apply to Form No. 1 should be made mutatis mutandis to apply to this form.

The above clauses 23, 24, 25 and 26 together with the above part of Schedule A contain all the enactments in the Printworks Act that relate to the School attendance of children.

The above alterations would in a great measure remove the objections of those Occupiers of Printworks who are willing that School attendance should be required before a child can be employed in a Printwork.

II.—As to attendance at School five days a week during employment.

Many of the most considerable occupiers of Printworks in Scotland without being in any way opposed to School attendance being made obligatory on the children they employ strongly object . . . to its being made preliminary to employment and a considerable majority of those in Scotland have suggested a modification of the Law which in their opinion would make the education of children more effective and thus better fulfil the object of the legislature. The plan they propose is in substance as follows:—

That a new clause be framed to enable children to be employed in Printworks without a preliminary School attendance provided that from the first day of their employment and during the whole continuance of their employment while under 13 years of age the children attend School a part of every day exclusive of Saturdays and Sundays, to be certified by the Schoolmaster weekly as in the case of children employed in Factories.

This clause ought to contain the following provisions:—

1. That the children after the first day of their being employed in any manner within the premises of the Printwork shall attend a School every Monday, Tuesday, Wednesday, Thursday and Friday (excepting certain holidays to be provided for and excepting on occasions of sickness or other allowable cause as in the Factory Act) for at least 1½ hour continuously after the hour of 6 o'clock in the evening.

2. That the attendance shall be certified weekly by the Schoolmaster according to a form to be given in a Schedule to the amending Act.

III.—As to attendance at School alternately by days or by weeks with employment.

Mr. Saunders in his report of the 7th Nov. last suggested that children might in places where a sufficient number could.be obtained be employed by relays not on the same day but on alternate days or weeks without requiring proof of any preliminary attendance at School, provided they attend School on the days excepting Saturdays and Sundays that they are not at work. This it is feared will not be practicable in many cases at present because of the greater number of children required, but all the Inspectors agree in conceiving that where it is possible and the occupier is willing to adopt it, it would be in all respects so far as regards the education of the children between 8 and 13 years of age to be employed in Printworks for half time the same as in the Factory Act or for each alternate day or each alternate week at the option of the occupier of a Printwork without preliminary attendance at School on condition that such children attend School regularly during the intermediate periods under regulations similar to those for such children in Mills subject to the Factory Acts, and that the Form of Certificate in proof of such attendance be similar to that prescribed by those Acts.

That for the protection of the Schoolmaster against loss of his Fees we further submit that a clause be framed to provide for the payment of School Fees in the same manner as provision is made for this purpose in the Factory Acts whenever the occupier of a Printwork shall determine to employ children under either of the last two propositions.

In submitting for your consideration the above amendments in the Printworks Act we have brought under your notice only such alterations of the Educational Clauses as appear to us capable of being reduced to practice. We have been guided in the plan we have submitted to you respecting preliminary attendance at School by the Instructions conveyed to us from you to retain that principle, we have endeavoured also in conformity with those instructions to remedy the difficulties which " have stood in the way of carrying that principle into effect."

We have however further laid before you two other plans under which children may in our opinion be employed while their attendance at School is required to at least the same extent as under the present Act: but Mr. Saunders begs to state he cannot concur as fully as his colleagues in the propriety of adopting the second plan as he considers it in many respects injurious to the children themselves.

—Minutes, Vol. II, pp. 299-304.

THE PRINTWORKS AMENDMENT ACT, 1847.

10 & 11 Vict., c. 70.

Sec. 3.—After the first day of August the occupier of every printwork shall, before employing any child therein, obtain from a schoolmaster a certificate according to one of the forms and according to the directions given in the schedule to this Act annexed, that such child had attended for at least thirty days and not less than one hundred and fifty hours during the half-year immediately preceding the first day of the employment of such child or if it shall have left the said printworks and shall be again employed therein, the said school attendance shall have been during the half-year immediately preceding the first day of such re-employment, and such school attendance shall be after the hour of eight o'clock in the morning, and before the hour of six o'clock in the evening, but no attendance of less than two and a half hours on any one day shall be reckoned as any part of the said one hundred and fifty hours, nor shall any attendance on any one day for more than five hours; and a like certificate shall be obtained at the beginning of each period of six calendar months during which the employer of such child shall keep every such certificate so long as such child shall continue in his employment for twelve calendar months after the date thereof, and shall produce the same to any Inspector or Sub-Inspector when required during such period.

SCHEDULE (A).

I.—FORM OF SCHOOL CERTIFICATE FOR ONE CHILD.

I hereby certify, That the child *A.B.*, Son [*or* Daughter] of *C.D.*, and *E.F.*, residing in   attended the School kept by me at   for the Number of Hours and at the Time on each Day specified in the Columns opposite to his [*or* her] Name During the several Weeks ending the Day, Month and Year stated in the First Column.

| Week ending Saturday | | Monday | | Tuesday | | Wednesday | | Thursday | | Friday | | Saturday | | Total No. of Hours during this week | Signature of Schoolmaster | Date of Signing |
Month	Year	From	To	From	To	From	To	From	To	From	To	From	To			
Day																

II.—FORM OF SCHOOL CERTIFICATE WHICH MAY BE USED WHEN TWO OR MORE CHILDREN EMPLOYED IN THE SAME PRINTWORK ATTEND THE SAME SCHOOL.

I hereby certify, That the Children whose Names are underwritten, employed in the Print-Work of   at   in the Parish of   and County of   attended for the Number of Hours and at the Time specified in the Columns opposite to their respective Names, at the School kept by me at   in the Parish of   and County of   .

DURING THE WEEK ENDING ON SATURDAY THE   DAY OF   18   .

Child's Name		Monday		Tuesday		Wednesday		Thursday		Friday		Saturday		Total No. of hours during this week
Sur-name	Christian Name	From	To	From	To	From	To	From	To	From	To	From	To	

Signed...

Schoolmaster.

This   Day of   18   .

XVI.—FENCING.

SAUNDERS' PROPOSALS.

The regulations I respectfully beg to recommend to your Lordship's consideration are the following:—

1. That every steam-engine and water-wheel, situated in or about a factory where children and young persons are liable to come in contact with the same, and every fly-wheel, and bevil-wheel, directly connected with the steam-engine or water-wheel, or other mechanical power, and whether in the engine-house or not, should be well and securely boxed or fenced off to the height of at least six feet; and every wheel-race not otherwise secured should be surrounded by a fence to the height of at least four feet immediately adjoining to such wheel-race.

2. That all mill-gearing and the driving-shafts of any machine-gearing revolving in or near to a passage, gangway, or frame gate, or within six feet perpendicular height from the floor of such passage, gangway, or frame-gate, should be boxed-off or secured in such manner that no person working or passing near thereto, or under the same, can come in contact therewith.

3. That every main-shaft, on which any drum or pulley is fixed, should be arranged in such manner that the shaft can, while in motion, be thrown out of gear in the room where the shaft works; or provision made in every room in which a main or other principal shaft is at work, either by means of connexion with a stop-valve in the main steam-pipe of the steam-engine to stop the engine, or by means of a communication with an external bell not less than seven inches diameter at the mouth, to give warning to the person in charge of the steam-engine, water-wheel, or other mechanical moving power to stop the same with the least possible loss of time.

4. That every driving-drum or pulley over which any strap or band is employed in communicating motion from one part of the machinery to another, and with which is not conjoined a loose drum or pulley and guide-hook, by which the strap or band can be traversed from one drum or pulley to the other, should be provided with a flange, strap-hanger, catch-hook, or other sufficient protection on either side of the said drum or pulley, or the shaft shall be provided on either side the said drum with a case or boxing, so that the strap or band, when it shall have been accidentally or intentionally moved from the drum or pulley, shall not come in contact with the shaft: and every such driving-drum or pulley which shall give motion to more than one strap or band should be provided with a sufficient number of flanges on such drum, or with guide-hooks within three inches of such drum, so that one strap shall not come in contact with another strap.

5. That every strap or band employed in driving any machinery in a factory, and not boxed-off at least six feet in height, should be arranged in such manner that it shall not pass obliquely across any passage, gangway, or frame-gate, at a less height from the floor than six feet, excepting when such strap shall be of less width than one inch, and shall give motion only to a single reeling or winding-frame; and every strap or band, when passing through the floor of a room, should be cased round to the height of six inches, at least, on the upper side of the floor through which it passes.

6. That every shaft and drum, and every strap or band, driving any machine in a factory, and being next a passage, gangway, or frame-gate, of less width, clear of all obstructions, than 24 inches between the working parts of two machines, or of less width, clear of all obstructions, than 18 inches between the working parts of a machine, and a wall or partition, should be fenced off or separated from the passage, gangway, or frame-gate, by a partition, so that no person working or passing near thereto shall come in contact therewith.

7. That any strap or band accidentally or intentionally moved from a drum or pulley revolving on a main or other principal shaft, should not be replaced by hand on the said drum or pulley while the drum or pulley is in motion by action of the steam-engine or water-wheel, except by a male person above 21 years of age, nor should any such strap be replaced, except in the presence of the overlooker or other person in charge of the persons working in the part of a factory where such drum is situated.

8. That the several parts of the machine-gearing, where any two wheels work inwards, should be secured by a case of wood, iron, brass, tin-plate or other adequate material, so that no person can come in contact with such parts.

9. That any space, being more than six inches and less than twelve inches wide, between the working parts of two machines, or between the working parts of a machine and a wall or partition, should be closed up in such manner that no person can pass through such space while any part of the machinery is in motion.

10. That all machinery to be fixed in any factory after the passing of this Act should be arranged in such manner that no passage, gangway, or frame-gate, should be of less width between the working parts of two machines than 30 inches; and no passage, gangway, or frame-gate, between the working parts of a machine and a wall or partition, shall be less than 24 inches.

—*Parl. Papers (1841) X, pp. 240-241.*

XVII.—FACTORIES REGULATION ACT, 1844.

NOTICE OF DANGEROUS MACHINERY.

SCHEDULE (D).

FORM OF NOTICE to be given to the Occupier of a Factory, by an Inspector or Sub-Inspector, of such Part of the Machinery, or such Driving Strap or Band, in the Factory, as appears to him to be dangerous to the Workers.

To [*Name of Occupier*], Occupier of a [*Description of the Manufacture*] Factory, situated in the Parish of   and County of   .

I hereby give you Notice, that the following Parts of the Machinery in your Factory, namely [*here enumerate the Parts*], appear to me to be dangerous, and likely to cause bodily Injury to the Workers employed in the Factory; and I am of opinion that they ought to be immediately well and securely fenced. And I hereby further give you Notice, that by the Act made in the   Year of Her Majesty's Reign, intituled [*here set forth the Title of this Act*], it is provided, that if, after receiving this Notice, you shall neglect or fail to fence the above-enumerated Machinery, and if any Person shall suffer any bodily Injury in consequence of such Neglect or Failure, you will be liable to a Penalty of One Hundred Pounds, over and above all Damages, Costs, and Charges to which you may be found liable in any Action brought against you by or on behalf of the Person so injured.

Given under my Hand, this   Day of   in the Year One thousand eight hundred and

(*Signed*)...……..

Inspector [*or* Sub-Inspector].

XVIII.—THE HALIFAX CASE.

FENCING AND JOINT OCCUPATION.

DEFINITION OF A FACTORY.

Counsel's opinion was as follows:—

"I am on the whole of opinion that the room in which the accident occurred cannot be considered as a 'Factory' within the meaning of the Act.

"The definition of the word Factory in the dictionary clauses of the Act consists of two branches.

"1st. The word signifies all buildings, &c., within which or within the close or curtilage of which any mechanical power is used to work any machinery employed in certain processes.

"But within this leading definition of the word I think the room in question clearly cannot be brought. For in the room itself there is no such user of mechanical power and the rest of the building though adjacent to it cannot obviously be considered as within the close or curtilage of an interior room constituting merely a dependent part of that which surrounds it. For the close or curtilage of a building is something appurtenant as well as adjacent to the building.

"2nd. Any room situate within the outward boundary wall of any Factory *wherein* children or young persons are employed in any process incident to the manufacture carried on in the Factory shall be taken as part of the Factory; and any part of such Factory may be taken to be a Factory within the meaning of the Act.

"Now to be strictly grammatical the relative word 'wherein' should be referred to its last antecedent which would be the word 'Factory' and not 'room' and this construction is confirmed by the subsequent phrase 'such Factory' which seems to refer to some class of Factories recently defined.

"And if the whole building of which the room in question is a part is a 'Factory' within the meaning of the Act it would consequently appear that this room may be considered also in itself as a 'Factory' by virtue of the second branch of the definition, as being part of a Factory in which young persons are employed, &c., and as a part of such Factory being capable of being considered as a Factory.

"But this construction of the Act would lead to such extraordinary results that I am inclined to think it must bear a more limited construction.

"There is a certain improbability too in the grammatical construction I have just given for it seems senseless to make a class of Factories of those in which young persons are employed if as I imagine the case to be there be no factories in which young persons are not employed whilst on the other hand if the word 'wherein' were referred to the 'room' within the outer boundary of the Factory, and not to the Factory itself there would appear to be a sensible object in the enactment.

"I think it doubtful which of these constructions a Court of Law would decide to be the correct one, the latter one would clearly take the room in question out of the category of Factories. But supposing that they decided upon the one more strictly grammatical and which would at first sight appear to lead to the conclusion that the room is to be considered as a Factory. A solution of the difficulty may still I think be found in this, that the Act in its definition of a 'Factory' does not contemplate several occupations. Thus the whole building in this case would not be considered a 'Factory' but a collection of Factories and consequently this room would not merely as a part of the whole building answer to the term a 'Factory' although each part of the building might or might not according to its occupation come within the definition.

"If some such limit of interpretation be not imposed the following may serve as an example of the consequences which would ensue—a man by occupying in a certain manner one room only in any building however large might make the whole building a 'Factory' *for all the purposes of the Act* except so far as the rest of the building might come within the express exception to the term contained in the dictionary clause.

"It will be noticed that all through the Act mention is made of 'the occupier of a Factory' a phrase pointing to the same conclusion which I have suggested.

"The owner as such does not seem to come at all within the scope of the Act the whole duty being thrown upon the occupier."

—*Minutes, 2nd June, 1846, Vol. II, pp. 242-243.*

XIX.—THE UNFIT SCHOOLMASTER.

A Case in Mr. Redgrave's District.

By section 39 of the Factories Regulation Act, 1844, the Inspectors were empowered to annul the certificates of school attendance granted by incompetent schoolmasters. In his report for 31st October, 1853, Alexander Redgrave stated that he had taken action against Charles Cooke, of Stanningley, near Leeds.

" Upon visiting that School at 20 minutes to 12 o'clock in the forenoon, the children were playing in the open yard, and the master was engaged in sawing up the blackboard, for fittings, he said, for a new house to which he proposed to move his school . . . . The children were summoned into the schoolroom: they entered disorderly and careless, ranging themselves against the wall with a show of obedience, influenced more by the presence of the Sub-Inspector, Mr. Baker, and myself, than from regard to the directions of the master. In the meantime, two girls, lying at length upon the top of the inner porch of the door, and amusing themselves with their playmates, were ordered down to join the others. The master drew from his pocket a whistle, and blew the signal for attention: he then produced his books and materials for teaching, which consisted of six dilapidated Bibles, some copy-books, one slate, half a dozen loose and ragged leaves of a ' Reading Made Easy,' and the remains of the blackboard. The pretence of discipline and system in the exhibition of his pocket-whistle,—the only whole and unbroken implement of his calling,—contrasted with the deplorable aspect of his room, containing twenty boys and girls ranged along the wall, though capable of accommodating 150, the miserable remnants of his books, and the surviving fragments of the blackboard, supported on either side by a hand-saw and a hammer, was in itself intensely ludicrous: but the injury this man was inflicting upon his scholars by the daily repetition of this farce of teaching might be incalculable."

—Parl. Papers (1854) XIX, p. 306.

XX.—FALSE RELAYS.

Plans for Relays.

Circulated by Leonard Horner to the mill-occupiers in his district on 6th July, 1836.

I.—Where the work begins at 6, and breakfast is from 8 to 8½, dinner from 12½ to 1½, tea from 5½ to 6, and the mill stops at 8 o'clock.

Suppose three sets of children of thirty each, called A., B., and C.

	A. Work from	6 to 8	...	2 hours
		8½ to 10½	...	2
		1½ to 5½	...	4
				—
				8

Go to school from 10½ to 12½, two hours, and have the evening for recreation.

	B. Work from	10½ to 12½	..	2 hours
		1½ to 5½	...	4
		6 to 8	...	2
				—
				8

Go to school from 8½ to 10½, and have the morning before breakfast for recreation.

	C. Work from	6 to 8	...	2 hours
		8½ to 12½	...	4
		6 to 8	...	2
				—
				8

And go to school from 1½ to 3½, and have the afternoon for recreation.

By this system, those working 12 hours a day have—

A. and C. from	6 o'clock	till	8	...	2 hours
and	8½	„	10½	...	2
B. and C.	10½	„	12½	...	2
A. and B.	1½	„	5½	...	4
B. and C.	6	„	8	...	2
					—
					12

All the changes take place at meal-hours except one, *viz.,* between breakfast and dinner, when a half of the number at work go out, to be replaced by others.

By this arrangement, the schoolmaster is employed only from 8½ to 3½, with an hour's interval for dinner.

II.—When the work begins at 6, and breakfast is from 9 to 9½, dinner from 2 to 3, and the mill stops at half-past 7 o'clock.

A. Work from 6 to 9 in the morning, and from half-past 9 till 2. $\Big\}$ =7½ hours for 5 days=37½

Ditto work on 6th day from 6 to 9, from half-past 9 till 2, and from 3 till half-past 4. $\Big\}$ =9 hours for 1 day = 9

$\left.\right\}$ hours 46½

B. Work from 6 to 9, and from 3 till half-past 7. $\Big\}$ =7½ hours for 5 days=37½

Ditto work on 6th day from 6 to 9, from half-past 9 till 2, and from 3 till half-past 4. $\Big\}$ =9 hours for 1 day = 9

$\left.\right\}$ 46½

C. Work from half-past 9 till 2, and from 3 till half-past 7. $\Big\}$ =9 hours for 5 days   ...   = 45

Thus leaving the time of A. and B. one hour and a half, and C. three hours, in each week, at the disposal of the mill-owner, for cleaning, etc.

By this system, those working 12 hours a day have

A. and B. from 6 o'clock till 9   ...   3
A. and C. from half-past 9 till 2 ...   4½ $\Big\}$ five days of the week.
B. and C. from 3 till half-past 7 ...   4½

and A. and B. for 9 hours on Saturday.

A. go to school from 3 to 5 in the afternoon, and have the evening for recreation.

B. go to school from 10 to 12 and have the forenoon for recreation.

C. go to school from 7 to 9 in the morning; they have little time for recreation, except Saturday, when they have several hours.

If it were thought advisable to equalise the labour of all the children, a change of the hours of attendance at the mill of the different sets might be made once a fortnight, or once a month.

—*Parl. Papers* (1837) *XXXI, p. 68.*

Plan II had been included in Horner's Report of 21st July, 1834 (*Parl. Papers*, 1834, XLIII, p. 441). It had been communicated to him by Hy. Houldsworth, a Glasgow cotton-spinner. Houldsworth, however, apparently found some difficulty in operating his own scheme, for Stuart, Horner's successor in the north, reported on 31st December, 1836 (*Parl. Papers*, 1837, XXXI, p. 120) "Mr. Houldsworth, of Glasgow, who gave Mr. Horner the plan of relays . . . had no more than 11 children employed when I visited his factory on the 29th October last."

FALSE RELAYS IN 1838.

CARD ROOM.

18 minutes before   6 to 18 minutes after   7
                    8 to 12 minutes before 12
                    1 to 24 minutes before   8

PIECERS (EXCEPT SEVEN).

18 minutes before 6 to 12 minutes before 8
30 minutes after   8 to 12 minutes before 1
                   2 to 24 minutes before 8

TWO PIECERS.

30 minutes before 6 to 30 minutes before 9
24 minutes before 10 to 30 minutes before 2
30 minutes before 3 to 24 minutes before 8

ONE PIECER.

30 minutes before 6 to 30 minutes before 9
                   9 to 30 minutes before 2
6 minutes after   3 to 24 minutes before 8

ONE PIECER.

6 minutes after   6 to 8
30 minutes before 9 to 1
                   2 to 24 minutes before 8

ONE PIECER.

30 minutes before 6 to 8
30 minutes before 9 to 24 minutes before 12
                   2 to 24 minutes before 8

ONE PIECER.

30 minutes before 6 to 8
30 minutes after   8 to 1
                   2 to 4
24 minutes before 5 to 24 minutes before 8

ONE PIECER.

30 minutes before 6 to 30 minutes before 9
                   9 to 30 minutes before 2
30 minutes before 3 to 4
24 minutes before 5 to 24 minutes before 8

"The above is the most elaborate contrivance I have yet met with, although all are more or less upon the same principle, by assigning different intervals to different persons for rest and refreshment, in which intervals those who are present, besides doing their own work, do the work of those who are absent."—*Howell's* Report, 6th July, 1838. Quoted *Parl. Papers* (1849) XXII, pp. 221-222.

FALSE RELAYS IN 1848.

Stuart's District.

Young persons and women were employed in six sets, A, B, C, D, E, F. All took their meals at the same times—9.30-10.15, and 2.15-3.

A, B, C, D, E	...	5.30— 7.30	... 2 hours
B, C, D, E, F	...	7.30— 9.30	... 2 hours
A, C, D, E, F	...	10.15—12.15	... 2 hours
A, B, D, E, F	...	12.15— 2.15	... 2 hours
A, B, C, E, F	...	3 — 5	... 2 hours
A, B, C, D, F,	...	5 — 7	... 2 hours

Factory works 12 hours

These sets were varied each week for six successive weeks, when the rotation began afresh.
—*Stuart's Report 31st October, 1848. Parl. Papers (1849) XXII, p. 266.*

Howell's District.

Loom No.	6—8	Breakfast	8.30-10.30	10.30-12.30	Dinner	1.30-3.30	3.30-5.30	5.30-7.30
1	**Man**		Woman	Woman		Woman	Woman	Woman
2	Woman		**Man**	Woman		Woman	Woman	Woman
3	Woman		Woman	**Man**		Woman	Woman	Woman
4	Woman		Woman	Woman		**Man**	Woman	Woman
5	Woman		Woman	Woman		Woman	**Man**	Woman
6	Woman		Woman	Woman		Woman	Woman	**Man**

—*Howell's Report, 30th April, 1848.*

Parl. Papers (1847-1848) XXVI, p. 170.

FACTORIES REGULATION ACT, 1844.

ATTEMPTED PROHIBITION OF RELAYS.

Sec. 26.—And be it enacted, that the Hours of Work of Children and young Persons in every Factory shall be reckoned from the Time when any Child or young Person shall first begin to work in the morning in such Factory, and shall be regulated by a public Clock, or by some other Clock open to the public View, to be approved of in either Case in writing under the Hand of the Inspector or Sub-Inspector of the District.

Sec. 28.—And be it enacted, that it shall not be necessary to hang up in any Mill or Factory any Copy of any Abstract of the Factory Act, or of any Regulations made in pursuance of the said Act, other than is herein-after provided; and that such Abstract of the Factory Act as amended by this Act as shall be directed by One of Her Majesty's Principal Secretaries of State shall be fixed on a moveable Board, and be hung up as soon as received by the Occupier of the Factory or his Agent in the Entrance of the Factory, and in such other Places as the Inspector or Sub-Inspector of the District may direct; and Notices of the Names and Addresses of the Inspector and Sub-Inspector of the District in which the Factory is situated, of the Name and Address of the Surgeon who grants Certificates of Age for the Factory, of the Clock by which the Hours of

Work in the Factory are regulated, of the Times of beginning and ending daily Work of all Persons employed in the Factory, and any Alteration thereof, of the Times of the Day and Amount of Time allowed for their several Meals, of all Time lost which is intended to be recovered, and of all Time which shall be recovered, together with every other Notice required by this Act, written or printed in legible Characters, and fixed on moveable Boards, (each particular Notice being signed by the Occupier of every Factory or his Agent) shall be hung up in the Entrance of the Factory, where they may be easily read by the Persons employed in the Factory, and in such other Places as the Inspector or Sub-Inspector of the District may direct, and whence they shall not be removed while the Factory is at work; and in case any such Abstract of the Factory Act as amended by this Act, or Notice, shall become illegible in any Part, the Occupier of the Factory shall cause a new Copy thereof to be provided and hung up as aforesaid; but the Notice of lost Time need not remain after the whole of the lost Time intended to be recovered shall have been recovered; and every Notice required to be hung up shall be in the Forms and according to the Directions given in the Schedule (C.) hereunto annexed.

Sec. 36.—And be it enacted, that the Times allowed for Meal Times as provided by the Factory Act shall be taken between the Hours of Half-past Seven in the Morning and Half-past Seven in the Evening of every Day, and One Hour thereof at the least shall be given, either the whole at one Time or at different Times, before Three of the Clock in the After-noon; and no Child or young Person shall be employed more than Five Hours before One of the Clock in the afternoon of any Day without an Interval for Meal Time of at least Thiry Minutes; and during any Meal Time which shall form any Part of the Hour and a Half allowed for Meals no Child or young Person shall be employed or allowed to remain in any Room in which any manufacturing Process is then carried on; and all the young Persons employed in a Factory shall have the Time for Meals at the same Period of the Day, unless some Alteration for special Cause shall be allowed in Writing by an Inspector.

Sec. 52.—And be it enacted, that in any Complaint of the Employ-ment of any Person in a Factory otherwise than is allowed by this Act the Time of beginning Work in the Morning which shall be stated in any Notice fixed up in the Factory, signed by the Occupier or his Agent, shall be taken to be the Time when all Persons in the Factory, except Children beginning to work in the Afternoon, began work on any Day subsequent to the Date of such Notice, so long as the same continued fixed up in the Factory; and if any Person shall be allowed to enter or be in any Factory, except at meal Times, or during the Stoppage of the whole Machinery of the Factory, or for the sole Purpose of bringing Tea or other Articles of Food to the Workers in a Factory, between the Hours of Four and Five of the Clock in the Afternoon, it shall be Evidence, unless the contrary shall be proved, that such Person was then employed in that Factory; but Yards, Play Grounds, and Places open to the public View, Schoolrooms, Waiting Rooms and other Rooms belonging to the Factory, in which no Machinery is used or manufacturing Process carried on, shall not be taken to be any Part of the Factory, with reference to this Enactment.

SCHEDULE C.

See page 352.

THE INTERPRETATION OF THE LAW.

20th January, 1845. The Inspectors to Manners Sutton.

By the Act to amend the Laws relating to Labour in Factories, 7 Vict., c. 15, it is enacted " That the *hours of work* of children and young persons *in every Factory* shall be reckoned from the time when *any Child or Young Person* shall *first begin to work in the morning* in such Factory."

By Sec. 28 it is enacted, that notice of the Clock by which the hours of work in the Factory are regulated and " of the *times of beginning and ending daily work of all persons* employed in the Factory " and any alteration thereof, of the times of the day and amount of time allowed for their several meals " shall be hung up in the entrance of every Factory; and that the notices shall be in the Forms and according to the directions given in Schedule C. hereunto annexed." The form of notice of the hours of work given in Schedule C. is entitled " The hours of work of all *young persons* and females above 18 years of age employed in this Factory," and at the end of the Form are these words " In every silk Factory in which children above 11 years of age are employed more than seven hours in any one day, a *separate* notice in the *above Form* shall be fixed up of the hours such children are employed." Attention is requested to the Forms in Schedule C. of the notice of the hours of work and of the times allowed for meals. Attention is also requested to the regulations as to Meal Times in S. 36.

By Sec. 52, It is enacted " that in any complaint of the employment of any person in a Factory otherwise than as allowed by this Act the *Time of beginning work in the morning which shall be stated in any notice* fixed up in the Factory, signed by the occupier or his agent shall be taken to be the time when all persons in the Factory, except children beginning to work in the afternoon, began on any day subsequent to the date of such notice, so long as the same continued fixed up in the Factory," &c.

Upon the construction of S. 52 taken in connexion with S. 26 doubts have arisen upon which the Inspectors desire to be advised. On the one hand it is held that S. 52 makes the notice (even if it should be inconsistent with the fact) the sole evidence of the things therein stated; so that altho' some children or young persons may actually have begun at 6 a.m. or even at 5 a.m. (see 3 & 4 Wm. IV, c. 103, S. 1) yet if the notice state 7 a.m. as the hour of beginning, the latter by S. 52 " shall be taken to be the time when all persons except children beginning to work in the afternoon (see S. 30) began," and that the Mill occupier can in such case only be prosecuted under S. 64 for not having put up " a notice of the hours of beginning work " correctly. On the other hand it is held that the notice required by S. 28 and recognized by S. 52 must be in conformity with the provisions of S. 26: but that if the notice be *inconsistent with the fact* it will not be in conformity with those provisions and cannot be set up to defeat them.

The Inspectors therefore desire to be advised as to the true legal intent and meaning of the 26th and 52nd Sections construed together, as they bear upon the employment of children and young persons respectively, upon the power of the Inspector to enforce regularity in the observance of time, and more particularly upon the mode of reckoning the hours of work of children employed in the forenoon under S. 30, for ten hours on alternate days under S. 31, or for ten hours daily under S. 72.[1]

It may be proper to remark that by the Factory Act 3 & 4 Wm. IV, c. 103, S. 1 and 2 young persons were limited to 12 hours work in the day, but as these 12 hours might be taken between $5\frac{1}{2}$ a.m. and $8\frac{1}{2}$ p.m. a practice arose in some places of working by a species of relay, whereby altho' no young person worked more than 12 hours, yet by assigning different meal hours to different individuals, and in like manner varying the hours of commencing and concluding work, the whole machinery could be kept going for the whole period of 15 hours between $5\frac{1}{2}$ a.m. and $8\frac{1}{2}$ p.m. It is believed to have been the object of the 26th, 28th, 36th, and 52nd Sections of the 7 Vict., c. 15 to prevent the employing of either children or young persons in this manner, and, if such was the object of the legislature, we are desirous of being instructed how far it has been accomplished by the Sections referred to. As regards the hours of work of young persons the 1st and 2nd Sections of the 3 & 4 Wm. IV, c. 103 remain unrepealed. If some young persons in a Factory begin at 6 a.m. and finish at 7 p.m. having had an hour and a half for meals and other young persons begin at 7 a.m. and finish at $8\frac{1}{2}$ p.m. having had the same time for meals and at the same periods of the day, or if all young persons begin at 6 a.m. but some are absent from work between 10 and 11 a.m., and then resume work but continue after the rest have left the Factory from $7\frac{1}{2}$ to $8\frac{1}{2}$ having had the same time for meals and at the same periods of the day as the others; no young person will have worked more than 12 hours but the machinery will have worked 13 hours; for in the first case, those who began at 6 did double work the first hour, and those who came at 7 did double work the last hour of the day, and in the other case young persons remaining in the Factory between 10 and 11 did double work during that hour and the others during the last hour. If the notice states the hours at which certain young persons begin to be 7 a.m., is the operation of S. 52 such as to prevent the Inspector from compelling the hours of labour being reckoned from 6 a.m. the period when other young persons first began work in the morning of the same day; if it is not, then he could make the labour of all young persons cease at $7\frac{1}{2}$ instead of $8\frac{1}{2}$ p.m. and the working of the machinery would be restricted, as it is believed it was meant to be, to 12 hours.

Again with respect to children employed in the process of winding and throwing of raw silk and who are permitted to work 10 hours in every day by S. 72, for whom it has been shewn that a separate notice, but in the same form as directed in Sch. C. is required. The Inspectors wish to be instructed, whether the work of such children is to be reckoned from the hour at which *any* child or young person first began work in the morning or whether their 10 hours of work are to be reckoned from the hour at which any of themselves first began to work, or in what other manner their hours are to be reckoned. For example in a factory in which children may be employed 10 hours in virtue of S. 72, and in which the hours of young persons are

$$5\frac{1}{2} \text{ to } 9\frac{1}{2} - 10 \text{ to } 12 - 3 \text{ to } 7 \quad \text{Total } 12$$

will the occupier by putting up a separate notice in the same form be entitled to employ the children for 10 hours in either of the two following ways: —

$$5\frac{1}{2} \text{ to } 9\frac{1}{2} - 10 \text{ to } 12 - \text{ and } 3 \text{ to } 7 \quad \text{Total } 10, \text{ or}$$
$$9 \text{ to } 9\frac{1}{2} - 10 \text{ to } 2 - 3 \text{ to } 8\frac{1}{2} \quad \text{Total } 10$$

---

1 *i.e.* Children employed in silk factories.

in either of which cases the machinery will have worked 13½ hours, but the children only 10 hours, and in the one case the children will have begun work at the same hour in the morning as the other children and young persons.

The Inspectors request to be informed whether in a Factory, in which the notice of the hours of work and of meals of all persons employed are in the form required by S. 28 and by Sch. C., and have been duly fixed up, and such notices shall shew the hours of work to be as follows:—

5½ to 9½ — 10 to 2 — and 3 to 7   Total 12

if by reason of accident to the machinery or from any other cause the whole or any part of the machinery and persons employed do not work during a part of the above-mentioned hours, the occupier by putting up a new notice, varying the hours of work and the times allowed for meals, before the work which was interrupted shall be renewed, can postpone the hour of closing his Factory on that day to such period between 7 p.m. and 8½ p.m. as will be equal to the period during which the work was interrupted to complete their full period of 12 hours; or whether the labour of all the persons employed in the Factory on that day must be restricted to 12 hours, reckoning from the time when *any* child or young person first began work in the morning of that day, over and above the hour and a half allowed for meals.

Sec. 4 of 3 & 4 Wm. IV, c. 103 gave a power of making up time lost by accidents to the machinery, but it was repealed by S. 33 of 7 Vict., c. 15 because it had been found to open a door to fraudulent overworking to a very considerable extent; and it is believed to have been the intention of the restriction in the beginning of S. 33, that such fraudulent overworking should be prevented. But if the occupier of a Factory can by the mere fixing up of an altered notice work after the expiration of 13½ hours from the time of starting his Mill in the morning (of which 1½ hours shall have been given for meals) alleged accidents will be of perpetual occurrence without the possibility of the Inspector detecting a fraud, or being able to prove that no time was lost.

—*Minutes, Vol. II, pp. 113-117.*

[To this letter Manners Sutton replied on 21st January, asking if any difficulty had actually arisen in consequence of the decisions of legal tribunals. The Inspectors informed him that there had been no decisions, but they desired an opinion because different owners interpreted the law in different ways. On 27th January Sutton told them that Sir James Graham, the Home Secretary, saw no necessity for taking the opinion of the Law Officers. (*Minutes, Vol. II, pp. 118, 119, 124.*) On 6th March, 1845, the Inspectors accordingly addressed another letter to the Home Office.]

6th March, 1845.   The Inspectors to Manners Sutton.

As uniformity of practice in all the districts is not only desirable but enjoined by the 45th Sec. of the Act 3 & 4 Wm. IV, c. 103, and as there are some important parts of the Law on which we differ in opinion as to the interpretation to be put upon them, we beg you, respectfully, to lay these points before Sir J. Graham.

We stated at some length the cases of want of uniformity of practice, to which we now refer, in our communication of the 20th Jan., on which occasion we expressed a desire to have a *legal opinion* upon the several points, but this you, in your Letter of the 27th Jan. informed us, Sir J.G. did not see a necessity for. Our object now in again troubling you is to have Sir J.G.'s. instructions in order to establish the desired uniformity of practice. We beg to refer you to our Letter of the 20th Jan., but for your convenience we now briefly state the points as follows:—

1. We take different views as regards the application of Section 26 and 52, coupled with the direction at the foot of the Form of notice of the hours of work in Sc. C. as applied to Silk Mills.

It is held on the one hand, that children working 10 hours in Silk Mills, must (as in other Mills) have their hours of work reckoned from the time when *any* child or young person first began work in the Factory in the morning of the same day.

On the other hand, that it is legal for the hours of work of children working 10 hours in Silk Mills to begin at a later hour than that at which the other hands in the Mill began.

2. We take different views as to the power of altering the hours of work during the day, when the Machinery is stopped by an accident or other cause of interruption.

It is contended on the one hand, that except in case of a water wheel being so stopped by drought or flood, that 12 hours work during the day cannot be obtained, in which case the time lost may be recovered in the manner pointed out in Sections 33 & 34, in no case can a Factory work more than 12 hours to be reckoned from the time when any child or young person first began work in the Factory on the same day.

On the other hand, that if in a Factory where the moving power is Steam only, and beginning work at 6 a.m. an accident happened in the course of the day causing an interruption to the work, it is legal to alter the hours of work on that day before 8½ p.m., the hour and a half having been allowed for meals,and a corresponding altered form having been fixed up before commencing work after the interruption which caused a deviation from the hours of work stated in the notice fixed up in the Mill on that day when any child or young person first began to work.

Having thus stated the different opinions held by us, we respectfully request that Sir J.G. will instruct us as to what interpretation we in his opinion ought to follow.

—Minutes, Vol. II, pp. 142-143.

4th April, 1845. Manners Sutton to the Inspectors.

I have laid your Letter of the 6th ult. before Sec. Sir J.G., and I am to inform you that he thinks that the permission for the hours of work of children working ten hours in Silk Mills to begin at a later hour than that at which the other hands in the Mill begin, should be allowed.

It appears to Sir J.G. from sections 26 and 52 of the 7 Vict., c. 15, that the opinion is correct, that in no case can a Factory work more than 12 hours to be reckoned from the time when any child or young person *first* began work in the Factory in the same day, except when lost time is recovered in the manner pointed in Sections 33 & 34.

—Minutes, Vol. II, p. 160.

7th June, 1848. The Inspectors to Cornewall Lewis.

By the Factory Act 3 & 4 Wm. IV, c. 103, S. 2 no person under 18
years of age shall be employed more than 12 hours in any one day or
than 69 hours in any one week.

By the same Statute S. 6 there shall be allowed in the course of every
day not less than one and a half hours for meals to every such person
restricted to the performance of 12 hours work daily.

Upon this 6th Section the Law Officers of the Crown in 1837, now
Lord Campbell and Mr. Baron Rolfe reported to Secretary Lord John
Russell their opinion " that the meaning of the Act was that at least an
hour and a half should be allowed for meals in the course of the Factory
working-day and that no part of such hour and a half should be taken
before the commencement or after the termination of the actual employment of the party."

By the Factory Act Amendment Act 7 Vict., c. 15, c. 36 " the times
allowed for Meal Times as provided by the *Factory Act* shall be taken
between the hours of 7½ in the morning, and 7½ in the evening of every
day, and one hour thereof at least shall be given either the whole at one
time or at different times before 3 o'clock in the afternoon."

By the 10 Vict., c. 29, S. 2 (commonly called the Ten-hours Bill) the
employment of Young Persons under the age of 18 years is from the
1st May, 1848 further limited to 10 hours in any one day and 58 hours in
any one week. And by S. 4 the two preceding Acts and this Act shall be
construed together as one Act.

It will be observed that the Factory Act 3 & 4 Wm. IV, c. 103 had
not specified any periods of the day when the Meal hours were to be
allowed and it is assumed that the fixing of these was therefore optional
with the master and might be so arranged by him within the Factory
working-day as to have admitted of *11 hours continuous work* and still
no part of the hour and a half be taken before the commencement or
after the termination of the actual employment of the party; in like manner
upon this assumption under the restricted period of 10 hours work, a
Mill owner might legally employ the Young Persons and females 9 hours
continuously.

On the commencement of the Ten Hours Bill one of the Inspectors,
Mr. Horner, issued a Circular instructing the several occupiers of Factories
in his District as to the principal provisions of the Law.

Of these instructions the 8th & 9th were as follows:—

" VIII.—The hour and a half for meals, required to be given in each
day, must be between HALF-PAST SEVEN in the morning, and HALF-
PAST SEVEN in the evening; and no Child, Young Person, or Woman
can be legally employed more than five hours before ONE O'CLOCK in
the afternoon of any day without an interval for meal time of at least
THIRTY MINUTES; and ONE HOUR of the said hour and half must be
given, either the whole at one time or at different times, before THREE
O'CLOCK in the afternoon; and during any meal time which forms any
part of the hour and a half, no Child, Young Person, or Woman, must be
employed or even allowed to remain in any room in which any manufacturing process is *then,* that is during the said meal time, carried on.
—(7 Vict., c. 15, sect. 36).

" IX.—Within the above limits of half-past seven in the morning and
half-past seven in the evening, a part of the hour and a half allowed for

meals may be given before commencing work in the morning, and after leaving off work in the evening, provided the work be not continued more than five hours without an interval of 30 minutes before One o'clock, and provided one hour be given before three o'clock in each day.

" I have been asked whether the following mode of working would be legal: —

		H.	M.	
Five Days ...	From 8 a.m. to 12.30 ...	4	30	
	1 p.m. to 6.30 ...	5	30	
				10.0
Saturday ...	8 a.m. to 12.30 ...	4	30	
	1 p.m. to 4.30 ...	3	30	
				8.0

" My answer was, that it would be legal; for I consider that, in such a case, the work people have 30 minutes for breakfast after half-past seven; that they do not work five hours continuously before one o'clock; that they have had an hour for meals before three o'clock; and, by stopping half an hour sooner in the evening, that they get the remainder of the hour and half."

In the example put in the 9th Instruction it will be seen that half an hour only would be allowed for meals between the commencement and the termination of the actual employment of the party. Doubts having been expressed to Mr. Horner whether the words of the Act would bear out the above construction, he applied for the opinion of the present Law Officers of the Crown, and on the 29th April last, he was informed by Sir Denis Le Marchant, that the Law Officers were of opinion " that the rules proposed by Mr. Horner in regard to the hours of work and meal times are in accordance with the Factory Acts as they will be in force on and after the 1st May next."

Applications have since been made to know whether it be permissible to commence working at 9 a.m. and terminate at 7 p.m. without any interval for meals on the assumption that the one hour and a half would have been allowed between the hours of $7\frac{1}{2}$ and 9 a.m., i.e., before the commencement of the working day: that the hour and a half would therefore be taken between the hours of $7\frac{1}{2}$ a.m. and $7\frac{1}{2}$ p.m.: that one hour thereof at least would be given before 3 p.m.; and that no person would be employed more *than five hours* before one o'clock p.m. without an interval for meal time of at least 30 minutes; these it is contended being the only provisions of the Law which now can be enforced.

The Inspectors are in these circumstances desirous of being instructed what is the true construction of the 3 & 4 Wm. IV, c. 103, S. 6 as amended by the 7 Vict., c. 15, S. 36 and taken in connexion with the 10 Vict., c. 29, S. 2 whereby the working day is reduced from 12 to 10 hours, and particularly whether it be lawful to work for ten hours continuously from 9 a.m. to 7 p.m. without any interval for meals in the manner proposed to us.

—*Minutes, Vol. II, pp. 352-354.*

22nd June, 1848. *Cornewall Lewis to the Inspectors.*

The Law Officers state that . . . they think the true construction of the Statute is, that time should be allowed for three Meals, breakfast, dinner and tea;—That the time for the first may be taken before the work begins. and the time for the last after the work has ceased, but the time for dinner must be in the interval during the working hours, and it will not be lawful to work for ten hours continuously from 9 a.m. to 7 p.m. without any interval for meals in the manner proposed.

—*Minutes, Vol. II, p. 367.*

9th June, 1848. Cornewall Lewis to the Inspectors.

I am directed by Sec. Sir George Grey to inform you that by his desire a case has been laid before the Law Officers of the Crown as to the construction of the Act 7 Vict. c. 15 in regard to working by relays. The Law Officers having been applied to for their opinion as to the true construction of the 26th Sec. of the above Act, and whether there is any mode by which the question can be brought before a Court of Law so as to obtain a decision upon the points, state that they are of opinion that the time of working for young persons, women and children (except children beginning to work in the afternoon) begins to run from the time specified in the Notice fixed up in the Factory as the time for beginning daily work. This is in their opinion the true construction of the 26th Section of the Act when taken in conjunction with the 52nd Section.

They further state, that as by the 69th Section the order cannot be appealed against or removed by Certiorari, there is no means of raising the question hostiley; but if the parties can so arrange that a Magistrate shall refuse to convict, the question may be raised by an application to the Court of Queen's Bench for a Mandamus.

As it appears that conflicting decisions upon the 26th Section have been made by different Benches of Magistrates, Sir George Grey thinks it would be desirable that the question should, if possible, be raised in such a manner as to obtain the opinion of a Superior Court upon it.

—*Minutes, Vol. II, pp. 361-362.*

21st July, 1848. The Inspectors to Cornewall Lewis.

We have received from our colleague Mr. Horner the enclosed letter respecting some points of very great legal nicety as to the true interpretation of different Sections of the Factory Acts upon which we do not feel ourselves competent to give a decided opinion and request your instructions thereon:—

Dear Sirs,

It was to be expected that some Millowners would endeavour by various contrivances to elude without intending to act illegally the restrictions of the Ten-hours Act; some as you are already aware have already tried relays of Young Persons, and if Trade goes on as it has begun to improve such expedients will be multiplied. I have this morning been investigating a plan on which a mill is working having been called upon by the owner to say whether it is legal. I have not been able to come to a clear decision on the point, and I have now to request my Colleagues to favour me with their several or joint opinions thereon.

John Bright (M.P.) & Co. of Rochdale work the larger portion of their hands (Spinning & Power Loom weaving of Cotton) as follows:—

From 6 a.m. to 8	=2			
8½ to 12½	=4	Breakfast — 8 to 8½	=	30
1½ p.m. to 5½	=4	Dinner —12½ to 1½	=	1.0
	10			1.30

and they have a notice accordingly.

But they have about 50 young persons who work as follows:—

From 6 a.m. to 8	=2			
8½ to 11½	=3	Breakfast — 8 to 8½	=	30
1½ to 6½	=5	Dinner —11½ to 1½	=	2.0
	10			2.30

and they have a second notice accordingly, but without the names of the said 50 persons.

These 50 persons are Tenters, that is assistants to adult males who work 12 hours a day from 6 a.m. to 7½ p.m. with 1.30 for meals, weavers. The reason for the adoption of the above plan is that it is inconvenient to the weavers to be without their Tenters so long as 2 hours at a time, viz., from 5½ to 7½ p.m. but they can continue to do without them for one hour at a time twice a day, viz., from 11½ to 12½ in the forenoon and from 6½ to 7½ in the evening.

I stated to them that these 50 persons by the 26th and 52nd Clause of 7 Vict. work 11 hours a day: they replied that they were allowed 2 hours for dinner.

I referred them to the 36th Sect. that all the Young Persons shall have the Times for meals at the same period of the day: they replied—the 50 Tenters have their Meals at the same period of the day with the rest, and they have one hour more. They referred to Sec. 6 of 3 & 4 Wm. IV, c. 103 that there shall be allowed not less than 1½ hours for meals.

The question turns upon what interpretation a lawyer will give to the word " period "? Can the interpretation put upon it by Bright & Co. be sustained? I have no doubt that the intention was that all workers in the Mill, i.e., Young Persons and women should not only have their meals at the same time but that they should all have the same number of minutes for each meal, neither more nor less.

Is it your opinion that I could take Bright & Co. into Court for working these 50 persons 11 hours a day. You will observe that there is no system of relays properly so called, no substitution of one Set of workers for another and that their hours of work are reckoned from the time when any Young Person first begins to work in the Factory.

What is the legal construction of the word period as used in the 36th Sect. of 7 Vict.? If all the workers in a Mill have their breakfast from 8 to 8½ and dinner from 12½ to 1½ must all be held to be working from the time when the Mill starts in the morning until it closes at night with the exception of those intervals; or is it legal to allow to some of the workers to have an hour at breakfast time and an hour at dinner in addition to the above-named intervals and make them work 2 hours later than those who have only 1½ hours for meals?

I objected to the two notices, the heading being " The hours of work of all young persons " &c., one notice of the following kind being suggested.

"The hours of work of all Young Persons and Females above 18 years of age employed in this Factory."

All except those named in ⎱ Monday — 6   to   8
    the annexed List *A*.   ⎰   8½ to 12½
                                        1½ to 5½ = 10

The above repeated for each day. Tuesday.—The above repeated for each day and at the bottom of the paper the names and the number of their Certificates.

Can I legally object to this notice? I think not, for it does give the hours of work of all, and the 28th Sect. says Notices of the Times of beginning and ending daily work of all persons employed, &c.

Although I see that such a mode of working and such an interpretation of the word "period" may lead to much fraudulent overworking which it would be almost impossible to detect, my present impression is that it is not contrary to the *words* of the Act and that I could not obtain a conviction, as Magistrates do not trouble themselves about the intention of the legislature, if that intention is not clearly set forth by the words of the Act.

Kennedy & Co. are working by relays as follows:—

They have one notice of which the following is a copy:—

"The hours of work of all Young Persons and Females above 18 years of age employed in this Factory."

	Morning	Forenoon	Aftern'n	Evening	Total	Breakfast	Dinner	Tea
1st Set (Names as in Time Book below)	Absent	9.20–12.40	1.40–5	5.10–8.30	10⎫			
2nd Set ,,	5.30–8.50	Absent	1.40–5	5.10–8.30	10⎬			
3rd Set ,,	5.30–8.50	9.20–12.40	Absent	5.10–8.30	10	8.50–9.20	12.40–1.40	5–5.10
4th Set ,,	5.30–8.50	9.20–12.40	1.40–5	Absent	10⎭			
Saturday								
1st Set (Names as in Time Book below)	Absent	8.20–10.40	10.40–1	2–4.30	⎫			
2nd Set ,,	5.30–7.50	Absent	10.40–1	2–4.30	⎬	7.50–8.20	1–2	
3rd Set ,,	5.30–7.50	8.20–10.40	Absent	2–4.30	⎭			
4th Set ,,	5.30–7.50	8.20–10.40	10.40–1	Absent				

To this notice is attached a Book containing the names of the persons included in the several sets.

The notice has also the days of the week as in the Schedule: I do not consider that the notice is contrary to the Act, but I have no doubt that the plan of working is contrary to the interpretation of the 26th and 52nd Clauses which we have all held and which has been given to us by the Secretary of State to enforce. I therefore yesterday determined to have an information laid against them for employing a Young Person and a Woman (taken from the 1st Set) more than 10 hours a day, and shall prove this by the evidence of two from the second set who begin at $5\frac{1}{2}$ a.m. It will be an amicable suit to try the question of legality, and the case will be heard by Mr. Maude.

But since I have been to Bright's Factory at Rochdale this morning, having for the first time heard such an interpretation of the word period in the 36th Sect. as Bright is acting upon, a doubt has arisen in my mind whether I shall obtain a conviction. For if Kennedy adopts Bright's interpretation of the word period he may say:—

" All my workers have their meals at the same period but to the 1st Set, I allow 3 hours 20 minutes for breakfast in addition to the 30 minutes from 8.50 to 9.20, viz., from 5.30 to 8.50. To the 2nd Set I allow 3 hours and 20 minutes for breakfast in addition to the 30 minutes from 8.50 to 9.20, viz., from 9.20 to 12.40. To the 3rd Set I allow 3 hours and 20 minutes for dinner in addition to the hour from 12.40 to 1.40, viz., from 1.40 to 5."

To this I should reply that no time for meals can be reckoned before $7\frac{1}{2}$ in the morning and therefore even upon the interpretation put upon the word period by the 26th Section they worked the first set from $5\frac{1}{2}$ to $7\frac{1}{2}$, which together with their subsequent time makes 12 hours.

Do you think that I have grounds for maintaining this last position?

I am, &c.,

LEONARD HORNER.

—*Minutes, Vol. II, pp. 376-379.*

[Acknowledging this letter, the Home Secretary replied, on 26th July, 1848, that if the Inspectors desired the opinion of the Law Officers upon any specific point, a case would be submitted if it was distinctly stated. (*Minutes, Vol. II, p. 380*). In the meantime Horner had resolved to reject the view put forward by Messrs. Bright].

29th July, 1848. Leonard Horner to Messrs. Bright.

Having fully considered the question of the legality of your employing certain young persons from 6 a.m. to $6\frac{1}{2}$ p.m. with an interval of half an hour from 8 to $8\frac{1}{2}$ a.m. and another interval of 2 hours from $11\frac{1}{2}$ to $1\frac{1}{2}$ p.m., while you also employ other young persons and women from 6 a.m. to $5\frac{1}{2}$ p.m. with an interval of half an hour from 8 to $8\frac{1}{2}$ a.m. and another interval of *one* hour from $12\frac{1}{2}$ to $1\frac{1}{2}$ p.m.; I am of opinion that such a mode of working the first named young persons is contrary to Ss. 26, 28, 36, & 52 of the Act 7 Vict. c. 15 and to the forms of notice referred to in Ss. 28 & 52.

If you were to allow the two hours from $11\frac{1}{2}$ to $1\frac{1}{2}$ to *all* the young persons and women you employ you would be then acting in conformity with the Law.

Any one young person and woman must be held to have been employed on any one day from the time that any other Young Person or woman first began to work in the morning and to the time that the first named young person or woman left off work the same day, deducting such number of minutes as shall have been allowed for meal times on that day to *all* the Young Persons and women and to all at the same time of the day. I therefore hold that the young persons who begin at 6 a.m. and leave off at $6\frac{1}{2}$ p.m. according to the mode of computing their hours of work laid down in the 26th & 52nd Ss. and to the regulation of S. 36 as to one time for meals for all, have been employed for a longer time than 10 hours a day.

I request you to inform me what alteration if any you propose to make in your mode of working in consequence of the above statement of what I believe to be the true construction of the enactments referred to.

—*Minutes, Vol. II, p. 381.*

THE CASE OF MESSRS. JONES.

21st July, 1848. From the Chairman of the Tyldersley Bench to the Home Office.

As Chairman of the Bench of the Magistrates sitting at Tyldersley, I have the honour to acknowledge the receipt of your letter of the 15th Inst, requesting us to state the grounds on which we declined to hear the cases against Messrs. Jones & Co. on the information laid by Mr. Jones, Sub-Inspector of Factories, and in reply thereto I have to state that similar cases to those brought before the Tyldersley Bench on the 7th Inst, had been decided by a Bench of Magistrates sitting at Atherton only a short distance from this place and in the same district.

Those Magistrates (4 in number) came to the Tyldersley Bench on the 7th Inst, evidently with the intention of carrying out the decision given by them at Atherton, they being the majority then present, and Mr. Greene who had delivered the decision of the Magistrates at Atherton stated they attended only to support their former decision, they interfered with no other cases and left the Court as soon as Messrs. Jones' cases were disposed of.

Under these circumstances we being the minority considered it only a waste of time to go into the cases . . . . If the cases had come before the Tyldersley Bench of Magistrates only, they would have conceived it their duty to have gone into them.

—*Minutes, Vol. II, pp. 383-384.*

THE CASE OF MESSRS. KENNEDY.

2nd August, 1848. Horner to Cornewall Lewis.

I laid an information against Messrs. Kennedy & Co. for working Young Persons (by relays) more than 10 hours in one day, computing their hours of work by the enactments in Ss. 26, 28 & 52 of 7 Vict., c. 15, as interpreted by the Law Officers of the Crown.

The case was heard this day in the Borough Court by Daniel Maude, Esqre., Stipendiary Magistrate, and ten other Magistrates. It was argued by Counsel on both sides at considerable length—the Magistrates retired for some time, and on their return Mr. Maude announced that Messrs. Kennedy were convicted of the offence laid in the information. This decision will probably carry great weight throughout my District.

But Messrs. Jones & Co. against whom an Information was laid for the same offence at Tyldersley on the 7th July last, and which the Magistrates there refused to hear, have intimated to me since the above decision (they

were in Court the whole time) in answer to a question put to them that
notwithstanding the conviction of Messrs. Kennedy & Co. they will go on
working as they were doing when the Information was laid against them.
I am therefore desirous of knowing, before I decide as to the course I shall
take with respect to Messrs. Jones . . . whether you have any instructions
to give relative to that case.

—Minutes, Vol. II, p. 382.

THE POLICY OF THE HOME OFFICE.

5th August, 1848.   Cornewall Lewis to Horner.

In reply to your enquiry whether Sir G. Grey has any instructions to
give you relative to this case, I am to state that Sir G. Grey does not wish
to interfere in particular cases with the discretion vested in the Inspectors:
but I am to add that as a general rule he thinks it inexpedient to lay
informations against Millowners for a breach of the letter of the Act as to
the employment of young persons by relays, in cases in which there is no
reason to believe that such young persons have been actually employed for
a longer period than that sanctioned by law.

Sir G. Grey requests you will communicate a copy of this letter to
your Colleagues.

—Minutes, Vol. II, p. 383.

THE POLICY OF THE INSPECTORS.

10th August, 1848.   Horner to Cornewall Lewis.

I have had the honour to receive your letter of the 5th Inst, ...
intimating to me that Sir G. Grey thinks it inexpedient that I should lay
informations against Millowners for a breach of the letter of the Act as
to the employment of Young Persons by relays in cases in which there is
no reason to believe that such young persons have been actually employed
for a longer time than that sanctioned by law.

I beg you will assure Sir George Grey that I have every disposition to
follow any instructions he may think it advisable to give me as far as I
am able; but believing that he is not fully aware of the consequences that
must result from my allowing the employment of young persons by relays
in a manner contrary to the 26th and 52nd Sections of the Act of 1844 I
feel it my duty to make the following statement.

My firm conviction is that under any modification which I have ever
seen or can imagine, the employment of young persons by relays must
virtually render nugatory the main purpose of the law which imposes
restriction upon their hours of work, and that acting contrary to the above
named Sections is not a mere disobedience of the " letter of the Act," but
a violation of its spirit and scope, and of enactments which form necessary
and indispensable adjuncts of the main restrictive enactment.   All my
experience up to the present hour, has satisfied me that a license to work
young persons by relays and a law restricting their labour to a given
number of hours, evasions of which can practically be prevented, are two
things which cannot co-exist.   I cannot illustrate what I have now stated
better than by the case of Messrs. Jas. Kennedy & Co, which was heard

last week by the Manchester Bench of Magistrates. So far as I know, the young persons in their Mill do not, technically, work more than 10 hours a day, but practically they are engaged in their occupation nearly $13\frac{1}{2}$ hours exclusive of their mealtimes. I restricted the information to the case of one person only as my object was to have a decision of the Magistrates on the point of law.

Sarah Overend, the young person named in the Information, a girl between 14 and 15 years of age (it might have been a boy of 13 years of age) worked as follows:—

From	5.30 to 8.50 a.m.	...	=	3.20
	1.40 to 5 p.m.	...	=	3.20
	5.10 to 8.30 p.m.	...	=	3.20
				10 hours

She was thus absent from the mill from 8.50 a.m. to 1.40 p.m.= 4 hours and 50 minutes, and if the half hour for breakfast and an hour for dinner be deducted, she was unoccupied 3 hours and 20 minutes; she was in the Mill from 1.40 to 8.30 p.m., the steam engine stopping at 5 p.m. for 10 minutes to allow the workpeople to take any food they may bring with them.

Now it is obvious that Sarah Overend (and still less a boy of 13 years of age) could not turn the 3 hours and 20 minutes in the forenoon that by the above arrangement she was not at work in the Mill, to any purpose of moral improvement. Besides according to the system followed in the Mill, her unoccupied hours varied every week, being sometimes before breakfast, sometimes in the forenoon, sometimes in the afternoon. But if the requirements of the law had been observed, her work for the day would have entirely ceased at 5 o'clock in the evening. She could then have thrown off her working dress and gone for two hours to an evening school, and thus she would have been in a position to profit by the restricted hours of labour.

I have stated my belief that Messrs. Kennedy & Co. were not employing any young persons more than 10 hours a day, but had they been acting differently it would not have been possible to convict them. For I found on going to their mill last week that the persons composing their four sets of relays did not work together, that is, each set distinct and at the same time of the day continuously. The four sets included above 150 persons, were working promiscuously in different rooms in five different stories, and they were changing their hours of work from week to week, and the persons changed from one set into another as convenience required.

Information may be given to me that a mill owner is working young persons more than ten hours a day and on the strongest prima facie evidence, viz., that they are seen going to their work at half past 5 in the morning and leaving off at half past 8 at night. But it would be impossible for me to know whether the charge were true or otherwise, unless I could prove to my own satisfaction that each individual young person in the Mill (and there might be 500) had been unemployed such a number of hours in the course of the day between the two extremes as to leave no more than 10 hours of work, a thing manifestly impossible.

I see no medium course which I can take: I must allow all or none to act contrary to the enactments in the 26th and 52nd Sections. I cannot with consistency allow A to work by relays because the young persons are not actually employed more than 10 hours between $5\frac{1}{2}$ a.m. and $8\frac{1}{2}$ p.m. and prosecute B from having been told and having reason to believe that he is by an ingenious contrivance working young persons more than 10 hours a day because the only proof to which I can have recourse, with any hope of being able to prove the offence is that given to the Inspectors for the express purpose, *viz.*, the violation of the 26th & 52nd Sections; so that I should be prosecuting B for doing that which I had allowed his neighbour A to do.

If Sir G. Grey deems it advisable to direct me not to enforce the 26 & 52 Sections as interpreted by the Law Officers of the Crown, I shall of course completely obey his instruction; but for the reasons above stated I cannot undertake to exercise any discretionary power.

I therefore respectfully request that you will inform me whether I am to continue to enforce the observance of the Law according to the interpretation of the 26th and 52nd Sections by the Law Officers of the Crown, by means of such powers as the Act itself gives me, or if I am to cease to interfere with Millowners, who are working by relays of Young Persons in a manner that is contrary to that interpretation.

—Minutes, Vol. II, pp. 384-387.

12th August, 1848. Howell to Cornewall Lewis.

My colleague Mr. Horner has sent to me the copy of a letter from you to him dated the 10th Inst., wherein you inform him that Sir G. Grey thinks it inexpedient to bring informations against Millowners for a breach of the letter of the Act as to the employment of Young Persons by relays in cases where there is no reason to believe that such Young Persons have been actually employed for a longer period than that sanctioned by law . . .

I am of opinion that there is no alternative between a strict enforcement of Ss. 26 and 52 and their total abandonment. Their strict enforcement would compel those masters who might wish to run their machinery or any part thereof longer than 10 hours to employ for that purpose Males of 18 years of age whose labour is not restricted by law. I should not venture to trespass upon Sir G. Grey's indulgence by obtruding an unasked opinion on this subject did I not know that the strongest feeling pervades the working classes in favour of the strict enforcement of the Sections in question: it is in fact notorious that when Kennedy's case was decided the other day at Manchester Deputies from the surrounding Districts were in attendance to watch the proceedings on behalf of the operatives, and I believe they would view any relaxation of the sections in question as a virtual repeal of the Ten Hours Act for which they have been striving for so many years and as to which I believe their feelings to be sensitive if not inflammable. Further experience of the Factory system teaches them to know that in Towns the practical effect of this spurious relay system would be (whatever may be said to the contrary) that the hands would be really worked in one Factory or another for the whole time the machinery runs, and that in rural Districts where Factories are thinly scattered so that all the hands could not readily be transferred from one to another, the intervals interposed to prolong the working day would from the distance of their homes from the Factory be valueless to the working people and would (in those cases where the 10 hours are not surreptitiously exceeded) be spent in idling about waiting for the moment when they are wanted to resume work with the additional discomfort of exposure to the severity of the weather in inclement seasons so that for any useful purpose these intervals might as well not be granted at all but employed with the ordinary work of the Factory. This causes the working classes to view the project of working by spurious relays of young persons however speciously recommended as artful devices for cheating them out of the results of their

Ten Hour Bill which the strict enforcement of the section under consideration would secure to them; for they know that by protracting the working day for Young Persons by these devices, though for the sake of argument it be admitted that no one of them shall be employed on manual labour more than ten hours yet in consequence of their constant attendance to be ready to resume their work at the precise moment when they are wanted after their intervals which are interposed to protract the working day, they are really as much employed at the Factory from the beginning to the end of the working day as a player who performs in the first in the last and in all the intermediate scenes of a comedy save three or four is deemed to be and in fact is employed from the beginning to the end of the performance. In my District there has been and doubtless will continue to be after the recent decisions a constant pressure on the part of the operatives for the enforcement of the Sections under consideration and I cannot help apprehending that any appearance of a disposition to shirk their enforcement would awaken the energies of the now dormant Short time Committees and revive the agitation of former days with an activity soured by disappointment.

—*Minutes, Vol. II, pp. 393-397.*

CHANGING VIEWS OF THE HOME OFFICE.

12th August, 1848. Cornewall Lewis to Horner.

I have laid before Secretary Sir George Grey your letter of the 10th Instant, and I am to inform you in reply that although in consequence of your enquiring whether he had any instructions to give you relative to the case of Messrs. Jones & Co. mentioned in your letter of the 2nd Instant, he stated his general opinion as to the course to be pursued in such matters, Sir George Grey had no intention of interfering with the discretion of the Inspectors in regard to particular instances of a violation of the law which might come under their notice; nor would he consider it to be consistent with his duty to instruct you to abstain generally from enforcing any of the provisions of the Laws respecting employment in Factories.

—*Minutes, Vol. II, p. 387.*

9th January, 1849. Cornewall Lewis to Horner.

Sir George Grey sees no way of settling the question but by an Act of Parliament, and it is his intention to bring in a Bill for that purpose at the commencement of the Session.

—*Minutes, Vol II, p. 412.*

OFFICIAL COPY OF THE JUDGES' DECISION ON THE FACTORY ACT.

RYDER v. MILLS.

Judgment delivered in the Court of Exchequer, Friday, February 8th, 1850.

(From Mr. Gurney's Shorthand Notes).

Mr. Baron Parke.—The question raised by this special case, by the agreement between the Crown and the defendant, is, whether it is an offence against the Factory Acts, or any of them, to employ a young person in a factory for ten hours and no more in one day, such ten hours ending at a period which is more than ten hours from the time when another child or young person first began to work in the morning of such day in such factory, if such last-mentioned ten hours are counted consecutively from that time, omitting only the meal times?

This question depends entirely on the proper construction to be put on those Acts, and more particularly on the 7th Victoria, cap. 15. These Acts must be construed according to the established rules for the construction of statutes. In a court of law we have only to ascertain the meaning of the words used by the Legislature, and when that is ascertained we have to carry it into effect, and we are not to enquire whether the enactments are dictated by sound policy or not; that question is exclusively for the consideration of Parliament. We agree also with the Attorney General that though the immediate question in this case did relate to adult females, who are more capable of taking care of themselves, and of continued labour, than children, and consequently need less protection, and on whom the restriction from employing themselves as they may think best appears more of a hardship, the point to be decided is the same as if we were considering the case of children and young persons only, for the Legislature has clearly put all females on the same footing as they are. Indeed, the case as agreed on by both parties states that to be the question. Is, then, the owner of a factory liable to the penalty in respect of the employment of a child or young person in the manner stated?

The Act imposes a penalty, and therefore according to the established rule, must be construed strictly; that is, a man is not to be restrained from the liberty which he has by acting as he pleases, and rendered liable to a punishment, unless the law has plainly said that he shall. It is not enough that we conjecture, even strongly, that it was the intention of the Legislature to have prohibited the act. There must be words indicating plainly and clearly that it has done so, and, applying this rule of construction, we do not think that there are words in the statutes sufficiently plain and clear to render the conduct of the defendant in the case above-mentioned liable to punishment.

On the opening of the argument by the Attorney General, we thought the defendant meant to contend that the time limited by the 26th section of the 7th Victoria, cap. 15, was to be calculated for each child or young person from the time that such child or young person first began to work in the morning; and that argument seemed to us to be altogether untenable, as being against the ordinary and grammatical sense of the words in that section.

But such is not the construction contended for by the learned counsel for the defendant. He admits, and properly, that it is clearly the ordinary meaning of the words in that section, that the period from which the time is to be reckoned for all children and young persons working at the factory is that time when the first child or young person that was employed therein began to work. Both sides are agreed upon this limit of the time, and there can be not the least doubt about it. So, also, it is perfectly clear that the times for meals for all young persons must all be at the same period of the day, according to the plain words of the 36th section, which may be explained by the convenience of all the women and children and young persons having their meals prepared at the same time.

But it is contended for the defendant, that the other limit—the end of the time of working for all children and young persons—has not been prescribed, and that it has not been enacted that the time for the cessation of labour for all should be that when the first ceased labour. Certainly this has not been done in express words and nothing was more easy than to have said, in the 26th section, that the 12 hours—reduced to 11 and 10 by the subsequent statute, the 10th Vicoria, cap. 29—should end when any one had worked that time; or to have said, in the 36th section, that all young persons should have the time for labour as well as for meals at the same period of the day.

We must, then, consider whether, in the absence of express words to this effect, we can collect from other parts of the Act that this was the meaning of the Legislature so clearly and unequivocally as to call upon us to give effect to it, and punish the defendant.

Undoubtedly if there was such an enactment it would have the effect of securing to the children and young persons, whom it was most certainly the object of the Legislature to protect against their own improvidence, or that of their parents, the more effectual superintendence and care of the inspectors. Without question it would more effectually prevent them from being overworked, and secure to them more completely the benefit of some education in public schools which the Legislature meant them to enjoy; it would advance the intended remedy. But then this result could only have been obtained by a larger sacrifice of the interest of the owners of factories, and we cannot assume that Parliament would disregard so important a consideration.

At any rate, a court of justice cannot render a man liable to a penalty merely because it might think that it would better promote the supposed object of the Legislature than the provisions of the statute according to their ordinary construction.

The words used must plainly and clearly show that the act complained of is punishable. On the part of the prosecution it was contended that the intention of the Legislature could be clearly collected, partly from the words in the Act itself, and partly from the schedules. Some reliance was placed upon the term " reckoned," in the 26th section, as meaning that it was to be continuously reckoned from the time when any one should begin to work; that is, that the next 12 hours after the time (with the intervals mentioned in the 36th section) should be the only hours of work; but we think that such is not the ordinary construction of that word: it means only that the computation of time shall then begin. It does not state when it shall end.

An argument was also drawn from the wording of the 52nd section, which provides, it is said, for the beginning of work, and therefore the 26th section must have been intended, and ought to be construed to mean, to provide for the whole time—the beginning and ending, otherwise that section would be unnecessary. But the 52nd section provides only for the evidence of the time of commencement—no more.

The principal reliance was placed on the schedules which are required to be adopted by section 28, as showing the intention of the framers of the Act, that the times of all should begin and end simultaneously; for, in the first form, it is clear that no names are intended to be mentioned. In the last, where particular individuals are to be named, the form expressly provides that it shall be so.

It cannot be denied that the forms appear to have been constructed on the supposition that all would work the same time, but they are capable of being reconciled with the other supposition, for there seems certainly to be nothing expressly to forbid the blanks from being filled up so as to provide for the time of part ending at one hour, and that of the other part at another.

Indeed, if it were not so, no factory owner could employ some young persons for four hours, some for five, some for nine (which he unquestionably may); for the schedules if they are to be filled up strictly according to the forms, stating all as beginning and ending at the same time, are not adapted to such a case, and they must, therefore, undergo some alteration.

On the other hand, some argument in favour of the defendant was deduced from the peculiar language of the 28th section, which requires notice of the "times" of beginning and ending daily work of all persons, as if they might end at different times, and as if in such a case the Act required each to be named with his allotted time in the notice. But the distinction between the use of the term "times" instead of "time" is by no means satisfactory to our minds, and we do not at all rest upon it.

The ground upon which we proceed is, that though the Act of Parliament (taken in conjunction with the 10th Victoria, cap. 29) does distinctly forbid the employment of young persons, and therefore all females, for more than ten hours, and those to be taken between half-past 5 in the morning and half-past eight at night; though it distinctly requires that the time of all is to begin to be computed from the beginning of the first to work, and that an hour and a half shall be allowed for meals, and for all at the same time, it has not imposed in sufficiently clear terms any other restriction on the employment of young persons, and they are therefore at liberty to agree together for working for less than for the whole of that time within the limits before-mentioned, ending at half-past eight, or any previous time that they please, and with any intervals of leisure that may be thought convenient.

Mr. Baron Alderton.—I have no doubt that that was the meaning of the word "reckoned," that it was to distinguish the hour at which the first person began to work from the half-past five o'clock, which was the limit of all. Instead of reckoning from half-past five, you must reckon from the time when the first person began.

Quoted in *The Champion*, Vol. I, No. 18. March 9th, 1850, pp. 280-283.

RELAYS IN 1850.

Number of Factories worked on the 15th of July, 1850, by male persons above eighteen years of age, after the young persons and women who are employed in those Factories for Ten Hours continuously (exclusive of meal times) have ceased to work for the day, and in which Factories children are employed as assistants to the said male persons during such extra time of work; together with the number of children so employed.

	Number of Factories	Number of Children employed		
		Boys	Girls	Total
In Mr. Horner's district	148	1405	544	1949
In Mr. Howell's district	11	72	15	87
In Capt. Kincaid's district	8	30	9	39
In Mr. Saunders' district	90	871	796	1667
	257	2378	1364	3742

—*Parl. Papers* (1850) *XLII*, p. 477.

XXI.—GROWTH OF TOWNS.

		1821	1831	1841	1851
Cheshire					
Bidston	... ...	1,014	3,434	9,236	25,818
Stockport	... ...	44,957	66,610	84,301	91,423
Wallasey	... ...	1,169	2,737	6,261	8,339
Lancashire					
Ashton-under-Lyne		25,967	33,597	46,304	56,959
Blackburn	... ...	53,350	59,791	71,711	84,919
Bury	... ...	34,335	47,627	62,125	70,143
Chorley	... ...	7,315	9,282	13,139	12,684
Manchester	...	187,031	270,963	353,390	455,158
Preston	... ...	27,300	36,336	53,482	72,136
Rochdale	... ...	47,109	58,441	67,889	80,214
Wigan	... ...	38,318	44,486	51,988	63,287
Yorkshire					
Bradford	... ...	52,954	76,986	105,257	149,543
Halifax	... ...	93,050	109,899	130,743	140,257
Leeds	... ...	83,796	123,393	151,874	172,023

(*Commerce and Industry, ed. W. Page (1919), pp. 4-18*).

XXII—STATUTORY AND SPECIAL MEETINGS OF THE FACTORY INSPECTORS.

Day	Date	Inspectors present			
		Horner	Howell	Saunders	Stuart
Half Yearly Meeting					
Thursday	8 Sept., 1836	*	*	*	*
Friday	9 Sept., 1836	*	*	*	*
Saturday	10 Sept., 1836	*		*	*
Monday	12 Sept., 1836	*		*	
Tuesday	13 Sept., 1836	*		*	
Wednesday	14 Sept., 1836	*		*	*
Thursday	15 Sept., 1836	*		*	*
Friday	16 Sept., 1836	*		*	*
Wednesday	21 Sept., 1836	*		*	*
Thursday	22 Sept., 1836	*		*	*
Thursday	29 Sept., 1836	*		*	*
Friday	30 Sept., 1836	*		*	*
Tuesday	4 Oct., 1836	*		*	*
Wednesday	5 Oct., 1836	*		*	*
Thursday	6 Oct., 1836	*		*	*
Monday	10 Oct., 1836	*		*	*
Wednesday	12 Oct., 1836	*		*	
Half Yearly Meeting					
Monday	16 Jan., 1837	*		*	*
Tuesday	17 Jan., 1837	*	*	*	*
Wednesday	18 Jan., 1837	*	*	*	*
Thursday	19 Jan., 1837	*	*	*	*
Tuesday	24 Jan., 1837	*	*	*	*
Wednesday	25 Jan., 1837	*	*	*	*
Thursday	26 Jan., 1837	*	*	*	*
Friday	27 Jan., 1837	*	*	*	*
Monday	30 Jan., 1837	*	*	*	*
Tuesday	31 Jan., 1837	*	*	*	*
Half Yearly Meeting					
Tuesday	18 July, 1837	*	*	*	*
Wednesday	19 July, 1837	*	*	*	*
Thursday	20 July, 1837	*	*	*	*
Saturday	22 July, 1837	*	*	*	*
Monday	24 July, 1837	*		*	*
Thursday	27 July, 1837	*		*	*
Tuesday	1 Aug., 1837	*	*	*	*
Wednesday	2 Aug., 1837	*	*	*	*
Monday	7 Aug., 1837	*		*	*
Wednesday	9 Aug., 1837	*		*	
Half Yearly Meeting					
Tuesday	16 Jan., 1838	*		*	*
Wednesday	17 Jan., 1838	*	*	*	*
Thursday	18 Jan., 1838	*	*	*	*
Monday	22 Jan., 1838	*	*	*	*
Half Yearly Meeting					
Thursday	5 July, 1838	*	*	*	*
Friday	6 July, 1838	*	*	*	*
Half Yearly Meeting					
Thursday	17 Jan., 1839	*	*	*	*
Friday	18 Jan., 1839	*	*	*	*
Saturday	19 Jan., 1839	*	*	*	*
Monday	21 Jan., 1839	*	*	*	*
Wednesday	23 Jan., 1839	*	*	*	*
Friday	25 Jan., 1839	*	*	*	*
Saturday	26 Jan., 1839	*	*	*	*
Tuesday	29 Jan., 1839	*	*	*	*
Wednesday	30 Jan., 1839	*	*	*	*
Thursday	31 Jan., 1839	*	*	*	*

Day	Date	Inspectors present			
		Horner	Howell	Saunders	Stuart
Half Yearly Meeting					
Tuesday	16 July, 1839	*	*	*	*
Wednesday	17 July, 1839	*	*	*	*
Thursday	18 July, 1839	*	*	*	*
Friday	19 July, 1839	*	*	*	*
Saturday	20 July, 1839	*	*	*	*
Monday	22 July, 1839	*	*	*	*
Wednesday	24 July, 1839	*	*	*	*
Thursday	25 July, 1839	*	*	*	*
Friday	26 July, 1839	*	*	*	*
Saturday	27 July, 1839	*	*	*	*
Monday	29 July, 1839	*		*	*
Tuesday	30 July, 1839	*		*	*
Thursday	1 Aug., 1839	*		*	*
Monday	5 Aug., 1839	*		*	*
Monday	12 Aug., 1839	*		*	*
Monday	19 Aug., 1839	*		*	*
Half Yearly Meeting					
Tuesday	14 Jan., 1840	*	*	*	*
Saturday	18 Jan., 1840	*	*	*	*
Monday	20 Jan., 1840	*	*	*	*
Friday	24 Jan., 1840	*	*	*	*
Half Yearly Meeting					
Tuesday	7 July, 1840	*	*	*	*
Friday	10 July, 1840	*	*	*	*
Monday	13 July, 1840	*	*	*	*
Tuesday	14 July, 1840	*	*	*	*
Wednesday ...	15 July, 1840	*	*	*	*
Half Yearly Meeting					
Tuesday	2 Feb., 1841	*	*	*	*
Wednesday	3 Feb., 1841	*	*	*	*
Monday	8 Feb., 1841	*	*	*	*
Thursday	11 Feb., 1841	*	*	*	*
Half Yearly Meeting					
Tuesday	29 June, 1841	*	*	*	*
Friday	2 July, 1841	*	*	*	*
Half Yearly Meeting					
Tuesday	1 Feb., 1842	*	*	*	*
Thursday	3 Feb., 1842	*	*	*	*
Half Yearly Meeting					
Tuesday	28 June, 1842		*	*	*
Wednesday	29 June, 1842	*	*	*	*
Tuesday	5 July, 1842	*	*	*	*
Half Yearly Meeting					
Tuesday	7 Feb., 1843	*	*	*	*
Friday	10 Feb., 1843	*	*	*	*
Half Yearly Meeting					
Thursday	20 July, 1843	*	*	*	*
Friday	21 July, 1843	*	*	*	*
Half Yearly Meeting					
Friday	12 Jan., 1844	*	*	*	*
Saturday	13 Jan., 1844	*	*	*	*
Monday	15 Jan., 1844	*	*	*	*
Tuesday	16 Jan., 1844	*	*	*	*
Wednesday	17 Jan., 1844	*	*	*	*
Friday	19 Jan., 1844	*	*	*	*
Half Yearly Meeting					
Tuesday	16 July, 1844	*	*	*	*
Wednesday	17 July, 1844	*	*	*	*
Thursday	18 July, 1844	*	*	*	*
Friday	19 July, 1844	*	*	*	*
Monday	22 July, 1844	*	*	*	*
Tuesday	23 July, 1844	*	*	*	*
Wednesday	24 July, 1844	*	*	*	*

Day	Date	Inspectors present			
		Horner	Howell	Saunders	Stuart
Thursday	25 July, 1844	*	*	*	*
Friday	26 July, 1844	*	*	*	*
Monday	29 July, 1844	*	*	*	*
Tuesday	30 July, 1844	*	*	*	*
Wednesday	31 July, 1844	*	*	*	*
Thursday	1 Aug., 1844	*	*	*	*
Friday	2 Aug., 1844	*	*	*	*
Tuesday	6 Aug., 1844	*		*	*
Wednesday	7 Aug., 1844	*		*	*
Thursday	8 Aug., 1844	*		*	*
Friday	9 Aug., 1844	*		*	*
Monday	12 Aug., 1844	*		*	*
Tuesday	13 Aug., 1844	*		*	*
Wednesday	14 Aug., 1844	*		*	*
Thursday	15 Aug., 1844	*		*	*
Friday	16 Aug., 1844	*		*	*
Saturday	17 Aug., 1844	*		*	*
Monday	19 Aug., 1844	*		*	*
Tuesday	20 Aug., 1844	*		*	*
Wednesday	21 Aug., 1844	*		*	*
Thursday	22 Aug., 1844	*	*	*	*
Friday	23 Aug., 1844	*	*	*	*
Tuesday	27 Aug., 1844	*		*	*
Special Meeting					
Tuesday	26 Nov., 1844	*	*	*	*
Wednesday	27 Nov., 1844	*	*	*	*
Thursday	28 Nov., 1844	*	*	*	*
Friday	29 Nov., 1844	*	*	*	*
Monday	2 Dec., 1844	*		*	*
Wednesday	4 Dec., 1844	*		*	*
Friday	6 Dec., 1844	*		*	*
Thursday	12 Dec., 1844	*		*	*
Tuesday	17 Dec., 1844	*		*	*
Friday	20 Dec., 1844	*		*	*
Tuesday	24 Dec., 1844	*		*	*
Friday	27 Dec., 1844	*		*	*
Tuesday	31 Dec., 1844	*		*	*
Friday	3 Jan., 1845	*		*	*
Monday	6 Jan., 1845	*		*	*
Wednesday	8 Jan., 1845	*		*	*
Wednesday	15 Jan., 1845			*	*
Wednesday	22 Jan., 1845			*	*
Monday	27 Jan., 1845			*	*
Monday	3 Feb., 1845			*	*
Thursday	6 Feb., 1845	*		*	*
Monday	10 Feb., 1845	*		*	*
Monday	17 Feb., 1845	*		*	*
Thursday	20 Feb., 1845	*		*	*
Monday	24 Feb., 1845	*		*	*
Thursday	27 Feb., 1845	*		*	*
Monday	3 Mar., 1845	*		*	*
Thursday	6 Mar., 1845	*		*	*
Monday	10 Mar., 1845	*			
Extraordinary Meeting					
Saturday	22 Mar., 1845	*		*	*
Monday	31 Mar., 1845	*	*	*	*
Tuesday	1 April, 1845	*	*	*	*
Half Yearly Meeting					
Tuesday	27 May, 1845	*	*	*	*
Saturday	31 May, 1845	*	*	*	*
Monday	2 June, 1845	*	*	*	*
Wednesday	4 June, 1845	*	*	*	*
Friday	6 June, 1845	*		*	*
Monday	9 June, 1845	*		*	*
Thursday	12 June, 1845	*		*	*
Monday	16 June, 1845			*	*
Thursday	19 June, 1845			*	*
Monday	23 June, 1845			*	*
Monday	30 June, 1845	*		*	*
Friday	4 July, 1845	*		*	*
Tuesday	8 July, 1845	*		*	*

Day	Date	Inspectors present			
		Horner	Howell	Saunders	Stuart
Tuesday	15 July, 1845	*		*	*
Saturday	19 July, 1845	*		*	*
Monday	28 July, 1845			*	*
Wednesday	6 Aug., 1845			*	*
Half Yearly Meeting					
Tuesday	25 Nov., 1845	*		*	*
Friday	28 Nov., 1845	*		*	*
Tuesday	2 Dec., 1845	*	*	*	*
Friday	5 Dec., 1845	*	*	*	*
Wednesday	10 Dec., 1845	*	*	*	*
Friday ... , ...	12 Dec., 1845	*	*	*	*
Tuesday	16 Dec., 1845	*	*	*	*
Thursday	18 Dec., 1845	*	*	*	*
Tuesday	23 Dec., 1845	*	*	*	*
Tuesday	30 Dec., 1845	*		*	*
Tuesday	6 Jan., 1846	*		*	*
Tuesday	13 Jan., 1846	*		*	*
Tuesday	20 Jan., 1846	*		*	*
Tuesday	27 Jan., 1846	*		*	*
Tuesday	3 Feb., 1846	*		*	*
Tuesday	10 Feb., 1846	*		*	*
Tuesday	17 Feb., 1846			*	*
Monday	23 Feb., 1846			*	*
Half Yearly Meeting					
Tuesday	2 June, 1846	*	*	*	*
Thursday	4 June, 1846	*	*	*	*
Friday	5 June, 1846	*	*	*	*
Tuesday	9 June, 1846	*	*	*	*
Thursday	11 June, 1846	*	*	*	*
Tuesday	16 June, 1846	*		*	*
Thursday	18 June, 1846	*		*	*
Wednesday	24 June, 1846			*	*
Thursday	25 June, 1846			*	*
Friday	26 June, 1846			*	*
Monday	29 June, 1846		*	*	*

They met 1 July and on several subsequent dates not recorded in Minutes.

Day	Date	Inspectors present			
		Horner	Howell	Saunders	Stuart
Half Yearly Meeting					
Tuesday	8 Dec., 1846	*		*	*
Thursday	17 Dec., 1846	*	*	*	*
Wednesday	23 Dec., 1846	*	*	*	*
Tuesday	29 Dec., 1846	*		*	*
Thursday	31 Dec., 1846	*	*	*	*
Saturday	2 Jan., 1847	*	*	*	*
Thursday	7 Jan., 1847	*	*	*	*
Thursday	21 Jan., 1847	*		*	*
Thursday	28 Jan., 1847	*	*	*	*
Thursday	4 Feb., 1847	*	*		
Thursday	18 Feb., 1847	*		*	*
Wednesday	24 Feb., 1847	*		*	*
Friday	26 Feb., 1847	*	*	*	*
Saturday	27 Feb., 1847	*	*	*	*
Half Yearly Meeting					
Thursday	20 May, 1847	*	*	*	*
Saturday	22 May, 1847	*	*	*	*
Tuesday	25 May, 1847	*	*	*	*
Thursday	27 May, 1847	*	*	*	*
Friday	28 May, 1847	*	*	*	*
Tuesday	2 June, 1847		*	*	*
Friday	4 June, 1847		*	*	*
Thursday	10 June, 1847		*	*	*
Monday	14 June, 1847			*	*
Tuesday	22 June, 1847		*	*	*
Wednesday	23 June, 1847		*	*	*
Wednesday	7 July, 1847	*	*	*	*
Saturday	24 July, 1847		*	*	*
Friday	30 July, 1847	*	*	*	
Monday	2 Aug., 1847	*	*	*	

Day	Date	Inspectors present			
		Horner	Howell	Saunders	Stuart
Half Yearly Meeting					
Monday	6 Dec., 1847	*		*	*
Monday	13 Dec., 1847	*	*	*	*
Monday	20 Dec., 1847	*	*	*	*
Monday	27 Dec., 1847	*	*	*	*
Tuesday	4 Jan., 1848	*	*	*	*
Monday	10 Jan., 1848	*	*	*	
Monday	17 Jan., 1848	*	*	*	
Monday	24 Jan., 1848	*		*	
Monday	7 Feb., 1848	*		*	
Monday	21 Feb., 1848	*	*	*	*
Half Yearly Meeting					
Tuesday	30 May, 1848	*	*	*	*
Monday	5 June, 1848	*	*	*	*
Wednesday ...	7 June, 1848	*	*	*	*
Friday	9 June, 1848	*	*	*	*
Wednesday ...	14 June, 1848	*	*	*	*
Monday	19 June, 1848	*		*	*
Friday	23 June, 1848	*		*	*
Tuesday	27 June, 1848	*		*	*
Monday	3 July, 1848	*		*	*
Half Yearly Meeting					
Monday	4 Dec., 1848	*	*	*	*
Wednesday ...	6 Dec., 1848	*	*	*	*
Thursday	14 Dec., 1848	*	*	*	*
Friday	15 Dec., 1848	*	*	*	*
Thursday	21 Dec., 1848	*	*	*	*
Wednesday ...	27 Dec., 1848	*	*	*	*
Tuesday	2 Jan., 1849	*	*	*	*
Thursday	4 Jan., 1849	*	*	*	*
Tuesday	9 Jan., 1849	*	*	*	*
Thursday	11 Jan., 1849	*	*	*	*
Monday	15 Jan., 1849	*	*	*	*
Monday	22 Jan., 1849	*	*	*	*
Monday	29 Jan., 1849	*	*	*	*
Wednesday ...	31 Jan., 1849	*	*	*	*
Thursday	1 Feb., 1849	*	*	*	*
Monday	5 Feb., 1849	*	*	*	*

BIBLIOGRAPHY

Minutes of the statutory and special Meetings of the Factory Inspectors.

Vol. I.   8th September, 1836—17th January, 1844.

Vol. II.   16th July, 1844—5th February, 1849.

Letters from the Home Office to the Factory Inspectors.

Home Office Papers.   H.O. 87 (1).

PARLIAMENTARY PAPERS.

Parliamentary Bills.

For preserving the Health and Morals of Apprentices in Cotton Mills and other Factories.   1801-2.   I, 225, 369.

To preserve the Health and Morals of Apprentices in the Cotton Trade. 1814-15.   II, 735, 739.

To amend the Act for preserving the Health and Morals of Apprentices and others employed in Cotton Mills.   1818.   I, 87, 91.

For regulating Cotton Factories, and for the preservation of the Health of Young Persons employed therein.   1819.   I-B, 857.

To amend the Act respecting Children employed in Cotton Factories. 1819-20.   I, 97.

To make further Provision for the Regulation of Cotton Mills and Factories, and for the better Preservation of the Health of Young Persons employed therein.   1825.   I, 297, 303.

To amend the Law relating to the Employment of Children in Cotton Mills and Factories.   1829.   I, 483.

To repeal the Laws relating to Apprentices and Young Persons in Cotton and other Factories and Mills, and to make further Provision in lieu. 1830-31.   I, 121, 127, 135.   1831.   I, 345, 353.

To restrain the Labour of Children in Factories throughout the Kingdom. 1831-2.   II, 1.

To regulate the Labour of Children in Mills and Factories. 1833.   II, 263, 281.

To explain the Act of last Session for regulating the Labour of Children. 1834.   II, 347.

To repeal the Act 3 & 4 Will. IV, relating to the Labour of Children in Factories, and to make other Provisions.   1835.   II, 781.

To amend the Act 3 & 4 Will IV, for regulating the Labour of Children, &c., in Mills and Factories of the United Kingdom.   1836.   IV, 1.

To regulate the Employment of Children and young Persons in Factories. 1837-38. IV, 1. 1839. III, 467, 485. 1841. II, 425.

To regulate the Employment of Children and Young Persons in Silk Factories. 1841. II, 459.

To regulate the Employment of Children and Young Persons in Factories, and for the better Education of Children in Factory Districts. 1843. II, 495, 549, 607.

To regulate the Employment of Children, young Persons, and Women in Factories. 1844. II, 149.

To amend the Laws relating to Labour in Factories. 1844. II, 187, 223. 1846. II, 173.

To regulate the Labour of Children in the Calico Print Works of Great Britain and Ireland. 1845. I, 227, 235.

To amend a Clerical Error in an Act of last Session for regulating the Labour of Children, young Persons, and Women in Print Works. 1846. III, 167.

To limit the Hours of Labour of young Persons and Females in Factories. 1847. I, 321.

To amend the Act 7 Vict. relating to Labour in Factories 1850. III, 159.

To regulate the Employment of Children in Factories. 1852-53. III, 409.

Select Committees & Commissions.

Report of Minutes of Evidence respecting the state of health and morals of children employed in manufactories; chiefly as to cotton factories. (Peel's Committee). 1816. III.

Reports from the Select Committee on the Bill for the regulation of factories. (Sadler's Committee). 1831-32. XV.

First Report from Commissioners appointed to collect information in the manufacturing districts, relative to the employment of children in factories; with Minutes of Evidence and Reports of District Commissioners. (Commission of 1833). 1833. XX.

Second Report from Commissioners. 1833. XXI.

Supplementary Reports of Commissioners. 1834. XIX, XX.

Reports from the Select Committee on the Act for the regulation of factories, together with Minutes of Evidence. (Ashley's Committee). 1840. X. 1841. IX.

Second Report of the Commissioners for inquiring into the employment of children in mines and manufactories. (Children's Employment Commission). 1843. XIII.

Appendix to Report, with Reports and Evidence from Sub-Commissioners. 1843. XIV, XV.

Reports of the Factory Inspectors.

1834		XLIII,	423.
1835		XL,	689.
1836		XLV,	155.
1837		XXXI,	53.
1837-8		XXVIII,	81, 139.
		XLV,	55.
1839		XIX,	433, 539.
1840		XXIII,	1, 27.
1841		X,	161.
1841	(sess. 2)	VI,	213.
1842		XXII,	337, 441.
1843		XXVII,	289, 335.
1844		XXVIII,	533, 565.
1845		XXV,	431.
1846		XX,	565, 611.
1847		XV,	441, 489.
1847-8		XXVI,	105, 149.
1849		XXII,	131, 283.
1850		XXIII,	181, 261
1851		XXIII,	217, 293.
1852		XXI,	353, 377.
1852-3		XL,	461, 533.
1854		XIX,	257, 373.

Miscellaneous.

Instructions from the Central Board of Factory Commissioners to the District and Medical Commissioners. 1833. XXXI, 349.

Regulations issued by Leonard Horner. 1836. XLV, 215.

Directions to Factory Inspectors relative to the Regulation of Factories. 1837. XXXI, 123.

Rules and Regulations issued by the Factory Inspectors since May, 1836. 1837. L, 35.

First Memorial of the Manchester Short-time Committee. 1837. L, 203.

Second Memorial of the Manchester Short-time Committee. 1837-8. XLV, 79.

Particulars of remuneration and employment of Superintendents. 1837-8. XLV, 69.

Reports on the effects of the Educational Provisions of the Factories Act. 1839. XLII, 353.

Instructions by Leonard Horner for Superintendents of Factories. 1840. X, 153.

Special Reports on the practicability of legislative interference to diminish accidents to children and young persons, arising from the machinery being cleaned when in motion, and from being left unguarded. 1841. X, 199.

Report of R. J. Saunders upon the establishment of schools in the Factory Districts. February, 1842. 1843. XXVII, 385.

Judgment of the Court of Exchequer in the case of Ryder v. Mills. 1850. XLII, 479.

STATUTES.

42 Geo. III, c. 73.   22nd June, 1802.

An Act for the preservation of the health and morals of apprentices and others, employed in cotton and other mills, and cotton and other factories.

59 Geo. III, c. 66.   2nd July, 1819.

An Act to make further Provisions for the Regulation of Cotton Mills and Factories, and for the better Preservation of the Health of young Persons employed therein.

60 Geo. III, c. 5.   23rd December, 1819.

An Act to amend an Act of the last Session of Parliament to make further Provision for the Regulation of Cotton Mills and Factories, and for the Preservation of the Health of young Persons employed therein.

6 Geo. IV, c. 63.   22nd June, 1825.

An Act to make further Provisions for the Regulation of Cotton Mills and Factories, and for the better Preservation of the Health of young Persons employed therein.

10 Geo. IV, c. 51.   19th June, 1829.

An Act to amend the Law relating to the Employment of Children in Cotton Mills and Factories.

10 Geo. IV, c. 63.   24th June, 1829.

An Act to render valid an Act to amend the Law relating to the Employment of Children in Cotton Mills and Factories.

1 & 2 Will. IV, c. 39.   15th October, 1831.

An Act to repeal the Laws relating to Apprentices and other young Persons employed in Cotton Factories and in Cotton Mills, and to make further Provisions in lieu thereof.

3 & 4 Will. IV, c. 103.   29th August, 1833.

An Act to regulate the Labour of Children and young Persons in the Mills and Factories of the United Kingdom.

4 & 5 Will. IV, c. 1.   20th February, 1834.

An Act to explain and amend an Act of the last Session of Parliament, for regulating the Labour of Children and young Persons in the Mills and Factories of the United Kingdom.

7 & 8 Vict., c. 15.   6th June, 1844.

An Act to amend the Laws relating to Labour in Factories.

8 & 9 Vict., c. 29.   30th June, 1845.

An Act to regulate the Labour of Children, young Persons and Women, in Print Works.

9 & 10 Vict., c. 18.   18th June, 1846.

An Act to amend Two clerical Errors in an Act of the last Session, for regulating the Labour of Children, young Persons, and Women in Print Works.

9 & 10 Vict., c. 40.   3rd August, 1846.

An Act to declare certain Ropeworks not within the operation of the Factory Acts.

10 & 11 Vict., c. 29.   8th June, 1847.

An Act to limit the Hours of Labour of young Persons and Females in Factories.

10 & 11 Vict., c. 70.   22nd July, 1847.

An Act to amend the Law as to the School Attendance of Children employed in Print Works.

13 & 14 Vict., c. 54.   5th August, 1850.

An Act to amend the Acts relating to Labour in Factories.

16 & 17 Vict., c. 104.   20th August, 1853.

An Act further to regulate the Employment of Children in Factories.

BOOKS & PAMPHLETS.

A few Arguments in Favour of Mr. Sadler's Bill for Shortening the Hours of Labour in Factories: and against Oppression in general. Huddersfield. 1833.

A Letter to Sir John Cam Hobhouse, Bart., M.P., on " The Factories Bill " by a Manufacturer. London. 1832.

Address to the Friends of Justice and Humanity in the West Riding of York from the Meeting of Delegates of the Short Time Committees, established to promote the legislative Adoption of the Ten Hour Factory Bill, Assembled at the Yew Tree Inn, Birstall, October 28th, 1833. Bradford. 1833.

An Address on the State of the Cotton Trade, to the Master Spinners and Weavers of Lancashire. Manchester. 1829.

An Analytical Digest of the Education Clauses of the Factories Bill. London. 1843.

An Inquiry into the Principle and Tendency of the Bill now pending in Parliament for imposing Certain Restrictions on Cotton Factories. 1818.

Answers to certain objections made to Sir Robert Peel's Bill for Ameliorating the Conditions of Children employed in Cotton Factories. Manchester. 1819.

Catechism of the Society for Promoting National Regeneration. Bradford. 1833.

Don Quixote and his Esquires. Leeds. 1833.

Exposition of the Factory Question. Manchester. 1832.

Great Meeting in Leeds, on Thursday the 16th of May, 1833, of the Factory Children, to present their Protest to the Commissioners appointed through Mr. Wilson Patten's Motion for further Enquiry, etc., etc. Leeds. 1833.

Letter to the Right Hon. Lord Althorp, on the Factory Bill, by a Scotch Mill Spinner. Montrose. 1833.

On the Factory Question. Ashton. 1836.

Protest of the Bradford Short-time Committee against the Proceedings of Mr. Rickards, the Factory Inspector, and of the Mill Owners of the Neighbourhood. Bradford. 1835.

The Commissioners' Vade Mecum whilst engaged in collecting Evidence for the Factory Masters. Leeds. 1833.

The Condition of the West India Slave contrasted with that of the Infant Slave in our English Factories.

The Factories. [*The London and Westminster Review*. October, 1836].

The Factory Child. A Poem. London. 1831.

The Factory System; or, Frank Hawthorn's Visit to his Cousin, Jemmy Cropper, of Leeds. Leeds. 1831.

The Justice, Humanity, and Policy, of restricting the Hours of Children and Young Persons in the Mills & Factories, of the United Kingdom, illustrated in the Letters, Speeches, etc., of Persons of the highest Respectability and the most correct and extensive Information, of various religious Creeds, and political Views, and of various Stations in Life, many of them resident in the midst of those Districts, where the Evils exist, which it is sought to mitigate, by Mr. Saddler's Ten Hour Bill. Leeds. 1833.

The Reform Ministry, and the Reformed Parliament. [*The Edinburgh Review*. No. CXVII. 1833].

The Sayings and Doings of Daniel O'Connell, Esq. London. 1836.

The Ten Hour Bill.—Report of the Proceedings of the great Leeds Meeting to petition Parliament in favour of Mr. Sadler's Bill for the Regulation of the Hours of Children's Labour in Factories, held on Monday, January 9, 1831.

View Extraordinary of Sir John's Huddersfield Menagerie of political Houhynims, Ourang Outangs, Kangaroos, Lizards, Camelions, Crocadiles, Locusts, and Hyaenas: with a variety of other sectarian Oddities of Dissent, Cantwells, Mawworms, Boobies, Humbugs, and Hypocrites. Leeds. 1837.

AIKIN, J.
A Description of the Country from thirty to forty Miles round Manchester.
London. 1795.

" ALFRED " (SAMUEL KYDD).
The History of the Factory Movement from the year 1802, to the enactment of the Ten Hours' Bill in 1847.
2 vols. London. 1857.

ANDERSON, GEORGE.
The Half-Time System and the Educational Test.
[Transactions of the National Association for the Promotion of Social Science. 1860].

ASHLEY, LORD.
The Factory System.
[Quarterly Review. Vol. 57. 1836].

BABBAGE, CHARLES.
On the Economy of Machinery and Manufactures.
London. 1832.

BAINES, EDWARD
History of the Cotton Manufacture in Great Britain.
London. 1835.

BAKER, ROBERT.
On the Physical Effects of Diminished Labour.
[Transactions of the National Association for the Promotion of Social Science. 1859].

BIRLEY, J.
Sadler's Bill—Cotton Branch.
Manchester. 1832.

BISCHOFF, JAMES.
A Comprehensive History of the Woollen and Worsted Manufactures.
London. 1842.

BLELLOCH, D. H.
A Historical Survey of Factory Inspection in Great Britain.
[International Labour Review. November, 1938.]

BOWLEY, MARION.
Nassau Senior.
London. 1937.

BROWN, JOHN.
A Memoir of Robert Blincoe, an Orphan Boy; sent from the Work-house of St Pancras, London, to endure the Horrors of a Cotton Mill. through his infancy and youth with a minute detail of his sufferings, being the first memoir of the kind published.
Manchester. 1832.

BULL, G. S.
The Evils of the Factory System, illustrated in a respectful and faithful Appeal to the Inhabitants of the Parish of Bradford on the behalf of the Factory Children.
Bradford. 1832.

CARPENTER, WILLIAM.
Machinery as it affects the Industrial Classes.
London. 1844.

CARR-SAUNDERS, A. M. *and* WILSON, P. A.
   The Professions.

                                        Oxford. 1933.

CHAPMAN, S. J.
   The Lancashire Cotton Industry.

                           Manchester. 1904.

CLAPHAM, J. H.
   An Economic History of Modern Britain.
   Vol. I: The Early Railway Age, 1820-1850.

                         Cambridge. 1930.

CONDY, GEORGE.
   An Argument for placing Factory Children within the Pale of the Law.
                         London. 1833.

CRABTREE, GEOFFREY.
   Factory Commission: The Legality of its Appointment questioned, and
   the Illegality of its Proceedings proved.

                         London. 1833.

CROFT, W. R.
   History of the Factory Movement.

                         London. 1888.

DANIELS, G. W.
   The Early English Cotton Industry.

                         London. 1920.

DICEY, A. V.
   Law and Public Opinion in England.

                         London. 1905.

DJANG, T. K.
   Factory Inspection in Great Britain.

                         London. 1942.

DOBBS, A. E.
   Education and Social Movements 1700-1850.

                         London. 1919.

DODD, GEORGE.
   Days at the Factories, or the Manufacturing Industry of Great Britain
   Described.

                         London. 1843.

DODD, WILLIAM.
   The Factory System Illustrated in a Series of Letters to Lord Ashley.
                         London. 1842.

ENGELS, FREDERICK.
   The Condition of the Working-Class in England in 1844.
                         London. 1892.

FALLAS, T.
   The People's Rights and how to get them.

                                     1844.

FAUCHER, LEON.
   Etudes sur l'Angleterre.

                            Paris. 1856.

FAY, C. R.
    Great Britain from Adam Smith to the Present Day.
                                        London.   1929.

FAY, C. R.
    Life and Labour in the Nineteenth Century.
                                        Cambridge.   1920.

FIELDEN, JOHN.
    The Curse of the Factory System.
                                        London.   1836.

FINLAY, KIRKMAN.
    Letter to the Right Hon. Lord Ashley on the Cotton Factory System,
    and the Ten Hours' Factory Bill.
                                        Glasgow.   1833.

GASKELL, P.
    Artisans and Machinery: The Moral and Physical Condition of the
    Manufacturing Population.
                                        London.   1836.

GASKELL, P.
    The Manufacturing Population of England.
                                        London.   1833.

GREG, ROBERT HYDE.
    The Factory Question.
                                        London.   1837.

GREG, WILLIAM RATHBONE.
    An Enquiry into the state of the Manufacturing Population and the
    Causes and Cures of the Evils therein existing.
                                        London.   1831.

GUEST, RICHARD.
    Compendious History of Cotton Manufacture.
                                        Manchester.   1823.

GUEST, RICHARD.
    The British Cotton Manufactures.
                                        Manchester.   1828.

HALEVY, ELIE.
    A History of the English People.   1830-1841.
                                                   1927.

HAMMOND, J. L. and B.
    Life of Lord Shaftesbury.
                                        London.   1923.

HAMMOND, J. L. and B.
    The Skilled Labourer.   1760-1832.
                                        London.   1927.

HAMMOND, J. L. and B.
    The Town Labourer.   1760-1832
                                        London.   1917.

HOOLE, HOLLAND.
    A Letter to the Right Honourable Lord Viscount Althorp, M.P.,
    Chancellor of the Exchequer; in defence of the Cotton Factories
    of Lancashire.
                                        Manchester.   1832.

HORNER, LEONARD.
The Factories Regulation Act Explained, with some Remarks on its Origin, Nature and Tendency.
Glasgow. 1834.

HORNER, LEONARD.
On the Employment of Children in Factories and other Works in the United Kingdom and in some Foreign Countries.
London. 1840.

HUTCHINS, B. L. and HARRISON, A.
A History of Factory Legislation.
London. 1926.

HUTT, W. H.
The Factory System of the early 19th Century.
[Economica. March, 1926].

KAY, JAMES PHILLIPS.
The Moral and Physical Condition of the Working Classes employed in the Cotton Manufacture in Manchester.
London. 1832.

KEELING, F.
Child Labour in the United Kingdom.
London. 1914.

KENNEDY, JOHN.
Miscellaneous Papers.
Manchester. 1849.

LEACH, JAMES.
Stubborn Facts from the Factories, by a Manchester Operative, published by Wm. Rashleigh, M.P.
1844.

LEADER, R. E.
Life and Letters of John Arthur Roebuck.
London. 1897.

LUDLOW, J. M. and JONES, L.
Progress of the Working Class, 1832-1867.
London. 1867.

LYELL, KATHARINE M.
Memoir of Leonard Horner.
London. 1890.

MANTOUX, PAUL.
The Industrial Revolution in the Eighteenth Century.
London. 1928.

MARSTON, MAURICE.
Sir Edwin Chadwick (1800-1890).
London. 1925.

MARTINEAU, HARRIET.
The Factory Controversy: a Warning against meddling legislation.
Manchester. 1855.

MORLEY, JOHN.
The Life of Richard Cobden.
London. 1905.
(First published in 2 volumes, 1879).

NICHOLSON, J.
    The Factory Child's Mother; the Voice of true humanity; a Poem.
                                                         Leeds. 1832.

OASTLER, RICHARD.
    A Letter to the Bishop of Exeter.
                                                  Manchester. 1838.

OASTLER, RICHARD.
    A Letter to Mr. Holland Hoole in reply to his letter to the Right
    Hon. Lord Viscount Althorp, M.P., Chancellor of the Exechequer,
    in Defence of the Cotton Factories of Lancashire.
                                                  Manchester. 1832.

OASTLER, RICHARD.
    A Letter to those Millowners who continue to oppose the Ten Hours'
    Bill, and who impudently dare to break the present Factories Act.
                                                  Manchester. 1836.

OASTLER, RICHARD.
    A Speech delivered by Richard Oastler, at a Meeting held in the
    Manor Court-room, Manchester, on Wednesday Evening, April 27th,
    1833, to consider the Propriety of petitioning the Legislature to pass
    the Ten Hours Factories' Regulation Bill, without waiting for the
    Report of that " Mockery of Iniquity," the Millowners Commission.
                                                  Huddersfield. 1833.

OASTLER, RICHARD.
    Facts and Plain Words on every-day Subjects.
                                                         Leeds. 1833.

OASTLER, RICHARD.
    More Work for the Leeds new Thief Catchers.
    A Letter to George Goodman, Esq., Mayor of Leeds.
                                                  Huddersfield. 1836.

OASTLER, RICHARD.
    The Factory Question and the Factory Agitation, calmly considered,
    in a Letter to those Millowners, who are the Friends of the Factory
    Children, and who are endeavouring, as far as possible to obey the
    present Factories' Regulation Act.
                                                         London. 1836.

OASTLER, RICHARD.
    The Law or the Needle.
                                                         London. 1836.

OASTLER, RICHARD.
    The Rejected Letter, with a Dedication to the Man wot would not
    have it read.
                                                         Leeds. 1836.

OASTLER, RICHARD.
    The Unjust Judge or the " Sign of the Judge's Skin." A Letter to
    George Goodman, Esq., Mayor of Leeds, on His Worship's recent
    Refusal to imprison a Criminal under the Factories' Regulation Act.
                                                         Leeds. 1836.

OASTLER, RICHARD.
    Slavery in Yorkshire. Monstrous Barbarity!!!
    To Edward Baines, Esq., M.P.
                                                         Bradford. 1835.

OASTLER, RICHARD.
Yorkshire Slavery. The " Devil-to-do " amongst the Dissenters in Huddersfield. A Letter addressed to E. Baines, Esq., M.P.
Leeds. 1835.

OASTLER, RICHARD.
The Huddersfield Dissenters in a Fury. And why? Because the Mask is falling! A third Letter addressed to Edward Baines, Esq., M.P.
Leeds. 1835.

OASTLER, RICHARD.
The Huddersfield Dissenters stark, staring mad!!! Because the Mask has fallen!!! The fourth Letter to Edward Baines, Esq., M.P.
Leeds. 1835.

PAGE, WILLIAM.
Commerce and Industry.
London. 1919.

PARKER, CHARLES STUART.
Life and Letters of Sir James Graham, 1792-1861.
London. 1907.

VON PLENER, ERNST.
The English Factory Legislation.
London. 1873.

RADCLIFFE, W.
Origin of the New System of Manufacture, commonly called " Power-Loom Weaving."
Stockport. 1828.

RICHARDSON, C.
A Short Description of the Factory System.
Bawtrey. 1832.

ROBSON, ADAM HENRY.
The Education of Children engaged in Industry in England. 1833-1876
London. 1931.

ROYLE, VERNON.
The Factory System Defended.
Manchester. 1833.

RUSSELL, ROLLO.
Early Correspondence of Lord John Russell.
London. 1913.

SADLER, MICHAEL THOMAS.
Factory Statistics.
London. 1836.

SADLER, MICHAEL THOMAS.
Protest against the Secret Proceedings of the Factory Commission in Leeds.
Leeds. 1833.

SAUNDERS, EDWIN.
The Teeth a Test of Age considered with reference to the Factory Children.
London. 1837.

SENIOR, NASSAU W.
Letters on the Factory Act addressed to the Right Honourable the
President of the Board of Trade.
London. 1837.

SHAFTESBURY, EARL OF
Speeches.
London. 1868.

SMART, WILLIAM.
Economic Annals of the Nineteenth Century.
London. 1910.

STEPHEN, LESLIE.
The English Utilitarians.
London. 1900.

SYMONS, JELLINGER C.
Arts and Artisans at Home and Abroad.
Edinburgh. 1839.

SYMONS, JELLINGER C.
Light and Life for the People.
London. 1843.

TAYLOR, W. COOKE.
Factories and the Factory System.
London. 1844.

TAYLOR, W. COOKE.
Notes of a Tour in the Manufacturing Districts of Lancashire.
London. 1842.

THORPE, FRANCIS.
The Factory Bill overstocks the Trade with Hands and thereby
reduces Wages and ruins the Work People.
Knaresbrough. 1843.

URE, ANDREW.
The Cotton Manufacture of Great Britain.
London. 1836.

URE, ANDREW.
Foreign Competition and the Ten Hours' Bill.
Bradford. 1836

URE, ANDREW.
The Philosophy of Manufactures: or, an Exposition of the Scientific,
Moral, and Commercial Economy of the Factory System of Great
Britain.
London. 1835.

WALKER, J. K.
Some observations on the Peculiarities of Diseases of Infants &
Children.
Worcester. 1835.

WALPOLE, SPENCER.
The Life of Lord John Russell.
London. 1889.

WEIR, A. C.
   The Inexpediency of compelling Employers to educate their Work-children.
   [*Transactions of the National Association for the Promotion of Social Science.* 1860].

WING, CHARLES.
   Evils of the Factory System Exposed.
                                                    London.   1837.

WOOD, JAMES.
   Right of Labour to Legislative Protection.
                                                    London.   1832.

INDEX